Applied
Mathematics I

Also by the same authors:
APPLIED MATHEMATICS II
PURE MATHEMATICS I
PURE MATHEMATICS II

Applied Mathematics I

L. Bostock, B.Sc.
Senior Mathematics Lecturer,
Southgate Technical College.

S. Chandler, B.Sc.
Lecturer in Mathematics,
Southgate Technical College.

Stanley Thornes (Publishers) Ltd.

First published in 1975 by Stanley Thornes (Publishers) Ltd.,
EDUCA House, Liddington Estate, Leckhampton Road,
CHELTENHAM GL53 0DN

Reprinted 1977
Reprinted 1978
Reprinted 1979
Reprinted 1980

ISBN 0 85950 019 5 Student edition

Typeset by Alden Press (London and Northampton) Ltd.,
and printed in Great Britain at The Pitman Press, Bath

PREFACE

How is the subject matter treated? and *For what examinations is it suitable?*
are the two questions which students of mathematics and their teachers ask when
a new book on Applied Mathematics makes its appearance. It is to these questions
that we now turn our attention.

Our aim is to present a sound but simple treatment of Mechanics as an
experimental science whose 'laws' are based on deductive and experimental
evidence. No previous knowledge of the subject is assumed and the use of Pure
Mathematics is kept to a minimum although we do not recommend anyone to
study Applied Mathematics without covering some Advanced Level Pure Mathematics. Our development is based on the fundamental difference between the
properties and effects of concurrent forces on the one hand and those of non-concurrent forces on the other. This allows for a full traditional treatment of mechanical principles, using vector notation and simple vector methods where applicable,
followed by the use of rigorous cartesian vector analysis as an alternative method
of solving appropriate problems. The text is straightforward and is illustrated by
a large number of worked examples. S.I. units have been used in most of the
examples but in some we have introduced other units and symbols, the knot for
example, which we feel are likely to remain in use despite metrication.

Questions which can be solved with an understanding of basic principles are
set throughout the text and, with new examining techniques in mind, we have
incorporated a variety of types of multiple choice questions. Problems requiring
more thought and application appear in the Miscellaneous Examples at the end
of each chapter. Some of these are quite demanding and should appeal to students
of 'Special Paper' calibre.

The topics dealt with in the first volume have been carefully selected to serve
the needs of a wide variety of students. In terms of the existing examinations
Volume 1 caters for the applied mathematics part of combined mathematics
papers, such as 'Pure and Applied Mathematics', for the first year of a full two-
year course in Applied Mathematics and for a basic mechanics course for students
with an engineering career in mind. With an eye to the future this volume will be
suitable for the Syllabus D of the University of London or for a general post-O-
level course at N-level. Volume 2 completes the work necessary for the existing
Applied Mathematics syllabuses of most of the examining boards and will satisfy

the demands of the new Further Mathematics Syllabus D of the University of London.

We wish to express our sincere thanks to friends and colleagues for their advice and constructive criticism during the preparation of this book and to those students of Southgate Technical College who assisted by checking solutions. We are particularly indebted to Mr. B Nour-Omid for his valuable criticism and correction of the work and to Miss E Clarke for her co-operation in typing the manuscript.

We are grateful to the following Examination Boards for their permission to reproduce questions from past examination papers:

The Associated Examining Board
Joint Matriculation Board
University of London University Entrance and School Examination Council
University of Cambridge Local Examinations Syndicate
Oxford Delegacy of Local Examinations
Southern Universities' Joint Board
Welsh Joint Education Committee

L. Bostock
S. Chandler

simple Harmonic Motion
relative motion

CONTENTS

Preface   v

Notes on Use of the Book   xi

Chapter 1. **Introduction**   1 ×

    Basic Concepts of Force and Motion.

Chapter 2. **Vectors. Components and Resultants**   12 ✗

    Vector representation. Properties of Vectors. Resolution.
    Resultant of Concurrent Coplanar forces.

Chapter 3. **Forces in Equilibrium. Friction**   41

    Equilibrium of three coplanar forces. Triangle of forces.
    Lami's Theorem. Contact forces between solid bodies.
    Laws of friction. Equilibrium of more than three con-
    current forces.

Chapter 4. **Velocity and Acceleration**   70

    Motion in a straight line. Velocity. Acceleration.
    Displacement-time and velocity-time graphs. Equations
    of motion for constant linear acceleration. Vertical
    motion under gravity. Angular motion. Equations of
    motion for constant angular acceleration.

Chapter 5. **Newton's Laws of Motion**   102

    The effect of a constant force on a body.
    Motion of connected particles.

Chapter 6. **Work and Power**   133

Chapter 7. **Hooke's Law. Energy**   149

    Properties of elastic strings and springs.
    Work done in stretching a string. Mechanical energy.
    Conservation of Mechanical energy.

Chapter 8. **Momentum. Direct Impact**   180

Impulse. Inelastic impact. Conservation of linear
momentum. Elastic impact. Law of restitution.

Chapter 9. **General Motion of a Particle in One Plane**   212

Motion in a straight line with acceleration being a function
of time; velocity; displacement.
Graphical methods. Motion in two dimensions. The effect
of a variable force on a body.

Chapter 10. **Projectiles**   242

General equations of motion of a projectile.
Equation of the path of a projectile. Special properties.

Chapter 11. **Motion in a Circle**   267

Circular motion with constant speed. Conical
pendulum. Banked tracks. Motion in a vertical circle.

Chapter 12. **Simple Harmonic Motion**   309

Basic equations of linear and angular S.H.M.
Associated circular motion. Simple pendulum.
Moving particle attached to an elastic string or spring.
Incomplete oscillations.

Chapter 13. **Relative Motion**   347

Relative velocity. Relative position. Line of closest approach.
Interception.

Chapter 14. **Turning Effect. Non-Concurrent Forces**   374

Moment of a force. Resultant moment.
Equilibrium of non-concurrent forces.

Chapter 15. **Resultants of Coplanar Forces. Equivalent Force Systems.** 403

Coplanar forces reducing to a single force. Resultant of
parallel forces. Couple. Properties of a couple.
Resultant of forces represented by line segments.
Replacement force systems.

Chapter 16. **Centre of Gravity** 445

Uniform triangular lamina. Composite bodies. Methods using integration. Body hanging freely. Body resting on a plane.

Chapter 17. **Problems Involving Rigid Bodies** 485

Equilibrium of a rigid body under the action of (a) three forces (using cotangent rule) (b) more than three forces. Sliding and overturning. Composite bodies. Heavy jointed rods.

Chapter 18. **Frameworks** 516

Calculation of stress in light rods.
Bow's Notation. Method of sections.

Appendix 535

Answers 537

Index 551

NOTES ON USE OF THE BOOK

1. Notation Used in Diagrams

Force

Velocity

Acceleration

Dimensions

Where components and resultant are shown in one diagram the resultant is denoted by the larger arrow-head thus:

2. Useful Pure Mathematics

In any triangle ABC

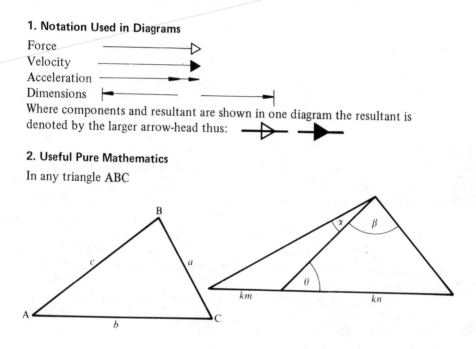

Sine Rule
$$\frac{\sin A}{a} = \frac{\sin B}{b} = \frac{\sin C}{c}$$

Cosine Rule
$$a^2 = b^2 + c^2 - 2bc \cos A$$

Cotangent Rule
$$(m + n) \cot \theta = m \cot \alpha - n \cot \beta$$

Compound Angle Formulae

$$\sin (A \pm B) = \sin A \cos B \pm \cos A \sin B$$

$$\cos (A \pm B) = \cos A \cos B \mp \sin A \sin B$$

xi

Small Angles

$$\text{As } \theta \longrightarrow 0, \quad \frac{\sin \theta}{\theta} \longrightarrow 1$$

Integrals

$$\int \frac{f'(x)}{f(x)} \, dx = \ln kf(x)$$

$$\int \frac{1}{\sqrt{(a^2 - b^2 x^2)}} \, dx = \frac{1}{b} \arcsin \frac{bx}{a} + k$$

3. Instructions for Answering Multiple Choice Exercises

These exercises are at the end of most chapters. The questions are set in groups, each group representing one of the variations that may arise in examination papers. The answering techniques are different for each type of question and are classified as follows:

TYPE I

These questions consist of a problem followed by several alternative answers, only *one* of which is correct.
Write down the letter corresponding to the correct answer.

TYPE II

In this type of question some information is given and is followed by a number of possible responses. *One or more* of the suggested responses follow(s) directly from the information given.
Write down the letter(s) corresponding to the correct response(s).
e.g.: PQR is a triangle.
(a) $\hat{P} + \hat{Q} + \hat{R} = 180°$.
(b) PQ + QR is less than PR.
(c) If $\hat{P}$ is obtuse, $\hat{Q}$ and $\hat{R}$ must both be acute.
(d) $\hat{P} = 90°, \hat{Q} = 45°, \hat{R} = 45°$.
The correct responses are (a) and (c).
(b) is definitely incorrect and (d) may or may not be true of the triangle PQR. There is not sufficient information given to allot a particular value to each angle. Responses of this kind, which require more information than is given, should not be regarded as correct.

TYPE III

Each problem contains two independent statements (a) and (b).
1) If (a) implies (b) but (b) does not imply (a)   write *A*.
2) If (b) implies (a) but (a) does not imply (b)   write *B*.

3) If (a) implies (b) *and* (b) implies (a)   write *C.*

4) If (a) denies (b) *and* (b) denies (a)   write *D.*

5) If none of the first four relationships apply   write *E.*

TYPE IV

A problem is introduced and followed by a number of pieces of information. You are not required to solve the problem but to decide whether:

1) the total amount of information given is insufficient to solve the problem. If so write *I*,

2) the given information is *all* needed to solve the problem. In this case write *A*,

3) the problem can be solved without using one or more of the given pieces of information. In this case write down the letter(s) corresponding to the items not needed.

TYPE V

A single statement is made. Write *T* if the statement is true and *F* if the statement is false.

CHAPTER 1

INTRODUCTION

This book is about Mechanics and the solving of mechanical problems with the help of Pure Mathematics.

Mechanics, which deals with the effects that forces have on bodies, is a science. So the laws of Mechanics are scientific laws. They come from observation and experiments and so can never be considered as universally true. The most that can be said of several of these laws is that they agree with observed results to the extent that they are accurate enough for most purposes. Pure Mathematics, on the other hand, is an art and its theorems are universally true. When Pure Mathematics is used to solve a Mechanical problem it is important to distinguish clearly between the use of a scientific law and a mathematical theorem.

CONVENTIONS

Certain factors which have a negligible effect on a problem are often ignored. This has the advantage of simplifying the problem without sacrificing much accuracy, and is best illustrated by an example: consider a heavy bob suspended from a fixed point by means of a thin wire.

The weight of the wire is negligible compared with the weight of the bob, and can be ignored. In such a case it would be described as a *light* wire.

If the dimensions of the bob are small compared with the length of the wire, the bob can be considered as a point and will be described as a *particle*.

If the bob is swinging in still air, then *air resistance* to its motion will be negligible. In fact air resistance is ignored in all problems unless specific mention is made of it.

1

If the bob is in the shape of a flat disc, where the surface area is large compared to its thickness, the thickness is ignored and the bob is described as a circular *lamina*.

If the bob is a spherical shape and the thickness of the material it is made from is small compared to its surface area, this thickness is again ignored and the bob is described as a *hollow* sphere.

If the bob is made to slide across a table, then there will be some frictional resistance to its motion. Although it is rare to find a frictionless surface the amount of friction is often small enough to be ignored and such a surface is described as *smooth*.

Summary of Conventions

Light . . . . Considered weightless
Particle. . . . . . . Object having no dimensions (considered as a point)
Lamina. . . . . . . Flat object, having dimensions of area only
Hollow . . . . 3-dimensional shell of no thickness
Smooth . . . . Frictionless
Air resistance . . . Ignored, unless mention is made of it.

UNITS

Most quantities used in this book are measured in the S.I. system of units. The three basic quantities are *mass*, *length* and *time*. All the other quantities are derived from these three but their definitions are left until the appropriate chapters.

Quantity	Unit	Symbol
mass	kilogramme	kg
length	metre	m
time	second	s
force	newton	N
work	joule	J
power	watt	W

Mechanics deals with the effect of forces acting on bodies, and one effect is that motion is produced. Before the relationship between force and the resulting motion is discussed we will consider them separately.

MOTION

The following quantities are needed to describe the motion of a body:
Distance is the *length* of a given path.

The *unit* of *distance* is the metre (m).

Displacement is the *position* of one point relative to another point: displacement includes both the distance between two points and the direction of the first point from the second point.

Speed is the rate at which a moving body covers its path, no account being taken of the direction of motion.

Unit of speed. The unit of distance is the metre and the unit of time is the second, hence the unit of speed is one metre per second (ms^{-1}).

Velocity is the rate of motion *and* the direction of motion.

Acceleration. When a velocity changes, it can be that either the speed changes, or the direction of motion changes, or both change. Acceleration measures this change either in speed or in direction of motion or both: so acceleration involves direction as well as a magnitude.

Unit of acceleration. The unit of speed is one metre per second, so the unit of acceleration is one metre per second per second (ms^{-2}).

Note that distance and speed involve magnitude only, but displacement, velocity and acceleration involve direction as well as magnitude.

EXAMPLES 1a

1) A particle moves round a square ABCD in the sense indicated by the letters. B is due north of A and C is due west of B and the side of the square is 10 m. If the particle starts from A, what distance has it travelled when it is mid-way between B and C, and what is its displacement then from A?

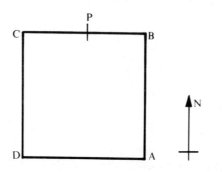

When the particle is at P, the distance travelled = AB + PB   = 15 m

The distance between P and A $\qquad = \sqrt{10^2 + 5^2}$ m $= 5\sqrt{5}$ m
∠ BAP $\qquad\qquad\qquad\qquad\qquad = $ arc tan $\frac{5}{10}$ $= 26°34'$
Therefore the displacement of P from A is $5\sqrt{5}$ m in the direction N26° 34'W.

2) If the particle in example 1 is covering its path at the constant rate of 2 ms^{-1}, what is its speed when travelling along (i) AB, (ii) BC?
State also its velocity when travelling along (i) AB, (ii) BC.

Speed along AB   = 2 ms^{-1}
Speed along BC   = 2 ms^{-1}
Velocity along AB = 2 ms^{-1} due north
Velocity along BC = 2 ms^{-1} due west

Note that although the speed along AB is equal to the speed along BC, the velocity along AB is *not* equal to the velocity along BC.

3) If the particle in example 1 moves so that when moving from C to D its speed increases at the rate of 2 ms^{-2}, while when moving from D to A its speed decreases at the rate of 2 ms^{-2}, what is its acceleration along CD and along DA?

When the particle is moving along CD (the direction of motion is given by the order of the letters: i.e. C to D) the speed is increasing at a rate of 2 ms^{-2}.
Therefore the acceleration = 2 ms^{-2} in the direction CD.
When the particle is moving along DA the speed is decreasing at the rate of 2 ms^{-2}.
Therefore the acceleration = 2 ms^{-2} but in the direction AD, because the speed is decreasing.

EXERCISE 1a

1) A particle moves round the sides of a regular hexagon ABCDEF of side 3 m. The particle starts from A and moves in the sense ABC. What is the distance travelled by the particle and its displacement from A when it is:
(a) at C,
(b) at the midpoint of DE?

2) If the particle in question 1 covers its path at the constant rate of 2 ms^{-1}, what is its displacement from A after 12 s?

3) What is the velocity of the particle in question 2 after:
(a) 5 s,
(b) 10 s?

4) A particle moves with constant speed on the circumference of a circle. Is the velocity constant?

5) A particle moves with a constant speed along the track shown in the diagram.

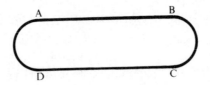

For which sections of its journey is the velocity constant?

FORCE

Most people have an intuitive idea of force: consider a book lying on a horizontal table. We know that force must be applied to the book to move it along the table. Force may be applied directly to the book by pushing it or indirectly by, for example, tying a string to the book and pulling the string. Obviously the movement of the book is related to the amount of force used. The direction in which the force is applied will also affect the movement of the book: with the string horizontal the book will move along the table, with the string vertical the book will be lifted off the table. The point at which the force is applied to the book also affects the result: if the string is attached to one edge of the book and pulled vertically the book will tilt about the opposite edge, but if the string is attached to the middle of the book and pulled vertically no tilting will take place.

So three factors determine the effect that a force has on a body to which it is applied:-

1) The amount, or the *magnitude*, of the applied force. The unit of magnitude is the newton (N).

2) The direction in which the force is applied.

3) The point of application of the force. An alternative way of expressing the direction and point of application of a force is to give its *line of action* and the *sense* of the force along that line.

We also know that the book will not move on its own account. From many such observations it is deduced that: *Force is necessary to make an object begin to move.* Conversely, if an object starts to move then there is a force causing that motion.

WEIGHT

If a body is dropped it will start to fall, so we deduce that there must be a force acting on that body which attracts it to the ground. This force is called the gravitational force or the *weight* of the body; thus the weight of a body is a force and is measured in force units (newton).

If we hold a heavy object we can still feel this gravitational pull, even though the object is not moving: so the weight of a body acts on it at all times, regardless of whether the object is moving or not.

MASS

It is a well known phenomenon that the force with which an object is attracted to the surface of the moon is less than the force with which the same object is attracted to the surface of the earth. It is also found that the weight of an object varies slightly in different places on the surface of the earth. So, although the amount of matter which constitutes an object is an absolute property of that object, its weight is not absolute.

Mass is a measure of the matter contained in an object. The unit of mass is the kilogramme (kg).

Forces Acting on Bodies

Consider again a book lying on a horizontal table.

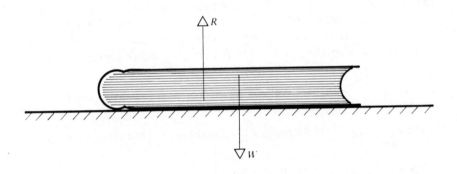

The book is not moving, but there is at least one force acting on it - its weight. If the table was not there the book would fall, so the table must be exerting an upward force on the book to counteract its weight; this force is called the reaction. A reaction force acts on a body whenever that body is in contact with another body which is supporting it.

Consider the book being pulled along the table by a horizontal string attached to the book.

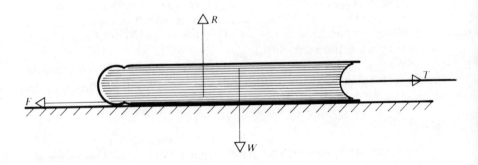

The weight and the reaction will be acting on the book, together with a pull from the string. The pull that the string is exerting on the book is referred to as the tension in the string. If there is friction between the book and the table there will be some resistance to the movement of the book along the table. This resistance is called the frictional force and it will act on a body whenever there is a tendency for that body to move over a rough surface.

SUMMARY

The forces which act on a body come mainly from three sources.

1) Gravitational pull (weight).

2) Contact with another body.

3) Attachment to another body.

(There are other sources, such as wind force, engines etc. which we shall meet later on.)

DIAGRAMS

Before attempting the solution of any problem concerned with the action of forces on a body, it is important to draw a diagram which shows clearly all the forces acting on that body.
The points to remember are:

1) The weight always acts on a body unless it is described as light.

2) If there is contact with another body there will be reaction and possibly friction.

3) If there is attachment to another body (by means of a string, hinge, pivot etc.) there will be a force acting on the body at the point of attachment.

4) Check that there are no other sources of force.

5) Only the forces which are acting on the body itself are considered. A common fault is to include forces which are acting on an object with which the body is in contact.

6) Do not make the diagram too small.

EXAMPLES 1b

1) Draw a diagram to show the forces acting on a block which is sliding down a smooth plane inclined at 20° to the horizontal.

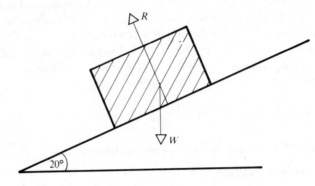

The plane is smooth so there is no friction.

2) Draw a diagram to show the forces acting on a block which is being pulled up a rough plane by a string attached to the block. The plane is inclined at $15°$ to the horizontal and the string is inclined at $30°$ to the horizontal.

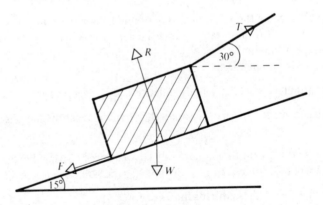

As the plane is rough there will be a frictional force acting down the plane (friction opposes motion).

3) Draw a diagram showing the forces acting on a ladder which is standing with one end on rough horizontal ground and the other end against a rough, vertical wall.

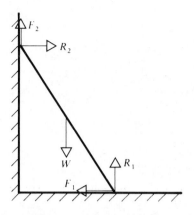

The lower end of the ladder has a tendency to slide away from the wall, so the frictional force acts towards the wall. The upper end of the ladder has a tendency to slide down the wall, so the frictional force acts up the wall.

4) A particle is suspended from a fixed point by a string and it is swinging in a horizontal circle below that point. Draw a diagram to show the forces which are acting on the particle.

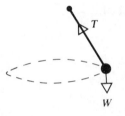

5) A cylindrical tin stands on a smooth table and two smooth spheres rest inside the tin as shown in the sketch.

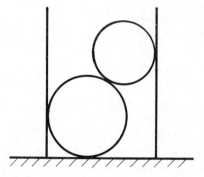

Draw diagrams to show (a) the forces acting on the large sphere, (b) the forces acting on the small sphere, (c) the forces acting on the tin.

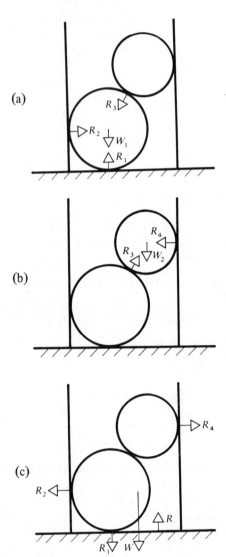

(a)   the forces acting on the large sphere.

(b)   the forces acting on the small sphere.

(c)   the forces acting on the tin.

EXERCISE 1b

1) Draw diagrams to show the forces which are acting on a **block** which is:
(a) at rest on a smooth horizontal surface,
(b) at rest on a rough horizontal surface,
(c) at rest on a rough surface inclined at an angle $20°$ to horizontal,
(d) sliding down a smooth surface inclined at an angle $30°$ to horizontal,
(e) sliding down a rough surface inclined at an angle $30°$ to horizontal ,
(f) pulled down a smooth surface inclined at an angle $10°$ to horizontal by a string parallel to the plane,

(g) pulled down a rough surface inclined at an angle 20° to horizontal by a string parallel to the plane,

(h) pulled along a smooth horizontal surface by a string at an angle 20° to horizontal,

(i) pulled up a rough surface inclined at an angle of 20° to horizontal by a string inclined at an angle of 40° to horizontal.

2) Draw a diagram to show the forces acting on a ladder which is leaning with one end against a smooth vertical wall and the other end standing on rough horizontal ground.

3) Draw a diagram to show the forces acting on a particle which is suspended from a fixed point by a string when:

(a) it is hanging at rest,

(b) it is turning in a vertical circle about the fixed point,

(c) it is turning in a horizontal circle below the fixed point,

(d) the string has broken and it is falling.

4) A ball is thrown in the air. Draw a diagram to show the forces acting on it at any point in its flight.

5) A ladder rests in a vertical plane with one end against a rough vertical wall, and the other end on rough horizontal ground. There is a block tied to the ladder by a string one-third of the way up the ladder. Draw diagrams to show:

(a) the forces acting on the ladder,

(b) the forces acting on the block.

(6) A plank is supported in a horizontal position by two vertical strings, one attached at each end. A block rests on the plank a quarter of the way in from one end. Draw diagrams to show:

(a) the forces acting on the plank,

(b) the forces acting on the block.

7) Two bricks, one on top of the other, rest on a horizontal surface. Draw diagrams to show:

(a) the forces acting on the bottom brick,

(b) the forces acting on the top brick.

8)

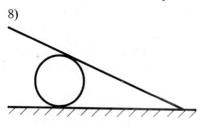

The diagram shows a rough plank resting on a cylinder with one end of the plank on rough ground.

Draw diagrams to show:

(a) the forces acting on the plank,

(b) the forces acting on the cylinder.

CHAPTER 2

VECTORS. COMPONENTS
AND RESULTANTS

DEFINITIONS

Certain quantities are described completely when their magnitude is stated in appropriate units:

e.g. A speed of 50 kmh^{-1}

A mass of 10 kg

A temperature of 30° C

A time of 3 seconds.

Such quantities are called *scalar* quantities.

Other quantities possess both magnitude and direction and are not completely defined unless both of these are specified:

e.g. A velocity of 5 ms^{-1} vertically upward

A force of 10 N vertically downward

A displacement of 8 km due East.

The name for this type of quantity is *vector*.

Vector Representation

Because a vector quantity has both magnitude and direction it can be represented by a segment of a line. The *length* of the line represents the *magnitude* of the vector quantity and the *direction* of the line shows which way the quantity

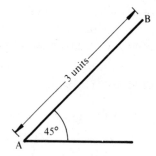

goes. Thus the line AB can be used to represent a displacement vector of 3 m North East.

To indicate that a line segment represents a vector, any of the *vector symbols* AB, $\overrightarrow{AB}$, **r** may be used. In the first two cases the sense of the vector is given by the *order* of the letters but as the single symbol **r** does not include any indication of sense, it must be accompanied by an arrow on the diagram.

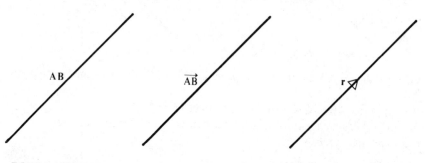

EQUAL VECTORS

Two vectors of *equal magnitude* and with the *same direction* are said to be *equal*.

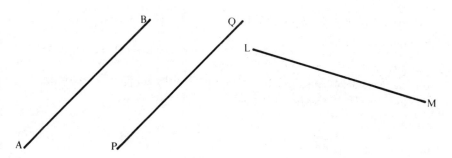

In the diagram the lines AB and PQ are parallel and equal in length hence $\overrightarrow{AB} = \overrightarrow{PQ}$.

Although LM is equal in length to AB these lines are not parallel so $\overrightarrow{AB} \neq \overrightarrow{LM}$. It is, however, correct to write AB = LM since AB and LM are *scalar symbols* referring only to the magnitude of the lines and not to their direction.

PARALLEL VECTORS

Consider two parallel vectors which are in the same sense but have different magnitudes

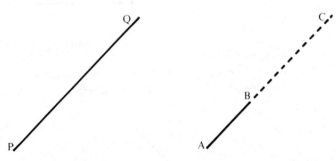

PQ is parallel to AB and the length (magnitude) of PQ is k times the length of AB.

If we produce AB to C so that AC = PQ then AC = kAB.

But AC and PQ are identical in magnitude, direction and sense and therefore represent equal vectors.

Therefore $\overrightarrow{AC} = \overrightarrow{PQ}$

and $k\overrightarrow{AB} = \overrightarrow{PQ}$.

In general the equation $\mathbf{a} = k\mathbf{b}$ means that $\mathbf{a}$ and $\mathbf{b}$ are parallel vectors, the magnitude of $\mathbf{a}$ being k times the magnitude of $\mathbf{b}$.

EQUAL AND OPPOSITE VECTORS

Two parallel vectors of equal magnitude but opposite sense are said to be *equal and opposite*.

Considering a displacement vector $\overrightarrow{AB}$ and the equal and opposite vector $\overrightarrow{BA}$ it is clear that these two together result in zero displacement.

i.e. $\overrightarrow{AB} + \overrightarrow{BA} = \vec{0}$

or $\overrightarrow{AB} = -\overrightarrow{BA}$.

A negative sign in vector work therefore indicates a reversal of sense.

In general if $\mathbf{a} = -\mathbf{b}$ then $\mathbf{a}$ and $\mathbf{b}$ are parallel vectors of equal magnitude but opposite sense.

FREE VECTORS

The representation of a vector by a line segment includes magnitude, direction and sense, but not, in general, the actual location of the vector (its line of action) i.e. if a line AB represents a vector, then any line parallel and equal to AB represents the same vector.

Vectors represented in this way are *free vectors*.

In some circumstances it will be necessary to extend the linear representation of a vector to include its line of action. In this case we shall be dealing with a *tied vector*. e.g. a force acting along a particular line is a tied vector.

EQUIVALENT VECTORS

Consider a displacement $\overrightarrow{AB}$ of 2 m due E followed by a displacement $\overrightarrow{BC}$ of 2 m due N.

The combined effect of these two displacements is the same as a single displacement $\overrightarrow{AC}$ of $2\sqrt{2}$ m NE. Hence

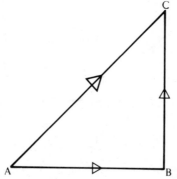

$$\overrightarrow{AB} + \overrightarrow{BC} \equiv \overrightarrow{AC}$$

In this vector equation

\+ means "*together with*"

$\equiv$ means "*is equivalent to*".

We say that $\overrightarrow{AC}$ is the *resultant* of $\overrightarrow{AB}$ and $\overrightarrow{BC}$, or that $\overrightarrow{AB}$ and $\overrightarrow{BC}$ are the *components* of $\overrightarrow{AC}$. The triangle ABC is a vector triangle.

It is possible to find the resultant (or equivalent) vector of more than two components using a similar argument.

Displacements of $\overrightarrow{AB}$, $\overrightarrow{BC}$, $\overrightarrow{CD}$ and $\overrightarrow{DE}$ are equivalent to the single displacement $\overrightarrow{AE}$

i.e. $\overrightarrow{AE} \equiv \overrightarrow{AB} + \overrightarrow{BC} + \overrightarrow{CD} + \overrightarrow{DE}$.

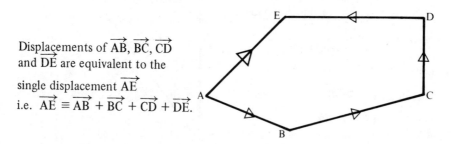

In this case the figure ABCDE is a vector polygon.

N.B. A is the starting point and E the end point both for the set of components and for the resultant.

In most of the illustrations so far, displacement vectors have been used because they are easy to visualise. Other vector quantities can, however, be dealt with in the same way. In fact it was from the results of experiments with force vectors that the concept of vector geometry and algebra first arose. Again it will be noticed that the vectors considered so far have always been in the same plane (coplanar vectors). The principles explained do, however, apply equally well to vectors in three dimensions. The detailed study of vector analysis is dealt with in Volume Two. At this stage it is sufficient to understand how to add and subtract coplanar vectors using the concept of equivalent vectors.

EXAMPLES 2a

1) What is the resultant of displacements 2 m E, 3 m N and 6 m W?

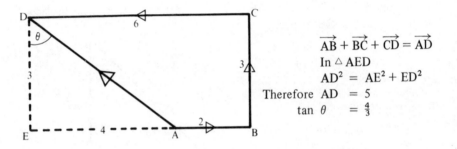

$$\overrightarrow{AB} + \overrightarrow{BC} + \overrightarrow{CD} = \overrightarrow{AD}$$

In $\triangle$ AED

$$AD^2 = AE^2 + ED^2$$

Therefore $AD = 5$

$\tan \theta = \frac{4}{3}$

Therefore the resultant, $\overrightarrow{AD}$, is 5 m in the direction N arctan $\frac{4}{3}$ W.

2) A vector a of magnitude 8 units has two components. One is perpendicular to a and is of magnitude 6 units. What is the magnitude of the other component?

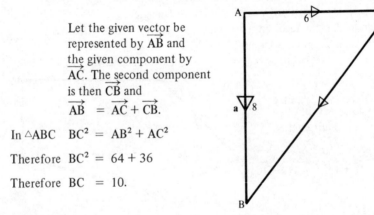

Let the given vector be represented by $\overrightarrow{AB}$ and the given component by $\overrightarrow{AC}$. The second component is then $\overrightarrow{CB}$ and

$$\overrightarrow{AB} = \overrightarrow{AC} + \overrightarrow{CB}.$$

In $\triangle ABC \quad BC^2 = AB^2 + AC^2$

Therefore $BC^2 = 64 + 36$

Therefore $BC = 10$.

The magnitude of the other component is 10 units.

3) In a quadrilateral ABCD, the sides $\overrightarrow{AB}$; $\overrightarrow{BC}$ and $\overrightarrow{DC}$ represent vectors p, q and r respectively. Express in terms of p, q and r the vectors represented by $\overrightarrow{AC}$, $\overrightarrow{AD}$ and $\overrightarrow{DB}$.

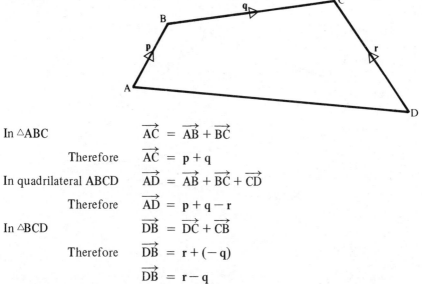

In △ABC	$\overrightarrow{AC} = \overrightarrow{AB} + \overrightarrow{BC}$
	Therefore $\overrightarrow{AC} = p + q$
In quadrilateral ABCD	$\overrightarrow{AD} = \overrightarrow{AB} + \overrightarrow{BC} + \overrightarrow{CD}$
	Therefore $\overrightarrow{AD} = p + q - r$
In △BCD	$\overrightarrow{DB} = \overrightarrow{DC} + \overrightarrow{CB}$
	Therefore $\overrightarrow{DB} = r + (-q)$
	$\overrightarrow{DB} = r - q$

4) ABCDEF is a regular hexagon in which AB represents a vector p and BC represents a vector q.
Express in terms of p and q the vectors which the remaining sides represent.

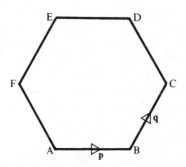

ED is equal and parallel to AB   therefore $\overrightarrow{ED} = p$

FE is equal and parallel to BC   therefore $\overrightarrow{FE} = q$

AD is twice as long as and parallel to BC therefore $AD = 2q$

$$\overrightarrow{CD} = \overrightarrow{CB} + \overrightarrow{BA} + \overrightarrow{AD}$$

Therefore $\overrightarrow{CD} = -q - p + 2q = q - p$ $\overrightarrow{CD} = q - p$

AF is equal and parallel to CD   therefore $\overrightarrow{AF} = q - p$

5) In a pentagon ABCDE:
(a) find the resultant of (i) $\overrightarrow{AB}$, $\overrightarrow{BC}$ and $\overrightarrow{CD}$ (ii) $\overrightarrow{BC}$ and $\overrightarrow{AB}$ (iii) $\overrightarrow{AB} - \overrightarrow{AE}$,
(b) find two sets of components of $\overrightarrow{AD}$.

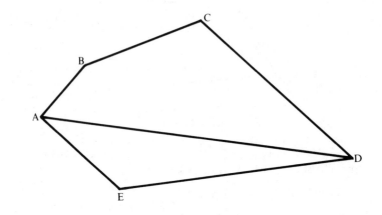

(a) (i) In ABCD $\overrightarrow{AB} + \overrightarrow{BC} + \overrightarrow{CD} = \overrightarrow{AD}$

    (ii) In ABC $\overrightarrow{BC} + \overrightarrow{AB} = \overrightarrow{AB} + \overrightarrow{BC}$

                                                  $= \overrightarrow{AC}$

    (iii) In ABE $\overrightarrow{AB} - \overrightarrow{AE} = \overrightarrow{AB} + \overrightarrow{EA}$

                                                  $= \overrightarrow{EA} + \overrightarrow{AB}$

                                                  $= \overrightarrow{EB}$

(b) In ABCD $\overrightarrow{AD} = \overrightarrow{AB} + \overrightarrow{BC} + \overrightarrow{CD}$

    and in ADE $\overrightarrow{AD} = \overrightarrow{AE} + \overrightarrow{ED}$

These are both suitable sets of components for $\overrightarrow{AD}$.
(We could equally well have chosen the set $\overrightarrow{AB} + \overrightarrow{BD}$ or $\overrightarrow{AC} + \overrightarrow{CD}$).

EXERCISE 2a

1) What is the resultant of the following vectors:- 5 m N, 3 m E and 2 m S?

2) In a quadrilateral ABCD what is the resultant of:
(i) $\overrightarrow{AB} + \overrightarrow{BC}$ (ii) $\overrightarrow{BC} + \overrightarrow{CD}$ (iii) $\overrightarrow{AB} + \overrightarrow{BC} + \overrightarrow{CD}$ (iv) $\overrightarrow{AB} + \overrightarrow{DA}$?

3) ABCDEF is a regular hexagon in which BC represents a vector **b** and FC represents a vector 2**a**. Express in terms of **a** and **b** the vectors represented by AB, CD and BE.

4) Draw diagrams illustrating the following vector equations:
(i) $\overrightarrow{AB} - \overrightarrow{CB} = \overrightarrow{AC}$ (ii) $\overrightarrow{AB} = 2\overrightarrow{PQ}$ (iii) $\overrightarrow{AB} + \overrightarrow{BC} = 3\overrightarrow{AD}$ (iv) **a** + **b** = − **c**.

5) If $\overrightarrow{AB} = \overrightarrow{DC}$ and $\overrightarrow{BC} + \overrightarrow{DA} = \vec{0}$, prove that ABCD is a parallelogram.

6) ABCD is a rectangle. Which of the following statements are true?
(i) $\overrightarrow{BC} = \overrightarrow{DA}$ (ii) $\overrightarrow{BD} = \overrightarrow{AC}$ (iii) $\overrightarrow{AB} + \overrightarrow{CD} = \vec{0}$ (iv) $\overrightarrow{AB} + \overrightarrow{BC} = \overrightarrow{CA}$
(v) $\overrightarrow{AC} + \overrightarrow{CD} = \overrightarrow{AD}$ (vi) $\overrightarrow{AB} + \overrightarrow{BC} = \overrightarrow{AD} + \overrightarrow{DC}$.

7) In an isosceles triangle ABC in which AB = BC and D is the mid-point of AC, show that $\overrightarrow{BA} + \overrightarrow{BC} = 2\overrightarrow{BD}$.

RESOLVING A VECTOR

When a vector is replaced by an equivalent set of components, it has been *resolved.* One of the most useful ways in which to resolve a vector is to choose only two components which are at right angles to each other. The magnitude of these components can be evaluated very easily using trigonometry

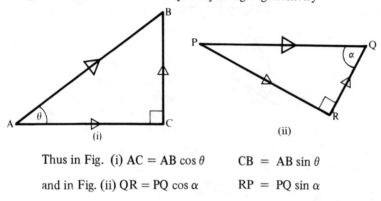

(i)   (ii)

Thus in Fig. (i) $AC = AB \cos \theta$ $CB = AB \sin \theta$

and in Fig. (ii) $QR = PQ \cos \alpha$ $RP = PQ \sin \alpha$

The use of such components is referred to as *resolving in a pair of perpendicular directions.*

EXAMPLES 2b

1) Resolve a weight of 10 N in two directions which are parallel and perpendicular to a slope of inclination $30°$ to the horizontal.

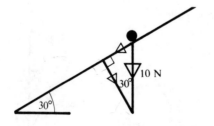

The component parallel to the slope is of magnitude $10 \sin 30°$ N $= 5$ N. The component perpendicular to the slope is of magnitude $10 \cos 30°$ N $= 5\sqrt{3}$ N.

2) Resolve horizontally and vertically a force of 8 N which makes an angle of $45°$ with the horizontal.

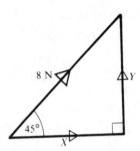

If X and Y are the magnitudes of the two components then

$$X = (8 \cos 45°)N = 4\sqrt{2}\,N$$

$$Y = (8 \sin 45°)N = 4\sqrt{2}\,N$$

3) A body is supported on a rough plane inclined at $30°$ to the horizontal by a string attached to the body and held at an angle of $30°$ to the plane. Draw a diagram showing the forces acting on the body and resolve each of these forces:
(a) horizontally and vertically,
(b) parallel and perpendicular to the plane.

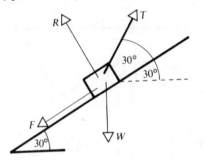

The forces are:

Tension in string	T
Reaction with plane	R
Weight of body	W
Friction	F

(a) Resolving horizontally and vertically

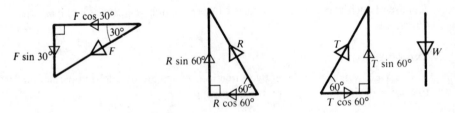

(b) Resolving parallel and perpendicular to the plane

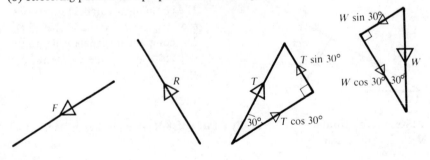

(Note that any force already in one of the directions specified is unchanged and has no component perpendicular to itself).

Sense of Resolved Parts

In the answer to Question (3) above it is worth noticing that, without diagrams, the sense of each component would be unknown. This is because the specification of the required components was not precise enough. The description *parallel to the plane* does not differentiate between the uphill sense and the downhill sense. This ambiguity is avoided if the positive sense of the required components is stated at the outset. A component in the opposite sense is then negative. Using Question 3 to demonstrate this approach, the answer could be given as follows:

(a) Resolving horizontally and vertically in the senses Ox and Oy as shown, the components are:

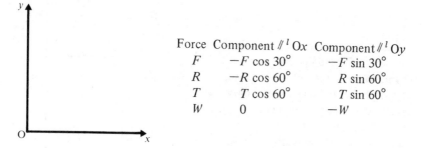

Force	Component $/\!/^{1} Ox$	Component $/\!/^{1} Oy$
F	$-F \cos 30°$	$-F \sin 30°$
R	$-R \cos 60°$	$R \sin 60°$
T	$T \cos 60°$	$T \sin 60°$
W	0	$-W$

(b) Resolving parallel and perpendicular to the plane in the sense Ox' and Oy' as shown:

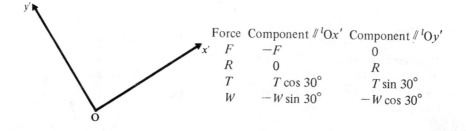

Force	Component $/\!/^{1}Ox'$	Component $/\!/^{1}Oy'$
F	$-F$	0
R	0	R
T	$T \cos 30°$	$T \sin 30°$
W	$-W \sin 30°$	$-W \cos 30°$

CARTESIAN VECTOR NOTATION

Components in perpendicular directions can be expressed more simply if we use the symbols **i** and **j** where

i is a vector of magnitude one unit in the direction Ox
and **j** is a vector of magnitude one unit in the direction Oy.

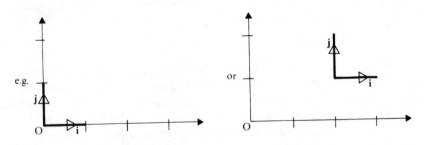

Thus 3i means a vector of magnitude 3 units in the direction Ox and 4j means a vector of magnitude 4 units in the direction Oy.

If a force vector **F** has components parallel to Ox and Oy of magnitudes 3 and 4 units respectively then using the symbols **i** and **j** we can say more simply that **F** has components 3i and 4j. As **F** is equivalent to the vector sum of its components, $F = 3i + 4j$.

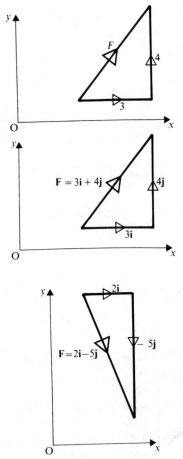

Conversely if a force **F** is such that $F = 2i - 5j$, this means that **F** has components of magnitude 2 units in the direction Ox and 5 units in the direction $-Oy$. The diagram shows how **F** can be represented.

EXAMPLE

Forces F_1, F_2, F_3 and F_4 have magnitudes 6, 2, 3 and $3\sqrt{2}$ N respectively and act in direction as shown in the diagram below. By finding the components of each force in the directions Ox and Oy, express each force in the form $ai + bj$.

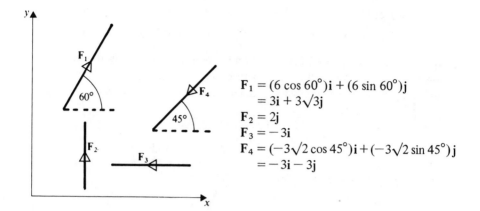

$$F_1 = (6 \cos 60°)i + (6 \sin 60°)j$$
$$= 3i + 3\sqrt{3}j$$
$$F_2 = 2j$$
$$F_3 = -3i$$
$$F_4 = (-3\sqrt{2} \cos 45°)i + (-3\sqrt{2} \sin 45°)j$$
$$= -3i - 3j$$

EXERCISE 2b

1) Calculate the magnitude of the horizontal and vertical components of:
(a) A force of 6 N inclined at $20°$ to the horizontal.
(b) A velocity of 20 ms^{-1} inclined at $30°$ to the vertical.
(c) A tension of 8 N in a string of length 10 m which has one end fastened to the top of a flagpole of height 6 m and the other end fixed to the ground.

2) What are the components parallel and perpendicular to an incline of $30°$ of a weight of 4 N?

3) An object of weight W is fastened to one end of a string whose other end is fixed and is pulled sideways by a horizontal force P until the string is inclined at $20°$ to the vertical. Draw a diagram showing the forces acting on the object and resolve each force parallel and perpendicular to the string.

4) Figure 1 shows the forces acting on a body. Express each force in terms of components parallel to AP (i) and AQ (j).

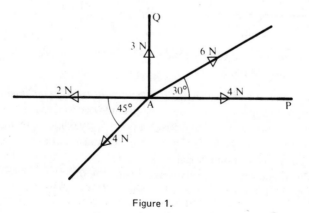

Figure 1.

5) Using axes Ox and Oy, mark on a diagram the following force vectors.

$$\mathbf{F}_1 = \mathbf{i} + \mathbf{j}; \quad \mathbf{F}_2 = 2\mathbf{i} - \mathbf{j}; \quad \mathbf{F}_3 = -3\mathbf{i} + 4\mathbf{j}; \quad \mathbf{F}_4 = -\mathbf{i} - 3\mathbf{j}.$$

6) A boat is steering due North at 24 kmh^{-1} in a current running at 6 kmh^{-1} due West. A wind is blowing the boat North East at 10 kmh^{-1} (Figure 2). What are the components of each velocity in the directions East and North?

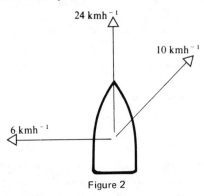

24 kmh^{-1}

10 kmh^{-1}

6 kmh^{-1}

Figure 2

DETERMINATION OF RESULTANT VECTORS

A single vector **R** equivalent to a set of vectors is the resultant of those vectors (which are, themselves, the components of **R**). The method of evaluating **R** depends upon the number and type of vectors in the given set.

CASE 1 *The resultant of two perpendicular vectors of magnitudes X and Y*

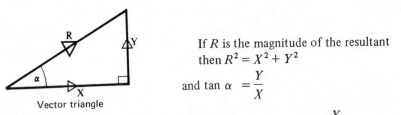

R

Y

α

X

Vector triangle

If R is the magnitude of the resultant then $R^2 = X^2 + Y^2$

and $\tan \alpha = \dfrac{Y}{X}$

Therefore the resultant is of magnitude $\sqrt{X^2 + Y^2}$ and makes $\arctan \dfrac{Y}{X}$ with the component of magnitude X.

CASE 2 *The resultant of two vectors of magnitudes P and Q inclined at an angle θ* At this point it becomes important to understand what is meant by the angle between two vectors. Suppose that, from a point O, two line segments are drawn representing the vectors **P** and **Q**. Then if both vectors point away from O as in Fig. (i), or both vectors point towards O as in Fig. (ii), the angle between the lines at O is θ. But if one vector points towards O and the other points away from O as in Fig. (iii) then the angle between the lines at O is $(180° - \theta)$.

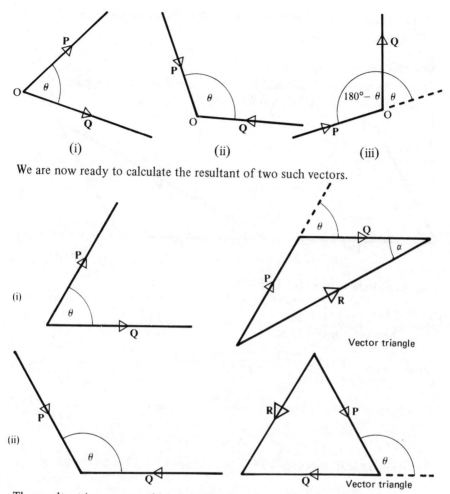

We are now ready to calculate the resultant of two such vectors.

Vector triangle

Vector triangle

The resultant is represented by the third side of a triangle formed by drawing a line representing the vector of magnitude P followed by a line representing the vector of magnitude Q (note that θ is an exterior angle of this triangle). Then the magnitude R of the resultant can be found using the cosine formula

$$R^2 = P^2 + Q^2 - 2PQ \cos (180° - \theta)$$

or
$$R^2 = P^2 + Q^2 + 2PQ \cos \theta.$$

The direction of the resultant can next be determined using the sine rule

$$\frac{\sin \alpha}{P} = \frac{\sin (180° - \theta)}{R}$$

or
$$\sin \alpha = \frac{P \sin \theta}{R}$$

These formulae for calculating the values of R and α are valid whether θ is acute {fig. (i)} or obtuse {fig. (ii)}.

EXAMPLES 2c

1) Find the resultant of two vectors of magnitudes 8 units and 10 units if the angle between them is (a) $60°$ (b) $90°$ (c) $120°$.

(a)

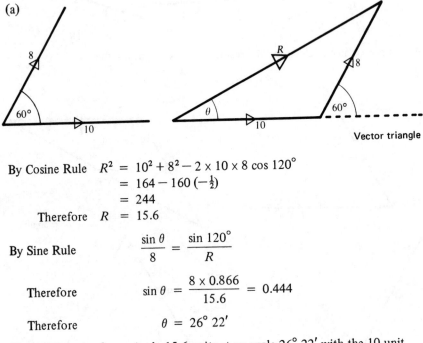

Vector triangle

By Cosine Rule $\quad R^2 = 10^2 + 8^2 - 2 \times 10 \times 8 \cos 120°$
$$= 164 - 160 \left(-\tfrac{1}{2}\right)$$
$$= 244$$
Therefore $\quad R = 15.6$

By Sine Rule $\qquad \dfrac{\sin \theta}{8} = \dfrac{\sin 120°}{R}$

Therefore $\qquad \sin \theta = \dfrac{8 \times 0.866}{15.6} = 0.444$

Therefore $\qquad \theta = 26° \, 22'$

The resultant is of magnitude 15.6 units at an angle $26° \, 22'$ with the 10 unit vector.

(b)

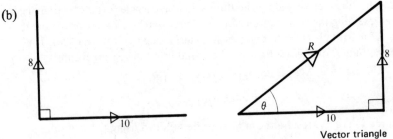

Vector triangle

Using Pythagoras' Theorem $\quad R^2 = 8^2 + 10^2 = 164$
Therefore $\quad R = 12.8$
and $\quad \tan \theta = \dfrac{8}{10}$
Therefore $\quad \theta = 38° \, 39'$.

The resultant is of magnitude 12.8 units at an angle 38° 39′ with the 10 unit vector.

(c)

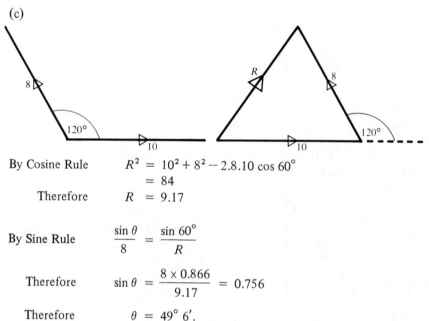

By Cosine Rule $R^2 = 10^2 + 8^2 - 2.8.10 \cos 60°$
                                $= 84$

Therefore $R = 9.17$

By Sine Rule $\dfrac{\sin \theta}{8} = \dfrac{\sin 60°}{R}$

Therefore $\sin \theta = \dfrac{8 \times 0.866}{9.17} = 0.756$

Therefore $\theta = 49° 6′$.

The resultant is of magnitude 9.17 units at an angle 49° 6′ with the 10 unit vector.

2) When two vectors of magnitudes P and Q are inclined at an angle θ the magnitude of their resultant is $2P$. When the inclination is changed to $(180° - \theta)$ the magnitude of the resultant is halved. Find the ratio of $P:Q$.

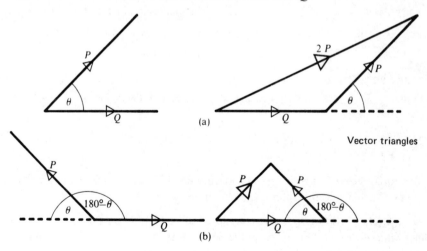

(a)

Vector triangles

(b)

In(a) $(2P)^2 = P^2 + Q^2 + 2PQ \cos \theta$

In (b) $(P)^2 = P^2 + Q^2 - 2PQ \cos \theta$

Therefore $2PQ \cos \theta = 3P^2 - Q^2$

and $2PQ \cos \theta = Q^2$

Therefore $Q^2 = 3P^2 - Q^2$

                        $2Q^2 = 3P^2$

Therefore $P:Q = \sqrt{2}:\sqrt{3}.$

3) Find the magnitude and inclination to Ox of a force vector **F** if
(a) **F** = 3**i** + 4**j** (b) **F** = −**i** + **j**

(a)

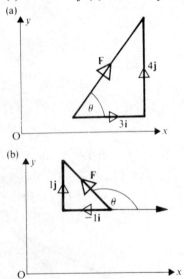

Since **F** has components of 3 and 4 units in perpendicular directions the magnitude of **F** (which is indicated by |F|) is given by

$$|F| = \sqrt{(3^2 + 4^2)} = 5$$

The inclination of **F** to Ox is θ where $\tan \theta = 4/3$

(b)

The magnitude of **F** is given by
$$|F| = \sqrt{(1^2 + 1^2)} = \sqrt{2}$$
The inclination of **F** to Ox is θ where
$$\theta = 180° - \arctan(1/1)$$
i.e. $\theta = 180° - 45° = 135°$

EXERCISE 2c

1) Find the resultant of forces of magnitudes 3 N and 4 N if they are at right angles.

2) Two forces of magnitudes 10 N and 6 N are inclined at 60°. What is the magnitude and direction of their resultant?

3) A force vector **F** = p**i** + 12**j** has a magnitude of 13 units. Find the two possible values of p and the corresponding inclinations of **F** to Ox.

4) An aircraft is flying with an engine speed of 400 kmh^{-1} on a course due North in a wind of speed 60 kmh^{-1} from the South West. At what speed is the aircraft covering the ground?

5) Two vectors have magnitudes of 4 units and 6 units. Find the angle between

them if their resultant is of magnitude (a) 8 units (b) 4 units.

6) A force of 8 N together with a force P have a resultant of magnitude 17 N. Find the value of P if the angle between the two forces is (a) 90° (b) 60°.

7) Two forces of magnitudes P and $2P$ are inclined at an angle θ. Find θ if the resultant is of magnitude (a) $2P$ (b) $3P$ (c) P. (It should not be necessary to use the cosine rule in all three cases).

CASE 3 *The resultant of more than two vectors.*
Consider a set of four vectors whose magnitudes and directions are shown in diagram (i). The resultant can be found by drawing consecutive lines representing the given vectors in magnitude and direction; the line which completes the polygon represents the resultant (diagram (ii)).

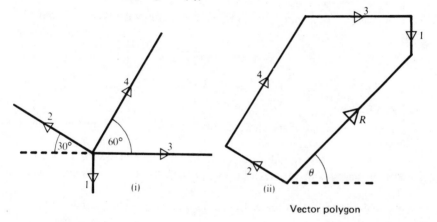

Vector polygon

Careful drawing to scale and measurement give values for the magnitude R and the direction θ of the resultant. The values obtained in this way however are only as accurate as the drawing; more precise values will be given by calculation as follows:

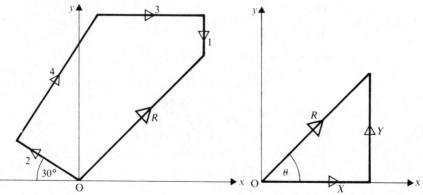

Suppose that the components of R in the directions Ox and Oy are X and Y. The value of X is the sum of the components of the original vectors in the direction Ox and the value of Y is their sum in the direction Oy.

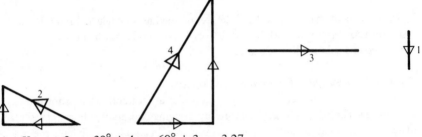

i.e. $X = -2 \cos 30° + 4 \cos 60° + 3 = 3.27$
$Y = 2 \sin 30° + 4 \sin 60° - 1 = 3.46$

Now the resultant of X and Y (two perpendicular components) can be found using

$$R = \sqrt{X^2 + Y^2} = \sqrt{22.66} = 4.76$$

$$\text{and } \tan \theta = \frac{Y}{X} = \frac{3.46}{3.27} = 1.06$$

Therefore the resultant of the given vectors is a vector of magnitude 4.76 units inclined at $46° \, 40'$ to Ox.

X and Y are very easily found if the forces are expressed in the form $\mathbf{F} = p\mathbf{i} + q\mathbf{j}$ since p and q represent the components of $\mathbf{F}$ in the directions Ox and Oy.

Suppose, for instance, that forces $\mathbf{F_1}$, $\mathbf{F_2}$, $\mathbf{F_3}$ and $\mathbf{F_4}$ act on a particle P as shown in the diagram, and

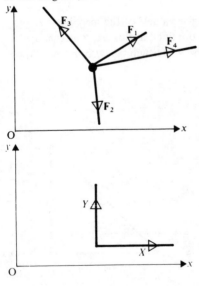

$$\mathbf{F_1} = 2\mathbf{i} + \mathbf{j}$$
$$\mathbf{F_2} = \mathbf{i} - 3\mathbf{j}$$
$$\mathbf{F_3} = -3\mathbf{i} + 4\mathbf{j}$$
$$\mathbf{F_4} = 4\mathbf{i} + \mathbf{j}$$

Their resultant can be expressed in the form $X\mathbf{i} + Y\mathbf{j}$ where

$$X = (2 + 1 - 3 + 4)$$
$$\text{and } Y = (1 - 3 + 4 + 1)$$

The resultant force can hence be represented by $4\mathbf{i} + 3\mathbf{j}$

EXAMPLES 2d

1) Find the resultant of forces of magnitudes 5, 4, 3, 2 and 1 newton, the angle between consecutive pairs being 30°.

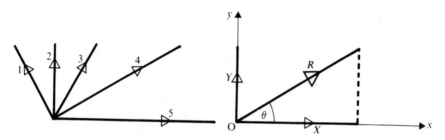

Let the resultant have components X and Y newtons parallel to Ox and Oy as shown. Resolving all forces along Ox and Oy we have:

$$\rightarrow X = 5 + 4 \cos 30° + 3 \cos 60° - 1 \cos 60° = 9.46$$

$$\uparrow Y = 4 \sin 30° + 3 \sin 60° + 2 + 1 \sin 60° = 7.46$$

Then

$$R = \sqrt{X^2 + Y^2} = \sqrt{(9.46)^2 + (7.46)^2} = \sqrt{145.2}$$

$$R = 12.1$$

and $\tan \theta = \dfrac{Y}{X} = \dfrac{7.46}{9.46} = 0.789$

Therefore the resultant is a force of 12.1 N making an angle of 38° 16′ with the 5 N force.

2) A river is flowing due East at a speed of 3 ms^{-1}. A boy in a rowing boat who can row at 5 ms^{-1} in still water starts from a point O on the South bank and steers the boat at right angles to the bank. The boat is also being blown by the wind at 4 ms^{-1} South West. Taking axes Ox and Oy in the directions East and North respectively find the velocity of the boat in the form $p\mathbf{i} + q\mathbf{j}$ and hence find its resultant speed.

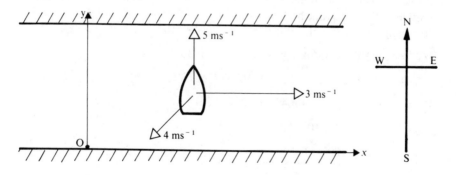

The velocity of the river can be written as $3\mathbf{i}$
The velocity due to rowing can be written as $5\mathbf{j}$
The velocity of the wind can be written as $-4\cos 45°\,\mathbf{i} - 4\cos 45°\,\mathbf{j}$
i.e. $-2\sqrt{2}\mathbf{i} - 2\sqrt{2}\mathbf{j}$

The resultant velocity $\mathbf{v}$ is then given by

$$\mathbf{v} = 3\mathbf{i} + 5\mathbf{j} + (-2\sqrt{2}\mathbf{i} - 2\sqrt{2}\mathbf{j})$$
$$\text{i.e. } \mathbf{v} = (3 - 2\sqrt{2})\,\mathbf{i} + (5 - 2\sqrt{2})\mathbf{j}$$

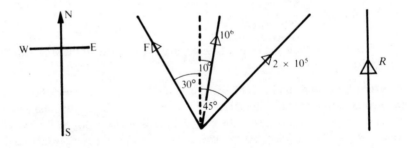

$(5 - 2\sqrt{2})\mathbf{j}$

$(3 - 2\sqrt{2})\mathbf{i}$

The resultant speed is the magnitude of the resultant velocity (i.e. $|\mathbf{v}|$) where

$$|\mathbf{v}| = \sqrt{(3 - 2\sqrt{2})^2 + (5 - 2\sqrt{2})^2} = \sqrt{50 - 32\sqrt{2}}$$

3) Three tugs are pulling a liner due North into a harbour. The ropes attaching the liner to the tugs are in the directions NE, N 10° E and N 30° W. If the tensions in the first two ropes are 2×10^5 N and 10^6 N, find the tension in the third rope and the resultant pull on the liner.

[Since the liner is being moved due North, the resultant pull R newton is in that direction (there is no overall component in the East-West direction)]. Let the tension in the third rope be F newton.
Resolving all forces in the directions East and North

$$\rightarrow 0 = 2 \times 10^5 \sin 45° + 10^6 \sin 10° - F \sin 30° \qquad (1)$$

$$\uparrow R = 2 \times 10^5 \cos 45° + 10^6 \cos 10° + F \cos 30° \qquad (2)$$

From (1) $\tfrac{1}{2}F = 10^5 (2\sin 45° + 10\sin 10°)$

$$F = 2 \times 10^5 (1.414 + 1.736)$$

$$F = 10^5 \times 6.3$$

From (2) $R = 10^5 (2 \cos 45° + 10 \cos 10° + 6.3 \cos 30°)$

$\qquad = 10^5 (1.414 + 9.848 + 5.456)$

$\qquad R = 10^5 \times 16.718.$

Therefore the tension in the third rope is 6.3×10^5 N and the resultant pull on the liner is 1.67×10^6 N.

4) A passenger walks directly across the deck of a ship from starboard to port at a speed of 6 kmh^{-1}. The ship which is travelling through the water at 20 kmh^{-1} is steering due North in a current running South East at 4 kmh^{-1}. In what direction is the passenger actually moving?

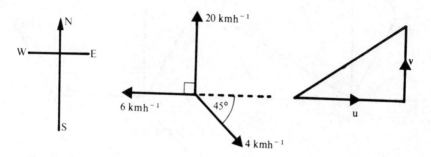

Let the velocity of the passenger have components u and $v \text{ kmh}^{-1}$ in the directions East and North.
Resolving all velocities East and North we have:

$$\rightarrow u = 4 \cos 45° - 6 = -3.17$$

$$\uparrow v = 20 - 4 \sin 45° = 17.17$$

A velocity of -3.17 kmh^{-1} Eastward is really a velocity of $+3.17 \text{ kmh}^{-1}$ Westward.

Passenger's velocity therefore has components as shown and:-

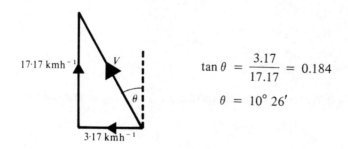

$$\tan \theta = \frac{3.17}{17.17} = 0.184$$

$$\theta = 10° 26'$$

Therefore the passenger moves in a direction N 10° 26′ W.

5) ABCDEF is a regular hexagon. Forces of magnitudes $3F$, $4F$, $2F$, $6F$ act along $\overrightarrow{AB}$, $\overrightarrow{AC}$, $\overrightarrow{EA}$, $\overrightarrow{AF}$, respectively. Find the magnitude and direction of their resultant. (*N.B. Only the direction* of the forces is denoted by $\overrightarrow{AB}$ etc. The magnitudes are given separately and are *not* represented by the lengths of the lines AB, etc.)

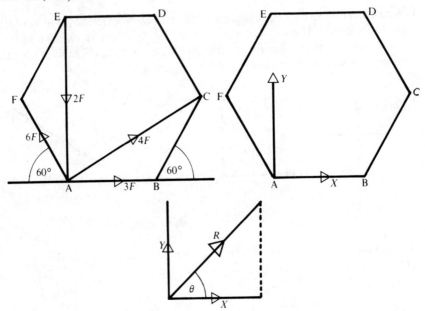

Let the resultant have components X and Y parallel to AB and AE as shown. Resolving all forces along AB and AE we have:

$$X = 3F + 4F\cos 30° - 6F\cos 60° = 2\sqrt{3}F$$

$$Y = 4F\sin 30° - 2F + 6F\sin 60° = 3\sqrt{3}F$$

Then

$$R = \sqrt{X^2 + Y^2} = F\sqrt{3}\sqrt{2^2 + 3^2}$$

$$R = F\sqrt{39}$$

and $\tan\theta = \dfrac{Y}{X} = \dfrac{3\sqrt{3}}{2\sqrt{3}} = 1.5$

Therefore the resultant is a force of magnitude $F\sqrt{39}$ making an angle arctan 1.5 with AB.

EXERCISE 2d

1) Find the resultant of forces of magnitudes 4, 3 and 6 newton acting in the directions AB, BC and CA respectively, where ABC is an equilateral triangle.

2) Starting from O, a point **P** traces out consecutive displacement vectors of $2\mathbf{i} + 3\mathbf{j}$; $-\mathbf{i} + 4\mathbf{j}$; $7\mathbf{i} - 5\mathbf{j}$ and $\mathbf{i} + 3\mathbf{j}$. What is the displacement of **P** from O?

3) Three boys are pulling a heavy trolley by means of three ropes. The boy in the middle is exerting a pull of 100 N. The other two boys, whose ropes both make an angle of $30°$ with the centre rope, are pulling with forces of 80 N and 140 N. What is the resultant pull on the trolley and in what direction will it move?

4) A surveyor starts from a point O and walks 200 m due North. He then turns clockwise through $120°$ and walks 100 m after which he walks 300 m due West. What is his resultant displacement from O?

5) An object A is subjected to forces of 5 N, 2 N and 3 N inclined at $30°, 90°$ and $150°$ respectively to the line AB. Taking AB as the x-axis, express their resultant in the form $a\mathbf{i} + b\mathbf{j}$.

6) A small boat is travelling through the water with an engine speed of 8 kmh^{-1}. It is being steered due East but there is a current running South at 2 kmh^{-1} and wind is blowing the boat South West at 4 kmh^{-1}. Find the resultant velocity of the boat.

7) Rain, which is falling vertically, makes streaks on the vertical sides of a van travelling at 80 kmh^{-1}. If the streaks are at $30°$ to the vertical, calculate the speed of the raindrops.

8) Forces of magnitudes $2P, 3P, 4P, 5P$, act along $\overrightarrow{AB}, \overrightarrow{AC}, \overrightarrow{AD}, \overrightarrow{AE}$, respectively. Find the magnitude and direction of their resultant if:
(a) ABCDEF is a regular hexagon,
(b) ABCDE is made up of a square ABCE together with an equilateral triangle CDE (D is outside the square).

Turning Effect of Forces

(a) Consider two equal and opposite forces each of magnitude F acting at the centre of a rod AB.

Resolving // to AB

$X = 0$

Resolving ⊥r to AB

$Y = F - F = 0$

$\sqrt{X^2 + Y^2} = 0$

We know from experience that the rod will not be moved and this is consistent with the results of resolving the forces parallel and perpendicular to the rod; viz. the resultant force is zero.

(b) Now consider the same two forces acting one at A and one at B.

This time we notice that the rod will rotate, although the method of resolving the forces again indicates that the resultant force is zero. Clearly then the turning effect (if any) of a set of forces cannot be found by the method of resolving in two perpendicular directions.

Resolving $\parallel^1$ to AB

$X = 0$

Resolving $\perp$r to AB

$Y = 0$

$\sqrt{X^2 + Y^2} = 0$

The detailed study of turning effect is dealt with in Chapter 14. At this stage it is sufficient to appreciate that in some cases a set of forces may exert not only a linear effect but also a turning effect on the body to which the forces are applied. *Concurrent forces however have no turning effect (see (a) above).*

SUMMARY

1) Two parallel vectors of equal magnitude are:
(a) *equal* if they have the same sense,
(b) *equal and opposite* if they have opposite senses.

2) When lines representing vectors in magnitude and direction are drawn consecutively the line which completes the polygon represents the resultant vector.

3) The resultant of two vectors **P** and **Q** inclined at an angle θ has magnitude R given by $R^2 = P^2 + Q^2 + 2PQ \cos \theta$.

4) The resultant of more than two vectors is calculated by resolving in two perpendicular directions.

5) In general a set of forces *may* exert a turning effect on a body but if all the forces pass through the same point there can be no turning effect.

MULTIPLE CHOICE EXERCISE 2

The instructions for answering these questions are given on page (xii)

TYPE I

1) The resultant of displacements 2 m South, 4 m West, 5 m North is of magnitude:
(a) 3 m   (b) 7 m   (c) 5 m   (d) $\sqrt{65}$ m   (e) 11 m.

2) If ABCD is a quadrilateral whose sides represent vectors, $\overrightarrow{AB}$ is equivalent to:
(a) $\overrightarrow{CA} + \overrightarrow{CB}$ (b) $\overrightarrow{CD}$ (c) $\overrightarrow{AD} + \overrightarrow{DC} + \overrightarrow{CB}$ (d) $\overrightarrow{AD} + \overrightarrow{BD}$ (e) $\overrightarrow{AC} - \overrightarrow{CB}$.

3) The horizontal component of a force of 10 N inclined at $30°$ to the vertical is:

(a) 5 N   (b) $5\sqrt{3}$ N   (c) 3 N   (d) $\dfrac{10}{3}$ N   (e) $\dfrac{10}{\sqrt{3}}$ N

4) Two vectors inclined at an angle θ have magnitudes 3 N and 5 N and their resultant is of magnitude 4 N. The angle θ is:

(a) $90°$ (b) $\arccos \dfrac{4}{5}$ (c) $\arccos \dfrac{3}{5}$ (d) $\arccos \dfrac{-3}{5}$ (e) $60°$

5) Two forces $\mathbf{F_1}$ and $\mathbf{F_2}$ have a resultant $\mathbf{F_3}$. If $\mathbf{F_1} = 2\mathbf{i} - 3\mathbf{j}$ and $\mathbf{F_3} = 5\mathbf{i} + 4\mathbf{j}$ then $\mathbf{F_2}$ is:

(a) $7\mathbf{i} + \mathbf{j}$ (b) $-3\mathbf{i} - 7\mathbf{j}$ (c) $3\mathbf{i} + 7\mathbf{j}$ (d) $7\mathbf{i} + 7\mathbf{j}$

TYPE II

6) $\overrightarrow{AB}$ and $\overrightarrow{PQ}$ are two vectors such that $\overrightarrow{AB} = 2\overrightarrow{PQ}$.
(a) AB is parallel to PQ.
(b) PQ is twice as long as AB.
(c) A, B, P and Q must be collinear.

7) The vector equation $\overrightarrow{AC} = \overrightarrow{AB} + \overrightarrow{BC}$ applies to:

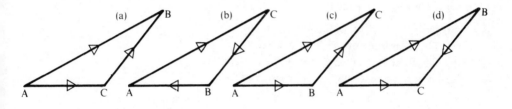

8) ABCD is a parallelogram.
(a) $\overrightarrow{AB} = \overrightarrow{CD}$ (b) $\overrightarrow{AD} = \overrightarrow{BC}$ (c) $\overrightarrow{AB} + \overrightarrow{BC} = \overrightarrow{CD} + \overrightarrow{DA}$ (d) $\overrightarrow{BC} + \overrightarrow{CD} = \overrightarrow{BA} + \overrightarrow{AD}$.

9) A force $\mathbf{F} = 3\mathbf{i} + 4\mathbf{j}$.
(a) The magnitude of the force is 5 units.
(b) The component of magnitude 3 units must be horizontal.
(c) The direction of the force is at $\arctan \frac{4}{3}$ to the x axis.

TYPE III

10) (a) A force $\mathbf{F} = 2\mathbf{i} + 3\mathbf{j}$.
   (b) A force has perpendicular components of magnitudes 2 and 3 units.

11) AB and PQ are two lines in the same plane:
(a) $\underline{AB} = 3\underline{PQ}$.
(b) $\overrightarrow{AB} = 3\overrightarrow{PQ}$.

12) ABC is a triangle:
(a) $\overrightarrow{AC} = \overrightarrow{AB} + \overrightarrow{BC}$.
(b) $\overrightarrow{AB} = \overrightarrow{AC} + \overrightarrow{CB}$.

TYPE IV

13) Calculate the magnitude of the resultant of two forces F_1 and F_2.
(a) $F_1 = 3i + 7j$.
(b) $F_2 = i - 4j$.
(c) Both forces act at a point $2i + j$.

14) ABCDEF is a hexagon. Find, in terms of a and b, the vectors which the remaining sides represent if:
(a) $\overrightarrow{AB} = a$,
(b) the hexagon is regular,
(c) $\overrightarrow{FC} = b$.

15) Six forces acting on a particle have directions parallel to the sides AB, BC, CD, DE, EF, FA of a hexagon. Find the magnitude and direction of their resultant if:
(a) the forces have magnitudes $F, 2F, 3F, 2F, 2F, F$ respectively,
(b) the sense of each force is indicated by the order of the letters,
(c) the hexagon is regular.

16) Express a force F in the form $ai + bj$.
(a) The magnitude of the force is 5 N.
(b) The force is inclined at $60°$ to the horizontal.
(c) j is in the direction of the upward vertical.

TYPE V

17) The resultant of $\overrightarrow{AB}$ and $\overrightarrow{BC}$ is $\overrightarrow{CA}$.

18) Two vectors of equal magnitude and which are in the same direction are equal vectors.

19) A particle of weight W is on a plane inclined at α to the horizontal. The component of the weight parallel to the plane is $W \cos \alpha$.

20) The resultant of two vectors of magnitudes P and Q and inclined at $60°$ is $\sqrt{P^2 + Q^2 - PQ}$.

21) If $F_1 = 2i + 3j$ and $F_2 = 2i - 3j$ then F_1 and F_2 are equal and opposite.

MISCELLANEOUS EXERCISE 2

1) A force of 30 N is inclined at an angle θ to the horizontal. If its vertical component is 18 N, find the horizontal component and the value of θ.

2) Resolve a vector into two perpendicular components so that:
(i) the components are of equal magnitudes,
(ii) the magnitude of one component is twice that of the other.

3) Forces of magnitudes 2, 3, 2 and 5 newton act at a point. The angles

between them are $30°$, $60°$ and $30°$ respectively. Calculate their resultant and verify your results by drawing a suitable scale diagram.

4) Forces represented by $3i + 5j$, $i - 2j$ and $-3i + j$ together with a fourth force F act on a particle. If the resultant force is represented by $4i + j$, find F.

5) ABCDEF is a regular hexagon. Forces acting along $\overrightarrow{CB}$, $\overrightarrow{CA}$, $\overrightarrow{CF}$ and $\overrightarrow{CD}$ are of magnitudes 2, 4, 5 and 6 newton respectively. What is the inclination of their resultant to CF?

6) If a represents a velocity of 4 ms^{-1} North East and b represents a velocity of 6 ms^{-1} West, what velocities are represented by:
(i) $-2a$ (ii) $a + b$ (iii) $3b - a$?

7) In a regular pentagon ABCDE:
(a) what is the resultant of: (i) $\overrightarrow{AB} + \overrightarrow{BC}$ (ii) $\overrightarrow{EA} - \overrightarrow{BA}$,
(b) prove that $\overrightarrow{AD} + \overrightarrow{DC} = \overrightarrow{AB} - \overrightarrow{CB}$.

8) ABCD is a parallelogram. What represents the resultant of forces represented by $\overrightarrow{AB}$, $\overrightarrow{BC}$, $\overrightarrow{BD}$ and $\overrightarrow{CA}$?

9) ABC is an equilateral triangle and D is the mid-point of BC. Forces of 1, 2, 4 and $3\sqrt{3}$ newton act along $\overrightarrow{BC}$, $\overrightarrow{BA}$, $\overrightarrow{CA}$ and $\overrightarrow{AD}$ respectively. Resolve each of the forces in the directions BC and DA and verify that the sum of the components in each direction is zero.

10) A force of $2\sqrt{2} \text{ N}$ acts along the diagonal AC of a square ABCD and another force P acts along AD. If the resultant force is inclined at $60°$ to AB find the value of P.

11) Forces of magnitudes $2P$, $4P$, $3P$ and P act on a particle in directions parallel to the sides $\overrightarrow{AB}$, $\overrightarrow{BC}$, $\overrightarrow{CD}$ and $\overrightarrow{DE}$ of a regular hexagon. Find the magnitude and direction of their resultant.

12) Forces of 9, 2, 5 and 1 newton act along the sides OA, AB, BC and CO of a rectangle OABC and a force of 15 newtons acts along AC. $OA = 4a$ and $AB = 3a$. Taking OA and OC as x and y axes respectively find an expression for the resultant force vector in the form $Xi + Yj$.

13) A quadrilateral ABCD has opposite sides AB and DC parallel. Angle $ABC = 150°$ and angle $BAD = 60°$. Forces $2P, P, P, 2P$ act along $\overrightarrow{AB}$, $\overrightarrow{BC}$, $\overrightarrow{CD}$, $\overrightarrow{AD}$ respectively. Prove that the resultant has magnitude $P(8 + 3\sqrt{3})^{\frac{1}{2}}$ and find the tangent of the angle it makes with AB.   (U of L)

14) Forces P and Q act along lines OA and OB respectively and their resultant is a force of magnitude P. If the force P along OA is replaced by a force $2P$ along OA, the resultant of $2P$ and Q is also a force of magnitude P. Find:
(a) the magnitude of Q in terms of P,
(b) the angle between OA and OB,

(c) the angles which the two resultants make with OA.

(Oxford)

15) A plane lamina has perpendicular axes Ox and Oy marked on it, and is acted upon by the following forces:

$5P$ in the direction Oy,

$4P$ in the direction Ox,

$6P$ in the direction OA where A is the point $(3a, 4a)$,

$8P$ in the direction AB where B is the point $(-a, a)$.

Express each force in the form $p\mathbf{i} + q\mathbf{j}$ and hence calculate the magnitude and direction of the resultant of these forces.

16) A speedboat which can travel at 20 knots in still water starts from the corner X of an equilateral triangle XYZ of side 10 nautical miles and describes the complete course XYZX in the least possible time. A tide of 5 knots is running in the direction $\overrightarrow{ZX}$. Find:

(a) the speed of the boat along XY,

(b) to the nearest minute the time taken by the speedboat to traverse the complete course XYZX.

    (1 knot is one nautical mile per hour).

(U of L)

17) The diagonals of the plane quadrilateral ABCD intersect at O and X, Y are the mid-points of the diagonals AC, BD respectively. Show that:

  (i) $\overrightarrow{BA} + \overrightarrow{BC} = 2\overrightarrow{BX}$

 (ii) $\overrightarrow{BA} + \overrightarrow{BC} + \overrightarrow{DA} + \overrightarrow{DC} = 4\overrightarrow{YX}$

(iii) $2\overrightarrow{AB} + 2\overrightarrow{BC} + 2\overrightarrow{CA} = 0$

If $\overrightarrow{OA} + \overrightarrow{OB} + \overrightarrow{OC} + \overrightarrow{OD} = 4\overrightarrow{OM}$, find the location of M.

(A.E.B)

18) Given two vectors $\overrightarrow{OP}$ and $\overrightarrow{OQ}$ show how to construct geometrically the sum $(\overrightarrow{OP} + \overrightarrow{OQ})$ and the difference $(\overrightarrow{OP} - \overrightarrow{OQ})$.

If X, Y, Z are the mid-points of the lines BC, CA, AB respectively and O is any point in the plane of the triangle ABC, show that $\overrightarrow{OA} + \overrightarrow{OB} + \overrightarrow{OC} = \overrightarrow{OX} + \overrightarrow{OY} + \overrightarrow{OZ}$ and find the position of the point D such that $\overrightarrow{OA} + \overrightarrow{OB} - \overrightarrow{OC} = \overrightarrow{OD}$.

(U of L)

CHAPTER 3

FORCES IN EQUILIBRIUM.
FRICTION

THE STATE OF EQUILIBRIUM

A set of forces acting on an object can be reduced (using methods discussed in Chapter 2) to a single resultant force. The effect of this linear resultant on the object would be to move it in a straight line. In addition the set of forces may also have a resultant turning effect which would cause the object to rotate. Forces which have zero linear resultant and zero turning effect will not cause any change in the motion of the object to which they are applied.
Such forces (and the object) are said to be in *equilibrium*.
The turning effect of a set of concurrent forces is always zero, consequently:-
Concurrent forces are in equilibrium if their linear resultant is zero.
(It is important to remember however that non-concurrent forces with zero linear resultant are not necessarily in equilibrium).

Equilibrium of Concurrent Forces

We have already seen that there are basically two ways of finding the linear resultant of a set of forces:-
(a) by drawing a vector diagram in which lines representing the given forces form all but one side of a polygon. The last side then represents the resultant.
(b) by resolving and collecting the forces in each of two perpendicular directions.

When the forces are in equilibrium their resultant is zero and the above methods can be adapted as follows:-

(i) The side representing the resultant is now of zero length, i.e. the given forces themselves can be represented by the sides of a closed polygon.

e.g. If the forces in diagram (i) are in equilibrium, the corresponding vector diagram will be as in diagram (ii)

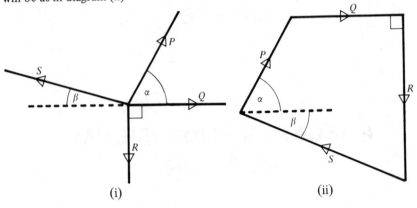

(i)   (ii)

(ii) When the given forces are resolved and collected in two perpendicular directions, the magnitude of the resultant, F, is normally calculated using $F = \sqrt{X^2 + Y^2}$.

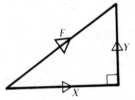

Neither X^2 nor Y^2 can ever be negative. So F is zero only if $X = 0$ and $Y = 0$.

e.g. In diagram (i) above, resolving parallel and perpendicular to the force Q we have:-

$$\rightarrow X = Q + P \cos \alpha - S \cos \beta = 0$$

$$\uparrow Y = P \sin \alpha + S \sin \beta - R = 0$$

These two equations are the condition for P, Q, R and S to be in equilibrium. Either of the methods above can be used to solve problems where the forces are in equilibrium.

EXAMPLES 3a

1) ABCDEF is a regular hexagon and O is its centre. Forces of 1, 2, 3, 4, P, Q newton act at O in the directions OA, OB, OC, OD, OE, OF respectively. If the six forces are in equilibrium find the values of P and Q.

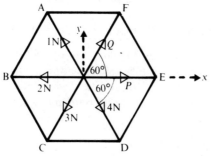

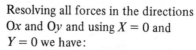

Resolving all forces in the directions Ox and Oy and using $X = 0$ and $Y = 0$ we have:

$$\rightarrow X = P + Q \cos 60° + 4 \cos 60° - 1 \cos 60° - 2 - 3 \cos 60° = 0 \qquad (1)$$

$$\uparrow Y = Q \sin 60° + 1 \sin 60° - 4 \sin 60° - 3 \sin 60° \qquad = 0 \qquad (2)$$

From (1) $P + \tfrac{1}{2}Q = 2$
From (2) $Q = 6$

Therefore the required values are $P = -1$ and $Q = 6$.
($P = -1$ indicates a force of $1\,\text{N}$ along EO).

2) Four forces of magnitudes $4\,\text{N}$, $3\,\text{N}$, $1\,\text{N}$ and $3\sqrt{2}\,\text{N}$ act on a particle as shown in the diagram. Prove, using a polygon of forces, that the particle is in equilibrium.

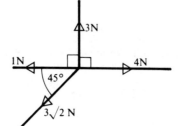

The polygon ABCDE is constructed so that AB, BC, CD, DE represent the forces $4\,\text{N}$, $3\,\text{N}$, $1\,\text{N}$ $3\sqrt{2}\,\text{N}$ respectively in magnitude and direction.

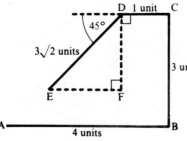

But $DF = 3\sqrt{2} \cos 45° = 3$ units

and $EF = 3\sqrt{2} \sin 45° = 3$ units

Therefore $DF = CB$

Therefore   E and F are both on AB

Also $EF + DC = AB$

Therefore   E coincides with A.

The four given concurrent forces therefore form a closed vector polygon and are in equilibrium.

(A scale drawing of the polygon ABCDE would verify that E coincides with **A**).

Note. A set of forces which is not in equilibrium may be reduced to equilibrium by the introduction of one extra force. This force is then called the *equilibrant* of the original set. Since it counteracts the resultant effect of the original set of forces, *the equilibrant of a system is equal and opposite to the resultant of that system.*

3) Four forces acting on a particle are represented by $2i + 3j$, $4i - 7j$, $-5i + 4j$ and $i - j$. Find the resultant force vector **F**. A fifth force $pi + qj$ is added to the system which is then in equilibrium. Find p and q and check that $pi + qj = -\mathbf{F}$.

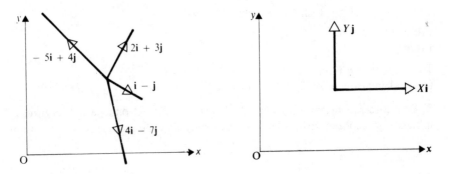

$\mathbf{F} = Xi + Yj = (4 + 1 + 2 - 5)\,i + (-7 - 1 + 3 + 4)j$
$\mathbf{F} = 2i - j.$

Now considering the set of five forces which are in equilibrium and hence have a resultant $0i + 0j$, we have:

$$(2i + 3j) + (4i - 7j) + (-5i + 4j) + (i - j) + (pi + qj) \equiv 0i + 0j$$

Therefore $2 + 4 - 5 + 1 + p = 0$ $p = -2$

and $3 - 7 + 4 - 1 + q = 0$ $q = +1$

The fifth force is therefore $-2i + j = -(2i - j) = -\mathbf{F}$

EXERCISE 3a

1) ABCD is a square. A force of 2 N acts along **AB**. Find the magnitude of forces acting along AC and AD if the three forces are in equilibrium.

2) In a regular hexagon ABCDEF, forces of magnitudes 2 N, 4 N, 3 N and 2 N act along the lines AB, AC, AD and AF respectively. Find the equilibrant of the given forces and verify that it is equal and opposite to their resultant.

3) A ring of weight 2 N is threaded on to a string whose ends are fixed to two points A and B in a horizontal line. The ring is pulled aside by a horizontal force

P newton parallel to AB. When the ring is in equilibrium the two sections of the string are inclined to the vertical at angles of 40° and 20°. Find the two possible values of *P*.

4) ABCDEF is a regular hexagon. Forces represented by $\overrightarrow{AB}$, $\overrightarrow{FA}$, $\overrightarrow{BC}$ and $2\overrightarrow{DE}$ act on a particle. Prove that the particle is in equilibrium.

Three Forces in Equilibrium

The methods already discussed can be applied to problems on any number of forces, including three. The situation where three forces only are in equilibrium, however, is of particular interest and special methods are applicable. Consider three forces *P*, *Q* and *R* which are in equilibrium. Lines representing, in magnitude and direction, a set of vectors in equilibrium form a closed polygon. In this case the polygon is a triangle often referred to as the *triangle of forces*. The formal statement of this property is:-
Three forces which are in equilibrium can be represented in magnitude, direction and sense by the sides of a triangle taken in order.

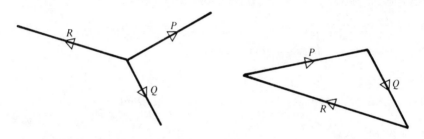

Conversely, if a triangle can be found whose sides, in order, have the same direction and sense as three concurrent forces in equilibrium, then the magnitudes of the forces are proportional to the sides of the triangle.

EXAMPLE I

One end of a string 0.5 m long is fixed to a point A and the other end is fastened to a small object of weight 8 N. The object is pulled aside by a horizontal force until it is 0.3 m from the vertical through A. Find the magnitudes of the tension in the string and the horizontal force.

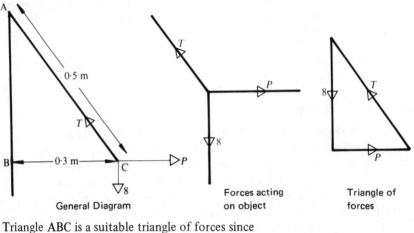

General Diagram   Forces acting on object   Triangle of forces

Triangle ABC is a suitable triangle of forces since
AB is in the same direction as the weight
BC is in the same direction as P, the horizontal force
CA is in the same direction as T, the tension

Then $\dfrac{8}{AB} = \dfrac{P}{BC} = \dfrac{T}{CA}$

But the length of AB is 0.4 m (Pythagoras).

Therefore $\dfrac{8}{0.4} = \dfrac{P}{0.3} = \dfrac{T}{0.5}$

The tension in the string is therefore 10 N and the horizontal force is 6 N.

LAMI'S THEOREM

Consider again three forces P, Q and R which are in equilibrium, and the corresponding triangle of forces ABC.

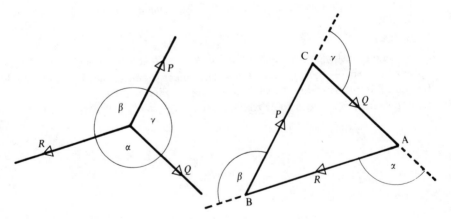

If the angles between P, Q and R are α, β and γ as shown in the diagram, then α, β and γ are exterior angles of triangle ABC.

Applying the Sine Rule to the vector triangle ABC we have:

$$\frac{P}{\sin(180° - \alpha)} = \frac{Q}{\sin(180° - \beta)} = \frac{R}{\sin(180° - \gamma)}$$

But since $\sin(180° - \alpha) = \sin\alpha$, a simpler form is

$$\frac{P}{\sin\alpha} = \frac{Q}{\sin\beta} = \frac{R}{\sin\gamma}$$

This property of three forces in equilibrium is known as *Lami's Theorem* and is a very neat method of solving many *three force* problems.

EXAMPLE 2

One end of a string is fixed to a point **A** and the other end is fastened to a small object of weight 8 N. The object is pulled aside by a horizontal force until the string is inclined at 30° to the vertical through **A**. Find the magnitudes of the tension in the string and the horizontal force.

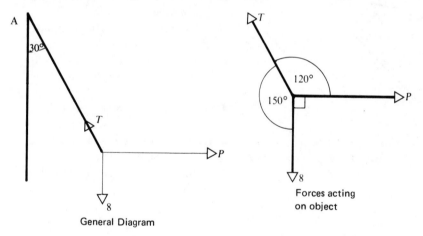

General Diagram

Forces acting on object

Applying Lami's Theorem we have:

$$\frac{8}{\sin 120°} = \frac{P}{\sin 150°} = \frac{T}{\sin 90°}$$

i.e.

$$\frac{8}{\sqrt{\frac{3}{2}}} = \frac{P}{\frac{1}{2}} = \frac{T}{1}$$

Therefore the tension is $\dfrac{16\sqrt{3}\,\text{N}}{3}$

and the horizontal force is $\dfrac{8\sqrt{3}\,\text{N}}{3}$

Note the similarity between Examples 1 and 2.

The *lengths* given in Example 1 were useful in the triangle of forces method whereas the *angles* in Example 2 suggested the use of Lami's Theorem.

It is also interesting to observe that either problem could have been solved by resolving the forces horizontally and vertically as in the earlier examples.

Concurrence Property

In order to be in equilibrium, three non-parallel forces must be concurrent.

This property can be confirmed by considering three forces P, Q and R which are to be in equilibrium. If P and Q meet at a point A, then their resultant, S, also passes through A.

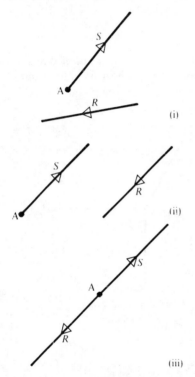

The original three forces have now been reduced to two (diagram (i)) and these two are to be in equilibrium. R and S therefore have zero linear resultant and zero turning effect.

Hence R and S are equal in magnitude, parallel and in opposite directions. If the positions of R and S are as shown in diagram (ii) however, they will have a turning effect.

This turning effect will be zero only when R and S are collinear (diagram (iii)) and in this case R also passes through A. Therefore in order that P, Q and R shall be in equilibrium all three forces pass through A.

This property is of considerable value in solving problems where one of three forces in equilibrium would otherwise have an unknown direction.

EXAMPLE

A uniform rod AB of weight 12 N is hinged to a vertical wall at A. The end B is pulled aside by a horizontal force until it is in equilibrium inclined at $60°$ to the wall. Find the magnitude of the horizontal force and the direction of the force acting at the hinge.

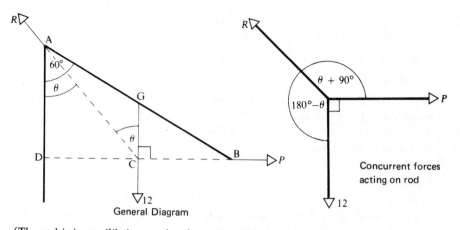

General Diagram

Concurrent forces acting on rod

(The rod is in equilibrium under the action of three forces which must therefore be concurrent. The weight and the horizontal force P meet at C so the direction of the hinge force must be CA).

First we must deal with the mensuration of the general diagram.

G is the mid-point of AB and GC is parallel to AD.

Hence C is the mid-point of DB

Now
$$\tan \theta = \frac{DC}{AD} = \frac{\frac{1}{2}DB}{AD} = \tfrac{1}{2}\tan 60° = \frac{\sqrt{3}}{2}$$

Hence
$$\theta = 40° 54'$$

Applying Lami's Theorem we have:-

$$\frac{12}{\sin (\theta + 90°)} = \frac{P}{\sin (180° - \theta)} = \frac{R}{\sin 90°}$$

Then
$$P = \frac{12 \sin 139° 6'}{\sin 130° 54'} = 10.4$$

Therefore the horizontal force is of magnitude 10.4 N and the hinge force is inclined at 40° 54' to the wall.

Problem Solving

The methods available for solving problems involving three forces in equilibrium use:-

(a) the 'triangle of forces',

(b) Lami's Theorem,

(c) resolution in two perpendicular directions.

In attempting to select the best approach to a particular problem the following points should be noted:-

1) A diagram including a suitable triangle whose sides are given (or are simple

to calculate) suggests the use of method (a). It is, however, not worth introducing special construction to create a suitable triangle.

2) When the angles between pairs of forces are known, Lami's Theorem is usually the best method.

3) If two of the three forces are in perpendicular directions, resolving in these directions gives a quick and easy solution.
It is important in all cases to remember that *three non-parallel forces in equilibrium must be concurrent.*

EXAMPLES 3b

1) A small block of weight of 20 N is suspended by two strings of lengths 0.6 m and 0.8 m from two points 1 m apart on a horizontal beam. Find the tension in each string.

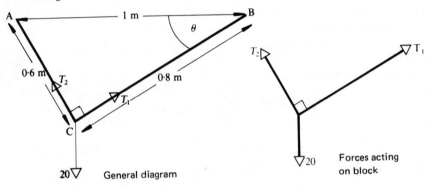

General diagram   Forces acting on block

First dealing with mensuration of the figure we see that:

$$AB^2 = AC^2 + BC^2 \text{ so that angle } ACB = 90°$$

Then $\cos \theta = 0.8$ and $\sin \theta = 0.6$

Resolving in the directions of T_1 and T_2

$$T_1 - 20 \sin \theta = 0 \quad T_1 = 0.6 \times 20$$

$$T_2 - 20 \cos \theta = 0 \quad T_2 = 0.8 \times 20.$$

The tensions in the strings are 12 N and 16 N.

2) A particle of weight W rests on a smooth plane inclined at 30° to the horizontal and is held in equilibrium by a string inclined at 30° to the plane. Find, in terms of W, the tension in the string.

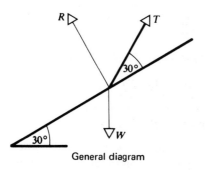 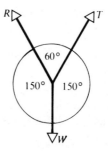

General diagram

Applying Lami's Theorem we have:

$$\frac{W}{\sin 60°} = \frac{T}{\sin 150°} = \left(\frac{R}{\sin 150°}\right)$$

Therefore

$$T = \frac{W \sin 150°}{\sin 60°} = \frac{W\sqrt{3}}{3}$$

3) A uniform rod **AB** of weight 10 N is hinged to a fixed point at **A** and maintained in a horizontal position by a string attached to **B** and to a point C vertically above A. If $AC = AB = l$, find the magnitude and direction of the force at the hinge and the tension in the string.

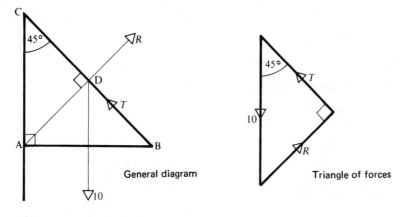

General diagram   Triangle of forces

The lines of action of the weight of the rod and the tension in the string meet at D. Therefore the third force also passes through D.
D is the mid-point of **CB** (since AG = GB and DG //^{l} to CA).
Therefore angle ADC = 90°.
In triangle CAD, $\overrightarrow{CA}$ is parallel to the weight
$\qquad\qquad\overrightarrow{AD}$ is parallel to the hinge force
$\qquad\qquad\overrightarrow{DC}$ is parallel to the tension

Therefore $$\frac{10}{CA} = \frac{R}{AD} = \frac{T}{DC}$$

But $$AD = DC = l \cos 45°$$

Therefore $$R = 10 \cos 45° = T$$

The tension in the string is of magnitude 7.07 N and the reaction at the hinge, also of magnitude 7.07 N is inclined at 45° to the vertical.

4) A point A on a sphere of radius a rests in contact with a smooth vertical wall and is supported by a string of length a joining a point B on the sphere to a point C on the wall. Find the tension in the string in terms of W, the weight of the sphere.

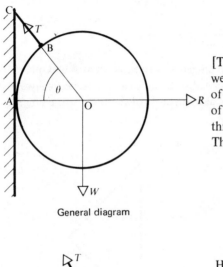

General diagram

[The reaction at the wall and the weight both pass through O (the centre of the sphere). Hence the line of action of the tension in the string also passes through O].

Then OBC is a straight line and OC = $2a$.

Hence $\cos \theta = \dfrac{a}{2a} = \dfrac{1}{2}$

and $\theta = 60°$

Using Lami's Theorem

$$\frac{T}{\sin 90°} = \frac{W}{\sin 120°} = \frac{R}{\sin 150°}$$

Therefore $$T = \frac{2W}{\sqrt{3}}$$

EXERCISE 3b

1) A particle of weight 24 N is attached to one end of a string 1.3 m long whose other end is fastened to a point on a vertical pole. A horizontal force acting on the particle keeps it in equilibrium (a) 0.5 m from the pole (b) so that the string is inclined at 20° to the vertical. Calculate the tension in the string and the magnitude of the horizontal force in both cases.

2) A small object of weight 10 N rests in equilibrium on a rough plane inclined at $30°$ to the horizontal. Calculate the magnitude of the frictional force.

3) A weight of 26 N is supported by two strings AB and AC of lengths 0.5 m and 1.2 m respectively. If BC is horizontal and of length 1.3 m, calculate the tension in AC and the angle BCA.

4) A small block of weight W rests on a smooth plane of inclination θ to the horizontal. Find the value of θ if:

(a) a force of $\dfrac{W}{2}$ parallel to the plane is required to keep the block in equilibrium,

(b) a horizontal force of $\dfrac{W}{3}$ keeps the block in equilibrium.

5) A uniform rod AB of weight 20 N is hinged to a fixed point at A. A force acts at B holding the rod in equilibrium at $30°$ to the vertical through A. Find the magnitude of this force if:
(a) it is perpendicular to AB,
(b) it is horizontal.

6) A uniform rod AB of weight W rests in equilibrium with the end A in contact with a smooth vertical wall and the end B in contact with a smooth plane inclined at $45°$ to the wall. Find the reactions at A and B in terms of W.

7) Three forces P, Q and R act on a particle. P and Q are perpendicular to each other and the angle between Q and R is $150°$. If the magnitude of P is 12 N find the magnitudes of Q and R.

8) A uniform rod AB, hinged to a fixed point at A is held in a horizontal position by a string attached to B and to a point C vertically above A so that angle ACB is $45°$. Find the magnitude and direction of the force acting at the hinge.

CONTACT FORCES

Two solid objects in contact exert equal and opposite forces upon each other. The two forces due to frictionless contact are perpendicular to the common surface of contact and are known as *normal contact forces*, or *normal reactions*, or simply *normals*. If however the objects are in rough contact and have a tendency to move relative to each other (without losing contact) then frictional forces arise which oppose such potential motion. Again each object exerts a frictional force on the other and the two forces are equal and opposite. Consider two wooden blocks A and B being rubbed against each other.

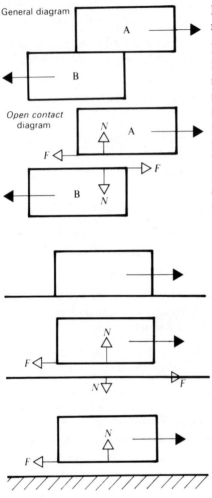

In the diagram, A is being moved to the right while B is being moved leftward.

In order to see more clearly which forces act on A and which on B, a second diagram is drawn showing a space between the blocks but they are still supposed to be in contact. The two normal contact forces are perpendicular to the surface of contact between the blocks. The two frictional forces *F* act along that surface each in a direction opposing the motion of the block upon which it acts.

Now consider one block being pushed along the ground as shown. Again each solid object exerts a normal force and a frictional force on the other and these are marked separately on the second diagram. In this case however, the ground is *fixed* and the two forces which act upon it do not have any effect. Consequently they are rarely included in the diagrams drawn to illustrate problems, the *fixed* surface often being indicated by shading.

Fixed Objects

The earth is our *frame of reference*, i.e. it is treated as absolutely stationary (fixed) and all movement is observed relative to it. Other objects which are immovably attached to the earth become virtually part of its surface and are therefore also fixed. e.g. A wall built on the ground; a pole with its foot bedded in the ground.

A fixed object cannot be moved relative to the earth.

Contact between a moveable object and fixed one is described as *external* contact and the contact force acting on the moveable object is an *external force*.

Contact between two moveable objects is *internal* and the contact forces acting on both objects are *internal forces*.

EXAMPLE

A block rests on a smooth horizontal plane and a smooth rod is placed against the block with one end on the ground. Draw diagrams showing the forces acting on the block and on the rod indicating which contacts are internal and which external.

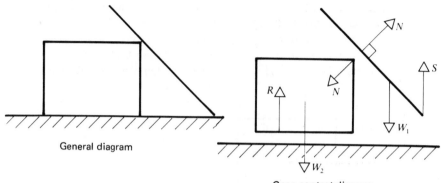

General diagram

Open contact diagram

Forces acting on the rod are:-
Weight W_1
Normal reaction with plane S (external contact)
Normal reaction with block N (internal contact)

Forces acting on the block are:-
Weight W_2
Normal reaction with plane R (external contact)
Normal reaction with rod N (internal contact)
(Forces $\downarrow R$ and $\downarrow S$ which act on the fixed plane are disregarded).
Note that the line of action of N is perpendicular to the *rod*.

FRICTION

Friction is a property of contact between solid objects.
Two surfaces which can move one across the other without encountering any resistance are in frictionless (called *smooth)* contact.
Conversely two objects whose relative surface movement is resisted have friction between them and their contact is *rough.*
(*Note*. It is now appreciated that the existence of friction between surfaces does not depend on their roughness or smoothness in the everyday sense of these words. In fact there can be very large frictional forces between two highly polished flat metal surfaces. Consequently it is important, in Mechanics, to interpret smooth as *frictionless* rather than *free from projections*.)
The results of experimental investigation into the behaviour of frictional forces confirm that:

(1) friction opposes the movement of an object across the surface of another with which it is in rough contact.

(2) the direction of the frictional force is opposite to the potential direction of motion.

(3) the magnitude of the frictional force is only just sufficient to prevent movement and increases as the tendency to move increases, up to a limiting value. When the limiting value is reached, the frictional force cannot increase any further and motion is about to begin (limiting equilibrium). The value of the limiting frictional force is related to the normal reaction N in the following way:

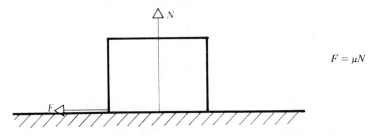

$$F = \mu N$$

The constant μ is called the *coefficient of friction* and each pair of surfaces has its own value for this constant.
In limiting equilibrium then, $F = \mu N$.
In general, $F \leqslant \mu N$.

The Angle of Friction

At a point of rough contact, where slipping is about to occur, the two forces acting on each object are the normal reaction N and friction μN.

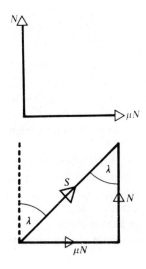

The resultant of these two is of magnitude $\sqrt{N^2 + (\mu N)^2}$
$$= N\sqrt{1 + \mu^2}$$
and the resultant makes $\arctan \dfrac{\mu N}{N}$

with the normal.

If this angle is called λ, then $\tan \lambda = \mu$.

At a point of rough contact, therefore, we can use either:-

Components N and μN at right angles

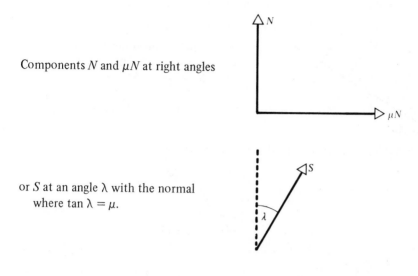

or S at an angle λ with the normal
where $\tan \lambda = \mu$.

S is the resultant contact force or *total reaction*.
λ is the angle of friction.
Note. The use of S instead of N and μN reduces the number of forces in a problem and can often lead to a *three force problem*.

SUMMARY

1) When the surfaces of two objects in rough contact tend to move relative to each other, equal and opposite frictional forces act on the objects opposing the potential movement.

2) Up to a limiting value, the magnitude of each frictional force, F, is just sufficient to prevent motion.

3) When the limit is reached $F = \mu N$ where N is the normal reaction and μ is the coefficient of friction for the two surfaces in contact.

4) At all times $F \leqslant \mu N$.

5) The resultant of N and μN makes an angle λ with the normal where $\tan \lambda = \mu$ and λ is the angle of friction.

EXAMPLES 3c

1) A particle of weight 10 N rests in rough contact with a plane inclined at 30° to the horizontal and is just about to slip. Find the coefficient of friction between the plane and the particle.

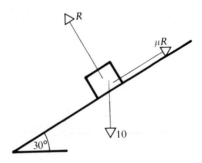

(The particle tends to slide down the plane so friction acts up the plane and is limiting so $F = \mu R$).

Resolving in the directions of μR and R we have

$$\nearrow \ \mu R - 10 \sin 30° = 0$$

$$\nwarrow \ R - 10 \cos 30° = 0$$

Hence

$$\mu = \frac{10 \sin 30°}{10 \cos 30°} = \tan 30°$$

$$\mu = \frac{1}{\sqrt{3}}.$$

2) A particle of weight W rests on a horizontal plane with which the angle of friction is λ.

A force P inclined at an angle θ to the plane is applied to the particle until it is on the point of moving. Find the value of θ for which the value of P will be least.

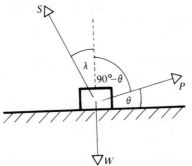

(Using the total contact force S inclined at λ to the normal only three forces act on the particle).

Using Lami's Theorem we have:-

$$\frac{P}{\sin (180° - \lambda)} = \frac{W}{\sin (90° - \theta + \lambda)} = \left[\frac{S}{\sin (90° + \theta)} \right]$$

Therefore

$$\frac{P}{\sin \lambda} = \frac{W}{\cos (\theta - \lambda)}$$

and
$$P = \frac{W \sin \lambda}{\cos (\theta - \lambda)}.$$

P will be least when $\cos (\theta - \lambda)$ is greatest (since W and $\sin \lambda$ are constant).
i.e. when $\cos (\theta - \lambda) = 1$ and $\theta - \lambda = 0$.
Therefore P is least when $\theta = \lambda$ and its value is then $W \sin \lambda$.

3) A uniform ladder rests against a smooth vertical wall and on rough horizontal ground. The weight of the ladder is 10 N and it is just about to slip when inclined at $30°$ to the verical. Calculate the coefficient of friction.

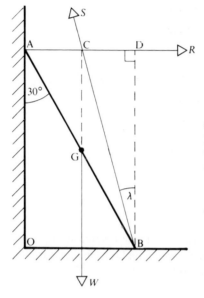

[Three forces keep the ladder in equilibrium:-
Normal reaction R with the smooth wall.
Weight W.
Total reaction S with the rough ground.

The three forces must be concurrent, so S passes through C, the point of inter-section of R and W].

S is inclined at λ to the normal BD and $\tan \lambda = \dfrac{CD}{DB}$.
But the coefficient of friction $\mu = \tan \lambda$.
Therefore $\mu = \dfrac{CD}{DB} = \dfrac{\frac{1}{2}AD}{DB}$ $\left(\begin{array}{l} \text{since CG } /\!/^l \text{ DB} \\ \text{and   AG} = \text{GB} \end{array} \right)$

i.e. $\mu = \frac{1}{2} \tan 30° = \dfrac{1}{2\sqrt{3}}$

The coefficient of friction is $\dfrac{\sqrt{3}}{6}$.

4) A small block of weight 10 N rests on a rough plane inclined at $30°$ to the horizontal. The coefficient of friction is $\frac{1}{2}$. Find the horizontal force required:
(a) to prevent the block from slipping down,
(b) to make it just about to slide up the plane.

(a)

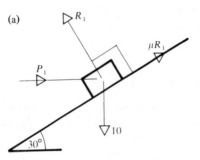

(In this case, as the block is about to slip downward, friction acts up the plane and is limiting).

Resolving in the directions of friction and normal.

$$\nearrow \tfrac{1}{2}R_1 + P_1 \cos 30° - 10 \sin 30° = 0$$

$$\nwarrow R_1 - P_1 \sin 30° - 10 \cos 30° = 0$$

Hence $20 \sin 30° - 2P_1 \cos 30° = P_1 \sin 30° + 10 \cos 30°$

$$10 - 1.73 P_1 = 0.5P_1 + 8.66$$

$$1.34 = 2.23P_1$$

The horizontal force required is of magnitude 0.6 N.

(b)

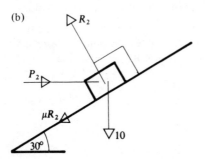

(This time the block is about to slip upward and the limiting friction acts downward).

Resolving as before:

$$\nearrow P_2 \cos 30 - \tfrac{1}{2}R_2 - 10 \sin 30° = 0$$

$$\nwarrow R_2 - P_2 \sin 30° - 10 \cos 30° = 0$$

Hence $1.73 P_2 - 10 = 0.5 P_2 + 8.66$

$$1.23 P_2 = 18.66$$

This time the magnitude of the horizontal force is 15.2 N.

An alternative solution could be given using the resultant contact force S in

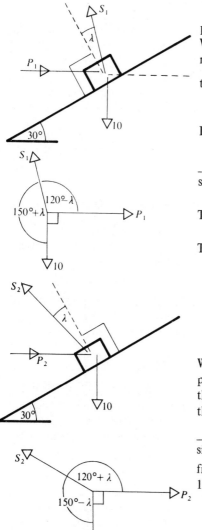

place of R and μR.
Where S makes an angle λ with the
normal such that

$$\tan \lambda = \mu = 0.5$$
$$\lambda = 26° \, 34'.$$

Lami's Theorem gives:

$$\frac{P_1}{\sin(150° + 26°34')} = \frac{10}{\sin(120° - 26°34')}$$

Therefore $P_1 = \dfrac{10 \sin 176° \, 34'}{\sin 93° \, 26'}$

The magnitude of P_1 is then 0.6 N.

When the frictional force is down the
plane, S is on the *downward* side of
the normal, so that Lami's Theorem
this time gives:

$$\frac{P_2}{\sin 123° \, 26'} = \frac{10}{\sin 146° \, 34'}$$

from which the magnitude of P_2 is
15.2 N.

Note. In examples 3 and 4 a phrase frequently encountered in examination
questions is used, viz. "a body rests on a rough plane ....".
This implies, incorrectly, that friction is a property of *one surface*.
The description "a body rests in rough contact with a plane ...." is better
because it conveys the idea of friction *between two surfaces*.

EXERCISE 3c   4, 5, 7, 8.

1) A small block of weight W is placed on a plane inclined at an angle θ to the

horizontal. The coefficient of friction between the block and the plane is μ.

(a) When $\theta = 20°$ the block is in limiting equilibrium. Find μ.

(b) When $\mu = \frac{1}{3}$ and $\theta = 30°$ a horizontal force of 6 N is required to prevent the block from slipping down the plane. What is the weight of this block?

(c) A force of 10 N up the plane causes the block to be on the point of sliding up. If $W = 20$ N and $\mu = \frac{1}{4}$ find θ.

(d) If $\theta = 40°$ and $\mu = \frac{1}{2}$ find the magnitude and direction of the least force required to prevent the block from sliding down the plane when $W = 12$ N.

2) A block of weight 20 N rests on a rough plane of inclination $30°$, the coefficient of friction being 0.25. Find what horizontal force will be required:

(a) just to prevent it from slipping down,

(b) to make it just begin to slide up.

3) A sledge whose weight is 4000 N is pulled at constant speed along level ground by a rope held at $30°$ to the ground. If $\mu = \frac{1}{4}$ find the pulling force required.

4) A uniform ladder rests on rough ground with its top against a smooth wall. If the angle of friction is $15°$ find the least possible inclination of the ladder to the horizontal.

5) A small block of weight 8 N is standing on rough horizontal ground. A horizontal force P is applied to the block. If the coefficient of friction between block and ground is 0.5, what is the value of the frictional force when:

(a) $P = 1$ N   (b) $P = 4$ N   (c) $P = 5$ N

State in each case whether or not the block would move.

6) A uniform rod AB of length $2a$ and weight W is inclined at $30°$ to the horizontal with its lower end A on rough horizontal ground, the angle of friction being $30°$. The rod rests in contact with a smooth peg C (AC < AB). Calculate the height of the peg above the ground and the reaction at the peg if the rod is in limiting equilibrium.

7) A uniform ladder is placed with its foot on horizontal ground and its upper end against a vertical wall. The angle of friction at both points of contact is $30°$. Find the greatest possible inclination of the ladder to the vertical. (The ladder will not slip until limiting friction has been reached at both ends).

8) A uniform rod AB of weight 200 N is lying on rough horizontal ground when a string attached to B begins to lift that end of the rod. When AB is inclined at $30°$ to the ground the end A is about to slip. If at this instant the string is inclined to the vertical at $30°$ calculate the tension in the string and the angle of friction between the rod and the ground.

MULTIPLE CHOICE EXERCISE 3

The instructions for answering these questions are given on page (xii)

TYPE I

1) Two perpendicular forces have magnitudes 5 N and 4 N. The magnitude of

their resultant is:

(a) $3\,\text{N}$ (b) $\sqrt{11}\,\text{N}$ (c) $\sqrt{41}\,\text{N}$ (d) $1\,\text{N}$.

2) A block of weight $12\,\text{N}$ rests in rough contact with a horizontal plane and $\mu = \frac{1}{3}$. A force of $3\,\text{N}$ is applied horizontally to the block. The frictional force acting on the block is:

(a) $4\,\text{N}$ (b) $3\,\text{N}$ (c) $-4\,\text{N}$ (d) zero because the block does not move.

3) Forces represented by $2i + 5j$, $i - 8j$ and $pi + qj$ are in equilibrium, therefore:

(a) $p = 3$ and $q = -3$ (b) $p = -3$ and $q = 3$ (c) $p = -2$ and $q = 3$
(d) $p = 2$ and $q = -40$

4) A light string is attached at one end to a point on a vertical wall and at the other end to a smooth sphere. When the sphere rests in equilibrium against the wall the direction of the string is:

(a) at $45°$ to the wall,   (b) horizontal,   (c) tangential to the sphere,
(d) through the centre of the sphere.

5) A particle rests in equilibrium on a rough plane inclined at $30°$ to the horizontal therefore:

(a) $\mu = \dfrac{1}{2}$ (b) $\mu = \dfrac{1}{\sqrt{3}}$ (c) $\mu \leqslant \dfrac{1}{2}$ (d) $\mu \geqslant \dfrac{1}{\sqrt{3}}$

TYPE II

6) Three forces F_1, F_2 and F_3 are in equilibrium, therefore:

(a) $F_1 = F_2 + F_3$
(b) $F_1 + F_2 + F_3 = 0$
(c) $F_1 - F_2 - F_3 = 0$
(d) $-F_1 = F_2 + F_3$.

7) Three concurrent forces represented by $2i + 3j$, $i - 4j$ and $-3i + j$:
(a) are in equilibrium,
(b) have zero linear resultant,
(c) have an equilibrant,
(d) exert a turning effect.

8) ABCD is a rectangle. Forces represented in magnitude and direction by $\overrightarrow{AB}$, $\overrightarrow{BC}$, $\overrightarrow{CD}$ and $\overrightarrow{DA}$:
(a) are in equilibrium,
(b) obey Lami's Theorem,
(c) have zero linear resultant,
(d) have a resultant $2\overrightarrow{AC}$.

9) A ladder is resting at $30°$ to a rough vertical wall with its foot on a horizontal plane.
(a) Friction acts on the ladder.
(b) The plane is smooth.

(c) The ladder is about to slip.

(d) Friction acts on the wall.

TYPE III

10) (a) Three non-parallel forces are concurrent.

(b) Three non-parallel forces are in equilibrium.

11) (a) The resultant of a set of forces is **F**.

(b) An extra force $-$**F** added to a set of forces produces a state of equilibrium.

12) (a) Two objects are in rough contact with each other.

(b) Two objects are in contact and each exerts a frictional force on the other.

13) (a) A force of 2 N is applied to a block of weight 4 N in an attempt to move it across a rough table.

(b) The coefficient of friction between a block and a table is $\frac{1}{2}$.

14) (a) A supporting force just prevents a particle from slipping down a rough inclined plane.

(b) A particle is in a state of limiting equilibrium on an inclined plane.

TYPE IV

15) Three forces P, Q and R act on a particle. Find the magnitude of P.

(a) P is inclined at $120°$ to R.

(b) P is inclined at $150°$ to Q.

(c) the magnitude of Q is 10 N.

16) A block rests on a rough inclined plane. Find the coefficient of friction between block and plane:

(a) the weight of the block is 8 N,

(b) the elevation of the plane is $30°$,

(c) friction is limiting.

17) Determine whether or not three forces are in equilibrium:

(a) the magnitudes of the forces are $P = 3, Q = 4, R = 5$,

(b) the angle between P and Q is $60°$,

(c) the angle between Q and R is $150°$.

18) A ladder is placed with its foot on horizontal ground and the other end leaning against a smooth vertical wall. Find the angle between the ladder and the wall when the ladder is about to slip:

(a) the weight of the ladder is 500 N,

(b) the ground is rough and $\mu = \frac{1}{2}$,

(c) the length of the ladder is 5 m.

TYPE V

19) Three forces acting along the sides of a triangle are in equilibrium.

20) Lami's Theorem states that when three forces act on a particle each force is proportional to the sine of the angle between the other two forces.

21) If a frictional force acts on a body, it is not necessarily of value μR where R is the normal contact force.

22) The angle of friction is the angle between the frictional force and the normal reaction.

23) Three forces in equilibrium must be concurrent.

MISCELLANEOUS EXERCISE 3

16, 20, 23

1) ABCD is a square. CD is produced to E so that DE = CD. Forces of magnitudes 2, $3\sqrt{2}$, 4 and $2\sqrt{2}$ units act along **AB**, **AC**, **DA** and **AE** respectively. Find the magnitude and direction of their resultant. A fifth force acting at A is added so that the system is in equilibrium. What is the magnitude and direction of the extra force?

2) O is any point in the plane of a regular hexagon ABCDEF. Prove that forces $\overrightarrow{OA}$, $\overrightarrow{OE}$, $\overrightarrow{CD}$, $\overrightarrow{CB}$ and $2\overrightarrow{FO}$ are in equilibrium.

3) A uniform rod AB of weight W is freely hinged at A. The rod is in equilibrium at an angle θ to the vertical when a horizontal force $\frac{1}{2}W$ acts at B. Calculate θ and the reaction of the hinge on the rod.

4) A small object of weight $4W$ in rough contact with a horizontal plane is acted upon by a force inclined at 30° to the plane. When the force is of magnitude $2W$ the object is about to slip. Calculate the magnitude of the normal reaction and the coefficient of friction between the object and the plane.

5) Three telegraph cables are attached to the top of a telegraph pole. Their tensions, in order, are 2500, 3000 and 3500 N and the cables are separated by angles of 20°. A fourth cable is to be attached to the same point on the post in order to ensure that the post is in equilibrium. Assuming that all the cables are horizontal find the tension which the fourth cable must take.

6) ABCDEF is a regular hexagon. Forces of 2, $4\sqrt{3}$, 10 and 6 N act along the sides AB, AC, DA and AF respectively. Show that these forces are in equilibrium.

7) A sphere of radius 9 cm rests on a smooth inclined plane (angle 30°). It is attached by a string fixed to a point on its surface to a point on the plane 12 cm from the point of contact and on the same line of greatest slope. Find the tension in the string if the weight of the sphere is 100 N.

8) Find the values of the unknown forces in each of the following cases. Each

set of forces is in equilibrium.

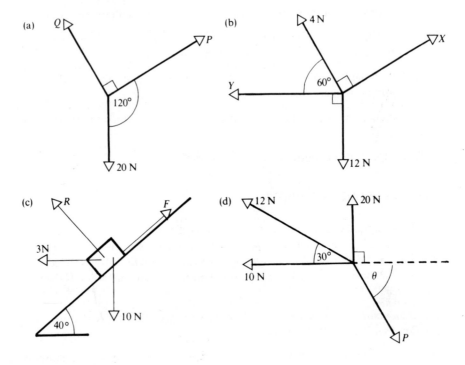

(a) Q P 120°   20 N

(b)   4 N   X   60° Y 12 N

(c) R F 3N   40°   10 N

(d)   12 N   20 N   30°   10 N θ P

In each case use calculation to solve the problem but in addition sketch the vector polygon.

9) A weight W is suspended by two ropes which make 30° and 60° with the horizontal. If the tension in the first rope is 20 N, find the tension in the other and the value of W.

10) A uniform rod of length l rests over the rim of a fixed hemispherical bowl of radius r, with one end in contact with the surface of the bowl. If all contacts are smooth and the inclination of the rod to the horizontal is θ, prove that the value of θ is given by the equation $8r \cos^2\theta - l \cos\theta - 4r = 0$.

11) A uniform rod AB of weight 12 N is free to turn in a vertical plane about a smooth hinge at its upper end A. It is held at an angle θ to the vertical by a force P acting at B.
(a) P is 5 N applied horizontally. What is the force at the hinge?
(b) P is horizontal and θ is arctan $\frac{3}{4}$. What is the force at the hinge?
(c) P is at right angles to AB and of magnitude 3 N. What is the force at the hinge?
(d) P is at right angles to AB and θ is arctan $\frac{3}{4}$. Find P and the hinge force.

12) A cylinder of weight 100 N rests in the angle between a smooth vertical wall

and a smooth plane inclined at $30°$ to the wall. Find the thrusts of the cylinder on the wall and the plane.

13) A heavy bead is threaded on a smooth circular wire whose plane is vertical. The bead is tied to the highest point of the wire by a string which in the position of equilibrium is inclined to the vertical at $30°$. Calculate the tension in the string and the reaction of the wire on the bead.

14) A uniform rod AB of length l is in equilibrium at $60°$ to the horizontal, with its end A on a horizontal plane, and resting against a fixed smooth sphere which has its lowest point C on the plane. The vertical plane containing the rod passes through the centre of the sphere. If the rod is on the point of slipping in the vertical plane, calculate the coefficient of friction between the rod and the plane when:

(a) $AC = \frac{1}{2}l$,   (b) $AC = \frac{5}{8}l$.   (U of L)

15)

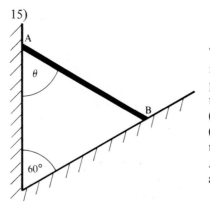

The diagram shows a uniform rod AB resting in the angle between a vertical plane and a plane inclined at $60°$ to the vertical. Find the angle θ if:
(a) both planes are smooth,
(b) the inclined plane is smooth but the vertical plane is rough,
A is on the point of slipping down and $\mu = \frac{1}{2}$.

16) One end of a light string is fixed and the other end is attached to the end A of a uniform rod AB of weight W. The rod is at rest, at an angle α to the horizontal, under the action of a horizontal force P applied to the end B. Calculate the magnitude of P and show that θ, the angle the string makes with the horizontal, is given by

$$\tan \theta \ = \ 2 \tan \alpha.$$

Calculate the magnitude of the least force through B which will maintain the rod in equilibrium, inclined at an angle α to the horizontal (the direction of the least force is at right angles to the rod). If, in this case, the string is inclined at an angle ϕ to the horizontal, show that

$$\tan \phi \ = \ 2 \tan \alpha + \cot \alpha. \qquad \text{(A.E.B.)}$$

17) A uniform rod of length $2a$ has one end on rough horizontal ground and is supported by a smooth horizontal rail perpendicular to the rod at a height h above the ground. When the rod is on the point of slipping it makes an angle θ with the horizontal. Prove that the coefficient of friction between the rod and

the ground is

$$\frac{a \cos \theta \sin^2 \theta}{h - a \cos^2 \theta \sin \theta}.$$ (U of L)

18) A uniform ladder of weight W rests on rough horizontal ground against a smooth vertical wall. The vertical plane containing the ladder is perpendicular to the wall and the ladder is inclined at an angle α to the vertical. Prove that, if the ladder is on the point of slipping and μ is the coefficient of friction between it and the ground, then $\tan \alpha = 2\mu$.   (Oxford)

19) (i) A uniform rod AB is suspended from a fixed point O by two light inextensible strings OA and OB which join the ends of the rod to O. Prove that the tensions in these strings are proportional to their lengths.

(ii) A uniform rod is suspended from a smooth fixed peg by a single light inextensible string tied to the ends of the rod and passing over the peg. If the tension in the string is two-thirds of the weight of the rod, calculate the angle between the two portions of the string.   (U of L)

20) A uniform rod AB of weight W is in limiting equilibrium at an angle of $45°$ to the horizontal with its end A on a rough horizontal plane and with a point C in its length against a horizontal rail. This rail is at right angles to the vertical plane containing AB. The coefficient of friction between the rod and the plane is $\frac{1}{2}$ and between the rod and the rail is $\frac{1}{3}$. Calculate the magnitude and direction of the resultant reaction at A.   (A.E.B.)

21) A uniform ladder of weight W rests inclined at an angle θ to the horizontal, with one end against a smooth vertical wall and the other end on rough horizontal ground. Find, in terms of W, the magnitude of the frictional force when $\theta = \arctan \frac{12}{5}$. If the angle of friction between the ladder and the ground is $\arctan \frac{3}{8}$, find the value of θ when the ladder is about to slip.

22) A heavy uniform sphere of radius a has a light inextensible string attached to a point on its surface. The other end of the string is fixed to a point on a rough vertical wall. The sphere rests in equilibrium touching the wall at a point distant h below the fixed point. If the point of the sphere in contact with the wall is about to slip downwards and the coefficient of friction between the sphere and the wall is μ, find the inclination of the string to the vertical.

If $\mu = \frac{h}{2a}$ and the weight of the sphere is W, show that the tension in the string is $\frac{W}{2\mu} (1 + \mu^2)^{\frac{1}{2}}$.   (U of L)

23) The figure shows a uniform rod AB of weight W resting with one end A against a rough vertical wall. One end of a light inextensible string is attached at B and the other end is attached at a point C, vertically above A. The points A, B and C lie in the same vertical plane with $AB = BC = 4a$ and $AC = a$. If

equilibrium is limiting, calculate:
  (i) the tension in the string,
 (ii) the angle of friction between the rod and the wall,
(iii) the magnitude of the resultant force acting at A.

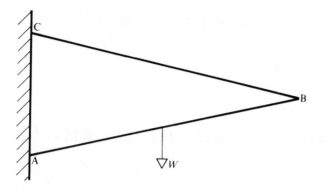

(A.E.B.)

24) A particle rests on a rough plane inclined at an angle θ to the horizontal. The coefficient of friction between the particle and the plane is μ. When the weight of the particle is W, a horizontal force of magnitude P just prevents the particle from slipping down the plane. If however a force of magnitude $2P$ acts parallel to the plane, the particle is on the point of slipping up the plane. The same force acting on a particle of weight $2W$ just prevents it from slipping down the same plane. Find the values of θ and μ, and express P in terms of W.

CHAPTER 4

VELOCITY AND ACCELERATION

MOTION IN A STRAIGHT LINE

When a particle moves in a straight line its displacement, velocity and acceleration can have one of only two possible directions. Positive and negative signs are used to differentiate between the two directions by taking one sense as positive and the other as negative.

UNIFORM VELOCITY

In Chapter 1 speed was defined as the rate at which a moving body covers its path and velocity as the speed of the body together with the direction in which the body is moving. So a particle moving with *uniform velocity* has a *constant speed in a fixed direction.*

Consider a particle moving with uniform velocity along a line as shown in the diagram, O being a fixed point on that line.

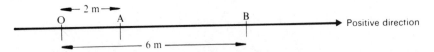

(i) If at some instant the particle is at A and 2 s later it is at B it has covered a distance of 4 m in 2 s: therefore its speed is $2\,\mathrm{ms}^{-1}$. It is moving in the positive direction: therefore its velocity is $\pm 2\,\mathrm{ms}^{-1}$.

Alternatively the displacement from O has increased by $+4\,\mathrm{m}$ in 2 s. Therefore its displacement from O is increasing at the rate of $\pm 2\,\mathrm{ms}^{-1}$: this is its velocity.

(ii) If at some instant the particle is at B and 2 s later it is at A it has again

covered a distance of 4 m in 2 s: therefore its speed is 2 ms^{-1}. This time it is moving in the negative direction: therefore its velocity is -2 ms^{-1}.
Alternatively the displacement from O has decreased by 4 m or increased by -4 m in 2 s. Therefore its displacement from O is increasing at the rate of -2 ms^{-1}: this is its velocity.

So in both examples the *velocity is the rate of increase of displacement* and the velocity of any moving object, whether uniform or not is defined in the same way.

Displacement - Time Graph

When a particle is moving along a straight line a graph of its displacement (s) from a fixed point on the line plotted against time (t) is often a useful way of representing the motion. When the velocity is uniform, equal distances will be covered in equal intervals of time, so the graph will be a straight line.

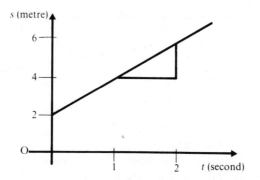

This is a displacement–time graph for the motion discussed in example (i). The gradient of the line is $+2$: this is the velocity of the particle.

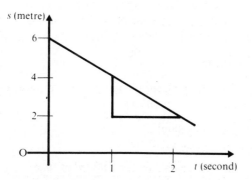

This is a displacement–time graph for the motion discussed in example (ii). The gradient of this line is -2: this is the velocity of the particle. Thus in both examples the gradient of the line represents the velocity. In general, for uniform velocity the *gradient of the displacement–time graph represents the velocity.*

Average Velocity

A cyclist starting from a point **A** travels 200 m due North to a point **B** at a constant speed of 5 ms^{-1}. He rests at **B** for 30 s and then travels 300 m due South to a point **C** at a constant speed of 10 ms^{-1}.

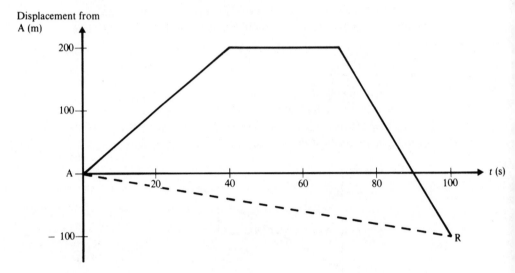

The time taken for the whole journey is 100 s.

Total distance travelled is 500 m.

The *average speed* for the whole journey is the constant speed that would be required to cover the total distance in the same time.

Thus the average speed for the journey is $\dfrac{500}{100} \text{ ms}^{-1} = 5 \text{ ms}^{-1}$.

The *average velocity* for the whole journey is the uniform velocity that would be required to achieve the final increase in displacement from A in the time of 100 s. The increase in displacement from A after 100 s is -100 m. Thus the average velocity for the journey is $\dfrac{-100}{100} \text{ ms}^{-1} = -1 \text{ ms}^{-1}$.

On the displacement–time graph for the journey this average velocity is represented by the gradient of the chord AR.

In general for any type of motion:

Average speed for a given interval of time

$$= \frac{\textit{distance covered in that interval of time}}{\textit{interval of time}}$$

Average velocity for a given interval of time

$$= \frac{\textit{increase in displacement in that interval of time}}{\textit{interval of time}}$$

In a displacement–time graph the *gradient of the chord represents the average velocity*.

EXERCISE 4a   1 , 5

1) A cyclist rides his bicycle along a straight road for 30 minutes at 10 ms^{-1} and then gets off and pushes his bicycle for 10 minutes at 1.5 ms^{-1}. Draw a displacement–time graph and find his average velocity for the whole journey.

2) A man walks up a hill at constant speed taking 10 minutes to cover a distance of 800 m. He rests for 2 minutes and then walks down again at constant speed in 6 minutes. Draw a displacement–time graph and find his average speed for the whole journey.

3) A ball is rolled along a line on the floor at a constant speed of 3 ms^{-1} towards a wall which is 5 m from its starting point. It bounces on the wall and returns at a constant speed of 2 ms^{-1} along the same line and is caught when it is 7 m from the wall. Draw a displacement–time graph showing the displacement of the ball from its starting point and find the average speed and the average velocity of the ball for its complete journey.

4) A particle is made to move along a straight line at constant speeds in such a way that, measuring from a fixed point O on the line, it goes forward a distance of 12 m at 1.5 ms^{-1}, then backward a distance of 5 m at 2.5 ms^{-1} and then forward again a distance of 3 m at 1 ms^{-1}. Draw a graph plotting the displacement of the particle from O against time and find the average speed and the average velocity of the particle for its complete journey.

5) A particle is moving along a straight line and O is a fixed point on that line. The table shows the displacement (s) of the particle from O at given instants of time (t)

t (second)	0	1	2	3	4	5	6
s (metre)	0	2	4	6	6	2	−2

Assuming that the particle has constant speeds over the intervals of time $t = 0$ to $t = 3$, $t = 3$ to $t = 4$, $t = 4$ to $t = 6$, draw a displacement–time graph and find the average velocity of the particle over the interval of time
(a) $t = 0$ to $t = 3$,   (b) $t = 1$ to $t = 5$,   (c) $t = 2$ to $t = 6$.

VELOCITY AT AN INSTANT

A particle is moving along a straight line where O is a fixed point on that line. The table below gives the displacement of the particle from O at given instants of time.

t (second)	0	1	2	3	4	5
s (metre)	0	1	4	9	16	25

The displacement–time graph will not be a straight line as varying distances are covered in equal intervals of time.

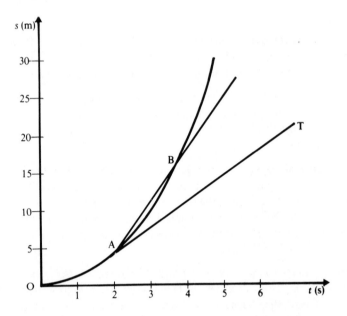

The gradient of the chord $AB = 6$: therefore the average velocity over the interval of time $t = 2$ to $t = 4$ is $6\,\text{ms}^{-1}$.
This can be taken as an approximate value for the actual velocity at the instant when $t = 2$. (It is not a very good approximation; better approximations can be found by taking smaller intervals of time).
The actual velocity at the instant when $t = 2$ is represented by the gradient of the tangent to the curve at A and this can be estimated from the graph.
From the graph the gradient of AT is 4.
Therefore the velocity at the instant $t = 2$ is $4\,\text{ms}^{-1}$.
In general *the velocity at an instant can be found by determining the gradient of the tangent to the displacement–time graph at that instant.*

EXAMPLE 4b

A particle moves along a straight line and O is a fixed point on that line. The displacement s metre of the particle from O at time t second is given by
$s = (t - 1)(t - 5)$.
Draw a displacement–time graph for the interval of time $t = 0$ to $t = 6$. From the graph find:
(a) the average velocity over the interval $t = 0$ to $t = 4$,
(b) the distance covered in the interval $t = 0$ to $t = 4$,
(c) the time at which the velocity is zero.

t (s)	0	1	2	3	4	5	6
s (m)	5	0	-3	-4	-3	0	5

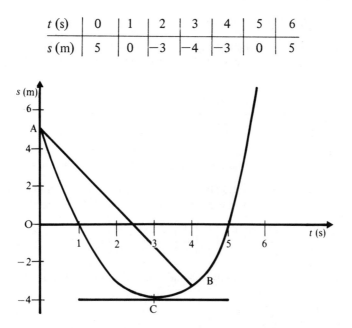

(a) the gradient of the chord $AB = -2$

Therefore the average velocity over the interval $t = 0$ to $t = 4$ is -2 ms^{-1}.

(b) From $t = 0$ to $t = 3$ the particle is moving in the negative sense along the line. When $t = 0$ its displacement from O is 5 m.

When $t = 3$ its displacement from O is -4 m.

Therefore the *distance* covered from $t = 0$ to $t = 3$ is 9 m.

From $t = 3$ to $t = 4$ the particle is moving in the positive sense along the line.

When $t = 3$ its displacement from O is -4 m.

When $t = 4$ its displacement from O is -3 m.

Therefore the distance covered from $t = 3$ to $t = 4$ is 1 m. Therefore the distance covered from $t = 0$ to $t = 4$ is 10 m.

(c) The gradient of the tangent to the curve represents the velocity at an instant. From the graph the gradient of the tangent is zero at the point C (when $t = 3$). Therefore the velocity is zero when $t = 3$.

EXERCISE 4b

1) A particle is moving along a straight line and O is a point on that line. The displacements (s) of the particle from O at given instants of time (t) are shown in the table.

t (second)	0	1	2	3	4	5	6
s (metre)	0	3	4	3	0	-5	-12

Draw a displacement–time graph and find the average velocity over the interval of time (a) $t = 0$ to $t = 2$,   (b) $t = 0$ to $t = 6$.

2) A particle is moving along a straight line where O is a fixed point on the line. The displacement (s) of the particle from O at given instants of time (t) is shown in the table.

t (second)	0	1	2	3	4
s (metre)	0	2	2	0	−4

Draw a displacement–time graph, find the average velocity over the interval of time $t = 1$ to $t = 2$ and estimate the velocity at the instant when $t = 1$.

3) A particle moves along a straight line and O is a fixed point on that line. The displacements from O at given instants of time are shown in the table.

t (second)	0	1	2	3	4	5
s (metre)	0	3	8	9	0	−25

Draw a displacement–time graph and find over the interval of time $t = 1$ to $t = 4$:
(a) the increase in displacement,
(b) the distance covered,
(c) the average speed,
(d) the average velocity.
Estimate the velocity when $t = 4$.

4) A particle moving along a straight line has its displacement s metre from a fixed point O on the line at time t second given by $s = t - 5t^2$.
Draw a displacement–time graph for the interval $t = 0$ to $t = 6$.
From your graph find:
(a) the average velocity over the interval $t = 2$ to $t = 5$,
(b) the velocity when $t = 4$,
(c) the time at which the velocity is zero.

5) A particle is moving along a straight line and O is a fixed point on that line. Its displacement s metre from O at time t second is given by $s = 6 + t - t^2$.
Draw a displacement–time graph for the interval $t = -1$ to $t = 5$ and from your graph find:
(a) the distance travelled in the interval $t = 0$ to $t = 2$,
(b) the displacement of the particle from O when $t = 0$,
(c) the velocity when $t = 0$,
(d) the time at which the velocity is zero.

ACCELERATION

If a particle moving in a straight line has a velocity of 2 ms^{-1} at one instant and 4 seconds later it has a velocity of 10 ms^{-1} its velocity has increased by

8 ms^{-1} in 4 seconds. If the velocity is increasing steadily, its rate of increase is 2 ms^{-1} each second (written 2 ms^{-2}) and the particle is said to have a constant acceleration of 2 ms^{-2}.

If on the other hand the particle has a velocity of 10 ms^{-1} at one instant and 4 seconds later it has a velocity 2 ms^{-1} its velocity has decreased by 8 ms^{-1} in 4 seconds or increased by -8 ms^{-1} in 4 seconds. If this increase is steady then the rate of increase of velocity is -2 ms^{-1} each second so the acceleration is -2 ms^{-2}. In general *acceleration is the rate of increase of velocity.*

EXAMPLE 4c

A particle moving in a straight line with a constant acceleration of -2 ms^{-2} has a velocity of -4 ms^{-1} at one instant. Find its velocity 3 seconds later.

The acceleration is -2 ms^{-2}.
Therefore the velocity is increasing at the rate of -2 ms^{-1} each second.
Therefore the increase in the velocity after 3 seconds is -6 ms^{-1}.
The initial velocity is -4 ms^{-1}.
Therefore the velocity after 3 seconds is -10 ms^{-1}.

EXERCISE 4c

1) A particle moving in a straight line with constant acceleration has a velocity of 8 ms^{-1} at one instant and 3 seconds later it has a velocity of 2 ms^{-1}. Find its acceleration.

2) A particle moving in a straight line with a constant acceleration of 3 ms^{-2} has a velocity of 2 ms^{-1} at one instant. Find its velocity 2 seconds later.

3) A particle moving in a straight line with a constant acceleration of -3 ms^{-2} has a velocity of 15 ms^{-1} at one instant. Find its velocity:
(a) 4 seconds later,
(b) 5 seconds later,
(c) 6 seconds later.

4) A particle moving in a straight line with constant acceleration has a velocity of -8 ms^{-1} at one instant. If the acceleration of the particle is 2 ms^{-2}, find its velocity after 5 seconds.

5) A particle is moving in a straight line with constant acceleration. If it has a velocity of -10 ms^{-1} at one instant and a velocity of -2 ms^{-1} 4 seconds later, find its acceleration.

Velocity-Time Graph

A graph of velocity plotted against time is a useful way of representing motion in a straight line. When the acceleration is constant the increase in velocity will be the same for equal intervals of time so the graph will be a straight line. Consider a particle moving in a straight line with constant acceleration. It has a velocity of 2 ms^{-1} at one instant and a velocity of 8 ms^{-1} 3 seconds later.

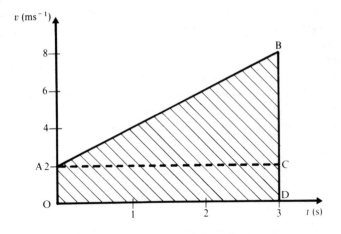

The acceleration is $\frac{6}{3}\,\text{ms}^{-2} = 2\,\text{ms}^{-2}$.

This is represented on the graph by the fraction $\dfrac{\text{BC}}{\text{AC}}$ which is the gradient of the line **AB**.

In general *the gradient of the velocity–time graph represents the acceleration.*
As the graph is a straight line the average velocity over the interval of 3 seconds is the numerical average of the initial velocity $(2\,\text{ms}^{-1})$ and the final velocity $(8\,\text{ms}^{-1})$.
Therefore the average velocity in the interval $t = 0$ to $t = 3$ is $\frac{1}{2}(2 + 8)\text{ms}^{-1} = 5\,\text{ms}^{-1}$.

In general *when a particle is moving in a straight line with constant acceleration the average velocity over an interval of time is the algebraic average of the initial and final velocities in that interval of time.*

From the definition on page (72), for the interval $t = 0$ to $t = 3$:

$$\text{Average velocity} = \frac{\text{increase in displacement}}{\text{time}}$$

From the graph the average velocity is represented by $\frac{1}{2}(\text{AO} + \text{BD})$
the interval of time is represented by OD
Therefore the increase in displacement is represented by $\frac{1}{2}(\text{AO} + \text{BD}) \times \text{OD}$
This is the area of the trapezium OABD.
In general *the area between the velocity–time graph, the time axis and the ordinates t_1 and t_2 represents the increase in displacement over the interval of time $t = t_1$ to $t = t_2$.*

EXAMPLES 4d

1) A car is moving along a straight line. It is brought from rest to a velocity of $20\,\text{ms}^{-1}$ by a constant acceleration of $5\,\text{ms}^{-2}$. It then maintains this constant velocity of $20\,\text{ms}^{-1}$ for 5 seconds and then is brought to rest again by a constant

acceleration of -2 ms^{-2}. Draw a velocity–time graph and find the distance covered by the car.

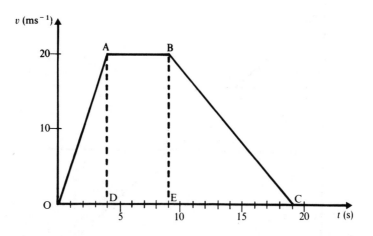

[When the velocity decreases ($t = 9$ to $t = 19$ on the graph) this is sometimes referred to as a deceleration or a retardation.]

The increase in displacement while accelerating is represented by the area of $\triangle$ OAD.

The increase in displacement at uniform velocity is represented by the area of rectangle ABED.

The increase in displacement while decelerating is represented by the area of $\triangle$ BEC.

Therefore the total increase in displacement is represented by the area of the trapezium OABC which is $\frac{1}{2}$(AB + OC) × AD

$$= \tfrac{1}{2}(5 + 19) \times 20$$
$$= 240$$

Therefore the increase in displacement is 240 m.

As the car is travelling in the same sense along the line at all times the distance covered is equal to the increase in displacement.

Therefore the distance covered = 240 m.

2) A particle is travelling in a straight line. It has a velocity of 10 ms^{-1} when it is subjected to an acceleration of -2 ms^{-2} for 8 seconds. Draw a velocity–time graph for this interval of 8 s and find:
(a) the increase in displacement,
(b) the distance covered for the interval of 8 s.

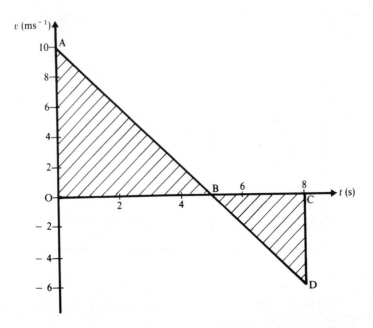

From $t = 0$ to $t = 5$ the velocity is positive: so the particle is travelling in a positive sense along the line.

Therefore the area of $\triangle OAB$ represents an increase in displacement of 25 m.

From $t = 5$ to $t = 8$ the velocity is negative: so the particle is travelling in a negative sense along the line.

Therefore the area of $\triangle BCD$ represents a decrease in displacement of 9 m,

or an increase in displacement of -9 m.

Therefore the increase in displacement from $t = 0$ to $t = 8$ is $25 - 9$ m $= \underline{16\,m}$.

The distance covered from $t = 0$ to $t = 5$ is 25 m.

The distance covered from $t = 5$ to $t = 8$ is 9 m.

Therefore the distance covered from $t = 0$ to $t = 8$ is $25 + 9$ m $= \underline{34\,m}$.

EXERCISE 4d

1) A car is uniformly accelerated from a velocity of $10\ \mathrm{ms}^{-1}$ to a velocity of $40\ \mathrm{ms}^{-1}$ in a time of 10 s. Draw a velocity–time graph and find the acceleration and the distance covered by the car in this time of 10 s.

2) A train is brought to rest from a velocity of $24\ \mathrm{ms}^{-1}$ by a constant acceleration of $-0.8\ \mathrm{ms}^{-2}$. Draw a velocity–time graph and find the distance covered by the train while it is decelerating.

3) A particle moving in a straight line is uniformly accelerated from rest by an acceleration of $4\ \mathrm{ms}^{-2}$ for 4 seconds. It is then uniformly brought to rest again by an acceleration of $-2\ \mathrm{ms}^{-2}$. Draw a velocity–time graph and find the total distance covered by the particle.

4) A particle moving in a straight line is accelerated from rest by an acceleration of $4\,\text{ms}^{-2}$ acting for a time of 3 s. It then maintains a uniform velocity for 6 seconds and is then brought to rest again in a time of 4 seconds by a uniform retardation. Draw a velocity–time graph and find the final acceleration and the final displacement of the particle from its starting point.

5) A particle moves in a straight line with a constant velocity of $5\,\text{ms}^{-1}$ for 2 s. It is then subjected to a constant acceleration of $-2\,\text{ms}^{-2}$ for a time of 8 seconds. Draw a velocity–time graph and find:
(a) the final velocity,
(b) the distance covered by the particle,
(c) the increase in displacement of the particle,
for the interval of 10 s.

6) A particle moves in a straight line. It has a velocity of $6\,\text{ms}^{-1}$ when it is subjected to an acceleration of $-3\,\text{ms}^{-2}$ for 3 s. It then maintains a uniform velocity for 2 s and is then brought to rest in a time of 2 s.
Draw a velocity–time graph and find:
(a) the final acceleration,
(b) the distance covered,
(c) the increase in displacement,
for the interval of 7 s.

EQUATIONS OF MOTION FOR A PARTICLE MOVING IN A STRAIGHT LINE WITH CONSTANT ACCELERATION

Motion in a straight line with constant acceleration occurs frequently enough to justify obtaining general equations which can then be applied to a particular problem.

Consider a particle which is moving in a straight line with a constant acceleration a and has an initial velocity u and a final velocity v after an interval of time t.

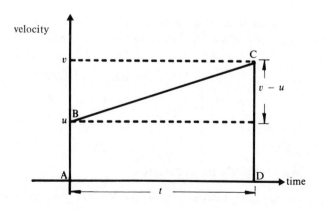

In the velocity–time graph the acceleration is represented by the gradient of the line BC:

Therefore
$$a = \frac{v - u}{t}$$

rearranging:
$$v = u + at \qquad (1)$$

Let the increase in displacement in time t be denoted by s: this is represented by the area of ABCD.

Therefore
$$s = \tfrac{1}{2}(u + v)t \qquad (2)$$

Eliminating v from equations (1) and (2):
$$s = \tfrac{1}{2}[u + (u + at)]\, t$$
$$s = ut + \tfrac{1}{2}at^2 \qquad (3)$$

Eliminating u from equations (1) and (2):
$$s = \tfrac{1}{2}[(v - at) + v]\, t$$
$$s = vt - \tfrac{1}{2}at^2 \qquad (4)$$

Eliminating t from equations (1) and (2):
$$s = \tfrac{1}{2}(u + v)(v - u)$$
$$v^2 = u^2 + 2as \qquad (5)$$

Equations (1), (2), (3), (4), (5) can now be used for any motion in a straight line with constant acceleration and they should be memorised. When deciding which of these equations to use in solving a particular problem it helps if a list is made of the information given and that required.

EXAMPLES 4e

1) A particle is moving along a straight line with a constant retardation of $3\ \mathrm{ms}^{-2}$. If initially it has a velocity $10\ \mathrm{ms}^{-1}$ find the time when the velocity is zero.

Information given: $u = 10$ therefore using the equation

$v = 0$ $v = u + at$

$a = -3$ $0 = 10 - 3t$

Information required: t $\therefore t = 3\tfrac{1}{3}$

Therefore the velocity is zero after $3\tfrac{1}{3}$ seconds.

2) A particle is moving along a straight line with a constant acceleration of $-2\ \mathrm{ms}^{-2}$. It passes through a point A on the line with a velocity of $6\ \mathrm{ms}^{-1}$, find

the displacement of the particle from A after 5 seconds and the distance travelled
by the particle in this time.

Given: $\quad\quad u = 6 \quad\quad$ therefore using the equation

$\quad\quad\quad\quad\quad a = -2$

$$s = ut + \tfrac{1}{2}at^2$$

$\quad\quad\quad\quad\quad t = 5 \quad\quad\quad\quad s = 30 - 25$

Required: $\quad s \quad\quad\quad\quad\quad\quad s = 5.$

Therefore the displacement of the particle from A after 5 s is 5 m. A velocity–
time graph for a problem often leads to quick solutions especially when distances
or displacements are involved, so a sketch graph should always be drawn.

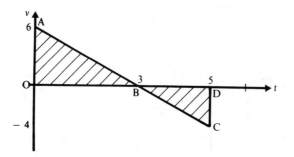

From the sketch we can see that the distance covered in 5 s is represented by the
area of $\triangle$ OAB + area of $\triangle$ BDC.
Therefore the distance covered in 5 s is $9 + 4\,\text{m} = \underline{13\,\text{m}}$.
(Note that the increase in displacement is represented by the area of $\triangle$ OAB –
$\triangle$ BCD.)

3) A train travelling along a straight line with constant acceleration is observed
to travel consecutive distances of 1 km in times of 30 s and 60 s respectively.
Find the initial velocity of the train.

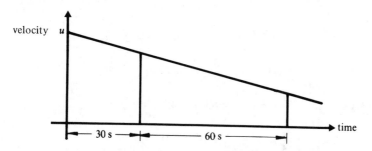

If we let u metre/second be the initial velocity then as units must be consistent,
distance must be measured in metres.

Required: u

Given: when $s = 1000, t = 30$
       when $s = 2000, t = 90$ $\Big\}$ use $s = ut + \frac{1}{2}at^2$ twice

$$1000 = 30\,u + 450\,a \qquad\qquad (1)$$
$$2000 = 90\,u + 4050\,a \qquad\qquad (2)$$

Eliminating a from equations (1) and (2):

$$200 - 9\,u = 9(100 - 3\,u)$$

Therefore $u = 38.9$

Therefore the initial velocity of the train is 38.9 ms^{-1}.
Alternatively:

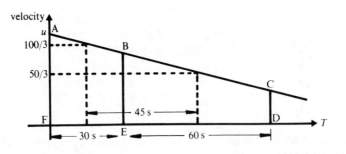

For the first 1000 m: area of **ABEF** represents a distance of 1000 m.

Therefore the average velocity $= \dfrac{1000}{30}$ ms^{-1}

Therefore the velocity is $\dfrac{100}{3}$ ms^{-1} when $T = 15$.

For the second 1000 m: area of **ABEF** represents a distance of 1000 m.

Therefore the average velocity $= \dfrac{1000}{60}$ ms^{-1}

Therefore the velocity is $\dfrac{50}{3}$ ms^{-1} when $T = 60$.

For the interval of time $T = 15$ to $T = 60$: $t = 45, u = \dfrac{100}{3}, v = \dfrac{50}{3}$.

using $v = u + at$, $\dfrac{50}{3} = \dfrac{100}{3} + 45\,a$.

Therefore $a = -\dfrac{10}{27}$

For the interval of time $T = 0$ to $T = 15$: $t = 15, a = \dfrac{10}{27}, v = \dfrac{100}{3}$.

$$\text{using } v = u + at,$$

$$\frac{100}{3} = u - \frac{50}{9}$$

Therefore $u = 38.9$

Therefore the initial velocity of the train is 38.9 ms^{-1}.

4) A particle starts from a point O with an initial velocity of 2 ms^{-1} and travels along a straight line with a constant acceleration of 2 ms^{-2}. Two seconds later a second particle starts from rest at O and travels along the same line with an acceleration of 6 ms^{-2}. Find how far from O the second particle overtakes the first.

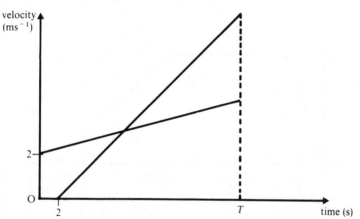

When the second particle overtakes the first they will both have the same displacement from O: let the displacement be d metre.
If the first particle takes T seconds to reach this point
    the second particle takes $(T - 2)$ seconds to reach the same point.

For the first particle $s = d$

$$\left. \begin{array}{l} u = 2 \\[4pt] t = T \\[4pt] a = 2 \end{array} \right\} \quad \begin{array}{l} \text{using } s = ut + \tfrac{1}{2}at^2 \\[4pt] d = 2T + T^2 \end{array} \qquad (1)$$

For the second particle $s = d$

$$\left. \begin{array}{l} u = 0 \\[4pt] t = T-2 \\[4pt] a = 6 \end{array} \right\} \quad \begin{array}{l} \text{using } s = ut + \tfrac{1}{2}at^2 \\[4pt] d = 3(T - 2)^2 \end{array} \qquad (2)$$

Eliminating d from (1) and (2): $2T + T^2 = 3(T-2)^2$

$$T^2 - 7T + 6 = 0$$

$$(T-6)(T-1) = 0$$

$$T = 6 \qquad \text{($T=1$ is before the}$$

Substituting into (2) $\qquad d = 48 \qquad \text{second particle starts)}$

Therefore the second particle overtakes the first 48 m from O.

5) A train takes 5 minutes to cover a distance of 3 km between two stations P and Q. Starting from rest at P it accelerates at a constant rate to a speed of 40 km/h and maintains this speed until it is brought uniformly to rest at Q. If the train takes three times as long to decelerate as it does to accelerate find the time taken by the train to accelerate.

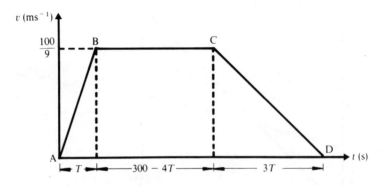

(Units must be consistent: as the time involved is fairly small we choose 1 s and 1 ms^{-1} as the units of time and velocity).
Let the time taken to accelerate be T seconds
then the time taken to decelerate is $3T$ seconds
Therefore the time for which the speed is constant is $300 - 4T$ seconds.
The area of ABCD represents the distance travelled by the train

The area of ABCD $= \frac{1}{2}(300 + (300 - 4T)) \times \dfrac{100}{9}$

$$3000 = \tfrac{1}{2}(600 - 4T) \times \dfrac{100}{9}$$

$$540 = 600 - 4T$$

$$T = 15$$

Therefore the time taken to accelerate is 15 s.

EXERCISE 4e

1) A particle with an initial velocity of 2 ms^{-1} moves in a straight line with a

constant acceleration of 3 ms^{-2} for 5 seconds. Find the final velocity and the distance covered.

2) A particle is moving in a straight line with a constant acceleration of -4 ms^{-2}. If the initial velocity is 10 ms^{-1} find the increase in displacement after (a) 2 s (b) 4 s.

3) A particle moving in a straight line with constant acceleration has a velocity of 5 ms^{-1} at one instant and 4 seconds later it has a velocity of 15 ms^{-1}. Find the acceleration and the distance covered by the particle in the 4 seconds.

4) A particle is moving in a straight line with constant acceleration. Initially it is at rest and after 6 s its velocity is 15 ms^{-1}. Find the acceleration and the distance covered in the 6 seconds.

5) A particle which is moving in a straight line with constant acceleration 2 ms^{-2} is initially at rest. Find the distance covered by the particle in the third second of its motion.

6) A particle moving in a straight line with a constant acceleration -5 ms^{-2} has an initial velocity of 15 ms^{-1}. Find when the velocity is zero.

7) A particle moving in a straight line with a constant retardation of 3 ms^{-2} has an initial velocity of 10 ms^{-1}. Find after what time it returns to its starting point.

8) A particle which is moving in a straight line with constant acceleration covers distances of 10 m and 15 m in two successive seconds. Find the acceleration.

9) A particle moving in a straight line with constant acceleration takes 3 s and 5 s to cover two successive distances of 1 m. Find the acceleration.

10) A particle moving in a straight line with constant acceleration of -3 ms^{-2} has an initial velocity of 15 ms^{-1}. Find the time at which its displacement from the starting point is (a) 15 m (b) -15 m.

11) A particle starts from rest at a point O on a straight line and moves along the line with a constant acceleration of 2 ms^{-2}. Three seconds later a second particle starts from rest at O and moves along the line with constant acceleration 4 ms^{-2}. Find when the second particle overtakes the first particle.

12) Two particles are travelling along a straight line AB of length 20 m. At the same instant one particle starts from rest at A and travels towards B with a constant acceleration of 2 ms^{-2} and the other particle starts from rest at B and travels towards A with a constant acceleration of 5 ms^{-2}. Find how far from A the particles collide.

13) A particle starts from rest and moves along a straight line with a constant acceleration until it reaches a velocity of 15 ms^{-1}. It is then brought to rest again by a constant retardation of 3 ms^{-2}. If the particle is then 60 m from its starting point, find the time for which the particle is moving.

14) A car takes 60 s to travel between two sets of traffic lights, starting from rest at the first set and coming to rest again at the second set. It accelerates uniformly to a speed of 12 ms⁻¹ and then uniformly decelerates to rest. Find the distance between the two sets of lights.

15) A train stops at two stations P and Q which are 2 km apart. It accelerates uniformly from P at 1 ms⁻² for 15 seconds and maintains a constant speed for a time before decelerating uniformly to rest at Q. If the deceleration is 0.5 ms⁻² find the time for which the train is travelling at a constant speed.

VERTICAL MOTION UNDER GRAVITY

Before the time of Galileo it was thought that if two objects of different masses were dropped the heavier object would fall faster than the light one. In a famous series of experiments Galileo showed that this was not true. (He allegedly dropped objects from the top of the leaning tower of Pisa and timed their descent by the Cathedral clock opposite).

The results that Galileo observed are that if air resistance is ignored *all bodies (whatever their mass) have the same constant acceleration towards the centre of the earth when they are moving under the action of their weight only.*

This acceleration is denoted by the letter g, and a good approximation to its value is 9.8 ms⁻².

When a body is thrown vertically upward or is dropped it will move in a straight line. The only force acting on it will be its weight causing a constant acceleration g along the line, so the equations for motion in a straight line with constant acceleration will apply. In some problems it is convenient to take the downward direction as positive, in which case the acceleration is $+g$, but in other problems it is convenient to take the upward direction as positive, in which case the acceleration is $-g$.

EXAMPLES 4f

1) A stone is thrown vertically upward from the top of a tower and hits the ground 10 seconds later with a speed of 51 ms⁻¹. Find the height of the tower.

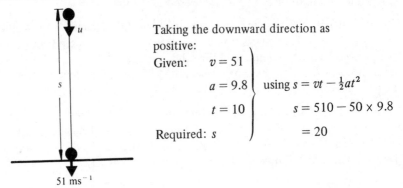

Taking the downward direction as positive:

Given: $v = 51$

$a = 9.8$ using $s = vt - \frac{1}{2}at^2$

$t = 10$ $s = 510 - 50 \times 9.8$

Required: s $= 20$

Therefore the tower is 20 m high.

2) A ball is thrown vertically upward from a point 0.5 m above ground level with a speed of 7 ms^{-1}. Find the height above this point reached by the ball and the speed with which it hits the ground.

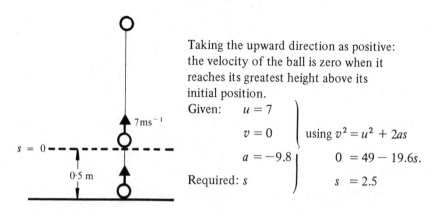

Taking the upward direction as positive: the velocity of the ball is zero when it reaches its greatest height above its initial position.

Given: $u = 7$

$v = 0$ using $v^2 = u^2 + 2as$

$a = -9.8$ $0 = 49 - 19.6s$.

Required: s $s = 2.5$

Therefore the stone reaches a height of 2.5 m above its initial position. When the stone hits the ground it is 0.5 m below its initial position.

Given: $u = 7$

$s = -0.5$ using $v^2 = u^2 + 2as$

$a = -9.8$ $v^2 = 49 + 9.8$

Required: v $v = \pm 7.66$

Therefore the stone hits the ground with a speed of 7.66 ms^{-1}.

3) A ball is thrown vertically upward with a speed of 14 ms^{-1}. Two seconds later a second ball is dropped from the same point. Find where the two balls meet.

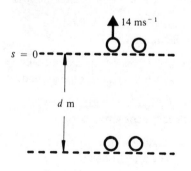

The balls will meet when they have the same displacement (d metre) from the starting point. If the time taken by the first ball to achieve this displacement is T second, the time taken by the second ball is $(T - 2)$ second.

Taking the upward direction as positive:

For the first ball: Given $\quad u = 14$

$$
\left.\begin{array}{l}
a = -9.8 \\
t = T \\
s = d
\end{array}\right\} \quad \text{using } s = ut + \tfrac{1}{2}at^2
$$

$$d = 14T - 4.9T^2 \qquad (1)$$

For the second ball: Given $u = 0$

$$
\left.\begin{array}{l}
a = -9.8 \\
t = T{-}2 \\
s = d
\end{array}\right\} \quad \text{using } s = ut + \tfrac{1}{2}at^2
$$

$$d = -4.9\,(T{-}2)^2 \qquad (2)$$

Eliminating d from (1) and (2): $2T - 0.7T^2 = -0.7(T-2)^2$

$$T = 3.5$$

Substituting into (2): $\qquad\qquad\qquad d = -11.0$

Therefore the balls meet 11.0 m below their initial position.

EXERCISE 4f

1) A stone is dropped from a cliff 100 m above the sea. Find the speed with which it hits the sea.

2) A stone is thrown vertically upward with a speed of 10 ms^{-1}. Find the greatest height reached by the stone.

3) A ball is thrown vertically upward to a height of 10 m. Find the time taken to reach this height and the initial speed of the ball.

4) A particle is projected vertically upward from ground level with a speed of 20 ms^{-1}. Find the time for which the particle is in the air.

5) A stone is thrown vertically upward with a speed of 7 ms^{-1} from the top of a cliff which is 70 m above sea-level. Find the time at which the stone hits the sea.

6) A stone is projected vertically upward with a speed of 21 ms^{-1}. Find the distance travelled by the stone in the first 3 s of its motion.

7) A ball is thrown vertically upward with a speed of 15 ms^{-1} from a point which is 0.7 m above ground level. Find the speed with which the ball hits the ground.

8) A particle is projected vertically upward from ground level with a speed of 50 ms^{-1}. For how long will it be more than 70 m above the ground?

9) A falling stone takes 0.2 seconds to fall past a window which is 1 m high. From how far above the top of the window was the stone dropped?

10) A stone is projected vertically upward with a speed of 7 ms^{-1} and one second later a second stone is projected vertically upward from the same point with the same speed. Find where the two stones meet.

11) A stone is dropped from the top of a building and at the same time a second stone is thrown vertically upward from the bottom of the building with a speed of 20 ms^{-1}. They pass each other 3 seconds later. Find the height of the building.

ANGULAR VELOCITY

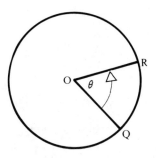

Consider a particle P which is moving round the circumference of a circle: it can rotate about O in only two senses, clockwise or anticlockwise. The positive and negative signs are used to differentiate between these two senses and it is customary to take the anticlockwise sense as positive.

If initially the particle is at Q and after an interval of time it is at R, then if angle QOR is θ, *the angular velocity of P is defined as the rate of increase of θ*. Angular velocity is usually denoted by ω.

If θ is increasing at a constant rate then the angular velocity (ω) is uniform.

Unit of Angular Velocity. Angles are measured in radians so the unit of angular velocity is one radian per second (1 rad s^{-1}).

EXAMPLE 4g   *particularly this example*

The hour and minute hands of a clock coincide at exactly 12.00 hours. Find when they next coincide.

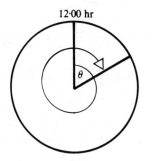

12·00 hr

The hour hand rotates through 1 revolution in 12 hours, i.e. 2π rad in 12 hours.
∴ the angular velocity of the hour hand is $\frac{\pi}{360}$ rad/min. (This is a more convenient

unit than rad s^{-1} in this problem).

The minute hand rotates at the steady rate of 2π rad per hour.

Therefore the angular velocity of the minute hand is $\frac{\pi}{30}$ rad/min.

If they next coincide after t minutes when they make an angle of θ rad with their initial position then the hour hand will have turned through an angle of θ rad and the minute hand through an angle of $(2\pi + \theta)$ rad.

For the hour hand:
$$\frac{\pi}{360}t = \theta. \tag{1}$$

For the minute hand:
$$\frac{\pi}{30}t = \theta + 2\pi. \tag{2}$$

Eliminating θ from (1) and (2)
$$\frac{\pi}{30}t = \frac{\pi}{360}t + 2\pi.$$

$$12t = t + 720$$

$$t = 65.45$$

Therefore they next coincide 65.5 minutes after 12.00 hours: i.e. at 13.05 hours.

Relationship Between Angular Velocity and Linear Velocity

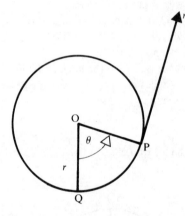

Consider a point P which is rotating in a circle of radius r with a constant angular velocity ω.

If P turns through an angle θ from its initial position in a time t then

$$\theta = \omega t \tag{1}$$

The length of the arc PQ is $r\theta$ (θ being measured in radians).

Therefore P has covered a distance of $r\theta$ in time t

Therefore the speed of P is
$$\frac{r\theta}{t} \tag{2}$$

Eliminating θ from (1) and (2).

The speed of P is $r\omega$ and its *velocity is $r\omega$ in the direction of the tangent to the circle at P.*

Thus a point which is rotating in a circle of radius 2 m with an angular velocity of $4\,\text{rad s}^{-1}$ has a speed of $8\,\text{ms}^{-1}$.

EXERCISE 4g $1, 5$.

1) Find the angular velocity in rad s^{-1} of a record which is rotating at the rate of:

(a) 33 revolutions per minute,
(b) 45 revolutions per minute.

2) Find the angular velocity in rad s^{-1} of the second hand of a clock.

3) A wheel of radius 2 m is rotating at the constant rate of $20\,\text{rad s}^{-1}$. Find the speed of a point on its circumference in ms^{-1}.

4) Find the speed in kmh^{-1} of a point on the equator of the earth assuming it to be a sphere of radius 6400 km.

5) The minute and hour hand of a clock coincide exactly at 12 o'clock. Find the time between 3 o'clock and 4 o'clock when they coincide.

Constant Angular Acceleration

Angular acceleration is defined as the rate of increase of angular velocity.
The *unit* of angular acceleration is one radian per second per second (rad s^{-2}). When the angular velocity increases at a steady rate the angular acceleration is constant. In this case if angular velocity is plotted against time the graph will be a straight line.

Consider a particle describing a circle with constant angular acceleration α.

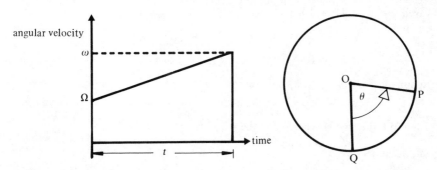

If initially the particle is at Q with an angular velocity Ω and after an interval of time t it is at P with angular velocity ω
then the increase in angular velocity is $\qquad\qquad \omega - \Omega$

Therefore the rate of increase of angular velocity is $\qquad \dfrac{\omega - \Omega}{t}$

Therefore $$\alpha = \frac{\omega - \Omega}{t}$$

Rearranging $$\omega = \Omega + \alpha t \tag{1}$$

As the angular acceleration is constant the average angular velocity for this interval of time is

$$\tfrac{1}{2}(\Omega + \omega).$$

If θ is the angle turned through by the particle in time t then

$$\theta = \tfrac{1}{2}(\Omega + \omega)t \tag{2}$$

Eliminating ω from (1) and (2) $\theta = \Omega t + \tfrac{1}{2}\alpha t^2$ (3)

Eliminating Ω from (1) and (2) $\theta = \omega t - \tfrac{1}{2}\alpha t^2$ (4)

Eliminating t from (1) and (2) $\omega^2 = \Omega^2 + 2\alpha\theta$ (5)

These five equations are the equations for circular motion with constant angular acceleration and can be used for any particular problem on circular motion with constant acceleration.

(Note the similarity to the equations for motion in a straight line with constant acceleration. This should be a help in recalling them.)

EXAMPLE 4h

A wheel rotates with constant angular acceleration and starting from rest it is observed to make 5 complete revolutions in 3 seconds. What is the angular velocity (rad s^{-1}) at the end of the 3 seconds?

The wheel makes 5 revolutions in 3 s, so it turns through an angle of 10π rad in this time.

Given: $\theta = 10\pi$

$t = 3$ using $\theta = \tfrac{1}{2}(\Omega + \omega)t$

$\Omega = 0$ $10\pi = \tfrac{1}{2}\omega \times 3$

Required: ω therefore $\omega = \dfrac{20\pi}{3}$

Therefore the angular velocity of the wheel is $\dfrac{20\pi}{3}$ rad s^{-1}.

EXERCISE 4h

1) A wheel rotates with a constant angular acceleration of 3 rad s^{-2}. If it starts from rest find its angular velocity 2 s later.

2) A particle describes a circle with constant angular acceleration. It makes one complete revolution in 2 seconds starting from rest. What is its angular acceleration?

3) A rotating wheel changes its angular velocity from 2 rad s^{-1} to 4 rad s^{-1} in 5 s.

Assuming that the angular acceleration is constant find the angle the wheel turns through in this time and its angular acceleration.

4) A flywheel rotates with constant angular acceleration. If its angular velocity changes from 10 revolutions per second to 4 revolutions per second in one revolution of the flywheel find its angular acceleration.

5) A wheel makes 4 complete revolutions in 3 s. If at the end of the 3 s it has an angular velocity of π rad s^{-1} find its angular acceleration assuming this to be constant.

6) A particle starting from rest moves in a circle with a constant angular acceleration of $\frac{\pi}{4}$ rad s^{-2}. Find the angle it turns through in the third second of its motion.

SUMMARY

DEFINITIONS: *Velocity* is the rate of increase of linear displacement.
Acceleration is the rate of increase of velocity.
Angular velocity is the rate of increase of angular displacement.
Angular acceleration is the rate of increase of angular velocity.

Equations of motion with constant acceleration

1. Motion in a straight line: $v = u + at$

$$s = \tfrac{1}{2}(u + v)t$$

$$s = ut + \tfrac{1}{2}at^2$$

$$s = vt - \tfrac{1}{2}at^2$$

$$v^2 = u^2 + 2as$$

2. Circular motion: $\omega = \Omega + \alpha t$

$$\theta = \tfrac{1}{2}(\omega + \Omega)t$$

$$\theta = \Omega t + \tfrac{1}{2}\alpha t^2$$

$$\theta = \omega t - \tfrac{1}{2}\alpha t^2$$

$$\omega^2 = \Omega^2 + 2\alpha\theta.$$

MULTIPLE CHOICE EXERCISE 4

The instructions for answering these questions are given on page (xii).

TYPE I

1)

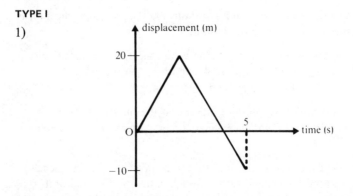

The diagram shows the displacement-time graph for a particle moving in a straight line. The average velocity for the interval $t = 0$ to $t = 5$ is:

(a) 0   (b) $6\,\text{ms}^{-1}$ (c) $-2\,\text{ms}^{-1}$ (d) $2\,\text{ms}^{-1}$ (e) $-4\,\text{ms}^{-1}$

2)

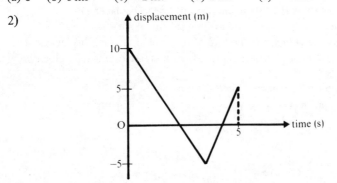

The diagram shows the displacement-time graph for a particle moving in a straight line. The distance covered by the particle in the interval $t = 0$ to $t = 5$ is:

(a) 20 m   (b) 25 m   (c) 15 m   (d) 5 m   (e) 10 m

3)

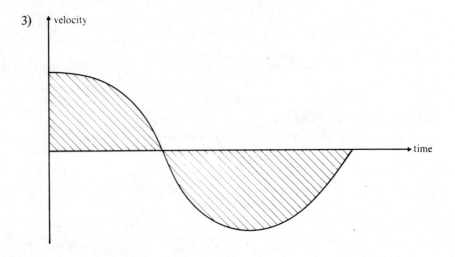

The diagram shows the velocity-time graph for a particle moving in a straight line. The sum of the two shaded areas represents:
(a) the increase in displacement of the particle,
(b) the average velocity of the particle,
(c) the average acceleration of the particle,
(d) the distance moved by the particle,
(e) the average speed of the particle.

4) A particle moving in a straight line with a constant acceleration of 3 ms^{-2} has an initial velocity of -1 ms^{-1}. Its velocity two seconds later is:
(a) 5 ms^{-1} (b) 6 ms^{-1} (c) 4 ms^{-1} (d) 0 (e) -7 ms^{-1}.

5) A particle moves in a straight line and passes through O, a fixed point on the line with a velocity of 6 ms^{-1}. The particle moves with a constant retardation of 2 ms^{-2} for four seconds and thereafter moves with constant velocity. How long after leaving O does the particle return to O?
(a) 3 s (b) 8 s (c) never   (d) 4 s (e) 6 s.

TYPE II

6) When a number of particles, each of different weight, are dropped the acceleration of each particle:
(a) is constant but different for each particle, depending on its weight,
(b) is constant and the same for each particle,
(c) increases as the particle falls.

7) If a particle is moving in a straight line with constant acceleration and a velocity-time graph is drawn for the motion, the gradient of the graph represents:
(a) the acceleration,
(b) the rate of increase of velocity,
(c) the rate of decrease of velocity.

8) A particle is rotating in a circle with constant angular acceleration. With the usual notation, the speed of the particle at any time t is:
(a) $r(\Omega + \alpha t)$

(b) $\dfrac{r\theta}{t}$

(c) $r\omega$

TYPE III

9) (a) A particle is moving in a straight line with constant acceleration.
   (b) The average velocity of a particle moving in a straight line is the algebraic average of the initial and final velocities.

10) (a) A particle is moving in a straight line with a constant acceleration of 2 ms^{-2}.
   (b) A particle moving in a straight line with a constant acceleration has a velocity of 2 ms^{-1} at one instant and a velocity of 8 ms^{-1} three seconds later.

11) Using the standard notation for a particle moving in a straight line with constant acceleration:
(a) The particle covers a distance s in time t where $s = ut + \frac{1}{2}at^2$
(b) $u > 0$ and $v < 0$.

TYPE IV

12) A particle is moving in a straight line. Find when the particle returns to its initial position.
(a) The particle is thrown vertically upwards.
(b) The initial velocity of the particle is 10 ms^{-2}.
(c) The weight of the particle is 20 N.

13) A particle is moving in a circle. Find the speed of the particle when it returns to its initial position.
(a) The acceleration is constant and equal to α.
(b) The initial angular velocity is Ω.
(c) The radius of the circle is r.

14) Two particles A and B are moving along a straight line and initially B is behind A. Determine whether B overtakes A.
(a) B moves with a constant velocity of 6 ms^{-1}.
(b) B is 4 m behind A initially.
(c) A moves with a constant acceleration of 3 ms^{-2}.

15)

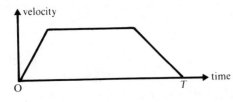

The diagram shows a sketch of a velocity-time graph for a particle moving in a straight line. Find the value of T.

(a) The distance covered is 100 m.
(b) The maximum velocity reached is 10 ms^{-1} and is maintained for five seconds.
(c) The acceleration is twice the retardation.

TYPE V

16) Velocity is the rate of increase of distance.

17) A particle moving in a straight line with a constant acceleration of -2 ms^{-2} has a velocity of 3 ms^{-1} at one instant and a velocity of -3 ms^{-1} three seconds later.

18) A particle moving under the action of its weight only has a constant acceleration g vertically downwards.

19) A particle is moving with constant acceleration in a straight line. At one instant it has a velocity u and t seconds later it has a velocity v. Its acceleration is $\dfrac{u-v}{t}$.

20) A particle is moving in the positive sense on the circumference of a circle of radius 2 m. The particle has a constant angular acceleration of 3 rad s^{-2}. At one instant the speed of the particle is 2 ms^{-1} and one second later it is 8 ms^{-1}.

21) A particle is moving in a straight line. A displacement-time graph is drawn for its motion. The gradient of the tangent to the graph at time T represents the velocity of the particle at time T.

22) A car travels from A to B at a constant speed of 30 kmh^{-1} and returns to A immediately at a constant speed of 40 kmh^{-1}. The average speed for the journey is 35 kmh^{-1}.

23) If a particle moving in a straight line has a negative acceleration then this always means that the speed is decreasing.

MISCELLANEOUS EXERCISE 4 $1, 12, 18$

1) A stone is dropped from the top of a building 20 m high. A second stone is dropped from half-way up the same building. Find the time that should elapse between the release of the two stones if they are to reach the ground at the same time.

2) A particle is describing a circle of radius 4 m with a constant angular acceleration. At one instant it has a speed of 2 ms^{-1} and 4 s later it has a speed of 10 ms^{-1}. Find its angular acceleration and the distance it has travelled in this time.

3) A particle is describing a vertical circle of radius 2 m with a constant angular acceleration of $\frac{\pi}{6}$ rad s^{-2}. If it is initially at rest at the lowest point of the circle find its speed 2 seconds later and its displacement from its original position.

4) A toy train is moving along a straight length of track. It accelerates uniformly from rest to a velocity of 0.5 ms^{-1} and maintains this velocity for a time before decelerating uniformly to rest again. If the time taken for this journey is 2 seconds and it moves a distance of 0.8 m along the track, find the time for which the speed of the train is uniform.

5) A car has a maximum acceleration of 6 ms^{-2} and a maximum deceleration of 8 ms^{-2}. Find the least time in which it can cover a distance of 0.2 km starting from rest and stopping again. What is the maximum speed reached by the car in this time?

6) A particle moving in a straight line covers distances of 90 m and 240 m in

successive times of 2 s and 4 s. Show that the particle has a constant acceleration and find it.

7) A particle P moves along the x-axis and a particle Q moves along the y-axis. P starts from rest at the origin and moves with a constant acceleration of 2 ms^{-2}. At the same time Q is at the point $(0, 3)$ with a velocity of 2 ms^{-1} and is moving with a constant acceleration of -3 ms^{-2}. Find the distance between P and Q 4 seconds later.

8) A particle P starts from rest from a point A and moves along a straight line with a constant acceleration of 2 ms^{-2}. At the same time a second particle Q is 5 m behind A and is moving in the same direction as P with a speed of 5 ms^{-1}. If Q has a constant acceleration 3 ms^{-2} find how far from A it overtakes P.

9) A particle P which is moving along a straight line with a constant acceleration of 0.3 ms^{-2} passes a point A on the line with a velocity of 20 ms^{-1}. At the time when P passes A a second particle Q is 20 m behind A and is moving with a constant velocity of 30 ms^{-1}. Prove that the particles collide.

10) A bus moves away from rest at a bus stop with an acceleration of 1 ms^{-2}. As the bus starts to move a man who is 4 m behind the stop runs with a constant speed after the bus. If he justs manages to catch the bus find his speed.

11) A model aeroplane is constrained to fly in a circle by a guide line which is 3 m long. It accelerates from a speed of 2 ms^{-1} with a constant angular acceleration of $\frac{\pi}{10} \text{ rad s}^{-1}$ for $2\frac{1}{2}$ revolutions. The guide line then breaks. Find the speed of the aeroplane when the guide line breaks.

12) A stone is thrown vertically upward with a speed of u metre per second. A second stone is thrown vertically upward from the same point with the same initial speed but T seconds later than the first one. Prove that they collide at a distance of $\left(\dfrac{4u^2 - g^2 T^2}{8g}\right)$ metre above the point of projection.

13) A stone is dropped from the top of a tower. In the last second of its motion it falls through a distance which is $\frac{1}{5}$ of the height of the tower. Find the height of the tower.

14) A particle moving in a straight line OD with uniform retardation leaves point O at time $t = 0$, and comes to instantaneous rest at D. On its way to D the particle passes points A, B, C at times $t = T, 2T, 4T$, respectively after leaving O, where $AB = BC = l$. Find, in terms of l, (i) the length of CD and (ii) the length of OA.
(J.M.B.)

15) Three points A, B, C on a motor racing track are such that B is 1 km beyond A and C is 2 km beyond B. A car X, moving with uniform acceleration takes 1 minute to travel from A to B and $1\frac{1}{2}$ minutes to travel from B to C. Find its acceleration in km/h/min and show that its speed at C is 92 km/h. Another car

Y, which is moving with uniform acceleration of 8 km/h per min. passes C 15 seconds earlier than X, and its speed is then 75 km/h. Find where X passes Y.

(Cambridge)

16) In a motor race, a car A is 1 km from the finishing post, and is travelling at 35 m per second with a uniform acceleration of $\frac{2}{3}$ m per sec^2. At the same instant a second car B is 200 m behind A and is travelling at 44 m per second with a uniform acceleration of $\frac{1}{2}$ m per sec^2. Show that B passes A 220 m before the finish.

Show also that, if these accelerations are maintained, B arrives at the finishing post 1 sec. before A.

(Cambridge)

17) A flywheel is brought to rest by a constant retarding torque. From the instant this torque is applied, the flywheel is observed to make 200 revolutions in the first minute and 120 revolutions in the next minute. Calculate how many more revolutions the wheel makes before coming to rest and the time taken to stop the wheel.

(A.E.B)

18) A flywheel starts from rest and is uniformly accelerated to an angular speed of 120 revolutions per minute. It maintains this speed until it is uniformly retarded to rest again. The magnitude of the retardation is three times the value of the starting acceleration. Between starting and coming to rest again the flywheel completes N revolutions in five minutes. Sketch the angular speed–time graph and hence find, in terms of N, the time for which the flywheel is travelling at the maximum speed. Show that $300 < N < 600$.

If $N = 480$, find the starting acceleration and the number of revolutions completed in the first two minutes.

(A.E.B)

CHAPTER 5

NEWTON'S LAWS OF MOTION

The study of mechanics is based on three laws which were first formulated by Newton:
1. *Every body will remain at rest or continue to move with uniform velocity unless an external force is applied to it.*

2. *When an external force is applied to a body of constant mass the force produces an acceleration which is directly proportional to the force.*

3. *When a body A exerts a force on a body B, B exerts an equal and opposite force on A.*

NEWTON'S FIRST LAW

This law in effect defines force: it states that if a body is travelling with uniform velocity there is no external force acting on the body; conversely if there is an external force acting on the body its velocity changes: i.e. force is the quantity that, when acting on a body, changes the velocity of that body. There is usually more than one external force acting on a body, so to cause the body to accelerate there must be a resultant force acting on it. Conversely there will be no acceleration if there is no resultant force acting on the body. Thus summarising:
1. *If a body has an acceleration there is a resultant force acting on that body.*
2. *If a body has no acceleration the forces acting on the body are in equilibrium.*
[*Note:* if a body has zero acceleration it can either be at rest *or* moving with uniform velocity - this should dispel the notion that because a body is moving with uniform velocity there is a force responsible for the maintenance of that velocity: there is not.]

EXAMPLE 5a

1) The diagram shows the forces that are acting on a particle. Has the particle an acceleration?

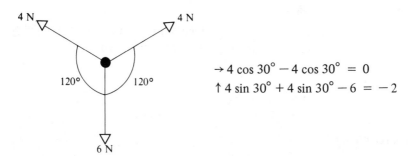

$$\rightarrow 4 \cos 30° - 4 \cos 30° = 0$$
$$\uparrow 4 \sin 30° + 4 \sin 30° - 6 = -2$$

Therefore there is a resultant force acting on the particle.
Therefore it has an acceleration.

2) A particle of weight 4 N is suspended from a vertical string. If the particle is moving upward with a uniform velocity find the tension in the string.

As the particle is moving with uniform velocity the forces acting on it are in equilibrium.
$$\uparrow T - 4\,\text{N} = 0$$
$$T = 4\,\text{N}$$

EXERCISE 5a

The diagram shows the forces acting on a particle. In questions 1–4 determine whether or not the particle has an acceleration.

1) $P = Q = R = 6\,\text{N}$, $\theta = 120°$

2) $P = Q = R = 4\,\text{N}$, $\theta = 150°$

3) $P = 8\,\text{N}, Q = R = 4\,\text{N}, \theta = 120°$

4) $P = Q = 3\,\text{N}, R = 4\,\text{N}, \theta = 135°$

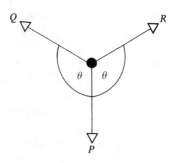

5) The diagram shows the forces acting on a particle:

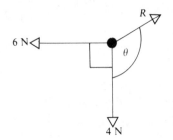

Find R and θ if the particle is moving with uniform velocity.

NEWTON'S SECOND LAW

This law gives the relationship between force, mass and acceleration. It states that when a force is applied to a body causing it to accelerate, the acceleration is directly proportional to the force. Experimental evidence also shows that the acceleration is inversely proportional to the mass of the body, so if the force is F, the mass is m and the acceleration is a:

$$a \propto \frac{F}{m} \quad \text{or} \quad F \propto ma.$$

Introducing a constant of proportion this relationship becomes $F = k\,ma$. Thus the force which gives a mass of 1 kg an acceleration of 1 ms^{-2} is of magnitude k (since $F = k \times 1 \times 1$). If we choose to make this force the unit of force then $k = 1$ so that

$$F = ma$$

and the *unit of force* is now defined as that force which gives a mass of 1 kg an acceleration of 1 ms^{-2}. This unit of force is called a *newton* (N).

The equation $F = ma$ is the basic equation of motion and it is of fundamental importance to the study of the motion of a body with constant mass. It should be noted that as force and acceleration are both vector quantities the equation $F = ma$ is a vector equation: therefore as well as the magnitudes of both sides being equal, force and acceleration have the same direction. If the force is constant the acceleration will also be constant and conversely if the force varies so does the acceleration. There is usually more than one force acting on a body and in this case F represents the resultant force acting on the body. Summarising:

1. *The resultant force acting on a body of constant mass is equal to the mass of the body multiplied by its acceleration:*
   F (newton) $= m$ (kilogramme) $\times a$ (metre/second^2)
2. *The resultant force acting on a body and the acceleration of the body are both in the same direction.*
3. *A constant force acting on a constant mass produces a constant acceleration.*

Weight and Mass

Consider a body of mass m which is falling under the action of its weight only: it has an acceleration g ms^{-2} downwards.

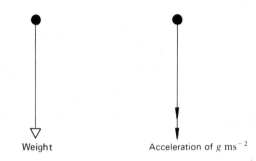

Weight   Acceleration of g ms^{-2}

Using $F = ma$: Weight $= mg$ newton

Therefore a body of mass m kilogramme has a weight of mg newton

$\left(\begin{array}{l}\text{It is interesting to note that an average sized apple has a mass of about 0.1 kg:}\\ \text{so it has a weight of about 1 N!}\end{array}\right)$

Problem Solving

When using Newton's Laws to solve a problem it is helpful to draw a diagram showing the forces that are acting on the body under consideration and the acceleration of the body. It must also be remembered that:
(a) the resultant force and the acceleration are both in the same direction,
(b) if there is no acceleration the forces are in equilibrium.
In problems which involve a large body (as opposed to a particle) the body is treated as a particle of equal mass.

EXAMPLES 5b

1) A particle of mass 5 kg slides down a smooth plane inclined at 30° to the horizontal. Find the acceleration of the particle and the reaction between the particle and the plane.

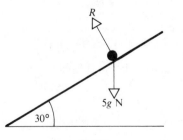

Forces

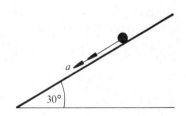

Acceleration

As the acceleration is down the plane, the resultant force is also down the plane. (It is the resultant force that causes the acceleration.)

The resultant force down the plane = $5\,g\sin 30°$

Using $F = ma$:

$$5\,g\sin 30° = 5a$$

Therefore

$$a = \frac{g}{2}$$

Therefore the acceleration of the particle is $\dfrac{g}{2}\,\text{ms}^{-2}$ down the plane.

There is no component of acceleration perpendicular to the plane: so there is no component of force perpendicular to the plane.

Therefore resolving perpendicular to the plane, $R - 5\,g\cos 30° = 0$

Therefore

$$R = \frac{5g\sqrt{3}}{2}$$

Therefore the reaction between the particle and the plane is $\dfrac{5g\sqrt{3}}{2}\,\text{N}.$

2) A block of mass 2 kg rests on the floor of a lift which has an acceleration of $5\ \text{ms}^{-2}$ upwards. Find the reaction between the block and the lift.

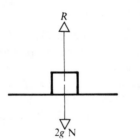

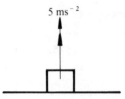

The resultant upward force on the block is $R - 2g$

Using $F = ma$

$$R - 2g = 2 \times 5$$

Therefore $R = 10 + 2g$

$$= 29.6$$

Therefore the reaction between the block and the lift is 29.6 N.

3) A particle of mass 5 kg is pulled along a rough horizontal surface by a string which is inclined at $60°$ to the horizontal. If the acceleration of the particle is $\dfrac{g}{3}\,\text{ms}^{-2}$ and the coefficient of friction between the particle and the plane is $\tfrac{2}{3}$, find the tension in the string.

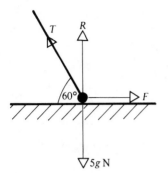

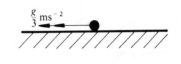

As there is no component of acceleration vertically there is no resultant force vertically:

Therefore ↑ $R + T \sin 60° - 5g = 0$ (1)

As friction is limiting $\qquad F = \frac{2}{3} R$ (2)

← Resultant force $= T \cos 60° - F$

Using $F = ma$: $\qquad T \cos 60° - F = \frac{5g}{3}$ (3)

Eliminating F and R from (1), (2) and (3):

$$T \cos 60° - \frac{2}{3}(5g - T \sin 60°) = \frac{5g}{3}$$

$$T = 10g\sqrt{3}\,(2 - \sqrt{3}).$$

4) A car of mass 1000 kg is brought to rest from a speed of 40 ms^{-1} in a distance of 80 m. Find the braking force of the car assuming that it is constant and that there is a constant resistance to motion of 100 N.

As the braking force is constant the acceleration of the car is constant. Taking the direction of motion as positive we are given:

$$u = 40, \quad v = 0, \quad s = 80$$

Therefore using $v^2 = u^2 + 2as$: $\;0 = 1600 + 160a$
Therefore $\qquad\qquad\qquad\qquad a = -10$
Therefore the car has an acceleration of -10 ms^{-2}.

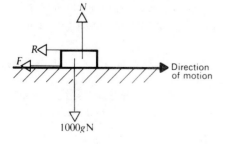

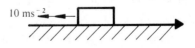

In the diagram F is the braking force and R is the resistance.
The resultant horizontal force is $F + R$.

Using Newton's Law $F + R = 1000 \times 10$
But $R = 100$ Therefore $F = 10\,000 - 100$
                                      $= 9\,900$

Therefore the braking force of the car is 9 900 N.

EXERCISE 5b

1) A particle of mass 2 kg has an acceleration of 5 ms^{-2}: find the magnitude of the resultant force acting on the particle.

2) A particle has a resultant force of magnitude 8 N acting on it. If the mass of the particle is 3 kg, find the magnitude of its acceleration.

3) A particle of mass 5 kg is pulled along a smooth horizontal surface by a horizontal string. If the acceleration of the particle is 3 ms^{-2} find the tension in the string.

4) A particle of mass 10 kg is pulled up a smooth slope inclined at $60°$ to the horizontal by a string parallel to the slope. If the acceleration of the particle is $\frac{g}{10}$ ms^{-2} find the tension in the string.

5) A particle of mass 8 kg is pulled along a smooth horizontal surface by a string inclined at $30°$ to the horizontal. If the tension in the string is 10 N find the acceleration of the particle.

6) A particle of mass 4 kg is pulled along a rough horizontal surface by a string parallel to the surface. If the tension in the string is 20 N and the coefficient of friction between the particle and the plane is $\frac{1}{5}$ find the acceleration of the particle.

7) A particle of mass 8 kg slides down a rough plane which is inclined at arcsin $\frac{1}{6}$ to the horizontal. If the acceleration of the particle is $\frac{g}{10}$ ms^{-2} find the coefficient of friction between the particle and the plane.

8) A block of mass 15 kg rests on the floor of a lift. Find the reaction between the block and the floor of the lift if the lift is accelerating down at 4 ms^{-2}.

9) A block of mass 12 kg rests on the floor of a lift. If the reaction between the block and the lift floor is 20 N find the acceleration of the lift.

10) A bullet of mass 0.02 kg is fired into a wall with a velocity of 400 ms^{-1}. If the bullet penetrates the wall to a depth of 0.1 m find the resistance of the wall assuming it to be uniform.

11) A lift of mass 500 kg is drawn up by a cable. It makes an ascent in three stages: it is brought from rest to its maximum speed by a constant acceleration of $\frac{g}{2}$ ms^{-2}, it then moves with its maximum speed for an interval of time and is then brought to rest by a deceleration of g ms^{-2}. Find the tension in the cable in each of the three stages.

12) A car of mass 300 kg is brought to rest in a time of 4 s from a speed of 20 ms^{-1}. If there is no resistance to motion find the force exerted by the brakes assuming it to be constant.

13) A car of mass 500 kg is capable of braking with a deceleration of $\frac{g}{2}$ ms^{-2}. If the resistance to motion is constant and equal to 50 N find the braking force assuming this to be constant.

14) The diagram shows the forces that are acting on a wedge which is in contact with a rough horizontal table.

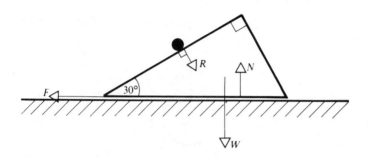

If the mass of the wedge is 10 kg, $R = 6g$ N and the coefficient of friction between the wedge and the table is $\frac{1}{7}$ find the acceleration of the wedge.

NEWTON'S THIRD LAW

This states that action and reaction are equal and opposite:

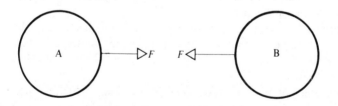

i.e. if a body A exerts a force on a body B then B exerts an equal and opposite force on A. This is true whether A and B are in contact with each or if they are some distance apart; it is also true if A and B are moving or if they are stationary. However, we are mainly concerned with the forces between two bodies which are in contact and the statements in Chapter 3 on contact and internal forces are based on this law. A rigid body may be considered as a collection of particles that are held together by forces of attraction between the particles. Newton's Third Law states that these forces occur in equal and opposite pairs; thus their net effect on the whole body is zero: this justifies the fact that only the external forces acting on a body are considered.

Note: Most of us have an intuitive idea of what a force is and the effect that it produces but it required Newton's genius to express these ideas in such basically simple terms. Under normal conditions the results that are obtained from the use of Newton's Laws agree very closely indeed with observed results and this is justification enough for their use. Although it is now known that they do not represent the whole truth, significant errors arising from their use cannot be found unless conditions are extreme (very high temperatures, very small masses such as atomic particles etc.).

MOTION OF CONNECTED PARTICLES

Consider two particles connected by a light string passing over a fixed pulley as shown in the diagram.

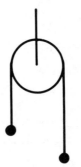

If the pulley is smooth the tension in the string will be the same throughout its length.

If the pulley is rough the tensions in the portions of the string on either side of the pulley will be different.

If the string is inelastic (i.e. does not alter its length under tension) the acceleration of the particles attached to it will have the same magnitude. Also at a given instant of time the speeds of the particles will be equal and they will have covered equal distances.

To analyse the motion of the system the forces acting on each particle must be considered separately and the equation $F = ma$ applied to each particle in turn.

EXAMPLES 5c

1) Two particles of mass 5 kg and 3 kg are connected by a light inelastic string passing over a smooth fixed pulley. Find the accelerations of the particles and the tension in the string when the system is moving freely.

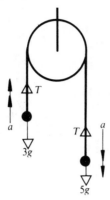

For the 3 kg mass the resultant upward force is $T - 3g$
Applying $F = ma$ to the 3 kg mass: $T - 3g = 3a$ (1)
For the 5 kg mass the resultant downward force is $5g - T$
Applying $F = ma$ to the 5 kg mass: $5g - T = 5a$ (2)
(1) + (2): $2g = 8a$

Therefore $a = \dfrac{g}{4}$

Substituting into (1): $T = \dfrac{3g}{4} + 3g = \dfrac{15g}{4}$

Therefore the acceleration of the system is $\dfrac{g}{4}$ ms^{-2}

and the tension in the string is $\dfrac{15g}{4}$ N.

2) A particle of mass 2 kg rests on the surface of a rough plane which is inclined
at $30°$ to the horizontal. It is connected by a light inelastic string passing over
a light smooth pulley at the top of the plane, to a particle of mass 3 kg which is
hanging freely. If the coefficient of friction between the 2 kg mass and the plane
is $\frac{1}{3}$ find the acceleration of the system when it is released from rest and find the
tension in the string. Find also the force exerted by the string on the pulley.

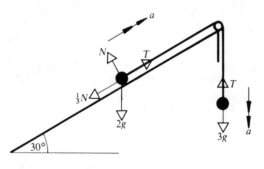

For the 2 kg mass:
There is no component of acceleration perpendicular to the plane.

Therefore resolving perpendicular to the plane: $N - 2g \cos 30° = 0$, $N = g\sqrt{3}$.
There is an acceleration a up the plane.
The resultant force parallel to the plane $= T - \frac{1}{3}N - 2g \sin 30°$

Applying $F = ma$:
$$T - \tfrac{1}{3}N - 2g \sin 30° = 2a$$

$$T - \frac{g}{3}(\sqrt{3} + 3) \qquad = 2a \qquad (1)$$

For the 3 kg mass: $\downarrow$ Resultant force $= 3g - T$

Applying $F = ma$:
$$3g - T = 3a \qquad (2)$$

Adding (1) and (2):
$$3g - \frac{g}{3}(\sqrt{3} + 3) = 5a$$

$$\text{Therefore } a = \frac{(6 - \sqrt{3})}{15}g$$

Substituting in (2):
$$T = \frac{(9 + \sqrt{3})}{5}g$$

Therefore the acceleration of the system is $\dfrac{(6 - \sqrt{3})}{15}g$ ms^{-2} and the tension in
the string is $\dfrac{(9 + \sqrt{3})}{5}g$ N.

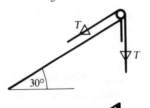

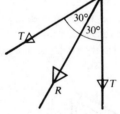

The components of force acting on the
pulley are T acting down the plane and
T acting vertically downward.

These two forces are equal so their
resultant R bisects the angle between
them. $\therefore R$ acts at an angle of $30°$ to
the vertical.
Resolving in the direction of R:
$$2T \cos 30° = R$$
$$R = T\sqrt{3}$$
$$= \frac{3(3\sqrt{3} + 1)}{5}g$$

so the force acting on the pulley is $3(3\sqrt{3} + 1)g/5$ N acting at $30°$ to the vertical.
(As the pulley is light, the force exerted on the top edge of the plane is the same
as the force exerted by the string on the pulley).

3) The diagram shows a particle of mass 8 kg connected to a light scale pan by

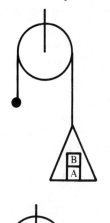

a light inextensible string which passes over a smooth fixed pulley. The scale pan holds two blocks A and B of masses 3 kg and 4 kg respectively with B resting on top of A. Find the acceleration of the system and the reaction between A and B.

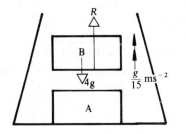

The reaction forces between A and B and between A and the scale pan are internal forces when considering the scale pan and its contents as one unit. For the scale pan and its contents:

$$\uparrow T - 7g$$

Applying $F = ma$ $T - 7g = 7a$ (1)

For the 8 kg mass: $\downarrow 8g - T$

Applying $F = ma$: $8g - T = 8a$ (2)

Adding (1) and (2): $g = 15a$

Therefore $a = \dfrac{g}{15}$

To find the reaction between A and B let us consider the forces that are acting on B

B has an upward acceleration of $\dfrac{g}{15}$ ms^{-2}

$$\uparrow R - 4g$$

Applying $F = ma$: $R - 4g = \dfrac{4g}{15}$

$$R = \dfrac{64}{15}g$$

Therefore the reaction between A and B is $\dfrac{64}{15}g$ N.

4) Two particles of masses 5 kg and 8 kg are connected by a light inelastic string passing over a fixed pulley. The system is released from rest with both portions of the string vertical and both particles at a height of 3 m above the ground. In the subsequent motion the 8 kg mass hits the ground and does not rebound. Find the greatest height reached by the 5 kg mass if the pulley is of such height that the mass never reaches the pulley.

Before the 8 kg mass reaches the ground the two particles are moving as a connected system but when the 8 kg mass hits the ground there is a sudden change in the conditions of the system: after the 8 kg mass has hit the ground the 5 kg mass is moving on its own with the string slack. These two conditions must be considered separately.

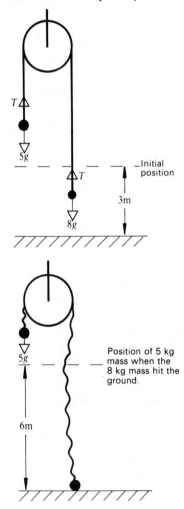

For 5 kg mass: ↑ $T - 5g = 5a$ $(F = ma)$
For 8 kg mass: ↓ $8g - T = 8a$ $(F = ma)$
Adding: $3g = 13a$
                           $a = 3g/13$

As the 8 kg mass moves down a distance 3 m, the 5 kg mass moves up the same distance.
Therefore considering the motion of the 5 kg mass we have:
$a = 3g/13$, $u = 0$, $s = 3$
Therefore using $v^2 = u^2 + 2as$:
$$v^2 = 18g/13$$
$$v = \sqrt{18g/13}$$

Therefore the 5 kg mass has an upward velocity of $\sqrt{18g/13}$ ms^{-1} at the instant when the 8 kg mass hits the ground. After that the string goes slack and the 5 kg mass moves under the action of its weight only:
i.e. it has a downward acceleration of g.
When it reaches its highest position its velocity is zero
i.e. $v = 0$, $u = \sqrt{18g/13}$, $a = -g$

Using $v^2 = u^2 + 2as$: $0 = \dfrac{18}{13}g - 2gs$

$$s = \frac{9}{13}$$

Therefore the 5 kg mass rises a distance $\frac{9}{13}$ m after the 8 kg mass hits the ground. Therefore it reaches a height of $6\frac{9}{13}$ m above the ground.

EXERCISE 5c   1, 7, 14

1) Two particles of mass 5 kg and 10 kg are connected by a light inextensible string which passes over a smooth fixed pulley. Find the acceleration of the system and the tension in the string.

2) Two particles of mass 9 kg and 10 kg are connected by a light inelastic string which passes over a smooth fixed pulley. Find the acceleration of the system and the tension in the string.

3) Two particles of mass m and M are connected by a light inelastic string which passes over a smooth fixed pulley. Find the acceleration of the system and the tension in the string.

4) A particle of mass 4 kg rests on a smooth plane which is inclined at $60°$ to the horizontal. The particle is connected by a light inelastic string passing over a smooth pulley at the top of the plane to a particle of mass 2 kg which is hanging freely. Find the acceleration of the system and the tension in the string.

5) A particle of mass 4 kg rests on a smooth horizontal table. It is connected by a light inextensible string passing over a smooth pulley at the edge of the table to a particle of mass 2 kg which is hanging freely. Find the acceleration of the system and the tension in the string.

6) A particle of mass 5 kg rests on a rough horizontal table. It is connected by a light inextensible string passing over a smooth pulley at the edge of the table to a particle of mass 6 kg, which is hanging freely. The coefficient of friction between the 5 kg mass and the table is $\frac{1}{3}$. Find the acceleration of the system and the tension in the string.

7)

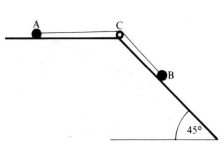

In the diagram particles A and B are of mass 10 kg and 8 kg respectively and rest on planes as shown. They are connected by a light inextensible string passing over a smooth fixed pulley at C. Find the acceleration of the system and the tension in the string if:

(a) the planes the particles are in contact with are smooth,

(b) the planes are rough and the coefficient of friction between each particle and the plane is $\frac{1}{4}$.

8)
Two particles A and B of mass 10 kg and 5 kg are connected by a light inextensible string passing over a smooth fixed pulley C and rest on inclined planes as shown in the diagram. Find the acceleration of the system and the tension in the string if:

(a) both planes are smooth,
(b) if both planes are rough and the coefficient of friction is $\frac{1}{10}$ for both particles.

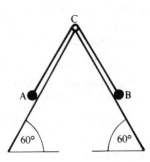

9)

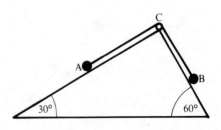

A particle A of mass 5 kg is connected by a light inextensible string passing over a smooth fixed light pulley to a light scale pan C as shown in the diagram. C holds a block B of mass 8 kg. Find the tension in the string and the reaction between B and C.

10)
Two particles A and B rest on the inclined faces of a fixed triangular wedge as shown in the diagram. A and B are connected by a light inextensible string which passes over a light smooth pulley at C. The faces of the wedge are smooth and A and B are both of mass 7 kg. Find the force exerted by the string on the pulley at C when the system is moving freely with both particles in contact with the wedge.

11) A particle of mass 10 kg lies on a rough horizontal table and is connected by a light inextensible string passing over a fixed smooth light pulley at the edge of the table to a particle of mass 8 kg hanging freely. The coefficient of friction between the 10 kg mass and the table is $\frac{1}{4}$. The system is released from rest with

the 10 kg mass a distance of 1.5 m from the edge of the table. Find:
(a) the acceleration of the system,
(b) the resultant force on the edge of the table,
(c) the speed of the 10 kg mass as it reaches the pulley.

12) Two particles of mass 3 kg and 4 kg are connected by a light inextensible string passing over a smooth fixed pulley. The system is released from rest with the string taut and both particles at a height of 2 m above the ground. Find the velocity of the 3 kg mass when the 4 kg mass reaches the ground.

13) Two particles of mass 5 kg and 7 kg are connected by a light inelastic string passing over a smooth fixed pulley. The system is released from rest with the string taut and both particles at a height of 0.5 m above the ground. Find the greatest height reached by the 5 kg mass, assuming that the pulley is of such height that the 5 kg mass does not reach the pulley, and that the 7 kg mass does not rebound when it hits the ground.

14)

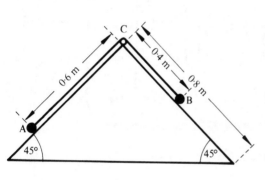

Two particles A and B of mass 5 kg and 9 kg respectively rest on the smooth faces of a fixed wedge as shown in the diagram. They are connected by a light inextensible string passing over a smooth pulley at C and are released from rest from the position shown in the diagram. In the subsequent motion B hits the ground and does not rebound. Find:

(a) the speed of the particles when B hits the ground,
(b) the acceleration of A after B hits the ground,
(c) the distance of A from C when A first comes to rest.

Related Accelerations

In problems concerned with connected particles and moveable pulleys or bodies in contact where each body is free to move, the accelerations of different parts of the system will not necessarily have the same magnitude. However, a relationship between the accelerations can be found by considering the physical properties of the system. As before, Newton's Law must be applied to each body of the system. However, it is not always convenient to apply the law in the direction of the acceleration. As $F \cos \theta = ma \cos \theta$ the equation can be applied in any direction in this form: i.e. the component of the resultant force in a chosen direction is equal to the mass multiplied by the component of the acceleration in the same direction.

EXAMPLES 5d

1)

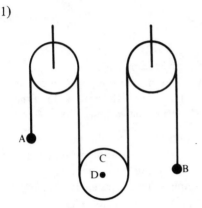

The diagram shows two particles A and B of masses 3 kg and 5 kg connected by a light inextensible string passing over two fixed smooth pulleys and under a light smooth moveable pulley C, which carries a particle D of mass 6 kg. The system is released from rest. Find:

(a) the acceleration of the particle A,
(b) the acceleration of the pulley C,
(c) the tension in the string.

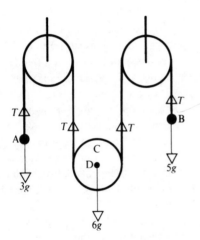

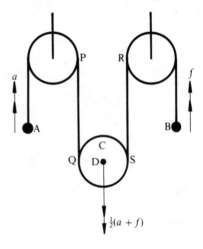

Suppose that A moves up with an acceleration a
and B moves up with an acceleration f
then the portion of the string PQ moves down with acceleration a
and the portion of the string RS moves down with acceleration f.
Then the pulley C moves down with acceleration equal to the average of a and f,
i.e. $\frac{1}{2}(a + f)$.
(If we are wrong about the directions we have chosen for the various accelerations, the answers we obtain will be negative).
Applying $F = ma$ to each part of the system.

For A: ↑	$T - 3g = 3a$	(1)
For B: ↑	$T - 5g = 5f$	(2)
For C: ↓	$6g - 2T = 3(a + f)$	(3)
$5 \times (1) + 3 \times (2)$:	$8T - 30g = 15(a + f)$	(4)

Eliminating T from (3) and (4): $-6g = 27(a+f)$

Therefore $$\tfrac{1}{2}(a+f) = -\frac{g}{9} \qquad (5)$$

Therefore the pulley C moves *up* with an acceleration $\dfrac{g}{9}$ ms^{-2}

Substituting (5) in (3): $6g - 2T = -\dfrac{2}{3}g$

Therefore $$T = \frac{10}{3}g \qquad (6)$$

Therefore the tension in the string is $\dfrac{10}{3}g$ N.

Substituting (6) in (1): $\dfrac{10}{3}g - 3g = 3a$

Therefore $$a = \frac{g}{9}$$

Therefore the mass A has an upward acceleration of $\dfrac{g}{9}$ ms^{-2}

2) A particle A of mass 6 kg is connected by a light inextensible string passing over a fixed smooth pulley to a light smooth moveable pulley B. Two particles C and D of masses 2 kg and 1 kg are connected by a light inextensible string passing over the pulley B. When the system is moving freely find the acceleration of the 1 kg mass and the tensions in the strings.

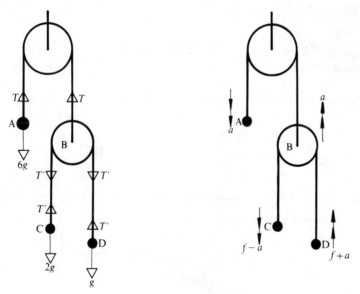

(There are two strings involved in this problem: their tensions will not necessarily be the same).

If A moves down with an acceleration a, B moves up with an acceleration a.
If B were stationary, C would accelerate downwards and D would have an equal acceleration upward. But as B has an acceleration a upward then D has an acceleration $(f + a)$ upward and C an acceleration $(f - a)$ downward.

Applying $F = ma$ to each part of the system:

For A ↓	$6g - T = 6a$	(1)
For B ↑	$T - 2T' = 0$ (B has zero mass)	(2)
For C ↓	$2g - T' = 2(f - a)$	(3)
For D ↑	$T' - g = (f + a)$	(4)
$(1) + (2)$:	$6g - 2T' = 6a$	
	$T' = 3g - 3a$	(5)
(5) in (3):	$-g = 2f - 5a$	(6)
(5) in (4):	$2g = f + 4a$	(7)

Eliminating f from (6) and (7): $a = \dfrac{5}{13}g$, therefore $f = \dfrac{6}{13}g$,

Therefore $a + f = \dfrac{11}{13}g$

Substituting into (4): $T' = \dfrac{24}{13}g$

Substituting into (2): $T = \dfrac{48}{13}g$

Therefore D moves up with acceleration $\dfrac{11}{13}g$ ms^{-2}, the tension in CD is $\dfrac{24}{13}g$ N and in AB is $\dfrac{48}{13}g$ N.

3) A particle of mass m is in contact with a smooth sloping face of a wedge which is itself standing on a smooth horizontal surface. If the mass of the wedge is M and the sloping face of the wedge is inclined at an angle $30°$ to the horizontal find the acceleration of the wedge in terms of m and M.

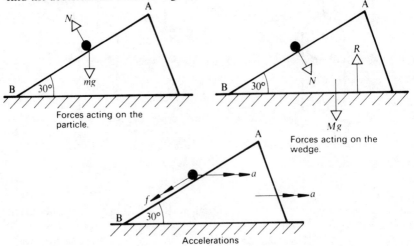

Forces acting on the particle.

Forces acting on the wedge.

Accelerations

The wedge will move horizontally: therefore let the wedge have an acceleration a in the horizontal direction.

The particle will move down the slope AB, so if the wedge were stationary it would have an acceleration in the direction AB, but as it remains in contact with the wedge as the wedge moves the particle has an acceleration of a horizontally and an acceleration of f in the direction AB.

Applying $F = ma$ to each part of the system:

For the particle:

resolving perpendicular to AB: $\searrow$ $mg \cos 30° - N = ma \sin 30°$ (1)

For the wedge:

$$\rightarrow \qquad N \sin 30° = Ma \qquad (2)$$

Eliminating N from (1) and (2):

$$\frac{1}{2}\left(\frac{mg}{2}\sqrt{3} - \frac{ma}{2}\right) = Ma$$

Therefore

$$a = \frac{mg\sqrt{3}}{(m + 4M)}$$

Therefore the acceleration of the wedge is $\dfrac{mg\sqrt{3}}{(m + 4M)}$ horizontally.

$\left(\begin{array}{l}\text{As has already been stated, Newton's Law } (F = ma) \text{ can be applied in any} \\ \text{direction: the direction perpendicular to AB was chosen so that } f \text{ does not} \\ \text{appear in any equation as it was not required.}\end{array}\right)$

4)

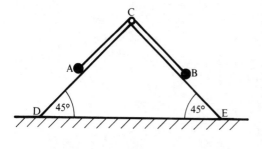

Two particles A and B of mass 3 kg and 2 kg are connected by a light inextensible string. The particles are in contact with the smooth faces of a wedge DCE of mass 10 kg resting on a smooth horizontal plane. When the system is moving freely find the acceleration of the wedge and the acceleration of B.

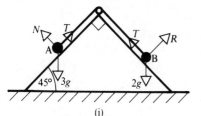

(i)
Forces acting on A and B.

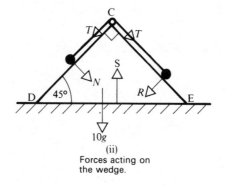

(ii)
Forces acting on the wedge.

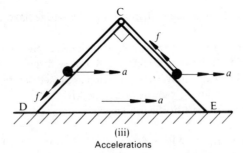

(iii)

Accelerations

If the wedge were stationary, A would have an acceleration down CD and, as A and B are connected by a string, B would have an equal acceleration up EC. But the wedge has an acceleration a horizontally, therefore the accelerations of A and B are made up of components as shown in diagram (iii).

Applying $F = ma$ to each part of the system:

For A: ↘ $3g \cos 45° - N = 3a \cos 45°$: $\qquad\qquad 3g - N\sqrt{2} = 3a \qquad$ (1)

$\qquad$ ↓ $3g - N \cos 45° - T \cos 45° = 3f \cos 45°$: $\quad 3g\sqrt{2} - N - T = 3f \qquad$ (2)

For B: ↗ $R - 2g \cos 45° = 2a \cos 45°$: $\qquad\qquad R\sqrt{2} - 2g = 2a \qquad$ (3)

$\qquad$ ↑ $T \cos 45° + R \cos 45° - 2g = 2f \cos 45°$: $\quad T + R - 2g\sqrt{2} = 2f \qquad$ (4)

For the wedge:

$\qquad$ → $N \cos 45° + T \cos 45° - T \cos 45° - R \cos 45° = 10a$: $N - R = 10a\sqrt{2}$ (5)

Adding (1) and (3): $\qquad\qquad\qquad\qquad\qquad g - (N-R)\sqrt{2} = 5a$

Substituting from (5): $\qquad\qquad\qquad\qquad\quad g - (10a\sqrt{2})\sqrt{2} = 5a$

$$\text{Therefore } a = \frac{g}{25}$$

Therefore the acceleration of the wedge is $\dfrac{g}{25}$ ms^{-2}.

Adding (2) and (4): $\qquad\qquad\qquad\qquad\qquad g\sqrt{2} - (N-R) = 5f$

Substituting from (5): $\qquad\qquad\qquad\qquad\quad g\sqrt{2} - 10a\sqrt{2} = 5f$

$$g\sqrt{2} - \frac{10g\sqrt{2}}{25} = 5f$$

$$\text{Therefore } f = \frac{3g\sqrt{2}}{25}$$

The acceleration of B is composed of two components as shown:

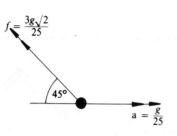

Resolving to find the magnitude and direction of the resultant

$$\rightarrow \quad \frac{g}{25} - \frac{3g}{25} = -\frac{2g}{25}$$

$$\uparrow \quad \frac{3g}{25}$$

Therefore magnitude of the

acceleration $= \dfrac{g\sqrt{13}}{25}$ ms^{-2} and the

direction is arctan $\frac{3}{2}$ with ED.

EXERCISE 5d

For all questions in this exercise: all strings are light and inextensible, all pulleys are light and smooth, all surfaces are frictionless, the wedges are free to move.

Find the acceleration of A and the tensions in the strings.

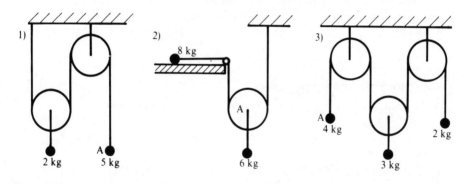

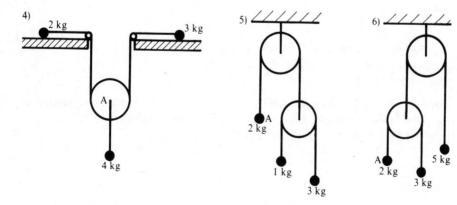

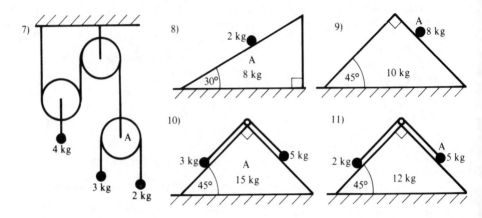

SUMMARY

Force is the quantity that changes the velocity of a body.

The resultant force acting on a body is equal to the mass of the body multiplied by the acceleration of the body: i.e. $F = ma$.

The resultant force and the acceleration are both in the same direction.

The weight of a body is its mass multiplied by g.

To analyse the motion of a system of bodies which are not rigidly connected Newton's Law ($F = ma$) must be applied to each separate part of the system.

MULTIPLE CHOICE EXERCISE 5

Instructions for answering these questions are given on page (xii)

TYPE I

1) A particle of mass 5 kg is pulled along a smooth horizontal surface by a horizontal string. The acceleration of the particle is $10\,\text{ms}^{-2}$. The tension in the string is:

(a) 2 N   (b) 50 N   (c) 5 N   (d) 15 N   (e) 10 N.

2) A particle of mass 3 kg slides down a smooth plane inclined at arcsin $\frac{1}{3}$ to the horizontal. The acceleration of the particle is:

(a) $\frac{g}{3}\,\text{ms}^{-2}$ (b) $g\,\text{ms}^{-2}$ (c) $1\,\text{ms}^{-2}$ (d) $3g\,\text{ms}^{-2}$ (e) 0.

3) A block of mass 10 kg rests on the floor of a lift which is accelerating upwards at $4\,\text{ms}^{-2}$. The reaction of the floor of the lift on the block is:

(a) 104 N   (b) 96 N   (c) 60 N   (d) 30 N   (e) 140 N.

4)

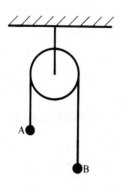

The pulley in the diagram is smooth and light. The masses of A and B are 5 kg and 2 kg. The acceleration of the system is:

(a) g

(b) $\frac{7}{3}g$

(c) $\frac{3}{7}g$

(d) $\frac{g}{7}$

(e) $\frac{5}{2}g$

5)

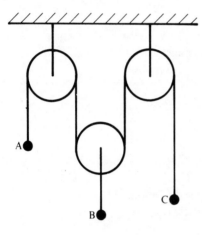

The pulleys in the diagram are all smooth and light. The acceleration of A is a upwards, the acceleration of C is f downwards. The acceleration of B is:

(a) $\frac{1}{2}(a-f)$ up.

(b) $\frac{1}{2}(a+f)$ up.

(c) $\frac{1}{2}(a+f)$ down.

(d) $\frac{1}{2}(f-a)$ up.

6)

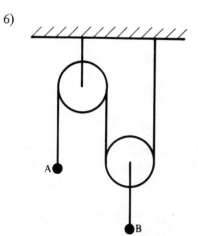

The two pulleys in the diagram are smooth and light. The acceleration of B is a downwards. The acceleration of A is :

(a) a up.

(b) $2a$ up.

(c) a down.

(d) $2a$ down.

(e) 0.

TYPE II

7) A particle is moving with uniform velocity.
(a) The forces acting on the particle are in equilibrium.
(b) The particle has zero acceleration.
(c) There is a resultant force acting on the body in the direction of the velocity.

8) A particle is moving horizontally with constant acceleration.
(a) The sum of the horizontal components of the forces acting on the particle is not zero.
(b) The sum of the vertical components of the forces acting is not zero.
(c) The forces acting on the particle are not in equilibrium.

9) A body of mass 10 kg has a resultant force of 20 N acting on it.
(a) The weight of the body is $10g$ N.
(b) The acceleration of the body is $2 \, \text{ms}^{-2}$.
(c) The body is moving in a straight line.

10) Two particles A and B of masses 3 and 4 kg are connected by a light inelastic string passing over a smooth fixed pulley.

(a) The acceleration of A is $\dfrac{g}{7} \, \text{ms}^{-2}$ upwards.

(b) The tension in the string is $\dfrac{24}{7} g$ N.

(c) The acceleration of B is $-\dfrac{g}{7} \, \text{ms}^{-2}$ upwards.

TYPE III

11) (a) A particle is moving with constant acceleration.
    (b) The resultant force acting on a particle is constant.

12) (a) A particle of mass 2 kg has a resultant force of 5 N acting on it.
    (b) A particle is moving with a constant acceleration of $5 \, \text{ms}^{-2}$.

13) (a) A particle is moving vertically downwards with a constant acceleration $g \, \text{ms}^{-2}$.
    (b) The only force acting on a particle is its weight.

14) (a) A particle is moving with a constant velocity.
    (b) The forces acting on a particle are in equilibrium.

TYPE IV

15) Two particles A and B are connected by a light inelastic string passing over a small smooth light fixed pulley. The particles are released from rest when both are at the same height above the ground. Find the speed of the particles when the heavier one hits the ground.
(a) The initial position of the particles is 1.5 m above the ground.
(b) The masses of A and B are 8 kg and 10 kg respectively.
(c) The length of the string is greater than 3 m.

16) A ring is free to slide down a rough straight wire. Find the acceleration of the ring.
(a) The coefficient of friction between the wire and the ring is μ.
(b) The wire is inclined at an angle θ to the horizontal.
(c) The mass of the ring is m.

17) A particle is placed on the inclined face of a wedge which is itself resting on a horizontal surface. Find the acceleration of the particle when the system is moving freely.
(a) The sloping face of the wedge is inclined at $\alpha°$ to the horizontal.
(b) The contact between the wedge and the horizontal surface is smooth.
(c) The mass of the particle is m.

18) A particle slides down a rough plane. Find the coefficient of friction between the particle and the plane.
(a) The plane is inclined at $\alpha°$ to the horizontal.
(b) The mass of the particle is m.
(c) The acceleration of the particle is a.

19) Two particles A and B are connected by a light inelastic string passing over a smooth pulley. Find the acceleration of A if the pulley is moving upwards with an acceleration of $2\,\text{ms}^{-2}$.
(a) The mass of A is $5\,\text{kg}$.
(b) The mass of B is $4\,\text{kg}$.
(c) The pulley is light.

20) A car is brought to rest by the action of its brakes which are assumed to exert a constant force on the car. Find the distance moved by the car before coming to rest.
(a) The mass of the car is $750\,\text{kg}$.
(b) The initial velocity of the car is $40\,\text{ms}^{-1}$.
(c) The time taken is 5 seconds.

21) A particle is projected up a rough plane. Find how far it moves up the plane.
(a) The mass of the particle is $2\,\text{kg}$.
(b) The coefficient of friction between the particle and the plane is $\frac{1}{2}$.
(c) The initial velocity of the particle is $10\,\text{ms}^{-1}$.

TYPE V

22) The S.I. unit of force (N) is that force which will give a body of mass 1 kg an acceleration of $1\,\text{ms}^{-2}$.

23) If a body has a resultant force acting on it the body will accelerate in the direction of the force.

24) Two bodies A and B are in contact. A exerts a force F on B and B exerts a force R on A. F and R are equal only if the bodies A and B are stationary.

25) A block A rests on a smooth horizontal table. It is pushed horizontally by

another block B. B exerts a force F on A. By Newton's third law the block A exerts an equal and opposite force on B, so the total horizontal force acting on A is zero.

26) A particle is hanging freely attached to a light inextensible string. The string is made to accelerate vertically upward. The tension in the string is greater than the weight of the particle.

27) Two particles of masses 3 kg and 5 kg are connected by a light inextensible string passing over a fixed rough pulley. The acceleration of the system is $\frac{g}{5}$.

MISCELLANEOUS EXERCISE 5

1) A bullet of mass $2m$ is fired horizontally into a fixed block of wood which offers a constant resistance R to the motion of the bullet. Find the deceleration of the bullet.

2) A ring of mass 2 kg slides down a wire which is inclined at $30°$ to the horizontal. If the ring has an acceleration of magnitude $\frac{g}{4}$ find the coefficient of friction between the ring and the wire.

3) A particle of mass 5 kg is projected up a rough plane inclined at $45°$ to the horizontal. The coefficient of friction between the particle and the plane is $\frac{1}{3}$. If the initial speed of the particle is 7 ms^{-1}, find how far it travels up the plane and the time it takes to return to its initial position.

4) A bullet of mass m is fired horizontally into a block of wood of mass M which is resting on a smooth horizontal surface. If the block offers a constant resistance R to the motion of the bullet, find the acceleration of the bullet and the acceleration of the block.

5) Two particles of mass 3 kg and 5 kg are connected by a light inextensible string passing over a smooth pulley which is fixed to the ceiling of a lift. Find the tension in the string when the system is moving freely and the lift has a downward acceleration $g \text{ ms}^{-2}$.

6)

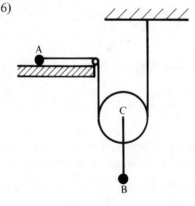

A particle A of mass m rests on a smooth horizontal table and is connected by a light inextensible string passing over a smooth fixed pulley at the edge of the table and under a smooth light pulley C to a fixed point on the ceiling as shown in the diagram. The pulley C carries a particle B of mass $2m$. Find the acceleration of C and the tension in the string.

7)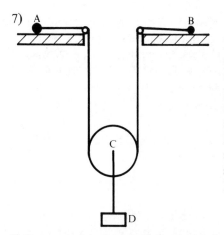

Particles A and B of mass 5 kg and 3 kg are connected by a light inextensible string passing under a smooth light pulley C which carries a particle D of mass 4 kg. A and B rest on horizontal rough surfaces as shown in the diagram. If the coefficient of friction is the same for both A and B and is just sufficient to stop A moving, but not B, find the coefficient of friction.

8) Two particles of mass 8 kg and 3 kg are connected by a light inelastic string passing over a smooth fixed pulley. The system is held at rest with the string taut and the 8 kg mass at a height of 0.8 m above the ground. The system is then released and the 8 kg mass hits the ground and does not rebound. Find the time for which the string is slack.

9)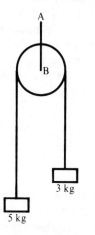

The diagram shows a smooth, weightless pulley suspended by a light support AB. A light, inextensible string passes over the pulley and carries masses of 5 kg and 3 kg at its ends. The masses are released from rest. Find the acceleration of each mass in ms^{-2} and the tension in the string in newtons. The support AB is now made to descend with an acceleration of $3\,ms^{-2}$. Find the magnitude and direction of the acceleration in space of each of the masses and the new tension in the string.   (Cambridge)

10)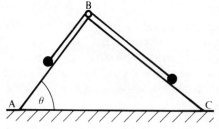

In Fig. 1, ABC is the right section of a prism; the angle BAC is θ ($< 45°$) and the angle ABC is $90°$. Two particles, each of mass m, are on the smooth sloping faces of the prism and are connected by a light inextensible string which passes over a smooth pulley in the top edge of the prism.

The prism stands on a horizontal plane which is rough enough to prevent the prism moving. The system is released from rest when the string is in the plane ABC. Find the acceleration of the particles and the tension in the string when the particles are moving freely. If the prism is of mass M, find the vertical component of the reaction between the prism and the horizontal plane.   (U of L)

11)

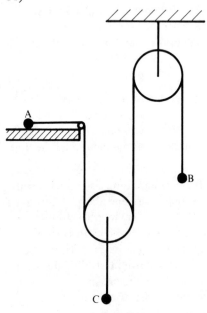

A particle A of mass 3 kg rests on a smooth horizontal table and is connected to a particle B of mass 7 kg by a light inextensible string which passes over a smooth pulley at the edge of the table, under a light, smooth moveable pulley and over a smooth fixed pulley as shown in the diagram. The moveable pulley carries a particle of mass M. Find M if the moveable pulley is stationary when the system is moving freely.

12) A light inextensible string passes over a smooth fixed pulley and has a particle of mass $5m$ attached to one end and a second smooth pulley of mass m attached to the other end. Another light inextensible string passes over the second pulley and carries a mass $3m$ at one end and a mass m at the other end. If the system moves freely under gravity, find the acceleration of the heaviest particle and the tension in each string.   (U of L)

13) One end of a light inextensible string is attached to a ceiling. The string passes under a smooth light pulley carrying a weight C and then over a fixed smooth light pulley. To the free end of the string is attached a light scale pan in which two weights A and B are placed with A on top of B as shown. The portions of the string not in contact with the pulleys are vertical. Each of the

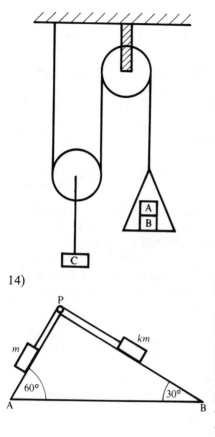

weights A and B has a mass M and the weight C has a mass kM. If the system is released from rest find the acceleration of the moveable pulley and of the scale pan and show that the scale pan will ascend if $k > 4$. When the system is moving freely find:

(a) the tension in the string,
(b) the reaction between the weights A and B.

(U of L)

14)

The diagram shows the cross-section of a wedge fixed to the horizontal ground. Its smooth faces PA and PB are inclined at 60° and 30° to the ground. A string passes over the small smooth pulley P, with particles of mass m and km attached at its ends. Show that the particle of mass m will accelerate towards P provided that $k > \sqrt{3}$.

If $k = 2$, find the tension in the string.
If $k = 2$, and the planes PA and PB are rough, μ being the coefficient of friction between each particle and the plane, show that the particle of mass m will move towards P if $\mu < \dfrac{2 - \sqrt{3}}{1 + 2\sqrt{3}}$.

(Cambridge)

15) Two wooden discs X and Y of thickness $2a$ and $4a$ respectively are fixed at a small distance apart with their plane faces vertical and parallel. A small bullet of mass m is fired horizontally into X with initial speed u at right angles to the plane faces. It emerges from X with speed v and then enters Y into which it penetrates a distance a before being brought to rest. If the motion of a bullet through X and Y is opposed by constant forces R_1, R_2 respectively, find expressions for R_1 and R_2 in terms of u, v, a and m.
A second bullet of mass m is now fired horizontally into Y with initial speed u at right angles to the plane faces in a direction towards X. Show that this bullet will emerge from Y if $v < \frac{1}{2}u$.

If $v = \frac{1}{3}u$ and the second bullet enters X after emerging from Y, find the distance which it penetrates into X before being brought to rest. (The effect of gravity may be ignored).   (Cambridge)

16) Two points A and B on a rough horizontal table are at a distance a apart. A particle is projected along the table from A towards B with speed u, and simultaneously another particle is projected from B towards A with speed $3u$. The coefficient of friction between each particle and the table is μ. By considering the distance travelled by each particle before coming to rest, show that the particles collide if $u^2 \geqslant \frac{1}{5}\mu\,ag$.
If $u^2 = \frac{4}{7}\mu\,ag$, show that the collision occurs after a time $[a/(7\mu g)]^{\frac{1}{2}}$ and at a distance $\frac{3}{14}a$ from A.   (Cambridge)

17) A smooth wedge of mass $6m$ has a normal cross-section ABC such that AB = AC and the angle BAC is a right angle. The face containing BC is in contact with a horizontal plane, and a light taut string joining two particles of mass $3m$, m lies in the plane ABC so that each particle is in contact with one inclined face of the wedge. The centroid of the wedge lies in the plane ABC. If the system is released from rest, determine the acceleration of the wedge.
                                                                        (U of L)

CHAPTER 6

WORK AND POWER

WORK

When a body moves under the action of a force it is useful to study the combination of the force and the distance moved by the body, and from this study arises the concept of work which is defined as follows:

When a body is moved under the action of a constant force *the work done* by that force is *the component of the force in the direction of motion multiplied by the distance moved by the point of application of the force.*

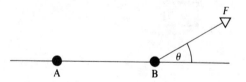

So when a particle is moved from A to B by a constant force F
the work done by $F = F \cos \theta \times$ **AB**.

Note: This definition applies only to the work done by a constant force. The work done by variable forces is dealt with in volume 2.

Unit of work. The unit of force is the newton and the unit of distance is the metre so that the unit of work done by a force is the newton metre: this unit is called the *joule.* (J)

When a body moves under the action of several forces, the work done by each force acting on the body can be found.

133

Consider a block which is pulled a distance *s* along a rough horizontal surface by a string inclined at an angle θ to the horizontal.

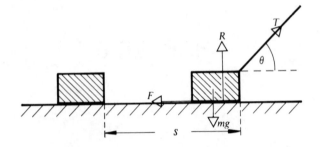

The point of application of each force moves a distance *s*.

The work done by the tension in the string	$= T \cos \theta \times s$	$= Ts \cos \theta$
The work done by the frictional force	$= -F \times s$	$= -Fs$
The work done by the weight	$= 0 \times s$	$= 0$
The work done by the normal reaction	$= 0 \times s$	$= 0$

These equations show that when an object moves under the action of several forces, not all of these forces do positive work. Those forces that have no effect on the speed (the weight and the normal reaction in the example) do no work. When the work done by a force is negative, work is said to be done against that force. i.e. *Fs* is the work done against the frictional force in the example.

Work done against gravity

Consider a body of mass *m* which is raised a vertical distance *h*.

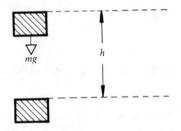

The work done by the weight $= -mgh$.

mgh is called the work done against gravity.

If an agent, such as a crane, is responsible for lifting the body, then *mgh* is referred to as the work done by the crane against gravity.

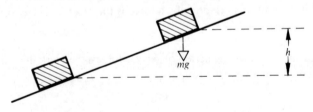

Similarly if a vehicle of mass m climbs a hill and in doing so raises itself a vertical distance h, then mgh is called the work done by the vehicle against gravity.

Work done by a moving vehicle

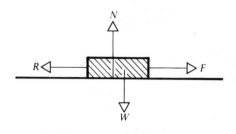

The diagram shows the forces that commonly act on a moving vehicle. R is the resistance to motion (this is always in the direction opposite to the direction of motion) and F is the driving force of the engine.

The work done by F is referred to as the work done by the vehicle.

(Note that if the vehicle is not accelerating the forces acting on it are in equilibrium).

EXAMPLES 6a

1) A man lifts 20 boxes each of mass 15 kg to a height of 1.5 m. Find the work done by the man against gravity.

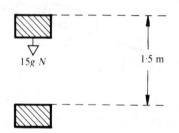

The work done against gravity in lifting one box $= 15g \times 1.5$ J
$$= 22.5g \text{ J}$$
The work done against gravity in lifting 20 boxes $= 20 \times 22.5g$ J
$$= 450g \text{ J.}$$

2) A light tank, of mass 9 tonne, travels a distance of 10 m up a bank which is inclined at arcsin $\frac{1}{3}$ to the horizontal. If the average resistance to motion is 200 N, find the total work done by the tank against the resistance and gravity.

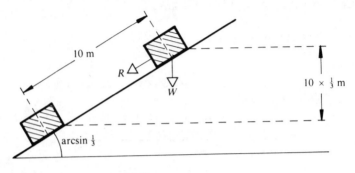

Resistance to motion, R = 200 N
Work done against R = 200 × 10 J   = 2000 J
The weight of the tank, W = 9000g N
Height risen by tank = 10 × $\frac{1}{3}$ m
Work done against gravity = 9000g × 10 × $\frac{1}{3}$ J = 294 000 J
Therefore total work done   = 296 000 J.

3) A car of mass 1500 kg climbs a hill at a constant speed of 20 ms^{-1}. If the hill is inclined at arcsin $\frac{1}{10}$ to the horizontal, find the work done by the car against gravity in one minute. If the total work done by the car in this time is 24 × 10^5 J, find the resistance to motion.

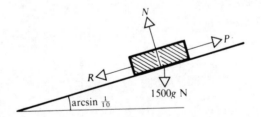

In one minute the distance moved up the slope by the car = 20 × 60 m
Therefore vertical distance raised in one minute = 1200 × $\frac{1}{10}$ m = 120 m
Therefore work done against gravity in one minute = 1500g × 120 J
= 1 764 000 J

As the car is not accelerating the forces acting on it are in equilibrium.
Therefore resolving parallel to the hill $P = R + 1500g \times \frac{1}{10}$.
The work done by the car in one minute = work done by P in one minute
= P × 1200 J
= $(R + 1470)$ × 1200 J
Therefore   24 × 10^5 = 1200 $(R + 1470)$
Therefore $R = 530$ N.

EXERCISE 6a

1) A block is pulled a distance x along a rough horizontal table by a horizontal string. If the tension in the string is T, the weight of the block is W, the normal reaction is R and the frictional force is F, write down expressions for the work done by each of these forces.

2) A particle is pulled a distance l down a rough plane inclined at an angle α to the horizontal by a string inclined at an angle β to the horizontal $(\alpha + \beta < 90°)$. If the tension in the string is T, the normal reaction between the particle and the plane is R, the frictional force is F and the weight of the particle is W, write down expressions for the work done by each of these forces.

3) A block of mass 500 kg is raised a height of 10 m by a crane. Find the work done by the crane against gravity.

4) A block of mass 10 kg is pulled a distance 5 m up a plane which is inclined at $15°$ to the horizontal. Find the work done against gravity.

5) A train travels 6 km between two stations. If the resistance to motion averages 500 N, find the work done against this resistance.

6) A cable car travelling at a steady speed moves a distance of 2 km up a slope inclined at $20°$ to the horizontal. If the mass of the cable car is 1200 kg and the resistance to motion is 400 N, find the work done by the tension in the cable.

7) A man climbs a mountain of height 2000 m. If the weight of the man is 700 N, find the work he does against gravity.

8) A man pushes his bicycle a distance of 200 m up a hill which is inclined at arcsin $\tfrac{1}{15}$ to the horizontal. If the man and his bicycle together weigh 850 N, find the work he does against gravity. If the average resistance to motion is 30 N, find the total work done by the man.

9) A block is pulled along a rough horizontal surface by a horizontal string. If the string pulls the block at a steady speed and does work of 100 J in moving the block a distance of 5 m, find the tension in the string.

10) A block is pulled at a constant speed of 5 ms^{-1} along a horizontal surface by a horizontal string. If the tension in the string is 5 N, find the work done by the string in ten seconds.

11) A block is pulled up an incline of arcsin $\tfrac{1}{20}$ to the horizontal at a steady speed of 6 ms^{-1}. If the work done against gravity in one second is 400 J, find the weight of the block.

12) A particle of mass 5 kg is pulled up a rough plane by a string parallel to the plane. If the plane is inclined at $30°$ to the horizontal, and if the work done by the tension in the string in moving the block a distance of 3 m at a steady speed is 90 J, find the coefficient of friction between the block and the plane.

POWER

Power is the rate at which a force does work.
If a force does 10 J of work in five seconds, the average rate at which it is working
is 2 Js^{-1}.

Unit of Power. The unit of power is one joule per second and this is called the
watt (W). So the power of the force in the example above is 2 W.

Power of a moving vehicle

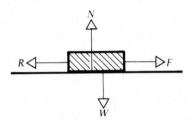

The power of a vehicle is the rate at which the driving force (*F*) is working.

Note: If the velocity of the vehicle is constant the forces acting on the vehicle
are in equilibrium.
If the vehicle is accelerating there is a resultant force in the direction of that
acceleration.

Relationship between power, driving force and velocity. If a force *F* newton
moves a body with a velocity *v* metre per second in the direction of the force
then

the distance moved in 1 s $= v$ metre
the work done by the force in 1 s $= Fv$ joule
therefore the power $= Fv$ watt
Therefore if *P* is the power $\underline{P = Fv}$

When the velocity is not constant this relationship gives the power at the instant
when the velocity is *v*.

EXAMPLES 6b

1) A train has a maximum speed of 40 ms^{-1} on the level against frictional
resistances to motion of magnitude 30 000 N. Find the maximum power of the
engine.

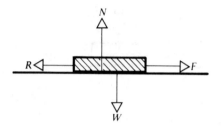

At the maximum speed there is no acceleration: therefore the forces acting on the train are in equilibrium.

Therefore $F = R$

$$F = 30\,000\,\text{N}$$

$$P = Fv$$

Therefore maximum power $= 30\,000 \times 40\,\text{W} = 1200\,\text{kW}$

2) A train of mass 200 tonne has a maximum speed of $20\,\text{ms}^{-1}$ up a hill inclined at arcsin $\frac{1}{50}$ to the horizontal when the engine is working at 800 kW. Find the resistance to the motion of the train.

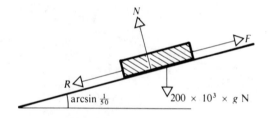

since $P = Fv$,

$$F = \frac{P}{v}$$

$$= \frac{800 \times 10^3}{20} = 40\,000\,\text{N}.$$

At maximum speed, the forces acting on the train are in equilibrium.

Resolving parallel to the hill: $F = R + 200 \times 10^3 g \times \frac{1}{50}$

$$40\,000 = R + 39\,200$$

Therefore $\qquad\qquad R = 800\,\text{N}.$

3) A cyclist moves against a resistance to motion which is proportional to his speed. At a power output of 75 W he has a maximum speed of $5\,\text{ms}^{-1}$ on a level road. If the cyclist and his machine together weigh 800 N, find the maximum speed he reaches when travelling down a hill inclined at arcsin $\frac{1}{40}$ to the horizontal when he is working at the rate of 25 W.

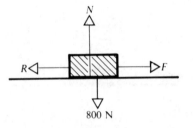

When travelling at any speed v, $F = \dfrac{P}{v}$ and $R = kv$

When travelling on the level $F = \dfrac{75}{5}$ N

Also $F = R$ as there is no acceleration
But $R = k \times 5$
Therefore $15 = k \times 5$ therefore $k = 3$
Therefore $R = 3v$ at any velocity v.

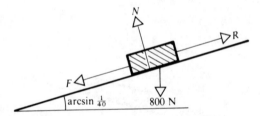

When travelling down the hill at maximum speed V, $F = \dfrac{P}{V}$ and $R = 3V$

$$= \frac{25}{V}.$$

There is no acceleration, so resolving parallel to the hill:

$$F + 800 \times \tfrac{1}{40} = R$$

$$\frac{25}{V} + 20 = 3V$$

$$3V^2 - 20V - 25 = 0$$

$$V = 7.7 \text{ ms}^{-1} \text{ (the negative root is not applicable).}$$

4) A car of mass 1500 kg has a maximum speed of 150 kmh^{-1} on the level when working at its maximum power against resistances of 60 N. Find the acceleration

of the car when it is travelling at $60 \, \text{kmh}^{-1}$ on the level with the engine working at maximum power assuming that the resistance to motion remains constant.

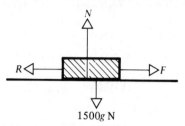

$$1500g \, \text{N}$$

At maximum speed there is no acceleration: therefore $F = R$

$$F = 60 \, \text{N}$$

$$P = Fv$$

$$= 60 \times 150 \times \tfrac{5}{18} \, \text{W} \qquad = 2500 \, \text{W}$$

When the speed is $60 \, \text{kmh}^{-1}$ $F = \dfrac{P}{V}$

$$= \dfrac{2500 \times 18}{60 \times 5} \, \text{N} \qquad = 150 \, \text{N}$$

As the car is accelerating, the resultant force in the direction of this acceleration is $F - R = 150 - 60 \, \text{N} = 90 \, \text{N}$
If the acceleration is a, $90 = 1500a$ (Newton's Law)

Therefore $$a = \dfrac{90}{1500} \, \text{ms}^{-2} = 0.06 \, \text{ms}^{-2}.$$

5) An engine of mass 100 tonne pulls a train of mass 400 tonne. The resistance to motion of the engine is $1000 \, \text{N}$ and the resistance to motion of the train is $20\,000 \, \text{N}$. Find the tension in the coupling between the engine and the train at the instant when the speed of the train is $80 \, \text{kmh}^{-1}$ and the engine is exerting a power of $4000 \, \text{kW}$.

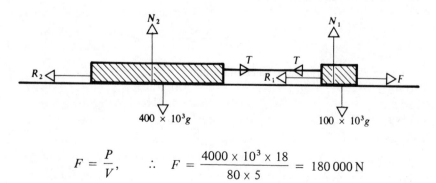

$$F = \dfrac{P}{V}, \qquad \therefore \quad F = \dfrac{4000 \times 10^3 \times 18}{80 \times 5} = 180\,000 \, \text{N}$$

By considering the forces acting on both the engine and train, T is not brought into the calculations as it is an internal force.

The resultant force in the direction of motion $= F - (R_1 + R_2)$
$$= (180\,000 - 21\,000) = 159\,000\,\text{N}$$

Therefore the train is accelerating. If this acceleration is a

$$159\,000 = 500 \times 10^3 \times a \quad \text{(Newton's Law)}$$

$$\therefore \quad a = \frac{159\,000}{500 \times 10^3} = 0.318\,\text{ms}^{-2}$$

Now that the acceleration of the engine and train is known, T can be found by considering the forces acting on either the train or the engine.

Considering the forces acting on the train: the resultant force in the direction of motion $\qquad = T - R_2$

$$\therefore \quad T - R_2 = (400 \times 10^3 \times 0.318) \quad \text{(Newton's Law)}$$
$$T = 400 \times 10^3 \times 0.318 + 20\,000 = 147\,200\,\text{N}.$$

6) The resistance to motion of a car is proportional to the square of its speed. The car has a mass of 1000 kg and can maintain a steady speed of 30 ms^{-1} when travelling up a hill inclined at arcsin $\frac{1}{20}$ to the horizontal with the engine working at 60 kW. Find the acceleration of the car when it is travelling down the same hill with the engine working at 40 kW at the instant when the speed is 20 ms^{-1}.

The resistance to motion at any speed v is given by $R = kv^2$.

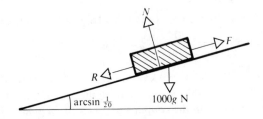

When the car is travelling up the hill $F = \dfrac{P}{v}$

$$= \frac{60 \times 10^3}{30} = 2000\,\text{N}$$

The forces acting on the car are in equilibrium

Therefore $\qquad\qquad\qquad F = R + 1000g \times \tfrac{1}{20}$

Therefore $\qquad\qquad\qquad R = 2000 - 490\,\text{N} = 1510\,\text{N}$

But as $R = kv^2$: $\qquad\qquad 1510 = k \times 900$

Therefore $\qquad\qquad\qquad k = \dfrac{151}{90}$

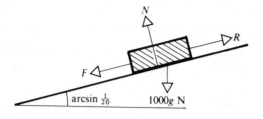

When the car is travelling down the hill: $F = \dfrac{P}{v}$

$$= \frac{40 \times 10^3}{20} = 2000 \text{ N}$$

The resultant force down the hill $= F + 1000g \times \tfrac{1}{20} - R$

$$= 2000 + 490 - \frac{151}{90} \times 20^2$$

$$= 1819 \text{ N}$$

If the acceleration of the car is a, $\quad 1819 = 1000a \quad$ (Newton's Law)

Therefore $\qquad\qquad a = 1.82 \text{ ms}^{-2}$

EXERCISE 6b

1) A train has a maximum speed of 80 kmh^{-1} on the level against resistance of 50 000 N. Find the power of the engine.

2) A car has a maximum speed of 100 kmh^{-1} on the level with the engine working at 50 kW. Find the resistance to motion.

3) A train of mass 500 tonne has a maximum speed of 90 kmh^{-1} up an incline of arcsin $\tfrac{1}{50}$ against frictional resistances of 100 000 N. Find the power of the engine.

4) A cyclist working at 20 W has a maximum speed of 30 kmh^{-1} down an incline of arcsin $(\tfrac{1}{20})$ to the horizontal. Find the frictional resistance to motion if the mass of the cyclist and his machine is 100 kg.

5) A car of mass 750 kg has a maximum power of 30 kW and moves against a constant resistance to motion of 800 N. Find the maximum speed of the car:
(a) on the level,
(b) up an incline of arcsin $\tfrac{1}{10}$ to the horizontal,
(c) down the same incline.

6) An engine of mass 75 tonne moves against a resistance to motion which is proportional to its speed. It has a maximum speed of 40 ms^{-1} on the level with the engine working at 1500 kW. Find the maximum speed of the engine up an incline of arcsin $\tfrac{1}{50}$ to the horizontal with the engine working at the same power.

7) A hoist with a power input of 220 W can lift a block of weight 600 N to a height of 10 m in 30 seconds. Find the resistance to the motion of the hoist.

8) A constant force of 6 N moves a particle of mass 12 kg from rest through a distance of 30 m. Find the work done by the force and the maximum power achieved.

9) A car of mass 2000 kg has a constant frictional resistance to motion of 2000 N. Find the acceleration of the car when it has a speed of 20 kmh^{-1} on a level road with the engine working at 100 kW.

10) A car of mass 1000 kg has a constant resistance to motion of 3000 N. If the maximum power of the car is 50 kW find the acceleration when travelling at 20 kmh^{-1} up a hill inclined at arcsin $(\frac{1}{20})$ to the horizontal.

11) A train of mass 400 tonne is travelling down an incline of arcsin $\frac{1}{50}$ to the horizontal against resistances of 30 000 N. Find the acceleration of the train when it is travelling at 20 ms^{-1} and the power output of the engine is 50 kW.

12) A car of mass 2000 kg pulls a caravan of mass 400 kg. The resistance to motion of the car is 1000 N and the resistance to motion of the caravan is 100 N. Find the acceleration of the car and the caravan at the instant when their speed is 40 kmh^{-1} with the power output of the engine equal to 100 kW. Find also the tension in the coupling between the car and the caravan at this instant.

13) A cyclist moves against resistance to motion of $(3 + kv^2)$N where k is a constant and his speed is v ms^{-1}. If his maximum speed on the level is 10 ms^{-1} when he is working at the rate of 75 W, find his acceleration on the level at the instant when his speed is 5 ms^{-1} and he is working at the same rate. The mass of the cyclist and his machine is 90 kg.

14) A car of mass 1500 kg tows another car of mass 1000 kg up a hill inclined at arcsin $\frac{1}{10}$ to the horizontal. The resistance to motion of the cars is 0.5 N per kg. Find the tension in the tow rope at the instant when their speed is 10 ms^{-1} and the power output of the towing car is 150 kW.

SUMMARY

Work: The work done by a constant force is the product of the component of the force in the direction of motion and the distance moved by the point of application of the force.

Power: Power is the rate at which a force does work.
The power of a vehicle is the rate at which the driving force works.
Power = driving force × velocity.

MULTIPLE CHOICE EXERCISE 6

Instructions for answering these questions are given on page (xii).

TYPE I

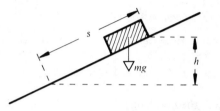

The work done against gravity in moving the block a distance s up the slope is:
(a) mh (b) mgs
(c) ms (d) mgh ✓
(e) gh.

2) A block of weight W is pulled a distance l along a horizontal table. The work done by the weight is:

(a) Wl ✓   (b) 0   (c) Wgl (d) $\dfrac{Wl}{g}$ (e) W.

3) A child builds a tower from three blocks. The blocks are uniform cubes of side 2 cm. The blocks are initially all lying on the same horizontal surface and each block has a mass of 0.1 kg. The work done by the child is:
(a) 4 J   (b) 0.04 J   (c) 6 J   (d) 0.6 J   (e) 0.06 J.

4) A car is moving with a constant speed of 20 ms^{-1} against a resistance of 100 N. The power exerted by the car is:
(a) 2 kW   (b) 5 W   (c) 200 W   (d) 1 kW   (e) 20 kW.

5) A particle of mass m moves from rest under the action of a constant force F which acts for two seconds. The maximum power attained is:
(a) $2Fm$ (b) $\dfrac{F^2}{m}$ (c) $\dfrac{2F}{m}$ (d) $\dfrac{2F^2}{m}$ (e) $\dfrac{F^2}{2m}$

TYPE III

6) (a) A train is moving with its engine working at constant power.
 (b) A train is moving with its engine exerting a constant driving force.

7) A particle is pulled by a string a distance s along a horizontal surface. The tension in the string is T.
(a) The work done by the tension in the string is Ts.
(b) The string is inclined at an angle θ to the horizontal.

TYPE IV

8) Find the work done by a forklift truck in lifting two uniform boxes which are stacked vertically.
(a) The boxes are cubes of side 0.6 m.

(b) The mass of each box is 20 kg.

(c) The boxes are lifted vertically a distance of 3 m.

9) A car tows a caravan. Find the tension in the coupling between the car and caravan at the instant when their speed is 15 ms^{-1}.

(a) The mass of the car is 900 kg.

(b) The car is working at a steady rate of 50 kW.

(c) The resistance to motion of the car and caravan is 1000 N.

10) A car is climbing a hill against a resistance to motion which is proportional to its speed. Find the maximum power of the car.

(a) The car has a maximum speed of 20 ms^{-1} up the hill and a maximum speed of 40 ms^{-1} on the level.

(b) The inclination of the hill is arcsin $\frac{1}{10}$ to the horizontal.

(c) The mass of the car is 1000 kg.

11) Find the maximum power at which a cyclist can work.

(a) The cyclist has a maximum speed of 70 kmh^{-1} on the level.

(b) The resistance to the motion of the cyclist is constant at 10 000 N.

(c) The mass of the cyclist and his machine is 90 kg.

TYPE V

12) Work is a scalar quantity.

13) If the engine of a car is working at constant power the acceleration of the car must be constant.

14) The unit of work is one newton metre per second.

15) A car is towing a van at constant speed. The resistance to the motion of the car is R and the driving force of the car is F. F and R are in equilibrium.

16) A car is towing a van and is accelerating. The tension in the tow rope is greater than the resistance to the motion of the van.

17) A train covers a distance of 20 m in two seconds at a constant speed, with the engine exerting a driving force of 2000 N. The engine is working at the rate of 20 kW.

MISCELLANEOUS EXERCISE 6

1) A car of mass 900 kg accelerates uniformly from rest to a speed of 60 km/h in a time of two seconds when travelling on a level road. If there is a constant resistance to motion of 20 N find the maximum power exerted by the engine in this time.

2) A car of mass 1500 kg has a maximum speed of 150 km/h on a level road when the engine is exerting its maximum power of 200 kW. Find the resistance to motion at this speed. If this resistance is proportional to the speed of the car find the maximum speed of the car up a road inclined at arcsin $\frac{1}{10}$ to the horizontal.

3) A car of mass 1000 kg has a maximum speed of 90 km/h up a slope inclined at arcsin $\frac{1}{7}$ to the horizontal and a maximum speed of 180 km/h down the same slope. If the resistance to motion varies as the speed of the car find the maximum power of the car.

4) A cyclist and his machine have a total mass of 100 kg. When travelling up a hill inclined at arcsin $\frac{1}{50}$ to the horizontal against a resistance to motion of 20 N the cyclist can maintain a speed of 12 km/h. Find the rate at which he is working. If the resistance to motion is unchanged, find the acceleration of the cyclist when travelling at 10 km/h on a level road and working at the same rate.

5) A car has a maximum power of 200 kW. Its maximum speed on a level road is twice its maximum speed up a hill inclined at arcsin $\frac{1}{15}$ to the horizontal against a resistance to motion of 1600 N in each case. Find the mass of the car. Find also the acceleration of the car at the instant when its speed is 30 km/h on the level with the engine working at full power, assuming the resistance to motion is unchanged.

6) A car of mass 1000 kg is travelling on a level road against a resistance to motion which varies as the square of its speed. If the maximum power of the engine is 60 kW and the car has a maximum speed of 150 km/h, find an expression for the resistance to motion at any speed. Find also the acceleration when the engine is working at three-quarters full power and the speed is 30 km/h.

7) An engine of mass 5 tonne pulls a train of mass 50 tonne against a constant resistance to motion of R newton per tonne. The train has a maximum speed of 110 km/h on the horizontal when the engine is working at its maximum power of 1500 kW. Find R.
Find also the tension in the coupling between the engine and the train at the instant when it is travelling at 30 km/h on the horizontal with the engine working at half power.

8) A car of mass 1200 kg tows another car of mass 800 kg, the frictional resistances being 120 N and 80 N respectively. If the tow rope has a breaking tension of 2000 N find the maximum acceleration possible, and the maximum power the towing car can use at the instant when the speed is 10 km/h.

9) A car of mass 1000 kg has a maximum speed of 15 m/s up a slope inclined at an angle θ to the horizontal where $\sin \theta = 0.2$. There is a constant frictional resistance equal to one tenth of the weight of the car. Find the maximum speed of the car on a level road.
If the car descends the same slope with its engine working at half its maximum power, find the acceleration of the car at the moment when its speed is 30 m/s.

(U of L.)

10) A lorry of mass 10 000 kg has a maximum speed of 24 km/h up a slope of 1 in 10 against a resistance of 1200 newtons. Find the effective power of the engine in kilowatts.

If the resistance varies as the square of the speed, find the maximum speed on the level to the nearest km/h.

[Take g as 9.8 m/s^2]   (U of L.)

11) A car of mass 1000 kg whose maximum power is constant at all speeds experiences a constant resistance R newtons. If the maximum speed of the car on the horizontal is 120 km/h and the maximum speed up a slope of angle θ where $\sin \theta = 1/100$ is 60 km/h, calculate the power of the car. Calculate also the maximum speed of the car (a) on the horizontal and (b) up the slope when it is pulling a caravan of mass 1000 kg if the total resistance to the motion of the car and the caravan is $3R$ newtons.

[Take g to be 9.8 m/s^2]   (U of L.)

12) At the instant a car of mass 840 kg passes a sign post on a level road its speed is 90 km/h and its engine is working at 70 kW. If the total resistance is constant and equal to 2100 N, find the acceleration of the car in m/s^2 at the instant it passes the sign post. Calculate the maximum speed in km/h at which this car could travel up an incline of arcsin (1/10) against the same resistance with the engine working at the same rate.   (A.E.B.)

13) A car of mass 1000 kg is moving on a level road at a steady speed of 100 km/h with its engine working at 60 kW. Calculate in newtons the total resistance to motion, which may be assumed to be constant.

The engine is now disconnected, the brakes are applied, and the car comes to rest in 100 metres. Assuming that the total resistance remains the same, show that the retarding force of the brakes is about 1700 newtons.

If the engine is still disconnected, find the distance the car would run up a hill of inclination arcsin $\frac{1}{10}$ before coming to rest, starting at 100 km/h when the same resistance and braking force are operating.   (Cambridge.)

14) A car of weight W has maximum power H. In all circumstances there is a constant resistance R due to friction. When the car is moving up a slope of 1 in n (arcsin $\frac{1}{n}$) its maximum speed is v and when it is moving down the same slope it maximum speed is $2v$. Find R in terms of W and n.

The maximum speed of the car on level road is u. Find the maximum acceleration of the car when it is moving with speed $\frac{1}{2}u$ up the given slope.   (A.E.B.)

15) When a car of mass M kilograms is ascending a hill of inclination α against a constant resistance of R newtons, its engine is working at P kilowatts. Prove that:

$$1000P = (R + 9.8M\sin \alpha + Mf)v.$$

where v m/sec is the velocity of the car and f m/sec^2 its acceleration.

If $\sin \alpha = \frac{1}{8}, P = 20, R = 400, M = 500$, find the maximum speed attained by the car.

When the car has attained this speed the power of the engine is suddenly increased to 25 kilowatts. Show that the immediate acceleration is about $\frac{1}{2}$ m/sec^2.   (Cambridge.)

CHAPTER 7

HOOKE'S LAW. ENERGY

ELASTIC STRINGS

A string whose length changes when forces are applied to its ends is said to be *elastic*.

The length of the string when no forces are acting on it is its *natural length*.

In order to stretch an elastic string, equal and opposite extending forces must be applied outwards to the ends of the string. The string is then in tension and exerts an inward pull (tension) at each end, equal in magnitude to the extending force.

The difference between the natural length of the string and its stretched length is the *extension*.

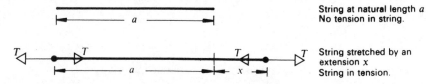

String at natural length *a*
No tension in string.

String stretched by an extension *x*
String in tension.

It can be shown experimentally that, up to a point, the tension in the string is directly proportional to the extension i.e.

$$T \; \alpha \; x.$$

This relationship, discovered in C17 by Hooke, is known as *Hooke's Law* and is used in the form

$$T = \lambda \frac{x}{a}$$

where T is the tension in the string,

  a is the natural length,

  x is the extension,

and λ is the *modulus of elasticity* of the string.

Elastic limit

If x is progressively increased, there comes a stage when the string becomes *overstretched* and will not return to its natural length when released. The string has then exceeded its *elastic limit* and no longer obeys Hooke's Law. In this state the string is no longer of any mathematical interest to us and, at this level, we study only those strings which have not reached their elastic limit and which do therefore obey Hooke's Law.

Modulus of Elasticity

For an elastic string of natural length a, Hooke's Law can be arranged in the form

$$\lambda = \frac{Ta}{x}$$

If $x = a$, i.e. if the length of the string is doubled, then

$$\lambda = T$$

From this we see that λ, although a constant of proportion, has the dimensions of force and is equal to the tension in an elastic string whose length has been doubled.

Because λ has the dimensions of force it is measured in newtons.

SPRINGS

A spring is very similar to an elastic string with one important difference; a spring can be compressed as well as stretched.

When stretched, a spring behaves in exactly the same way as a stretched elastic string.

When the spring is compressed (i.e. has its length reduced from the natural length) the forces in the spring are an outward push (thrust) at each end. These forces again tend to restore the spring to its natural length and the spring is *in thrust* or *in compression*.

The reduction in length is the *compression*.

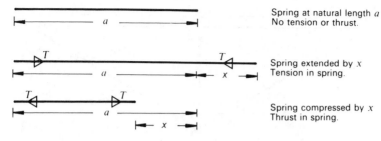

Spring at natural length a
No tension or thrust.

Spring extended by x
Tension in spring.

Spring compressed by x
Thrust in spring.

In compression as well as in tension a spring obeys Hooke's Law

$$T = \lambda \frac{x}{a}$$

where T is now the thrust in the spring
and x is the compression.

SUMMARY

Elastic strings and springs obey Hooke's Law $T = \lambda \dfrac{x}{a}$

λ is the Modulus of Elasticity and has the dimensions of force.
λ is equal to the force required to double the length of the string or spring.

EXAMPLES 7a

1) An elastic string of natural length 2 metre is stretched to 2.8 metre in length
by a force of 4 N. What is its modulus of elasticity?

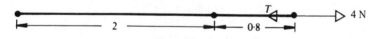

Tension = Extending Force

$$T = 4\,\text{N}$$

Using Hooke's Law

$$T = \lambda \left(\frac{0.8}{2.0} \right)$$

Therefore

$$\lambda = 4 \left(\frac{2.0}{0.8} \right) \text{N}$$

Modulus of Elasticity = 10 N

2) An elastic string of natural length 4l and modulus of elasticity 4 mg is stretched
between two points A and B which are on the same level, where AB = 4l. A particle
attached to the mid point of the string hangs in equilibrium with both portions
of string making 30° with AB. What is the mass of the particle?

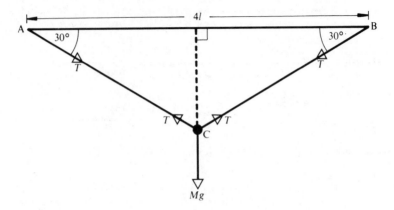

Let M be the mass of the particle and C the mid-point of the string.

Resolving vertically $2T \sin 30° = Mg$

$\therefore$ $T = Mg$

Stretched length of string $2AC = 2(2l \sec 30°)$

$2AC = 4.62l$

Extension in string $2AC - 4l = 0.62l$

Using Hooke's Law $T = \lambda \left(\dfrac{0.62l}{4l}\right)$

$\therefore$ $Mg = 4mg \left(\dfrac{0.62l}{4l}\right)$

$M = 0.62\,m$

Mass of particle is $0.62\,m$

3) An elastic spring is fixed at one end. When a force of 4N is applied to the other end the spring extends by 0.2 m. If the spring hangs vertically supporting a mass of 1 kg at the free end, the spring is of length 2.49 m. Find the natural length and modulus of elasticity of the spring.

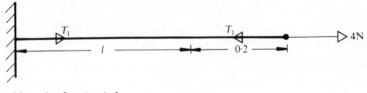

Natural length of spring is l

Extending Force $=$ Tension

$T_1 = 4\,N$

Hooke's Law:-

$$T_1 = \lambda \left(\frac{0.2}{l}\right)$$

$$\therefore \quad \lambda = \frac{4l}{0.2} = 20l$$

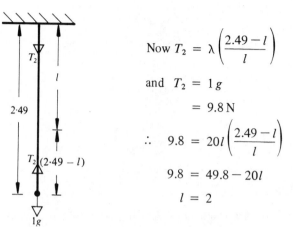

Now $T_2 = \lambda \left(\frac{2.49 - l}{l}\right)$

and $T_2 = 1g$

$\qquad = 9.8\,\text{N}$

$\therefore \quad 9.8 = 20l \left(\frac{2.49 - l}{l}\right)$

$\qquad 9.8 = 49.8 - 20l$

$\qquad l = 2$

Natural length of spring $= 2\,\text{m}$
Modulus of Elasticity $\quad = 40\,\text{N}$

4) Two springs AB and BC are joined together end to end to form one long spring. The natural lengths of the separate springs are 1.6 m and 1.4 m and their moduli of elasticity are 20 N and 28 N respectively. Find the tension in the combined spring if it is stretched between two points 4 m apart.

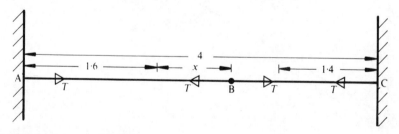

Measuring all lengths in metres,

let the extension in spring AB be x $\qquad\qquad \therefore AB = (1.6 + x)$

Then length of spring BC is $4 - (1.6 + x)$ $\qquad \therefore BC = (2.4 - x)$

But natural length of spring BC is 1.4

$\therefore$ Extension in spring BC is $(2.4 - x - 1.4)$ $\qquad\qquad = (1 - x)$

Because the end B is in equilibrium, the tensions in AB and BC are equal.

Using Hooke's Law $T = 20 \dfrac{x}{1.6}$ for AB   (1)

$$T = 28 \dfrac{(1-x)}{1.4} \text{ for BC}$$ (2)

$$\therefore \quad \frac{20x}{1.6} = 28 \frac{(1-x)}{1.4}$$

$$\therefore \quad x = 1.6\,(1-x)$$

$$\therefore \quad x = \frac{1.6}{2.6}$$

$$\therefore \quad \text{In (1) } T = \frac{20}{1.6}\left(\frac{1.6}{2.6}\right) = \frac{100}{13}$$

Tension in spring is $7\frac{9}{13}$ N

5) A uniform rod AB, length $4a$, weight W rests at $60°$ to a smooth vertical wall. It is supported with the end A in contact with the wall by an elastic string connecting a point C on the rod to a point D on the wall vertically above A. If the natural length of the string is $\dfrac{3a}{4}$ and the distances AC and AD are a, find the modulus of elasticity of the string.

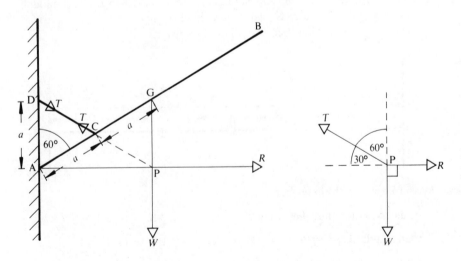

In $\triangle$ DAC DA = AC $\therefore$ $A\hat{D}C = A\hat{C}D$ But $D\hat{A}C = 60°$

$\therefore$ $\triangle$ DAC is equilateral

$\therefore$ String makes $60°$ with wall and DC = a.

The rod is in equilibrium under the action of three forces which must therefore be concurrent. The line of action of the tension in the string must therefore pass through P, the point of intersection of R and W.

Using Lami's Theorem $\qquad \dfrac{T}{\sin 90°} = \dfrac{W}{\sin 30°}$

$$\therefore \quad T = 2W$$

For the string $\qquad$ Natural length $\quad = \dfrac{3a}{4}$

$\qquad\qquad\qquad\qquad$ Stretched length $= a$

$\qquad\qquad\qquad\qquad$ Extension $\qquad = \dfrac{a}{4}$

$\qquad\qquad\qquad\qquad$ Modulus $\qquad = \lambda$

Using Hooke's Law $\qquad 2W = \dfrac{\lambda \dfrac{a}{4}}{\dfrac{3a}{4}} = \dfrac{\lambda}{3}$

Modulus of Elasticity $= 6W$

6) When an elastic string of natural length 2 m is fixed at one end and hangs vertically supporting a particle of mass 4 kg at the other end, it stretches to a length of 2.8 m. A horizontal force of 28 N is then applied gradually to the mass until it is once again in equilibrium. Calculate the length and the inclination to the vertical of the string in this position.

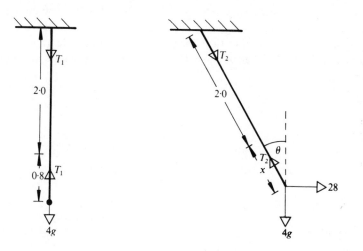

1st Case: Hooke's Law $T_1 = \lambda \left(\dfrac{0.8}{2.0} \right)$

Mass is in Equilibrium $\therefore\ T_1 = 4g$

$$\therefore\ \lambda = 4g \left(\frac{2.0}{0.8} \right) = 10g$$

2nd Case: Lami's Theorem gives

$$\frac{T_2}{\sin 90°} = \frac{28}{\sin (180° - \theta)} = \frac{4g}{\sin (90° + \theta)}$$

or

$$\frac{T_2}{\sin 90°} = \frac{28}{\sin \theta} = \frac{4g}{\cos \theta}$$

$\therefore$

$$\tan \theta = \frac{28}{4g} = \frac{7}{9.8} = \frac{1}{1.4}$$

$\therefore$

$$\theta = 35° \, 32'$$

Hence

$$T_2 = \frac{28}{\sin 35° \, 32'} = 48.17\,\text{N}$$

Using Hooke's Law $T_2 = \lambda \dfrac{x}{2}$

$$\therefore\ x = \frac{2T_2}{\lambda} = \frac{2}{98} \left(\frac{28}{\sin 35° \, 32'} \right)$$

Length of string $= (2.0 + 0.9831)\,\text{m} = 2.9831\,\text{m}$
Inclination of string to vertical $= 35° \, 32'$

7) Two identical elastic strings AB and BC of natural length a and modulus of elasticity $2\,mg$ are fastened together at B. Their other ends A and C are fixed to two points $4a$ apart in a vertical line (A above C). A particle of mass m is attached at B. Find the height above C at which the particle rests in equilibrium.

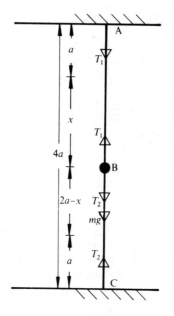

Let the extension in AB be x

Then the extension in BC is $(4a-2a-x)$

i.e. $(2a - x)$

The particle at B is in equilibrium

$$\therefore \quad T_1 = T_2 + mg \qquad (1)$$

Using Hooke's Law

$$T_1 = \lambda \frac{x}{a} = 2mg \frac{x}{a} \qquad (2)$$

$$T_2 = \lambda \frac{(2a-x)}{a} = 2mg \frac{(2a-x)}{a} \qquad (3)$$

Combining (1), (2) and (3)

$$2mg \frac{x}{a} = 2mg \frac{(2a-x)}{a} + mg$$

$$\therefore \quad 2\frac{x}{a} = 4 - 2\frac{x}{a} + 1$$

$$4\frac{x}{a} = 5$$

$$x = \frac{5a}{4}$$

Height of B above C is $2a - x + a = \dfrac{7a}{4}$

Particle rests in equilibrium at a height $\dfrac{7a}{4}$ above C

EXERCISE 7a

1) A force of 2 N is applied to an elastic string of natural length 3 m so as to stretch it. To what length will the string extend if its modulus of elasticity is:
(a) 0.3 N   (b) 2 N   (c) 4 N?

2) The length of an elastic spring whose modulus of elasticity is 25 N is reduced by 0.5 m when a force of 20 N compresses it. What is the natural length of the spring?

3) A string will break if the tension in it exceeds 10 N. If the maximum extension it can be given is $\frac{1}{4}$ of its natural length, find its modulus of elasticity.

4) A spring of unstretched length l and modulus λ hangs with a scale pan of mass m at its free end. If a mass M is placed gently on the scale pan find how far the new equilibrium position is below the old one.

5) What is the length and modulus of elasticity of an elastic string which has length a_1 when supporting a mass M_1 and length a_2 when supporting a mass M_2?

6) A spring is fixed at one end. When it hangs vertically, supporting a mass of 2 kilogramme at the free end, its length is 3 metre. The mass of 2 kilogramme is then removed and replaced by a particle of unknown mass. The length of the spring is then 2.5 metre. If the modulus of elasticity of the spring is 9.8 newton, find the mass of the second load.

7) A particle of mass M is attached to the midpoint of an elastic spring whose modulus is $2Mg$ and whose unstretched length is $2a$. One end P of the spring is attached to the ceiling and the other end Q to the floor of a room of height $4a$. If P is vertically above Q find the distance from the ceiling of the particle when it is in equilibrium.

8) A mass of 4 kilogramme rests on a smooth plane inclined at $30°$ to the horizontal. It is held in equilibrium by a light elastic string attached to the mass and to a point on the plane. Find the extension in the string if it is known that a force of 49 newton would double the natural length of 1.25 metre.

9) The end A of an elastic string AB of natural length a and modulus of elasticity $2mg$ is fastened to one end of another elastic string AC of natural length $2a$ and modulus of elasticity $3mg$. The ends B and C are stretched between two points $6a$ apart in a horizontal line. Find the length of AB.

10) A light spring of natural length l is fixed at one end to a point O on a smooth horizontal table. The other end is attached to a particle P of mass m which rests on the table. The particle is pulled away from O until $OP = 5l/2$. If the modulus of elasticity of the spring is $2mg$ find the tension in the spring and the initial acceleration of the particle when released.

WORK DONE IN STRETCHING AN ELASTIC STRING

If a force is applied to the end of an elastic string so that the string stretches, the force is moving the object to which it is applied and is therefore doing work. Let us consider an elastic string of natural length a which is fixed at one end. A force is applied to the other end until the extension in the string is x.

Calculation of Amount of Work Done

The extending force will not be constant because it is always equal to the restoring tension in the string, which varies uniformly with the extension. The extending force $\left(\lambda \dfrac{x}{a}\right)$ is therefore directly proportional to the extension.

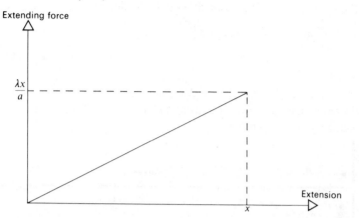

Extending force

$\dfrac{\lambda x}{a}$

Extension

The initial force T_o is zero and the final force T_x when the extension is x, is $\lambda \dfrac{x}{a}$. The average force therefore, throughout the whole of the stretching is

$$\frac{1}{2}\left(0 + \lambda \frac{x}{a}\right) \text{ or } \frac{1}{2}(T_o + T_x)$$

The work done in stretching the string can be calculated using
Average Force × Extension

Therefore:-　Work Done $= \dfrac{\lambda x^2}{2a}$　or　$\left(\dfrac{T_o + T_x}{2}\right) x$

Those students who are sufficiently familiar with Calculus may prefer to derive the expression for the work done in stretching an elastic string by using integration, as follows:

The magnitude of the extending force when the extension is s is $\dfrac{\lambda s}{a}$

The work done in producing a further small extension δs is therefore

approximately $\left(\dfrac{\lambda s}{a}\right)(\delta s)$

Total work done in stretching the string from a to $(a + x)$ is now given by

$$\int_0^x \frac{\lambda s}{a} \, ds = \frac{\lambda x^2}{2a}$$

N.B. The work done when a spring of modulus λ and natural length a is compressed a distance x is also given by $\dfrac{\lambda x^2}{2a}$

EXAMPLES 7b

1) An elastic string of natural length 2 m and modulus of elasticity 6 N is stretched until the extending force is of magnitude 4 N. How much work has been done and what is the final extension?

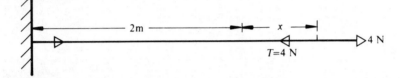

At maximum extension x, Tension = Extending Force

Using Hooke's Law $\qquad\qquad\qquad T = \lambda \dfrac{x}{a}$

We have $\qquad\qquad\qquad\qquad 4 = 6 \dfrac{x}{2}$

$$\therefore \quad x = \frac{4}{3} \text{ m}$$

Average Force is $\qquad\qquad\qquad \dfrac{0+4}{2} \text{N} = 2 \text{ N}$

$$\therefore \qquad \text{Work Done} = 2 \times \frac{4}{3} \text{J} = \frac{8}{3} \text{ J.}$$

$$\text{Work Done} = 2\tfrac{2}{3} \text{J}$$

$$\text{Maximum Extension} = 1\tfrac{1}{3} \text{ m}$$

2) An elastic spring of modulus λ and natural length a is fixed at one end and is attached to a load of mass m at the other end. How much work is done in stretching the spring slowly from its natural length to the position of equilibrium of the load?

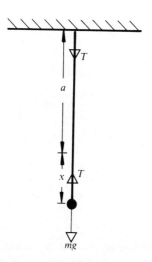

When the load is in equilibrium

$$T = mg$$

But using Hooke's Law

$$T = \lambda \frac{x}{a}$$

$$\therefore \quad x = \frac{mga}{\lambda}$$

Work done in stretching the spring is

$$\frac{\lambda x^2}{2a} = \frac{\lambda}{2a} \left(\frac{mga}{\lambda} \right)^2$$

Work done $= \dfrac{m^2 g^2 a}{2\lambda}$

3) If the work done in compressing a spring of natural length $2l$ and modulus of elasticity mg to a length l is equal to the work done in stretching an elastic string of modulus $2mg$ to a length $\dfrac{3l}{2}$, find the natural length of the string.

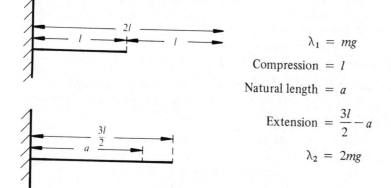

$$\lambda_1 = mg$$

$$\text{Compression} = l$$

$$\text{Natural length} = a$$

$$\text{Extension} = \frac{3l}{2} - a$$

$$\lambda_2 = 2mg$$

Work done in compressing spring $= \dfrac{\lambda_1 l^2}{2(2l)} = \dfrac{mgl}{4}$

Work done in stretching string $= \lambda_2 \dfrac{\left(\dfrac{3l}{2} - a \right)^2}{2a} = \dfrac{2mg}{2a} \left(\dfrac{3l}{2} - a \right)^2$

But these are equal, therefore $\dfrac{mgl}{4} = \dfrac{mg}{a} \left(\dfrac{3l}{2} - a \right)^2$

$$\therefore \quad al = 4 \left(\frac{3l}{2} - a \right)^2$$

$$\Rightarrow al = 9l^2 - 12al + 4a^2$$

$$\Rightarrow 0 = 4a^2 - 13al + 9l^2$$

$$\Rightarrow 0 = (4a - 9l)(a - l)$$

$$\therefore a = l \text{ or } \frac{9l}{4}$$

But $\frac{9l}{4}$ cannot be the natural length of the string as it is greater than the stretched length $\frac{3l}{2}$.

The natural length of the string therefore is l

EXERCISE 7b

1) An elastic string breaks if the tension in it exceeds 3 N. The unstretched length of the string is 4 m and its modulus of elasticity is 2 N. Find the work done in stretching it to breaking point and the length of the string at that moment.

2) If the work done in halving the length of a spring of modulus 4 N is 1.2 joule what is the natural length?

3) Two elastic strings AB and CD are each fixed with one end fastened to the ceiling and the other to the floor of a room of height 2.6 m.
For AB $\lambda = 2$ N and natural length = 1.4 m.
For CD $\lambda = 3$ N and natural length = 1.8 m.
If both strings are vertical find the ratio of the work done in stretching them.

4) Find the work done in stretching a rubber band round a roll of papers of radius 4 centimetre if the band when unstretched will just go round a cylinder of radius 2 centimetre and its modulus of elasticity is 0.5 N.

5) The work done in compressing a spring of natural length $3l$ to a length $2l$ is twice as great as the work done in doubling the length of a string of natural length $2l$. Show that the moduli of elasticity are in the ratio 12:1.

ENERGY

A body is said to possess energy if it has the capacity to do work.
When a body possessing energy does some work part of its energy is used up. Conversely if work is done to an object the object will be given some energy. Energy and work are mutually convertible and are measured in the same unit (joule), i.e.

$$\text{Work Done} = \text{Change in Energy}$$

There are various forms of energy. Heat, Electricity, Light, Sound and Chemical Energy are all familiar forms. In studying Mechanics however we are concerned chiefly with *Mechanical Energy*. This type of energy is a property of movement or position.

KINETIC ENERGY (KE) is the capacity of a body to do work by virtue of its motion.

If a body of mass m has a velocity v its kinetic energy is equivalent to the work which an external force would have to do to bring the body from rest up to its velocity v.

The numerical value of the kinetic energy can be calculated from the formula

$$KE = \tfrac{1}{2}mv^2$$

This formula can be derived as follows:

Consider a constant force F which, acting on a mass m initially at rest, gives the mass a velocity v. If, in reaching this velocity, the particle has been moving with an acceleration a and has been given a displacement s, then:-

$$F = ma \text{ (Newton's Law)}$$

$$v^2 = 2as \text{ (Equation of Motion of a particle moving}$$
$$\text{with uniform acceleration.)}$$

$$Fs = \text{Work done by force}$$

Combining these relationships we have:-

$$\text{Work done} = (ma)\left(\frac{v^2}{2a}\right)$$

$$= \tfrac{1}{2}mv^2$$

But the KE of the body is equivalent to the work done in giving the body its velocity.

$$\therefore \quad KE = \tfrac{1}{2}mv^2$$

N.B. Since both m and v^2 are always positive, KE is always positive and does not depend upon the direction of motion of the body.

POTENTIAL ENERGY is energy due to position.

If a body is in such a position that if it were released it would begin to move, it has potential energy.

TYPE I

Gravitational Potential Energy is a property of height.

When an object is allowed to fall from one level to a lower level it gains speed due to gravitational pull, i.e. it gains kinetic energy. Therefore, in possessing height, a body has the ability to convert its height into kinetic energy, i.e. it possesses *potential* energy.

The magnitude of its gravitational potential energy (PE) is equivalent to the amount of work done by the weight of the body in causing the descent.

If a mass m is at a height h above a lower level the PE possessed by the mass is $(mg)(h)$.

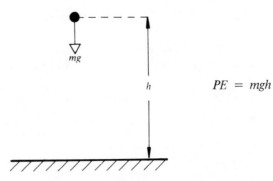

$$PE = mgh$$

Since h is the height of an object *above* a specified level, an object *below* the specified level has negative potential energy

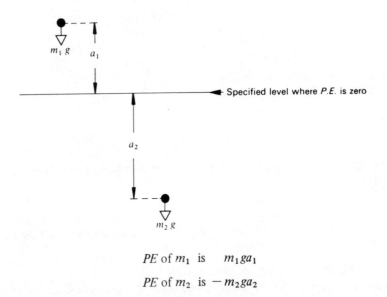

PE of m_1 is $\quad m_1 g a_1$

PE of m_2 is $\ - m_2 g a_2$

N.B. The chosen level from which height is measured has no absolute position. It is important therefore to indicate clearly the zero PE level in any problem in which PE is to be calculated.

TYPE 2

Elastic Potential Energy is a property of stretched strings and springs or compressed springs.
The end of a stretched elastic string will begin to move if it is released. The string therefore possesses potential energy due to its elasticity.

The amount of elastic potential energy (*EPE*) stored in a string of natural length *a* and modulus of elasticity λ when it is extended by a length *x* is equivalent to the amount of work necessary to produce the extension. Earlier in the chapter we saw that the work done was $\dfrac{\lambda x^2}{2a}$

$$\therefore \quad EPE = \frac{\lambda x^2}{2a}$$

N.B. EPE is always positive whether due to extension or to compression.

SUMMARY

Energy is the ability to do work.

Energy and work are mutually convertible.

The *unit of energy* is the Joule.

Kinetic energy (KE) is $\frac{1}{2}mv^2$ and is always positive.

Gravitational Potential Energy (PE) is *mgh*. It is positive for objects above a specified level but negative for objects below this level.

Elastic Potential Energy (EPE) is $\dfrac{\lambda x^2}{2a}$ and is always positive.

EXAMPLES 7c

1) A body of mass 2 kg is held 3 m above the floor of a room. Find the potential energy of the body relative to:
(a) the floor,
(b) a table of height 0.8 m.

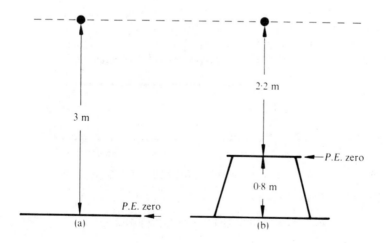

(a) $PE = mgh_1$ and $h_1 = 3$ m (relative to floor)

$\therefore PE = (2)(9.8)(3)$ J $= 58.8$ J

(b) $PE = mgh_2$ and $h_2 = 2.2$ m (relative to table)

$\therefore PE = (2)(9.8)(2.2)$ J $= 43.12$ J.

2) A force acts on a body of mass 3 kilogramme causing its speed to increase from 4 metre per second to 5 metre per second. How much work has the force done?

$$\text{Initial } KE = \tfrac{1}{2}mv_1^2 = \tfrac{1}{2}(3)(4)^2 \text{J} = 24 \text{ J}$$

$$\text{Final } KE = \tfrac{1}{2}mv_2^2 = \tfrac{1}{2}(3)(5)^2 \text{J} = 37.5 \text{ J}$$

$$\text{Work Done} = \text{Change in Energy}$$

$$\therefore \text{Work done by force} = (37.5 - 24) \text{J} = 13.5 \text{ J}.$$

3) A stone of mass 3 kg is thrown so that it just clears the top of a wall 2 m high when its speed is 4 ms^{-1}. What is its total mechanical energy as it passes over the wall?

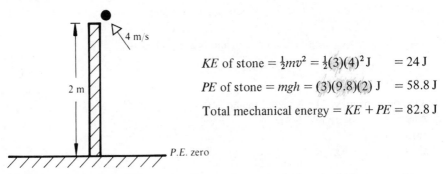

$$KE \text{ of stone} = \tfrac{1}{2}mv^2 = \tfrac{1}{2}(3)(4)^2 \text{J} \quad = 24 \text{ J}$$

$$PE \text{ of stone} = mgh = (3)(9.8)(2) \text{ J} \quad = 58.8 \text{ J}$$

$$\text{Total mechanical energy} = KE + PE = 82.8 \text{ J}$$

4) Water is being raised by a pump from a storage tank 4 metre below ground and delivered at 8 metre per second through a pipe at ground level. If the cross sectional area of the pipe is 0.12 square metre find the work done per second by the pump (1 cubic metre of water has mass 1000 kilogramme).

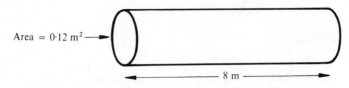

Volume of water delivered per second $= (8)(0.12) \text{ m}^3 = 0.96 \text{ m}^3$

Mass of water delivered per second $= (0.96)(10^3) \text{ kg} = 960 \text{ kg}$

PE gained by water per second $(mgh) = (960)(9.8)(4)$ J

$$= 37\,632 \text{ J}$$

KE gained by water per second $(\frac{1}{2}mv^2)$ $= \frac{1}{2}(960)(8^2)$ J

$$= 30\,720\,J$$

Total mechanical energy gained per second $= PE + KE$

$$= 68\,352\,J$$

Work done = Change in Energy

∴ Work done by pump = 68 352 joule per second.

EXERCISE 7c

1) Complete the following table by calculating the missing items.

Mass	Velocity	Kinetic Energy
3 kg	6 m/s	54 J
8 kg	5 m/s	100 J
1 kg	4 m/s	8 J

2) How much energy is stored in a spring of natural length 1 m and modulus 2 N when it is:

(a) stretched to a length of 1.4 m,

(b) compressed to half its length?

3) An athlete of mass 80 kilogramme starts from rest and sprints until his speed is 10 metre per second. He then takes off for a high jump and clears the bar with his body centre at a height of 2.2 metre. How much work has he done up to the moment when he clears the bar?

4) An elastic string whose modulus is 4 N is stretched from 3 m to 4 m in length. What is its increase in energy if its natural length was 2 m?

5) A machine picks up a stationary block of mass m, lifts it through a height h and projects it with velocity v. This operation is carried out 20 times every minute. How much work does the machine do each minute?

CONSERVATION OF MECHANICAL ENERGY

Kinetic and Potential Energy are both forms of Mechanical Energy. The total Mechanical Energy of a body or system of bodies will be changed in value if:-

(a) an external force other than weight causes work to be done. (Work done by weight is Potential Energy and is therefore already included in the total Mechanical Energy),

(b) some Mechanical Energy is converted into another form of energy (e.g. sound, heat, light etc). Such a conversion of energy usually takes place when a sudden change in the motion of the system occurs. For instance when two moving objects collide, some Mechanical Energy is converted into Sound Energy which is heard as a *bang* at impact.

If neither (a) nor (b) occurs then the total Mechanical Energy of a system remains constant. This is the *Principle of Conservation of Mechanical Energy* and can be expressed in the form:-

> *The total Mechanical Energy of a system remains*
> *constant provided that no external work is done*
> *and no sudden changes occur.*

When this principle is used in solving problems, a careful apparaisal must be made of any external forces which are acting. Some external forces do work and hence cause a change in the total energy of the system. Others, however, can be present without doing any work and these will not cause any change in energy.

e.g. Consider a mass m moving along a rough horizontal surface.

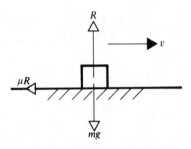

The normal reaction R is perpendicular to the direction of motion and does no work. The frictional force μR, acting in the line of motion, does cause the velocity of the mass to change. The frictional force therefore does do work and the total Mechanical Energy will change.

The Conservation of Mechanical Energy Principle is a very powerful weapon to use in problem solving. It is applicable to any problem where the necessary conditions are satisfied and which is concerned with position and velocity. Problems involving acceleration, however, are usually better approached by applying Newton's Law of Motion.

EXAMPLES 7d

1) A smooth heavy bead is threaded on to a wire in the shape of a circle of radius 0.6 m and centre C. The circular wire is fixed in a vertical plane with the bead at rest at the lowest point A. If the bead is projected from A with a velocity of 4.2 ms^{-1} find its height above A when it first comes to rest.

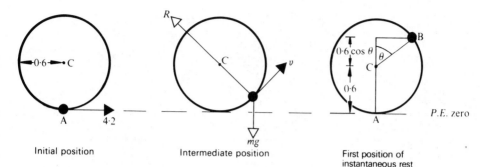

Initial position   Intermediate position   First position of
instantaneous rest

Let the mass of the bead be m kg.

If the bead first comes to rest at B, let BC make an angle θ with the upward vertical, so that the height of B above A is $0.6 + 0.6 \cos \theta$

$$\text{or } 0.6 (1 + \cos \theta)$$

In the initial position $PE = 0$

$$KE = \tfrac{1}{2} mv^2 \qquad = \tfrac{1}{2} m (4.2)^2 \, \text{J}$$

Total Mechanical Energy $= PE + KE = \tfrac{1}{2} m (4.2)^2 \, \text{J}$

In the first rest position:- $\qquad PE = mgh = mg(0.6)(1 + \cos \theta)$

$$= m(9.8)(0.6)(1 + \cos \theta)$$

$$KE = 0$$

Total Mechanical Energy $= PE + KE = m(9.8)(0.6)(1 + \cos \theta) \, \text{J}$

[During the intermediate motion no work is done by the normal reaction because it is always perpendicular to the direction of motion]

Using Conservation of Mechanical Energy,

$$\text{Initial Energy} = \text{Final Energy}$$

$$\therefore \quad \frac{m}{2} (4.2)^2 = m(9.8)(0.6)(1 + \cos \theta)$$

$$\Rightarrow \quad 1 + \cos \theta = \frac{(4.2)(4.2)}{2(9.8)(0.6)} = \tfrac{3}{2}$$

$$\Rightarrow \qquad \cos \theta = \tfrac{1}{2}.$$

Height of B above A $= 0.6(1 + \cos \theta)$

$$= \underline{0.9 \, \text{m}}$$

2) Two particles of equal mass m are connected by a light inelastic string. One particle A rests on a smooth plane inclined at $30°$ to the horizontal. The string passes over a smooth pulley at the top of the plane and then hangs vertically supporting the second particle. Initially particle A is held at a point A_1 on the plane and is released from this position. Find the speed of either particle when A has travelled a distance l up the plane.

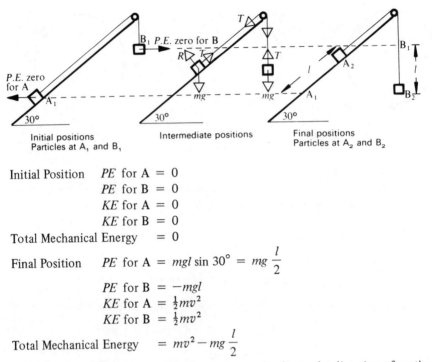

Initial positions
Particles at A₁ and B₁

Intermediate positions

Final positions
Particles at A₂ and B₂

Initial Position	PE for A = 0
	PE for B = 0
	KE for A = 0
	KE for B = 0
Total Mechanical Energy	= 0

Final Position PE for A $= mgl \sin 30° = mg\dfrac{l}{2}$

PE for B $= -mgl$
KE for A $= \frac{1}{2}mv^2$
KE for B $= \frac{1}{2}mv^2$

Total Mechanical Energy $= mv^2 - mg\dfrac{l}{2}$

[No external work is done as R is always perpendicular to the direction of motion and T is an internal force]

Using Conservation of Mechanical Energy

$$0 = mv^2 - mg\frac{l}{2}$$

$$\therefore \quad v^2 = \frac{gl}{2}$$

Velocity of either mass is $\left(\dfrac{gl}{2}\right)^{\frac{1}{2}}$

3) A light elastic string of natural length $2a$ has its ends fixed to two points A and B in a horizontal line where $AB = 2a$. A particle P of mass m is fastened to the midpoint of the string and is held midway between A and B. When released, the particle first comes to instantaneous rest when both portions of string are at $60°$ to AB. Find the modulus of elasticity of the string.

[In this problem, mechanical energy includes elastic potential energy]

Initial Position:-	$PE = mga \tan 60°$	$= mga\sqrt{3}$
	KE	$= 0$
	EPE (string unstretched)	$= 0$
	Total Mechanical Energy	$= mga\sqrt{3}$

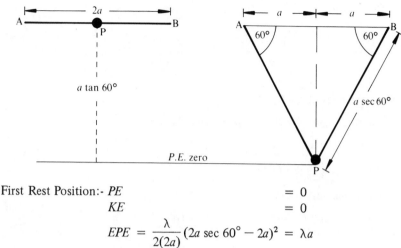

First Rest Position:- *PE*   = 0

KE = 0

$$EPE = \frac{\lambda}{2(2a)}(2a \sec 60° - 2a)^2 = \lambda a$$

Total Mechanical Energy   = λa

Using Conservation of Mechanical Energy

$$mga\sqrt{3} = \lambda a$$

$$\lambda = \sqrt{3}\, mg$$

Modulus of Elasticity of string is $\sqrt{3}\, mg$

4) An elastic string has one end fixed to a point A. The other end B, which is attached to a particle of mass 2 kg is pulled vertically down from A until AB is 3 m and then released. If the modulus of elasticity of the string is 21.6 N and its natural length is 1 m find:

(a) the velocity of the particle when the string first becomes slack,

(b) the distance from A of the particle when it first comes to rest.

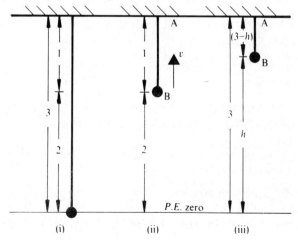

(i) Initial Position $PE = 0$

$KE = 0$

$$EPE = \frac{\lambda}{2l}x^2 = \frac{(21.6)(2)^2}{2(1)} \text{ J}$$

Total Mechanical Energy $= 43.2 \text{ J}$

(ii) String first slack $PE = mgh = 2(9.8)(2) \text{ J}$

$KE = \frac{1}{2}mv^2 = v^2 \text{ J}$

$EPE = 0$

Total Mechanical Energy $= (39.2 + v^2) \text{ J}$

(iii) Particle first at rest $PE = mgh = 2(9.8)h$

$KE = 0$

$EPE = 0$

Total Mechanical Energy $= 19.6\,h \text{ J}$

Using Conservation of Mechanical Energy throughout

$$43.2 = 39.2 + v^2 = 19.6\,h$$

$$\therefore \quad v^2 = 43.2 - 39.2 = 4$$

and $$h = \frac{43.2}{19.6}\,\text{m} = 2.2\,\text{m}$$

$\therefore$ Velocity of particle when string becomes slack is $\underline{2\,\text{ms}^{-1}}$.
Depth of particle below A when first at rest is $\underline{0.8\,\text{m}}$.

EXERCISE 7d

1) A particle falls freely from rest until its speed is 7 metre per second. How far has it fallen?

2) A truck of mass M is pulled up a smooth track inclined at $30°$ to the horizontal. Its speed increases from u to $3u$ in a distance d. Find the work done by the engine.

3) One end of an elastic string is fixed to a point A on a smooth horizontal table. The other end is attached to a heavy particle P. The particle is pulled away from A until AP is of length $3l/2$ and is then released. If the natural length of the string is l and its modulus of elasticity is mg find the velocity of the particle when the string reaches its natural length, if the mass of the particle is m.

4) Two identical particles of mass m are connected by a light inelastic string of length $2l$. One particle A rests on a smooth horizontal table and the other particle B hangs freely over the edge. Initially A is held at a distance l from the edge of

the table and the string attached to A is perpendicular to the edge. If A is released find its velocity when it reaches the table edge.

5) A particle of mass 0.5 kilogramme is attached to a light elastic string of natural length 2 metre and modulus of elasticity 1 N. The other end of the string is fixed at point P on a smooth horizontal plane. The particle is projected from P along the plane with a velocity of 4 metre per second. Find its greatest distance from P during the following motion.

6) The end A of a light elastic string AB is fixed. A particle of mass m is attached to the end B. The particle is held as close as possible to A and is released from that position. Find the length of **AB** when the particle is in its lowest position if the natural length of the string is l and its modulus of elasticity is $2\,mg$.

7) A particle of mass m is suspended from a fixed point A by a light elastic string of natural length l and modulus of elasticity $4\,mg$. The particle is pulled down from its equilibrium position a distance d and then released. If the particle just reaches the height of A, find d.

8) Two equal scale pans each of mass M are connected by a light inelastic string which passes over a smooth pulley. The two pans are at the same level. If a load of mass $2M$ is gently placed on one pan and the system is released, find through what distance each pan has moved when their velocity is 2.1 ms^{-1}.

MULTIPLE CHOICE EXERCISE 7
The instructions for answering these questions are given on page (xii)

TYPE I

1) A force of 4 N is applied to an elastic string in order to stretch it. The string has natural length 3 m and modulus 12 N. The extension is:
(a) 9 m   (b) 3 m   (c) 1 m   (d) 4 m.

2) A spring is compressed to half its natural length by a force of 6 N. Its modulus of elasticity is:
(a) 12 N   (b) 3 N   (c) 6 N   (d) 4.5 N.

3) The potential energy of a body of mass m is mgh where h is:
(a) the distance from a chosen level,
(b) the height above the ground,
(c) the height above a chosen level,
(d) the vertical distance moved.

4) A particle of mass m slides a distance d down a plane inclined at θ to the horizontal. The work done by the normal reaction R is:
(a) Rd (b) $mgd\cos\theta$ (c) 0   (d) $mgd\sin\theta$.

5) A particle falls freely from rest through a distance d. Its speed is then:
(a) $\sqrt{gd}$ (b) $-\sqrt{2gd}$ (c) $-\sqrt{\dfrac{gd}{2}}$ (d) $\sqrt{2gd}$.

TYPE II

6) A particle of mass $2m$ is attached to one end of an elastic string of modulus mg whose other end is fixed to a point P. The particle is dropped from P. It will first come to rest:
(a) when the tension in the string $= 2\,mg$,
(b) when the kinetic energy is zero,
(c) below the equilibrium position,
(d) when the length of the string has doubled.

7) A particle travelling in a horizontal straight line has an acceleration of $+2\,\mathrm{ms}^{-2}$:
(a) Its total mechanical energy is constant.
(b) The particle is doing work.
(c) Its potential energy is constant.
(d) Work is being done on the particle.

8) The modulus of elasticity of an elastic string is:
(a) the ratio of the extension to the natural length,
(b) equal to the force stretching the string,
(c) measured in joules,
(d) equal to the tension when the string is twice its natural length.

TYPE III

9) (a) The tension in a string of length 1 m is 2 N.
   (b) An elastic string of natural length 0.5 m and modulus of elasticity 2 N is extended by 0.5 m.

10) (a) The energy stored in an elastic string of natural length a modulus λ is $\dfrac{\lambda a}{2}$.

   (b) An elastic string of natural length a and modulus λ is stretched to a length $2a$.

11) (a) In a system the total work done, other than by weight, is zero.
   (b) The total mechanical energy of a system is constant.

12) (a) A block is set moving across a horizontal surface and as it moves the temperature of the block rises.
   (b) The kinetic energy of a block moving on a horizontal surface is constant.

TYPE IV

13) Calculate the extension in an elastic string:
(a) the natural length is 2 m,
(b) the elastic potential energy is 3 J,
(c) the string is hanging vertically.

14) A particle is sliding down an inclined plane. Calculate its speed when it reaches the foot of the plane:
(a) the length of the plane is 4 m,

(b) contact is smooth,
(c) the inclination of the plane is $20°$,
(d) the mass of the particle is 3 kg.

15) A particle is hanging in equilibrium at one end of an elastic string whose other end is fixed. Find the distance between the particle and the fixed end:
(a) the particle weighs 10 N,
(b) the modulus of elasticity is 8 N,
(c) the natural length of the string is 2 m.

16) A particle is released from rest at the top of a tower. Find its speed at the bottom:
(a) the tower is 50 m high,
(b) the mass of the particle is 2 kg,
(c) the particle moves vertically.

TYPE V

17) The energy stored in an elastic string is proportional to the extension.

18) As long as no external forces act on a system the kinetic energy must be constant.

19) Some external forces which act on a moving body do not do any work.

20) A spring obeys Hooke's Law when it is stretched but not when it is compressed.

MISCELLANEOUS EXERCISE 7

1) Two particles A and B are connected by a light inelastic string which passes over a smooth pulley. A is of mass m and B is of mass $2m$. Initially both particles are at rest at a depth $2l$ below the pulley. If they are released from rest find their velocity when each has moved a distance l.

2) Two springs AB and BC are fastened together at B. The ends A and C are fastened to two fixed points on a smooth horizontal table where AC is 2 m. AB and BC have natural lengths of 0.6 and 0.8 m and moduli of elasticity 2 and 4 N respectively. Find the stretched lengths of AB and BC.

3) A body of mass 2.5 kilogramme is attached to the end B of a light elastic string AB of natural length 2 metre and modulus $5g$ newton. The mass is suspended vertically in equilibrium by the string whose other end A is attached to a fixed point.
 (i) Find the depth below A of B when the body is in equilibrium.
(ii) Find the distance through which the body must be pulled down vertically from its equilibrium position so that it will just reach A after release.

4) An engine is pumping water from a large tank and delivering it through a pipe of diameter 0.04 metre at a rate of 100 litre per second. Find the work done by the engine in one second.

(The mass of 1 litre of water is taken as 1 kilogramme).

5) A ring is threaded on to a smooth wire in the form of a circle fixed in a vertical plane. The ring is projected from the lowest point on the wire with a velocity of 4.2 ms^{-1}. If the radius of the circular wire is 0.6 m, find the height above the centre at which the particle first comes to instantaneous rest. If, instead, the ring had been projected with a velocity of 5.6 ms^{-1} describe its motion.

6) A light elastic string, of unstretched length a and modulus of elasticity W, is fixed at one end to a point on the ceiling of a room. To the other end of the string is attached a particle of weight W. A horizontal force P is applied to the particle and in equilibrium it is found that the string is stretched to three times its natural length. Calculate:

(a) the angle the string makes with the horizontal,

(b) the value of P in terms of W.

   If, instead, P is not applied horizontally find the least value of P which in equilibrium will make the string have the same inclination to the horizontal as before. Deduce that the stretch length of the string is $\frac{3}{2}a$ in this case and find the inclination of P to the vertical.   (U of L)

7) Prove that the work done in stretching a light elastic string from its natural length a to a length $(a + x)$ is proportional to x^2.

   One end of this string is fastened to a fixed point A, and at the other end a particle of mass m is attached. The particle is released from rest at A, and first comes to rest when it has fallen a distance $3a$. Show that at the lowest point of its path the acceleration of the particle is $2g$ upwards.

   Find in terms of g and a the speed of the particle at the instants when the magnitude of its acceleration is $\frac{1}{2}g$.   (U of L)

8) In the diagram AC, BC and CD are three elastic strings with the same modulus of elasticity. The ends A and B are attached to a horizontal support and the end D of the string CD carries a particle of mass 2 kg hanging freely under gravity. The natural lengths of the strings AC and CD are 0.24 and 0.18 m respectively, and in the equilibrium position AC is extended by 0.03 m and the angles ACD and BCD are $120°$ and $150°$ respectively. Calculate:

  (i) the modulus of elasticity of the strings,

 (ii) the natural length of BC,

(iii) the depth of D below AB.

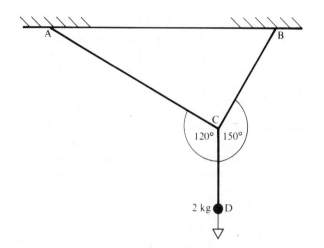

9) Two identical elastic strings of length 1 metre and modulus 4.9 N are each fastened to a particle of mass 0.5 kilogramme. Their other ends are fixed to two points 4 metres apart in a vertical line. Find the height of the particle above the lower fixed point A in the equilibrium position. The particle is now pulled down to A and released from rest. Find the greatest height above A to which the particle rises.

10) A particle P of mass 2 kg is attached to two strings PA and PB. PA is an elastic string of natural length 0.5 m and modulus of elasticity 9.8 N, and PB is an inelastic string. A and B are fixed points in a horizontal line. If P rests in equilibrium with PA making 30° with AB and PA perpendicular to PB find the lengths of PA and PB and the tension in the inelastic string.

11) A ring of mass m can slide freely on a smooth wire in the shape of a circle of diameter $2a$, which is fixed in a vertical plane. The ring is fastened to one end of a light elastic string of natural length a and modulus of elasticity mg. The other end of the string is attached to the lowest point of the wire. The ring is held at the highest point of the wire and is slightly disturbed from rest. Find the velocity of the ring:
(a) when it is level with the centre of the circular wire,
(b) when the string first becomes slack,
(c) when the string makes an acute angle θ with the upward vertical.

12) A particle of weight W is attached by two light inextensible strings each of length a to two fixed points distant a apart in a horizontal line. Write down the tension in either string.

One of the strings is now replaced by an elastic string of the same natural length, and it is found that in the new position of equilibrium this string has stretched to a length $5a/4$. Prove that the modulus of elasticity of this string is $7W/\sqrt{39}$, and show that the tension in the other string has been increased in the ratio $5: \sqrt{13}$.

(U of L)

13) One end O of an elastic string OP is fixed to a point on a smooth plane inclined at 30° to the horizontal. A particle of mass m is attached to the end P and is held at O. If the natural length of the string is a and its modulus is $2mg$, find:
(a) the distance down the plane from O at which the particle first comes to instantaneous rest after being released from rest at O.
(b) the velocity of the particle as it passes through its equilibrium position.

14) In the diagram BAC is a rigid fixed rough wire and angle BAC is 60°. P and Q are two identical rings of mass m connected by a light elastic string of natural length $2a$ and modulus of elasticity mg. If P and Q are in equilibrium when PA = AQ = $3a$ find the least coefficient of friction between the rings and the wire.

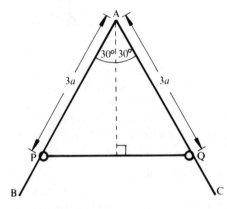

15) Water is pumped at the rate of 1.2 cubic metre per minute from a large tank on the ground, up to a point 8 metre above the level of the water in the tank. It emerges as a horizontal jet from a pipe of cross-section 5×10^{-3} square metre. If the efficiency of the apparatus is 60%, find the energy supplied to the pump per second.

16) A particle of weight W is attached to a point C of an unstretched elastic string AB, where AC = $4a/3$, CB = $4a/7$. The ends A and B are then attached to the extremities of a horizontal diameter of a fixed hemispherical bowl of radius a and the particle rests on the smooth inner surface, the angle BAC being 30°. Show that the modulus of elasticity of the string is W and determine the reaction of the bowl on the particle.   (U of L)

17) Prove that the potential energy of a light elastic string of natural length l and modulus λ when stretched to a length of $(l + x)$ is $\dfrac{1}{2} \lambda \dfrac{x^2}{l}$.

Two points A and B are in a horizontal line at a distance $3l$ apart. A particle P of mass m is joined to A by a light inextensible string of length $4l$ and is joined to B by a light elastic string of natural length l and modulus λ. Initially P is held at a point C in AB produced such that BC = l, both strings being just taut, and is then released from rest. If $\lambda = \dfrac{mg}{4}$ show that when AP is vertical the speed of the particle is $2\sqrt{gl}$ and find the instantaneous value of the tension in the elastic string in this position.   (J.M.B)

18) Two fixed points A and B on the same horizontal level are 20 cm apart. A light elastic string, which obeys Hooke's Law, is just taut when its ends are fixed at A and B. A block of mass 5 kg is attached to the string at a point P where AP = 15 cm. The system is then allowed to take up its position of equilibrium with P below AB and it is found that in this position the angle APB is a right angle. If $\angle$ BAP $= \theta$, show that the ratio of the extensions of AP and BP is

$$\frac{4\cos\theta - 3}{4\sin\theta - 1}.$$

Hence show that θ satisfies the equation

$$\cos\theta\,(4\cos\theta - 3) = 3\sin\theta\,(4\sin\theta - 1). \qquad \text{(U of L)}$$

19) A ring A of mass m is threaded on to a smooth fixed horizontal straight wire. The ring is attached to one end of a light elastic string whose other end is fixed to a point B at a height h above the wire. Initially the ring is vertically below B. In this position it is given a velocity v along the wire. The string has a natural length h and modulus of elasticity mg. Show that the angle θ between AB and the wire when the ring first comes to instantaneous rest, is given by

$$\sin\theta\left(\frac{v}{\sqrt{gh}} + 1\right) = 1.$$

20) A mass of 3 kilogramme is connected by an elastic string of natural length 1 metre and modulus of elasticity 14.7 N to a fixed point. A horizontal force equal to the weight of 1 kilogramme acts on the mass maintaining it in equilibrium. Find the inclination of the string to the vertical. If the horizontal force is removed, what is the least force which must act on the particle to ensure that the string shall be inclined at the same angle as before.
Calculate in each case the extension of the string.

CHAPTER 8

MOMENTUM. DIRECT IMPACT

The momentum of a body is the product of its mass and its velocity.

$$\text{Momentum} = mv$$

Because velocity is a vector quantity, momentum also is a vector whose direction is the direction of the velocity.

If a body is moving with constant velocity, its momentum is constant. In order to cause a change in velocity a force must act on the body. It follows, then, that a force must act in order to change momentum.

Properties of motion already established can be used to determine the relationship between a force applied to an object and the change in momentum which it produces. Consider a constant force F which acts for a time t on a body of mass m, thus changing its velocity from u to v. Because the force is constant the body will travel with constant acceleration a where:

$$F = ma \qquad \text{(Newton's Law)}$$

and $\quad at = v - u \qquad$ (Chapter 4　Equation 1)

hence $\quad \dfrac{F}{m} t = v - u$

or $\quad Ft = mv - mu$

The product of a constant force F and the time t for which it acts is called the *impulse* of the force and the relationship above can be written:

The impulse of a force is equal to the change in momentum which it produces.
(Impulse of a variable force is discussed in Chapter 9).

Units

The unit of impulse is the newton second, Ns.

Momentum (mv) can be measured in kilogram metre per second (kgms^{-1}) units but it is better to use the impulse unit Ns as the unit for momentum also.

Instantaneous Impulse

There are many occasions when a force acts for so short a time that the effect is instantaneous e.g. a bat striking a ball. In such cases, although the magnitude of the force and the time for which it acts may each be unknown, the change in momentum produced is still equal to the instantaneous impulse.

EXAMPLES 8a

1) A truck of mass 10^3 kg travelling at 3 ms^{-1} is brought to rest in 2 seconds when it strikes a buffer. What force (assumed constant) is exerted by the buffer?

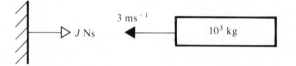

If the impulse exerted by the buffer is $+J$ newton second then the initial velocity of the truck is -3 ms^{-1} and its final velocity is zero.

Then
$$J = mv - mu$$
$$J = 0 - 10^3(-3) = 3 \times 10^3 \text{Ns}$$

But
$$J = Ft = 2F$$

Hence
$$F = \frac{J}{2} = 1500 \text{ N}$$

2) What constant force acting in the direction of motion of a particle of mass 2 kg will increase its speed from 4 ms^{-1} to 20 ms^{-1} in 4 seconds?

The constant force F, u and v are all in the same sense i.e. all are positive.

Since
$$Ft = mv - mu$$
$$F \times 4 = 2 \times 20 - 2 \times 4$$
$$F = 8$$

The required force is 8 N

3) A ball of mass 0.5 kg is thrown towards a wall so that it strikes the wall normally with a speed of 10 ms^{-1}. If the ball bounces at right angles away from the wall with a speed of 8 ms^{-1}, what impulse does the wall exert on the ball?

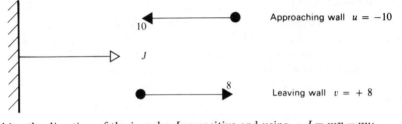

Taking the direction of the impulse J as positive and using

$$J = mv - mu$$

we have

$$J = \tfrac{1}{2} \times 8 - \tfrac{1}{2}(-10)$$
$$= 9$$

Therefore the wall exerts an impulse of 9 Ns on the ball.

4) A nozzle is discharging water at a rate of 200 litre per second, with a speed of 10 metre per second. If the water strikes a wall at right angles and does not bounce off the wall, find the force F newton exerted by the wall on the water. (Mass of 1 litre of water is 1 kilogram).

Mass of water discharged per second $= 200 \text{ kg}$

Momentum destroyed per second $= 200 \times 10 \text{ kgms}^{-1}$.

Impulse exerted by wall in one second $= F \times 1 \text{ Ns}$

But   Impulse $=$ Change in Momentum

Hence $F \times 1 = 2000$

and $F = 2 \times 10^3 \text{N}$

Therefore the wall exerts a force of 2 kN on the water.

5) A bullet of mass m strikes an obstruction and ricochets off at $120°$ to its original direction. If its speed also is changed from u to v, find the magnitude of the impulse acting on the bullet.

This time the velocities before and after the impulse are not in line and it is necessary to consider components of impulse and velocities in two perpendicular directions. (Parallel and perpendicular to the initial velocity are convenient directions).

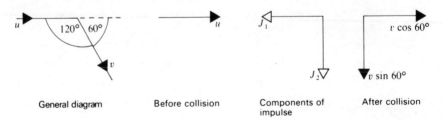

General diagram   Before collision   Components of impulse   After collision

Consider components parallel to J_1 taking the sense of J_1 as positive

$$J_1 = m(-v\cos 60°) - m(-u)$$

Similarly, parallel to J_2 we have

$$J_2 = m(v\sin 60°) - 0$$

Hence

$$J_1 = m\left(u - \frac{v}{2}\right)$$

and

$$J_2 = mv\frac{\sqrt{3}}{2}$$

The magnitude of the resultant impulse is given by

$$\sqrt{J_1^2 + J_2^2}$$

$$= m\sqrt{\left(u - \frac{v}{2}\right)^2 + \left(\frac{v\sqrt{3}}{2}\right)^2}$$

$$= m\sqrt{u^2 - uv + v^2}.$$

EXERCISE 8a

1) A constant force of 12 N acts on a particle of mass 4 kg whose initial speed is 8 ms^{-1}, the direction of the force being in the direction of motion. Find its speed at the end of 3 seconds.

2) In what time will a force of 8 N reduce the speed of a particle of mass 3 kg from 21 ms^{-1} to 6 ms^{-1}?

3) A hammer of mass 1.2 kg travelling at 15 ms^{-1} is brought to rest when it strikes a nail. What impulse acts on the hammer?

4) A dart of mass 0.12 kg flying at a speed of 20 ms^{-1} hits the dartboard and comes to rest in 0.1 seconds. What is the average force exerted by the dartboard on the dart?

5) A batsman strikes a cricket ball at right angles to the bat so that its direction is reversed. If the ball approaches the bat with a speed of 30 ms^{-1} and leaves it at 50 ms^{-1}, what is the magnitude of the impulse exerted by the bat on the ball if the mass of the ball is 0.13 kg?

6) Sand falls steadily through a hole on to a conveyor belt moving horizontally. 4 kg of sand falls every second, striking the belt at 10 ms^{-1}. Find the vertical force exerted by the belt on the sand (assuming that the sand does not bounce on impact).

7) An object of mass 2 kg is diverted from its path through 90° by collision with a solid obstruction. Find the magnitude and direction of the impulse incurred at impact if the speed is changed from 20 ms^{-1} to 10 ms^{-1}.

8) A football travels horizontally at $12 \, \text{ms}^{-1}$ towards a player who diverts its path horizontally through $60°$ and passes it at $18 \, \text{ms}^{-1}$ to a team mate. Find the impulse given to the ball:
(a) if it is passed horizontally,
(b) if it is kicked at an angle of $30°$ to the ground.
The mass of the football is $0.4 \, \text{kg}$.

9) A jet of water travelling with a speed of $12 \, \text{ms}^{-1}$ impinges on a plane at right angles to the jet. If the force (assumed constant) exerted by the water on the plane is $400 \, \text{N}$, calculate the volume of water being discharged per minute. (The water does not bounce off the plane and its mass per litre is $1 \, \text{kg}$).

Constant Momentum

When a force affects the velocity of an object, momentum changes in the direction of that force.
It follows that, if in a certain direction *no* force affects the motion, there is no change in momentum in that direction.
Consider, for example, a football which is travelling along the ground at $16 \, \text{ms}^{-1}$. A player kicks the ball at right angles to its direction of motion. The impulse of the kick changes the momentum in the direction of the kick but the ball continues with an unchanged velocity component of $16 \, \text{ms}^{-1}$ in the original direction since no impulse has acted in this direction.

Internal Impact

Whenever two solid objects are in contact they exert *equal and opposite forces* on each other (Newton's Law)
It is clear that, regardless of the length of time for which they are in contact, each is in contact with the other for the *same time.*
Consequently they exert *equal and opposite impulses* on each other.
Since change in momentum is equal to the impulse which produces the change, it follows that equal and opposite impulses produce equal and opposite changes in momentum. The resultant change in momentum of the two objects is therefore zero and their *total* momentum remains constant although internal forces have affected the motion of both objects.

This property can be combined with our earlier observations to form
the **PRINCIPLE OF CONSERVATION OF LINEAR MOMENTUM.**
*If, in a specified direction, no external force affects the motion of a system, the
total momentum in that direction remains constant.*

EXAMPLES 8b

1) A truck of mass 1200 kg is moving with a speed of 7 ms^{-1} when it collides
with a second truck of mass 1600 kg which is stationary. If the two trucks are
automatically coupled together at impact, with what speed do they move on
together?

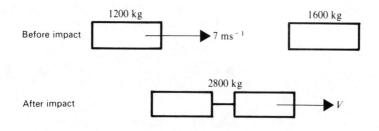

Let the velocity of the coupled trucks (total mass 2800 kg) be V.
In the direction of motion:-
Momentum before impact $= 1200 \times 7 + 1600 \times 0$
Momentum after impact $\quad = 2800\,V$
A pair of equal and opposite internal impulses act at impact, therefore, using
Conservation of Momentum:
$$1200 \times 7 = 2800\,V$$
$$\text{Therefore } V = 3\text{ ms}^{-1}$$
Therefore speed of coupled trucks is 3 ms^{-1}.

2) A bullet of mass 0.04 kg travelling horizontally at 100 ms^{-1} hits a stationary
block of wood of mass 8 kg, passes through it and emerges horizontally with a
speed of 40 ms^{-1}. If the block is free to move on a smooth horizontal plane find
the speed with which it is moving after the bullet has passed through it.

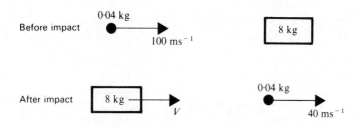

If the speed of the block is V, then using Conservation of Momentum (in the direction of motion) we have:

$$0.04 \times 100 = 8 \times V + 0.04 \times 40$$

$$4 - 1.6 = 8V$$

$$V = \frac{2.4}{8} = 0.3 \text{ ms}^{-1}$$

Therefore the block has a speed of 0.3 ms^{-1}.

3) Two particles, each of mass m, collide head on when their speeds are $2u$ and u. If they stick together on impact, find their combined speed in terms of u.

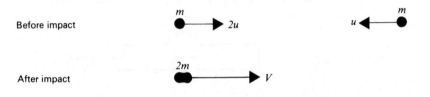

Using Conservation of Momentum (in the direction of the velocity $2u$) we have:

$$m \times 2u - m \times u = 2m \times V$$

$$V = \frac{u}{2}$$

The combined mass will travel at speed $\frac{u}{2}$.

(Note that the momentum of the second particle before impact is negative because its sense is opposite to that specified).

4) A gun of mass M fires a shell of mass m and recoils horizontally. If the shell travels along the barrel with speed v find the speed with which the barrel begins to recoil if:
(a) the barrel is horizontal,
(b) the barrel is inclined at an angle $30°$ to the horizontal.
State in each case the constant force required to bring the gun to rest in 2 seconds.

(a)

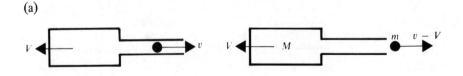

[The speed of the shell is $v - V$ as it leaves the barrel because the barrel is recoiling with speed V].

Before firing the shell, the gun is at rest and the total momentum is zero.

Using Conservation of Momemtum (in the direction of the shell's motion)

$$0 = m(v - V) - MV$$

$$MV = m(v - V)$$

$$(M + m)V = mv$$

$$V = \frac{mv}{M + m}$$

Therefore the initial velocity of recoil is $\dfrac{mv}{M + m}$

If a constant force F_1 brings the gun to rest it must exert an impulse equal to the initial momentum of the gun.

Therefore

$$2F_1 = M \frac{mv}{M + m}$$

The force required is

$$\frac{Mmv}{2(M + m)}$$

(b)

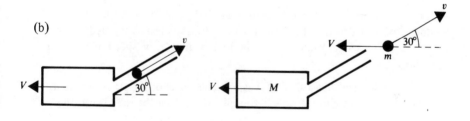

[This time the shell leaves the barrel with a velocity which is the resultant of two inclined components]

Using Conservation of Momentum (in the direction of recoil)

$$0 = MV + m(V - v \cos 30°).$$

$$mv \frac{\sqrt{3}}{2} = (M + m)V$$

$$V = \frac{mv\sqrt{3}}{2(M + m)}$$

Therefore the initial velocity of recoil is $\dfrac{mv\sqrt{3}}{2(M + m)}$ and the force F_2 required to stop the gun in two seconds is given by

$$2F_2 = M\left(\frac{mv\sqrt{3}}{2(M+m)}\right)$$

Required force is $\dfrac{Mmv\sqrt{3}}{4(M+m)}$

EXERCISE 8b

1) Two particles A and B of equal mass are travelling along the same line with constant speeds 4 ms^{-1} and 3 ms^{-1} respectively. If they collide and coalesce find their common speed just after impact:
(a) if they collide head-on,
(b) if they were originally travelling in the same sense.

2) A truck of mass 400 kg runs at a speed of 2 ms^{-1} into a stationary truck. They become coupled together and move on with speed 0.8 ms^{-1}. What is the mass of the second truck.

3) A gun of mass 2000 kg fires horizontally a shell of mass 25 kg. The gun's horizontal recoil is controlled by a constant force of 8000 N which brings the gun to rest in 1.5 seconds. Find the initial velocity of the shell:
(a) relative to the gun,
(b) in the air.

4) A boy of mass 40 kg is on a sledge of mass 10 kg travelling at 5 ms^{-1} when another boy comes from behind moving three times as fast as the sledge and jumps on to the sledge. What is the second boy's mass if the speed of the sledge is doubled?

5) A gun of mass km fires a shell of mass m. The barrel of the gun is elevated at an angle α and the gun recoils horizontally. Show that the shell leaves the barrel at an angle β to the horizontal where $\tan \beta = \dfrac{k+1}{k} \tan \alpha$.

6) A bullet of mass m is fired with a horizontal speed $2u$ into a stationary block of wood of mass $50m$ which is free to move horizontally. Find the velocity of the block if:
(a) the bullet goes right through it and emerges with speed u,
(b) the bullet becomes embedded in the block.

7) A vertical post of mass M is to be driven into the ground. A pile-driver of mass m strikes the post vertically with a velocity v. Assuming that the pile-driver does not bounce off the post, find the velocity with which the post enters the ground. If the combined mass comes to rest when the post has been driven into the ground to a depth h find the constant force with which the ground resists penetration.

8) A particle travelling horizontally with speed u collides and coalesces with a particle of equal mass hanging at rest at the end of a light inextensible string of length $2l$. If the string rotates through an angle of $60°$ before first coming to rest, show that $u^2 = 8gl$.

IMPULSIVE TENSIONS

When a string jerks, equal and opposite tensions act suddenly at each end. Consequently equal and opposite impulses act on the objects to which the two ends of the string are attached. There are two cases to consider.

(a) *One end of the string is fixed.* The impulse which acts at the fixed end of the string cannot affect the momentum of the fixed object there. A moveable object attached to the free end however will undergo a change in momentum equal in magnitude to the impulsive tension.

In such cases the momentum of the system does change in the direction of the string but is unchanged in the perpendicular direction where no impulse acts.

EXAMPLE

A string AB of length $2l$ is fixed at A to a point on a smooth horizontal table. A particle of mass m attached to B is initially at a point C distant l from A. The particle is projected horizontally with speed u at right angles to AC. Find its velocity just after the string becomes taut.

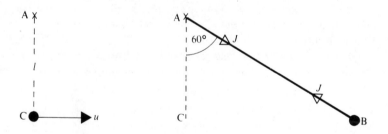

When the string becomes taut $AB = 2l$ and $\cos \hat{CAB} = \frac{1}{2}$. Hence angle $\hat{CAB} = 60°$ when the instantaneous impulses act. Parallel and perpendicular to AB, just before the string jerks taut, the particle has velocity components

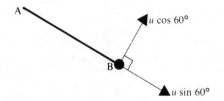

When the string becomes taut the length of AB is fixed and B can no longer travel in the direction $\overrightarrow{AB}$. After the jerk the velocity of the particle is therefore perpendicular to AB

Using Impulse = Change in Momentum

(i) Along BA:-

$$J = 0 - (-mu \sin 60°)$$

$$J = mu \frac{\sqrt{3}}{2}$$

(ii) Perpendicular to BA (no impulse)

$$0 = mv - mu \cos 60°$$

therefore

$$v = \frac{u}{2} \text{ (no change)}$$

(b) *Both ends of the string attached to moveable objects.*
In this case equal and opposite impulses act on the two objects, producing equal and opposite changes in momentum.
The total momentum of the system therefore remains constant, although the momentum of each individual object is changed in the direction of the string. Perpendicular to the string however, no impulse acts and the momentum of *each* particle in this direction is unchanged.
The velocities of two objects moving at the ends of a taut string are not independent. The important relationship between them can be illustrated as follows:

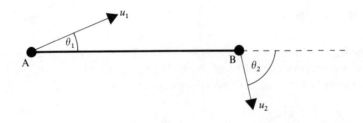

At A and B are particles moving with velocities as shown in the diagram. AB is a taut string. Resolving the velocities along and perpendicular to AB we have

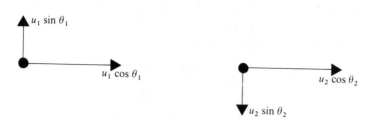

The noteworthy components are those along **AB** since:

if $u_1 \cos \theta_1 > u_2 \cos \theta_2$ the string is not taut,

if $u_2 \cos \theta_2 > u_1 \cos \theta_1$ the string has snapped.

Hence for the string to remain taut and unbroken $u_1 \cos \theta_1 = u_2 \cos \theta_2$.

EXAMPLE

A particle of mass m is attached to each end of a string **AB** of length $2l$. The whole system lies on a smooth horizontal table with **B** initially at a point **C** distant l from **A**. The particle at the end **B** is projected across the table with speed u perpendicular to **AC**. Find the velocity with which each particle begins to move after the jerk and the magnitude of the impulsive tension.

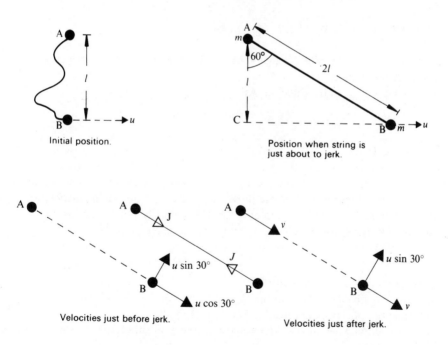

Initial position.

Position when string is just about to jerk.

Velocities just before jerk.

Velocities just after jerk.

When the string jerks tight, both particles begin to move in the direction **AB** with equal speeds v.

Perpendicular to AB there is no impulse on either particle; velocities in this direction are therefore unchanged.

Using Conservation of Momentum in the direction AB:

$$0 + mu \cos 30° = mv + mv$$

giving
$$v = \frac{u\sqrt{3}}{4}$$

Just after the jerk therefore:-

velocity of mass at A $= \dfrac{u\sqrt{3}}{4}$ along AB

velocity of mass at B $= \sqrt{\left(\dfrac{u}{2}\right)^2 + \left(\dfrac{u\sqrt{3}}{4}\right)^2}$

$$= \frac{u}{4}\sqrt{7}$$

in a direction inclined at $\arctan \dfrac{u \sin 30°}{v}$ with AB

i.e. $\arctan \dfrac{2}{\sqrt{3}}$ with AB.

The magnitude of J can be calculated by considering the change in momentum of *one* of the particles.

For the mass at A, in the direction AB

$$J = mv - 0$$

Therefore
$$J = \frac{mu\sqrt{3}}{4}$$

[*Note:* It is important to appreciate that, in analysing the effect of an instantaneous impulse, the velocities involved are those *immediately* before and *immediately* after the impact or jerk. The subsequent motion depends, not on the impulse, but upon whatever forces act after the impulse has taken place.]

SUMMARY

1) Momentum = mass × velocity
2) Impulse = Change in Momentum
3) Momentum increases in the direction of the Impulse
4) In a direction where no external force acts, the momentum of a system remains constant
5) Particles moving at the ends of a taut string have equal velocity components in the direction of the string.

EXAMPLES 8c

1) Three equal particles A, B and C lie on a smooth horizontal table. Light inextensible strings which are just taut connect AB and BC and angle ABC is 135°. An impulse J is applied to the particle C in the direction BC. Find the initial speed of each particle.

The external impulse applied to C causes both strings to jerk exerting internal impulses J_1 and J_2.

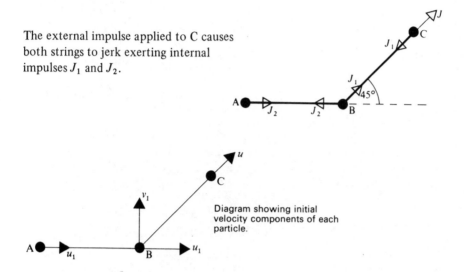

Diagram showing initial velocity components of each particle.

Using Impulse = Change in Momentum in the directions parallel and perpendicular to AB we have:-

For particle A
$$J_2 = mu_1 \qquad (1)$$

For particle B
$$J_1 \cos 45° - J_2 = mu_1 \qquad (2)$$

$$J_1 \sin 45° = mv_1 \qquad (3)$$

For particle C along BC
$$J - J_1 = mu \qquad (4)$$

Also velocities of B and C along BC are equal

$$v_1 \cos 45° + u_1 \cos 45° = u \qquad (5)$$

Equations (1) and (2) give
$$\frac{1}{\sqrt{2}} J_1 - mu_1 = mu_1$$

i.e.
$$J_1 = 2\sqrt{2}mu_1$$

Equation (3) gives
$$mv_1 = 2\sqrt{2}mu_1 \frac{1}{\sqrt{2}}$$

i.e.
$$v_1 = 2u_1$$

Equation (5) gives

$$\frac{1}{\sqrt{2}}v_1 + \frac{1}{\sqrt{2}}u_1 = u$$

i.e.

$$\frac{1}{\sqrt{2}}2u_1 + \frac{1}{\sqrt{2}}u_1 = u$$

i.e.

$$u = \frac{3}{\sqrt{2}}u_1$$

Equation (4) gives

$$J - 2\sqrt{2}mu_1 = \frac{3}{\sqrt{2}}mu_1$$

i.e.

$$J = \left(\frac{3\sqrt{2}}{2} + 2\sqrt{2}\right)mu_1$$

$$J = \frac{7\sqrt{2}}{2}mu_1$$

Hence initial speed of A

$$= \frac{2J}{7\sqrt{2}m} = \frac{J\sqrt{2}}{7m}$$

and initial speed of C

$$= \frac{3}{\sqrt{2}}\frac{2J}{7\sqrt{2}m} = \frac{3J}{7m}$$

and initial speed of B

$$= \sqrt{u_1^2 + v_1^2} = \frac{2J\sqrt{5}}{7\sqrt{2}m} = \frac{J\sqrt{10}}{7m}$$

2) A mass $2m$ rests on a horizontal table. It is attached to a light inextensible string which passes over a smooth pulley and carries a mass m at the other end. If the mass m is raised vertically through a distance h and is then dropped, find the speed with which the mass $2m$ begins to rise.

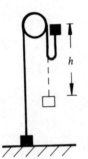

Mass m about to be dropped.

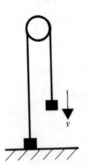

Just before string jerks.

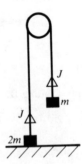

Impulses when string jerks.

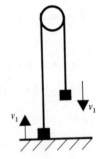

Just after string jerks.

When mass m falls $\downarrow$ $u = 0, a = g, s = h$ (Vertical motion under gravity)

$$v^2 - u^2 = 2as$$

Therefore $$v = \sqrt{2gh}$$

Using impulse = change in momentum for each mass.

For mass $2m$ $J = 2mv_1 - 0$

For mass m $J = mv - mv_1$.

From these equations $v_1 = \dfrac{v}{3}$

Hence particle of mass $2m$ begins to rise with speed $\frac{1}{3}\sqrt{2gh}$.

EXERCISE 8c

1) Two particles, each of mass m, are connected by a light inextensible string of length $2l$. Initially they lie on a smooth horizontal table at points A and B distant l apart. The particle at A is projected across the table with velocity u. Find the speed with which the second particle begins to move if the direction of u is:
(a) along BA,
(b) at an angle of $120°$ with AB,
(c) perpendicular to AB.
In each case calculate (in terms of m and u) the impulsive tension in the string.

2) A particle A of mass 2 kg lies on the edge of a table of height 1 m. It is connected by a light inelastic string of length 0.65 m to a second particle B of mass 3 kg which is lying on the table 0.25 m from the edge (AB is perpendicular to the edge). If A is pushed gently over the edge find the velocity with which B begins to move. Find also the impulsive tension in the string.

3) Three particles A, B and C all of mass m rest on a smooth horizontal plane so that angle ABC is $120°$. B is connected to both A and C by light inextensible strings which are initially just taut. An impulse J is then applied to particle B in a direction making an angle of $150°$ with BC and $90°$ with BA. Find the impulsive tension in each string and the initial velocity of each particle.

4) Two particles, A of mass $2m$ and B of mass m, are connected by a light inextensible string which passes over a smooth fixed pulley. Initially the particles are held so that they are both at a height 0.81 m above a fixed horizontal plane, and the string is just taut. The system is then released from rest. Find:
(a) the impulse exerted by the plane when A strikes it (without bouncing),
(b) the velocity with which A next leaves the plane.

5) Three identical particles A, B and C lie close together on a smooth plane. A is connected to B and to C by light inextensible strings. If B is set moving with velocity v across the table find:
(a) the first impulsive tension in the string AB,

(b) the initial velocity of A,
(c) the initial velocity of C.

6)

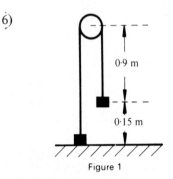

Figure 1

Figure 1 shows two particles connected by a light inextensible string passing over a pulley fixed at a height of 1.05 m above a horizontal plane. A is of mass 2 kg and is initially at rest on the plane B is of mass 1 kg and hangs at a depth of 0.9 m below the pulley. B is then raised to the height of the pulley and released from rest from that position. Calculate:

(i) the speed of B when the string is about to tighten,
(ii) the impulsive tension in the string,
(iii) the speed with which A leaves the plane,
(iv) the speed of either particle when B reaches the plane,
(v) the impulse which B exerts when it strikes the plane (without bouncing).
Is there an impulsive tension in the string when B hits the plane?

DIRECT ELASTIC IMPACT

When two objects collide and *bounce,* the impact between them is *elastic* (if, instead, they coalesce upon collision, the impact is *inelastic*).
A pair of equal and opposite impulses act at the moment of impact. If, just before impact, the objects were moving along the line of action of these impulses, the impact is *direct.*

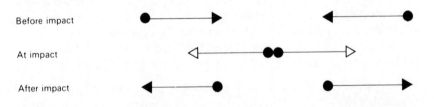

After impact the particles again begin to move along the line of action of the impulses since no impulse acted in the perpendicular direction.

NEWTON'S LAW OF RESTITUTION

When two objects are in direct elastic impact the speed with which they separate after impact is usually less than their speed of approach before impact.

Experimental evidence suggests that the ratio of these relative speeds is constant. This property, first discovered by Newton, is known as the *Law of Restitution* and can be written in the form

$$\frac{\text{Separation speed}}{\text{Approach speed}} = e$$

The ratio e is called the *coefficient of restitution* and is constant for two particular objects.

Impact between objects which coalesce is *inelastic* and in this case $e = 0$.

A collision between two objects whose relative speed is unchanged by the impact is said to be *perfectly elastic*. For two such objects $e = 1$

In general $0 \leqslant e \leqslant 1$.

Direct impact can occur between two moveable objects or between one fixed and one moveable object. In both cases the Law of Restitution is valid. The Principle of Conservation of Linear Momentum applies to impact between two moveable objects (equal and opposite internal impulses) but not when one of the objects in collision is fixed (external impulse).

EXAMPLES 8d

1) A smooth sphere of mass 0.5 kg moving with horizontal speed of 3 ms^{-1} strikes at right angles a vertical wall and bounces off the wall with horizontal speed of 2 ms^{-1}. Find the coefficient of restitution between the sphere and the wall and the impulse exerted on the wall at impact.

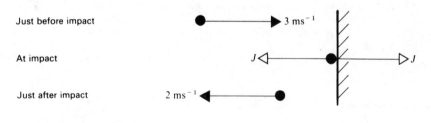

$$e = \frac{\text{Separation speed}}{\text{Approach speed}} = \frac{2}{3}$$

Therefore the coefficient of restitution is 0.67.

Using Impulse = Change in Momentum for the sphere we have:-

$$J = 0.5 \times 2 - 0.5(-3) = 2.5.$$

The equal and opposite impulse acting on the wall is therefore 2.5 Ns.

2) A smooth sphere of mass 2 kg is moving with speed 3 ms^{-1} on a horizontal plane when it collides with a stationary smooth sphere of equal size but mass 4 kg. If the coefficient of restitution between the spheres is $\frac{1}{2}$ find the velocities of both spheres after impact.

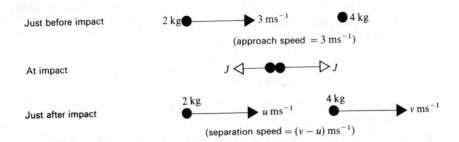

Using the Law of Restitution in the form
$e \times$ approach speed = separation speed
and the Principle of Conservation of Linear Momentum we have:

$$\tfrac{1}{2} \times 3 = v - u \tag{1}$$

and
$$2 \times 3 = 2u + 4v \tag{2}$$

Hence
$$v = \tfrac{3}{2} \text{ and } u = 0$$

After impact the 2 kg mass is at rest and the 4 kg mass has a speed of 1.5 ms^{-1}.

3) Two identical smooth spheres of mass m collide directly head-on with speeds of 6 ms^{-1} and 2 ms^{-1}. If the coefficient of restitution is $\tfrac{1}{4}$ find the speed of both spheres after impact.

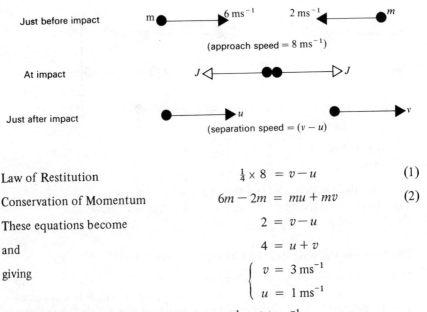

Law of Restitution	$\tfrac{1}{4} \times 8 = v - u$	(1)
Conservation of Momentum	$6m - 2m = mu + mv$	(2)
These equations become	$2 = v - u$	
and	$4 = u + v$	
giving	$\begin{cases} v = 3 \text{ ms}^{-1} \\ u = 1 \text{ ms}^{-1} \end{cases}$	

Therefore the speeds after collision are 3 ms^{-1} and 1 ms^{-1}.

4) Two identical smooth spheres A and B are free to move on a horizontal plane. B is at rest and A is projected with velocity u to strike B directly. B then collides with a vertical wall which is perpendicular to the direction of motion of the spheres. After rebounding from the wall B again collides with A and is brought to rest by this impact. If the coefficient of restitution has the same value at all impacts prove that $e = 1$.

First Impact: Between A and B.

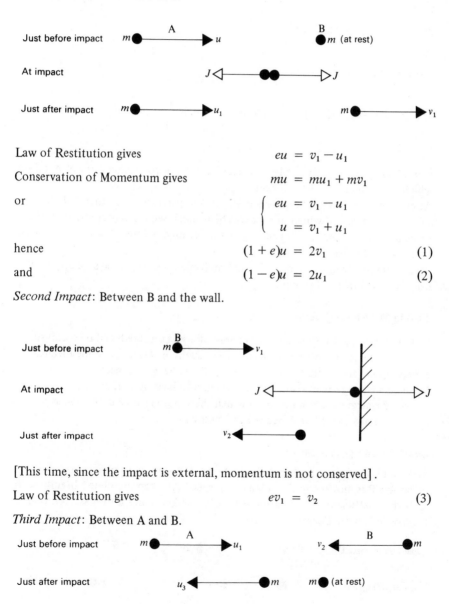

Law of Restitution gives

$$eu = v_1 - u_1$$

Conservation of Momentum gives

$$mu = mu_1 + mv_1$$

or

$$\begin{cases} eu = v_1 - u_1 \\ u = v_1 + u_1 \end{cases}$$

hence

$$(1 + e)u = 2v_1 \qquad (1)$$

and

$$(1 - e)u = 2u_1 \qquad (2)$$

Second Impact: Between B and the wall.

[This time, since the impact is external, momentum is not conserved].

Law of Restitution gives

$$ev_1 = v_2 \qquad (3)$$

Third Impact: Between A and B.

Law of Restitution gives $\qquad\qquad e(u_1 + v_2) = u_3$

Conservation of Momentum gives $\qquad mu_1 - mv_2 = -mu_3$

or $\qquad\qquad\qquad\qquad\qquad\qquad\quad v_2 - u_1 = u_3$

Eliminating u_3 gives $\qquad\qquad v_2 - u_1 = e(u_1 + v_2)$

i.e. $\qquad\qquad\qquad\qquad\qquad v_2(1 - e) = u_1(e + 1)$ $\qquad\qquad\qquad$ (4)

But $\quad v_2 = ev_1 = e(1 + e)\dfrac{u}{2}$ $\qquad\qquad\qquad\qquad\qquad$ from (3) and (1)

and $\quad u_1 = (1 - e)\dfrac{u}{2}$ $\qquad\qquad\qquad\qquad\qquad\qquad$ from (2)

Therefore in (4): $\quad e(1 + e)\dfrac{u}{2}(1 - e) = (1 - e)\dfrac{u}{2}(e + 1)$

from which $\qquad\qquad\qquad\qquad e = 1.$

Note: Example 4, which involved several impacts, introduced a form of notation which helps to clarify the solution.

At every impact the symbol u was used for A's speed and v for that of B. The suffix used indicated which impact was being analysed e.g. u_3 represented the speed of A after the third impact; u_2 was never used because A was not involved in the second impact.

A problem involving three particles and multiple impacts can be similarly treated using u, v, w for speed symbols.

Loss in Mechanical Energy

In practice the total mechanical energy of a system is reduced by a collision or a jerk. The explanation for this loss can usually be *heard* i.e. some mechanical energy is converted into the sound energy of the *bang* at impact.

Mechanical energy may also be transformed into heat or light energy.

Perfectly elastic impact however in which there is no change in relative speed, is not accompanied by any mechanical energy loss.

EXAMPLES 8d (continued)

5) A and B are smooth spheres of equal size. A is stationary on a horizontal plane and B is moving on that plane with speed $2u$ when it collides directly with A. If the coefficient of restitution is $\frac{1}{2}$, A is of mass m and B of mass $2m$, find the loss in Kinetic Energy at impact.

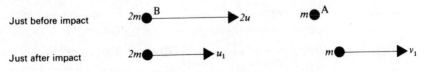

Law of Restitution	$\frac{1}{2} \times 2u = v_1 - u_1$
Conservation of Momentum	$2m \times 2u = 2mu_1 + mv_1$
hence	$u = v_1 - u_1$
	$4u = v_1 + 2u_1$
giving	$3u = 3u_1$
and	$6u = 3v_1$
Original $K.E$	$= \frac{1}{2}(2m)(2u)^2 = 4mu^2$
Final $K.E$	$= \frac{1}{2}(2m)u_1^2 + \frac{1}{2}mv_1^2$
	$= \frac{1}{2}(2m)u^2 + \frac{1}{2}m(2u)^2 = 3mu^2$
Loss in $K.E$	$= 4mu^2 - 3mu^2 = mu^2$

6) Repeating Example 1 with a coefficient of restitution of 1 instead of $\frac{1}{2}$.

Law of Restitution	$1 \times 2u = v_1 - u_1$
Conservation of Momentum	$2m \times 2u = 2mu_1 + mv_1$
hence	$2u = v_1 - u_1$
	$4u = v_1 + 2u_1$
giving	$2u = 3u_1$
and	$8u = 3v_1$
Original $K.E$	$= 4mu^2$
Final $K.E$	$= \frac{1}{2}(2m)\left(\frac{2u}{3}\right)^2 + \frac{1}{2}(m)\left(\frac{8u}{3}\right)^2$
	$= \frac{1}{2}m\frac{u^2}{9}(8 + 64) \qquad = 4mu^2$
Loss in $K.E$	$= 4mu^2 - 4mu^2 \qquad = 0$

(This confirms that perfectly elastic impacts involve no loss in mechanical energy).

EXERCISE 8d

In all questions involving spheres, these will be smooth and of equal size.

1) A sphere of mass 10 kg moving at 16 ms^{-1} impinges directly on another sphere of mass 5 kg moving in the opposite direction at 4 ms^{-1}. If $e = \frac{1}{2}$ find the speeds of both spheres after impact and the magnitude of the instantaneous impulses.

2) A ball of mass 2 kg moving at 6 ms^{-1} collides directly with another ball of mass

3 kg moving in the same direction at 4 ms^{-1}. Find the speed of each ball after impact and the loss in kinetic energy if $e = \frac{3}{4}$.

3) When two spheres of equal mass collide directly at speeds of 4 ms^{-1} and 8 ms^{-1} in opposite senses, half the original kinetic energy is lost upon impact. Prove that $e = \frac{2}{3}$.

4) A sphere A of mass 0.1 kg is moving with speed 5 ms^{-1} when it collides directly with a stationary sphere B. If A is brought to rest by the impact and $e = \frac{1}{2}$, find the mass of B, its speed just after impact and the magnitude of the instantaneous impulses.

5) Three perfectly elastic spheres A, B and C have masses $3m, 2m, m$ respectively. They are lying in a straight line on a horizontal plane and A is projected with speed u to collide directly with B which goes on to collide directly with C. Find the speed of each sphere after the second impact. Explain why there will be no further impacts.

6) Find, in terms of M, m, e, V and v, the instantaneous impulses which act when two spheres of masses M and m collide directly with speeds V and v respectively:
(a) if they collide head-on,
(b) if they are travelling in the same sense $(V > v)$.
The coefficient of restitution between the spheres is e.

7) A sphere of mass 2 kg falls from rest at a height 10 m above an elastic horizontal plane. Find the height to which the sphere will rise again after its first bounce, if the coefficient of restitution is $\frac{1}{2}$.

8) If a small sphere which is dropped from a height of 1.2 m on to a horizontal plane rebounds to a height of 1.0 m find the value of e and the loss in mechanical energy caused by the impact, if the mass of the sphere is 2 kg.

9) A light inextensible string AB has the end A fixed to a vertical wall. The end B is attached to a small elastic object which is drawn aside, from the wall, until the string makes an angle of $60°$ with the wall. The particle is then released from rest. Find the angle which the string makes with the wall when the particle next comes to instantaneous rest if the value of e is $\frac{3}{4}$.

10) A small sphere is dropped on to a horizontal plane from a height h. If the coefficient of restitution between the sphere and the plane is e find, in terms of h and e, the height to which the particle rises after each of the first, second and third impacts, showing that these heights are in geometric progression. Deduce the total distance travelled by the sphere before it comes to rest.

MULTIPLE CHOICE EXERCISE 8

The instructions for answering these questions are given on page (xii)

TYPE I

1) A ball of mass 0.4 kg hits a wall at right angles with a speed of 12 ms^{-1} and bounces off, again at right angles to the wall, with a speed of 8 ms^{-1}. The impulse exerted by the wall on the ball is:

(a) 1.6 Ns   (b) 20 Ns   (c) 4 Ns   (d) 8 Ns.

2) Two masses collide and coalesce as shown in the diagram. What is the speed V of the combined mass just after impact?

(a) $3v$ (b) $\frac{2}{3}v$ (c) v (d) $\frac{2}{3}v$.

3)

A gun which is free to recoil horizontally fires a bullet when the barrel is inclined at $30°$ to the horizontal. When the bullet leaves the barrel it will be travelling at an angle to the horizontal of:

(a) $30°$,
(b) a little less than $30°$,
(c) a little more than $30°$,
(d) zero.

4) Two smooth objects, with a coefficient of restitution e, collide directly and bounce as shown

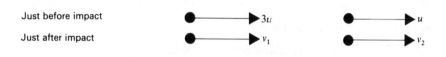

Newtons Law of Restitution gives:
(a) $e \times 4u = v_2 + v_1$
(b) $e \times 2u = v_1 - v_2$
(c) $e \times 2u = v_2 - v_1$
(d) it cannot be applied as the masses are not known.

5) A particle of mass 2 kg moving with speed 4 ms^{-1} is given a blow which changes the speed to 1 ms^{-1} without deflecting the particle from a straight line. The impulse of the blow is:
(a) 10 Ns,
(b) 6 Ns,
(c) we do not know whether it is 10 Ns or 6 Ns.

TYPE II

6) A body of mass m is moving with speed v when a constant force F newtons is applied to it in the direction of motion for t seconds:
(a) The impulse of the force is Ft newton second,
(b) $Ft = mv$,
(c) The body loses an amount of kinetic energy equal to Ft.
(d) The final speed of the body is $v + \dfrac{Ft}{m}$.

7) When a particle P of mass $2m$ collides with a particle Q of mass m:
(a) P exerts an impulse on Q,
(b) the mechanical energy of the system is unchanged,
(c) the impulse which P exerts on Q is twice the impulse which Q exerts on P,
(d) Q exerts an impulse on P.

8) Two moving particles are attached, one to each end of a string AB. If the string jerks tight, then immediately afterwards:
(a) both particles have the same speed,
(b) the particles have the same speed if they are of equal mass,
(c) the particles have equal velocity components in the direction AB.

9) A sphere A of mass m, travelling with speed v, collides directly with a stationary sphere B. If A is brought to rest by the collision and B is given a speed V, then:

(a) $e = \dfrac{v}{V}$,

(b) the mass of B is $\dfrac{mv}{V}$,

(c) $e = \dfrac{V}{v}$,

(d) the particles are of equal mass.

10) A particle of mass 1 kg is dropped from a height of 3 m on to a horizontal plane where it bounces and rises to a height of 2 m above the plane.
(a) the coefficient of restitution is $\frac{2}{3}$,
(b) just before striking the plane the speed is $\sqrt{6g}$ ms^{-1},
(c) the coefficient of restitution is $\sqrt{\frac{2}{3}}$,
(d) just after striking the plane, the speed of the particle is $\sqrt{\dfrac{8g}{3}}$ ms^{-1}.

TYPE III

11) (a) In a specified direction a body has a constant speed.
    (b) No resultant force acts on the body.

12) (a) The coefficient of restitution between two colliding objects is less than 1.

(b) Mechanical energy is lost when two objects collide.

13) (a) Two spheres collide directly.
   (b) Two spheres are travelling towards each other in the same straight line.

14) (a) Two spheres collide directly without loss of momentum.
   (b) Two perfectly elastic spheres collide directly.

15) (a) When two spheres collide directly half the original kinetic energy is lost.
   (b) Two spheres have a coefficient of restitution of $\frac{1}{2}$.

TYPE IV

16) Two particles A and B collide directly head-on and bounce. Find their speeds immediately after impact.
(a) The mass of A is twice the mass of B.
(b) Just before impact the speed of A is $4 \, \text{ms}^{-1}$ and that of B is $3 \, \text{ms}^{-1}$.
(c) No kinetic energy is lost by the impact.

17) A ball moving on a horizontal floor hits a smooth vertical wall normally. Calculate the speed with which it leaves the wall if:
(a) the speed when approaching the wall is $3 \, \text{ms}^{-1}$,
(b) the coefficient of restitution is $\frac{1}{2}$,
(c) the mass of the ball is 0.4 kg.

18) A ball falls vertically on to a horizontal plane and bounces. Find the impulse the ball exerts on the plane if:
(a) the ball is initially 2 m above the plane,
(b) it rises after bouncing to a height 1.2 m,
(c) the coefficient of restitution is $\sqrt{\frac{3}{5}}$,
(d) the mass of the ball is 0.5 kg.

19) Two particles A and B are travelling on the same straight line when they collide. Find the loss in kinetic energy due to impact if:
(a) A and B have equal mass,
(b) just before impact the speed of A is three times the speed of B,
(c) the coefficient of restitution is $\frac{2}{3}$.

20) An inelastic string has a particle A attached to one end and a particle B attached to the other end. If A is projected in the direction $\overrightarrow{BA}$ find the initial speed of B if:
(a) initially the string is slack,
(b) the speed of projection of A is $4 \, \text{ms}^{-1}$,
(c) the particles are of equal mass,
(d) the string is 2 m long.

TYPE V

21) The Law of Restitution applies to an elastic impact between a moving object and a fixed surface.

22) The coefficient of restitution is given by: relative speed before impact divided by relative speed after impact.

23) A perfectly elastic impact does not cause a loss in mechanical energy.

24) The momentum of a system remains constant in any direction in which no external force force acts.

25) Impulse means an impact between moving bodies.

MISCELLANEOUS EXERCISE 8

1) A force of 10 N acts on a mass of 2 kg for three seconds. If the initial velocity was 50 ms^{-1} what is the final velocity?

2) A stone weighing 5 N is thrown vertically upwards, with velocity 80 ms^{-1}. What is its velocity after two seconds and after twenty seconds? (take $g = 10$ ms^{-2}).

3) Water issues from a pipe, whose cross section is c m^2, in a horizontal jet with velocity v ms^{-1}. What force must be exerted by a shield placed perpendicular to the jet to bring the water to a horizontal stop? (The mass of 1 m^3 of water is 10^3 kg).

4) Two masses of 20 and 10 units, moving in the same direction at speeds of 16 and 12 units respectively collide and stick together. Find the velocity of the combined mass immediately afterwards.

5) A gun of mass 1000 kg can launch a shell of mass 1 kg with a horizontal velocity of 1200 ms^{-1}. What is the horizontal velocity of recoil of the gun?

6) A sphere of mass m falls from rest at a height h above a horizontal plane and rebounds to a height $\dfrac{h}{2}$. Find the coefficient of restitution, the impulse exerted by the plane and the loss in KE due to impact.

7) A sphere A, of mass $2m$ and velocity $2u$, overtakes and collides with sphere B, of mass m and velocity u travelling in the same line which is perpendicular to a vertical smooth wall. After being struck by A, sphere B goes on to strike the wall. If the coefficient of restitution between A and B is $\frac{1}{2}$ and that between B and the wall is $\frac{3}{4}$ show that there is a second collision between A and B and describe what happens after the second impact.

8) A sphere A, of mass m_1, and velocity u, collides with a stationary sphere B of mass m_2. If sphere A is brought to rest by the collision, find the velocity of B after impact, and the coefficient of restitution. If sphere B now collides with a stationary sphere C and is brought to rest find the mass of sphere C assuming the same coefficient of restitution between A and B, and B and C.

9) A smooth sphere A of mass $2m$, moving on a horizontal plane with speed u, collides directly with another smooth sphere B of equal radius and of mass m, which is at rest. If the coefficient of restitution between the spheres is e, find their speeds after impact.

The sphere B later rebounds from a perfectly elastic vertical wall, and then collides directly with A. Prove that after this collision the speed of B is $\frac{2}{9}(1 + e)^2 u$ and find the speed of A.
(U of L.)

10) State the law of conservation of linear momentum for two interacting particles. Show how the law of conservation of linear momentum applied to two particles which collide directly follows from Newton's laws of motion.

Three smooth spheres A, B, C, equal in all respects, lie at rest and separated from one another on a smooth horizontal table in the order A, B, C with their centres in a straight line. Sphere A is projected with speed V directly towards sphere B. If the coefficient of restitution at each collision is e, where $0 < e < 1$, find the velocity of each of the spheres just after C is set in motion. Show that A strikes B a second time.
(J.M.B.)

11) A pump raises water from a depth of 10 m and discharges it horizontally through a pipe of 0.1 m diameter at a velocity of 8 ms^{-1}. Calculate the work done by the pump in one second. If the water impinges directly with the same velocity on a vertical wall, find the force exerted by the water on the wall if it is assumed that none of the water bounces back (Take g as 9.81 ms^{-2}, π as 3.142 and the mass of 1 m^3 of water as 1000 kg).
(U of L.)

12) Two equal spheres B and C, each of mass $4m$, lie at rest on a smooth horizontal table. A third sphere A, of the same radius as B and C but of mass m, moves with velocity V along the line of centres of B and C. The sphere A collides with B which then collides with C. If A is brought to rest by the first collision show that the coefficient of restitution between A and B is $\frac{1}{4}$. If the coefficient of restitution between B and C is $\frac{1}{2}$ find the velocities of B and C after the second collision. Show that the total loss of kinetic energy due to the two collisions is $\dfrac{27mV^2}{64}$.
(J.M.B.)

13) A particle of mass m is projected vertically upward with speed u and when it reaches its greatest height a second particle, of mass $2m$, is projected vertically upward with speed $2u$ from the same point as the first. Prove that the time that elapses between the projection of the second particle and its collision with the first is $\dfrac{u}{4g}$, and find the height above the point of projection at which the collision occurs.

If, on collision, the particles coalesce, prove that the combined particle will reach a greatest height of $\dfrac{19u^2}{18g}$ above the point of projection.
(J.M.B.)

14) Two particles, each of mass m, are connected by a light inextensible string which passes over a smooth pulley at the top of a fixed plane inclined at an angle arctan $\frac{5}{12}$ to the horizontal. The particle A is on the plane and the particle B hangs freely (see figure). The system is released from rest with the string in a vertical plane through a line of greatest slope of the plane. The coefficient of friction between A and the plane is $\frac{1}{3}$. When B has fallen a distance h the string breaks. A comes to rest after travelling a further distance s up the plane. B falls a further distance h to strike a horizontal plane and rise to a height h above that plane. Find:

(i) the speed of the particles when the string breaks,

(ii) the value of s,

(iii) the coefficient of restitution between B and the horizontal plane and the impulse of the blow the particle B strikes this plane.

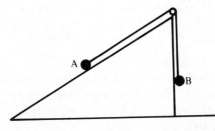

(A.E.B.)

15) Three particles A, B, C of masses m, $2m$, $3m$ respectively lie at rest in that order in a straight line on a smooth horizontal table. The distance between consecutive particles is a. A slack light inelastic string of length $2a$ connects A and B. An exactly similar slack string connects B and C. If A is projected in the direction CBA with speed V, find the time which elapses before C begins to move. Find also the speed with which C begins to move. Show that the ratio of the impulsive tensions in BC and AB when C is jerked into motion is $3:1$. Find the total loss of kinetic energy when C has started to move.   (J.M.B.)

16) A smooth plane is fixed at an inclination $30°$ with its lower edge at a height a above a horizontal table. Two particles P and Q, each of mass m, are connected by a light inextensible string of length $2a$, and P is held at the lower edge of the inclined plane while Q rests on the table vertically below P. The particle P is then projected with velocity u $(u > \sqrt{ga})$ upwards along a line of greatest slope of the plane. Find the impulsive tension in the string when Q is jerked into motion. Determine the magnitude of u if Q just reaches the lower edge of the plane, and the tension in the string while Q is moving.   (J.M.B.)

17) A hammer of mass $5m$, moving horizontally with velocity V, strikes a stationary horizontal nail of mass m. If the coefficient of restitution between the hammer and the nail is $\frac{3}{5}$ find the velocity of the nail just after the blow. Immediately after the blow the nail begins to penetrate a block of mass nm which

is free to move on a smooth horizontal table. Penetration is resisted by a constant force R. Find the common velocity of the block and the nail when the nail ceases to penetrate the block. Show that penetration ceases at a time $\dfrac{4mnV}{3(n+1)R}$ after the blow (it may be assumed that there is only one blow between the hammer and the nail.)

(J.M.B.)

18) Two particles of masses m and $3m$ are connected by a light inelastic string of length $2l$ which passes over a small smooth fixed peg. The particles are held in contact with the peg and then allowed, at the same instant, to fall from rest under gravity, one on either side of the peg. Prove that:
   (i) the speed of each particle just after the string tightens is $\sqrt{(gl/2)}$,
   (ii) the sudden tightening of the string causes a loss of energy equal to $3mgl$,
   (iii) the lighter particle reaches the peg again after a total time $\sqrt{6l/g}$.   (J.M.B.)

19) A golf ball, initially at rest, is dropped on to a horizontal surface and bounces directly up again with velocity v. If the coefficient of restitution between the ball and the surface is e, show that the ball will go on bouncing for a time $\dfrac{2v}{g(1-e)}$ after the first impact.
{You may assume $1 + e + e^2 + e^3 + ... = (1-e)^{-1}$}.
If the golf ball is dropped from a height of 19.62 m and comes to rest 12 seconds later, find the value of e. (Take g as 9.81 ms^{-2}).

(U of L.)

20) A particle of mass m is thrown vertically upwards with speed u from a point A on the ground. Simultaneously an identical particle is thrown vertically downwards also with speed u from a point B vertically above A and at a height h above the ground ($h < 4u^2/g$). On impact the particles adhere and move subsequently as a single particle. Calculate the loss in kinetic energy caused by the impact and the speed of the combined particle on reaching the ground.   (A.E.B.)

21) The barrel of a gun of mass M resting on a smooth horizontal plane is elevated at an angle α to the horizontal. The gun fires a shell of mass m and recoils with horizontal velocity U. If the velocity of the shell on leaving the gun has horizontal and vertical components v and w respectively, prove that $w = (v + U)\tan\alpha$, and hence or otherwise prove that the initial inclination of the path of the shell to the horizontal is $\arctan\left[\left(1 + \dfrac{m}{M}\right)\tan\alpha\right]$. Prove that the kinetic energy generated by the explosion is

$$\frac{U^2}{2m}(M+m)(M\sec^2\alpha + m\tan^2\alpha).$$

(J.M.B.)

22) A particle of mass 4 kg is attached to one end X of a light inextensible string which passes over a smooth light pulley and supports particles of masses 2 kg and 3 kg at the other end Y. The end X is held in contact with a horizontal table at a depth 6 m below the pulley, both portions of the string being vertical and the

particles at Y hanging freely. The system is released from rest. When Y has descended a distance of 2.5 m, the particle of mass 2 kg is disconnected and begins to fall freely. Calculate the greatest height reached by X above the table and the momentum of the 4 kg particle when it strikes the table.
Take g to be 9.81 m/s^2 (U of L.)

23) Two small spheres, A and B, of equal radii with masses $2m$ and m respectively, lie at rest on a smooth horizontal plane with A due north of B. The sphere B is projected towards A and after the collision A moves north with speed $5u$. Given that the coefficient of restitution between the spheres is 2/3, calculate the speed of B before and after the impact.
When the sphere A is moving north at $5u$ an impulse of magnitude $8mu$ is applied in the direction due south. As a result of this impulse the sphere A is split into two fragments, each of mass m, which move in the directions 330° (N 30° W) and 060° (N 60° E). Calculate the speeds of these fragments.

                                                                          (A.E.B.)

24) Two scale pans, each of mass m, are connected by a light inelastic string which passes over a small smooth fixed light pulley. On one scale pan there is an inelastic particle A of mass $2m$. The system is released from rest with the hanging parts of the string vertical. Find the tension in the string and the acceleration of either scale pan.
At the instant when motion begins, a particle of mass $3m$ is allowed to fall from rest and after t seconds it strikes, and adheres to, A. Find the impulsive tension in the string and the velocity of either scale pan immediately after the impact.

                                                                          (J.M.B.)

25) Two particles each of mass m are connected by a light inextensible string and a particle of mass M is attached to the midpoint of the string. The system is at rest on a smooth horizontal table with the string just taut and in a straight line. The particle M is given a velocity V along the table perpendicular to the string. Prove that, when the two end particles are about to collide:
 (i) the velocity of M is $VM/(M + 2m)$,
 (ii) the speed of each of the other particles is $V\{2M(M + m)\}^{\frac{1}{2}}/(M + 2m)$.

                                                                          (Oxford)

26) Three particles A, B and C, each of mass m, lie at rest on a smooth horizontal table. Light inextensible strings connect A to B and B to C. The strings are just taut with the angle $\overrightarrow{ABC} = 135°$, when a blow of impulse J is applied to C in a direction parallel to $\overrightarrow{AB}$. Prove that A begins to move with speed $(J/7)m$ and find the impulsive tension in the string BC.   (U of L.)

27) A bullet of mass m is fired with speed u into a fixed block of wood and emerges with speed $2u/3$. When the experiment is repeated with the block free to move the bullet emerges with speed $u/2$ *relative* to the block. Assuming the same constant resistance to penetration in both cases, find the mass and the

final speed of the block in the second case. (Neglect the effect of gravity through-out)

(U of L.)

28) The masses of three perfectly elastic spheres A, B and C are M, M and m respectively ($M > m$). The spheres are initially at rest with their centres in a straight line, C lying between A and B. If C is given a velocity towards A along the line of centres, show that after colliding first with A and then with B it will not collide a second time with A if $M < (\sqrt{5} + 2)m$. Find the ratios of the kinetic energies of the three spheres after the second collision and verify that no energy has been lost.

(U of L.)

CHAPTER 9

GENERAL MOTION OF A PARTICLE IN ONE PLANE

MOTION IN A STRAIGHT LINE

If a particle moves in a straight line such that, at time t, its displacement from a fixed point on that line is s, its velocity is v and its acceleration is a then, as velocity is the rate of increase of displacement; $$v = \frac{ds}{dt}$$

and acceleration is the rate of increase of velocity: $a = \dfrac{dv}{dt}$

$$\text{Conversely } v = \int a\, dt$$

$$\text{and} \qquad s = \int v\, dt$$

These equations give the basic relationship between a, v, s and t. If any one of them is given as a function of one of the others it is usually possible to find expressions for the remaining quantities. The analysis of the motion of a particle usually begins with applying Newton's Law ($F = ma$) which leads to an expression for the acceleration. If the acceleration is constant the equations derived in Chapter 4 may be used. If the acceleration is variable then the appropriate differential equations must be derived for each problem.

Acceleration as a Function of Time

Consider a particle moving along a straight line with an acceleration of a ms^{-2} at time t seconds where $a = 3t^2 - 2$. If initially the particle is at O, a fixed point on the line, with a velocity 2 ms^{-1} then

as $$a = 3t^2 - 2$$

and
$$v = \int a\, dt$$
$$v = \int (3t^2 - 2)\, dt = t^3 - 2t + c$$

but $v = 2$ when $t = 0$, therefore $c = 2$

Therefore
$$\underline{v = t^3 - 2t + 2}$$

Also:
$$s = \int v\, dt$$

$$s = \int (t^3 - 2t + 2)\, dt = \frac{t^4}{4} - t^2 + 2t + c_1$$

$s = 0$ when $t = 0$, therefore $c_1 = 0$

Therefore
$$\underline{s = \frac{t^4}{4} - t^2 + 2t}$$

A neater way of expressing this is as follows:

since
$$a = \frac{dv}{dt}, \quad \frac{dv}{dt} = 3t^2 - 2$$

Therefore
$$\int_2^v dv = \int_0^t (3t^2 - 2)\, dt$$
$$v - 2 = t^3 - 2t$$
$$v = t^3 - 2t + 2$$

$\left(\begin{array}{l}\text{The lower limits are the} \\ \text{initial conditions, the} \\ \text{upper limits are the gen-} \\ \text{eral velocity and time.}\end{array}\right)$

and
$$v = \frac{ds}{dt}, \quad \frac{ds}{dt} = t^3 - 2t + 2$$

Therefore
$$\int_0^s ds = \int_0^t (t^3 - 2t + 2)\, dt$$
$$s = \frac{t^4}{4} - t^2 + 2t$$

In general if $a = f(t)$, the velocity can be found as a function of time by using $\int dv = \int f(t)\, dt$.

EXAMPLES 9a

1) A particle moves in a straight line with an acceleration of $(3t - 4)$ ms^{-2} at time t seconds. The particle is initially 1 m from O, a fixed point on the line, with a velocity of 2 ms^{-1}. Find the times when the velocity is zero. Also find the displacement of the particle from O when $t = 3$.

$a = 3t - 4$, therefore $\dfrac{dv}{dt} = 3t - 4$, therefore $\displaystyle\int_2^v dv = \int_0^t (3t - 4)\, dt$

$$v - 2 = \frac{3t^2}{2} - 4t$$

$$v = \frac{3t^2}{2} - 4t + 2$$

The velocity is zero when $\dfrac{3t^2}{2} - 4t + 2 = 0$

$$(3t - 2)(t - 2) = 0$$

$$\text{i.e. when } t = \tfrac{2}{3} \text{ or } 2$$

$\dfrac{ds}{dt} = v$, therefore $\dfrac{ds}{dt} = \dfrac{3t^2}{2} - 4t + 2$, therefore $\displaystyle\int_1^s ds = \int_0^3 \left(\frac{3t^2}{2} - 4t + 2\right) dt$

$$s - 1 = \left[\frac{t^3}{2} - 2t^2 + 2t\right]_0^3 = 1\tfrac{1}{2}$$

$$s = 2\tfrac{1}{2}$$

Therefore the particle is $2\tfrac{1}{2}$ m from O when $t = 3$.

2) A particle starts from rest and travels in a straight line with an acceleration $\cos \pi t$ where t is the time. Find the distance covered by the particle in the interval of time $t = 2$ to $t = 3$.

$$a = \frac{dv}{dt} = \cos \pi t \text{ therefore } \int_0^v dv = \int_0^t \cos \pi t \, dt$$

$$v = \frac{1}{\pi} \sin \pi t$$

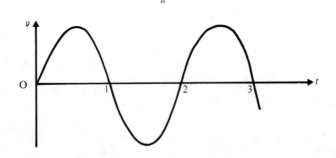

From the sketch of the velocity-time graph it can be seen that the velocity is positive for the interval of time $t = 2$ to $t = 3$: i.e. the particle is moving in the same direction throughout this interval of time. Therefore if s_2 is the displacement of the particle from its initial position when $t = 2$ and s_3 is its displacement when $t = 3$, then $s_3 - s_2$ is the distance travelled by the particle in the interval $t = 2$ to $t = 3$.

$$v = \frac{ds}{dt} = \frac{1}{\pi} \sin \pi t, \text{ therefore } \int_{s_2}^{s_3} ds = \int_{2}^{3} \frac{1}{\pi} \sin \pi t \, dt$$

$$s_3 - s_2 = \left[-\frac{1}{\pi^2} \cos \pi t \right]_{2}^{3} = \frac{2}{\pi^2}$$

Therefore the particle travels a distance $\frac{2}{\pi^2}$ units in the interval $t = 2$ to $t = 3$.

3) A particle moves in a straight line with acceleration which is inversely proportional to t^3 where t is the time (s). If the particle has a velocity of 3 ms^{-1} when $t = 1$ and the velocity approaches a limiting value of 5 ms^{-1}, find an expression for the velocity at any time t.

$$a = \frac{k}{t^3} \text{ where } k \text{ is a constant.}$$

Therefore $\frac{dv}{dt} = \frac{k}{t^3}$ therefore $\int_{3}^{v} dv = \int_{1}^{t} \frac{k}{t^3} dt$

$$v - 3 = -\frac{k}{2t^2} + \frac{k}{2}$$

$$v = 3 + \frac{k}{2} - \frac{k}{2t^2}$$

As $t \to \infty$, $\frac{k}{2t^2} \to 0$, therefore $v \to 3 + \frac{k}{2}$

therefore $3 + \frac{k}{2} = 5$

therefore $k = 4$

therefore $v = 5 - \frac{2}{t^2}$

EXERCISE 9a

1) A particle moving in a straight line starts from rest at a point O on the line and t seconds later has an acceleration $(t - 6)$ ms^{-2}. Find expressions for the velocity and displacement of the particle from O at time t and 6 seconds after leaving.

2) A particle moves in a straight line with an acceleration $2t$ ms^{-2} at time t. If it starts from rest at a point O on the line, find its velocity and displacement from O at time t.

3) A particle moves in a straight line with an acceleration $(3t - 1)$ ms^{-2} where t is the time. If the particle has a velocity of 3 ms^{-1} when $t = 2$ find its velocity at time t and when $t = 5$.

4) A particle moves in a straight line with velocity $v\,\mathrm{ms}^{-1}$ at time t seconds where $v = 3\,t^2 - 1$. Find the increase in displacement of the particle for the interval $t = 2$ to $t = 3$.

5) A particle moves in a straight line with an acceleration $(6\,t - 2)\,\mathrm{ms}^{-2}$ at time t seconds. If the particle has an initial velocity of $3\,\mathrm{ms}^{-1}$ find the distance travelled by the particle in the first second of its motion.

6) A particle moves in a straight line with acceleration $\dfrac{1}{t^3}\,\mathrm{ms}^{-2}$ at time t seconds.

If the particle is at rest at O, a fixed point on the line, when $t = 1$, find expressions for its velocity and displacement from O at time t and when $t = 2$.

7) A particle moves in a straight line with velocity $v\,\mathrm{ms}^{-1}$ where $v = \dfrac{1}{t^2} + 2$ at

time t seconds. Show that the velocity approaches a limiting value and find an expression for the displacement of the particle at time t.

8) A particle moves in a straight line with acceleration $\sin 2t\,\mathrm{ms}^{-2}$ at time t sec-

onds. If the particle is initially at rest when its displacement is $\dfrac{1}{2}$ m from a fixed

point O on the line find its velocity and displacement from O at any time t. Find also the time that elapses before the particle again comes to rest.

9) A particle moves in a straight line with an acceleration $a\,\mathrm{ms}^{-2}$ at time t seconds

where $a = -\dfrac{1}{t^2}$. If when $t = 1$ the particle has a velocity of $3\,\mathrm{ms}^{-1}$ find the velocity

when $t = 4$ and show that the velocity approaches $2\,\mathrm{ms}^{-1}$ as t increases.

10) A particle moves from rest in a straight line with an acceleration $(8 - 2t^2)\,\mathrm{ms}^{-2}$ at time t seconds. Find the maximum velocity of the particle and the distance covered by the particle in the first two seconds of its motion.

11) A particle moves from rest in a straight line with an acceleration $\cos \omega t\,\mathrm{ms}^{-2}$ at time t seconds. Find the maximum velocity of the particle and show that

this maximum velocity occurs periodically at equal intervals of $\dfrac{2\pi}{\omega}$ seconds.

12) A particle moves in a straight line with an acceleration $\cos \pi t\,\mathrm{ms}^{-2}$ at time t seconds. If the particle is initially at rest find the velocity of the particle when $t = 1$ and $t = 2$ and the distance travelled by the particle in the interval of time from $t = 1$ to $t = 2$.

13) A particle moves from rest in a straight line with acceleration $a\,\mathrm{ms}^{-2}$ at time t seconds. If a is proportional to t and the particle has a velocity of $2\,\mathrm{ms}^{-1}$ when $t = 3$, find an expression for its velocity at any time t.

14) A particle moves in a straight line with an acceleration which is inversely proportional to $(t + 1)^3$ where t is the time. Initially the particle is at rest at O and

3 seconds later it has a velocity of 2 ms^{-1}. Find the displacement of the particle from O at time t.

Acceleration as a Function of Velocity

Consider a particle which moves along a straight line with an acceleration $\dfrac{1}{v}$ where v is its velocity.

Since $\quad a = \dfrac{1}{v}$ $\qquad\qquad \dfrac{dv}{dt} = \dfrac{1}{v}$ $\qquad\qquad$ (1)

This can be integrated with respect to time by separating the variables:

$$\int v\,dv = \int dt$$
$$v^2 = 2t + c$$

giving a relationship between velocity and time.
Alternatively if a direct relationship between velocity and displacement is required then

since $\qquad\qquad \dfrac{dv}{dt} = \dfrac{ds}{dt}\dfrac{dv}{ds} = v\dfrac{dv}{ds} \quad$ equation (1) can be written

$$v\dfrac{dv}{ds} = \dfrac{1}{v}$$

Separating the variables: $\qquad \int v^2 dv = \int ds$

$$\dfrac{v^3}{3} = s + c$$

In general if $a = f(v)$ then either a relationship between v and t can be found by using $\int \dfrac{1}{f(v)}\,dv = \int dt$
or a relationship between v and s can be found by using $\int \dfrac{v}{f(v)}\,dv = \int ds$

Acceleration as a function of Displacement

Consider a particle moving along a straight line with acceleration s^2 where s is its displacement from a fixed point on the line: i.e. $a = s^2$. A relationship between v and s can be found by writing a as $v\dfrac{dv}{ds}$

i.e. $\quad v\dfrac{dv}{ds} = s^2$

Separating the variables $\int v\,dv = \int s^2\,ds$

$$\dfrac{v^2}{2} = \dfrac{s^3}{3} + c$$

A relationship between s and t can usually be found from the relationship between v and s by writing v as $\dfrac{ds}{dt}$ and separating the variables.

In general if $a = f(s)$ a relationship between v and s can be found by using
$$\int v\,dv = \int f(s)\,ds$$

EXAMPLES 9b

1) A particle moves in a straight line with acceleration $-\dfrac{1}{3v^2}$ where v is its velocity at time t. Initially the particle is at O, a fixed point on the line, with velocity u. Find in terms of u the time at which the velocity is zero and the displacement of the particle from O at this time.

$$a = -\frac{1}{3v^2} = \frac{dv}{dt}$$

To find the time at which the velocity is zero we want a relationship between v and t.

$$\int_u^0 -3v^2\,dv = \int_0^t dt \tag{1}$$

$$u^3 = t$$

Therefore the particle is at rest when $t = u^3$

To find the displacement we can either find a relationship between v and t from (1) and integrate again to find a relationship between s and t, or we can work more directly as follows:

As $a = -\dfrac{1}{3v^2}$, $\quad v\dfrac{dv}{ds} = -\dfrac{1}{3v^2}$

Therefore $\displaystyle\int_u^0 -3v^3\,dv = \int_0^s ds$

$$\tfrac{3}{4}u^4 = s$$

Therefore the particle has a displacement $\tfrac{3}{4}u^4$ from O when it is at rest

2) A particle moves in a straight line with an acceleration which is proportional to its distance from O, a fixed point on the line, and directed towards O. Initially the particle is at rest when its displacement from O is l. Show that the particle has a maximum velocity when passing through O and zero velocity when its displacement from O is $+l$ or $-l$.

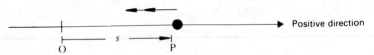

When the particle is at P with a displacement s from O it has an acceleration of magnitude ks (k is a positive constant). Its acceleration is in the negative sense:

Therefore $a = -ks$

The velocity is maximum when a is zero: i.e. when $s = 0$
Therefore the velocity is maximum when the particle is at O

$$a = v\frac{dv}{ds}$$

Therefore
$$\int_0^v v\,dv = \int_l^s -ks\,ds$$

$$v^2 = -ks^2 + kl^2$$

$$v^2 = k\,(l^2 - s^2)$$

when $v = 0$,
$$l^2 - s^2 = 0$$

$$s = \pm l$$

Therefore the particle is at rest when its displacement from O is $+l$ or $-l$.

EXERCISE 9b

1) A particle moves along a straight line with an acceleration a ms^{-2} where $a = \dfrac{3}{v}$, v ms^{-1} being the velocity of the particle at time t seconds. Initially the particle is at rest at O, a fixed point on the line. Find expressions for the velocity and displacement of the particle from O at time t, and find the velocity of the particle when its displacement from O is 5 m.

2) A particle moves in a straight line with acceleration a ms^{-2} where $a = -3v^3$, v ms^{-1} being the velocity of the particle at time t seconds. Initially the particle is at O, a fixed point on the line, with a velocity 2 ms^{-1}. Find the velocity of the particle 3 seconds later and the displacement of the particle from O at this time.

3) A particle moves in a straight line with an acceleration $\dfrac{1}{4v^2}$ ms^{-2} when the velocity of the particle is v ms^{-1}. The particle has a velocity 1 ms^{-1} as it passes through O, a fixed point on the line. Find the displacement of the particle from O when the velocity was zero.

4) A particle moves in a straight line with an acceleration $(12\,s^2)$ ms^{-2} where s metre is the displacement of the particle from O, a fixed point on the line, at time t seconds. The particle has zero velocity when its displacement from O is -2 m. Find the velocity of the particle as it passes through O.

5) A particle moves in a straight line and at time t its displacement from O, a fixed point on the line, is s. The acceleration of the particle is $-4s$, and the velocity is zero when $s = a$. Show that the velocity of the particle is $2\sqrt{(a^2 - s^2)}$ when its displacement from O is s.

6) A particle moves in a straight line with an acceleration which is proportional to its velocity. The particle has a velocity of 20 ms^{-1} when it passes through O,

a fixed point on the line, and a velocity of $4\,\text{ms}^{-1}$ when its displacement from O is 4 m. Show that subsequently the particle is always less than 5 m from O.

GRAPHICAL METHODS FOR MOTION IN A STRAIGHT LINE WITH VARIABLE ACCELERATION

Velocity-time Graph

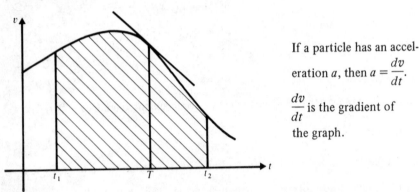

If a particle has an acceleration a, then $a = \dfrac{dv}{dt}$.

$\dfrac{dv}{dt}$ is the gradient of the graph.

Thus the acceleration can be estimated at time T by drawing the tangent to the velocity-time graph at that point and finding the gradient of the tangent.

Also since $s = \int v\,dt$, the increase in displacement in the interval of time $t = t_1$ to $t = t_2$ is $\int_{t_1}^{t_2} v\,dt$: this is the area shaded in the diagram.

Therefore the increase in displacement over an interval of time $(t_2 - t_1)$ can be estimated by finding the area between the velocity-time graph, the time axis and the ordinates t_1 and t_2.

Velocity-Displacement Graphs

A set of corresponding values of displacement and velocity can be used to plot graphs from which can be found:
(1) the acceleration at a particular velocity or displacement,
(2) the time taken to achieve a given increase in displacement.

(1) To find the acceleration:

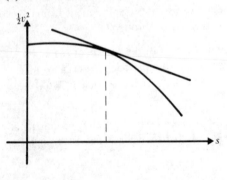

$$a = \frac{dv}{dt} = v\frac{dv}{ds} = \frac{d}{ds}\left(\frac{1}{2}v^2\right)$$

$\dfrac{d}{ds}\left(\dfrac{1}{2}v^2\right)$ is the gradient of the graph given by plotting

$\left(\dfrac{1}{2}v^2\right)$ against s.

Therefore the acceleration at a given displacement can be estimated by drawing the tangent to the curve of $\frac{1}{2}v^2$ plotted against s and finding the gradient.

(2) To find the time taken for a given increase in displacement:

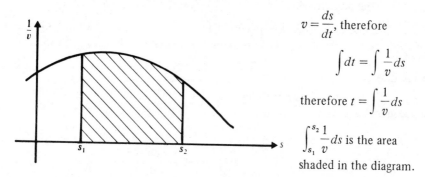

$$v = \frac{ds}{dt}, \text{ therefore}$$

$$\int dt = \int \frac{1}{v}ds$$

$$\text{therefore } t = \int \frac{1}{v}ds$$

$\int_{s_1}^{s_2} \frac{1}{v}ds$ is the area shaded in the diagram.

Therefore the time for an increase in displacement $(s_2 - s_1)$ can be found by estimating the area bounded by the graph of $\frac{1}{v}$ plotted against s, the s-axis and the ordinates s_1 and s_2.

EXAMPLE 9c

Values of velocity at given displacements for a particle moving in a straight line are given in the table

s (m)	0	2	4	6	8
v (ms^{-1})	2	3	5	8	12

Draw a suitable graph to find the time taken to cover a distance of 6 m from the initial position.
The time can be found by plotting $\frac{1}{v}$ against s

s	0	2	4	6	8
$\frac{1}{v}$	0.5	0.33	0.2	0.13	0.08

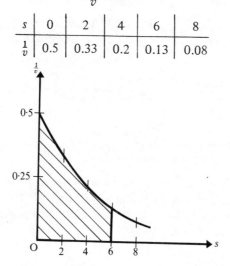

The time taken for the particle to travel 6 m from its initial position is $\int_0^6 \frac{1}{v}\,ds$ which is the area shaded in the diagram.

From the graph this area $\simeq 1.63$

Therefore the particle takes 1.63 seconds to travel 6 m from its initial position.

Note: The answer above was obtained by using Simpson's Rule with 3 ordinates, but any method for finding the approximate area under a curve can be used.

EXERCISE 9c

1) A particle moves in a straight line. Its velocity $v(\text{ms}^{-1})$ at given times $t(\text{seconds})$ is shown in the table.

t	0	1	2	3	4	5	6
v	5	10.5	14.5	16.5	13	5	0

Draw a velocity-time graph and find (a) the acceleration when $t = 3$, (b) the distance moved by the particle between $t = 2$ and $t = 5$.

2) The diagram shows the velocity-time graph for a particle which is moving in a straight line.

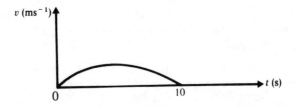

The scale for one unit is the same on both axes and the curve is exactly one quarter of the circumference of a circle. Find the time at which the acceleration is zero and the distance moved by the particle in the time of 10 seconds.

3) A particle moves in a straight line and O is a fixed point on that line. The velocity $v(\text{ms}^{-1})$ of the particle at given displacements $s(\text{metre})$ from O is shown in the table.

s	0	5	10	15	20	25
v	3	7	11	13	12	8

Draw suitable graphs to find:
(a) the acceleration when $s = 10$,
(b) the time taken to move a distance of 20 m from O.

4) The velocity of a particle moving in a straight line increases uniformly with the distance moved by the particle. The particle has an initial velocity of $2\,\text{ms}^{-1}$ and a velocity of $12\,\text{ms}^{-1}$ when it is 20 m from its initial position. Draw suitable

graphs to estimate:

(a) the acceleration of the particle when it is 10 m from its initial position,

(b) the time taken to cover the distance of 20 m.

5) Show that the area represented by $\int_0^t a\, dt$ represents the velocity at time t. A particle moves in a straight line and its acceleration a (ms^{-2}) at given times t (seconds) is shown in the table.

t	0	1	2	3	4	5
a	0	0.6	1.3	2.4	4	8

Draw a graph of a plotted against t and use it to find the velocity of the particle when $t = 2$ and when $t = 4$.

6) A particle moves in a straight line starting from rest. The diagram shows an acceleration-time graph for the first 10 s of its motion: both sections of the graph are straight lines.

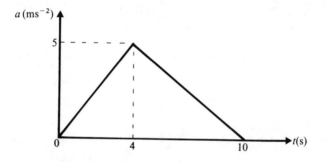

From the graph find the velocity of the particle at times $t = 2, 4, 6, 8, 10$ and hence draw a velocity-time graph for these 10 seconds. Use the velocity-time graph to find the distance travelled by the particle in the first 10 s of its motion.

MOTION IN TWO DIMENSIONS

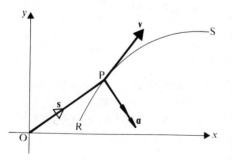

If a particle P is free to move in a plane then at any time its displacement, velocity and acceleration are likely to have different directions as well as different magnitudes. By taking the components of each of these quantities parallel to Ox and Oy we can use the methods for motion in a straight line in each of these directions.

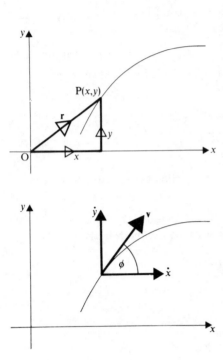

Consider a particle P moving along the curve RS. (The curve RS is referred to as the path of the particle). If the particle is at the point (x, y) at time t, its displacement from O is $\overrightarrow{OP}$ or **r**.

$\overrightarrow{OP}$ has components x in the direction Ox and y in the direction Oy

Therefore the velocity component in the direction Ox is $\dfrac{dx}{dt}$ (written $\dot{x}$) and the velocity component in the direction Oy is $\dfrac{dy}{dt}$ $(\dot{y})$

Therefore if **v** is the velocity of the particle at time t:

The magnitude of **v** is $\sqrt{(\dot{x}^2 + \dot{y}^2)}$
The direction of **v** makes an angle ϕ with Ox

where $\tan \phi = \dfrac{\dot{y}}{\dot{x}}$

$$= \frac{dy}{dt} \bigg/ \frac{dx}{dt}$$

$$= \frac{dy}{dx}$$

Therefore the direction of **v** = the direction of the tangent at P to the curve RS.

Therefore if a particle is moving on a curve and is at the point P on the curve at time t, *the velocity of the particle at time t is in the direction of the tangent to the curve at P.*

As the component of velocity in the direction Ox is $\dot{x}$

the component of acceleration in the direction Ox is $\dfrac{d\dot{x}}{dt}$ (written $\ddot{x}$).

Similarly the component of acceleration in the direction Oy is $\dfrac{d\dot{y}}{dt}$ $(\ddot{y})$

Therefore the acceleration, a, has magnitude $\sqrt{(\ddot{x}^2 + \ddot{y}^2)}$

and inclination $\arctan \left(\dfrac{\ddot{y}}{\ddot{x}} \right)$ to Ox

Equation of the path: If, at time t, the components of displacement of a particle are x and y then the equation of its path is the relationship between x and y. If x and y can both be expressed as functions of t, the equation of the path can be found by eliminating t from these equations.

Vector expressions for displacement, velocity and acceleration

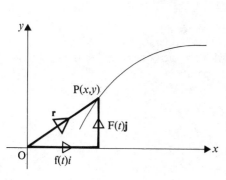

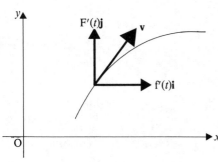

The components of displacement of a particle P projected from O are both functions of time and can therefore be written as

$$x = f(t) \quad y = F(t)$$

Then $\quad \mathbf{r} = f(t)\mathbf{i} + F(t)\mathbf{j}.$

Also, using $f'(t)$ to denote $\dfrac{d}{dt}[f(t)]$, the velocity components of P are:-

$$\dot{x} = f'(t) \quad \dot{y} = F'(t)$$

so that $\quad \mathbf{v} = f'(t)\mathbf{i} + F'(t)\mathbf{j}.$

It can now be seen that

$$\mathbf{v} = \frac{d}{dt}(\mathbf{r}).$$

Similarly by writing the acceleration components of P as

$$\ddot{x} = f''(t) \quad \ddot{y} = F''(t)$$

then $\mathbf{a} = f''(t)\mathbf{i} + F''(t)\mathbf{j}$ showing that

$$\mathbf{a} = \frac{d}{dt}(\mathbf{v}) = \frac{d^2}{dt^2}(\mathbf{r}).$$

EXAMPLES 9d

1) A particle moves in the xy plane such that its position vector at time t is given by $\mathbf{r} = (3t^2 - 1)\,\mathbf{i} + (4t^3 + t - 1)\,\mathbf{j}$. Find vector expressions for the velocity and acceleration of the particle at time t and when $t = 2$.

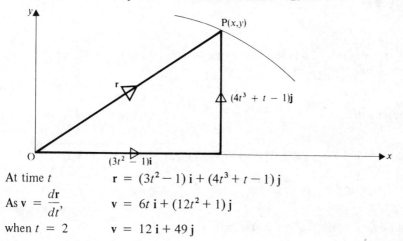

At time t $\qquad \mathbf{r} = (3t^2 - 1)\,\mathbf{i} + (4t^3 + t - 1)\,\mathbf{j}$

As $\mathbf{v} = \dfrac{d\mathbf{r}}{dt}$, $\qquad \mathbf{v} = 6t\,\mathbf{i} + (12t^2 + 1)\,\mathbf{j}$

when $t = 2$ $\qquad \mathbf{v} = 12\,\mathbf{i} + 49\,\mathbf{j}$

As a $= \dfrac{dv}{dt}$, $a = 6i + 24tj$

when $t = 2$ $a = 6i + 48j$

2) A particle moves in a plane with a constant acceleration of $2\ \text{ms}^{-2}$ in the direction Oy. Initially it is at the origin with a velocity of $6\ \text{ms}^{-1}$ in the direction Ox. Show that the path of the particle is a parabola.

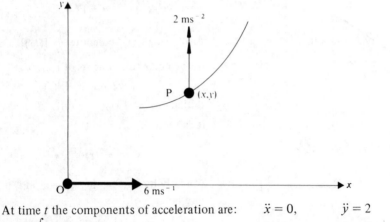

At time t the components of acceleration are: $\ddot{x} = 0$, $\ddot{y} = 2$

As $v = \int a\,dt$ $\dot{x} = c$, $\dot{y} = 2t + k$

As $\dot{x} = 6$ and $\dot{y} = 0$ when $t = 0$, $c = 6$ and $k = 0$, ∴ $\dot{x} = 6$, $\dot{y} = 2t$

As $s = \int v\,dt$ $x = 6t + c'$, $y = t^2 + k'$

As $x = 0, y = 0$ when $t = 0$, $c' = 0$ and $k' = 0$ ∴ $x = 6t$ $y = t^2$

Eliminating t: $x^2 = 36y$

But $36y = x^2$ is the equation of a parabola: therefore the path is a parabola.

Note: $\left.\begin{array}{l} x = 6t \\ y = t^2 \end{array}\right\}$ are the parametic equations of the path

Alternatively

As the components of acceleration at time t are $\ddot{x} = 0$ and $\ddot{y} = 2$, the acceleration can be written in the form

$$a = 2j.$$

As $v = \int a\,dt$, $v = ci + (2t + k)j$ where c and k are
constants of integration.

When $t = 0, v = 6i$,   ∴ substituting these values of v and t we get $c = 6, k = 0$.

$$∴\quad v = 6i + 2tj$$

As $r = \int v\,dt$, $r = (6t + c')i + (t^2 + k')j$

When $t = 0, r = 0$,   ∴ $c' = 0$ and $k' = 0$.

$$∴\quad r = 6t\,i + t^2 j.$$

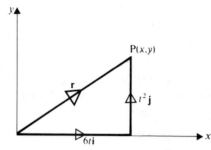

Therefore at time t the coordinates of P are $x = 6t, y = t^2$.
Eliminating t gives $36y = x^2$ which is the equation of a parabola.

3) A particle moves in the xy plane and at time t is at the point $(t^2, t^3 - 2t)$. Find the time at which the directions of the velocity and acceleration of the particle are perpendicular.

The components of displacement are $\quad\quad\quad\quad\quad x = t^2, \quad y = t^3 - 2t$

Therefore the components of velocity are $\quad\quad\quad \dot{x} = 2t, \quad \dot{y} = 3t^2 - 2$

and the components of acceleration are $\quad\quad\quad \ddot{x} = 2 \quad\quad \ddot{y} = 6t$

Therefore at time t the direction of the velocity is $\quad \dfrac{\dot{y}}{\dot{x}} = \dfrac{3t^2 - 2}{2t}$

and the direction of the acceleration is $\quad\quad\quad \dfrac{\ddot{y}}{\ddot{x}} = \dfrac{6t}{2} = 3t$

These are perpendicular when their product is -1

$$\text{i.e. when} \frac{(3t^2 - 2)}{(2t)} \times 3t = -1$$

$$t(9t^2 - 4) = 0$$

$$t = \tfrac{2}{3} \text{ or } 0$$

EXERCISE 9d

1) A particle moves in the xy plane such that its displacement from O at time t is given by $\mathbf{r} = 3t^2\mathbf{i} + (4t - 6)\mathbf{j}$. Find vector expressions for the velocity and acceleration of the particle at time t and when $t = 4$.

2) A particle moves in the xy plane such that it has an acceleration $\mathbf{a}$ at time t where $\mathbf{a} = 2\mathbf{i} - \mathbf{j}$. Initially the particle is at rest at the point whose position vector is $3\mathbf{i} + \mathbf{j}$. Find the position vector of the particle at time t.

3) A particle moves in the xy plane such that its velocity at time t is given by $\mathbf{v} = 3t^2\mathbf{i} + (t - 1)\mathbf{j}$. Find the acceleration vector and position vector of the particle when $t = 3$, if initially the particle is at the origin.

4) The position vector of a particle at time t is given by $\mathbf{r} = \cos \omega t\, \mathbf{i} + \sin \omega t\, \mathbf{j}$. Show that the speed of the particle is constant.

5) A particle moves in a plane with a constant acceleration vector. The velocity vector is zero when $t = 0$ and equal to $3\mathbf{i} - 2\mathbf{j}$ when $t = 1$. Find an expression for the velocity vector at any time t.

6) A particle moves in the xy plane and at time t has acceleration components $\ddot{x} = 2, \ddot{y} = 0$. Initially the particle is at the origin with a velocity of 1 ms^{-1} in the direction Oy. Find the velocity of the particle when $t = 1$ and show that the path of the particle is a parabola.

7) A particle moves in the xy plane and at time t is at the point $(\cos \omega t, \sin \omega t)$. Show that the path is a circle and find the velocity and acceleration of the particle at time t. Prove that the velocity and acceleration are always perpendicular.

8) A particle moves in the xy plane and at time t is at the point $(3 t^2 + 2, t - t^2)$. Prove that the particle has a constant acceleration and find it.

9) A particle moves in the xy plane and at time t it is at the point (x, y) with components of acceleration $\ddot{x}$ and $\ddot{y}$ where $\ddot{x} = x, \ddot{y} = 2$. Initially the particle is at rest at the point $(1, 0)$. By writing $\ddot{x}$ as $\dot{x}\dfrac{d\dot{x}}{dx}$ and $\ddot{y}$ as $\dot{y}\dfrac{d\dot{y}}{dy}$ find the components of velocity at time t in terms of x and y respectively. Hence show that the particle moves on a curve whose equation can be derived from
$$\frac{dy}{dx} = \frac{2\sqrt{y}}{\sqrt{(x^2 - 1)}}.$$

10) A particle moves in the xy plane and at time t it has velocity components $\dot{x}$ and $\dot{y}$ and acceleration components $\ddot{x}$ and $\ddot{y}$ where $\ddot{x} = \dfrac{2}{x}$ and $\ddot{y} = \dfrac{9}{y^2}$. Initially the particle is at rest at the origin. Find $\dot{x}$ and $\dot{y}$ as functions of t and hence show that the equation of the path is $\left(\dfrac{3x}{4}\right)^8 = \left(\dfrac{4y}{9}\right)^9$.

MOTION UNDER THE ACTION OF VARIABLE FORCES

(*Note:* examples in this section involve integration leading to logarithmic and inverse trigonometric functions)

Relationship between force and acceleration

Newton's Law of Motion applies to the motion of any particle, however it is caused: it applies whether the force causing the motion is variable or constant. Thus if a body of constant mass m is moving under the action of a force and at time t

$$\left.\begin{array}{r} \text{the force is } F \\ \text{and} \\ \text{the acceleration is } a \end{array}\right\} \text{then } \underline{F = ma}$$

EXAMPLES 9e

1) A particle of mass m moves in a straight line under the action of a variable force such that at time t the displacement of the particle is $\cos 2t$ from O, a fixed point on the line. Show that the force varies as the displacement of the particle from O.

If s is the displacement from O at time t, $s = \cos 2t$
Therefore $v = -2 \sin 2t$
                                                   $a = -4 \cos 2t$

If the force is F at time t
Applying Newton's Law: $F = -4m \cos 2t$
Therefore $F = -4ms$
i.e. the force varies as the displacement.

2) A particle of mass m falls from rest through a resisting medium where the resistance to motion is kv, v being the velocity of the particle at time t, and k a positive constant. Find the velocity of the particle at time t and show that the velocity approaches a limit of $\dfrac{mg}{k}$.

At time t the resultant downward force acting on the particle
is $mg - kv$
Applying $F = ma$: $mg - kv = ma$
$a = \dfrac{dv}{dt}$, therefore $mg - kv = m\dfrac{dv}{dt}$

$$\int_0^v \frac{m\,dv}{mg - kv} = \int_0^t dt$$

$$-\frac{m}{k}\ln(mg - kv) + \frac{m}{k}\ln mg = t$$

$$\frac{m}{k}\ln\frac{(mg - kv)}{(mg)} = t$$

$$\frac{mg - kv}{mg} = e^{-\frac{kt}{m}}$$

$$v = \frac{mg}{k} - \frac{mg}{k}e^{-\frac{kt}{m}}$$

As $t \to \infty$, $e^{-\frac{kt}{m}} \to 0$,   therefore $v \to \dfrac{mg}{k}$

Therefore the velocity approaches a limit of $\dfrac{mg}{k}$.

Impulse of a Variable Force

Consider a particle of mass m moving in a straight line under the action of a variable force. If, at time t, the particle has an acceleration a and the force acting on it is F, then applying Newton's Law:

At time t, $$F = ma \tag{1}$$

$$= m\frac{dv}{dt} \tag{2}$$

If the particle has a velocity u when $t = 0$ and a velocity v at time t then by separating the variables equation (2) becomes:

$$\int_0^t F\,dt = \int_u^v m\,dv$$

$$= mv - mu$$

$mv - mu$ is the increase in momentum of the particle over the interval of time t. The quantity $\int_0^t F\,dt$ is called the *impulse* of the force over the interval of time t. Thus *the impulse of a force (constant or variable) is equal to the increase in momentum.*

For a constant force: Impulse = Ft
For a variable force: Impulse = $\int_0^t F\,dt$

Work Done by a Variable Force

If we write equation (1) above in the form:

$$F = ma$$

$$= mv\frac{dv}{ds} \tag{3}$$

then by separating the variables equation (3) becomes $\int_0^s F\,ds = \int_u^v mv\,dv$ where s is the increase in displacement of the particle in time t

therefore $$\int_0^s F\,ds = \tfrac{1}{2}mv^2 - \tfrac{1}{2}mu^2.$$

$\tfrac{1}{2}mv^2 - \tfrac{1}{2}mu^2$ is the increase in the kinetic energy of the particle.

The quantity $\int_0^s F\,ds$ is called the work done by the force in increasing its displacement by s. (*Note*: F and s are both in the same direction).

The concepts of work and impulse sometimes lead to neat solutions although the methods in the previous section can also be used.

EXAMPLES 9f

1) A particle of mass m moves in a straight line under the action of a force F where $F = 2t$ at time t. If the particle has a velocity u when $t = 0$, find the velocity when $t = 3$.

If v is the velocity when $t = 3$, then by considering the impulse of F from $t = 0$ to $t = 3$ we have

$$mv - mu = \int_0^3 F\,dt$$

$$= \int_0^3 2t\,dt$$

$$= 9$$

Therefore
$$v = \frac{9 + mu}{m}$$

2) A particle of mass m slides from rest down a plane inclined at $30°$ to the horizontal. The resistance to the motion of the particle is ms^2 where s is the displacement of the particle from its initial position. Find the velocity of the particle when $s = 1$.

The resultant force down the plane is $\dfrac{mg}{2} - ms^2$.

By considering the work done by this force in displacing the particle 1 unit from O we have:

$$\int_0^1 F\,ds = \tfrac{1}{2}mv^2$$

$$\int_0^1 \left(\frac{mg}{2} - ms^2\right)ds = \tfrac{1}{2}mv^2$$

$$\frac{mg}{2} - \frac{m}{3} = \tfrac{1}{2}mv^2$$

Therefore
$$v = \sqrt{\frac{3g - 2}{3}}$$

SUMMARY

For Motion in a Straight Line:

If $a = f(t)$,
$$\int dv = \int f(t)\,dt$$

If $a = f(v)$
$$\int \frac{dv}{f(v)} = \int dt$$

or

$$\int \frac{v\,dv}{f(v)} = \int ds$$

If $a = f(s)$,

$$\int v\,dv = \int f(s)\,ds$$

The impulse of a variable
force F is

$$\int_0^t F\,dt = mv - mu$$

The work done by a variable
force F is

$$\int_0^s F\,ds = \tfrac{1}{2}mv^2 - \tfrac{1}{2}mu^2$$

For Motion in a Plane:
If the position vector of a particle at time t is $\mathbf{r} = f(t)\mathbf{i} + F(t)\mathbf{j}$

then $\mathbf{v} = \dfrac{d\mathbf{r}}{dt}$ and $\mathbf{a} = \dfrac{d\mathbf{v}}{dt}$

If a particle moves in a curved path, the velocity at time t is in the direction of
the tangent to the path at time t.

For any Motion
If a particle moves under the action of a force which is F at time t and has an
acceleration a at time t and a constant mass m then $F = ma$.

MULTIPLE CHOICE EXERCISE 9
Instructions for answering these questions are given on page (xii).

TYPE I

1) A particle moves along a straight line Ox such that $\ddot{x} = (6t - 4)\,\text{ms}^{-2}$ at time t.
Initially the particle is at O with a velocity of $-2\,\text{ms}^{-1}$. The displacement of the
particle from O at time t is:
(a) $t^3 - 2t^2 - 2t$　(b) $t^3 - 2t^2$　(c) 6　(d) $t^3 - 2t^2 + 2$　(e) 0.

2) A particle moves along a straight line such that at time t its displacement from
a fixed point O on the line is $3t^2 - 2$. The velocity of the particle when $t = 2$ is:
(a) $8\,\text{ms}^{-1}$　(b) $4\,\text{ms}^{-1}$　(c) $12\,\text{ms}^{-1}$　(d) $6t$　(e) $t^3 - 2t$.

3) A particle of mass 3 kg moves along a straight line Ox under the action of a
force F such that a time t, $x = t^2 + 3t$. The magnitude of F at time t is given by:
(a) 0　(b) 2 N　(c) $3(2t + 3)$　(d) 6 N　(e) -6 N.

4) A particle moves along a straight line with acceleration $a \sin \omega t$ at time t.
Initially the particle is at rest at O, a fixed point on the line. The displacement
of the particle from O at time t is given by:

(a) $\dfrac{a}{\omega^2} \sin \omega t + \dfrac{a}{\omega} t$　(b) $\dfrac{-a}{\omega^2} \sin \omega t + \dfrac{a}{\omega} t$　(c) $a\omega^2 \cos \omega t$　(d) $-a\omega^2 \sin \omega t$

(e) $-\dfrac{a}{\omega^2} \sin \omega t + \dfrac{a}{\omega^2} \cos \omega t$.

5) A particle moves along a straight line with an acceleration of $\dfrac{2}{v}$ where v is the
the velocity at any instant. Initially the particle is at rest. The velocity of the
particle at time t is:

(a) $2t$ (b) $4t$ (c) $\dfrac{2t}{v}$ (d) $2\sqrt{t}$ (e) $2\sqrt{t} + 2$.

6) A particle moves in a straight line with an acceleration $2s$ where s is its displacement from a fixed point on the line, and $v = 0$ when $s = 0$. Its velocity when
its displacement is s is:

(a) s (b) s^2 (c) $-s\sqrt{2}$ (d) $s\sqrt{2}$ (e) $\sqrt{2s}$.

7) A particle moves in the xy plane such that at time t it is at the point
$(2t^2, 3t - 1)$. At time t the acceleration components are given by:

(a) $\ddot{x} = 4t, \ddot{y} = 3$ (b) $\ddot{x} = \tfrac{2}{3}t^3, \ddot{y} = \dfrac{3t^2}{2} - t$ (c) $\ddot{x} = 4, \ddot{y} = 3$

(d) $\ddot{x} = 0, \ddot{y} = 0$ (e) $\ddot{x} = 4, \ddot{y} = 0$.

8) A particle moves in the xy plane such that at time t its displacement from O
is $(3t - 1)\mathbf{i} + (2t^2 + 1)\mathbf{j}$. The acceleration vector of the particle at time t is
given by:

(a) $4\mathbf{i}$ (b) $3\mathbf{i} + 4t\mathbf{j}$ (c) $4\mathbf{j}$ (d) $-\mathbf{i} + \mathbf{j}$ (e) $\mathbf{i} + 4\mathbf{j}$.

9) A particle of mass 2 kg moves in the xy plane under the action of a constant
force $\mathbf{F}$ where $\mathbf{F} = \mathbf{i} - \mathbf{j}$. Initially the velocity of the particle is $2\mathbf{i}$. The velocity
of the particle at time t is:

(a) $\tfrac{1}{2}(t + 4)\mathbf{i} - \tfrac{1}{2}t\mathbf{j}$ (b) $t(\mathbf{i} - \mathbf{j})$ (c) $\dfrac{t}{2}(\mathbf{i} - \mathbf{j})$ (d) $\tfrac{1}{2}t\mathbf{i} + \tfrac{1}{2}(t + 4)\mathbf{j}$ (e) $2\mathbf{i}$

10) A particle moves in the xy plane such that at time t its velocity vector is
$(3t^2 - 1)\mathbf{i} + 2\mathbf{j}$. Initially the particle is at the origin. The position vector of the
particle at time t is:

(a) $6\mathbf{i}$ (b) $6t\mathbf{i}$ (c) $(t^3 - t - 1)\mathbf{i} + (2t + 1)\mathbf{j}$ (d) $(t^3 - t)\mathbf{i} + 2t\mathbf{j}$ (e) $(3t^2)\mathbf{i}$.

TYPE II

11) A particle moves along a straight line Ox. Its velocity at time t is given by:

(a) $\dot{x}$ (b) $\dfrac{dx}{dt}$ (c) $\displaystyle\int_0^t a \, dt$.

12) A particle moves on the curve $y = f(x)$. If the particle is at the point $P(x, y)$
on the curve at time t, the direction of its velocity is given by:

(a) $\dfrac{d^2y}{dx^2}$ (b) $\dfrac{dy}{dt} \Big/ \dfrac{dx}{dt}$ (c) $\dfrac{dy}{dx}$.

13) The area shaded in the graph represents:

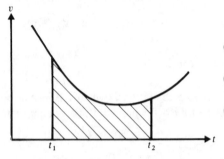

(a) the distance travelled in the time interval $(t_2 - t_1)$,

(b) the increase in the displacement in the time interval $(t_2 - t_1)$,

(c) the acceleration at time t_2.

14) A resultant force F of varying magnitude acts on a particle. The work done by F in moving the particle a distance s is:

(a) $\int_0^s F\,dt$,

(b) the increase in kinetic energy,

(c) $\int_0^s F\,ds$.

15) A particle moves along a straight line such that at time t its velocity is v and its displacement from a fixed point on the line is s. Its acceleration at time t is:

(a) $\dfrac{dv}{dt}$ (b) $v\dfrac{dv}{ds}$ (c) $\int v\,dt$.

TYPE III

16) (a) At time t the acceleration of a particle is given by $a = \dfrac{2}{v}$.

(b) The velocity of a particle at time t is given by $v = 2t^{\frac{1}{2}}$.

17) (a) $a = f(s)$.   (b) $\int v\,dv = \int f(s)\,ds$.

18) (a) $\mathbf{v} = (2t - 1)\mathbf{i} + 3t\mathbf{j}$.   (b) $a = 2\mathbf{i} + 3\mathbf{j}$.

19) (a) $\mathbf{r} = (3t^2 + 2)\mathbf{i} - (t + 1)\mathbf{j}$.   (b) $\mathbf{v} = 6t\mathbf{i} + \mathbf{j}$.

TYPE IV

20) A particle moves in a straight line. Find the distance covered by the particle in the third second of its motion.

(a) $s = 0$ when $t = 0$.

(b) $a = 3t - 4$ at time t.

(c) $v = 0$ when $t = 0$.

21) A particle moves on the line Ox with an acceleration which is proportional to $-x$. Find the maximum velocity of the particle.

(a) $v = 0$ when $t = 0$.

(b) $x = a$ when $t = 0$.

(c) $\ddot{x} = 3$ when $t = 1$.

22) A particle moves under the action of a force **F**. Find **F** in terms of t.
(a) $\dot{x} = 3t^2 - 4$.
(b) $\dot{y} = 6t + 3$.
(c) the mass of the particle is 2 kg.

23) A particle moves in the xy plane under the action of a force **F**. Find the position vector of the particle at time t.
(a) $\mathbf{F} = 3\mathbf{i} - 2\mathbf{j}$.
(b) $\mathbf{v} = \mathbf{i}$ when $t = 0$.
(c) $\mathbf{r} = \mathbf{0}$ when $t = 0$.

24) A particle moves in a straight line under the action of a force F. Find the impulse of F over the interval $t = 0$ to $t = t_1$.
(a) the mass of the particle is 5 kg.
(b) $t_1 = 3$.
(c) the initial velocity is 0 and the velocity when $t = t_1$ is 4 ms^{-1}.

TYPE V

25) A particle is moving along a straight line with variable acceleration. If, at some instant, the particle has a maximum velocity, the acceleration at that instant is zero.

26) If a particle has a constant acceleration is must be moving in a straight line.

27) If a particle moves in a straight line and the acceleration is plotted against the time, this graph can be used to find the velocity of the particle at any instant.

28) A particle moves in a plane under the action of a force **F**, where $\mathbf{F} = a(\cos \omega t\, \mathbf{i} + \sin \omega t\, \mathbf{j})$ at time t, so the speed of the particle is constant.

MISCELLANEOUS EXERCISE 9

1) A particle of mass m moves in a straight line under the action of a force F where $F = -mk \sin 3t$ at time t and k is a positive constant. The particle is at O, a point on the line, when $t = 0$, with a velocity u. Find expressions for the acceleration, velocity and displacement from O at time t.

2) A particle of mass m moves in a straight line under the action of a force F where $F = ms$, s being the displacement of the particle from O, a fixed point on the line. When $s = -a$ the velocity of the particle is u. Find the velocity of the particle when $s = 0$.

3) A particle of mass m moves in the xy plane such that its position vector at time t is $\mathbf{r} = (3t^2 + 2)\mathbf{i} + (4 - 6t)\mathbf{j}$. Prove that the particle is moving under the action of a constant force and find it.

4) A particle of mass 2 kg moves in the xy plane under the action of a force **F** where $\mathbf{F} = 2\mathbf{i} - 6\mathbf{j}$. Initially the particle is at the point whose position vector is

$\mathbf{i} + \mathbf{j}$ with a velocity vector $\mathbf{i} - \mathbf{j}$. Find the position vector of the particle at any time t.

5) A particle of mass m moves in a straight line against a resistance of $(mv + k)$ where v is the velocity of the particle and k is a positive constant. Initally the particle has a velocity of u. Find an expression for the velocity of the particle at any time t and show that the greatest displacement from the initial position occurs when $t = \ln\left(\dfrac{mu + k}{k}\right)$.

6) By writing a as $\dfrac{dv}{dt}$ show that $\displaystyle\int \frac{1}{a}\,dv = t$. Hence show that if $\dfrac{1}{a}$ is plotted against v, the area between the graph, the v axis and the ordinates $v = 0, v = V$ gives the time at which the velocity is V, if $t = 0$ when $v = 0$. A particle moves in a straight line with acceleration which decreases uniformly with the velocity. If the acceleration is 10 ms^{-2} when the velocity is zero and 4 ms^{-2} when the velocity is 6 ms^{-1}, find the times at which the velocity is 2 ms^{-1}, 8 ms^{-1}, if $t = 0$ when $v = 0$.

7) By writing a as $v\dfrac{dv}{ds}$ show that $\displaystyle\int a\,ds = \tfrac{1}{2}v^2$.

The table gives corresponding values of acceleration a (ms^{-2}) and displacement s (metre) for a particle moving in a straight line.

s	0	2	4	6	8
a	0	0.4	1.6	3.6	6.4

Draw a graph of a plotted against s and use it to find the velocity when $s = 4$ and when $s = 8$.

8) The figure shows the velocity-time graph of a particle which moves along a straight line from rest to rest in 30 seconds. The parts OA and AB are straight lines and the curve BC is an arc of the circle whose radius is equal to the chord BC. Find:

(i) The accelerations during the stages OA and AB,

(ii) the greatest and least retardations during the stage BC,

(iii) the total distance covered by the particle.

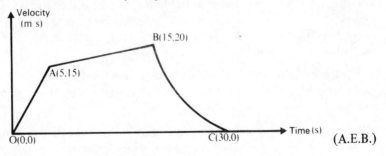

(A.E.B.)

9) As a car of mass 1000 kg travels along a level road its motion is opposed by a constant resistance of 100 N. The values of the pull of the engine for given values of the time, t seconds, are as follows:

Time t (seconds)	0	1	2	3	4	5	6
Pull (newtons)	1100	1200	1350	1550	1850	2300	3100

Find the acceleration of the car at each of the given values of t. When $t = 0$ the speed of the car is 50 km/h. Find graphically the speed of the car in km/h when $t = 6$.

State how you would find graphically the distance travelled by the car in the period from $t = 0$ to $t = 6$.   (A.E.B.)

10) A particle moves along a horizontal straight line with acceleration proportional to $\cos \pi t$, where t is the time. When $t = 0$ the velocity of the particle is u, and when $t = \frac{1}{2}$ its velocity is $2u$. Find the distance that the particle has travelled when $t = 2$, and draw the velocity-time graph for the interval $0 \leqslant t \leqslant 2$. (U of L)

11) A particle starts from rest at time $t = 0$ and moves in a straight line with variable acceleration f m/s²; where

$$f = \frac{t}{5} \qquad (0 \leqslant t < 5),$$

$$f = \frac{t}{5} + \frac{10}{t^2} \quad (t \geqslant 5)$$

t being measured in seconds. Show that the velocity is $2\frac{1}{2}$ m/s when $t = 5$ and 11 m/s when $t = 10$.

Show also that the distance travelled by the particle in the first 10 seconds is $(43\frac{1}{3} - 10 \ln 2)$ m.   (U of L)

12) A particle moves in a straight line with initial speed u at time $t = 0$, and with acceleration inversely proportional to $(t + t_0)^3$, where t_0 is positive and constant. Show that the speed of the particle approaches a limiting value. If this value is $2u$, show that after time t the particle will have travelled a distance

$$ut(2t + t_0)/(t + t_0).$$ (U of L)

13) A parachutist of mass m falls freely until his parachute opens. When it is open, he experiences an upward resistance kv where v is his speed and k is a positive constant. Prove that, after time t from the opening of his parachute, $m(dv/dt) = mg - kv$. Prove also that, irrespective of his speed when he opens his parachute, his speed approaches a limiting value mg/k, provided that he falls for a sufficiently long time.

The parachutist falls from rest freely under gravity for a time $m/2k$ and then opens his parachute. Prove that the total distance he has fallen when his velocity is $3mg/4k$ is $\frac{m^2 g}{8k^2}(8 \ln 2 - 1)$.   (Oxford)

14) A particle leaves a point A at time $t = 0$ with speed u and moves towards a point B with a retardation λv, where v is the speed of the particle at time t. The particle is at a distance s from A at time t. Show that:

(i) $v = u - \lambda s$,

(ii) $\ln (u - \lambda s) = \ln u - \lambda t$.

At $t = 0$ a second particle starts from rest at B and moves towards A with acceleration $2 + 6t$. The particles collide at the mid-point of AB when $t = 1$. Find the distance AB and the speeds of the particles on impact.   (A.E.B.)

15) A particle is projected horizontally with speed u across a smooth horizontal plane from a point O in the plane. The particle is subjected to a retardation of magnitude k times the speed of the particle. Find the distance of the particle from O and also its speed at time t after projection.

Another particle is projected vertically upwards with speed u. In addition to the retardation due to gravity this particle is also subjected to a retardation of k times its speed. Find the time this particle takes to reach its greatest height.
                                          (A.E.B.)

16) A particle moving on the x-axis starts from the origin at time $t = 0$ and moves with constant acceleration a_0 until it reaches a speed v_0. Subsequently its acceleration a is related to its speed v by $a = a_0 v_0/v$.

(i) Find expressions for the time t_0 and co-ordinate x_0 when the speed v_0 is reached.

(ii) Show that the speed v at any time $t > t_0$ is given by the equation

$$v = \{2a_0 v_0 t - v_0^2\}^{1/2}$$

and find an expression for the co-ordinate x at any time $t > t_0$.

If $v_0 = 5$ m/s and if the particle accelerates from 15 m/s to 25 m/s in 10 seconds find a_0 and also the total time taken to accelerate to 25 m/s from rest. (W.J.E.C.)

17) A particle P, of mass m, moves on a rough horizontal table, and is attracted towards a fixed point O on the table by a force whose magnitude is kmg/x^2, where x is the distance OP. The coefficient of friction between the particle and the table is μ. The particle is projected from a point A at a distance a from O with speed u in the direction directly away from O, and its velocity is first zero at a point B at a distance b from O. Show that

$$u^2 = 2g \left(\frac{k}{a} - \frac{k}{b} + \mu b - \mu a \right).$$

Show that, if $b^2 \geqslant k/\mu$, the particle remains at B. In the case $b^2 < k/\mu$ find the speed of the particle when it first returns to A.   (J.M.B.)

18) A particle moves on a straight line so that its distance s from a fixed point of the line is given by $s = l \sin \omega t$, where t is the time and l, ω are constants. Prove that its velocity v at any point is given by $v^2 = \omega^2 (l^2 - s^2)$.

Particles A and B move along a straight line, each starting from a point O with velocity u. A is acted on by a constant force directed towards O, and B by a force, also towards O, proportional to the distance from O.

(i) If they both cover the same distance l before starting back towards O, show that the times taken, t_A and t_B respectively, are in the ratio $4:\pi$; and that their velocities as they pass a point distant s from O are in a ratio given by

$$V_A{}^2 : V_B{}^2 = l : (l + s).$$

(ii) If they both take the same time T between leaving O and returning to O, show that their maximum distances from O are in a ratio given by

$$l_A : l_B = \pi : 4. \tag{S.U.}$$

19) A particle moves in the xy plane such that the acceleration of the particle at time t is $3\mathbf{i}$. At time $t = 0$ the particle is at the origin with velocity vector $-2\mathbf{j}$. Find the position vector of the particle at time t and hence find the cartesian equation of its path.

20) A particle is acted upon by two forces $\mathbf{F_1}$ and $\mathbf{F_2}$ where $\mathbf{F_1} = 2\mathbf{i} - t\mathbf{j}$ and $\mathbf{F_2} = \mathbf{i} + 4t\mathbf{j}$ at time t. The particle is initially at rest. Find the momentum of the particle 5 seconds later.

21) A particle of mass m moves under the action of a force $\mathbf{F}$ where $\mathbf{F} = m \cos t\mathbf{i} + m \sin t\mathbf{j}$. Initially the particle is at the point $-\mathbf{j}$ with velocity vector $-\mathbf{i}$. Prove that the path of the particle is a circle whose cartesian equation is $x^2 + y^2 = 1$.

22) A particle of unit mass is acted upon by a force which at time t is $4\mathbf{i} + 12t^2\mathbf{j}$. At time $t = 0$ the particle is at rest at the point $-\mathbf{i} + \mathbf{j}$. Find the position vector of the particle at time $t = T$, and deduce that the path of the particle is a parabola with vertex at the point $-\mathbf{i} + \mathbf{j}$. At time $t = 1$ the force acting on the particle becomes $4\mathbf{i}$. Find the position vector of the particle when $t = 2$.

(U of L)

23) A particle moves in the xy plane such that at time t it is at the point (x,y) where $x = 2 \cos \omega t, y = 2 \sin \omega t$. Prove that the particle moves in a circular path with constant angular velocity. Prove that the acceleration of the particle at time t is in the direction of the radius from the particle to the centre of its path.

24) A particle moves in the xy plane with acceleration components $\ddot{x}$ and $\ddot{y}$ where $\ddot{x} = (\dot{x})^2$ and $\ddot{y} = (\dot{y})^2$. Initially the particle is at the point $(1, 0)$ with velocity components $\dot{x} = 3$, and $\dot{y} = 3$. Find the direction of the velocity at time t and hence show that the particle moves in a straight line whose equation is $x - y - 1 = 0$.

25) Cartesian axes Ox, Oy are chosen with fixed origin O and Ox vertically downwards. A particle P of mass m moving in the x, y plane is acted on by its weight and another force $\mathbf{F}$ in the plane.

(a) If at time t the co-ordinates of P are $\frac{1}{2}gt^2 + V_1t + h\cos kt, b + V_2t + h\sin kt$ where b, h, V_1 and V_2 are all positive constants, find the magnitude and direction of **F** at time t, carefully indicating the direction and sense in a figure.

(b) If **F** is in a fixed horizontal direction and at time t is of magnitude $F(1 - e^{-nt})$, where F and n are positive constants, find the co-ordinates of P at time t if, at $t = 0$, P is at the origin and moving horizontally with speed U.   (W.J.E.C.)

26) Axes Ox and Oy are chosen with Ox vertically downwards. The point A moves in the x, y plane so that at time t, $\overrightarrow{OA}$ makes an angle ωt with Ox, where ω is a constant. A particle P of mass m moving in the xy plane experiences two forces: its weight and a varying force of constant magnitude F in the direction and sense of $\overrightarrow{OA}$. At $t = 0$, P is projected vertically downwards from the origin with speed U. Write down cartesian equations of motion for P. Show that at

time t its x co-ordinate is $\frac{1}{2}gt^2 + Ut + \dfrac{F}{m\omega^2}(1 - \cos\omega t)$ and find its y co-ordinate.

Find the time that elapses after projection before its direction of motion is again vertical. Show also that if the direction of motion of P is instantaneously horizontal when $t = 3\pi/2\omega$, then $F = \frac{1}{2}m(3\pi g + 2U\omega)$.   (W.J.E.C.)

27) If an engine works at a constant rate show that the driving force P is inversely proportional to the velocity v at time t.

A car moves along a straight road against a resistance to motion which is ten times the speed of the car. The car has a mass of 800 kg and the engine is working at the constant rate of 4 kW. Find an expression for the acceleration of the car as a function of the velocity at any time t. Hence find the distance covered by the car as it increases its velocity from 5 ms^{-1} to 10 ms^{-1}.

28) A car of mass m is moving in a straight line on a rough horizontal plane. At time t the car is moving with velocity v and the resistance to motion is kv where k is a constant. If the car works at a constant rate h, show that

$$mv\frac{dv}{dt} + kv^2 = h$$

If the car starts from rest, show that v is always less than $\left(\dfrac{h}{k}\right)^{\frac{1}{2}}$ and find the time taken for the car to reach the speed $\frac{1}{2}\left(\dfrac{h}{k}\right)^{\frac{1}{2}}$ (Oxford)

29) A mass m hangs at the end of a light string and is raised vertically by an engine working at a constant rate kmg. Derive the equation of motion of the mass in the form

$$v^2\frac{dv}{dx} = (k - v)g$$

where v is the upward velocity of the mass and x is its displacement measured upwards.

Initially the mass is at rest and when it has risen to a height h its speed is u. Show that

$$gh = k^2 \ln \frac{k}{k-u} - ku - \frac{1}{2}u^2.$$

Without further integration find, in terms of m, k and u, the increase in the total energy of the mass due to this motion and hence, by considering the work done by the engine, deduce that the time taken is

$$\frac{1}{g}\left\{k \ln\left(\frac{k}{k-u}\right) - u\right\}.$$

PROJECTILES

CHAPTER 10

PROJECTILES

A projectile is a particle which is given an initial velocity and then moves under the action of its weight only. In this chapter we analyse the motion of projectiles while they are in flight. For example, a ball which is thrown is a projectile and we are concerned with its flight from the moment it leaves the thrower's hand until its flight is interrupted.

If the initial velocity of a projectile is vertical it will move in a straight line (see Chapter 4).

If the initial velocity is not vertical the particle will move in a curve and its flight can be analysed by considering the vertical and horizontal components of its acceleration, velocity and displacement.

Consider a ball which is thrown with an initial velocity of $20\,\text{ms}^{-1}$ at an angle of $30°$ to the horizontal.

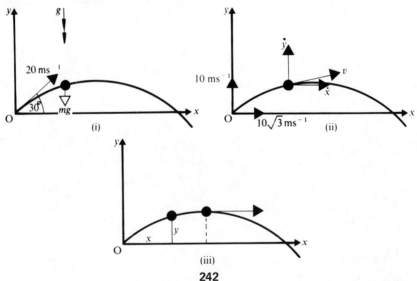

Taking the origin at the point of projection, Ox horizontally and Oy vertically upward, at any time during the flight the horizontal components of acceleration, velocity and displacement from O are $\ddot{x}, \dot{x}$ and x, (see Chapter 9, page 224) and the vertical components of acceleration, velocity and displacement from O are $\ddot{y}, \dot{y}$ and y.

Throughout the flight the only force acting on the ball is mg vertically downward: therefore *the ball has a constant acceleration g vertically downward.*

Therefore $\ddot{x} = 0$ and $\ddot{y} = -g$.

As the acceleration is constant we can use the equations
$v = u + at, s = ut + \frac{1}{2}at^2$
to find the components of velocity and displacement.

$$\dot{x} = 10\sqrt{3} \quad (1) \qquad \dot{y} = 10 - gt \qquad (2)$$

$$x = 10\sqrt{3}\,t \quad (3) \qquad y = 10t - \tfrac{1}{2}gt^2 \quad (4)$$

(Note that the horizontal component of velocity ($\dot{x}$) remains constant as there is zero acceleration horizontally).

Any information required about the flight of the ball can be found from these four equations; e.g.:-

(i) What is the velocity of the ball 2 seconds after projection?

From equations (1) and (2):

when $t = 2$, $\dot{x} = 10\sqrt{3}$, $\dot{y} = -9.6$

therefore the velocity $(v) = \sqrt{\dot{x}^2 + \dot{y}^2} = 19.8 \text{ ms}^{-1}$

at an angle $\arctan \dot{y}/\dot{x}$ to the horizontal

$$= \arctan\left(-\frac{9.6}{10\sqrt{3}}\right)$$

$$= -28°48' \text{ (i.e. } 28°48' \text{ below the horizontal)}$$

Note: this is the direction of the tangent to the path (see Chapter 9, page 224)

(ii) What is the distance of the ball from its point of projection 1 second after leaving O?

From equations (3) and (4): when $t = 1$

$$x = 10\sqrt{3}, y = 10 - 4.9$$

Distance from O

$$= \sqrt{x^2 + y^2}$$

$$= \sqrt{326}$$

$$= 18.1 \text{ m}$$

(iii) What is the equation of the path of the ball?

Equations (1) and (4) are the parametric equations of the path: eliminating t from these gives y in terms of x:

$$y = 10\left(\frac{x}{10\sqrt{3}}\right) - \tfrac{1}{2}g\left(\frac{x^2}{300}\right)$$

$$y = \frac{x}{\sqrt{3}} - g\frac{x^2}{600}$$

(*Note:* this is the equation of a parabola)

(iv) What is the greatest height reached by the ball above its point of projection? When the ball reaches its greatest height above the level of O it has no vertical component of velocity: (fig. iii)

i.e. $\dot{y} = 0$ \qquad Therefore \quad $10 - gt = 0.$

$$t = \frac{10}{g}$$

from (4) when $t = \dfrac{10}{g}$, \quad $y = \dfrac{100}{g} - \tfrac{1}{2}g\dfrac{100}{g^2}$

$$= \frac{50}{g} = 5.1$$

Therefore the greatest height reached by the ball is 5.1 m.

(v) If the ball hits the ground at a point which is level with O, for how long is it in the air?
When the ball is level with O, \quad $y = 0$
$$\text{i.e.: } 10t - \tfrac{1}{2}gt^2 = 0$$
$$t(10 - 4.9t) = 0$$
$$t = 0 \text{ or } t = 2.04$$

Therefore the ball is in the air for 2.04 seconds.
($t = 0$ is the time at which the ball is at O).

IN GENERAL if a particle is projected with initial velocity u at an angle α to the horizontal (α is called the angle of projection) then at any time t after leaving O, the only force acting on the particle is its weight:
Therefore *the particle has a constant acceleration g vertically downward.*

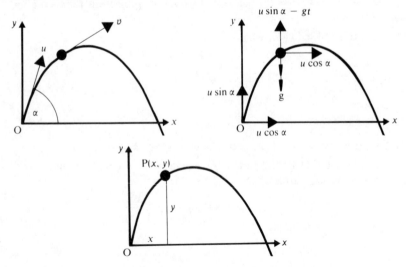

Taking axes as before:

$$\ddot{x} = 0 \qquad\qquad \ddot{y} = -g$$

$\dot{x} = u \cos \alpha$ $\quad$ (1) $\quad$ $\dot{y} = u \sin \alpha - gt$ $\qquad\qquad$ (2) $\quad$ $(v = u + at)$

$x = (u \cos \alpha)\, t$ $\quad$ (3) $\quad$ $y = (u \sin \alpha)\, t - \tfrac{1}{2} g t^2$ $\qquad$ (4) $\quad$ $(s = ut + \tfrac{1}{2} at^2)$

The last two equations are the parametric equations of the path of the particle (sometimes referred to as the trajectory)
Eliminating t from these two equations:

$$y = x \tan \alpha - \frac{x^2 g \sec^2 \alpha}{2 u^2} \tag{5}$$

These 5 equations can now be used to solve any problem on projectiles.

The following points should be noted.
Equation (5) is the equation of a parabola: thus the path of any projectile is a parabola.

The velocity (v) at any instant has magnitude $\sqrt{\dot{x}^2 + \dot{y}^2}$ and direction $\arctan \dfrac{\dot{y}}{\dot{x}}$ to the horizontal.

But $\qquad\qquad\qquad \dfrac{\dot{y}}{\dot{x}} = \dfrac{dy}{dt} \bigg/ \dfrac{dx}{dt} = \dfrac{dy}{dx}$

Therefore the direction of the velocity at any instant is along the tangent to the path at that instant.
Also the horizontal component of velocity $(\dot{x})$ remains constant since there is no acceleration horizontally.
If the angle of projection is below the horizontal it is sometimes more convenient to take the y axis vertically downward: thus if a particle is projected with initial velocity u at an angle α below the horizontal the acceleration of the particle is still constant and equal to g vertically downward.

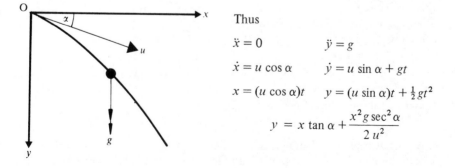

Thus

$$\ddot{x} = 0 \qquad\qquad \ddot{y} = g$$

$$\dot{x} = u \cos \alpha \qquad \dot{y} = u \sin \alpha + gt$$

$$x = (u \cos \alpha)t \qquad y = (u \sin \alpha)t + \tfrac{1}{2} g t^2$$

$$y = x \tan \alpha + \frac{x^2 g \sec^2 \alpha}{2 u^2}$$

PROBLEM SOLVING

Problems involving the velocity: equations (1) and (2) give the components of velocity as functions of time, thus if the direction of motion is required at a given time it can be found using $\dfrac{\dot{y}}{\dot{x}}$. If, however, the direction of motion at a given position is involved it can be found from equation (5) by finding $\dfrac{dy}{dx}$ without introducing time.

Problems involving position: if position and time are involved then equations (3) and (4) are useful as these give the co-ordinates as a function of time. Equation (5) relates the co-ordinates without involving time: this equation is very useful in solving a problem where time is not a factor to be taken into consideration.

EXAMPLES 10a

1) A particle is projected with a speed of $20\ \mathrm{ms}^{-1}$ and reaches its greatest height above the point of projection $\frac{1}{3}$ of a second later. Find the angle of projection.

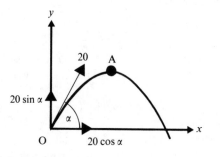

When the particle is at A (its greatest height above O) it is travelling horizontally
i.e. $\dot{y} = 0$

This occurs when $\quad t = \frac{1}{3}$
At any time t, $\quad \dot{y} = 20 \sin \alpha - gt$
Therefore $\quad\quad 0 = 20 \sin \alpha - 9.8 \times \frac{1}{3}$

$$\sin \alpha = \frac{9.8}{60} = 0.1633$$

$$\alpha = 9°\,24'$$

Therefore the angle of projection is $9°\,24'$.

2) A particle is projected from a point which is 2 m above ground level with a velocity of $40\ \mathrm{ms}^{-1}$ at an angle of $45°$ to the horizontal. Find its horizontal distance from the point of projection when it hits the ground.

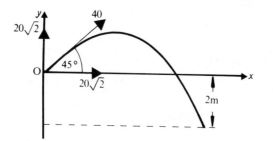

Using the equation of the path: $y = x \tan \alpha - \dfrac{gx^2 \sec^2 \alpha}{2u^2}$

$$y = x - \dfrac{gx^2}{1600}$$

We require the value of x when $y = -2$

$$-2 = x - \dfrac{gx^2}{1600}$$

$$49\,x^2 - 8000\,x - 16000 = 0$$

$$x = 165$$

Therefore the horizontal distance of the particle from O is 165 m when it hits the ground.

3) A stone is thrown from the top of a cliff 70 m high at an angle of 30° below the horizontal and hits the sea 20 m from the bottom of the cliff. Find the initial speed of the stone and the direction in which it is moving when it hits the sea.

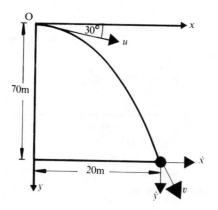

Let the initial speed be u ms^{-1}

Using the equation of the path: $y = x \tan 30° + \dfrac{x^2 g}{2u^2} \sec^2 30°$ (1)

The stone hits the sea when $y = 70$ and $x = 20$

Therefore $70 = \dfrac{20}{\sqrt{3}} + \dfrac{400 \times 9.8}{2\,u^2} \times \dfrac{4}{3}$

$u^2 = 44.7$

$u = 6.7$

Therefore the initial speed of the stone is 6.7 ms^{-1}.
As the stone moves in the direction of the tangent to the path at any time, from equation (1)

$$\frac{dy}{dx} = \tan 30° + \frac{x\,g \sec^2 30°}{u^2}$$

When the stone hits the sea, $x = 20$

Therefore $\dfrac{dy}{dx} = \dfrac{1}{\sqrt{3}} + \dfrac{20 \times 9.8 \times 4}{44.7 \times 3}$

$= 6.42$

Therefore the stone hits the sea at arctan 6.42 to the horizontal.

4) A particle is projected from a point O with an initial velocity of 60 ms^{-1} at an angle 30° to the horizontal. At the same instant a second particle is projected in the opposite direction with initial speed 50 ms^{-1} from a point level with O and 100 m from O. Find the angle of projection of the second particle if they collide and the time at which this occurs.

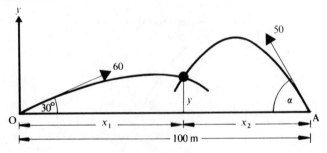

If the particles collide they must be at the *same point* at the *same time*: (and as time is an important consideration we do not use the equation of the path)

i.e. $\left. \begin{aligned} x_1 &= (60 \cos 30°)\,t \\ x_2 &= (50 \cos \alpha)\,t \end{aligned} \right\}$ $x_1 + x_2 = 100$:

therefore $100 = t(30\sqrt{3} + 50 \cos \alpha)$ (1)

$$y = 60 \sin 30°t - \tfrac{1}{2}gt^2 \atop = 50 \sin \alpha t - \tfrac{1}{2}gt^2 \Bigg\} \quad \text{therefore } 30 = 50 \sin \alpha \qquad (2)$$

From equation (2): $\sin \alpha = \tfrac{3}{5}$

Therefore the angle of projection of the second particle is $36°52'$. Substituting into equation (1):

$$100 = t(30\sqrt{3} + 40)$$

$$t = 1.09$$

Therefore the particles collide 1.09 s after projection.

5) A particle is projected from a point O with initial velocity vector $3\mathbf{i} + 4\mathbf{j}$. Find vector expressions for the velocity and position of the projectile at time t.

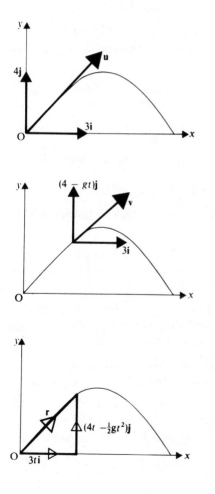

The initial horizontal component of velocity is 3: i.e. $u \cos \alpha = 3$.

The initial vertical component of velocity is 4: i.e. $u \sin \alpha = 4$.

$\therefore$ at time t, the horizontal component of velocity is $3\mathbf{i}$ $\qquad (\dot{x} = u \cos \alpha)$

and the vertical component of velocity is $(4 - gt)\mathbf{j}$ $\qquad (\dot{y} = u \sin \alpha - gt)$

$$\therefore \quad \mathbf{v} = 3\mathbf{i} + (4 - gt)\mathbf{j}$$

Similarly at time t the horizontal component of displacement is $3t\mathbf{i}$
$$(x = ut \cos \alpha)$$

and the vertical component of displacement is $(4t - \tfrac{1}{2}gt^2)\mathbf{j}$
$$(y = ut \sin \alpha - \tfrac{1}{2}gt^2)$$

$$\therefore \quad \mathbf{r} = 3t\mathbf{i} + (4t - \tfrac{1}{2}gt^2)\mathbf{j}$$

In general if a particle is projected with initial velocity $a\mathbf{i} + b\mathbf{j}$, then its velocity at any time t can be expressed in the form

$$\mathbf{v} = a\mathbf{i} + (b - gt)\mathbf{j}$$

and its position at any time t can be expressed in the form

$$\mathbf{r} = at\mathbf{i} + (bt - \tfrac{1}{2}gt^2)\mathbf{j}.$$

Any problem on projectiles may be solved using vector methods but in general it is unwise to do so unless the problem is phrased in vector terms.

EXERCISE 10a

1) A particle is projected with a velocity of 40 ms^{-1} at an angle of $60°$ to the horizontal. Find its velocity $1\frac{1}{2}$ seconds later.

2) A particle is projected with a velocity of 10 ms^{-1} at an angle of $30°$ to the horizontal. Find its distance from the point of projection $\frac{1}{2}$ second later.

3) A particle is projected with a velocity of 30 ms^{-1} at an angle $\arctan \frac{3}{4}$ to the horizontal. It hits the ground at a point which is level with its point of projection. Find the time for which it is in the air.

4) A particle is projected from a point on level ground with a velocity of 20 ms^{-1} and hits the ground $\frac{2}{3}$ of a second later. Find the angle of projection.

5) A particle is projected with a velocity of 10 ms^{-1} at an angle of $45°$ to the horizontal. It hits the ground at a point which is 3 m below its point of projection. Find the time for which it is in the air and the horizontal distance covered by the particle in this time.

6) A ball is thrown from ground level with a velocity of 15 ms^{-1} at an angle of $60°$ to the horizontal. Find when the ball hits the ground and the time at which it reaches its greatest height above the point of projection.

7) A particle is projected with a velocity of 70 ms^{-1} at an angle of $20°$ to the horizontal. Find the greatest height reached by the particle above its point of projection.

8) A ball is thrown with a velocity of 15 ms^{-1} at an angle of $30°$ to the horizontal from a point which is 1.5 m above ground level. Find when the ball hits the ground and the direction in which it is moving just before it hits the ground.

9) A ball is thrown from ground level so that it just clears a wall 3 m high when it is moving horizontally. If the initial speed of the ball is 20 ms^{-1}, find the angle of projection.

10) A particle is projected at an angle of $30°$ to the horizontal and 2 seconds later is moving in the direction $\arctan (\frac{1}{4})$ to the horizontal. Find its initial speed.

11) In question 10, if the direction of motion is $\arctan (-\frac{1}{4})$ 2 seconds after projection, what is the initial speed? Also what is the significance of $\arctan (-\frac{1}{4})$?

12) A particle is projected from ground level with an initial velocity of 35 ms^{-1} at an angle of arctan $\frac{3}{4}$ to the horizontal. Find the time for which the particle is more than 20 m above the ground.

13) A particle is projected from a point O which is 100 m above ground level. The initial velocity is 40 ms^{-1} horizontally. Find the time at which the particle hits the ground and the horizontal distance of this point from the point of projection.

14) A particle is projected from a point O at an angle of $-30°$. ($30°$ below the horizontal). If the particle hits the ground, which is 50 m below the level of O, 2 seconds later find the initial speed of the particle.

15) A particle is projected from a point O with initial velocity vector $\mathbf{i} + 2\mathbf{j}$. Find the velocity vector and position vector of the particle (a) after t seconds, (b) after $1\frac{1}{2}$ seconds. (Take g as 10 ms^{-2}).

16) A particle is projected from a point O and $1\frac{1}{2}$ seconds later it passes through the point whose position vector is $4\mathbf{i} + \mathbf{j}$. Find the initial velocity vector of the particle. (Take g as 10 ms^{-2}).

17) A particle is projected from a point O with initial velocity vector $3\mathbf{i} - \mathbf{j}$. Find the direction in which it is moving 2 seconds later. Find also the cartesian equation of its path. (Take g as 10 ms^{-2})

18) A particle is projected from a point O with velocity vector $20\mathbf{i} + 30\mathbf{j}$. Two seconds later a second particle is projected from O with velocity vector $60\mathbf{i} + 50\mathbf{j}$. Prove that the particles collide one second after the projection of the second particle. (Take g as 10 ms^{-2}).

19) Two particles are projected simultaneously from a point O in the same vertical plane with angles of projection $30°$ and $60°$ and with the same initial speed of $2\sqrt{3} \text{ ms}^{-1}$. Find the positions of the particles t seconds after projection and hence find the distance between them when $t = 2$.

20) A and B are two points on level ground, 60 m apart. A particle is projected from A towards B with initial velocity 30 ms^{-1} at $45°$ to the horizontal. At the same instant a particle is projected from B towards A with the same initial velocity. Find when the particles collide and the height above the level of AB at which they collide. (Take g as 10 ms^{-2})

21) A particle is projected from a point O with an initial velocity of 20 ms^{-1} and at an angle of arctan $\frac{3}{4}$ to the horizontal. Two seconds later a second particle is projected from O and it collides with the first particle 1 second after leaving O. Find the initial velocity of the second particle. (Take $g = 10 \text{ ms}^{-2}$).

22) A particle is projected from a point O with an initial velocity of 21 ms^{-1} at an angle of arctan $\frac{4}{3}$ to the horizontal and one second later another particle is projected from O with an initial velocity of 31.5 ms^{-1} at an angle arctan $\frac{3}{4}$ to the

horizontal. Prove that the particles collide and find when this occurs. Find also the direction in which each particle is moving when they collide.

PARTICULAR PROPERTIES OF PARABOLIC FLIGHT

Certain information about projectiles is required frequently enough to justify obtaining this in general terms.

Consider a particle which is projected from a point O on level ground with a velocity u at an angle α to the horizontal, reaching ground level again at a point A.

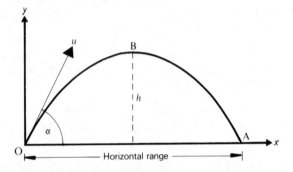

1. **Time of flight:** this is the time taken for the particle to travel along its path from O to A.

At any time t, $$y = (u \sin \alpha)t - \tfrac{1}{2}gt^2$$

When the particle is at **A**, $y = 0$

Therefore $(u \sin \alpha)t - \tfrac{1}{2}gt^2 = 0$

$$t = 0 \text{ or } t = \frac{2u \sin \alpha}{g}$$

Therefore the time of flight is $\dfrac{2u \sin \alpha}{g}$

2. **Greatest height:** this is h in the diagram.

At any time t, $$\dot{y} = u \sin \alpha - gt$$

When the particle is at **B**, it is moving horizontally: i.e. $\dot{y} = 0$

$$u \sin \alpha - gt = 0$$

$$t = \frac{u \sin \alpha}{g} \quad \text{(Note: this is half the total time of flight)}$$

Substituting into $y = u \sin \alpha t - \tfrac{1}{2}gt^2$

$$h = \frac{u^2 \sin^2 \alpha}{g} - \frac{1}{2} \cdot \frac{u^2 \sin^2 \alpha}{g}$$

Therefore $$h = \frac{u^2 \sin^2 \alpha}{2g}$$

3. **Horizontal range:** this is the distance from the initial position to the final position on a horizontal plane through the point of projection, i.e. OA.

At any time t, $\qquad x = ut \cos \alpha$

When $\qquad t = \dfrac{2 u \sin \alpha}{g}$ (time of flight)

$$x = \frac{2 u^2 \sin \alpha \cos \alpha}{g} = \frac{u^2 \sin 2\alpha}{g}$$

Therefore the range is $\dfrac{u^2 \sin 2\alpha}{g}$

4. **Maximum horizontal range:**

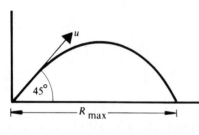

For a given value of u, the horizontal range is maximum when

$$\frac{u^2 \sin 2\alpha}{g} \text{ is maximum.}$$

This occurs when $\sin 2\alpha = 1$

$$\text{i.e. } \alpha = 45°$$

Therefore the maximum horizontal range is $\dfrac{u^2}{g}$ *and occurs when the angle of projection is 45°.*

5. **Angle of projection required to achieve a given horizontal range R_0 $(R_0 < R_{max})$**

For a given value of u, the horizontal range $R_0 = \dfrac{u^2 \sin 2\alpha}{g}$

Therefore $\sin 2\alpha = \dfrac{R_0 g}{u^2}$

Therefore $2\alpha = \arcsin\left(\dfrac{R_0 g}{u^2}\right)$ or $180° - \arcsin\left(\dfrac{R_0 g}{u^2}\right)$

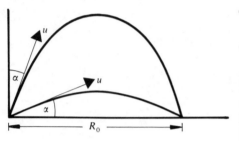

Therefore there are two values of α less than $90°$. If α_1 and α_2 are these two solutions

$$\alpha_1 = \tfrac{1}{2}\arcsin\left(\frac{R_0 g}{u^2}\right)$$

$$\alpha_2 = 90° - \tfrac{1}{2}\arcsin\left(\frac{R_0 g}{u^2}\right)$$

$$= 90° - \alpha_1$$

Thus there are two angles of projection which with initial speed u will give a horizontal range R_0 and they are equally inclined to the horizontal and vertical through the point of projection. The smaller angle of projection gives the larger horizontal component of velocity: and thus a shorter time of flight.

6. Equation of the path:

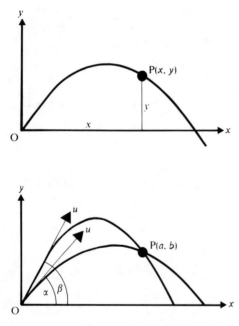

At any time t, if the particle is at the point $\mathrm{P}(x, y)$ on its path:

$$x = (u\cos\alpha)t,$$

$$y = (u\sin\alpha)t - \tfrac{1}{2}gt^2$$

Eliminating t from these two equations:

$$y = x\tan\alpha - \frac{x^2 g}{2u^2}\sec^2\alpha$$

If the path of a projectile has to pass through one particular point (a, b), then substituting into the equation of the path:

$$b = a\tan\alpha - \frac{a^2 g}{2u^2}\sec^2\alpha$$

Writing $\sec^2\alpha$ as $1 + \tan^2\alpha$ and rearranging

$$\frac{a^2 g}{2u^2}\tan^2\alpha - a\tan\alpha + \left(b + \frac{a^2 g}{2u^2}\right) = 0$$

This is a quadratic equation in $\tan\alpha$ so, provided it has two different positive roots, there are two angles of projection for which the path of the projectile will pass through a given point, with a given speed of projection.

EXAMPLES 10b

(g is taken as 10 ms^{-2} unless otherwise specified)

1) A gun has a muzzle velocity of 200 ms^{-1} (i.e. a shell leaves the gun with an initial speed of 200 ms^{-1}). Find the horizontal range of the gun when the angle of projection is $30°$. Find also the maximum horizontal range of the gun.

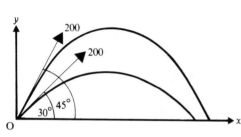

The horizontal range is $\dfrac{u^2 \sin 2\alpha}{g}$

when $\alpha = 30°$, range $= \dfrac{(200)^2 \sin 60°}{g}$

$$= 3460 \text{ m}$$

The maximum horizontal range occurs when $\alpha = 45°$

Therefore the maximum range is $\dfrac{u^2}{g}$

$$= \frac{(200)^2}{10} = 4000 \text{ m}$$

Therefore the horizontal range of the gun is 3460 m when the angle of projection is $30°$ and the maximum horizontal range is 4000 m.

2) A particle is projected from a point O with an initial speed of 30 ms^{-1} to pass through a point which is 40 m from O horizontally and 10 m above O. Show that there are two angles of projection for which this is possible. If these angles are α and β show that $\tan(\alpha + \beta) = -4$

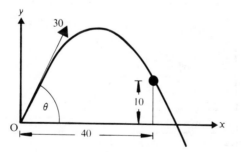

Let the angle of projection of the particle be θ

The path of the particle has to pass through the point $x = 40$

$$y = 10$$

The equation of the path of any projectile is $\qquad y = x \tan \alpha - \dfrac{x^2 g}{2u^2} \sec^2 \alpha$

Therefore the equation of the path of this projectile is $y = x \tan \theta - \dfrac{x^2}{180} \sec^2 \theta$

The point (40, 10) lies on this path

Therefore $\qquad\qquad\qquad\qquad\qquad\qquad\qquad\qquad 10 = 40 \tan \theta - \dfrac{80}{9} \sec^2 \theta$

$$9 = 36 \tan \theta - 8 \sec^2 \theta$$

$$8 \tan^2 \theta - 36 \tan \theta + 17 = 0 \qquad\qquad (1)$$

This is a quadratic equation in $\tan \theta$ with two positive roots. Therefore there are two values of $\theta < 90°$. Therefore there are two possible angles of projection. If these angles are α and β, $\tan \alpha$ and $\tan \beta$ are the roots of equation (1)

Now, $\qquad\qquad\qquad \tan(\alpha + \beta) = \dfrac{\tan \alpha + \tan \beta}{1 - \tan \alpha \tan \beta}$

From equation (1), $\tan \alpha + \tan \beta = \dfrac{36}{8} = \dfrac{9}{2}$

$$\tan \alpha \tan \beta = \dfrac{17}{8}$$

Therefore $\qquad\qquad\qquad \tan(\alpha + \beta) = \dfrac{\dfrac{9}{2}}{1 - \dfrac{17}{8}} = -4$

3) An arrow which has an initial speed of 40 ms^{-1} is aimed at a target which is level with it at a distance of 100 m from the point of projection. Find the minimum time of flight for the arrow to hit the target.

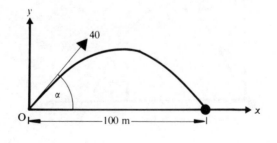

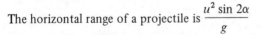

The horizontal range of a projectile is $\dfrac{u^2 \sin 2\alpha}{g}$

When the horizontal range is 100 m, $100 = 160 \sin 2\alpha$

$$\sin 2\alpha = \tfrac{5}{8}$$

Therefore $\alpha = 19°20'$ or $\alpha = 70°40'$.

Therefore there are two possible angles of projection for the arrow to hit the target.

The time of flight is $\dfrac{2u \sin \alpha}{g} = 8 \sin \alpha$

This is least when $\sin \alpha$ is least: i.e. when $\alpha = 19°20'$

Therefore the minimum time of flight is $8 \times 0.3308 \text{ s} = 2.6 \text{ s}$.

4) In example 3, if the target is a strip which is 3.75 m high, find the values between which the angle of projection must lie so that the arrow hits the target.

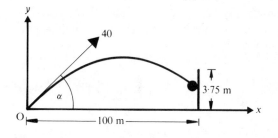

The equation of the path of the arrow is $y = 10^2 \tan \alpha - \dfrac{10^4 \sec^2 \alpha}{320}$

For the arrow to hit the target, $0 \leqslant y \leqslant 3.75$ when $x = 100$

i.e. $0 \leqslant 100 \tan \alpha - \dfrac{1000}{32} \sec^2 \alpha \leqslant 3.75$

$\quad 0 \leqslant 800 \tan \alpha - 250 \sec^2\alpha \leqslant 30$

If $y \leqslant 3.75$ $\qquad\qquad 800 \tan \alpha - 250 \sec^2\alpha \leqslant 30$

$\qquad\qquad\qquad\qquad 25 \tan^2\alpha - 80 \tan \alpha + 28 \geqslant 0$

$\qquad\qquad\qquad\qquad (25 \tan \alpha - 14)(5 \tan \alpha - 2) \geqslant 0$

$\qquad\qquad\qquad\qquad \tan \alpha \leqslant \tfrac{2}{5} \text{ or } \tan \alpha \geqslant \tfrac{14}{5}$

$\qquad\qquad\qquad\qquad \alpha \leqslant 21°48' \text{ or } \alpha \geqslant 70°21'$

If $y \geqslant 0$: $\qquad\qquad\quad 800 \tan^2\alpha - 250 \sec^2\alpha \geqslant 0$

$\qquad\qquad\qquad\qquad 5 \tan^2\alpha - 16 \tan \alpha + 5 \leqslant 0$

If $y = 0$, the two possible angles of projection are $19°20'$ and $70°40'$ (from example 3). Therefore $y \geqslant 0$, $19°20' \leqslant \alpha \leqslant 70°40'$.

Therefore to hit the target $19°20' \leqslant \alpha \leqslant 21°48'$

or $\qquad\qquad\qquad\qquad 70°21' \leqslant \alpha \leqslant 70°40'$.

5) A particle is projected from a point O on level ground towards a smooth vertical wall which is 50 m away from O. The particle hits the wall when travelling horizontally. If the coefficient of restitution between the particle and the wall is $\frac{1}{3}$ find the distance from O of the point where the particle hits the ground.

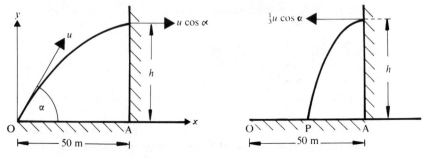

As the particle hits the wall directly, its speed the instant after hitting the wall is $\frac{1}{3}u \cos \alpha$ horizontally. (Newton's experimental Law)

> The time taken to reach the highest point (which is where the particle hits the wall) is $\dfrac{u \sin \alpha}{g}$
>
> The time taken to reach ground level from the greatest height, h, is $\sqrt{\dfrac{2h}{g}}$.
> (Using $v = u + at$ vertically)
>
> But $h = \dfrac{u^2 \sin^2 \alpha}{2g}$, therefore the time to reach ground level from the greatest height is $\dfrac{u \sin \alpha}{g}$
>
> i.e. time 'up' to greatest height and time 'down' from greatest height are the same.

If the particle hits the ground again at P then the time taken to cover the horizontal distance OA is equal to the time taken to cover the horizontal distance AP.

Therefore $\dfrac{AP}{50} = \dfrac{\frac{1}{3}u \cos \alpha}{u \cos \alpha}$

$AP = \frac{1}{3} \times 50 \, m$

$= 16.7 \, m$

Therefore the particle hits the ground again 33.3 m from O.

EXERCISE 10b

(Take g as $10 \, ms^{-2}$)

1) A gun has a maximum range of 200 m on the horizontal. Find the velocity of a shell as it leaves the muzzle of the gun.

2) The maximum range of a gun is 150 m. What is the muzzle velocity and what is the greatest height reached by the shot?

3) A particle is projected from a point O to pass through a point level with O and 50 m from O. Find the minimum velocity of projection for this to be possible and the greatest height reached with this velocity.

4) A particle is projected at 20° to the horizontal and just clears a wall which is 10 m high and 30 m from the point of projection. Find the initial speed of the particle.

5) A ball is thrown with an initial velocity of 30 ms^{-1} at 30° to the horizontal. It just clears a wall, the foot of which is 25 m from the point of projection. Find the height of the wall.

6) A particle is projected from a point O with an initial speed of 30 ms^{-1} to hit a target which is level with O and 60 m from O. Show that there are two possible angles of projection for which this is possible and find them.

7) A particle is projected from a point O with an initial speed of 50 ms^{-1}. The particle just clears a wall which is 50 m high and 100 m horizontally from O. Find the two possible angles of projection of the particle.

8) A particle is projected with an initial speed of 60 ms^{-1} towards a wall which is 100 m horizontally from the point of projection and 20 m high. Find the least angle of projection for which the particle will pass over the wall.

9) A particle is projected with an initial speed u to pass through a point which is $5u$ horizontally and u vertically from the point of projection. Show that if there are two angles of projection for which this is possible $u^2 > 20(u + 125)$. Find the value of u for which there is only one angle of projection.

10) A gun with a muzzle velocity of 100 ms^{-1} is fired from the floor of a tunnel which is 4 m high. Find the maximum angle of projection possible if a bullet is not to hit the roof, and the range of the gun with this angle of projection.

11) A gun is fired to hit a target level with it but 1000 m away. If the muzzle velocity of the gun is 200 ms^{-1} and the shell it fires has to pass over a tree 15 m high and 50 m from the gun, find the angle of projection necessary.

12) Show that, with an initial speed u, the maximum horizontal distance that a particle can travel from its point of projection is twice the maximum height it can reach above the point of projection.

13) A particle is projected from a point O with an angle of projection α. Find α if the horizontal range of the particle is five times the greatest height reached by it.

14) A particle is projected inside a tunnel which is 2 m high. If the initial speed is u show that the maximum range inside the tunnel is $4\sqrt{\dfrac{u^2 - 4g}{g}}$.

15) A particle is projected from a point O on level ground towards a smooth vertical wall which is 20 m from O. The particle hits the wall when travelling horizontally. If the speed of projection is 25 ms^{-1} find the two possible angles of projection. If the coefficient of restitution between the particle and the wall is $\frac{1}{2}$, find the distance from the foot of wall of the point where the particle hits the ground.

16) A particle is projected from a point O on level ground towards a smooth vertical wall 30 m from O. The particle hits the wall when travelling horizontally with a speed of 15 ms^{-1}. Find the initial velocity of the particle.
Show that the time taken by the particle to reach the ground again is independent of the coefficient of restitution between the particle and the wall.

17) A bomb is to be dropped from an aeroplane which is flying steadily at 1000 m with a speed of 200 ms^{-1}. How far (horizontally) should the plane be from the target before it releases the bomb and how long will it take the bomb to hit the target which is on the ground.

18) Two particles P and Q are fired simultaneously from two points A and B on level ground with speeds of projection u and $2u$ respectively. If AB is the maximum range of P, and the particles collide when both are moving horizontally, find the angle of projection of Q.

19) Two particles are projected simultaneously from two points A and B on level ground and a distance of 150 m apart. The first particle is projected vertically upwards from A with an initial speed of u ms^{-1} and the second particle is projected from B towards A with an angle of projection α. If the particles collide when they are both at their greatest height above the level of AB, prove that

$$\tan \alpha = \frac{u^2}{150 g}.$$

20) Two particles are projected simultaneously from a point O with the same initial speed but with angles of elevation α and $90° - \alpha$. Prove that the range of the two particles is the same and show that at any time during their flight the line joining them is inclined at $45°$ to the horizontal.

MULTIPLE CHOICE EXERCISE 10
Instructions for answering these questions are given on page (xii).

TYPE I

1) A ball is thrown with a speed of 20 ms^{-1} at an angle arctan $\frac{3}{4}$ to the horizontal. Its horizontal component of velocity two seconds later is:
(a) 4 ms^{-1} (b) 32 ms^{-1} (c) 0   (d) 12 ms^{-1} (e) 16 ms^{-1}.

2) A projectile is given an initial velocity of $i - 2j$. Its horizontal component of velocity three seconds later is:
(a) $\sqrt{5}$ ms^{-1} (b) -2 ms^{-1} (c) 1 ms^{-1} (d) -1 ms^{-1} (e) -29 ms^{-1}.

3) A projectile is thrown from a point which is 1 m above ground level. Taking Oy vertically upward it hits the ground when:

(a) $\dot{x} = 0$ (b) $y = -1$ (c) $y = 1$ (d) $\dot{y} = 0$ (e) $\dot{y} = 1$.

4) A projectile is thrown from ground level with an initial velocity $4\mathbf{i} + 3\mathbf{j}$. It reaches its greatest height above ground level after:

(a) 0.24 s   (b) 0.3 s   (c) 0.18 s   (d) 3 s   (e) 5 s.

5) A projectile is thrown with initial speed of 30 ms^{-1}. Its maximum horizontal range is:

(a) 900 m   (b) 30 m   (c) 300 m   (d) 90 m   (e) 9 m.

6) A projectile is given an initial velocity of $\mathbf{i} + 2\mathbf{j}$. The cartesian equation of its path is:

(a) $y = 2x - 5x^2$ (b) $4y = 2x - 5x^2$ (c) $3y = 6x - 25x^2$
(d) $y = 2x + 5x^2$ (e) $4y = 2x + 5x^2$.

7) A stone is thrown from a height of 10 m above the ground with an initial velocity of 10 ms^{-1} at $30°$ below the horizontal. Taking Oy vertically downward, it hits the ground when:

(a) $\dot{y} = 5$ (b) $\dot{y} = -5$ (c) $\dot{y} = 15$ (d) $\dot{y} = -15$ (e) $\dot{y} = 0$.

TYPE II

8) A particle is projected from ground level. Oy is taken vertically upward. When the particle reaches its greatest height above ground level:

(a) $\ddot{y} = -g$ (b) $\dot{y} = 0$ (c) $\dot{x} = 0$.

9) A projectile is fired with initial speed u so as to achieve the maximum horizontal range.

(a) The equation of its path is $y = x - \dfrac{10x^2}{u^2}$

(b) The horizontal component of its velocity is $\dfrac{u}{2}$

(c) The angle of projection is $45°$.

10) A particle is projected with initial speed u at an angle α to the horizontal. Its horizontal range is R.

(a) The particle would have the same horizontal range if the angle of projection was $90° - \alpha$

(b) The time of flight is $\dfrac{R}{u \cos \alpha}$

(c) The particle reaches a maximum height of $\dfrac{u^2 \sin^2 \alpha}{2g}$ above its point of projection.

11) A projectile is projected from a point O on level ground with initial velocity u at $45°$ to the horizontal. When it hits the ground:

(a) $y = 0$

(b) It has been in the air for a time $\dfrac{u\sqrt{2}}{10}$

(c) $x = 0$.

TYPE IV

12) A particle is projected from a point O on level ground towards a wall which it hits directly. Find how far from O the particle hits the ground again.
(a) The coefficient of restitution between the particle and the wall is $\frac{1}{3}$.
(b) The horizontal component of initial velocity is $10\,\text{ms}^{-1}$.
(c) The distance of the wall from O is $30\,\text{m}$.

13) A particle is projected from a point O to hit a target which is level with O. Find the two possible angles of projection.
(a) The target is $100\,\text{m}$ from O.
(b) The mass of the projectile is $0.005\,\text{kg}$.
(c) The initial speed of the projectile is $35\,\text{ms}^{-1}$.

14) A particle is projected towards a wall which it hits directly. Find the time taken by the particle to reach ground level again.
(a) The wall is $20\,\text{m}$ from the point of projection.
(b) The initial speed of the projectile is $30\,\text{ms}^{-1}$.
(c) The coefficient of restitution between particle and wall is $\frac{1}{2}$.

15) A particle is projected so that it just clears a wall. Find the initial velocity of the projectile.
(a) The wall is $5\,\text{m}$ high.
(b) The foot of the wall is $30\,\text{m}$ horizontally from the point of projection.
(c) The particle is moving at an angle of $\arctan \frac{1}{2}$ to the downward vertical as it passes over the wall.

16) Two particles A and B are fired simultaneously towards each other from two points on level ground. Determine whether the particles collide.
(a) The two points of projection are $50\,\text{m}$ apart.
(b) The initial speed of A is $15\,\text{ms}^{-1}$.
(c) The initial speed of B is $30\,\text{ms}^{-1}$.

17) A stone is thrown into the sea from the top of a cliff. Find how far from the base of the cliff the stone hits the sea.
(a) The stone is in the air for 1.5 seconds.
(b) The cliff is $20\,\text{m}$ high.
(c) The initial horizontal component of velocity is $10\,\text{ms}^{-1}$.

MISCELLANEOUS EXERCISE 10

1) A tile slides down a roof inclined at $20°$ to the horizontal starting $3\,\text{m}$ from

the edge of the roof. Assuming that the roof is smooth find the horizontal distance from the edge of the roof that the tile hits the ground if the edge of the roof is 8 m above ground level.

2) Two particles are projected simultaneously from the same point with angles of projection α and β and initial speeds u and v. Show that at any time during their flight the line joining them is inclined at $\arctan \left(\dfrac{u \sin \alpha - v \sin \beta}{u \cos \alpha - v \cos \beta} \right)$ to the horizontal.

3) At what point during its flight is the speed of a projectile a minimum? A particle is projected from a point O on a horizontal plane with an angle of projection α. Show that the ratio of the greatest speed to the least speed during the flight is $\dfrac{1}{\cos \alpha}$.

4) A ball has to be thrown over a small flat-roofed building which is 3 m high and 2 m wide. If the ball is thrown from ground level, find the minimum velocity of projection necessary and the distance of the point of projection from the nearest wall of the building.

5) A particle is projected from a point O with initial speed u to pass through a point which is at a horizontal distance a from O and a distance b vertically above the level of O. Show that there are two possible angles of projection. If these angles are α_1 and α_2 prove that $\tan (\alpha_1 + \alpha_2) = -(a/b)$.

6) A particle is projected with speed u ms^{-1} at an angle α to the horizontal. Find the direction in which it is moving after t sec. A particle is projected from a point O and after t sec passes through a point P travelling in a direction perpendicular to the direction of projection. Prove that $OP = \frac{1}{2}gt^2$.   (AEB)

7) A stone thrown upwards from the top of a vertical cliff 56 m high falls into the sea 4 seconds later, 32 m from the foot of the cliff. Find the speed and direction of projection. (The stone moves in a vertical plane perpendicular to the cliff). A second stone is thrown at the same time, in the same vertical plane, at the same speed and at the same angle to the horizontal, but downwards. Find how long it will take to reach the sea and the distance between the points of entry of the stones into the water. (Take g to be $10 \, \text{m/s}^2$).   (U of L)

8) A particle is to be projected under gravity from O, the centre of a horizontal circle of radius 70 m. Calculate the minimum velocity of projection of the particle if its trajectory is to pass through the circumference of the circle. Another particle is projected from O with a velocity of 108 km/h at an angle of 40° to the horizontal. This particle just clears the top of a vertical post on the circumference of the circle. Find, to the nearest tenth of a metre, the height of the post. (Take g as $9.81 \, \text{m/s}^2$).   (U of L)

9) A particle is projected from a point on the horizontal ground with velocity V

and angle of elevation α. Prove that the greatest height reached above the ground

is $\dfrac{V^2}{2g} \sin^2 \alpha$.

A bowler bowls a ball at the wicket which is 20 metres away from him measured horizontally. The ball leaves his hand 2 metres above the ground and without hitting the ground, passes through a point which is vertically above the wicket and $\frac{3}{4}$ metre vertically above the ground. The highest point reached by the ball is 3 metres above the ground. Find the angle of elevation at which the ball is projected. Show that the angle made with the horizontal by the direction of motion of the ball when it passes over the wicket is arctan $\frac{3}{8}$.

Find the time between the instant when the ball leaves the bowler's hand and the instant when it passes over the wicket.   (Cambridge)

10) A particle is projected under gravity with speed V from the point O, the angle of projection being α above the horizontal. The particle rises to a vertical height H above O and its range on the horizontal plane through O is R. Prove that

(i) $H = \dfrac{V^2}{2g} \sin^2 \alpha$ (ii) $R = \dfrac{V^2}{g} \sin 2\alpha$

Deduce that $16 H^2 - 8 R_0 H + R^2 = 0$ where R_0 is the maximum range for the given speed of projection.

Given that $R_0 = 200$ m and $R = 192$ m, find the two possible values of H, and the corresponding values of α.   (JMB)

11) A particle is projected with speed u at an elevation α to the horizontal. Calculate the greatest height reached and the horizontal range.

The maximum horizontal range a particle can achieve with an initial speed u is R. If a particle projected with speed u has a horizontal range $\frac{2}{3} R$, calculate the two possible angles of projection. Show that the difference in the maximum heights attained with these angles of projection is $\frac{2}{5} R$.   (AEB)

12) A particle is projected from the origin O with velocity V at an elevation θ to the horizontal. Show that its height y above O when it has travelled a distance x horizontally is given by $y = x \tan \theta - \dfrac{gx^2 \sec^2 \theta}{2 V^2}$.

A ball thrown from O with speed 1400 cm/s is caught at a point P, which is 1000 cm horizontally from O and 187.5 cm above the level of O. Find the two possible angles of projection. If the ball is thrown from O with the same initial speed to pass through a point 562.5 cm vertically above P, show that there is only one possible angle of projection.   (U of L)

13) A particle is projected with speed V at an angle α to the horizontal. Show that its greatest height above the point of projection during its flight is $(V^2 \sin^2 \alpha)/(2g)$. A ball is projected from a point at a height a above horizontal ground, with speed V at an angle α to the horizontal. At the highest point of its flight it impinges normally on a vertical wall and rebounds. Show that the horizontal distance from the point of projection to the wall is

$(V^2 \sin \alpha \cos \alpha)/g$ and that the time taken by the ball to reach the ground after the impact is $\sqrt{(V^2 \sin^2 \alpha + 2ga)}/g$.   (U of L)

14) If a particle is projected with speed u at an angle of elevation α show that the horizontal range is $u^2 \sin 2\alpha/g$ and the maximum height attained is $u^2 \sin^2\alpha/(2g)$.

A golf ball is struck so that it leaves a point A on the ground with speed 49 m/s at an angle of elevation α. If it lands on the green which is the same level as A, the nearest and furthest points of which are 196 m and 245 m respectively from A, find the set of possible values of α. Find also the maximum height the ball can reach and still land on the green.

There is a tree at a horizontal distance 24.5 m from A and to reach the green the ball must pass over this tree. Find the maximum height of the tree if this ball can reach any point on the green.

(Assume the point A, the green and the base of the tree to be in the same horizontal plane).   (AEB)

15) A vertical mast OP is h ft. high and stands with O on the horizontal ground.

(a) Two particles are projected simultaneously from P in the same vertical plane with the same speed, but with different angles of projection. Show that the distance between the particles increases uniformly with time.

(b) If a particle is projected vertically upwards from O with velocity V and a second particle is projected at the same instant from P with velocity V and angle of projection θ show that they are at their shortest distance apart after time $h/(2V)$, and find this shortest distance.   (Cambridge)

16) Two projectiles are fired simultaneously from points P and Q on horizontal ground and collide head on when travelling horizontally. The first projectile is fired with speed v m/s at an angle of elevation α and the second is fired with speed $v/2$ m/s at an angle of elevation β. If $PQ = \dfrac{v^2 \sin \beta}{2g}$ show that:

(a) $2 \sin \alpha = \sin \beta$,

(b) $2 = 2 \cos \alpha + \cos \beta$.

Hence show that $\cos \alpha = \frac{7}{8}$.   (U of L)

17) Two boys stand on horizontal ground at a distance a apart. One throws a ball from a height $2h$ with velocity V and the other catches it at height h. If θ is the inclination above the horizontal at which the first boy throws the ball, show that $ga^2 \tan^2 \theta - 2V^2 a \tan \theta + ga^2 - 2V^2 h = 0$.

When $a = 2\sqrt{2}h$ and $V^2 = 2gh$, calculate:

(i) the value of θ,

(ii) the greatest height attained by the ball above the ground, in terms of h.   (AEB)

18) Two particles are projected with the same speed from the same point. The angles of projection are 2α and α and a time T elapses between the instants of projection. If the particles collide in flight, find the speed of projection in terms of T and α.

If the collision occurs when one of the particles is at its greatest height, show that α is given by $4\cos^4\alpha - \cos^2\alpha - 1 = 0$. (AEB)

19) Two equal particles are projected at the same instant from points A and B at the same level, the first from A towards B with velocity u at $45°$ above AB, and the second from B towards A with velocity v at $60°$ above BA. If the particles collide directly when each reaches its greatest height, find the ratio $v^2:u^2$ and prove that $u^2 = ga(3 - \sqrt{3})$, where a is the distance AB.
After the collision the first particle falls vertically. Show that the coefficient of restitution between the particles is $(\sqrt{3} - 1)(\sqrt{3} + 1)$. (J.M.B)

CHAPTER 11

MOTION IN A CIRCLE

TYPES OF ACCELERATION

A body has an acceleration whenever its velocity is not constant. Velocity is a vector quantity however and may change either in magnitude (i.e. speed) or in direction or both. In all cases a force must act on the body to produce an acceleration, the direction of the force determining the particular type of acceleration.

(a) A *change in speed* occurs when a force acts *in the direction of motion* of the body to which it is applied. Such a force cannot cause any change in the direction of the velocity.

(b) A *change in direction* at constant speed is caused by a force *perpendicular to the direction of motion* of the body. Such a force will push or pull the body off its previous course but will not affect the speed since there is no force component in the direction of motion.

(c) If both speed and direction of motion are to be changed a force with components both parallel and perpendicular to the direction of motion is required.

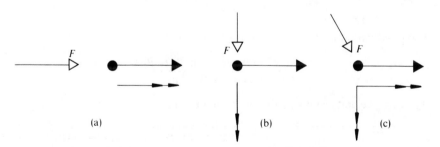

Type (a) Acceleration of this type has already been studied in Chapters 4 and 9 and needs no further analysis here.

Types (b) and (c) A body whose direction of motion is not constant traces out a curved path of some sort. The curve described depends upon the forces which are acting on the body.

In this chapter our analysis is concentrated on motion on one particular curve, the circle.

MOTION IN A CIRCLE WITH CONSTANT SPEED

Consider a particle P describing a circle, centre O and radius r, at constant speed v.

As there is no change in speed, no force component acts in the direction of motion, which is tangential at any instant.

A force must be acting on the particle however as the direction of motion is not constant.

This force must therefore act along the radius, producing a radial acceleration.

Magnitude of the Radial Acceleration

Suppose that the particle travels from P_1 to P_2 in time t and that angle P_1OP_2 is θ, then:

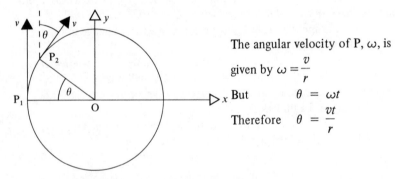

The angular velocity of P, ω, is

given by $\omega = \dfrac{v}{r}$

But $\qquad \theta = \omega t$

Therefore $\qquad \theta = \dfrac{vt}{r}$

An approximation to the acceleration at P_1 is given by

$$\frac{\text{increase in velocity from } P_1 \text{ to } P_2}{\text{time taken from } P_1 \text{ to } P_2}$$

Considering velocity components parallel to Ox and Oy we have:

	Parallel to Ox	Parallel to Oy
Velocity at P_1	0	v
Velocity at P_2	$v \sin \theta$	$v \cos \theta$
Increase in velocity	$v \sin \theta$	$v (\cos \theta - 1)$
Approximate Acceleration	$\dfrac{v \sin \theta}{t}$	$\dfrac{v (\cos \theta - 1)}{t}$

Now as $\theta \longrightarrow 0$ $\qquad$ $\sin \theta \longrightarrow \theta$ $\qquad$ and $\dfrac{v \sin \theta}{t} \longrightarrow \dfrac{v\theta}{t}$

$\qquad\qquad\qquad\qquad$ $\cos \theta \longrightarrow 1$ $\qquad$ and $\dfrac{v (\cos \theta - 1)}{t} \longrightarrow 0$

We deduce that the acceleration of P at any instant is $\dfrac{v^2}{r}$ towards the centre of the circle and is zero along the tangent.

(This confirms our argument that circular motion with constant speed involves an acceleration that is a rate of change of direction and which is perpendicular to the tangent).

THE RADIAL ACCELERATION IS **TOWARDS** THE CENTRE OF THE CIRCLE. TO PRODUCE IT A FORCE MUST BE ACTING **TOWARDS** THE CENTRE.

SUMMARY

A particle can describe a circle with constant speed only when it is acted upon by a *force of constant magnitude towards the centre* producing a radial acceleration whose constant magnitude is $\dfrac{v^2}{r}$ or $r\omega^2$.

EXAMPLES 11a

1) A particle of mass m is attached by a light inextensible string of length l to a fixed point A on a smooth horizontal table. If it is travelling with constant angular velocity ω in a circle what is the tension in the string and the reaction with the table?

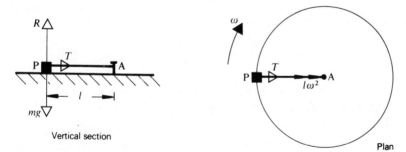

Vertical section $\qquad\qquad\qquad\qquad\qquad\qquad\qquad\qquad$ Plan

[In this problem the force acting on the particle towards the centre is T, the tension in the string. As the particle is travelling in a horizontal circle, its vertical acceleration is zero.]

Vertically $\qquad$ (zero acceleration) $\qquad\qquad\qquad$ $R = mg$ $\qquad\qquad$ (1)

Horizontally $\qquad$ (Force = mass × acceleration) $\qquad$ $T = ml\omega^2$ $\qquad\qquad$ (2)

Therefore $\qquad$ $\begin{cases} \text{Tension} = ml\omega^2 \\ \text{Reaction} = mg \end{cases}$

2) A car of mass M is turning a corner of radius r. The coefficient of friction between the wheels and the horizontal road surface is μ. What is the maximum speed at which the car can turn the corner without skidding?

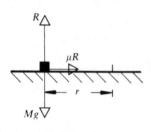

Vertical section

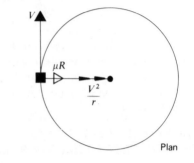

Plan

[At maximum speed the acceleration $\dfrac{v^2}{r}$ is also greatest and requires the maximum frictional force. Hence at maximum speed V, friction will be limiting.]

Vertically   (zero acceleration) $R = Mg$ (1)

Horizontally   (Force = mass × acceleration) $\mu R = \dfrac{MV^2}{r}$ (2)

Eliminating R, $\mu = \dfrac{MV^2}{rMg} = \dfrac{V^2}{rg}$

Therefore maximum speed $V = \sqrt{\mu rg}$

EXERCISE 11a

(where necessary use $g = 9.8$ ms^{-2})

1) A particle of mass m kg is travelling at constant speed v ms^{-1} round a circle of radius r m.
(a) If $v = 8$ and $r = 2$ find the magnitude of the central acceleration.
(b) If the force acting towards the centre of the circle is of constant magnitude 6 N, $m = 4$ and $v = 3$, find the value of r.

2) A circular tray of radius 0.2 m has a smooth vertical rim round the edge. The tray is fixed on a horizontal table and a small ball of mass 0.1 kg is set moving round the inside of the rim of the tray with speed 4 ms^{-1}. Calculate the horizontal force exerted on the ball by the rim of the tray.

3) A car of mass 400 kg can turn a corner at 40 kmh^{-1} without skidding but at 50 kmh^{-1} it does skid. If the corner is an arc of a circle of radius 20 m, find the values between which μ, the coefficient of friction between the wheels and the road surface, must lie.

4) A disc is free to rotate in a horizontal plane about an axis through its centre O. A small object P is placed on the disc so that OP = 0.2 m. Contact between

the particle and the disc is rough and the coefficient of friction is 0.5. The disc then begins to rotate. Find the angular velocity of the disc when the particle is about to slip.

5) A particle of mass 0.4 kg is attached to one end of a light inextensible string of length 0.6 m. The other end is fixed to a point A on a smooth horizontal table. The particle is set moving in a circular path.
(a) If the speed of the particle is 8 ms^{-1} calculate the tension in the string and and the reaction with table.
(b) If the string snaps when the tension in it exceeds 50 N, find the greatest angular velocity at which the particle can travel.

Conical Pendulum

An inextensible string of length l is fixed at one end, A. At the other end is attached a particle P of mass m describing a circle with constant angular velocity ω in a horizontal plane.

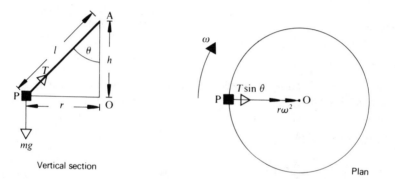

Vertical section   Plan

As P rotates, the string AP traces out the surface of a cone. Consequently the system is known as a *conical pendulum.*

Vertically $\qquad\qquad\qquad T \cos \theta = mg \qquad\qquad\qquad\qquad$ (1)

Horizontally $\qquad\qquad\quad T \sin \theta = mr\omega^2 \qquad\qquad\qquad\quad$ (2)

In triangle AOP $\qquad\qquad\quad r = l \sin \theta \qquad\qquad\qquad\qquad$ (3)

$\qquad\qquad\qquad\qquad\qquad h = l \cos \theta \qquad\qquad\qquad\qquad$ (4)

Several interesting facts can be deduced from these equations:
(i) It is impossible for the string to be horizontal. This is seen from equation (1) in which $\cos \theta = \dfrac{mg}{T}$ which cannot be zero.
Hence θ cannot be 90°.
(ii) The tension is always greater than mg. This also follows from equation (1) since $\cos \theta = \dfrac{mg}{T}$
and $\cos \theta < 1$ (θ is acute but not zero).

(iii) The tension can be calculated without knowing the inclination of the string. Since, from equations (2) and (3)

$$T \sin \theta = ml \sin \theta \, \omega^2$$

$$T = ml \, \omega^2$$

(iv) The vertical depth of P below A (i.e. h) is independent of the length of the string.

Since from equations (1) and (4)

$$T\frac{h}{l} = mg \text{ or } T = \frac{lmg}{h}$$

But

$$T = ml\omega^2 \quad \text{(iii)}$$

Therefore

$$ml\omega^2 = \frac{mlg}{h}$$

or

$$h = \frac{g}{\omega^2} \quad \text{(independent of } l)$$

EXAMPLES 11b

1) An inextensible string of length 2 m is fixed at one end **A** and carries at its other end **B** a particle of mass 3 kg which is rotating in a horizontal circle whose centre is 1 m vertically below A. Find the angular velocity of the particle and the tension in the string.

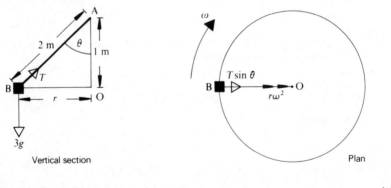

Vertical section   Plan

Vertically	(zero acceleration)	$T \cos \theta = 3g$	(1)
Horizontally	(Newton's Law)	$T \sin \theta = 3r\omega^2$	(2)
In triangle AOB		$\cos \theta = \frac{1}{2}$	(3)
		$r = 2 \sin \theta$	(4)

(3) and (4) $\longrightarrow \theta = \dfrac{\pi}{3}; \quad r = \sqrt{3}$

$(2) \div (1) \longrightarrow \tan \theta = \dfrac{r\omega^2}{g}$

Therefore $\quad \sqrt{3} = \sqrt{3}\,\dfrac{\omega^2}{g}$ $\qquad$ Therefore $\omega^2 = g$

In (1) $\qquad T \times \tfrac{1}{2} = 3g$ $\qquad\qquad\qquad T = 6g$

2) Two light inextensible strings **AB** and **BC** each of length l are attached to a particle of mass m at **B**. The other ends **A** and **C** are fixed to two points in a vertical line such that A is distant l above C. The particle describes a horizontal circle with constant angular velocity ω.
Find (i) the tension in **AB**,
$\qquad$ (ii) the least value of ω so that both strings shall be taut.

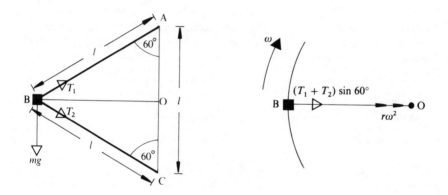

Vertically $\qquad\qquad\quad T_1 \cos 60° = T_2 \cos 60° + mg$ $\qquad$ (1)

Horizontally $\qquad (T_1 + T_2) \sin 60° = mr\omega^2$ $\qquad\qquad$ (2)

In triangle **AOB** $\qquad\qquad\quad r = l \sin 60°$ $\qquad\qquad\qquad$ (3)

Simplifying (1) $\qquad\longrightarrow\qquad T_1 - T_2 = 2mg$ $\qquad\qquad\qquad$ (4)

(2) and (3) $\qquad\longrightarrow\qquad T_1 + T_2 = ml\omega^2$ $\qquad\qquad\qquad$ (5)

(4) and (5) $\qquad\longrightarrow\qquad 2T_1 = 2mg + ml\omega^2$

$\qquad\qquad$ Therefore tension in **AB** $= mg + \tfrac{1}{2}ml\omega^2$

The string which could be slack is BC.
In order that it shall be taut, $T_2 \geqslant 0$.

(4) and (5) $\qquad\longrightarrow\qquad 2T_2 = ml\omega^2 - 2mg$

If $T_2 \geqslant 0$, then $ml\omega^2 \geqslant 2mg$.

Therefore in order that both strings shall be taut, $\omega^2 \geqslant \dfrac{2g}{l}$.

3) A light inextensible string of length $3l$ is threaded through a smooth ring and carries a particle at each end. One particle A of mass m is at rest at a distance l below the ring. The other particle B of mass M is rotating in a horizontal circle whose centre is A. Find the angular velocity of B and find m in terms of M.

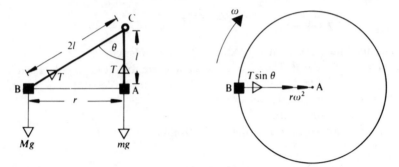

[Since two separate particles are involved we must analyse the state of each. As the ring is smooth, the tension is the same in both sections, BC and AC, of the string.]

For mass A (in equilibrium):-

$$T = mg \tag{1}$$

For mass B:

Vertically

$$T \cos \theta = Mg \tag{2}$$

Horizontally

$$T \sin \theta = Mr\omega^2 \tag{3}$$

In triangle ABC

$$\cos \theta = \frac{l}{2l} = \frac{1}{2} \tag{4}$$

$$r = 2l \sin \theta \tag{5}$$

(4) and (5) $\longrightarrow$ $\quad \theta = 60°; \quad\quad r = \sqrt{3}\,l$

In (2) $\quad\quad T(\tfrac{1}{2}) = Mg; \quad\quad T = 2Mg$

But $\quad\quad\quad\quad\quad\quad\quad\quad\quad\quad T = mg$

Therefore $\quad\quad m = 2M$

In (3) $\quad\quad T\dfrac{\sqrt{3}}{2} = M\sqrt{3}l\omega^2 = 2Mg\dfrac{\sqrt{3}}{2}$

Therefore $\quad\quad \omega = \sqrt{\dfrac{g}{l}}$

4) The base of a hollow right cone of semi vertical angle $30°$, is fixed to a horizontal plane. Two particles each of mass m are connected by a light inextensible string which passes through a small smooth hole in the vertex V of the cone. One particle, A, hangs at rest inside the cone. The other particle B moves on the outer smooth surface of the cone at a distance l from V, in a horizontal circle with centre A. Find the tension in the string, the angular velocity of B and the normal reaction between B and the cone.

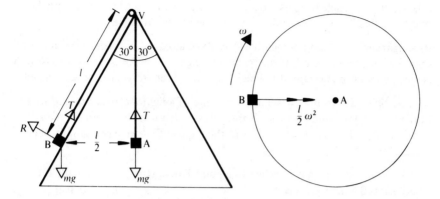

[The tension is the same in both portions of string since the hole is smooth. If the portion BV is of length l, then the radius of B's circular path is $l \sin 30° = \dfrac{l}{2}$]

For particle A (in equilibrium) $\hspace{3cm} T = mg$ $\hspace{2cm}$ (1)

For particle B $\hspace{2cm} T \cos 30° + R \sin 30° = mg$ $\hspace{2cm}$ (2)

$$T \sin 30° - R \cos 30° = m \frac{l}{2} \omega^2 \hspace{2cm} (3)$$

Simplifying, we have: $\hspace{3cm} T = mg$ $\hspace{2cm}$ (1)

$$\sqrt{3}\, T + R = 2mg \hspace{2cm} (2)$$

$$T - \sqrt{3}\, R = ml\omega^2 \hspace{2cm} (3)$$

Eliminating R from (2) and (3) $\hspace{2cm} 4T = 2\sqrt{3}\, mg + ml\omega^2$

From (1) $\hspace{3cm} 4mg = 2\sqrt{3}\, mg + ml\omega^2$

Hence $\hspace{3cm} \omega^2 = (4 - 2\sqrt{3})\dfrac{g}{l}$

From (1) and (2) $\hspace{2cm} R = 2mg - \sqrt{3}\, mg$

$$R = (2 - \sqrt{3})\, mg$$

Therefore: the tension in the string is mg

$\hspace{2cm}$ the angular velocity of B is $\left[\dfrac{2g}{l}(2 - \sqrt{3})\right]^{\frac{1}{2}}$

and $\hspace{2cm}$ the normal reaction at B is $(2 - \sqrt{3})\, mg$.

EXERCISE 11b

1) One end of a light inextensible string of length 1 m is fixed. The other end is

attached to a particle of mass 0.6 kg which is travelling in a horizontal circular path of radius 0.8 m. What is the angular speed of the particle?

2) A light inelastic string of length 1.2 m, fixed at one end, carries a particle P of mass 2 kg at the other end. If the tension in the string is not to exceed 40 N, what is the maximum angular speed at which the particle can travel in a horizontal circle?

3) A particle of mass m is attached to one end of a light inelastic string of length l the other end of which is fixed. If the particle is moving in a horizontal circle with the string inclined at an angle θ to the vertical find an expression for its angular velocity.

4) A ring of mass 0.6 kg is attached to a point P on a string AB of length 1.4 m, where AP is 0.8 m. The ends A and B are attached to two points 1.0 m apart in a vertical line, A being above B. The ring is made to travel in a horizontal circle with speed v ms^{-1}.
 (i) What is the smallest possible value of v if neither portion of string is slack?
 (ii) If $v = 4.2$ ms^{-1} calculate the tension in the portion AP of the string.

5) A particle of mass m, attached to the end A of a light inextensible string describes a horizontal circle on a smooth horizontal plane. The string is of length $2l$ and the other end B is fixed:
(a) to a point on the plane,
(b) to a point which is at a height l above the plane.
If the angular velocity of the particle is ω, find, in each case, the tension in the string and the reaction between the particle and the plane, giving your answers in terms of m, l and ω.

6) Two particles A and B of masses m and M respectively are connected by a light inelastic string of length $3l$ which passes through a smooth swivel at a fixed height. If A can be made to perform horizontal circles about B as centre while B is at rest at a depth l below the swivel, find the value of $M:m$ and find, in terms of l, an expression for the angular velocity of A.

7) Two particles of equal mass are connected by a light inextensible string of length 1 m which passes through a small smooth-edged hole in a smooth horizontal table. One particle hangs at rest at a depth 0.5 m below the hole. The other particle describes a horizontal circle on the table. What is its angular velocity?

8) A smooth ring of mass m is threaded on to a light inelastic string of length $8l$ whose ends are fixed to two points A and B distant $4l$ apart in a vertical line (A above B). Calculate the tension in the string when the ring describes horizontal circles about B as centre.
It is impossible for the ring to describe horizontal circles mid-way between the levels of A and B. Explain why this is so.

9) An elastic string AB of natural length a and modulus of elasticity $2 mg$, has one end, A, fixed. A particle of mass m is attached to the end B and performs

horizontal circles with angular velocity $\sqrt{\dfrac{3g}{4a}}$. Find the extension in the string and the cosine of the angle between the string and the vertical.

Banked Tracks

A vehicle which travels round a bend on horizontal ground relies entirely on the frictional force at the wheel base to provide the correct central force. Because the magnitude of the frictional force is limited, the central acceleration, $\dfrac{v^2}{r}$, and hence the speed of the vehicle, are also limited (see examples 11a/2.)
If, however, the road surface is not horizontal, this limitation can be overcome.
Consider a vehicle of mass m travelling at speed V round a bend of radius r on a road which is banked at an angle θ.

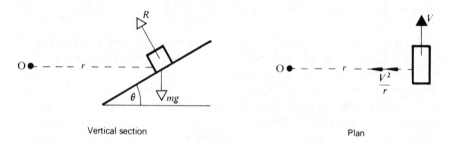

Vertical section   Plan

A force of $R \sin \theta$ acts towards O, the centre of the circular path.

Therefore $$R \sin \theta = \frac{mV^2}{r} \tag{1}$$

Vertically (no acceleration) $$R \cos \theta = mg \tag{2}$$

By eliminating R we see that $$V^2 = rg \tan \theta.$$

The vehicle can travel at a speed $V = \sqrt{rg \tan \theta}$ without any tendency to side-slip.
V is called the design speed.
The greater the value of θ, the faster the vehicle can round the bend without tending to slip.
If a speed v_1, greater than the design speed, is used, then the force $R_1 \sin \theta$ is insufficient to provide the necessary central acceleration. The vehicle will tend to slip outwards from the circular path and a frictional force will oppose this tendency, up to its maximum value μR_1.

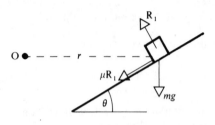

Vertical section   Plan

Towards O (Newton's Law) $R_1 \sin \theta + \mu R_1 \cos \theta = \dfrac{mv_1^2}{r}$ (1)

Vertically (no acceleration) $R_1 \cos \theta - \mu R_1 \sin \theta = mg$ (2)

Dividing (1) by (2) gives $v_1^2 = rg \left(\dfrac{\sin \theta + \mu \cos \theta}{\cos \theta - \mu \sin \theta} \right)$

The vehicle can therefore travel without slipping round the bend at a speed v_1, greater than the design speed $\sqrt{rg \tan \theta}$ when both friction and the banking of the track contribute to the central force.

At a speed v_2, less than $\sqrt{rg \tan \theta}$, the component of reaction $R_2 \sin \theta$ causes an acceleration greater than is required to keep the vehicle on a circular path. In this case the vehicle will tend to slip down the banked track; this tendency will be opposed by a frictional force acting outwards.

(i)

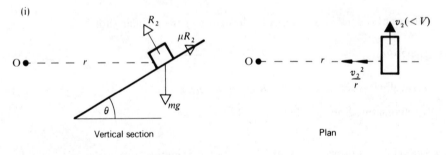

Vertical section   Plan

Towards O (Newton's Law) $R_2 \sin \theta - \mu R_2 \cos \theta = \dfrac{mv_2^2}{r}$ (1)

Vertically (no acceleration) $R_2 \cos \theta + \mu R_2 \sin \theta = mg$ (2)

Dividing (1) by (2) gives $v_2^2 = rg \left(\dfrac{\sin \theta - \mu \cos \theta}{\cos \theta + \mu \sin \theta} \right)$

This speed v_2 is the lowest speed possible at which the vehicle can travel round the track without slipping downwards.

EXAMPLES 11c

1) A car is travelling round a section of a race track which is banked at an angle of 15°. The radius of the track is 100 m. What is the speed at which the car can travel without tending to slip?

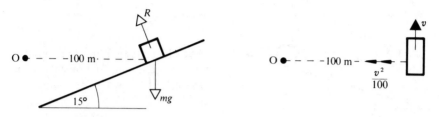

Let the mass of the car be m.

If there is no tendency to slip there will be no lateral frictional force.

Horizontally (Newton's Law) $\quad R \sin 15° = \dfrac{mv^2}{100}$

Vertically (no acceleration) $\quad R \cos 15° = mg.$

Hence $\qquad\qquad\qquad\qquad \tan 15° = \dfrac{v^2}{100g}$

i.e. $\qquad\qquad\qquad\qquad v^2 = 100 \times 9.8 \times 0.2679$

Therefore the design speed is 16.2 ms^{-1}.

2) A car travelling at 28 ms^{-1} has no tendency to slip on a track of radius 200 m banked at an angle θ. When the speed is increased to 35 ms^{-1} the car is just on the point of slipping up the track. Calculate the coefficient of friction between the car and the track.

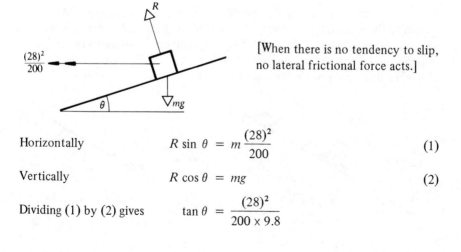

[When there is no tendency to slip, no lateral frictional force acts.]

Horizontally $\qquad\qquad R \sin \theta = m \dfrac{(28)^2}{200}$ $\qquad\qquad$ (1)

Vertically $\qquad\qquad\qquad R \cos \theta = mg$ $\qquad\qquad\qquad$ (2)

Dividing (1) by (2) gives $\qquad \tan \theta = \dfrac{(28)^2}{200 \times 9.8}$

or $\qquad\qquad\qquad\qquad \tan\theta = 0.4$

and $\qquad\qquad\qquad\qquad \theta = 21°\,48'$

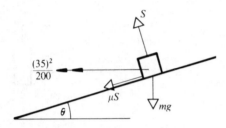

[At a higher speed the car is about to slip outwards and friction acts down the slope.]

Horizontally $\qquad\qquad S \sin\theta + \mu S \cos\theta = m\,\dfrac{(35)^2}{200}$ $\qquad$ (3)

Vertically $\qquad\qquad S \cos\theta - \mu S \sin\theta = mg$ $\qquad\qquad$ (4)

Dividing (3) by (4) gives $\qquad \dfrac{\sin\theta + \mu\cos\theta}{\cos\theta - \mu\sin\theta} = \dfrac{(35)^2}{200 \times 9.8}$

Dividing by $\cos\theta$ gives $\qquad \dfrac{\tan\theta + \mu}{1 - \mu\tan\theta} = \dfrac{35 \times 35 \times 10}{200 \times 98}$

But $\tan\theta = 0.4$ hence $\qquad \dfrac{0.4 + \mu}{1 - 0.4\,\mu} = \dfrac{5}{8}$

$$3.2 + 8\mu = 5 - 2\mu$$

$$10\mu = 1.8$$

The coefficient of friction between car and track is 0.18.

3) A railway line is taken round a circular arc of radius 1000 m, and is banked by raising the outer rail h m above the inner rail. If the lateral pressure on the inner rail when a train travels round the curve at 10 ms^{-1} is equal to the lateral pressure on the outer rail when the train's speed is 20 ms^{-1}, calculate the value of h. (The distance between the rails is 1.5 m.)

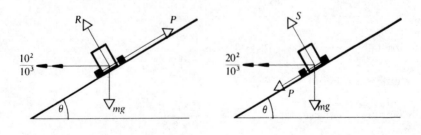

Let m be the mass of the train and θ the angle at which the rail track is banked.

(a) Horizontally $R \sin \theta - P \cos \theta = m \dfrac{10^2}{10^3}$ (1)

Vertically $R \cos \theta + P \sin \theta = mg$ (2)

or $R \sin \theta = \dfrac{m}{10} + P \cos \theta$

$R \cos \theta = mg - P \sin \theta$

Dividing $\dfrac{\sin \theta}{\cos \theta} = \dfrac{\frac{1}{10} m + P \cos \theta}{mg - P \sin \theta}$

Hence $mg \sin \theta - P \sin^2 \theta = \dfrac{m}{10} \cos \theta + P \cos^2 \theta$

and $mg \sin \theta - \dfrac{m}{10} \cos \theta = P$ $(\cos^2 \theta + \sin^2 \theta = 1)$

(b) Horizontally $S \sin \theta + P \cos \theta = m \dfrac{20^2}{10^3}$ (3)

Vertically $S \cos \theta - P \sin \theta = mg$ (4)

or $S \sin \theta = \dfrac{4m}{10} - P \cos \theta$

$S \cos \theta = mg + P \sin \theta$

Dividing $\dfrac{\sin \theta}{\cos \theta} = \dfrac{\frac{4}{10} m - P \cos \theta}{mg + P \sin \theta}$

Hence $mg \sin \theta + P \sin^2 \theta = \dfrac{4m}{10} \cos \theta - P \cos^2 \theta$

and $P = \dfrac{4m}{10} \cos \theta - mg \sin \theta$

Now from part (a) $P = mg \sin \theta - \dfrac{m}{10} \cos \theta$

Therefore $\qquad \dfrac{4m}{10} \cos\theta - mg\sin\theta = mg\sin\theta - \dfrac{m}{10}\cos\theta$

giving $\qquad\qquad\qquad \dfrac{m}{2}\cos\theta = 2\,mg\sin\theta$

hence $\qquad\qquad\qquad\quad \tan\theta = \dfrac{1}{4g} = 0.0255$

$$\theta = 1°\,28'$$

But the distance between the rails is 1.5 m.

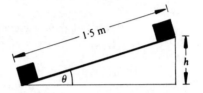

so that $h = 1.5\sin\theta = 1.5 \times 0.0255 = .0383$.
(*Note:* θ is a very small angle, hence $\sin\theta \simeq \tan\theta$.)

The outer rail is raised 0.0383 m above the inner rail.

EXERCISE 11c

1) A road banked at $10°$ goes round a bend of radius 70 m. At what speed can a car travel round the bend without tending to side-slip?

2) At what angle should an aircraft be banked when flying at $100\,\text{ms}^{-1}$ on a horizontal circle of radius 3000 m?

3) A motor car describes a curve of 120 m radius on a road sloping downwards towards the inside of the curve at arctan $\frac{1}{5}$. At what speed can the car travel with no tendency to side-slip?

4) On a level race track a car can just go round a bend of radius 80 m at a speed of $20\,\text{ms}^{-1}$ without skidding. At what angle must the track be banked so that a speed of $30\,\text{ms}^{-1}$ can just be reached without skidding, the coefficient of friction being the same in both cases? (Take $g = 10\,\text{ms}^{-2}$)

5) A circular race track is banked at $45°$ and has a radius of 200 m. At what speed does a car have no tendency to side-slip? If the coefficient of friction between the wheels and the track is $\frac{1}{2}$, find the maximum speed at which the car can travel round the track without skidding.

6) An engine of mass 80 000 kg travels at $40\,\text{kmh}^{-1}$ round a bend of radius 1200 m. If the track is level, calculate the lateral thrust on the outer rail. At what height above the inner rail should the outer rail be raised to eliminate lateral thrust at this speed if the distance between the rails is 1.4 m?

7) A bend on a race track is designed with variable banking so that cars on the inside of the track can corner at 80 kmh^{-1} and those on the outside at 160 kmh^{-1} without lateral friction. If the inner radius is 150 m and the outer radius 165 m, find the difference between the angles of banking at the inside and outside of the track.

8) The sleepers of a railway track which is turning round a bend of radius 60 m are banked so that a train travelling at 40 kmh^{-1} exerts no lateral force on the rails. Find the lateral force exerted on the rails by an engine of mass 10^5 kg:
(a) travelling at 30 kmh^{-1},
(b) travelling at 50 kmh^{-1},
(c) at rest.
State in each case whether the force acts on the inner or outer rail.

MOTION IN A CIRCLE WITH VARIABLE SPEED

The velocity of a particle P travelling on a circular path with varying speed, is changing both in magnitude and direction. The particle therefore has two acceleration components:

(i) towards the centre of the circle, a component which is the rate of change of direction of the velocity. Its magnitude at any instant is $\dfrac{v^2}{r}$ (or $r\omega^2$) but is not constant because v varies.

(ii) in the direction of motion, i.e. along the tangent to the circle at P, a component $\dfrac{dv}{dt}$ which is the rate of increase of magnitude of the velocity.

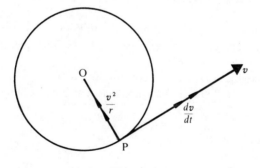

Motion of this type will result when the forces acting on the particle have both radial and tangential components. This situation arises when a particle is describing a circular path in a vertical plane.

MOTION IN A VERTICAL CIRCLE

A particle can be made to travel in a vertical circular path in a variety of ways. Some of these involve driving mechanism and can be fairly complex. Our study however is limited to simple cases in which the *speed* of the particle, once it is set moving, is not affected by any external force other than weight.
In problems of this type the total mechanical energy of the system remains constant.
Consider the motion of a small bead of mass m threaded on to a smooth wire in the shape of a circle of radius a and centre O. The circle is fixed in a vertical plane and the bead passes the lowest point A on the wire with speed u. It subsequently passes with speed v through another point B where angle BOA is θ.

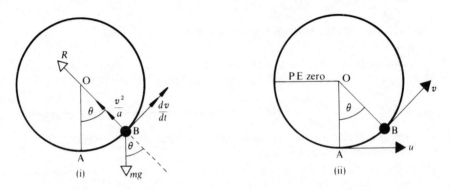

Diagram (i) shows the forces acting on the bead, and its acceleration components at B.
The normal reaction R is always perpendicular to the wire and is therefore perpendicular to the direction of motion and does no work. Consequently the total mechanical energy remains constant.
Diagram (ii) shows the velocities and positions of the bead.
Applying Newton's Law along radius and tangent at B (diagram (i)) we have:

Radially
$$R - mg \cos \theta = m \frac{v^2}{a} \qquad (1)$$

Tangentially
$$mg \sin \theta = -m \frac{dv}{dt} \qquad (2)$$

Using Conservation of Mechanical Energy (diagram (ii)):

Total M.E. at A is $\frac{1}{2} mu^2 - mga$

Total M.E. at B is $\frac{1}{2} mv^2 - mga \cos \theta$

Therefore $\frac{1}{2} mu^2 - mga = \frac{1}{2} mv^2 - mga \cos \theta \qquad (3)$

Equation (1) shows that R has its greatest value at A, since

$$R = mg \cos \theta + \frac{mv^2}{a}, \quad \cos \theta \leqslant 1 \text{ and } v \leqslant u.$$

Equation (3) gives, in terms of u, the speed v at any specified position. Using this expression in equation (1) gives the value of R at that position. Equation (2) (not often required in problem solving) gives the tangential acceleration at a specified position.

These three equations can be used to analyse the motion of a particle describing a vertical circle in slightly different circumstances:

1) A particle attached to one end of a light rod which is free to rotate about a smooth fixed axis through the other end of the rod. In this case the force, T, in the rod acts in the same way as the reaction, R, between the wire and the bead.

2) A particle rotating on the inside of a smooth circular surface. Again we have a normal reaction R between the surface and the particle.

3) A particle rotating at the end of a light string whose other end is fixed. The tension, T, in the string is the force towards the centre of the circle in this case.

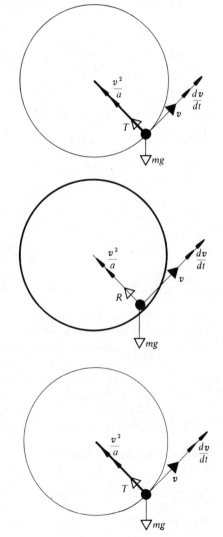

4) A particle moving on the outside of a smooth circular surface. This case is rather different from all the others, since the normal reaction, R, exerted on the particle acts always outward from the centre. The particle can remain in contact with the upper section only of the surface. Equations similar to those already derived can be found to analyse this form of circular motion however.

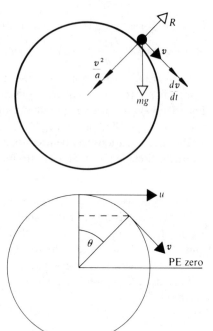

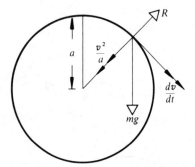

Newton's Law: ↙ $mg \cos \theta - R = \dfrac{mv^2}{a}$ (1)

↘ $mg \sin \theta = m \dfrac{dv}{dt}$ (2)

Conservation of M.E. $\tfrac{1}{2} mu^2 + mga = \tfrac{1}{2} mv^2 + mga \cos \theta$ (3)

Although the general analysis of all these cases is similar, there are in fact two different groups of problems which must now be considered separately.

(a) those in which the particle cannot move off the circular path e.g. the bead threaded on the wire and the particle attached to the light rod.

(b) those in which the particle can leave the circular path and travel in some other way e.g. the particle at the end of a string or moving on a circular surface. For these, circular motion is performed only while the string is taut or the particle is in contact with the surface.

Motion restricted to a Circular Path

Using the case of the bead threaded on the wire we see that the bead may:

(a) pass through the highest point of the wire and go on to describe complete circles,

(b) come momentarily to rest before reaching the highest point and subsequently oscillate.

(a) If the bead passes through the highes
point then $v > 0$ at the top.
Using Conservation of M.E.

$$\tfrac{1}{2} mu^2 = \tfrac{1}{2} mv^2 + 2\, mga$$
$$v^2 = u^2 - 4\, ga$$

But $v > 0$
Hence $u^2 > 4\, ga$

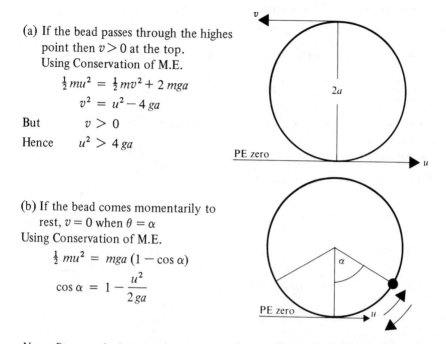

(b) If the bead comes momentarily to
rest, $v = 0$ when $\theta = \alpha$
Using Conservation of M.E.

$$\tfrac{1}{2} mu^2 = mga\,(1 - \cos \alpha)$$
$$\cos \alpha = 1 - \frac{u^2}{2\, ga}$$

Note: Because the bead cannot leave the wire, the only condition necessary for
it to describe complete circles is that *its velocity is greater than zero at the
highest point.*

EXAMPLES 11d

1) A particle of mass 2 kg is attached to the end **B** of a light rod **AB** of length
0.8 m which is free to rotate in a vertical plane about the end **A**. If the end **B**,
when vertically below **A**, is given a horizontal velocity of 3 ms⁻¹ show that the
particle will not describe complete circles. Find the angle through which it
oscillates and the greatest stress in the rod during the motion.

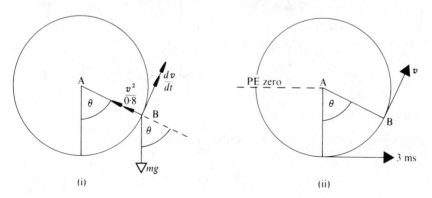

Using Conservation of Mechanical Energy (diagram (ii))

$$\tfrac{1}{2} \times 2 \times 3^2 - 2g\,(0.8) = \tfrac{1}{2} \times 2 \times v^2 - 2g\,(0.8)\cos\theta$$

If $v = 0$, $2g\,(0.8)\cos\theta = 2g\,(0.8) - 9$

$$\cos\theta = \frac{15.68 - 9}{15.7} = 0.425$$

Therefore $v = 0$ when $\theta = 64° \, 50'$ and the particle comes to rest before it reaches the top of the circular path.

The particle oscillates through $129° \, 40'$

Applying Newton's Law towards the centre

$$T - 2g\cos\theta = \frac{2 \times 3^2}{0.8}$$

T is greatest when $\theta = 0$

Therefore $$T_{max} = \left(\frac{18}{0.8} + 2g\right) \text{N}$$

$$T_{max} = 42.1 \text{ N}$$

2) A small bead of mass 2 kg is threaded on to a smooth circular wire which is fixed in a vertical plane. If the bead is slightly disturbed from rest at the highest point of the wire, find its speed when it reaches the lowest point and its reaction with the wire when the bead is level with the centre of the circle whose radius is 0.6 m.

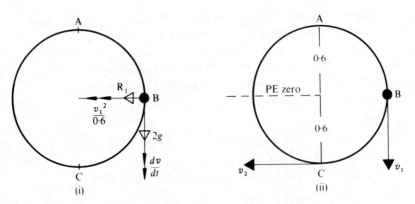

Applying Newton's Law radially at B (diagram (i))

$$R_1 = \frac{2v_1^2}{0.6} \tag{1}$$

Using Conservation of Mechanical Energy (diagram (ii))

From A to B $\qquad$ $0 + 2g\,(0.6) = \frac{1}{2}\,2v_1^2 + 0$ $\qquad$ (2)

From A to C $\qquad$ $0 + 2g\,(0.6) = \frac{1}{2}\,2v_2^2 - 2g\,(0.6)$ $\qquad$ (3)

From (3) $\qquad$ $v_2^2 = 4g\,(0.6)$

$\qquad\qquad\qquad v_2 = 4.84$

From (1) and (2) $\qquad$ $R_1 = \dfrac{2}{0.6}\,(1.2g)$

$\qquad\qquad\qquad R_1 = 39.2\,\text{N}$

The speed at the lowest point is $4.84\,\text{ms}^{-1}$ and the reaction when the bead is level with the centre is $39.2\,\text{N}$.

3) A light rod of length l is free to rotate in a vertical plane about one end. A particle of mass m is attached to the other end.
When the rod is hanging at rest vertically downward, an impulse is applied to the particle so that it travels in complete vertical circles. Find the range of possible values of the impulse and the tangential acceleration when the rod is inclined at $60°$ to the downward vertical.

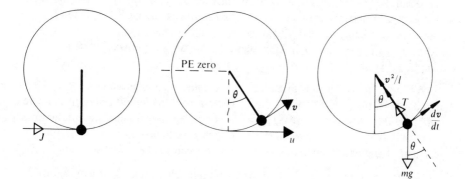

First using Impulse = Change in Momentum

$\qquad\qquad J = mu$ $\qquad\qquad$ (1)

Using Conservation of Mechanical Energy

$\qquad\qquad \frac{1}{2}\,mu^2 - mgl = \frac{1}{2}\,mv^2 - mgl\cos\theta$ $\qquad\qquad$ (2)

Applying Newton's Law tangentially

$\qquad\qquad -mg\sin\theta = m\dfrac{dv}{dt}$ $\qquad\qquad$ (3)

If the particle is to describe complete circles,

$$v > 0 \text{ when } \theta = 180°$$

In (2)
$$v^2 = u^2 - 2gl + 2gl \cos 180°$$
$$v^2 = u^2 - 4gl$$

But
$$v > 0$$

Therefore
$$u^2 > 4gl$$
$$u > 2\sqrt{gl}$$

Hence
$$J > 2m\sqrt{gl}$$

Therefore the value of the impulse must exceed $2m\sqrt{gl}$

When $\theta = 60°$

In (3)
$$mg \frac{\sqrt{3}}{2} = m \frac{dv}{dt}$$

Tangential Acceleration
$$= g \frac{\sqrt{3}}{2}$$

EXERCISE 11d

1) A light rod of length 1 m is smoothly pivoted about a horizontal axis through one end A. A particle of mass 2 kg attached to the other end B is released from the position when B is vertically above A. Find the tension in the rod and the velocity of the particle when AB makes an angle with the upward vertical of:
(i) 90°   (ii) 120°   (iii) 180°.

2) A bead of mass 1.5 kg is threaded on to a smooth circular wire of radius 1.5 m fixed in a vertical plane. The bead is projected from the lowest point on the wire with speed (i) $\sqrt{4g}$ ms^{-1} (ii) $\sqrt{6g}$ ms^{-1} (iii) $\sqrt{8g}$ ms^{-1}. In each case determine in what way the bead moves on the wire (giving particular care to part (ii)) and calculate the greatest value of the reaction between the bead and the wire.

3) A particle of mass m is attached to the end A of a light rod AB of length l, free to rotate in a vertical plane about the end B. The rod is held with A vertically above B and the particle is projected from this position with a horizontal velocity u. When the particle at A is vertically below B it collides with a stationary particle of mass $2m$ and coalesces with it. If the rod goes on to perform complete circles find the range of possible values of u.

4) A small bead of mass m is free to slide on a smooth circular wire of radius a fixed in a vertical plane. If the bead is slightly disturbed from rest at the highest point of the wire, find the reaction between the bead and the wire, the velocity of the bead and the resultant acceleration of the bead, when the bead has rotated through (i) 90°   (ii) 120°   (iii) 180°.

5) A light rod AB of length 1 m is free to rotate in a vertical plane about an axis

through A. A particle of mass 1 kg is attached to B. If the particle is projected from its lowest position with speed $3\sqrt{4.9}$ ms^{-1}, show that the particle describes complete circles. Find the vertical height above A of the end B when the stress in the rod is zero.

6) Two beads A and B of masses m and $2m$ respectively are free to slide in a vertical plane round a smooth circular wire of radius a and centre O. The bead A is at rest at the lowest point C of the wire while B is released from rest at a point on the same level as O. If the coefficient of restitution between the beads is $\frac{1}{2}$, find the height above C to which each particle rises after impact.

Motion not Restricted to a Circular Path

As an example of this case let us consider the motion of a particle rotating at one end of a light string fixed at its other end.

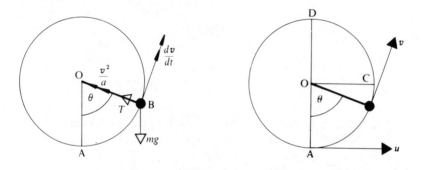

This time the particle can travel in one of three ways. It may:
(a) pass through D while the string is still taut and go on to describe complete circles,
(b) oscillate below the level of O, the string always being taut within this lower semi-circle,
(c) cease to travel on the circle at some point between C and D when the string becomes slack, subsequently moving as a projectile until the string becomes taut again.

Using Newton's Law and Conservation of M.E. in the diagrams above:

$$T - mg \cos \theta = \frac{mv^2}{a} \tag{1}$$

and

$$\tfrac{1}{2} mu^2 - mga = \tfrac{1}{2} mv^2 - mga \cos \theta \tag{2}$$

we see that

$$T = mg \cos \theta + \frac{mv^2}{a}$$

$$T = mg \cos \theta + \frac{m}{a} (u^2 - 2ga + 2ga \cos \theta)$$

$$T = m\left(\frac{u^2}{a} - 2g + 3g\cos\theta\right)$$

(a) For complete circles, the string must be taut in the highest position

i.e. $T \geqslant 0$ when $\theta = 180°$.

Hence $\dfrac{u^2}{a} \geqslant 2g - 3g\cos 180°$

$u^2 \geqslant 5ga$

Note: It is not sufficient in this case that $v > 0$ at the highest point, as the particle could be moving *inside* the circle with velocity v when $\theta = 180°$.

The essential condition is

$\underline{T \geqslant 0 \text{ when } \theta = 180°}$

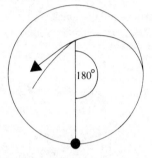

(b) For oscillations the particle comes momentarily to rest at a point on, or below, the level of the centre O. i.e. $v = 0$ when $\theta \leqslant 90°$.

In equation (2) $\cos\theta = 1 - \dfrac{u^2}{2ga}$ when $v = 0$

But $\theta \leqslant 90°$ so $\cos\theta \geqslant 0$

hence $u^2 \leqslant 2ga$.

Both in (a) and (b), the string is always taut. The ranges of values of u, the velocity at the lowest point, for which the string never goes slack (and the particle therefore never leaves a circular path) are:

$$u \leqslant \sqrt{2ga} \quad \text{and} \quad u \geqslant \sqrt{5ga}.$$

(c) Circular motion ceases at the instant when the string becomes slack, i.e. when $T = 0$. The angle θ at this instant is given by using

$$T = m\left(\frac{u^2}{a} - 2g + 3g\cos\theta\right) = 0$$

or $\cos\theta = \dfrac{2ga - u^2}{3ga}$

Once the string is slack, the only force acting on the particle is its own weight and the motion continues as that of a projectile.

This situation arises only if $90° < \theta < 180°$ (i.e. above the level of the centre).

In this case

$$0 > \cos \theta > -1$$

giving

$$0 > \frac{2ga - u^2}{3ga} > -1$$

Hence the range of values of u for which the string does go slack is

$$\sqrt{2ga} < u < \sqrt{5ga}$$

EXAMPLES 11e

1) A particle of mass 2 kg is moving on the inside surface of a smooth hollow cylinder of radius 0.2 m whose axis is horizontal. Find the least speed which the particle must have at the lowest point of its path if it travels in complete circles.

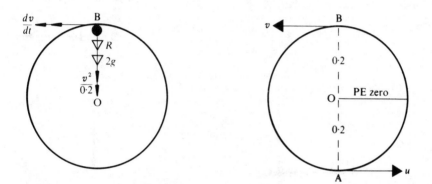

Applying Newton's Law along BO

$$R + 2g = 2\frac{v^2}{0.2} \tag{1}$$

Conservation of Mechanical Energy from A to B

$$\tfrac{1}{2}\, 2u^2 - 2g\,(0.2) = \tfrac{1}{2}\, 2\, v^2 + 2g\,(0.2) \tag{2}$$

From (1) and (2) $R + 2g = 10\,(u^2 - 0.8g)$

or $R = 10\,u^2 - 10g$

But, for complete circles, $R \geqslant 0$ at B (i.e. contact is not lost at any point).

Therefore $10\,u^2 - 10g \geqslant 0$ giving $u^2 \geqslant g$

Hence the least value of u is $\sqrt{g} = \sqrt{9.8} = \sqrt{\frac{98}{10}} = \sqrt{\frac{49}{5}}$

The least speed at A is $\dfrac{7\sqrt{5}}{5}$ ms^{-1}

2) A particle of mass $\frac{1}{2}$ kg is suspended from a fixed point A by a light inelastic string of length 1 m. When in its lowest position it is given a horizontal speed of 8 ms^{-1}.

(a) Prove that it performs complete circles.

(b) Find the ratio of the greatest to the least tension in the string.

(c) Calculate the tangential acceleration of the particle when the string is horizontal.

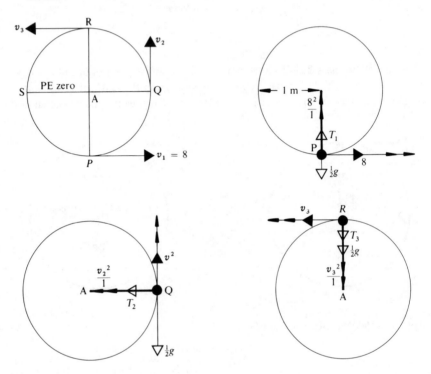

(a) Applying Newton's Law radially at R.

$$T_3 + \tfrac{1}{2}g = \tfrac{1}{2}\frac{v_3^2}{1} \qquad (1)$$

Conservation of M.E. from P to R

$$\tfrac{1}{2} \times \tfrac{1}{2} \times 8^2 - \tfrac{1}{2} \times g \times 1 = \tfrac{1}{2} \times \tfrac{1}{2} \times v_3^2 + \tfrac{1}{2} \times g \times 1 \qquad (2)$$

Hence $T_3 + \tfrac{1}{2}g = 32 - 2g$

or $T_3 = 32 - \tfrac{5}{2} \times 9.8 > 0$

Therefore the string is taut at the highest point on the circle and the particle will describe complete circles.

(b) Maximum tension, T_{max}, occurs at P (i.e. T_1)
and minimum tension T_{min}, occurs at R (i.e. T_3)
Applying Newton's Law radially at P

$$T_1 - \tfrac{1}{2}g = \tfrac{1}{2} \times \frac{8^2}{1}$$

Therefore $\hspace{3cm} T_{max} = (32 + 4.9)\,\text{N} = 36.9\,\text{N}$

We already know that $\hspace{1.5cm} T_{min} = (32 - 24.5)\,\text{N} = 7.5\,\text{N}$

Therefore $\hspace{1.5cm} T_{max} : T_{min} = 36.9 : 7.5 = 4.9 : 1$

(c) Applying Newton's Law tangentially at Q

$\uparrow \hspace{4cm} -\tfrac{1}{2}g = \tfrac{1}{2}\dfrac{dv}{dt}$

Hence $\hspace{3.5cm} \dfrac{dv}{dt} = -g$

The tangential acceleration when the string is horizontal is of magnitude g

3) A particle of mass m rests at the highest point of the outer surface of a smooth
cylinder of radius a whose axis is horizontal. If the particle is slightly disturbed
from rest so that it begins to travel in a vertical circle find the vertical distance
travelled by the particle before it leaves the surface of the cylinder.
After leaving the cylinder how far does the particle fall while travelling a distance
a horizontally?

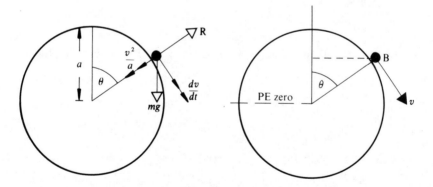

Applying Newton's Law radially at B

$$mg \cos \theta - R = \frac{mv^2}{a} \tag{1}$$

Conservation of M.E. from A to B

$$0 + mga = \tfrac{1}{2}mv^2 + mga \cos \theta \tag{2}$$

From (1) and (2) $R = mg \cos \theta - \dfrac{m}{a}(2ga - 2ga \cos \theta)$

The particle is about to leave the surface at C, when $R = 0$ and $\theta = \alpha$

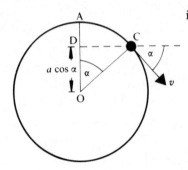

i.e. when $0 = 3\,mg \cos \alpha - 2\,mg$

or $\cos \alpha = \frac{2}{3}$

Then $AD = a - a \cos \alpha = \dfrac{a}{3}$.

The particle descends a vertical distance

$\dfrac{a}{3}$ before leaving the cylinder.

When $\cos \alpha = \frac{2}{3}$ equation 2 gives:

$$v^2 = 2ga\left(1 - \tfrac{2}{3}\right) = \dfrac{2ga}{3}$$

The particle now begins to travel as a projectile with velocity components

$$\begin{cases} v \cos \alpha \to \\ v \sin \alpha \downarrow \end{cases}$$

If $\cos \alpha = \frac{2}{3}$, $\sin \alpha = \sqrt{1 - \frac{4}{9}} = \dfrac{\sqrt{5}}{3}$

Hence the velocity components at C are

$$\frac{2}{3}\sqrt{\frac{2ga}{3}} \to$$

$$\frac{1}{3}\sqrt{\frac{10ga}{3}} \downarrow$$

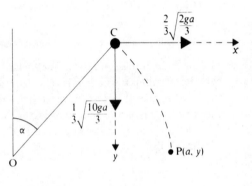

If the particle, travelling as a projectile, reaches a point P (a, y) in time t then:

$$a = \frac{2}{3}\sqrt{\frac{2ga}{3}}\,t \tag{3}$$

and $$y = \frac{1}{3}\sqrt{\frac{10ga}{3}}\,t + \frac{1}{2}gt^2 \tag{4}$$

Hence $$y = \frac{1}{3}\sqrt{\frac{10ga}{3}}\left(\frac{3a}{2}\sqrt{\frac{3}{2ga}}\right) + \frac{1}{2}g\left(\frac{3a}{2}\sqrt{\frac{3}{2ga}}\right)^2$$

or $$y = \frac{\sqrt{5}\,a}{2} + \frac{27a}{16}$$

The particle therefore travels a distance $\dfrac{8\sqrt{5} + 27}{16}\,a$ vertically while moving a distance a horizontally from C.

4) A particle P of mass m is attached by a light inextensible string of length $2a$, to a fixed point O. When vertically below O, P is given a horizontal velocity u. When OP becomes horizontal the string hits a small smooth rail, Q, distant a from O and the particle continues to rotate about Q as centre. If the particle just describes complete circles about the rail, find the value of u.

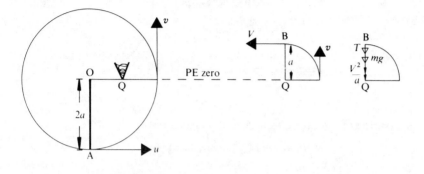

(There is no loss in mechanical energy when the string hits the rail Q because the sudden change in tension is perpendicular to the direction of motion of the particle and therefore has no effect on its speed).

Conservation of M.E. from A to B.

$$\tfrac{1}{2} mu^2 - mg(2a) = \tfrac{1}{2} mV^2 + mga \tag{1}$$

Applying Newton's Law radially at B.

$$T + mg = m\frac{V^2}{a} \tag{2}$$

Hence

$$T + mg = \frac{m}{a}(u^2 - 6ga)$$

or

$$T = \frac{m}{a}(u^2 - 7ga)$$

For complete circles about Q, $T \geqslant 0$ at B

i.e. $u^2 \geqslant 7ga$

If the particle *just* describes complete circles

$$u = \sqrt{7ga}$$

5) A smooth hollow cylinder of radius a and centre O, is fixed with its axis horizontal. A particle P of mass m is projected from a point on the inside surface of the cylinder, level with O, with speed $\sqrt{14ga}$ vertically downward. When P reaches the lowest point of the surface it collides with and adheres to a stationary particle Q also of mass m. Find the height above the centre of the cylinder at which the combined mass loses contact with the surface.

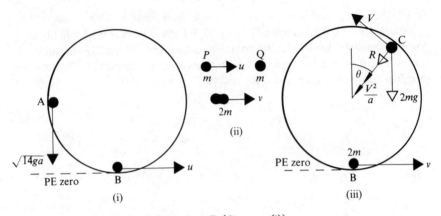

Conservation of M.E. for P from A to B (diagram (i))

$$\tfrac{1}{2}m\,(14ga) + mga \;=\; \tfrac{1}{2}mu^2$$

$$u^2 \;=\; 16ga$$

$$u \;=\; 4\sqrt{ga}$$

At impact between P and Q, (diagram (ii))
Conservation of Linear Momentum

$$m(4\sqrt{ga}) + 0 \;=\; 2mv$$

$$v \;=\; 2\sqrt{ga}$$

Now for the particle of mass $2m$ (diagram (iii))
Conservation of M.E. from B to C

$$\tfrac{1}{2}2m(2\sqrt{ga})^2 = \tfrac{1}{2}2mV^2 + 2mga + 2mga\cos\theta \qquad (1)$$

Applying Newton's Law radially at C

$$2mg\cos\theta + R \;=\; 2m\frac{V^2}{a} \qquad (2)$$

The particle leaves the surface when $R = 0$

so that $\qquad 2mg\cos\theta \;=\; 2m\dfrac{V^2}{a}$

In equation (1) $\qquad 4mga \;=\; m\,(ag\cos\theta) + 2mga + 2mga\cos\theta$

$$\cos\theta \;=\; \tfrac{2}{3}$$

When $\cos\theta = \tfrac{2}{3}$ the particle leaves the cylinder at a height $a\cos\theta = \tfrac{2}{3}a$ above the centre.

SUMMARY

1) A particle travelling in a vertical circle of radius r has two acceleration components:

$\dfrac{v^2}{r}$ towards the centre and $\dfrac{dv}{dt}$ along the tangent.

2) A particle which is restricted to the circular path will travel in complete circles if the velocity u at the lowest point satisfies $u^2 > 4gr$.

3) A particle which is free to leave the circular path must satisfy a condition which will ensure that the particle is always at a distance r from the centre of the circle e.g. contact with the inside of a circular surface must not be lost. In this case $u^2 \geqslant 5gr$.

EXERCISE 11e

1) A particle of mass 2 kg is attached to the end A of a light inextensible string AB fixed at B. Initially AB is horizontal and the particle is projected vertically downward from this position with velocity v. If the particle describes complete circles, find the possible values of v if the length of the string is 1 m.

2) A particle of mass m is projected horizontally from the highest point of a smooth solid sphere. If the particle loses contact with the surface after descending a vertical distance of one quarter of the radius a of the sphere, find the speed of projection.

3) A smooth hollow cylinder of radius 0.5 m is fixed with its axis horizontal. A particle of mass 1.2 kg is projected from the lowest point on the inner surface with speed (a) $3\,\text{ms}^{-1}$ (b) $4\,\text{ms}^{-1}$ (c) $5\,\text{ms}^{-1}$. Determine in each case whether the particle will oscillate, describe complete circles or lose contact with the cylinder.

4) A particle of mass m is free to rotate at the end of a light inextensible string fixed at its other end. If the length of the string is l and the particle is projected horizontally from its lowest position with speed $\sqrt{6gl}$, find the greatest and least tensions in the string during the ensuing motion. Find also the *resultant* acceleration of the particle when it is:
(a) at its lowest position,
(b) at its highest position,
(c) level with the fixed end of the string.

5) A particle of mass 1.5 kg is lying at the lowest point of the inner surface of a hollow sphere of radius 0.5 m when it is given a horizontal impulse. Find the magnitude of the impulse:
(a) if the particle subsequently describes complete vertical circles,
(b) if the particle loses contact with the sphere after rotating through 120°.

6) A light inextensible string AB of length l is fixed at A and is attached to a

particle of mass m at B. B is held a distance l vertically above A and is projected horizontally from this position with speed $\sqrt{2gl}$. When AB is horizontal a point C on the string strikes a fixed smooth peg so that the acceleration of the particle is instantaneously doubled. Express the length of AC in terms of l.

The particle continues to describe vertical circles about C as centre. Compare the greatest and least tensions in the string during this motion.

MULTIPLE CHOICE EXERCISE 11

The instructions for answering these questions are given on page (xii)

TYPE I

1) A particle of mass m is travelling at constant speed v round a circle of radius r. Its acceleration is:

(a) rv^2 (b) $\dfrac{mv^2}{r}$ (c) $\dfrac{v^2}{r}$ (d) mrv^2.

2) A string of length l has one end fixed and a particle of mass m attached to the other end travels in a horizontal circle of radius r. The tension in the string is:

(a) mg (b) $\dfrac{mgl}{\sqrt{l^2-r^2}}$ (c) $mg\dfrac{r}{l}$ (d) $mg\dfrac{l}{r}$

3) A bead is threaded on to a circular wire fixed in a vertical plane. The bead travels round the wire. The acceleration of the bead is:
(a) towards the centre and constant,
(b) towards the centre and varies,
(c) made up of two components one radial and one tangential,
(d) away from the centre and varies.

4) A vehicle can travel round a curve at a higher speed when the road is banked than when the road is level. This is because:
(a) banking increases the friction,
(b) banking increases the radius,
(c) the normal reaction has a horizontal component,
(d) when the track is banked the weight of the car acts down the incline.

5) A particle hanging at the end of a string of length a is given a horizontal velocity V so that it begins to travel in a vertical circle. The particle will describe complete circles if:
(a) $V \geqslant \sqrt{4ga}$ (b) $V < \sqrt{5ga}$ (c) $V > \sqrt{2ga}$ (d) $V \geqslant \sqrt{5ga}$.

TYPE II

6) A string of length l has one end fixed and a particle of mass m is attached to the other end. If the particle describes a horizontal circle at an angular speed ω:
(a) the tension in the string $= m/\omega^2$,
(b) the speed of the particle is $l\omega$,
(c) the resultant force acting on the particle has no vertical component.

7) A particle of mass m travelling in a vertical circle at the end of an inelastic string of length l will perform complete circles provided that:
(a) the kinetic energy at the lowest point is at least $2\,mgl$,
(b) the speed is zero only at the highest point,
(c) the string never goes slack,
(d) the string does not break until its tension exceeds $6\,mg$.

8) A bead is travelling on a smooth circular wire in a vertical plane and has a speed V at the lowest point.
(a) The mechanical energy of the bead is constant.
(b) No external forces act on the bead.
(c) The bead will oscillate if $V < 2\sqrt{ga}$.
(d) The bead will oscillate only if $V < \sqrt{2ga}$.

9) A particle of mass m is on a smooth table travelling with angular speed ω in a horizontal circle at the end of a string of length l whose other end is fixed. T is the tension in the string.
(a) T is constant.
(b) $T = ml\omega^2$.
(c) $T = mg$.
(d) T is the resultant force acting on the particle.

TYPE III

10) (a) A particle is travelling in a circle.
   (b) A particle is travelling with constant velocity.

11) A particle is describing a vertical circle of radius a and the speed V at the lowest point is such that $\sqrt{4ga} < V < \sqrt{5ga}$.
(a) The particle is not free to leave the circular path.
(b) Complete circles are described.

12) A light rod of length l is rotating in a vertical plane about an axis through one end. A particle is attached to the other end.
(a) The rod is at all times in tension.
(b) The greatest speed of the particle is between $\sqrt{2gl}$ and $\sqrt{5gl}$.

TYPE IV

13) A particle at the end of a string is travelling as a conical pendulum. Calculate the tension in the string if:
(a) the angular velocity is 2 rad s^{-1},
(b) the length of the string is 1.5 m,
(c) the inclination of the string to the vertical is $30°$.

14) Find the angle at which a race track should be banked to enable a car to go round at a speed V without tendency to side slip.
(a) The radius of the track is r,

(b) the mass of the car is m,
(c) the coefficient of friction is μ.

15) A particle is moving in a vertical plane on the inside of a smooth hollow cylinder. Determine where the particle loses contact with the cylinder.
(a) The velocity at the lowest point is $4\,\text{ms}^{-1}$,
(b) the mass of the particle is $2\,\text{kg}$,
(c) the radius of the cylinder is $1\,\text{m}$.

TYPE V

16) A particle travelling in a circle of radius r has an acceleration of constant magnitude $\dfrac{v^2}{r}$ towards the centre. Therefore the particle has a constant velocity.

17) A particle travelling in a vertical plane must either oscillate or describe complete circles.

18) Every particle describing a circle has a resultant acceleration towards the centre.

19) One end A of a light inextensible string is attached to a fixed point. A particle suspended at the other end B can describe horizontal circles about A as centre.

MISCELLANEOUS EXERCISE 11   1, 6, 9.

1) A race track has a circular bend of radius $50\,\text{m}$ and is banked at $40°$ to the horizontal. If the coefficient of friction between the car wheels and the track is $\frac{3}{5}$, find within what speed limits a car can travel round the bend without slipping either inwards or outwards.

2) A particle is held at a point P on the surface of a smooth fixed sphere of radius $2a$ and centre O, where PO makes an angle $30°$ with the upward vertical. If the particle is released from rest at P find the height above O of the point where the particle loses contact with the sphere. Find also the horizontal distance of the particle from O when it is level with O.

3) A particle A of mass m is held on the surface of a fixed smooth solid sphere centre O and radius a at a point P such that OP makes an acute angle $\arccos \frac{3}{4}$ with the upward vertical, and is then released. Prove that, when OA makes an angle θ with the upward vertical, the velocity v of the particle is given by

$$v^2 = \tfrac{1}{2}ga\,(3 - 4\cos\theta),$$

provided that the particle remains on the surface of the sphere, and find the normal reaction on the particle at this time.
Deduce that the particle leaves the surface when OA makes an angle $\frac{1}{3}\pi$ with the upward vertical.   (Oxford)

4) A light inextensible string AB has length $7a$ and breaking tension $4mg$. A particle of mass m is fastened to the string at a point P, where $AP = 4a$. The ends A and B are secured to fixed points, A being at a height $5a$ vertically above B. If the particle is revolving in a horizontal circle with both portions of the string taut, show that the time of one revolution lies between

$$3\pi \sqrt{\frac{a}{5g}} \quad \text{and} \quad 8\pi \sqrt{\frac{a}{5g}}. \qquad \text{(U of L)}$$

5) A light inextensible string of length l is threaded through a smooth bead of mass m and has one end fixed at a point A on a smooth horizontal table and the other at a point B at a height $\frac{1}{2}l$ vertically above A. The bead is projected so as to describe a circle in contact with the table with angular velocity ω. Find the radius of the circle. Prove that the tension in the string is $\frac{15}{64}ml\omega^2$, and that ω must not exceed a certain value. Find this value. (J.M.B.)

6) A heavy particle is projected horizontally with speed u from the lowest point on the inside of a hollow smooth sphere of internal radius a. Show that the least value of u for the particle to complete a vertical circle is $\sqrt{5ga}$. The particle, projected with this velocity, hits a rubber peg after travelling a distance $\frac{3}{2}\pi a$, the coefficient of restitution between the peg and the particle being $\frac{1}{2}$. Calculate the vertical height of the particle above the point of projection at the moment when it leaves the surface of the sphere. (A.E.B.)

7) A particle A of mass m hangs by a light inextensible string of length a from a fixed point O. The string is initially vertical and the particle is then given a horizontal velocity $\sqrt{(nga)}$. Show that it will move round a complete circle in a vertical plane provided $n \geqslant 5$.
If when the string OA reaches the horizontal the particle A collides and coalesces with a second particle at rest also of mass m, find the least value of n for the vertical circle to be completed. (U of L)

8) A light inelastic string of length l has one end fixed at O and a particle of mass m attached to the other end. The particle describes a circle in a horizontal plane below O with constant angular velocity ω so that the string makes an angle θ with the vertical through O. Write down the equations of motion and show that $\cos \theta = g/l\omega^2$.
The string is now replaced with an elastic string of unstretched length l and modulus λmg and the particle is set in motion so that it rotates in a horizontal circle with the same angular velocity ω as before. Prove that, if the string makes an angle ϕ with the vertical

$$\cos \phi = (\lambda g - l\omega^2)/\lambda l\omega^2. \qquad \text{(S.U.J.B.)}$$

9) Two light inelastic strings AP and BP connect a particle P to fixed points A and B. The point B is vertically above A and $AB = AP = l$ and $BP = l\sqrt{3}$. The particle P moves in a horizontal circle with constant speed. The least angular

speed of P for both strings to be taut is ω. At this speed calculate the angle between the strings and the value of ω. When the angular speed of P is ω_1 ($> \omega$) the tensions in the string are equal. Show that $\omega_1{}^2 = 2g/(l\sqrt{3})$.　　　(A.E.B.)

10) The sleepers on a railway line which rounds a circular bend are banked so that at speed V an engine would exert no lateral thrust on the rails. The thrust on the inner rail when the engine's speed is v_1 is equal to the thrust on the outer rail when the speed is v_2 ($v_2 > V > v_1$). Show that $2V^2 = v_1{}^2 + v_2{}^2$.

11) A particle moves in a vertical circle on the smooth inner surface of a fixed hollow sphere of radius a and centre O, the plane of the circle passing through O. The particle is projected from the lowest point of the sphere with initial velocity u, and leaves the surface of the sphere at a point P, where OP makes an angle θ with the upward vertical through O. Show that

$$\cos\theta = \frac{u^2 - 2ga}{3ga}$$

If $\cos\theta = \frac{4}{5}$, show that after leaving the sphere the particle will pass the vertical line through O at a distance above O of $\frac{115}{128} a$.　　　(Cambridge)

12) A particle P of mass m is attached by a light inelastic string of length $a \sec\alpha$ to a point A vertically above a point O of a smooth horizontal plane and at a distance a from it.
(a) If P moves in a circle of centre O on the plane with speed v, show that
　　$v^2 \leqslant ag \tan^2\alpha$.
(b) One end of a light elastic string of natural length a and modulus of elasticity $\frac{1}{4} mg$ is now attached to a fixed point below the plane at a distance a from O, and the other end is passed through a small smooth hole at O and attached to P. If P describes a circle on the plane with both strings taut, and if the reaction of P on the plane has magnitude equal to half of the weight of P, find an expression for the speed v of P in terms of a, g and α.　　　(W.J.E.C.)

13) Two rigid, light rods AB, BC, each of length $2a$, are smoothly jointed at B, and the rod AB is smoothly jointed at A to a fixed smooth vertical rod. The joint at B carries a particle of mass m. A small ring, also of mass m, is smoothly jointed to BC at C and can slide on the vertical rod below A. The ring rests on a smooth horizontal ledge fixed to the vertical rod at a distance $2a$ below A, as shown in the diagram.

The system rotates about the vertical rod with constant angular velocity ω. Find the force exerted by the ledge on the ring, and deduce that if the ring remains on the ledge, then $a\omega^2 \leqslant 3g$.

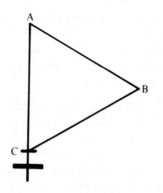

(J.M.B.)

14) A smooth hemispherical bowl with centre O and of radius a is fixed with its rim upwards and horizontal. A particle P of mass $3m$ describes a horizontal circle on the inner surface of the bowl with angular velocity ω. This mass is attached to one end of a light inextensible string of length $2a$. The string passes through a smooth hole at the lowest point of the bowl. At the other end of the string is attached a particle of mass m which moves as a conical pendulum in a horizontal circle with angular velocity ω. By considering the motion of the second particle show that the motion is only possible if $\omega^2 > g/b$, where b is the length of string outside the bowl.

If the angle made by OP with the vertical is $60°$, show that $\omega^2 = 6g/a$, and find, as a multiple of mg, the reaction between the first particle and the bowl.

(Cambridge)

15) A particle of mass m is attached to one end of a light inelastic cord of length l. The other end of the cord is held fixed at a height h (less than l) above a smooth horizontal table. If the particle is held on the table with the cord fully extended and projected along the table so that it moves in a horizontal circle with uniform speed v, prove that the force R that it exerts on the table is given by

$$R = m \left(g - \frac{v^2 h}{l^2 - h^2} \right).$$

Find an expression for T, the tension of the cord, in terms of m, v, l, h.
If $h = 0.3$ and $l = 0.5$ (both in metres) and $m = 2$ (kg),
(i) evaluate the force R, stating the units, when the speed is 1 ms^{-1}.
(ii) find the maximum velocity for which the particle will remain on the table, and the corresponding tension of the string.   (S.U.J.B.)

16) One end of a light inextensible string of length l is attached to a fixed point A and the other end to a particle B of mass m which is hanging freely at rest.
The particle is then projected horizontally with velocity $\sqrt{7gl/2}$. Calculate the height of B above A when the string goes slack.

The procedure is repeated but this time a small smooth peg C is placed at the same level as A so that when the string is horizontal it comes into contact with the peg. If the particle then describes a complete circle about C, find the least value of AC. When AC has this least value find the tension in the string immediately before and after the string strikes the peg.   (U of L)

17) A particle moves with constant speed v in a circle of radius r. Show that the acceleration of the particle is v^2/r directed towards the centre of the circle.
A rough horizontal plate rotates with constant angular velocity ω about a fixed vertical axis. A particle of mass m lies on the plate at a distance $5a/4$ from this axis. If the coefficient of friction between the plate and the particle is $\frac{1}{3}$ and the particle remains at rest relative to the plate, show that

$$\omega \leqslant \sqrt{\left(\frac{4g}{15a}\right)}$$

The particle is now connected to the axis by a horizontal light elastic string, of natural length a and modulus $3mg$. If the particle remains at rest relative to the plate and at a distance $5a/4$ from the axis, show that the greatest possible angular velocity of the plate is

$$\sqrt{\left(\frac{13g}{15a}\right)}$$

and find the least possible angular velocity.   (J.M.B.)

18) One end of a light inelastic string of length a is attached to a fixed point O and a particle of mass m is attached to the other end, A. The particle is held at the same level as O, at a distance of $a \sin \alpha$ away from O, and released. Find:
  (i) the impulse in the string when it becomes taut,
  (ii) the speed of the particle immediately after the string becomes taut,
  (iii) the cosine of the angle that OA makes with the vertical when the particle
      first comes to instantaneous rest.
When OA is next vertical it meets a peg placed at a distance of $3a/4$ below O. Show that, if the particle reaches the top of its new circular path, the tension in the string there is $mg(3 - 8 \cos^3 \alpha)$, g being the gravitational acceleration.
                    (S.U.J.B.)

19) A particle P of mass m moves in a vertical circle along the smooth inner surface of a fixed hollow sphere of internal radius a and centre O, the plane of the circle passing through O. The particle is projected from the lowest point of the sphere with a horizontal velocity u, where $u^2 > 2ga$. When OP makes an angle θ with upward vertical, the velocity of the particle is v and the normal reaction between the particle and the sphere is R. Find expressions for v and R in terms of m, a, u, θ and g.

Show that if $u^2 < 5ga$ the particle leaves the sphere where

$$\cos \theta = \frac{u^2 - 2ga}{3ga}$$

If the particle leaves the sphere at a point A and its trajectory meets the sphere again at a point B such that AB is a diameter of the sphere, show that OA makes an angle of 45° with the vertical, and find the requisite value of u.   (Cambridge)

20) Particles P and Q of equal mass are connected by a light inelastic string of length l threaded through a small hole O in a smooth horizontal table. The particle P is free to move on the table and describes a horizontal circle so that OP rotates with constant angular velocity ω. The particle Q moves below the table, with the string taut, in a horizontal circle with the same angular velocity ω. Prove that OP $= l/2$. Find the angle which OQ makes with the vertical and show that $\omega^2 > 2g/l$.
    (U of L)

21) A particle moves with constant speed v in a circle of radius r. Show that the acceleration of the particle is v^2/r directed towards the centre of the circle.
A particle P of mass $2m$ is attached by a light inextensible string of length a to a fixed point O and is also attached by another light inextensible string of length a to a small ring Q of mass $3m$ which can slide on a fixed smooth vertical wire passing through O. The particle P describes a horizontal circle with OP inclined at an angle $\frac{1}{3}\pi$ with the downward vertical.
  (i) Find the tensions in the strings OP and PQ.
 (ii) Show that the speed of P is $(6ga)^{\frac{1}{2}}$.
(iii) Find the period of revolution of the system.   (J.M.B.)

22) A circular cone of semi-angle α, made of thin smooth metal, is fixed with its axis vertical and its vertex O downwards. A particle P, of mass m, moving with constant speed V, describes a horizontal circle on the inner surface of the cone in a plane which is at a distance b above O.
(a) If P is free, show that $V^2 = gb$.
(b) If P is attached to one end of a light elastic string PA of natural length a
    ($a < b \sec \alpha < 2a$) and modulus of elasticity mg, find V^2 in the following two cases: (i) A is attached to O; (ii) A is passed through a small hole at O and attached to a particle of mass m that hangs freely in equilibrium.
    (W.J.E.C.)

23) A smooth wire bent into the form of a circle of radius a is fixed with its plane vertical. A small ring of mass m which can slide freely on the wire is attached to one end of a light elastic string of natural length a and modulus $4mg$, the other end of the string being tied to the highest point of the wire. The ring is held at the lowest point of the wire with the string taut and is then slightly displaced. Write down the equation of energy when the radius to the ring makes an angle θ

with the downward vertical and deduce that the maximum velocity occurs when $\cos \theta = -1/9$.

Find the velocity of the ring when the string first becomes slack.   (U of L)

24) Prove that the potential energy of a light elastic string of natural length l and modulus λ when stretched to a length $(l + x)$ is $\frac{1}{2}\lambda\, x^2/l$.

A bead of mass m can slide without friction along a circular hoop of radius a which is fixed in a vertical plane. The bead is connected to the highest point of the hoop by a light elastic string of natural length a and modulus $3mg$. Initially the bead is moving with speed u through the lowest point of the hoop. Given that $u^2 = ag$, show that the bead just reaches the highest point of the hoop. Show that the speed was u at the instant when the string first went slack and find the reaction of the hoop on the bead at that instant.   (J.M.B.)

25) The ends of a light string are fixed to two points A, B in the same vertical line, with A above B, and the string passes through a small smooth ring of mass m. The ring is fastened to the string at a point P, and when the string is taut the angle APB is a right angle, the angle BAP is θ and the distance of P from AB is r. The ring revolves in a horizontal circle with constant angular velocity ω and with the string taut. Find the tensions in the two parts of the string in terms of r, ω, m, g and θ.

Given that AB $= 5a$, AP $= 4a$, show that

$$16a\omega^2 > 5g.$$

If the ring is free to move on the string, instead of being fastened, show that it will remain in the same position on the string as before if the angular velocity Ω satisfies the equation

$$12a\, \Omega^2 \;=\; 35g.$$

In this case give the period of the motion in terms of a, g and π.   (J.M.B.)

CHAPTER 12

SIMPLE HARMONIC MOTION

DEFINITIONS

Simple Harmonic Motion (S.H.M.) is a particular type of oscillatory motion. It is defined in one of the following ways.
1. A particle moving in a straight line with a linear acceleration proportional to the linear displacement from a fixed point, and always directed towards that fixed point, is travelling with linear S.H.M.

2. A particle which oscillates on a circular arc with angular acceleration which is proportional to the angular displacement from a fixed line and always directed towards that fixed line is travelling with angular S.H.M.

BASIC EQUATIONS OF S.H.M.

1. LINEAR S.H.M.

Given a fixed point O and a particle P distant x from O at any time, the linear acceleration of P is $\dfrac{d^2x}{dt^2}$ or $\ddot{x}$ in the direction $\overrightarrow{OP}$.

But, by definition, the acceleration, f, of P is proportional to x and towards O. Using n^2 as a constant of proportion, $f = n^2x$ in the direction $\overrightarrow{PO}$

Therefore $\ddot{x} = -n^2x$
This differential equation is the basic equation of linear S.H.M.

2. ANGULAR S.H.M.

Given a fixed line OA and a particle P which is at an angular displacement θ from OA at any time t, the angular acceleration of P is $\dfrac{d^2\theta}{dt^2}$ or $\ddot{\theta}$ away from OA.

But by definition the angular acceleration α of P is proportional to θ and towards OA.

Therefore $\ddot{\theta} = -n^2\theta$ is the basic equation of angular S.H.M.

By integrating either basic equation it is possible to derive further relationships involving velocity, displacement and time.

Linear S.H.M.

The acceleration of P can be taken as $\dfrac{d^2x}{dt^2}, \dfrac{dv}{dt}$, or $v\dfrac{dv}{dx}$ (see Chapter 9), where v is the velocity of P at any time t.

The basic equation can be written

$$v\frac{dv}{dx} = -n^2x$$

Therefore

$$\int v\,dv = -n^2 \int x\,dx$$

Hence

$$\frac{v^2}{2} = -n^2\frac{x^2}{2} + K_1$$

If P is momentarily at rest when at a point A where OA $= a$, then $K_1 = \dfrac{n^2a^2}{2}$

so that

$$v^2 = n^2(a^2 - x^2)$$

But

$$v = \frac{dx}{dt}$$

Therefore

$$\frac{dx}{dt} = n\sqrt{a^2 - x^2}$$

Integrating
$$\int \frac{dx}{\sqrt{a^2 - x^2}} = n \int dt$$

Hence
$$\arcsin \frac{x}{a} = nt + K_2$$

If we choose to begin our analysis from point A, $t = 0$ when $x = a$;

then $K_2 = \dfrac{\pi}{2}$

so that
$$\arcsin \frac{x}{a} = nt + \frac{\pi}{2}$$

or
$$\frac{x}{a} = \sin\left(nt + \frac{\pi}{2}\right) = \cos nt$$

i.e.
$$x = a \cos nt$$

Summarising our results so far:

$$\frac{d^2x}{dt^2} = -n^2x \tag{1}$$

$$v = n\sqrt{a^2 - x^2} \tag{2}$$

$$x = a \cos nt \tag{3}$$

Now equation (2) shows that $v = 0$ when $x = \pm a$ confirming that the particle oscillates between two points A and A' on opposite sides of O and equidistant from O

The distance OA is the *amplitude* of the S.H.M.
The point O is the *centre* or *mean position* of the motion.
The time taken to travel from A to O is obtained from equation (3) when $x = 0$
giving $nt = \dfrac{\pi}{2}$ or $t = \dfrac{\pi}{2n}$.

It will take four times as long to travel from A to A' and back to A, i.e. to describe one complete oscillation. This is the *periodic time* (or period of oscillation), T, and

$$T = \frac{2\pi}{n} \tag{4}$$

Several interesting properties of S.H.M. can be observed from the four standard formulae which have just been derived.

1. The periodic time is independent of the amplitude of the motion (equation 4).
2. The greatest speed is na and occurs when $x = 0$ i.e. at the centre of the path. The speed is zero when $x = \pm a$, i.e. at the ends of the path.
3. The greatest acceleration is of magnitude $n^2 a$ and occurs when $x = \pm a$, while when $x = 0$, at the centre of the path, the acceleration is zero.

Angular S.H.M.

Using $\theta = \phi$ when $t = 0$ and the angular velocity $\omega = 0$, a similar set of relationships can be obtained for angular S.H.M. They are:

$$\frac{d^2\theta}{dt^2} = -n^2\theta \tag{1}$$

$$\omega = n\sqrt{\phi^2 - \theta^2} \tag{2}$$

$$\theta = \phi \cos nt \tag{3}$$

$$T = \frac{2\pi}{n} \tag{4}$$

Note: Unless their derivation is specifically asked for, the standard formulae (equations 1–4) can be quoted when solving problems on S.H.M. whether linear or angular.

EXAMPLES 12a

1) A particle is describing linear S.H.M. of amplitude 2 m. If its speed is 3 ms^{-1} when the particle is 1 m from the centre of the path find:
(a) the periodic time,
(b) the maximum velocity,
(c) the maximum acceleration.

Using

$$v^2 = n^2(a^2 - x^2)$$

gives

$$3^2 = n^2(2^2 - 1^2)$$

and

$$n = \sqrt{3}$$

(a) Periodic time $= \dfrac{2\pi}{n} = \dfrac{2\pi}{3}\sqrt{3}$ seconds.

(b) The velocity is greatest when $x = 0$ (equation 2)
    Therefore $v_{max} = na = 2\sqrt{3} \text{ ms}^{-1}$

(c) The acceleration is greatest when x is greatest
    i.e. when $x = a$ (equation 1)
    Therefore $f_{max} = n^2 a = 6 \text{ ms}^{-2}$.

2) A particle is travelling in a straight line with S.H.M. of period 4 seconds. If the greatest speed is $2\ \text{ms}^{-1}$, find the amplitude of the path and speed of the particle when it is $\dfrac{3}{\pi}$ m from the centre.

$$\text{Period} = 4 = \frac{2\pi}{n}$$

Therefore

$$n = \frac{\pi}{2}$$

$$v_{max} = na = 2\ \text{ms}^{-1}$$

Therefore

$$a = \frac{4}{\pi}\ \text{m}$$

Also

$$v = n\sqrt{a^2 - x^2}$$

When $x = \dfrac{3}{\pi}$,

$$v = \frac{\pi}{2}\sqrt{\left(\frac{4}{\pi}\right)^2 - \left(\frac{3}{\pi}\right)^2}$$

$$v = \frac{\sqrt{7}}{2}\ \text{ms}^{-1}.$$

3) A particle passes through three points, A, B, C in that order, with velocity 0, $2\ \text{ms}^{-1}$ and $-1\ \text{ms}^{-1}$ respectively. The particle is moving with S.H.M. in a straight line. What is the period and amplitude of the motin if $AB = 2\ \text{m}$ and $AC = 8\ \text{m}$?

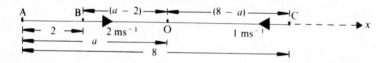

Since at A, $v = 0$, A must be one end of the path. Let O be the centre of the path where $AO = a$. The velocities at B and C, being opposite in sign are in opposite sense. Therefore B and C are on opposite sides of O.
Measuring x from O in the sense $\overrightarrow{AO}$ we have

$$v = 2 \text{ when } x = -(a-2)$$

$$v = -1 \text{ when } x = (8-a)$$

Using

$$v^2 = n^2(a^2 - x^2) \text{ gives:}$$

$$4 = n^2(a^2 - [2-a]^2) \tag{1}$$

$$1 = n^2(a^2 - [8-a]^2) \tag{2}$$

$(2) \div (1)$

$$\frac{1}{4} = \frac{16a - 64}{4a - 4} = \frac{4(a-4)}{(a-1)}$$

Therefore $\qquad\qquad\qquad\qquad\qquad\qquad\qquad$ $a = 4.2\,\text{m}$

From (1) $\qquad\qquad\qquad\qquad\qquad\qquad$ $4 = n^2\,[(4.2)^2 - (2.2)^2]$

$\qquad\qquad\qquad\qquad\qquad\qquad\qquad$ $4 = n^2\,(6.4 \times 2.0)$

Hence $\qquad\qquad\qquad\qquad\qquad\qquad\qquad$ $n = \dfrac{\sqrt{5}}{4}$

The periodic time $\qquad\qquad\qquad\qquad$ $T = \dfrac{2\pi}{n} = \dfrac{8\pi\sqrt{5}}{5}\ \text{seconds}$

And the amplitude $\qquad\qquad\qquad\qquad$ $a = 4.2\,\text{m}.$

Summary of Formulae and Terms Used in Linear S.H.M.

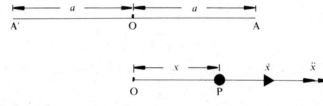

A A$'$ is the path
O $\quad$ is the centre or mean position
a $\quad$ is the amplitude
For a particle at a general point P

$$\ddot{x} = -n^2 x \quad \text{where } n \text{ is a constant}$$

$$\dot{x} = n\sqrt{a^2 - x^2}$$

$$x = a\cos nt$$

$$T = \frac{2\pi}{n} \qquad \text{where } T \text{ is the period of an oscillation}$$

The maximum acceleration has magnitude $n^2 a$ and occurs at A and A$'$.
The maximum speed is na and occurs at O.

EXERCISE 12a

1) A particle moves in a straight line with S.H.M. Find the periodic time if:
(a) the acceleration is of magnitude $2\,\text{ms}^{-2}$ when the particle is 1 m from the centre of oscillation,
(b) the maximum velocity is $4\,\text{ms}^{-1}$ and the maximum acceleration is $6\,\text{ms}^{-2}$.

2) The amplitude of oscillation of a particle describing linear S.H.M. is 1.5 m. The speed at a distance $\sqrt{2}\,\text{m}$ from the mean position is $2\,\text{ms}^{-1}$. Find:
(a) the velocity of the particle at the mean position,
(b) the maximum acceleration,
(c) the period of one oscillation.

3) A particle describing angular S.H.M. passes through its mean position with angular velocity 4 radians per second. If the amplitude is $\pi/6$ radians, find the angular velocity when the angular displacement from the mean position is $\pi/12$ radians.

4) A point is moving in a straight line with S.H.M. about a fixed point A. The point has speeds v_1 and v_2 when its displacements from A are x_1 and x_2 respectively. Find, in terms of x_1, x_2, v_1 and v_2 the periodic time of one oscillation.

5) A particle is describing angular S.H.M. of period π seconds. Its maximum angular acceleration is $4\pi/3$ rad s^{-2}. Find the maximum angular displacement of the particle from its mean position and the angular velocity of the particle when its angular displacement is half the maximum value.

6) A piston performing S.H.M. has a maximum speed of 0.5 ms^{-1} and describes four oscillations in one minute. Find the amplitude of the motion and the velocity and acceleration of the piston when it is 1 m from the centre of oscillation.

7) A particle performs two S.H.M. oscillations each second. Its speed when it is 0.02 m from its mean position is half the maximum speed. Find the amplitude of the motion, the maximum acceleration and the speed at a distance 0.01 m from the mean position.

ASSOCIATED CIRCULAR MOTION

A particle P is describing circular motion of radius a with constant angular velocity ω and Q is the foot of the perpendicular from P on to a diameter A A'. The velocity of P is $a\omega$ along the tangent and acceleration of P is $a\omega^2$ towards the centre O of the circle.

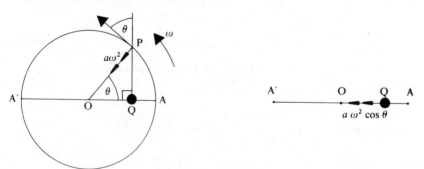

The components, parallel to A A', of the velocity and acceleration of P give the velocity and acceleration of Q.

Therefore, for Q,   velocity $= a\omega \sin \theta$ along $\overrightarrow{QO}$

$\qquad$ acceleration $= a\omega^2 \cos \theta$ along $\overrightarrow{QO}$

If the distance OQ is x, then $\cos \theta = \dfrac{x}{a}$

Therefore Q has an acceleration $a\omega^2 \left(\dfrac{x}{a}\right) = \omega^2 x$ towards O.

But ω^2 is constant. Therefore the acceleration of Q is proportional to the distance of Q from O and is always towards O.

Therefore Q describes S.H.M. about O as centre and with amplitude a.

The equations of Q's S.H.M. can now be derived by considering the associated circular motion of P (an alternative to the derivation by using calculus).

The velocity v of Q $= a\omega \sin \theta$

But $\sin \theta = \dfrac{\sqrt{a^2 - x^2}}{a}$

Therefore $v = \omega \sqrt{a^2 - x^2}$ (2a)

The period, T, of one oscillation of Q is the time taken for P to perform one revolution at angular velocity ω

Therefore $T = \dfrac{2\pi}{\omega}$ (4a)

Comparing equations (2a) and (4a) with equations (2) and (4) derived earlier by integration, we see that ω represents the same constant of proportion as n, and, in fact, the symbol ω is frequently used instead of n.

The time taken by Q to travel over any section of the diameter A A′ is equal to the time taken by P to travel round the corresponding arc,

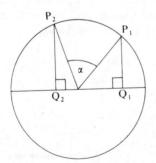

e.g. time taken from Q_1 to Q_2 with S.H.M. = time taken from P_1 to P_2 at constant angular velocity ω.

Required time $= \dfrac{\alpha}{\omega}$ (α must, of course, be measured in radians).

EXAMPLES 12b

1) A particle is performing linear S.H.M. about a centre O and with amplitude OA $= 4d$. B and C are two points on the path such that OB $= 2d$; OC $= d$. Find the time taken to travel (a) from A to B (b) from A to C, if one oscillation is completed in π seconds.

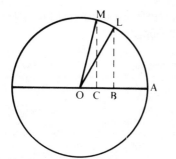

Project B and C on to the associated circle at L and M

As $T = \dfrac{2\pi}{\omega} = \pi$

then $\omega = 2$.

$\cos \text{L}\hat{\text{O}}\text{A} = \dfrac{2d}{4d} = \tfrac{1}{2}$ therefore $\text{L}\hat{\text{O}}\text{A} = \dfrac{\pi}{3}$ radians

$\cos \text{M}\hat{\text{O}}\text{A} = \dfrac{d}{4d} = \tfrac{1}{4}$ therefore $\text{M}\hat{\text{O}}\text{A} = 1.32$ radians

(a) From A to B time taken $= \dfrac{\pi}{3 \times 2} = \dfrac{\pi}{6}$ seconds

(b) From A to C time taken $= \dfrac{1.32}{2} = 0.66$ seconds

Alternatively, having evaluated ω as above, the problem can then be solved by using the formula $x = a \cos \omega t$.

(a) At B, $x = 2d$ and the time from A to B is given by
$$2d = 4d \cos 2t$$

i.e. $2t = \text{arcos } \tfrac{1}{2} = \pi/3$
$$t = \pi/6 \text{ seconds}$$

(b) At C, $x = d$ and the time from A to C is given by
$$d = 4d \cos 2t$$
$$2t = \text{arcos } \tfrac{1}{4} = 1.32 \text{ radians}$$
$$t = 0.66 \text{ seconds}$$

2) A particle travelling with linear S.H.M. of period T starts from the centre O of its path which is of length $2a$. The particle travels for a time t and is then at a point P. Find the distance OP if (i) $t = \tfrac{1}{6}T$ (ii) $t = \tfrac{1}{3}T$.

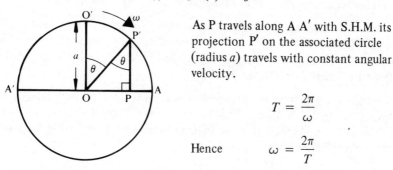

As P travels along A A′ with S.H.M. its projection P′ on the associated circle (radius a) travels with constant angular velocity.

$$T = \dfrac{2\pi}{\omega}$$

Hence $\omega = \dfrac{2\pi}{T}$

The time, t, taken to travel from O to P with S.H.M. is equal to the time taken to traverse the arc O′ P′ with constant angular velocity

i.e. $t = \dfrac{\theta}{\omega}$ or $\theta = \omega t$

But $OP = a \sin \theta = a \sin \omega t = a \sin \dfrac{2\pi t}{T}$

(i) If $t = \frac{1}{6}T$ $OP = a \sin \dfrac{\pi}{3} = a\dfrac{\sqrt{3}}{2}$

(ii) If $t = \frac{1}{3}T$ $OP = a \sin \dfrac{2\pi}{3} = a\dfrac{\sqrt{3}}{2}$

Therefore P is at the same distance from O when $t = \frac{1}{6}T$ and $t = \frac{1}{3}T$, but is travelling in the first case away from O and in the second case toward O.

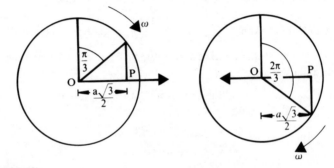

EXERCISE 12b

(The solutions to this exercise may be based either on the standard formulae for S.H.M. or on the use of the associated circular motion).

1) A particle is travelling between two points P and Q with linear S.H.M. If the distance PQ is 6 m and the maximum acceleration of the particle is $16\,\text{ms}^{-2}$, find the time taken to travel:
(a) a distance 1.5 m from P,
(b) from P to the mid-point O of PQ,
(c) from the mid-point of PO to the mid-point of OQ.

2) A particle describes linear S.H.M. of amplitude a about a fixed point O. The period of one complete oscillation is T seconds. If the particle passes through a point P, t seconds after passing through O, find in terms of a the length of OP if:
(i) $t = \frac{1}{6}T$ (ii) $t = \frac{1}{12}T$ (iii) $t = \frac{1}{3}T$.

3) A particle starts from rest at A and moves in a straight line with S.H.M. of periodic time $12\,T$. If the length of the path is $4l$ find the time taken to travel a distance l from A. Show that the velocity at a time T after leaving A is half the maximum velocity.

4) A particle is performing linear S.H.M. of amplitude 0.8 m about a fixed point O. A and B are two points on the path of the particle such that $AO = 0.6$ m and $OB = 0.4$ m. If the particle takes 2 seconds to travel from A to B find, correct to one decimal place, the periodic time of the S.H.M.:
(a) if A and B are on the same side of O,
(b) if A and B are on opposite sides of O.

5) A particle describes linear S.H.M. between two points A and B. The period of one oscillation is 12 seconds. The particle starts from A and after 2 seconds has reached a point distant 0.5 m from A. Find:
(a) the amplitude of the motion,
(b) the maximum acceleration,
(c) the velocity 4 seconds after leaving A.

The Simple Pendulum

Probably the commonest example of angular simple harmonic motion is that of a heavy particle oscillating through a small angle at the end of a light string fixed at its other end, a system known as a simple pendulum.

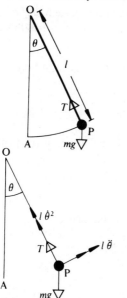

The particle P has mass m and the string, of length l, is fixed at O. OA is vertical and the angle made by the string to the vertical at any time t is θ.

The angular acceleration of P is $\dfrac{d^2\theta}{dt^2}$ away from OA (the sense in which θ *increases*) P also has an acceleration $l\dot{\theta}^2$ towards O. Applying Newton's Law along the tangent
$$mg \sin \theta = -ml\ddot{\theta}$$
Now the angle θ is always very small,

$$\sin \theta \simeq \theta$$

Hence $\qquad mg\theta \simeq -ml\ddot{\theta}$

or $\qquad \ddot{\theta} \simeq -\dfrac{g}{l}\theta$

But this is the basic equation of angular S.H.M. Therefore a particle oscillating through *small* angles at the end of a light string performs angular S.H.M. (to a good approximation).

The period, T, of such oscillations is $\dfrac{2\pi}{n}$ where $n^2 = \dfrac{g}{l}$

Therefore $T = 2\pi\sqrt{\dfrac{l}{g}}$

Note: T depends upon the length of the string and the value of gravitational acceleration but not upon the mass of the particle (often called the pendulum *bob*).

Seconds Pendulum

A simple pendulum which swings from one end of its path to the other end in exactly one second is called a *seconds pendulum* and is said to *beat seconds*. Since each half oscillation takes 1 second, the period of oscillation is 2 seconds, i.e. $T = 2$.

The length of string required for a seconds pendulum can then be calculated using

$$T = 2\pi \sqrt{\frac{l}{g}} \quad \text{or} \quad 2 = 2\pi \sqrt{\frac{l}{g}}$$

giving

$$l = \frac{g}{\pi^2}$$

EXAMPLES 12c

1) A simple pendulum which is meant to beat seconds (i.e. each *half oscillation* takes 1 second) gains 1 minute per day. By what fraction of its length should it be lengthened to make it accurate?

The pendulum makes $(24 \times 60 \times 60 + 60)$ half oscillations in 24 hours.

Time for one half oscillation $= \dfrac{24 \times \cancel{60} \times 60}{\cancel{60}\,(24 \times 60 + 1)}$ s

Time for one oscillation $= 2\pi \sqrt{\dfrac{l}{g}}$ where l is the length of the pendulum.

Therefore

$$\frac{24 \times 60}{1441} = \pi \sqrt{\frac{l}{g}} \tag{1}$$

Let the required *extra* length for an accurate 1 second beat be kl

Then

$$1 = \pi \sqrt{\frac{l + kl}{g}} \tag{2}$$

(2) ÷ (1) gives

$$\sqrt{1 + k} = \frac{1441}{1440}$$

Hence

$$k = \left(\frac{1441}{1440}\right)^2 - 1$$

$$= 0.0014$$

The fractional increase in length required is therefore $\dfrac{7}{5000}$.

2) At ground level where $g = 9.81$ ms^{-2} a simple pendulum beats exact seconds. If it is taken to a place where $g = 9.80$ ms^{-2} by how many seconds per day will it be wrong?

If l is the length of the pendulum then

$$\pi\sqrt{\frac{l}{9.81}} = 1 \quad \text{giving} \quad \sqrt{l} = \frac{\sqrt{9.81}}{\pi}$$

When $\qquad\qquad\qquad g = 9.80$ the time, t, of one beat is

$$\pi\sqrt{\frac{l}{9.8}} = \sqrt{\frac{9.81}{9.8}} \text{ s.}$$

Number of beats in 24 hours is now $(24 \times 60 \times 60) \div \sqrt{\dfrac{9.81}{9.8}}$

Number of beats lost in 24 hours is therefore

$$24 \times 60 \times 60 \left(1 - \sqrt{\frac{9.8}{9.81}}\right) = 24 \times 60 \times 60 \, (0.0005)$$

$$= 44$$

Therefore, where $g = 9.80$ the pendulum will lose 44 seconds per day.

EXERCISE 12c

1) By what length should a simple pendulum be shortened if it is meant to beat seconds but loses 40 seconds in 12 hours?

2) A pendulum which beats seconds where $g = 9.81$ ms^{-2} is taken up a mountain to a place where it loses 30 seconds per day. What is the value of g at the new location?

3) If a simple pendulum which beats exact seconds has its length changed by 1%, find the number of seconds by which it will be inaccurate if:
(a) the length is increased,
(b) the pendulum is shortened.

FORCES WHICH PRODUCE S.H.M.

Since linear S.H.M. is motion in which the acceleration is proportional to the distance from, and directed towards, a fixed point, such motion will be produced by the action of *a force directed towards a fixed point and proportional to the distance from that point.* If an elastic string is stretched, the tension in it is proportional to the extension and always acts to restore the string to its natural length.
Consequently we would expect a moving particle attached to a stretched elastic string to perform S.H.M. and will verify that this is so in several different cases.

EXAMPLES 12d

1) An elastic string, of natrual length a and modulus of elasticity λ, is stretched between two points A and B distant $2a$ apart on a smooth horizontal table. A particle of mass m, fastened to the mid-point M of the string, is pulled towards A through a distance less than $a/2$ and is then released. Analyse the subsequent motion.

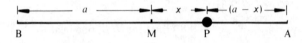

Consider the motion of the particle as it passes through a general point P distant x from M. For the portion of string AP

$$\text{Stretched length} = a - x$$

$$\text{Natural length} = \frac{a}{2}$$

$$\text{Extension} = (a - x) - \frac{a}{2} = \frac{a}{2} - x$$

$$\text{Therefore the tension } T_A = \frac{2\lambda}{a}\left(\frac{a}{2} - x\right) \quad \text{(Hooke's Law)}$$

$$= \frac{\lambda}{a}(a - 2x).$$

Similarly we can show that, for the portion of string BP in which the extension is $\left(\dfrac{a}{2} + x\right)$

$$\text{The tension } T_B = \frac{\lambda}{a}(a + 2x)$$

The particle will never be further from M than its initial displacement. Since this distance is less than $\frac{a}{2}$, neither string will ever go slack during the subsequent motion.

Therefore, for all positions of P, applying Newton's Law in the direction $\overrightarrow{MP}$ gives:

$$T_A - T_B = m\ddot{x}$$

Therefore

$$\frac{\lambda}{a}(a - 2x) - \frac{\lambda}{a}(a + 2x) = m\ddot{x}$$

Hence

$$-\frac{4\lambda x}{a} = m\ddot{x}$$

or
$$\ddot{x} = -\left(\frac{4\lambda}{ma}\right)x$$

Comparing with
$$\ddot{x} = -n^2 x$$

we see that the particle performs S.H.M. about M as centre (M being the fixed point from which x is measured)

The period of oscillation, $\frac{2\pi}{n}$, is $2\pi\sqrt{\frac{ma}{4\lambda}} = \pi\sqrt{\frac{ma}{\lambda}}$

2) One end of an elastic string of natural length l is fixed to a point A on a smooth horizontal table. A particle of mass m is attached to the other end of the string. The particle is pulled away from A and is then released. Investigate the subsequent motion.

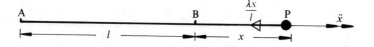

Consider the motion of the particle as it passes through a general point P distant x from B where $AB = l$.

The tension in the string is $\lambda\dfrac{x}{l}$.

Applying Newton's Law in the direction $\overrightarrow{BP}$

$$-\lambda\frac{x}{l} = m\ddot{x}$$

or
$$\ddot{x} = -\frac{\lambda}{ml}x.$$

This is the basic equation of linear S.H.M. where $n^2 = \dfrac{\lambda}{ml}$

The particle therefore initially performs S.H.M. with B as centre.
But as the particle passes through B the string becomes slack and no horizontal force then acts on the particle. It will therefore travel with constant speed until the string becomes taut again at B$'$ where $AB' = l$.

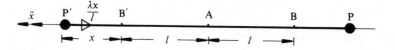

Once beyond B$'$ the string again has a tension $\dfrac{\lambda x}{l}$ towards B$'$ where $B'P' = x$.

The particle again moves with S.H.M. where $n^2 = \dfrac{\lambda}{ml}$ but about centre B'.

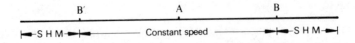

The particle therefore performs half an oscillation with S.H.M. at each end of its journey and covers the section between B and B' with constant speed.

3) Consider an elastic string of natural length a and modulus $2mg$ attached at one end to a fixed point A and hanging vertically with a particle of mass m at the other end. If the particle is pulled vertically downward a distance d below its equilibrium position and then released let us investigate the subsequent motion if $d < a/2$.

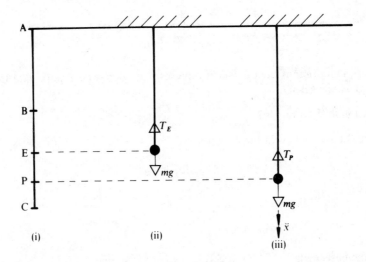

(i)   (ii)   (iii)

In diagram (i) AB is the natural length of the string

E is the position of equilibrium of the particle

P is a general point through which the particle passes

C is the lowest position of the particle.

In diagram (ii) where the extension in the string is e

The tension $T_E = \dfrac{\lambda e}{a} = \dfrac{2mge}{a}$ (Hooke's Law)

But the particle is in equilibrium

Therefore $T_E = mg$ and $e = \dfrac{a}{2}$

In diagram (iii) where the extension is $(e + x)$ and the acceleration of the particle is $\ddot{x}$ in the direction EP.

The tension $T_P = \dfrac{\lambda}{a}(e + x) = \dfrac{2mg}{a}(e + x)$

The maximum distance from E of the particle is the initial displacement d which is less than $a/2$. The particle therefore never rises above the level of B and the string never goes slack. For all positions of P, then, applying Newton's Law vertically downward at P gives:

$$mg - \frac{2mg}{a}(e + x) = m\ddot{x}$$

Therefore

$$mg - \frac{2mg}{a}\left(\frac{a}{2} + x\right) = m\ddot{x}$$

giving

$$-\frac{2mgx}{a} = m\ddot{x}$$

or

$$\ddot{x} = -\frac{2g}{a}x$$

Comparing with

$$\ddot{x} = -n^2 x,$$

we see that this is the basic equation of S.H.M. with centre E. The particle therefore travels throughout with linear S.H.M. about E as centre and with periodic time $2\pi\sqrt{\dfrac{a}{2g}}$. The amplitude of the motion is d since this is the maximum displacement from the centre E.

Note: We chose to measure x from E rather than from B because at E the resultant force, and hence the acceleration, is zero. Zero acceleration being a property of the centre point of the path of any S.H.M. we anticipated that E was a likely centre.

EXERCISE 12d

1) A particle of mass 2 kg is attached to one end of an elastic string of natural length 1 m whose other end is fixed to a point A on a smooth horizontal plane. The particle is pulled across the plane to a point C where AC = 1.5 m and is released from rest at C. B is a point on AC such that AB = 1 m. If the modulus of the string is 10 N show that:

(a) from C to B the particle performs S.H.M. with centre B (remember to analyse a general position),

(b) the time taken to travel from B to C is $\dfrac{\pi\sqrt{5}}{10}$ s,

(c) the speed at B is $\dfrac{\sqrt{5}}{2}$ ms^{-1},

(d) the particle then travels for $\frac{4}{5}\sqrt{5}$ s with constant speed.

2) A particle of mass 4 kg hangs at the end of a light elastic string of natural length 1 m attached at the other end to a fixed point A. The particle hangs in equilibrium at E where $AE = 1.4$ m. Calculate the modulus of elasticity of the string. If the particle is then pulled down to C where $EC = 0.2$ m and is released from rest at C prove that it performs S.H.M. State the centre and the period of the oscillations. What is the speed of the particle as it passes through E and what is the greatest height above E reached by the particle?

3) A particle P of mass m is ~~attahced~~ attached to one end of each of two light elastic strings. The other ends are attached to two fixed points A and B on a smooth horizontal table. The natural length of AP is $2a$ and its modulus is mg. The natural length of BP is a and its modulus is $2mg$.

If the distance AB is $8a$ find the distance from A of the point E at which the particle will rest in equilibrium.

When the particle is pulled a short distance towards A and is then released, show that it performs S.H.M. and find the periodic time.

4) A particle of mass $4m$ is attached to the mid-point of a light spring of modulus $2mg$ whose ends are attached to two fixed points distant $8a$ apart in a vertical line. If the spring is of natural length $2a$, find the depth below the upper fixed point, A, of the position of equilibrium of the particle. When the particle is slightly disturbed from rest in a vertical direction show that it performs S.H.M. of periodic time $2\pi\sqrt{(a/g)}$

5) A particle of mass 2 kg lies on a smooth horizontal table attached to one end of a light elastic spring whose other end is fixed to the table at a point A. The particle is at rest at E with the spring just taut when it is suddenly given a velocity of $4\,\text{ms}^{-1}$ towards A. The particle next comes to instantaneous rest at a point B where $AB = 0.8$ m. If the natural length of the spring is 1 m find its modulus of elasticity. Prove that the particle performs S.H.M. and find:

(a) its maximum acceleration,

(b) the time taken to travel from E to B,

(c) the velocity half way between E and B.

6) Prove that a particle of mass m, hanging from a fixed point at the end of a light elastic string, performs S.H.M. when given a vertical displacement from its equilibrium position. Find the period of oscillation in terms of m, l and λ where l and λ are the natural length and modulus of elasticity of the string. What is the maximum vertical displacement which the particle can be given if its subsequent motion is entirely S.H.M.?

INCOMPLETE OSCILLATIONS

There are some occasions in which a particle begins to move with S.H.M. but, before it reaches the end of its path, the character of its motion changes so that the simple harmonic oscillations are never completed. One way in which this can happen is illustrated in the following example.

Consider an elastic string of natural length a and modulus $4mg$ which is fixed at one end to a point A and hangs vertically with a mass m attached to the other end. If the particle is pulled down a distance a below its equilibrium position and is then released, show that the particle describes partial S.H.M. and investigate the subsequent motion.

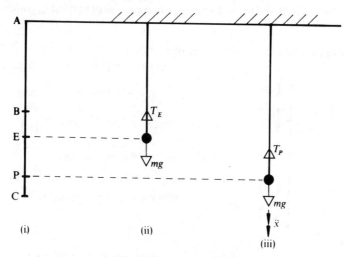

In diagram (i) AB is the natural length of the string

E is the equilibrium position of the particle

P is a general position of the particle

C is the lowest position of the particle.

In diagram (ii) where the extension is e, $T_E = \dfrac{4mge}{a}$

But the particle is in equilibrium

Therefore $\dfrac{4mge}{a} = mg$ giving $e = \dfrac{a}{4}$

In diagram (iii) the extension is $(e + x)$ so $T_P = \dfrac{4mg}{a}(e + x)$

But the string is in tension only while the particle is below the level of B.

Provided then that P is below B, applying Newton's Law vertically downwards gives:

$$mg - \frac{4mg}{a}(e + x) = m\ddot{x}$$

Hence $$-\frac{4mg}{a}x = m\ddot{x}$$

or

$$\ddot{x} = -\frac{4g}{a}x$$

Comparing with

$$\ddot{x} = -n^2 x$$

we see that the particle performs S.H.M. about E as centre, but only while the string is taut. As the particle passes through B the string becomes slack. The only force then acting on the particle is its own weight.

Above B, then, S.H.M. ceases and the particle travels with vertical motion under gravity.

In order to investigate this second type of motion in detail the velocity at B, v_B, is required and can be calculated using

$$v^2 = n^2(a^2 - x^2)$$

Hence $v_B{}^2 = \dfrac{4g}{a}\left(a^2 - \left[\dfrac{a}{4}\right]^2\right)$

or $v_B = \frac{1}{2}\sqrt{15ga}$

This is the initial velocity for the motion under gravity above B.

The oscillations performed by the particle are compound and the periodic time of one oscillation can be determined in two parts.

(a) Time t_1 taken from C to B with S.H.M.

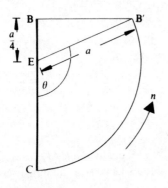

t_1 is equal to the time taken to describe arc CB' with constant angular velocity n.

i.e. $t_1 = \dfrac{\theta}{n}$

But $\theta = \pi - $ angle BEB'

or $\theta = \pi - \arccos\frac{1}{4}$

Therefore
$$t_1 = \sqrt{\frac{a}{4g}}\left(\pi - \arccos\frac{1}{4}\right)$$

(b) Time, t_2, taken to rise above B to instantaneous rest, with motion under gravity.

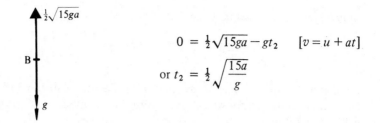

$$0 = \tfrac{1}{2}\sqrt{15ga} - gt_2 \qquad [v = u + at]$$

$$\text{or } t_2 = \tfrac{1}{2}\sqrt{\frac{15a}{g}}$$

Now one complete oscillation will take a time of $2(t_1 + t_2)$.
Therefore the period of compound oscillations is

$$\sqrt{\frac{a}{g}}\left(\pi - \arccos\tfrac{1}{4} + \sqrt{15}\right)$$

Solutions to problems of this type are inevitably rather complex. It is essential to deal systematically with the various sections of the motion, avoiding the temptation to take unsound 'short cuts'.
Further problems which illustrate the need for patience when working through such solutions are given in Examples 12e, below.
Fewer complications occur when analysing *oscillating springs*, because a spring never becomes slack.
When it is compressed to less than its natural length it continues to obey Hooke's Law exerting an outward push at each end.
A particle attached to one end of the spring will therefore continue to travel with S.H.M. even when the spring is reduced below its natural length.

EXAMPLES 12e

1) A particle of mass 2 kg lies, on a smooth horizontal table, at one end of an elastic string of length 1 m and modulus of elasticity 8 N. The other end of the string is attached to a fixed point A on the table. Initially the particle is at B where $\overrightarrow{AB} = 1$ m. It is then pulled in the direction $\overrightarrow{AB}$ to a point C such that $AC = 2AB$, and is then released from rest. Show that, as the particle moves back towards A, its motion is of two different types. Determine each type of motion and find the time taken to travel from C to A.

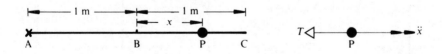

Consider the motion of the particle as it passes through a general point P distant x from B. If P is between B and C the string is taut and the tension is $8x$ (Hooke's Law)

Applying Newton's Law in the direction $\overrightarrow{BC}$,

$$-8x = 2\ddot{x}$$

or

$$\ddot{x} = -4x$$

Comparing with $\ddot{x} = -n^2 x$, we see that this is the basic equation of S.H.M. about B as centre and for which $n = 2$. Also the amplitude, a, of the motion is BC i.e. $a = 1$ m.

The time t_1 taken to travel from C to B, one quarter of a complete oscillation, is $\frac{1}{4}\left(\frac{2\pi}{n}\right)$

Therefore $$t_1 = \frac{\pi}{4} \text{ seconds.}$$

As the particle passes through B with velocity v_B, the string becomes slack. The particle no longer has any horizontal force acting on it and its horizontal velocity will therefore be constant.

Using $v^2 = n^2 (a^2 - x^2)$ at B where $x = 0$, gives

$$v_B = na = 2 \text{ ms}^{-1}.$$

The time t_2 taken to travel from B to A at this speed is therefore $\frac{1}{2}$ second. The two types of motion are (a) S.H.M. from C to B (b) constant velocity from B to A.

The total time, $(t_1 + t_2)$, taken to travel from C to A is $\left(\frac{\pi}{4} + \frac{1}{2}\right)$ s.

2) A particle of mass 2 kg is attached to one end of a light elastic string of natural length 1 m whose modulus of elasticity is $4g$ N. The other end of the string is fastened to a fixed point O. The particle is held at O and is then released from that position. Find the depth below O of the level where the particle first comes to instantaneous rest. Find also the period of oscillation of the subsequent motion.

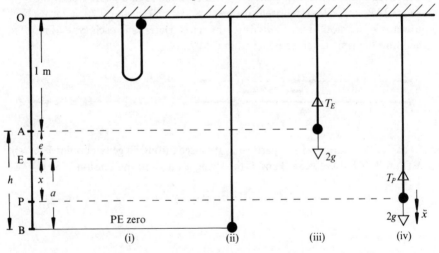

(i)　　　　(ii)　　　　(iii)　　　　(iv)

In the diagram OA is the natural length of the string

           E is the equilibrium position of the particle

           B is the lowest position of the particle

           P is a general position of the particle

From position (i) to (ii) we can use Conservation of Mechanical Energy (an elastic string does not 'jerk' when it becomes taut, since it immediately begins to stretch.)

$$(\text{P.E.} + \text{K.E.} + \text{E.P.E.})_{(i)} = (\text{P.E.} + \text{K.E.} + \text{E.P.E.})_{(ii)}$$

Therefore $\qquad 2g\,(1+h) + 0 + 0 = 0 + 0 + \dfrac{4g}{2}(h)^2 \qquad\qquad$ (1)

giving $\qquad\qquad\qquad h^2 - h - 1 = 0$

Therefore $\qquad\qquad\qquad h = \tfrac{1}{2}(1 \pm \sqrt{5})$

Taking the positive value for h (since B is below A) the depth $(1+h)$ below O where the particle first comes to instantaneous rest is $\dfrac{3+\sqrt{5}}{2}$ m.

When the particle is in equilibrium at E (diagram (iii))

$$T_E = \frac{4ge}{1} = 2g.$$

Therefore $\qquad\qquad\qquad e = \tfrac{1}{2}\text{m.}$

In a general position P where the extension $= e + x$ (diagram (iv))

$$T_P = \frac{4g}{1}(e+x) = 4g\,(\tfrac{1}{2}+x)$$

Applying Newton's Law ↓ (valid below A)

$$2g - 4g\,(\tfrac{1}{2}+x) = 2\ddot{x}$$

Therefore $\qquad\qquad\qquad \ddot{x} = -2gx \qquad\qquad\qquad (n^2 = 2g)$

This is the equation of linear S.H.M. about E as centre, showing that the particle moves with S.H.M. while it is below A.

The amplitude of the motion, EB, is $(h - e)$

i.e. $\qquad\qquad\qquad \dfrac{\sqrt{5}}{2}\text{m.}$

For the S.H.M. between B and A [using the associated circular motion and the equation $v^2 = n^2(a^2 - x^2)$]

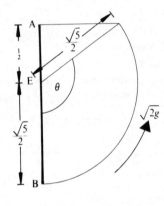

$$\theta = \pi - \arccos \frac{1}{\sqrt{5}}$$

Therefore time from B to A $= \dfrac{\theta}{n}$

$$= \frac{\pi - \arccos \dfrac{1}{\sqrt{5}}}{\sqrt{2g}}$$

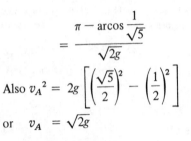

Also $v_A{}^2 = 2g\left[\left(\dfrac{\sqrt{5}}{2}\right)^2 - \left(\dfrac{1}{2}\right)^2\right]$

or $v_A = \sqrt{2g}$

Above A the time, t, taken before next coming to rest is given by

$$0 = \sqrt{2g} - gt \quad (v = u + at)$$

or
$$t = \sqrt{\frac{2}{g}} \text{ seconds}$$

The total time for one compound oscillation

is $2\left[\dfrac{\pi - \arccos \dfrac{1}{\sqrt{5}}}{\sqrt{2g}} + \sqrt{\dfrac{2}{g}}\right]$ seconds

3) A particle of mass m is attached to one end of a light elastic string whose other end is fixed to a point A on a smooth plane inclined at $30°$ to the horizontal. The length of the string is l and its modulus of elasticity is $2mg$. The particle is pulled down the line of greatest slope through A, to a point C where it is released from rest. If the particle just reaches A, find the time taken to travel from C to A.

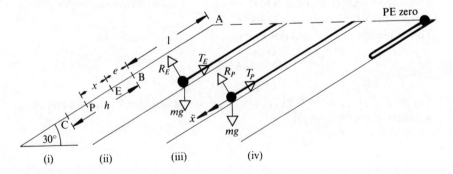

In diagram (i) **AB** is the natural length of the string

E is the equilibrium position of the particle

C is the lowest position of the particle

P is a general position of the particle

In diagram (ii) the particle is in equilibrium

Resolving parallel to the plane

$$T_E = mg \sin 30°$$

But

$$T_E = \frac{2mg}{l} e$$

Therefore

$$e = \frac{l}{4}$$

In diagram (iii)

$$T_P = \frac{2mg}{l}(e + x)$$

Applying Newton's Law down the plane

$$mg \sin 30° - \frac{2mg}{l}(x + e) = m\ddot{x}$$

hence

$$\frac{mg}{2} - \frac{2mg}{l}\left(x + \frac{l}{4}\right) = m\ddot{x}$$

giving

$$\ddot{x} = -\frac{2g}{l}x \qquad (\ddot{x} = -n^2 x)$$

This is the basic equation of S.H.M. about E as centre. It is valid while the string is taut, i.e. below **B**.

Using Conservation of Mechanical Energy between C and A (diagrams (i) and (iv)) we have:

Total M.E. at A $= 0$

Total M.E. at C $= -mg(h + l)\sin 30° + \dfrac{2mg}{2l}h^2$

Therefore $0 = -\dfrac{mg}{2}(h + l) + \dfrac{mg}{l}h^2$

Hence $0 = 2h^2 - hl - l^2$

$0 = (2h + l)(h - l)$

Therefore $h = -\dfrac{l}{2}$ or l

Taking the positive value since h is an extension, $h = l$; the amplitude of the

S.H.M. is then $h - e = \dfrac{3l}{4}$

Now, for the S.H.M. between C and B $\left(\text{at B } x = -\dfrac{l}{4}\right)$

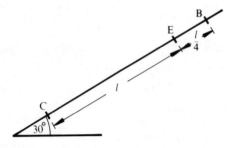

Using $v^2 = n^2\,(a^2 - x^2)$ the velocity at B, v_B is given by

$$v_B{}^2 = \frac{2g}{l}\left(\frac{9l^2}{16} - \frac{l^2}{16}\right)$$

$$v_B = \sqrt{gl}$$

Using $x = a\cos nt$, the time t_1 to travel from C to B is given by

$$-\frac{l}{4} = \frac{3}{4}l\cos t_1 \sqrt{\frac{2g}{l}}$$

$$t_1 = \sqrt{\frac{l}{2g}}\ \text{arcos}\left(-\tfrac{1}{3}\right)$$

Therefore

$$t_1 = \sqrt{\frac{l}{2g}}\left(\pi - \text{arcos}\,\tfrac{1}{3}\right).$$

For the motion above B with constant acceleration $g\sin 30°$ down the slope we have:

Initial velocity at B $= \sqrt{gl}$

Final velocity at A $= 0$

Acceleration $= -\dfrac{g}{2}$

Time from B to A $= t_2$

Therefore $0 = \sqrt{gl} - \dfrac{g}{2}t_2 \quad (v = u + at)$

giving $t_2 = 2\sqrt{\dfrac{l}{g}}$

The total time taken to travel from C to A is therefore

$$t_1 + t_2 = \sqrt{\frac{l}{2g}}\left(\pi - \text{arcos}\,\tfrac{1}{3} + 2\sqrt{2}\right)$$

4) A light elastic spring of natural length 1.2 m is attached at one end to a fixed point O and at the other end to a particle of mass 1 kg. The particle hangs in equilibrium at a depth 1.4 m below O. The particle is then lifted upwards through a vertical distance 0.4 m and released from rest. Show that the particle performs S.H.M. of period $2\pi/7$

If, as the particle passes through its equilibrium position on its upward path, it picks up a rider of mass 1 kg show that the combined mass continues to move with S.H.M. and find the amplitude and periodic time.

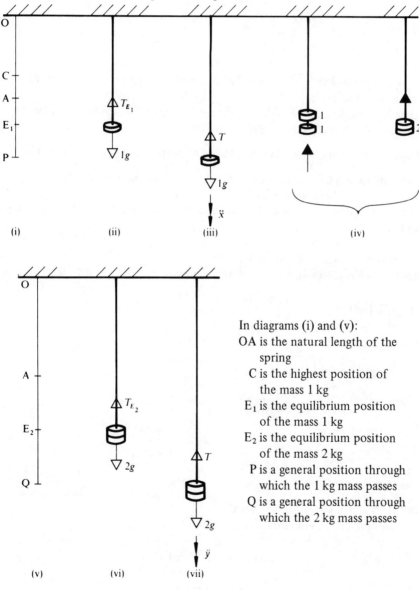

(i)   (ii)   (iii)   (iv)

(v)   (vi)   (vii)

In diagrams (i) and (v):
OA is the natural length of the spring
C is the highest position of the mass 1 kg
E_1 is the equilibrium position of the mass 1 kg
E_2 is the equilibrium position of the mass 2 kg
P is a general position through which the 1 kg mass passes
Q is a general position through which the 2 kg mass passes

In equilibrium (diagram (ii))

$$T_{E_1} = \frac{\lambda}{1.2}(0.2) = 1g$$

giving $$\lambda = 6g$$

Applying Newton's Law at P

(diagram (iii)) $$1g - T = 1\ddot{x}$$

Therefore $$g - \frac{6g(x + 0.2)}{1.2} = \ddot{x}$$

or $$\ddot{x} = -5gx$$

Comparing with $\ddot{x} = -n^2 x$ we see that this is the equation of S.H.M. about E_1 as centre and where $n = \sqrt{5g} = 7$.

Although the particle rises above A, the *spring* cannot become slack and the equation of S.H.M. is always valid.

Therefore the particle describes S.H.M. about centre E_1 of period $\frac{2\pi}{7}$ seconds.

The amplitude is $CE_1 = 0.4$ m, so the velocity of the particle at E_1 is
$$0.4 \times 7 = 2.8 \text{ ms}^{-1}$$

Using Conservation of Linear Momentum as the rider is picked up, (diagram (iv)) we have:
$$1 \times 2.8 + 0 = 2v$$
The combined mass at E_1 has speed 1.4 ms^{-1}.

But the new equilibrium position of the combined mass 2 kg is at E_2 where

(diagram (vi)) $$T_{E_2} = \frac{6ge}{1.2} = 2g$$

giving $$e = 0.4 \text{ m}$$

Applying Newton's Law at Q $$2g - T = 2\ddot{y}$$

(diagram (vii)) $$2g - \frac{6g}{1.2}(0.4 + y) = 2\ddot{y}$$

or $$\ddot{y} = -\frac{5g}{2}y$$

This is the equation of S.H.M. about E_2 as centre in which $n^2 = \frac{5g}{2}$ or $n = \frac{7}{\sqrt{2}}$

But at E_1 where $y = 0.2$, $v = 1.4 \text{ ms}^{-1}$
Therefore if a is the amplitude,

$$(1.4)^2 = \frac{49}{2}(a^2 - [0.2]^2)$$

giving $$a = 0.35 \text{ m}$$

The motion of the combined mass continues as S.H.M. with period $2\pi\sqrt{2/7}$ seconds and amplitude 0.35 metres.

5) A light vertical spring is fixed at its lower end O. A platform of mass m is attached to the upper end of the spring and a particle, also of mass m, rests on the platform. The length of the spring is $4a$ and its modulus of elasticity is $8mg$. If the platform together with the particle is gently depressed through a distance $2a$ below the equilibrium position and is then released from rest, show that the particle performs partial S.H.M. but also appears to bounce off the platform at some stage. Find the height above O when this occurs.

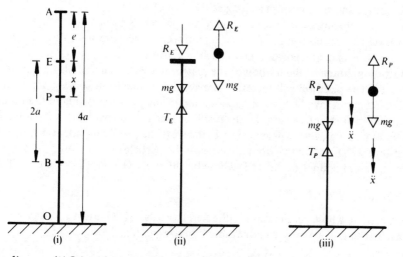

In diagram (i) OA is the natural length of the spring
E is the equilibrium position
B is the lowest position
P is a general position

In diagram (ii) both the platform and the particle are in equilibrium. There is a pair of normal reactions (R) between them.

The compression in the spring is $T_E = \dfrac{8mg}{4a} e$

Because the platform is in equilibrium $T_E = R_E + mg$

Because the particle is in equilibrium $mg = R_E$

Therefore $2mg = \dfrac{8mg}{4a} e$

$e = a$

In diagram (iii) $T_P = \dfrac{8mg}{4a}(e + x) = \dfrac{2mg}{a}(a + x)$

Applying Newton's Law vertically downward we have:

For the platform $\qquad\qquad mg + R_P - T_P = m\ddot{x}$

For the particle $\qquad\qquad\qquad mg - R_P = m\ddot{x}$

As long as the particle is in contact with the platform, these equations can be

combined to give $\qquad 2mg - \dfrac{2mg}{a}(a + x) = 2m\ddot{x}$

or $\qquad\qquad\qquad\qquad\qquad \ddot{x} = -\dfrac{g}{a}x$

This basic equation of S.H.M. about E as centre represents the motion of both the particle and the platform so long as they are in contact.

The maximum downward acceleration of the particle is g since the maximum downward force acting on it is mg. The platform has acceleration g downward when $x = -a$ i.e. at a position D of height a above E.

But the amplitude of the motion of the platform is $2a$ (the initial displacement from E). The platform will therefore rise above D where its downward acceleration will exceed g. Above D, then, the retardation of the platform is greater than that of the particle. Contact between them will be lost and the particle, as it continues to move under gravity, will appear to bounce off the platform (in fact it is the platform which withdraws from underneath the particle).

This apparent bounce occurs at D whose height above O is $4a$ (OD = OE + ED).

SUMMARY

1) A particle whose acceleration is directed towards a fixed origin and is proportional to the distance from that origin, moves with S.H.M.

2) The basic equation of S.H.M. is

$$\ddot{x} = -n^2x \quad \text{or} \quad \ddot{\theta} = -n^2\theta$$

3) Further relationships, which can usually be quoted, are:

$$v^2 = n^2(a^2 - x^2) \quad \text{where } a \text{ is the amplitude}$$

$$x = a\cos nt$$

$$T = \frac{2\pi}{n} \qquad\qquad \text{where } T \text{ is the periodic time.}$$

4) The projection on a diameter of a point describing a circle with constant angular velocity ω, travels with S.H.M. in which $\ddot{x} = -\omega^2 x$.

5) The motion of a particle moving on a stretched elastic string can be shown to be S.H.M. during the time that the string is taut. Attached to an oscillating spring however a particle always performs S.H.M. since the spring never becomes slack.

6) Remember that some problems about particles moving on elastic strings or springs can be solved without using the equations of S.H.M. When considering only velocity and position, the principle of Conservation of Mechanical Energy provides the best solution. Examples of this type were given in Chapter 7.

EXERCISE 12e

1) A particle of mass 1 kg is attached to one end of a light elastic string whose other end is fixed to a point O. The length of the string is 1 m and the particle hangs in equilibrium 1.2 m below O. If the particle is then pulled down a further 0.4 m and released show that it performs partial S.H.M. and find the time which elapses before the particle next comes to instantaneous rest.

2) A particle of mass m is attached to the mid-point of a light elastic string of length $2a$ and modulus mg whose ends are attached to two fixed points A and B on a smooth horizontal table distant $4a$ apart. The particle is drawn aside until it is at the point A and is then released from rest. Show that, as the particle moves from A to the mid-point of AB it performs S.H.M. of two different characteristics. Use the principle of conservation of mechanical energy to find the speed of the particle:
(a) when it is $\frac{1}{4}$ of the way from A to B,
(b) when it is halfway between A and B.

3) A particle of mass 2 kg hangs in equilibrium at the end of a light elastic string of length 1 m and modulus 10 N. The particle is projected vertically upwards from this position and just reaches the fixed upper end, A, of the string. Find the velocity of projection and time taken to rise to A. (take $g = 10\,\mathrm{ms}^{-2}$)

4) A particle of mass m rests on a smooth table, and is attached to one end of a light elastic string of natural length a and modulus mg. The other end of the string is attached to a fixed point O on the table. The particle is pulled away from O to a point B where $OB = 2a$ and is then released from rest. Find the time taken:
(a) to reach the point A where $OA = a$,
(b) to reach O,
(c) to return to B.

5) A particle of mass m hangs at the end of a light elastic string attached at the other end to a fixed point A. If the natural length of the string is a and its modulus is $4mg$, find the depth below A at which the particle rests in equilibrium. The particle is pulled down a further distance d below the equilibrium position and is released from rest. What is the greatest possible value of d if the particle's subsequent motion is entirely S.H.M? If d is given twice this value find the period of the compound oscillations which the particle will then perform.

MULTIPLE CHOICE EXERCISE 12

The instructions for answering these questions are given on page (xii)

TYPE I

1) A particle P describes S.H.M. of amplitude 1 m. In performing one complete oscillation, P travels a distance:
(a) 2 m   (b) 0   (c) 4 m   (d) – 2 m.

2) A particle performing S.H.M. has a speed of 4 ms^{-1} when it is 1 m from the centre. If the amplitude is 3 m what is the period of oscillation?

(a) $\sqrt{2}\pi$ (b) $\dfrac{\pi}{\sqrt{2}}$ (c) $\dfrac{\pi}{2}$ (d) $\dfrac{\pi}{2\sqrt{2}}$.

3)

A particle travels between A and A$'$ with S.H.M. of period 24 seconds. O is the centre and B is the mid-point of AO. The time taken to travel from A to B is:
(a) 3 s   (b) 8 s   (c) 6 s   (d) 4 s.

TYPE II

4) A particle is travelling with S.H.M. of amplitude 1 m and period π s.
(a) Its maximum velocity is 2 ms^{-1}.
(b) Its maximum acceleration is 2 ms^{-2}.
(c) The acceleration at a distance d from the centre is $4d$ ms^{-2}.

5) A particle of mass m is oscillating vertically at the end of an elastic string of length l and modulus $2mg$. The motion of the particle will be entirely simple harmonic if:
(a) the amplitude is less than l,
(b) the particle never rises above its equilibrium position,
(c) the string never goes slack,
(d) the amplitude is less than $\frac{1}{2}l$.

6) When a particle performs small oscillations at the end of a spring, the period depends upon:
(a) the mass of the particle,
(b) the modulus of elasticity of the spring,
(c) the natural length of the spring,
(d) the maximum extension of the spring.

TYPE IV

7) A particle P is moving with linear S.H.M. about a point O. Find the period of oscillation if:

(a) the acceleration is $6\,\mathrm{ms}^{-1}$ when $OP = 2\,\mathrm{m}$,

(b) the amplitude is $5\,\mathrm{m}$,

(c) the mass of the particle is $3\,\mathrm{kg}$.

8) Find the amplitude of the S.H.M. described by a particle if:

(a) its maximum velocity is $8\,\mathrm{ms}^{-1}$,

(b) its maximum acceleration occurs at O,

(c) the periodic time is $4\,\mathrm{s}$.

9) A particle is attached to a fixed point by an elastic string and is performing small vertical oscillations. Find the period if:

(a) the natural length of the string is l,

(b) the modulus of elasticity is $2mg$,

(c) the particle is of mass m.

TYPE V

10) A particle whose acceleration is proportional to its displacement from a fixed point is moving with S.H.M.

11) A particle hanging at the end of an elastic string is pulled down and then released. The motion of the particle must be entirely S.H.M.

12) A particle describing linear S.H.M. on a path AB with mid-point O has its greatest acceleration at either A or B.

13) A particle travelling in a circle with constant angular velocity ω is moving with S.H.M.

14) The period of oscillation of a particle travelling with angular S.H.M. is $\dfrac{2\pi}{\omega}$ therefore ω is the angular velocity at the centre of the path.

15) A particle which is oscillating is not necessarily performing S.H.M.

MISCELLANEOUS EXERCISE 12

1) A particle P moves with an acceleration which is proportional to its distance from a fixed point C, and is always directed towards C. If the particle starts from rest at a point A distant d from C, where the magnitude of its acceleration is $\lambda^2 d$, find an expression for the velocity of P when it is distant x from C. After what time does P next come to instantaneous rest? In what time does P travel from A to a point Q where $AQ = \dfrac{d}{2}$?

2) A particle of mass 1 kg is attached to the mid-point of a light elastic string of natural length 1 m and modulus of elasticity $4g\,\mathrm{N}$. The ends of the string are stretched between two points P and Q, 2 m apart in a vertical line (P above Q).

Find the height above Q of the position of equilibrium of the particle. Find also the period of *small* vertical oscillations when the particle is disturbed from rest.

3) A particle is moving with linear simple harmonic motion. Its speed is maximum at a point C and is zero at a point A. P and Q are two points on CA such that $4CP = CA$ while the speed at P is twice the speed at Q. Find the ratio of the accelerations at P and Q.
If the period of one oscillation is 10 seconds find, correct to the first decimal place, the least time taken to travel between P and Q.

4) Prove that, if a particle moving with linear simple harmonic motion of amplitude a has velocity v when distant x from the centre of its path, then $v = \omega \sqrt{a^2 - x^2}$ where ω is a constant.
A point travelling with linear S.H.M. has speeds 3 ms^{-1} and 2 ms^{-1} when distant 1 m and 2 m respectively from the centre of oscillations. Calculate the amplitude, the periodic time and the maximum velocity.

5) A particle of mass 10 grammes is moving along a straight line with simple harmonic motion. The particle has speeds of 9 centimetres per second and 6 centimetres per second at P and Q respectively, whose distances from the centre of oscillation are 1 centimetre and 2 centimetres respectively. Calculate the greatest speed and the greatest acceleration of the particle.
If the points P and Q are on the same side of the centre of oscillation, calculate:
  (i) the shortest time taken by the particle to move from P to Q,
  (ii) the work done during this displacement.   (A.E.B.)

6)

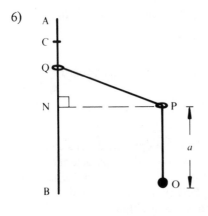

The diagram shows an elastic string OPQ of modulus λ and natural length a, one end of which is attached to a fixed point O. The string passes through a small smooth fixed ring at P, where $OP = a$. The other end of the string is attached to a small ring Q of mass m which can move on a smooth vertical wire AB. The perpendicular from P on to AB is PN. The ring is held at C, where $NC = c$, and is then released. Prove that the ring performs simple harmonic motion about a point on the wire distant mag/λ below N.

Find also the period of the motion and the speed of the ring when it passes through N.   (Cambridge)

7) A small sphere of mass m is suspended from a fixed point A by a light elastic string of modulus mg and natural length l. The sphere is pulled down to a point $\frac{1}{2}l$ vertically below its equilibrium position, and released from rest. As it passes

through its equilibrium position it picks up a rider, also of mass m, previously at rest, which adheres to the sphere. Find the depth below A at which the sphere and rider next come to rest.
(U of L)

8) One end of a light elastic string, of natural length a and modulus of elasticity kmg, is attached at a fixed point on a frictionless plane inclined at an angle θ to the horizontal. A heavy particle is attached to the other end of the string. The particle is at rest on the plane with the string along a line of greatest slope and extended by a length b. The particle is then pulled down a distance d in the line of the string and released. Show that the period of the simple harmonic motion with which the particle starts to move is independent of θ.
If $d = 2b$, find the time from release to the string going slack and find also the speed of the particle at the instant when the string goes slack.
(A.E.B.)

9) A particle of mass m is suspended from a ceiling by a light elastic string, of natural length a and modulus $12mg$. When the particle hangs at rest find the extension in the string. The particle is then pulled down vertically a distance x and released. If the particle just reaches the ceiling, find:
(a) the value of x,
(b) the maximum speed and the maximum acceleration during the motion.
(U of L)

10) A particle of mass m moves in a straight line in simple harmonic motion of period 4π s about a point O. It starts from rest at a point P, 4 m from O, and π s later a particle of mass $2m$ is released from rest at P and describes an exactly similar simple harmonic motion. Show that the two particles will collide $\frac{3}{2}\pi$ s after the second particle is released, and find how far from O the collision will occur.
Draw a rough graph of distance against time to illustrate your results.
If on colliding the two particles coalesce, find the magnitude and direction of the velocity of the composite particle immediately after the impact.
(Cambridge)

11) A light elastic spring, of modulus $8mg$ and natural length l, has one end attached to a ceiling and carries a scale pan of mass m at the other end. The scale pan is given a vertical displacement from its equilibrium position and released to oscillate with period T.

Prove that
$$T = 2\pi \sqrt{\left(\frac{l}{8g}\right)}$$

A weight of mass km is placed in the scale pan and from the new equilibrium position the procedure is repeated. The period of oscillation is now $2T$. Find the value of k.
Find also the maximum amplitude of the latter oscillations if the weight and the scale pan do not separate during the motion.
(A.E.B.)

12) A particle P, of mass m, is suspended from a fixed point O by an elastic string. When the particle is in equilibrium the extension of the string is a. Assuming that the string remains taut during the motion, prove that the period of vertical oscillations of P is $\frac{2}{3}\pi\sqrt{\left(\dfrac{a}{g}\right)}$.

A second particle Q, of mass $2m$, is attached to P. Find the extension of the string in the new equilibrium position and prove that, if Q now drops off, the string becomes slack after a time $2\pi\sqrt{\left(\dfrac{a}{g}\right)}$.   (Oxford)

13) (a) A mass of 5 kg describes Simple Harmonic Motion in a straight line moving from rest at P to rest at Q. It does 45 complete oscillations each each minute, and its speed as it passes through O, the mid-point of PQ, is $\pi\,\text{ms}^{-1}$. Find:

   (i) the distance PQ,

   (ii) the force on the mass when at P,

   (iii) the time taken to pass from the mid-point of PO to O after leaving P.

(b) A body of mass 5 kg is attached to the end B of a light elastic string AB of natural length 2 m and modulus $10g$ newtons, and is suspended vertically in equilibrium by the string whose other end A is attached to a fixed point.

   (i) Find the depth of B below A when the body is in equilibrium.

   (ii) Use energy principles to find the distance through which the body must be pulled down vertically from its equilibrium position so that it will just reach A after release.   (S.U.J.B.)

14) A light elastic spring AB of natural length b and modulus $2mg$ is secured to the floor at A. A light elastic string BC of natural length $4b$ and modulus mg is attached to the spring at B and to a point C vertically above A, where $AC = 5b$. When a particle of mass m is attached at B, find:

(a) the depth below C of its position of equilibrium,

(b) the period of its small vertical oscillations about the position of equilibrium.   (U of L)

15) A particle oscillates in a straight line in simple harmonic motion given by the differential equation

$$\frac{d^2x}{dt^2} = -\omega^2 x,$$

where ω is constant. Define the *amplitude* and *period* of the motion. Prove that the period is $2\pi/\omega$. (You may quote a general solution of the equation).

A light elastic string of natural length a and modulus λ has one end fixed at a point A and a particle of mass m is attached to the other end. The particle is held at a depth $a + b$ vertically below A and then released. Prove that if b lies within certain limits the whole motion of the particle is simple harmonic, and state the position of the centre of oscillation, the period and the amplitude of the motion. State the limits of b and explain why they are necessary.   (J.M.B.)

16) A particle P of mass m lies on a smooth horizontal table and is attached by two light elastic strings, of natural lengths $3a$, $2a$ and moduli λ, 2λ to two fixed points, S, T respectively, on the table. If $ST = 7a$, show that, when the particle is in equilibrium, $SP = \dfrac{9a}{2}$.

The particle is held at rest at the point in the line ST where $SP = 5a$, and then released. Show that the subsequent motion of the particle is simple harmonic of period $\pi \sqrt{\left(3\dfrac{ma}{\lambda}\right)}$. Find the maximum speed of the particle during this motion.   (J.M.B.)

17) The figure shows a straight smooth horizontal groove AB in which each of the perfectly elastic particles P and Q can move freely. The horizontal line OY is perpendicular to AB and passes through a fixed point M of the groove. Initially P and Q are at rest at distances a and $\dfrac{a}{2}$ respectively from OY. The masses of P and Q are m and $2m$ respectively. An attractive force $\lambda \overrightarrow{PO}$ where λ is a positive constant, acts continuously on particle P which starts to move towards Q which is unaffected throughout by this attraction. Show that:
 (i) P moves along the groove with simple harmonic motion about M as centre,

(ii) Q moves with speed $a\sqrt{\left(\dfrac{\lambda}{3m}\right)}$ after impact,

(iii) the amplitudes of the motion of the particle P before and after impact are in the ratio $\sqrt{3} : 1$

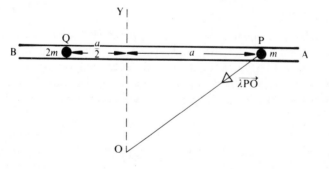

(A.E.B.)

18) One end of a light elastic string, of natural length l and modulus of elasticity $4mg$, is fixed to a point A and a particle of mass m is fastened to the other end. The particle hangs in equilibrium vertically below A. Find the extension of the string.

The particle is now held at the point B at a distance l vertically below A and projected vertically downwards with speed $\sqrt{(6gl)}$. If C is the lowest point reached by the particle, prove that the motion from B to C is simple harmonic motion of amplitude $\frac{5l}{4}$. Prove also that the time taken by the particle to move from B to C is

$$\frac{1}{2}\left(\frac{\pi}{2} + \arcsin\frac{1}{5}\right)\sqrt{\left(\frac{l}{g}\right)}.$$

(You may quote a solution of the equation of simple harmonic motion).

(J.M.B.)

19) A particle is attached to one end of a light elastic string, the other end of which is fastened to a fixed point A on a smooth plane inclined at an angle arcsin $\frac{1}{4}$ to the horizontal. The particle rests in equilibrium at a point O on the plane with the string stretched along a line of greatest slope and extended by an amount c. If the particle is released from rest at a point P on AO produced, show that so long as the string remains taut the particle will oscillate in simple harmonic motion about O as centre, and state the periodic time.
If OP = $2c$, find the velocity of the particle when it first reaches O after leaving P.

(U of L)

20) Two points A and B on a smooth horizontal table are at a distance $8l$ apart. A particle of mass m between A and B is attached to A by means of a light elastic string of modulus λ and natural length $2l$, and to B by means of a light elastic string of modulus 4λ and natural length $3l$. If M is the mid-point of AB, and O is the point between M and B at which the particle would rest in equilibrium, prove that $MO = \frac{2}{11}l$.
If the particle is held at M and then released, show that it will move with simple harmonic motion, and find the period of the motion.
Find the velocity V of the particle when it is at a point C distant $\frac{3}{11}l$ from M, and is moving towards B.

(Cambridge)

21) A light elastic spring, of natural length a, and modulus $8mg$, stands vertically with its lower end fixed and carries a particle of mass m fastened to its upper end. This particle is resting in equilibrium when a second particle, also of mass m, is dropped on to it from rest at a height $3a/8$ above it. The particles coalesce on impact. Show that the composite particle oscillates about a point which is at a height $\frac{3a}{4}$ above the lower end of the spring and that the equation of motion is

$$\frac{d^2x}{dt^2} = -\frac{4gx}{a}$$

where x is the displacement, at time t, of the composite particle from its centre of oscillation. State the period and find the amplitude of the resulting motion.
(Standard formulae for simple harmonic motion may be quoted without proof).

(J.M.B.)

CHAPTER 13

RELATIVE MOTION

RELATIVE VELOCITY

If one moving object, A, is viewed from another moving object, B, the *apparent* motion of A is the vector difference of their velocities, and is referred to as the velocity of A relative to B.

If $\quad\quad\mathbf{v_A}\quad\quad$ is the velocity of A

and $\quad\quad\mathbf{v_B}\quad\quad$ is the velocity of B

then $\quad\mathbf{v_A} - \mathbf{v_B}\quad$ is the velocity of A relative to B.

Similarly $\quad\mathbf{v_B} - \mathbf{v_A}\quad$ is the velocity of B relative to A and is the apparent velocity of B when viewed from A.

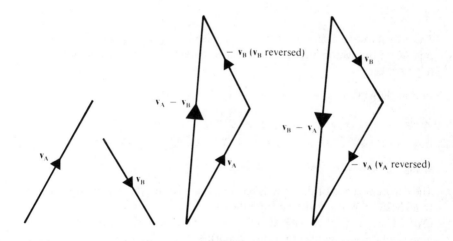

[Note that $\mathbf{v_A} - \mathbf{v_B}$ and $\mathbf{v_B} - \mathbf{v_A}$ have the same magnitude but opposite directions.]

$\mathbf{v_A}$ and $\mathbf{v_B}$ are velocities relative to the earth's surface, E, and are frequently written $_A\mathbf{v_E}$, $_B\mathbf{v_E}$

347

In this notation, the velocity of A relative to B would be written $_AV_B$
Problems involving relative velocity can be solved in a variety of ways. The
commonest methods are:
(a) the construction to scale of a velocity triangle in which sides and angles,
representing speeds and directions of motion, can be measured,
(b) the solution of a velocity triangle using trigonometry,
(c) resolving each velocity into components in a pair of perpendicular directions
and using relative velocity components.

EXAMPLES 13a

1) The driver of a car travelling due East on a straight road at 40 kmh^{-1} is
watching a train moving due North at 75 kmh^{-1}. What is the apparent speed and
direction of motion of the train?

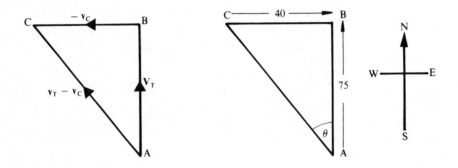

The velocity of the train relative to the car is $v_T - v_C$ and is represented by the
side AC of the vector triangle in which AB represents v_T and BC represents v_C
reversed, i.e. $-v_C$

In triangle ABC $(AC)^2 = (75)^2 + (40)^2$

giving $AC = 85$

Also $\tan \theta = \frac{40}{75} = 0.5333$

giving $\theta = 28° 4'$

The apparent speed of the train is 85 khm^{-1} and its direction of motion appears
to be N 28° 4' W when viewed from the car.
(*Note.* Instead of calculating AC and θ, a scale diagram of triangle ABC could
have been drawn and measurements taken).

2) To an observer in a boat moving North East at 20 kmh^{-1} an aeroplane appears
to be flying due West at 100 kmh^{-1}. What is the true course and speed of the
aeroplane?

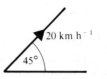

The velocity of the boat v_B is

The velocity of the plane v_A is not known
The velocity of the plane relative to the boat is $v_A - v_B$ and is

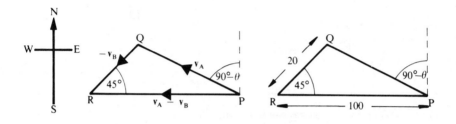

In the velocity triangle PQR the sides PR and QR represent $v_A - v_B$ and $-v_B$ (i.e. v_B reversed) respectively. Therefore PQ represents v_A

In triangle PQR $(PQ)^2 = 100^2 + 20^2 - 2 \times 100 \times 20 \cos 45°$

$= 10400 - 2828$

Hence $PQ = 87.02$

Also $\dfrac{\sin \theta}{20} = \dfrac{\sin 45°}{87.02}$

giving $\theta = 9° 21'$

so that $90° - \theta = 80° 39'$

The true speed of the aeroplane is $87.02 \, \text{kmh}^{-1}$ on a course N 80° 39' W (279° 21').

3) To a cyclist riding due South at $20 \, \text{kmh}^{-1}$ a steady wind appears to be blowing S 60° W. When he reduces his speed to $15 \, \text{kmh}^{-1}$, without changing direction, the wind appears to blow S 30° W. Find the true velocity of the wind.

If $_w v_E$ represents the true wind velocity and $_c v_E$ represents the cyclist's first velocity, the velocity of the wind relative to the cyclist is $_w v_{C_1} = {_w v_E} - {_c v_E}$
Let the true wind velocity have components u to the West and v to the South. Then considering components of each velocity towards West and South we have:
Case 1. (When the cyclist's speed is $20 \, \text{kmh}^{-1}$)

Velocity	$_W v_E$	$c_1 v_E$	$_W v_E - c_1 v_E$
Westward Component	u	0	$u - 0$
Southward Component	v	20	$v - 20$

The direction of $_W v_E - c_1 v_E$ is S $\alpha°$ W where

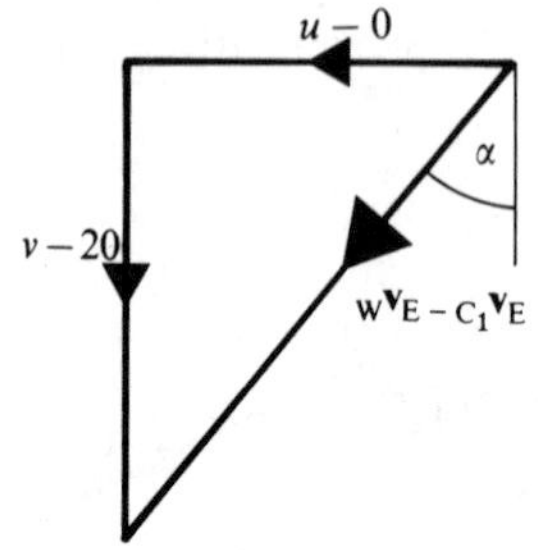

$$\tan \alpha = \frac{u - 0}{v - 20}$$

But α is known to be $60°$

Therefore $\dfrac{u - 0}{v - 20} = \tan 60°$

$$u = \sqrt{3}(v - 20) \qquad (1)$$

Case 2. (When the cyclist's speed is 15 kmh^{-1})

Velocity	$_W v_E$	$c_2 v_E$	$_W v_E - c_2 v_E$
Westward Component	u	0	$u - 0$
Southward Component	v	15	$v - 15$

The direction of $_W v_E - c_2 v_E$ is S $\beta°$ W where

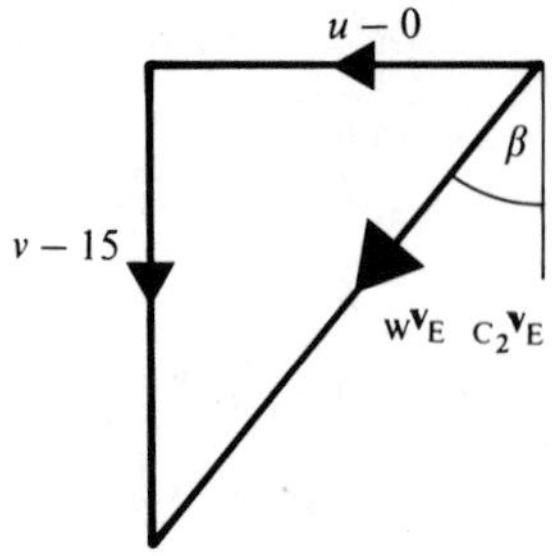

$$\tan \beta = \frac{u - 0}{v - 15}$$

But β is known to be $30°$

Therefore $\dfrac{u - 0}{v - 15} = \tan 30°$

$$\sqrt{3}u = v - 15 \qquad (2)$$

From (1) and (2)

$$3(v - 20) = v - 15$$
$$2v = 45$$

Therefore $\qquad v = 22.5$

and $\qquad u = 2.5 \times \sqrt{3}$

The actual wind speed is $\sqrt{u^2 + v^2}$

and

$$\sqrt{u^2 + v^2} = 2.5\sqrt{9^2 + (\sqrt{3})^2}$$
$$= 2.5\sqrt{84}$$
$$= 5\sqrt{21}$$
$$= 22.9$$

The direction of the wind is

$$\text{S } \theta° \text{ W where } \tan\theta = \frac{u}{v}$$

$$\text{i.e. } \tan\theta = \frac{2.5\sqrt{3}}{22.5}$$

$$\theta = 10° 54'$$

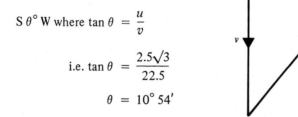

The true velocity of the wind is therefore 22.9 kmh^{-1} in the direction S 10° 54′ W (*Note.* Wind direction can be defined in two ways. In this problem we were told that 'the wind appears to be blowing S 60° W'. This information could equally well be expressed in the form 'the wind appears to be blowing *from* N 60° E'. Great care must always be taken, when reading questions involving wind direction, to interpret correctly the information given, since the two modes of expression are so similar).

Alternatively Example 3 can be solved graphically in the following way.

First sketch a velocity triangle showing the velocity of the wind relative to the cyclist in the first case (diagram i)

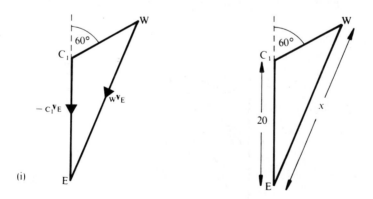

(Note that the prefix and suffix letters which identify a velocity can be used consistently for the vertices of the velocity triangle.)

i.e. $_W v_E$ is represented by the side WE;

$- c_1 v_E$ which is $c_1 v_E$ reversed, is represented by the side EC_1;

v is represented by WC_1).

In triangle WC_1E we know:

> the direction and length of C_1E
>
> the direction of WC_1

but neither the direction, θ, nor the length, x, of WE.

The true shape of the triangle is therefore not known at this stage, so it cannot be drawn to scale yet.

A similar sketch can be made for Case 2 (diagram ii)

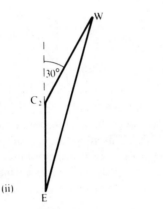

(ii)

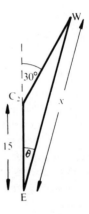

As in Case 1 the true shape of triangle WC_2E is not yet known.

The side WE has the same length and direction in both cases however so that the two triangles can be superimposed

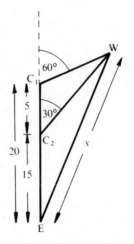

The figure EC_2C_1W can now be drawn to scale, in the order:
(a) draw EC_2 and C_2C_1 of lengths 15 and 5 units,
(b) draw lines from C_1 and C_2 making angles of $60°$ and $30°$ with EC_2 produced,
(c) join the point of intersection W, of these two lines, to E,
(d) measure x and θ.

4) From two reconnaissance vessels A and B observation is being kept on a foreign ship C.
To A, which is moving at 10 knots on a course $S\,30°\,E$ the ship C appears to be travelling $S\,60°\,E$. When viewed from B whose speed is 12 knots on a course $N\,30°\,E$, C appears to be travelling due East. What is the true velocity of the foreign ship?

Let C have velocity components u and v to the East and South respectively. Then, resolving the velocities v_A, v_B and v_C of the three ships, in the directions East and South we have:

	v_A	v_B	v_C	$v_C - v_A$	$v_C - v_B$
Component →	5	6	u	$u-5$	$u-6$
Component ↑	$-5\sqrt{3}$	$6\sqrt{3}$	v	$v-(-5\sqrt{3})$	$v-6\sqrt{3}$

The direction of $v_C - v_A$ is $S\,60°\,E$

Therefore
$$\tan 60° = \frac{u-5}{v+5\sqrt{3}}$$

hence
$$\sqrt{3}(v+5\sqrt{3}) = u-5$$

or
$$\sqrt{3}v = u-20$$

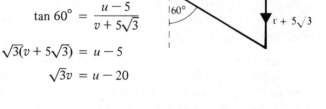

The direction of $v_C - v_B$ is due East

Therefore
$$v-6\sqrt{3} = 0$$

or
$$v = 6\sqrt{3}$$

In equation (1)
$$\sqrt{3}(6\sqrt{3}) = u-20$$

hence
$$u = 38$$

The speed of C is
$$\sqrt{u^2 + v^2} = \sqrt{(6\sqrt{3})^2 + (38)^2}$$
$$= 2\sqrt{388}$$
$$= 39.4$$

The direction of C's motion is $S\alpha^\circ$ E where $\tan\alpha = \dfrac{38}{6\sqrt{3}}$

The true velocity of the foreign ship C is therefore 39.4 knots on a course S 74° 42' E.

EXERCISE 13a

Answer questions 1 to 4 in two ways:
(a) by scale drawing and measurement,
(b) by calculation.

1) A girl is riding a horse along a straight path at $5\ kmh^{-1}$. A second rider is moving at $3\ kmh^{-1}$ along a perpendicular straight path. What is the velocity of the second rider relative to the first?

2) A passenger in a train travelling North East at $100\ kmh^{-1}$ watches a car moving on a straight road. The car seems to be travelling S 30° W at $125\ kmh^{-1}$. What is the true velocity of the car?

3) Two aircraft are flying at the same height on straight courses. The first is flying at $400\ kmh^{-1}$ due North. The true speed of the second is $350\ kmh^{-1}$ and it appears, to the pilot of the first aircraft, to be on a course S 40° W. Find the true course of the second aircraft.

4) A, B and C are three objects each moving with constant velocity. A's speed is $10\ ms^{-1}$ in a direction $\overrightarrow{PQ}$. The velocity of B relative to A is $6\ ms^{-1}$ at an angle of 70° with PQ. The velocity of C relative to B is $12\ ms^{-1}$ in the direction $\overrightarrow{QP}$. Find the velocity of B and of C.

5) A boy is walking due North along a straight road and the wind appears to be blowing South West. When he turns right at a cross roads the wind appears to be blowing S 80° W. If the boy walks at a constant $6\ kmh^{-1}$ and the two roads cross at right angles, find the true wind velocity.

6) Two aircraft, A and B, are flying at the same height. Both have speed $400\ kmh^{-1}$; A is flying in a direction N 30° W and B is flying due East. A third aircraft, also flying at the same height, appears to the pilot of A to be on a course due South while to the pilot of B its course seems to be S 60° W. In what direction is the third aircraft actually flying?

RELATIVE POSITION

When one moving object A is viewed from another moving object B, the displacement of A from B at any time t depends upon (a) the initial positions (b) the velocities, of both A and B.

Suppose that, when $t = 0$, A and B are at points A_0 and B_0 and are moving with constant velocities v_A and v_B.

After time t, A will be at a point A_t where $\overrightarrow{A_0A_t} = tv_A$

Similarly B will be at a point B_t where $\overrightarrow{B_0B_t} = tv_B$

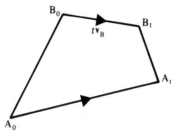

In the vector polygon $B_tB_0A_0A_t$,

$$\overrightarrow{B_tA_t} = \overrightarrow{B_tB_0} + \overrightarrow{B_0A_0} + \overrightarrow{A_0A_t}$$

i.e.
$$\overrightarrow{B_tA_t} = -tv_B + \overrightarrow{B_0A_0} + tv_A$$

$$= \overrightarrow{B_0A_0} + t(v_A - v_B) \tag{1}$$

But $\overrightarrow{B_tA_t}$ is the displacement of A from B at time t

$\overrightarrow{B_0A_0}$ is the displacement of A from B initially

$v_A - v_B$ is the velocity of A relative to B.

Therefore the displacement vector of A relative to B at any time t is the sum of the initial displacement vector and the product of t with the velocity of A relative to B.

Shortest Distance Apart

Equation (1) can be represented by a displacement vector triangle

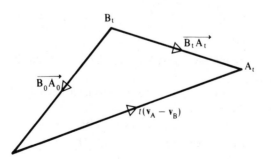

If the magnitude of $\overrightarrow{B_0 A_0}$ is d,
　the magnitude of $B_t A_t$ is l,
　the magnitude of $v_A - v_B$ is V
and $v_A - v_B$ makes angles α and θ with $A_0 B_0$ and $B_t A_t$, then the displacement triangle becomes

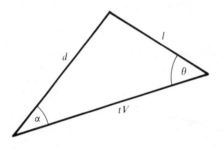

The values of θ and l are variable and depend upon the time but d and α are constant when the velocities of both objects are specified.

Using the Sine Rule

$$\frac{l}{\sin \alpha} = \frac{d}{\sin \theta}$$

Hence

$$l = \frac{d \sin \alpha}{\sin \theta}$$

l is least when $\sin \theta$ is greatest

i.e. when $\qquad \sin \theta = 1$ and $\theta = 90°$

The value of l is then $d \sin \alpha$, and the value of Vt is $d \cos \alpha$.

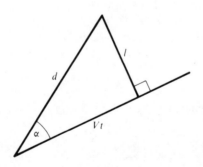

Therefore A and B are closest together after a time $\dfrac{d \cos \alpha}{V}$ and are then distant $d \sin \alpha$ apart.
(Where d is the initial distance apart and α is the angle between the relative velocity and the initial line $A_0 B_0$.)
Problems involving closest approach can be solved either by calculation or graphically (i.e. by scale drawing and measurement).

If a graphical method is chosen, two different scales are needed, one for speed and one for distance.

It is safer to draw separate figures, one to each scale, *the property they have in common being the direction of the relative motion.*

EXAMPLES

1) An aircraft P is 800 m due North of another aircraft Q. Both are flying at the same height with constant velocities 150 ms^{-1} due West and 200 ms^{-1} N 30° W. After what time will the aircraft be closest together and how far apart will they then be?

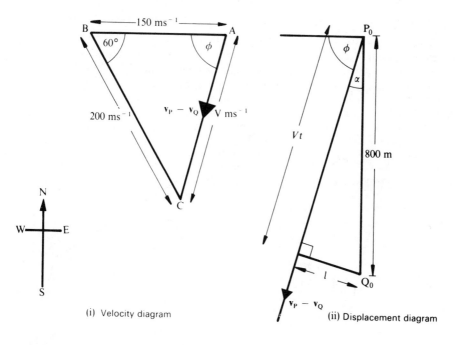

(i) Velocity diagram

(ii) Displacement diagram

In diagram (i) the side $\overrightarrow{AC}$ of the velocity triangle represents the velocity of P relative to Q. The length of AC represents their relative speed V.

In triangle ABC $V^2 = 200^2 + 150^2 - 2 \times 200 \times 150 \cos 60°$

Hence $V = 180$

Also $\dfrac{\sin \phi}{200} = \dfrac{\sin 60°}{180}$

Hence $\phi = 74° \, 11'$

In diagram (ii) P_0N represents the path of P relative to Q and is parallel to AC

Therefore $\qquad\qquad\qquad\qquad \alpha = 15°\,49'$

The shortest distance between P and Q is l where

$$l = 800 \sin \alpha = 218\,\text{m}$$

If t is the time taken to reach this position, then

$$Vt = 800 \cos \alpha$$

or $\qquad\qquad\qquad\qquad t = \dfrac{800 \cos 15°\,49'}{180} = 4.28 \text{ seconds.}$

Therefore the aircraft are closest together after 4.28 s and are then 218 m apart.

2) A ship moving at a speed of $15\,\text{kmh}^{-1}$, sights an enemy destroyer 10 km due South. The destroyer is travelling at $20\,\text{kmh}^{-1}$ North West. The captain of the ship is ordered to steer as far West of North as possible but the ship will be in range of the destroyer's guns if it approaches closer than 2 km. On what bearing can the ship steer so that it just stays out of range?

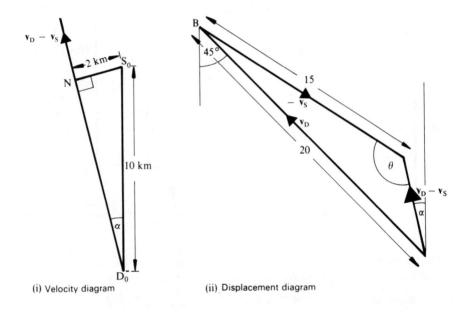

(i) Velocity diagram   (ii) Displacement diagram

In diagram (i) D_0N represents the path of the destroyer relative to the ship and is on a bearing $N\alpha°\,W$, where $\alpha = \arcsin \frac{2}{10} = 11°\,32'$.
In diagram (ii) the side AC of the velocity triangle represents the velocity of the destroyer relative to the ship.
Therefore AC is parallel to D_0N.

In triangle ABC
$$\frac{\sin \theta}{20} = \frac{\sin (45° - \alpha)}{15}$$

Therefore
$$\sin \theta = \tfrac{20}{15} \sin 33° 28'$$

Giving
$$\theta = 132° 40' \;(\theta \text{ is known to be obtuse})$$

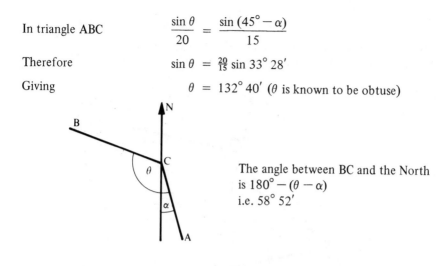

The angle between BC and the North
is $180° - (\theta - \alpha)$
i.e. $58° 52'$

The ship must not travel further to the West than N $58° 52'$ W.
Note. When graphical solutions are offered, explanation similar to that given in
these examples should be included. *Only the trigonometric calculations should
be replaced by measurement.*

Closest Approach (Choice of Course)

We have so far been considering the relative motion of two objects A and B,
both of which are moving with specified velocities, and have found that the
shortest distance between them is $d \sin \alpha$ where d is the initial distance apart and
α is the angle between the relative path and the initial line.

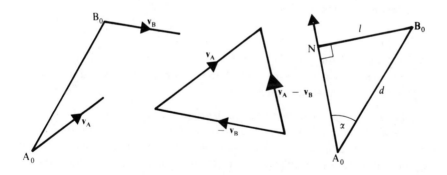

Suppose now, that while the speeds of both objects are fixed and B moves in a
specified direction, A is free to choose its bearing.
The angle α is no longer fixed and, as α varies, the shortest distance l between A
and B also varies.
If it is impossible for A to intercept B, i.e. l cannot be zero, then A will pass as

close to B as possible when l, and hence α, takes its smallest possible value.

Consider first a general case where the relative path makes angles β and γ with the directions of motion of B and A respectively.

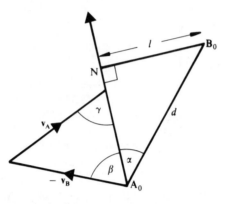

In this diagram, quantities which are constant are:
the magnitudes of v_A, v_B and d,
the directions of v_B and $\overrightarrow{A_0 B_0}$,
the compound angle $(\alpha + \beta)$.
Quantities which vary as A's bearing varies are: α, β, γ and l.
If α is to be as small as possible, β must be as large as possible ($\alpha + \beta$ is constant).
By applying the Sine Rule in the velocity triangle we see that β is greatest when $\gamma = 90°$.
Therefore, in order to approach as close as possible to B, the direction of motion of A should be perpendicular to the relative path.

EXAMPLE

A speedboat travelling due East at $100 \, \text{kmh}^{-1}$ is 500 m due North of a launch when the launch sets off to try to catch the speedboat. If the speed of the launch is $60 \, \text{kmh}^{-1}$ show that the launch cannot get closer to the speedboat than 400 m.

The launch cannot catch the speedboat because even when travelling due East at $60 \, \text{kmh}^{-1}$ the speedboat is pulling away at a relative speed of $40 \, \text{kmh}^{-1}$.
The launch will approach as close as possible to the speedboat when the velocity of the launch v_A is perpendicular to the relative velocity $v_A - v_B$ (v_B is the velocity of the speedboat).
If A_0 and B_0 are the initial positions of the launch and the speedboat, then:

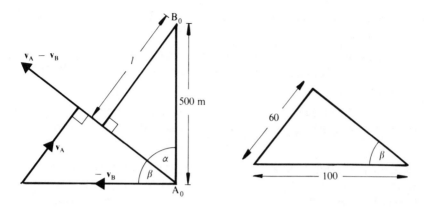

$$\sin \beta = \tfrac{60}{100} = \tfrac{3}{5}$$

Therefore $\sin \alpha = \sin (90° - \beta) = \cos \beta = \tfrac{4}{5}$

The shortest distance l between the launch and the speedboat is therefore given by

$$l = 500 \sin \alpha = 400 \, \text{m}$$

EXERCISE 13b

In questions 1–3, complete the table as indicated, given that A and B are two objects moving with constant velocities v_A and v_B from initial positions A_0 and B_0 respectively. A and B are closest together when a time t has elapsed after passing through A_0 and B_0. The distance AB is then of magnitude l.

Question	1	2	3
v_A magnitude direction	3 ms⁻¹ due S	10 ms⁻¹ perpendicular to $\overrightarrow{A_0B_0}$	20 kmh⁻¹ NE
v_B magnitude direction	4 ms⁻¹ due W	20 ms⁻¹	30 kmh⁻¹ due N
$\overrightarrow{A_0B_0}$ magnitude direction	20 m due S	40 m any convenient direction	SE
$v_A - v_B$ magnitude direction			
t			15 minutes
l		20 m	

4) Two straight paths, inclined to one another at 60°, intersect at a point O. A boy A is on one path 300 m from O, while a boy B is on the other path 400 m from O. (angle AOB = 60°). Simultaneously the boys begin to run towards O,

A with speed $15 \, \text{kmh}^{-1}$ and B with speed $12 \, \text{kmh}^{-1}$. What is the shortest distance between A and B.

5) At noon an observer on a ship travelling due East at $20 \, \text{kmh}^{-1}$ sees another ship 20 km due North which is travelling S 30° E at $8 \, \text{kmh}^{-1}$. At what time are the ships nearest together?

6) Two aircraft P and Q are flying at the same height at $300 \, \text{kmh}^{-1}$ SE and $350 \, \text{kmh}^{-1}$ N 60° E respectively. If P is initially 10 km North of Q, how close do they get to one another?

7) Two cyclists are riding one along each of two perpendicular roads which meet at A. At one instant both cyclists are 500 m from A and both are approaching A. If the speed of one cyclist is $8 \, \text{ms}^{-1}$ and the shortest distance between the cyclists is 50 m, find the two possible speeds of the second rider.

8) A and B are two ships which, at 1200 hours, are at P and Q respectively, where PQ = 26 nautical miles. A is steaming at 30 knots in a direction perpendicular to PQ and B is steaming on a straight course at 20 knots in such a direction as to approach A as closely as possible. Show that B steams at an angle arcsin $\frac{2}{3}$ with PQ.
Find when the ships are closest together.
(1 knot = 1 nautical mile per hour).

Interception

Interception or collision occurs if, at any time, A and B are in the same place at the same time i.e. A_t and B_t coincide.

In this case $\qquad\qquad\qquad\qquad B_t A_t \; = \; 0$

Therefore $\qquad\qquad \overrightarrow{B_0 A_0} + t(v_A - v_B) \; = \; 0 \qquad$ (Equation 1 Page 355)

Giving $\qquad\qquad\qquad\qquad t(v_A - v_B) \; = \; -\overrightarrow{B_0 A_0}$

Or $\qquad\qquad\qquad\qquad\quad t(v_A - v_B) \; = \; \overrightarrow{A_0 B_0}$

Therefore $t(v_A - v_B)$ and $\overrightarrow{A_0 B_0}$ have the same magnitude and direction.
But $v_A - v_B$ is the velocity of A relative to B and its magnitude is their relative speed.
Also $A_0 B_0$ is the line joining A to B initially and its magnitude is their initial distance apart.
Therefore: *A can intercept B if the velocity of A relative to B is parallel to the initial displacement $A_0 B_0$ and the time t at which interception occurs is given* by

$$t \; = \; \frac{\text{initial distance apart}}{\text{relative speed.}}$$

EXAMPLES 13c

1) A cruiser is travelling due East at 15 knots. At 1200 hours a destroyer which is 12 nautical miles South West of the cruiser sets off at 20 knots to intercept the cruiser. At what time will interception occur and on what bearing should the destroyer travel?

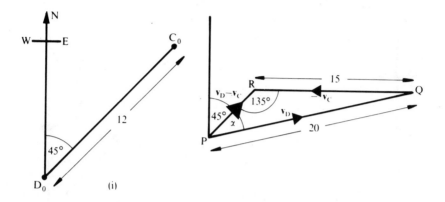

Diagram (i) shows the positions at noon of the destroyer and cruiser.
In diagram (ii) the side $\overrightarrow{PR}$ of the velocity triangle PQR, represents the velocity of the destroyer relative to the cruiser.
For interception $\overrightarrow{PR}$ is parallel to $\overrightarrow{D_0C_0}$, therefore angle PRQ = 135°.

In triangle PQR,
$$\frac{\sin 135°}{20} = \frac{\sin \alpha}{15}$$

Therefore
$$\sin \alpha = \frac{3}{4\sqrt{2}}$$

$$\alpha = 32° \, 02'$$

Giving $\qquad$ angle PQR = 12° 58'

And the destroyer's bearing, $\quad$ N(α + 45°)E = N 77° 02' E

Then
$$\frac{PR}{\sin 12° \, 58'} = \frac{20}{\sin 135°}$$

Therefore
$$PR = \frac{20 \times 0.2246}{0.7071}$$

Therefore speed of D relative to C $\qquad$ = 6.4 knots

Interception will take place after t hours where

$$t = \frac{12}{6.4} = 1.875$$

The destroyer will intercept the cruiser at 13.52 hours if it travels on a course N 77° 2′ E.

2) Two aircraft, P and Q, are flying at the same height. P is moving S 30° W at 300 kmh⁻¹ and Q is flying North West. When Q is 5 km due South of P the pilots find that they are on a collision course. What is the speed of Q and after what time will collision occur if neither pilot changes course?

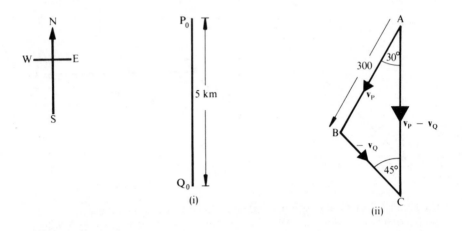

(i)   (ii)

Diagram (i) shows the initial positions of P and Q.
In diagram (ii) the side $\overrightarrow{AC}$ of the velocity triangle represents the velocity of P relative to Q.
For collision $\overrightarrow{AC}$ must be parallel to $\overrightarrow{P_0Q_0}$ i.e. $\overrightarrow{AC}$ runs due South.

In triangle ABC $\dfrac{BC}{\sin 30°} = \dfrac{300}{\sin 45°}$

Therefore $BC = 150\sqrt{2}$

                       $BC = 212$

Therefore the speed of Q is 212 kmh^{-1}

Also $\dfrac{AC}{\sin 105°} = \dfrac{300}{\sin 45°}$

Therefore $AC = 410$

But this represents the speed of P relative to Q. Therefore the time t before collision is expected is given by

$$t = \frac{5}{410} \text{ hours} \quad \left(t = \frac{\text{Initial distance apart}}{\text{Relative speed}} \right)$$

i.e. $\qquad\qquad\qquad\qquad\qquad t = 44$ seconds

Therefore Q is flying at $212 \, \text{kmh}^{-1}$ and collision is expected after 44 seconds.

EXERCISE 13c

1) A destroyer moving $N\,30°\,E$ at $50 \, \text{kmh}^{-1}$ observes at noon a cruiser travelling due North at $20 \, \text{kmh}^{-1}$. If the destroyer overtakes the cruiser one hour later find the distance and bearing of the cruiser from the destroyer at noon.

2) Two perpendicular roads intersect at P. Two cyclists are riding, one along each of the roads, towards P. One is 800 m from P and is riding at $18 \, \text{kmh}^{-1}$ and the other has a speed of $20 \, \text{kmh}^{-1}$ and is, at the same time, distant d from P. Find the value of d if:
(a) the cyclists meet at P,
(b) they are never nearer to each other than 50 m.

3) A yacht in distress is 8 km $S\,40°\,W$ of a harbour and is drifting $S\,10°\,E$ at $4 \, \text{kmh}^{-1}$. In what direction should a lifeboat travel to intercept the yacht if the speed of the lifeboat is $30 \, \text{kmh}^{-1}$.

4) A runaway horse is galloping across a field in a direction $N\,20°\,E$ at $40 \, \text{kmh}^{-1}$. It is already 300 m away in a direction due East, from a mounted rider who takes off in pursuit with a speed of $48 \, \text{kmh}^{-1}$. In what direction should he ride to catch the runaway?

5) Two aircraft A and B are flying at the same height in directions $N\,30°\,E$ and $N\,10°\,W$ respectively. At the instant when B is 10 km due East of A it is realised that they are on a collision course. If the speed of A is $500 \, \text{kmh}^{-1}$ find the speed of B.
If, at this instant, A changes course to $N\,45°\,E$ without altering speed, find the shortest distance between A and B.

SUMMARY

The motion of one object A relative to another object B is the motion it appears to have when viewed from B.
The velocity of A relative to B is the vector difference of velocities, $v_A - v_B$.
For interception or collision to occur, the relative velocity must be parallel to the initial displacement of A and B.
It is important to appreciate that several different methods are suitable for solving problems on relative motion. No one method is ideal for all problems and the student is advised to develop flexibility in choice of approach.

Although relative velocity is usually encountered in problems about moving vehicles, ships, aircraft etc., there are some questions of a less practical nature in which speeds are not necessarily constant and the paths are not always linear. The set of examples which follow are of this type.

EXAMPLES 13d

1) A particle P is moving in a clockwise sense at constant angular velocity ω round a circle whose equation is $x^2 + y^2 = a^2$. When $t = 0$, P is at the point $(-a, 0)$. A second particle Q moves along the x axis with constant velocity $a\omega$ in the positive sense. Q is at the origin when $t = 0$. Find, in terms of a, ω and t the speed of P relative to Q at time t. Find also the direction of the velocity of P relative to Q when $t = \dfrac{\pi}{\omega}$

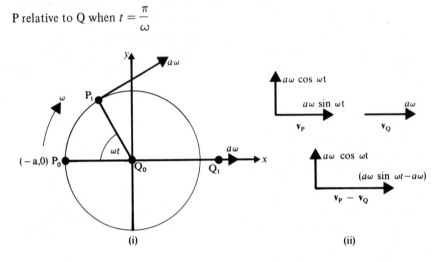

(i)   (ii)

Diagram (i) shows the positions of P and Q after t seconds. During this time, at angular velocity ω, P will describe an arc subtending an angle ωt at the centre, and will have a tangential speed of $a\omega$.

Diagram (ii) shows the components parallel to Ox and Oy of the velocities of P and Q and the velocity of P relative to Q at time t.

If V is the relative speed, then

$$V^2 = (a\omega \cos \omega t)^2 + (a\omega \sin \omega t - a\omega)^2$$
$$= a^2\omega^2 - 2a^2\omega^2 \sin \omega t + a^2\omega^2$$

The relative speed, $V = a\omega\sqrt{2(1 - \sin \omega t)}$.

When $t = \dfrac{\pi}{\omega}$, the components of the relative velocity, parallel to Ox and Oy, are:-

$$\rightarrow a\omega \sin \pi - a\omega = -a\omega$$
$$\uparrow a\omega \cos \pi \qquad = -a\omega$$

Therefore the direction of the velocity of P relative to Q when $t = \dfrac{\pi}{\omega}$ is parallel to the line $y = x$.

2) Two particles P and Q are projected simultaneously from a point O. P is

projected vertically with speed $V\sqrt{3}$ and Q is projected with speed V at 60° above the horizontal. Find the horizontal and vertical components of the velocity of P relative to Q at any time t. Hence find the vertical displacement between P and Q when the horizontal displacement between them is of magnitude $2V$. Find also the distance between P and Q when P is at its highest point.

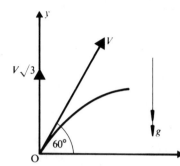

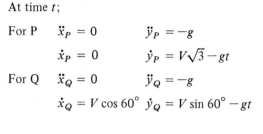

At time t;

For P $\ddot{x}_P = 0$ $\ddot{y}_P = -g$

        $\dot{x}_P = 0$ $\dot{y}_P = V\sqrt{3} - gt$

For Q $\ddot{x}_Q = 0$ $\ddot{y}_Q = -g$

        $\dot{x}_Q = V \cos 60°$ $\dot{y}_Q = V \sin 60° - gt$

Components of velocity of P relative to Q are

$$\dot{x}_P - \dot{x}_Q = 0 - V \cos 60° = -\frac{V}{2}$$

$$\dot{y}_P - \dot{y}_Q = (V\sqrt{3} - gt) - \left(V\frac{\sqrt{3}}{2} - gt\right) = V\frac{\sqrt{3}}{2}$$

Since both relative velocity components are constant, and the particles were initially at the same point O, the components of displacement of P relative to Q are

$$x_P - x_Q = (\dot{x}_P - \dot{x}_Q) \times t = -\frac{V}{2} \times t$$

$$y_P - y_Q = (\dot{y}_P - \dot{y}_Q) \times t = V\frac{\sqrt{3}}{2} \times t$$

Therefore the horizontal distance between P and Q is of magnitude $2V$ when

$$\left| -\frac{V}{2}t \right| = 2V$$

i.e. when $t = 4$

Then the vertical distance between P and Q is

$$V\frac{\sqrt{3}}{2} \times 4 = 2\sqrt{3}V.$$

P is at its highest point when $\dot{y}_P = 0$

This occurs when $t = \dfrac{V\sqrt{3}}{g}$

The displacement of P relative to Q then has components

$$x_P - x_Q = -\frac{V}{2} \times \frac{V\sqrt{3}}{g} = \frac{V^2\sqrt{3}}{2g}$$

$$y_P - y_Q = \frac{V\sqrt{3}}{2} \times \frac{V\sqrt{3}}{g} = \frac{3V^2}{2g}$$

The distance d between P and Q is given by

$$d^2 = \left(\frac{-V^2\sqrt{3}}{2g}\right)^2 + \left(\frac{3V^2}{2g}\right)^2$$

Hence
$$d = \frac{V^2}{2g}\sqrt{3+9} = \frac{V^2}{g}\sqrt{3}$$

Therefore when P is at its highest point, $PQ = \dfrac{V^2\sqrt{3}}{g}$

EXERCISE 13d

1) Two particles P and Q start simultaneously in the same sense from the origin O and both have constant speed v. P moves on the circle $x^2 + y^2 - 2x = 0$ and Q moves on the tangent to the circle through O. Find the relative speed of the particles when P has rotated through an angle (i) $\dfrac{\pi}{2}$ (ii) π (iii) $\dfrac{2\pi}{3}$

2) A point P moves so that its co-ordinates at time t are $x = t; y = 2t^2$. A second point Q moves along the x axis so that at time t its position is $x = 2t$. A third point R, moving on the y axis, is such that $y = t^2$. Find:
(a) the velocity of P relative to R,
(b) the velocity of P relative to Q, when $t = 3$.

3) Two particles are travelling round the circle $x^2 + y^2 = 4$. One particle, A, is initially at the point $(2, 0)$ and moves anticlockwise with constant angular velocity ω. The other particle, B, travels clockwise with constant angular velocity 2ω from its initial position at the point $(0, 2)$. Find:
(a) the speed of A relative to B at time t,
(b) the value of t when the particles are first travelling in the same direction,
(c) the acceleration of A relative to B when $t = 1$.

4) A particle P is moving along the line $y = x$ so that its speed at time t is $\sqrt{2}\,ut$ where u is a constant. A second particle Q moves along the positive y axis with constant speed u. If, when $t = 0$, P is at the point $(-4, -4)$ moving towards O, and Q is at the origin find:
(a) the velocity of P relative to Q at time t,
(b) the distance PQ when $t = 2$.

MISCELLANEOUS EXERCISE 13

1) A ship A is travelling due east at a speed of $8\,\mathrm{ms^{-1}}$, and a ship B is travelling due south at $10\,\mathrm{ms^{-1}}$. At an instant when A is 3 km from B in a direction N 60° E, a motor boat leaves A and travels in a straight line to B with speed $14\,\mathrm{ms^{-1}}$. Show that it reaches B in 500 seconds. On reaching the ship B, the motor boat immediately turns and travels back to A in a straight line, again with speed $14\,\mathrm{ms^{-1}}$. Find graphically (or otherwise) the time taken for the return journey.

(Cambridge)

2) At 1000 hours a pilot boat leaves the jetty to join a ship which is 4 nautical miles from the jetty on a bearing of 315°. The ship is steaming due east at a steady speed of 12 knots. Find the time at which the pilot boat reaches the ship and the distance and bearing of the ship from the jetty at that time if:
(i) the pilot boat travels at 15 knots,
(ii) the pilot boat travels at the least possible speed. (A.E.B.)

3) A ship P steaming at 20 km/h in the direction 050° is 120 km due west of ship Q steaming at 12 km/h in the direction 330°. If the ships do not alter course or speed, find by means of a scale drawing, or otherwise, the shortest distance between them in the subsequent motion. Find also the period of time during which the ships are within a range of 50 km of each other. (U of L)

4) A ship is moving due West at 20 knots and the wind appears to blow from $22\tfrac{1}{2}°$ West of South. The ship then steams due South at the same speed and the wind then appears to blow from $22\tfrac{1}{2}°$ East of South. Find the speed of the wind and the true direction from which it blows, assuming that they remain constant.

(J.M.B.)

5) An aircraft A flies horizontally at a constant speed $100\sqrt{2}$ km/h relative to the air, and its position at 1300 hours is at O. A wind speed 100 km/h blows from the West from 1300 to 1400 hours, after which the wind speed is 50 km/h blowing from the North. The aircraft adjusts its heading so as to maintain a course 45° East of North at all times. Find:
(i) the East and North components of the aircraft's velocity relative to the air, both before and after 1400 hours,
(ii) the aircraft's distance from O as a function of time t hours elapsed since 1400 hours, assuming $t > 0$. (W.J.E.C.)

6) The banks of a river 40 m wide are parallel and A and B are points on opposite banks. The distance AB is 50 m and B is downstream of A. There is a constant current of $4\,\mathrm{ms^{-1}}$ flowing. What is the minimum speed at which a motor boat must be able to move in still water in order to cross this river from A to B? If a boat sails from A to B with constant velocity in $7\tfrac{1}{2}$ seconds, find its speed relative to the water and the direction in which it is steered. Whilst this boat is sailing from A to B a man runs across a bridge which is at right angles to the

banks of the river. To this man the boat appears to be travelling parallel to the banks of the river. Find the speed at which the man is running.   (A.E.B.)

7) Relative to a ship which is travelling due north at a speed of 10 knots, the velocity of a speedboat is in the direction N 45° E. Relative to a second ship which is travelling due south at a speed of 10 knots, the velocity of the speedboat is in the direction N 30° E. Prove that the speedboat is travelling in the direction N θ° E where $\tan \theta = \sqrt{3} - 1$, and find its speed.   (U of L)

8) A cruiser sailing due N, at 12 knots sights a destroyer 24 sea-miles due E sailing at 28 knots on a course αW of N where $\cos \alpha = \frac{11}{14}$. Show that the destroyer's course relative to the cruiser is 60° W of N and find the relative speed. If the cruiser's guns have a maximum range of 15 sea-miles and both ships maintain course and speed, find for how long the destroyer will be within range. Immediately the destroyer is sighted an aircraft is despatched from the cruiser and flies in a straight line at a steady speed of 220 knots on an intersection course with the destroyer. Find the course on which the aircraft flies.
(A knot is one sea-mile per hour)   (J.M.B.)

9) A motorboat moving at 8 km/h relative to the water travels from a point A to a point B 10 km distant whose bearing from A is 150° (i.e. N 150° E). It then travels to a point C 10 km from B and due west of B. If there is a current of constant speed 4 km/h from north to south, find the two courses to be set, and prove that the total time taken to reach C is approximately 2 hours 20 minutes.
   (U of L)

10) A port X is 18 nautical miles due north of another port Y. Steamers A, B leave X, Y respectively at the same time, A travelling at 12 knots due east and B at 8 knots in a direction arcsin $\frac{1}{3}$ east of north. Find in magnitude and direction the velocity of B relative to A. Prove that subsequently the shortest distance between A and B is 14 nautical miles and find the time taken to reach this position.
If when the steamers are in this position a boat leaves A and travels due west so as to intercept B, find at what speed the boat must travel.   (J.M.B.)

11) Two aircraft are in horizontal flight at the same altitude. One is flying due north at 500 kmh^{-1} whilst the other is flying due west at 600 kmh^{-1}. Realising that they are on collision courses the pilots take avoiding action simultaneously when the aircraft are 10 km apart. The pilot of the first plane changes his course to 345° (N 15° W) maintaining his speed of 500 kmh^{-1} and the pilot of the second plane maintains his course but increases his speed to V kmh^{-1}. Find the value of V if:
 (i) the aircraft are still on collision courses,
(ii) the change of speed is the least possible to ensure that the distance between the planes is never less than 2 km.   (A.E.B.)

12) Two particles A and B are moving on a smooth horizontal plane in concentric circles with centre O. The lines OA and OB are rotating with constant angular velocities $+\omega$ and $+3\omega$ respectively and OA $= 2OB = 2r$. Find, in magnitude and direction, the velocity of B relative to A when the angle OB makes with OA is (i) $+90°$, (ii) $+60°$. When the angle AOB $= \theta$ the velocity of B relative to A is parallel to AO. Find the value of $\cos \theta$
When OB is at an angle $-90°$ to OA the forces acting on the particles are removed so that each particle then moves in a straight line. Find the shortest distance between the particles in the subsequent motion. (A.E.B.)

13) An equilateral triangular course is marked out by buoys A, B, C in a broad straight reach of a river, the buoy C being upstream and the line AB perpendicular to the current. A motor launch follows the course ABCA. If V is the speed of the launch in still water and u the speed of the current, show that while the launch is moving along AB it is pointed at an angle θ to AB on the upstream side, where $\sin \theta = u/V$.
Find the angle between BC and the direction in which the launch is pointed while it is moving along BC. Show that when it reaches C the launch turns through $120°$. (J.M.B.)

14) A ship A sails at $20\,\text{kmh}^{-1}$ on a course $60°$ E of N (actual speed and course). When A is 200 km W of a port, a ship B leaves the port and, after steaming on a straight course at its maximum speed of $V\,\text{kmh}^{-1}$ relative to the water, intercepts A.
(a) If there is no current in the sea, show that $V \geqslant V_0$, where V_0 should be given explicitly; and if $V = V_0$ find the time in hours (to 3 significant figures) before B reaches A after leaving port.
(b) If $V = 25$ and there is a steady current flowing from N to S at $5\,\text{kmh}^{-1}$, find the compass course that B should set as an angle W of N to the nearest minute of arc. (W.J.E.C.)

15) At a given instant, a ship P travelling due E at a speed of $30\,\text{kmh}^{-1}$ is 7 km due N of a second ship Q which is travelling $N\theta°\,W$ at a speed of $14\,\text{kmh}^{-1}$, where $\tan \theta = \frac{3}{4}$. Show that the speed of Q relative to P is $40\,\text{kmh}^{-1}$ and find the direction of the relative velocity.
The ships continue to move with uniform velicities. Find correct to three significant figures:
(i) the distance between the ships when they are nearest together,
(ii) the time taken, in minutes, to attain this shortest distance.
If initially, the course of Q had been altered to bring the ships as close as possible, the speed of Q and the speed and course of P being unchanged, find the direction of this new course. (J.M.B.)

16) At a particular instant a dinghy is observed to be at A, 200 m from a stationary buoy in a river estuary, and the bearing of A from the buoy is $240°$ (see figure). The River Board's regulations state that it is forbidden to approach

within 50 m of the buoy. In this part of the estuary there is a steady current of $1\frac{1}{2}$ ms^{-1} continuously flowing from due north. The dinghy, which can move at a maximum speed of 4 ms^{-1} in still water, moves in a straight line so that it passes as close to the buoy as the regulations allow. Show that there are two possible directions in which the dinghy can be steered and find the shortest time in each case for the dinghy to reach its closest approach to the buoy from A.

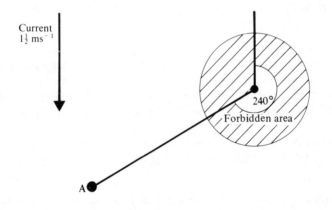

(A.E.B.)

17) A river of width a m with straight parallel banks flows due north with speed u ms^{-1}. The points O and A are on opposite banks and A is due east of O. Co-ordinate axes Ox, Oy are taken in the east and north directions respectively. A boat, whose speed V ms^{-1} relative to the water is constant, starts from O and crosses the river.

(i) If u is constant and equal to $\dfrac{V}{6}$ and the boat is steered so that it travels in a

straight line towards A, find the time taken for the boat to travel from O to A.

(ii) If u varies in such a way that

$$u = x(a-x)\frac{V}{a^2}$$

and if the boat is steered due east, show that the co-ordinates (x, y) of the boat satisfy the differential equation

$$\frac{dy}{dx} = \frac{x(a-x)}{a^2}$$

If the boat reaches the east bank at C, calculate the distance AC and find the time taken.   (J.M.B.)

18) The points X and Y are moving with the same speed u in the positive direction on the x axis and the y axis respectively. Find the velocity relative to X of the mid-point M of XY, and show that it is the reverse of the velocity of M relative to Y.

A particle P moves on the circle $x^2 + y^2 = 1$ with constant speed v. Show that at each instant when the acceleration of P is parallel to the line $x + y = 0$ the velocities of P relative to X and Y are equal in magnitude.

Find v in terms of u if the maximum value of the velocity of P relative to M is u.

(U of L)

CHAPTER 14

TURNING EFFECT.
NON-CONCURRENT FORCES

ROTATION OF A LAMINA

If a lamina is free to rotate in its own plane, the axis about which it turns is perpendicular to the plane of rotation, e.g. a wheel rotates in a plane perpendicular to its axle.

The lamina can be made to rotate by a force whose line of action is in the plane of rotation.

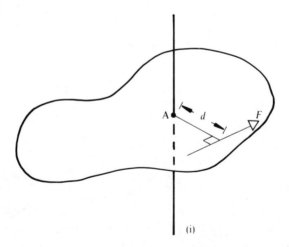

(i)

In diagram (i) a lamina is free to rotate about an axis through a point **A** of the lamina and perpendicular to the lamina. A force F which has its line of action in the lamina at a distance d from **A**, would cause the lamina to turn about **A**.

374

MOMENT OF FORCE

The turning effect C of the force F can be calculated by multiplying together the *magnitude* of the force and its perpendicular distance from the axis of rotation.

i.e. $$C = Fd$$

C is called the *moment of the force* or the *torque* about the specified axis.

Unit of Torque

Since torque = force × distance, the unit of torque is the newton metre, Nm. (*N.B.* Do not confuse this unit with the joule. The work done when a constant force moves through a distance is calculated from an apparently similar formula:-
Work done = Force × Distance
There are two major differences between Work and Torque however:
(i) Work is scalar and Torque is vector.
(ii) Work is interchangable with Energy and Torque is not.
Hence Work is measured in the energy unit, the joule, but Torque is measured in newton metres.)

Direction of Torque

The angular direction of a torque is the sense of the rotation it would cause.

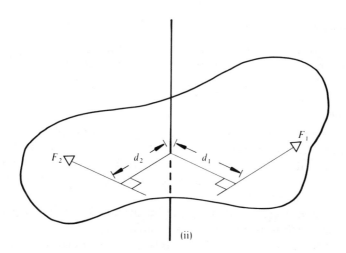

(ii)

In diagram (ii) the moment about **A** of the force F_1 is $F_1 d_1$ anticlockwise and the moment about **A** of the force F_2 is $F_2 d_2$ clockwise.
A convenient way to differentiate between clockwise and anticlockwise torques is to allocate a positive sign to one sense (usually, but not invariably, this is anticlockwise) and a negative sign to the other.
With this convention, the moments of F_1 and F_2 are $+ F_1 d_1$ and $- F_2 d_2$.

(When using a sign convention in any problem it is advisable to specify the chosen positive sense).

Graphical Representation of Torque

A force **F**, distant d from an axis through **A**, can be represented in magnitude, direction and position (i.e. completely) by a line $\overrightarrow{PQ}$

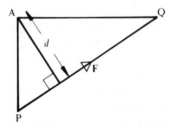

The magnitude of the torque about the axis is $|\mathbf{F}| \times d$ which is represented by $PQ \times d$. But $\frac{1}{2} \times PQ \times d$ is the area of triangle PAQ.

Therefore the magnitude of the moment about an axis through **A** of a force represented completely by a line PQ is represented by twice the area of triangle PAQ.

Zero Moment

If the line of action of a force passes through the axis of rotation, its perpendicular distance from the axis is zero. Therefore its moment about that axis is also zero.

Terminology

Whenever we refer to the moment of a set of coplanar forces about an axis, it is implicit that the axis is perpendicular to the plane in which the forces act. In a diagram of the forces in their plane of action, the axis of rotation, being perpendicular to that plane, can be indicated only by a point (its point of intersection with the plane).

Because of this it is common to refer to the moment of forces about a point. This is, of course, inaccurate, because forces do not cause turning about a point, but about a line. It should always be appreciated therefore that an expression such as 'the moment of force F about A' really means 'the moment of force F about an axis through A and perpendicular to the plane in which F acts'.

EXAMPLES 14a

1)

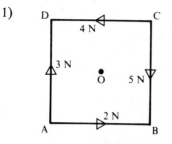

ABCD is a square of side 2 m and O is its centre. Forces act along the sides as shown in the diagram. Calculate the moment of each force about:
(a) an axis through A,
(b) an axis through O.

Taking anticlockwise moments as positive we have:

(a)

Magnitude of Force	2 N	5 N	4 N	3 N
Distance from A	0	2 m	2 m	0
Moment about A	0	− 10 Nm	+ 8 Nm	0

(b)

Magnitude of Force	2 N	5 N	4 N	3 N
Distance from O	1 m	1 m	1 m	1 m
Moment about O	+ 2 Nm	− 5 Nm	+ 4 Nm	− 3 Nm

2)

Forces act as indicated on a rod **AB** which is pivoted at **A**. Find the anticlockwise moment of each force about the pivot.

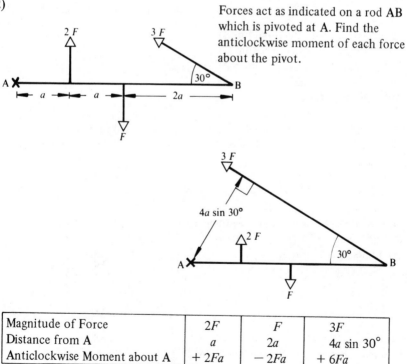

Magnitude of Force	2F	F	3F
Distance from A	a	$2a$	$4a \sin 30°$
Anticlockwise Moment about A	+ 2Fa	− 2Fa	+ 6Fa

3)

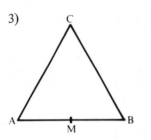

ABC is an equilateral triangle of side 2 m. Forces P, Q and R act along the sides AB, BC and CA respectively. If the anti-clockwise moments about axes perpendicular to the triangle through A, B and C are $+2\sqrt{3}$ Nm, $-4\sqrt{3}$ Nm and $+\sqrt{3}$ Nm respectively, calculate the magnitude and direction of P, Q and R.

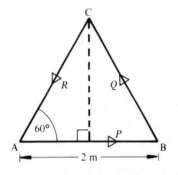

The altitude d of the triangle is $2\sin 60°$ i.e. $d = \sqrt{3}$.
The anticlockwise torque about A is Qd

Therefore	$Qd = +2\sqrt{3}$
Giving	$Q = +2$

About B the anti-clockwise torque $\qquad Rd = -4\sqrt{3}$
Giving $\qquad\qquad\qquad\qquad R = -4$
(the negative sign shows that R is in the direction $\overrightarrow{AC}$ and not $\overrightarrow{CA}$).
Similarly about C $\qquad Pd = +\sqrt{3}$
Giving $\qquad\qquad\qquad\qquad P = +1$

Therefore P is 1 N in the direction $\overrightarrow{AB}$
$\qquad\qquad Q$ is 2 N in the direction $\overrightarrow{BC}$ and
$\qquad\qquad R$ is 4 N in the direction $\overrightarrow{AC}$

POSITION VECTOR

Cartesian vector notation, which we have already used to describe free vectors (e.g. force, velocity, acceleration) can also be used to describe the position of a point.

If a point P has co-ordinates (2, 3) then the displacement of P *from the origin* has components 2i and 3j.

Thus $\qquad \mathbf{r} = 2\mathbf{i} + 3\mathbf{j}$

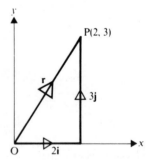

$\mathbf{r}$ is called the *position vector* of the point P.

4) Three coplanar forces F_1, F_2 and F_3 are defined as follows;

$F_1 = 2i + 3j$ and acts through the point $r_1 = i + 4j$
$F_2 = -i - 3j$ „   „   „   „   „ $r_2 = 2i - j$
$F_3 = 4i - j$ „   „   „   „   „ $r_3 = -3i$

Calculate the anticlockwise moment of each force about an axis through O.

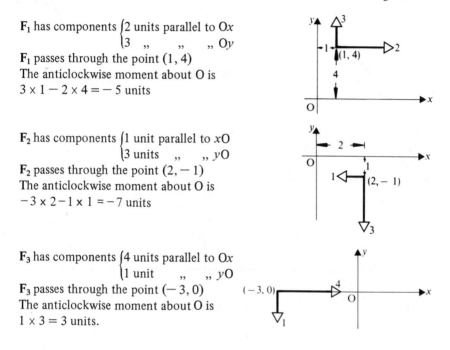

F_1 has components $\begin{cases} 2 \text{ units parallel to } Ox \\ 3 \text{ „ „ „ } Oy \end{cases}$
F_1 passes through the point $(1, 4)$
The anticlockwise moment about O is
$3 \times 1 - 2 \times 4 = -5$ units

F_2 has components $\begin{cases} 1 \text{ unit parallel to } xO \\ 3 \text{ units „ „ } yO \end{cases}$
F_2 passes through the point $(2, -1)$
The anticlockwise moment about O is
$-3 \times 2 - 1 \times 1 = -7$ units

F_3 has components $\begin{cases} 4 \text{ units parallel to } Ox \\ 1 \text{ unit „ „ } yO \end{cases}$
F_3 passes through the point $(-3, 0)$
The anticlockwise moment about O is
$1 \times 3 = 3$ units.

EXERCISE 14a

In questions 1 to 4, calculate the anticlockwise torque of each of the forces acting in the plane of the lamina shown in the diagram, about an axis perpendicular to the lamina, through A.

1)

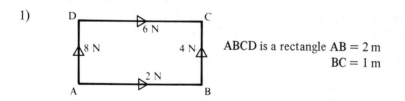

ABCD is a rectangle AB = 2 m
BC = 1 m

2)

ABCDEF is a regular hexagon of side 2*a*.

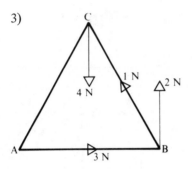

3)

ABC is an equilateral triangle of side 2 m

4)

BC is a rod pivoted about its
mid-point A
BM = MA = AN = NC = *a*.

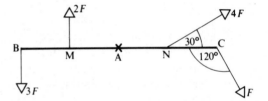

5)

The moment of *F* about A is 3 Nm
clockwise and about B is 1 Nm clockwise.
If AB = BC = 1 m find the moment of
F about C.

6) Calculate the anticlockwise moment of each of the following force vectors
about an axis through O.

$F_1 = 4i + 2j$ and acts through a point $r_1 = i + j$
$F_2 = 3i - 5j$,, ,, ,, ,, ,, $r_2 = 2i - j$
$F_3 = 4i$,, ,, ,, ,, ,, $r_3 = 3j$
$F_4 = -6j$,, ,, ,, ,, ,, $r_4 = i - 6j$

RESULTANT TORQUE

When several coplanar forces act on an object, their resultant turning effect about a specified axis is the algebraic sum of the moments of the individual forces about that axis (i.e. the sum of the separate moments taking into account the sign which indicates the sense).

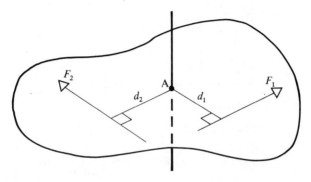

e.g. The resultant moment about the axis through A of forces F_1 and F_2 as shown in the diagram, is the sum of $+F_1d_1$ and $-F_2d_2$.
i.e. the torque about A is $F_1d_1 - F_2d_2$.

THE PRINCIPLE OF MOMENTS

Consider two coplanar forces F_1 and F_2 whose perpendicular distances from an axis through a point A in the plane are d_1 and d_2 respectively (diagram (i)). Let the forces intersect at an angle θ at a point O such that AO is of length l and AO makes an angle α with the line of action of the force F_2 (diagram (ii)).

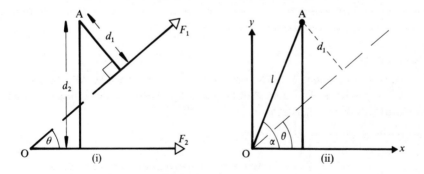

Since F_1 and F_2 meet at O, their resultant also passes through O and has components

$$F_2 + F_1 \cos \theta \qquad \text{along } Ox$$
$$F_1 \sin \theta \qquad \text{along } Oy$$

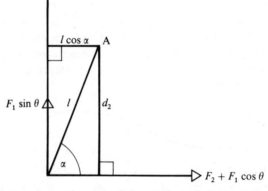

The anticlockwise torque about A of the resultant force is

$$(F_2 + F_1 \cos \theta)\, d_2 - F_1 \sin \theta\, (l \cos \alpha)$$

$$= F_2 d_2 + F_1 d_2 \cos \theta - F_1 \sin \theta \left(\frac{d_2}{\sin \alpha} \cos \alpha \right)$$

$$= F_2 d_2 + \frac{F_1 d_2}{\sin \alpha} (\cos \theta \sin \alpha - \sin \theta \cos \alpha)$$

$$= F_2 d_2 + F_1 \left(\frac{d_2}{\sin \alpha} \right) \sin (\alpha - \theta)$$

$$= F_2 d_2 + F_1 l \sin (\alpha - \theta)$$

But $d_1 = l \sin (\alpha - \theta)$ (diagram (ii))

Therefore the anticlockwise torque about A of the resultant force is $F_2 d_2 + F_1 d_1$ which is equal to the combined torque of the two separate forces.

This argument can be applied successively to include further forces and to establish the general principle that *the resultant moment of a set of forces is equal to the moment about the same axis of the resultant force.*

EXAMPLES 14b

1) Forces of magnitudes 2 N, 3 N, 1 N and 5 N act along the sides $\overrightarrow{AB}$, $\overrightarrow{BC}$, $\overrightarrow{DC}$ and $\overrightarrow{AD}$ respectively of a square ABCD of side 1 m. What is their resultant moment about (a) an axis through A (b) an axis through C?

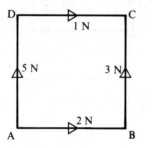

Giving a positive sign to a torque in the sense ABC (i.e. anticlockwise in the diagram) we have:

(a) About an axis through **A**

The individual moments are $+ 3\,\mathrm{Nm}$ and $- 1\,\mathrm{Nm}$ (the forces of 5 N and 2 N pass through **A** so their moment is zero).

Therefore the resultant moment is $(+ 3 - 1)\,\mathrm{Nm} = + 2\,\mathrm{Nm}$

i.e. 2 Nm in the sense **ABC**.

(b) About an axis through **C**

The individual moments are $+ 2\,\mathrm{Nm}$ and $- 5\,\mathrm{Nm}$

Therefore the resultant moment is $- 3\,\mathrm{Nm}$

i.e. 3 Nm in the sense **CBA**.

Note. In this problem the diagram can be lettered correctly in several different ways. A force which in one diagram has an anticlockwise moment may cause clockwise rotation in another.

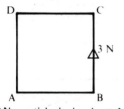

3 Nm anticlockwise about A

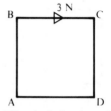

3 Nm clockwise about A

This ambiguity is avoided when the positive sense is specified by *letter order* (in either of the above diagrams the torque is 3 Nm in the sense **ABC**).

2)

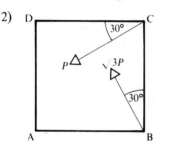

Two forces of magnitudes P and $\sqrt{3}P$ act in the plane of a square ABCD as shown in the figure. If $AB = a$ find the resultant moment about an axis perpendicular to the square, through **A**.

In this problem the perpendicular distance from **A** to the force P is not immediately obvious. On such occasions it is often preferable to resolve the force into components whose distances from the axis are easily obtained.

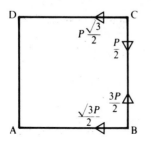

Resolving the force P along $\overrightarrow{CD}$ and $\overrightarrow{CB}$ and the force $\sqrt{3}P$ along $\overrightarrow{BA}$ and $\overrightarrow{BC}$ we have:

about an axis through **A** the individual moments (anticlockwise positive) are

$$+ Pa\,\frac{\sqrt{3}}{2}, \quad -\frac{Pa}{2}, \quad +\frac{3\,Pa}{2}, \quad \text{zero}$$

Therefore the resultant moment is $\dfrac{Pa}{2}(\sqrt{3} - 1 + 3)$

i.e. $\qquad\qquad\qquad\qquad (2 + \sqrt{3})\dfrac{Pa}{2}$ anticlockwise.

3) ABCD is a rectangle in which AB = 2 m and BC = 1 m. A force of 2 N acts along $\overrightarrow{BC}$. If the resultant torque about A is to be 6 Nm in the sense ABC find the extra forces needed if:
(a) only one more force acts along CD,
(b) two more forces of equal magnitude act along BC and CD.

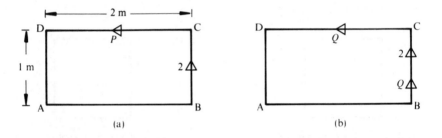

(a)　　　　　　　　　　　　　　　　(b)

(a) If the one extra force along CD is of magnitude P newton then the individual moments about A in the sense ABC are + 4 Nm and + P newton metre. But the resultant moment is + 6 Nm
Therefore $4 + P = 6$ and $P = 2$
Hence, a force of 2 N is required along $\overrightarrow{CD}$.

(b) If the two extra forces along BC and CD are both of magnitude Q newton, the individual moments are + 2Q newton metre and + Q newton metre.
Therefore $2Q + 4 + Q = 6$ and $Q = \frac{2}{3}$
Hence forces of magnitude $\frac{2}{3}$N are required along $\overrightarrow{BC}$ and $\overrightarrow{CD}$.

4) Find the resultant torque, about an axis through the point with position vector $\mathbf{i} + \mathbf{j}$, of the following forces.

$\begin{aligned}
\mathbf{F}_1 &= 4\mathbf{i} + 7\mathbf{j} \text{ acting through the point } \mathbf{r}_1 = -4\mathbf{i} + 3\mathbf{j} \\
\mathbf{F}_2 &= -\mathbf{i} - 2\mathbf{j} \quad ,, \qquad ,, \qquad ,, \quad ,, \quad \mathbf{r}_2 = \mathbf{i} - \mathbf{j} \\
\mathbf{F}_3 &= 6\mathbf{j} \qquad\quad ,, \qquad ,, \qquad ,, \quad ,, \quad \mathbf{r}_3 = 5\mathbf{i}
\end{aligned}$

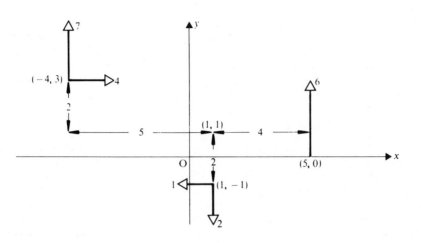

Taking the clockwise sense as positive, the moment of each force about the axis through $(1, 1)$ is

For $\mathbf{F_1}$ $7 \times 5 + 4 \times 2 \ = \ +43$ units
For $\mathbf{F_2}$ 1×2 $= + \ \ 2$ units
For $\mathbf{F_3}$ -6×4 $= -24$ units
The resultant torque is therefore 21 units clockwise.

EXERCISE 14b

In questions 1 — 4 all forces act in the plane of the lamina. Calculate the resultant torque about an axis through A perpendicular to the lamina, stating the sense in which it acts.

1)

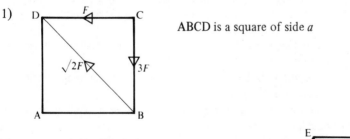

ABCD is a square of side a

2)

ABCDEF is a regular hexagon of side $2a$

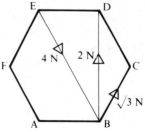

3)

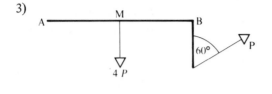

ABC is a metal rod bent at B
to a right angle.
AB = $4a$ and BC = a.
M is the mid-point of AB.

4)

LMN is an equilateral triangle of side
1 m and A bisects LN.

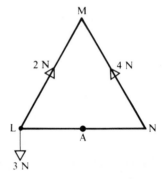

5) Forces represented by $5\mathbf{i}$, $4\mathbf{i} + 2\mathbf{j}$, $-3\mathbf{j}$, $\mathbf{i} - 6\mathbf{j}$ act respectively through points
with position vectors $\mathbf{i} + \mathbf{j}$, $\mathbf{i} - \mathbf{j}$, $3\mathbf{j}$, $4\mathbf{i}$. Find their resultant moment about an
axis through (a) the origin   (b) the point $-2\mathbf{i} - \mathbf{j}$.

6) O is the centre of a square **ABCD** of side 1 m. Calculate the magnitudes of
three forces which act along **AB**, **BC** and **CD** such that the resultant moment in
the sense ABC about A is -1 Nm, about B is $+3$ Nm and about O is $+5$ Nm.

RESULTANT MOMENT OF FORCES IN EQUILIBRIUM

Consider a stationary object upon which a number of forces begin to act.
If, about a certain axis, the forces have a resultant anticlockwise moment, the
object will begin to rotate anticlockwise about that axis.
Similarly the object will begin to rotate clockwise if the forces acting on it have
a resultant clockwise moment.
If, however, the object does not begin to rotate at all, there can be no resultant
torque in either sense about any axis.
But one of the conditions necessary for a set of forces to be in equilibrium is that
they cause no change in rotation.
It therefore follows that *if a set of forces is in equilibrium their resultant moment
about any axis is zero.*
This property can often be used to evaluate any of those forces acting on an
object in equilibrium, which are unknown.

EXAMPLES 14c

1) A uniform rod AB of length 2 m and weight 20 N rests horizontally on smooth

supports at A and B. A load of 10 N is attached to the rod at a distance 0.4 m from A. Find the forces exerted on the rod by the supports.

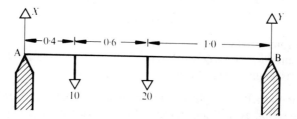

Let X and Y be the magnitudes (in newtons) of the supporting forces at A and B respectively.

Because the rod is at rest, the resultant moment of the forces acting on it is zero about any axis.

Using the symbol A) to indicate that the resultant moment about an axis through A is to be assessed in the sense indicated by the arrow, we have:

$$\text{A)} \qquad 10 \times 0.4 + 20 \times 1.0 - Y \times 2.0 = 0 \qquad (1)$$

$$\text{B)} \qquad X \times 2.0 - 10 \times 1.6 - 20 \times 1.0 = 0 \qquad (2)$$

Hence $\qquad\qquad X = 18 \quad \text{and} \quad Y = 12$

Therefore the supporting forces are 18 N at A and 12 N at B.

(*Note*. The sum of the supporting forces is equal to the sum of the loads confirming that the resultant of the vertical forces acting on the rod is zero.)

2) A uniform plank AB of weight 100 N and length 4 m lies on a horizontal roof, perpendicular to the edge of the roof and overhanging by 1.5 m. If a load of 200 N is to be attached to the overhanging end A, what force must be applied at the opposite end B just to prevent the plank from overturning?

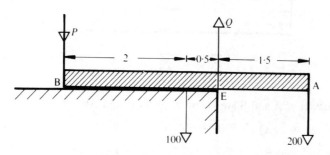

When the plank is just on the point of overturning it is in contact with the roof only at the edge E. The normal reaction therefore acts at E.

Let the normal reaction be Q and the force required at B be P (both in newtons).

Then

$$\text{E)} \qquad 200 \times 1.5 - 100 \times 0.5 - P \times 2.5 = 0$$

Hence $P = 100.$

Therefore a force of 100 N is needed at **B**.
(*Note.* The unknown force Q which is not required is avoided by choosing to take moments about an axis through which Q passes).

3) A uniform rod AB of weight W is hinged to a fixed point at **A**. It is held in a horizontal position by a string, one end of which is attached to **B** and the other end to a fixed point **C** such that angle ABC is $30°$. Find, in terms of W, the tension in the string.

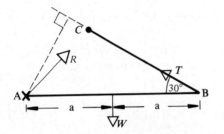

Let the length of the rod be $2a$.

$$\text{A)} \qquad Wa - T \times 2a \sin 30° = 0$$

i.e. $\qquad Wa - Ta \qquad\qquad = 0$
(The unknown force R at the hinge **A** is avoiding by taking moments about an axis through **A**.)

Therefore the tension in the string is of magnitude W.

4) A non-uniform rod AB of length 2 m is suspended in a horizontal position by two vertical strings, one at each end. The weight of the rod acts at **G** where $AG = 1.1$ m and is of magnitude 60 N. A load of 20 N is placed on the rod at a variable point **P**. If either string snaps when the tension in it exceeds 42 N, find the section of the rod in which P can lie.

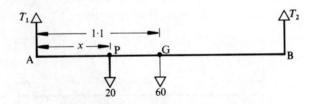

If the tensions at A and B are T_1 and T_2 newtons and $AP = x$ metres, then:

$$\text{A)} \qquad 20x + 60 \times 1.1 \; - 2\,T_2 \qquad = 0$$
$$\text{B)} \qquad 2\,T_1 - 20(2 - x) - 60 \times 0.9 = 0$$

Therefore $\qquad\qquad\qquad\qquad T_1 = 47 \; - 10x$

$$T_2 = 10x + 33$$

But $\qquad\qquad\qquad\qquad T_1 \leqslant 42 \quad \text{and} \quad T_2 \leqslant 42$

Therefore $47 - 10x \leqslant 42$

$$10x + 33 \leqslant 42$$

Giving $x \geqslant 0.5$ and $x \leqslant 0.9$

The load can therefore be placed anywhere within the section P_1P_2 without breaking either string, where $AP_1 = 0.5$ and $P_2B = 1.1$

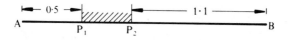

EXERCISE 14c

1) A uniform beam AB of length 1.6 m and weight 40 N rests on two smooth supports at C and D where $AC = BD = 0.3$ m. A load is attached to A so that the supporting force at C is twice the supporting force at D. Find the magnitude of the load.

2) A non-uniform rod of weight 40 N and length 1 m is suspended by a single string attached to the mid-point of the rod. If the rod is horizontal when a weight of 30 N is attached to one end of the rod, find the supporting force which would be required at the opposite end to keep the rod horizontal when the 30 N weight is removed.

3) A uniform beam 3 m long has weights 20 N and 30 N attached to its ends. If the weight of the beam is 50 N find the point on the beam where a support should be placed so that the beam will rest horizontally.

In questions 4–8 each diagram shows an object in equilibrium. Using the principle of moments calculate the forces or distances indicated (units are newtons and metres throughout).

4)

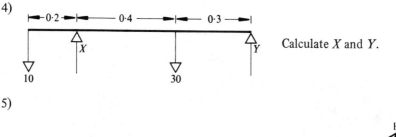

Calculate X and Y.

5)

A rod is hinged at A. Calculate the distance AB if the smooth support at B exerts a force 25 N on the rod.

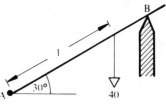

6)

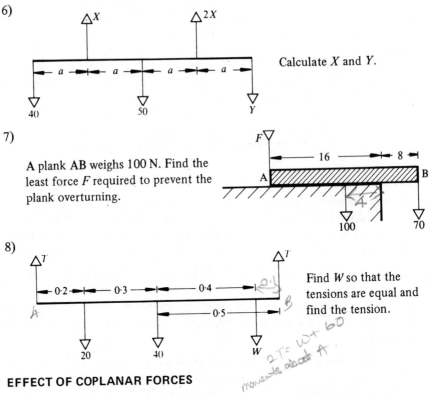

Calculate X and Y.

7)

A plank AB weighs 100 N. Find the
least force F required to prevent the
plank overturning.

16 ⊢— 8 ⊣

A ▨▨▨▨▨▨▨▨▨ B

100   70

8)

Find W so that the
tensions are equal and
find the tension.

$2T = W + 60$
moments about A.

EFFECT OF COPLANAR FORCES

We are now going to consider the general effect of a set of non concurrent
coplanar forces acting on an object (the simplest object to visualise is a lamina
in the plane of the forces).
For reference purposes let O be some point in the lamina and Ox, Oy be perpendicular lines through O in the plane of the lamina.

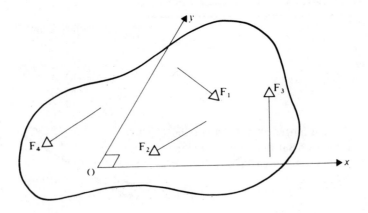

The movement of the lamina *in its own plane* may then be made up only of:
  (i) linear movement parallel to O*x*,
  (ii) linear movement parallel to O*y*,
(iii) rotation about some axis perpendicular to the lamina.
These three independent factors in the possible movement of the lamina are caused respectively by:-
  (i) the algebraic sum of the components parallel to O*x* of all the forces acting,
  (ii) the algebraic sum of all the components parallel to O*y*,
(iii) the resultant moment of all the forces about the axis of rotation.
The ability of a set of coplanar forces to generate movement made up of three independent factors is referred to as the *three degrees of freedom* of the force system.

COPLANAR FORCES IN EQUILIBRIUM

When a stationary object is in equilibrium under the action of a set of coplanar forces, each of the three independent factors which comprise the possible movement of the object must be zero. i.e. the object has:
  (i) no linear movement parallel to O*x*,
  (ii) no linear movement parallel to O*y*,
(iii) no rotation about any axis.
The set of forces must therefore be such that:
  (i) the algebraic sum of the components parallel to O*x* is zero,
  (ii) the algebraic sum of the components parallel to O*y* is zero,
(iii) the resultant moment of the forces about any specified axis is zero.
The use in a particular problem of this set of conditions for equilibrium leads to the formation of not more than three independent equations relating the forces in the system.

EXAMPLE

A rod AB rests with the end A on rough horizontal ground and the end B against a smooth vertical wall. The rod is uniform and of weight W. A mass also of weight W is attached at B. If the coefficient of friction at A is $\frac{3}{4}$ find the angle at which the rod is inclined to the vertical when it is just about to slip.

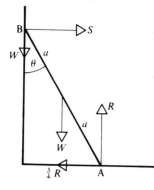

When the rod is about to slip the frictional force at A is $\frac{3}{4}R$.
Let the length of the rod be $2a$ and its inclination to the wall be θ.
Then, resolving parallel to the ground and to the wall and taking moments about an axis through A, we have:

$$\rightarrow \qquad\qquad S - \tfrac{3}{4}R = 0 \qquad\qquad (1)$$

$$\uparrow \qquad\qquad R - 2W = 0 \qquad\qquad (2)$$

$$\text{A)} \quad W \times a \sin\theta + W \times 2a \sin\theta - S \times 2a \cos\theta = 0 \qquad (3)$$

From (2)
$$R = 2W$$

From (1)
$$S = \tfrac{3}{4}(2W) = \frac{3W}{2}$$

From (3)
$$S = \frac{3W}{2}\tan\theta$$

Therefore
$$\frac{3W}{2} = \frac{3W}{2}\tan\theta$$

Giving
$$\tan\theta = 1$$

The rod is therefore inclined at $45°$ to the vertical.

Alternative Conditions for Equilibrium of Coplanar Forces

When a stationary object is in equilibrium it is not rotating about *any* axis or moving linearly in *any* direction. There are consequently many more equations which could be formed by equating to zero the resultant moment about various different axes or the collected force components in various different directions. But, as the *total number of independent equations is limited to three*, the various groups of equations which may be used are based on:
(a) resolving in any two directions and taking moments about one axis,
(b) resolving in one direction and taking moments about two axes,
(c) taking moments about three axes (which must not be collinear or the third resultant moment would simply be the combination of the first two, giving no extra information).

EXAMPLES 14d

1) A uniform rod AB of length $2a$ and weight W is smoothly pivoted to a fixed point at A. A load of weight $2W$ is attached to the end B. The rod is kept horizontal by a string attached to the mid-point G of the rod and to a point C vertically above A. If the length of the string is $2a$ find, in terms of W, the tension in the string and the magnitude of the reaction at the pivot.

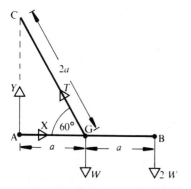

$$\cos A\hat{G}C = \frac{a}{2a} = \tfrac{1}{2}$$

Therefore $A\hat{G}C = 60°$

Let X and Y be the horizontal and vertical components of reaction at the hinge.

Then: Resolving horizontally and vertically and taking moments about an axis through A, we have:

$$\rightarrow \qquad\qquad X - T\cos 60° = 0 \qquad\qquad (1)$$

$$\uparrow \qquad\qquad Y + T\sin 60° - 3W = 0 \qquad\qquad (2)$$

$$A\rangle \quad Wa + 2W(2a) - Ta\sin 60° = 0 \qquad\qquad (3)$$

From (3) $\qquad\qquad T = \dfrac{10W}{\sqrt{3}} \qquad\qquad = \dfrac{10\sqrt{3}}{3}W$

From (1) $\qquad\qquad X = \left(\dfrac{10\sqrt{3}}{3}W\right)\left(\dfrac{1}{2}\right) \qquad = \dfrac{5\sqrt{3}}{3}W$

From (2) $\qquad\qquad Y = 3W - \left(\dfrac{10\sqrt{3}}{3}W\right)\left(\dfrac{\sqrt{3}}{2}\right) = -2W$

The reaction at the hinge is of magnitude

$$\sqrt{X^2 + Y^2} = \sqrt{\left(\frac{25}{3}W^2 + 4W^2\right)} = W\sqrt{\frac{37}{3}}$$

The tension in the string is $\dfrac{10\sqrt{3}}{3}W$

2) A ladder rests in limiting equilibrium against a rough vertical wall and with its foot on rough horizontal ground, the coefficient of friction at both points of contact being $\tfrac{1}{2}$. The ladder is uniform and weighs 300 N. Find the normal reaction at the wall and the angle θ which the ladder makes with the horizontal.

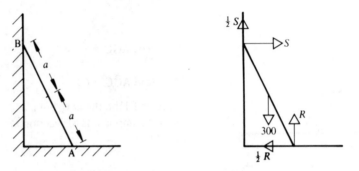

(The rod is in limiting equilibrium, so the frictional forces at A and B are $\frac{1}{2}R$ and $\frac{1}{2}S$ where R and S respectively are the normal reactions).

Let $2a$ be the length of the rod.

Taking moments about two axes, through A and B, and resolving horizontally we have:

A) $300 \times a \cos \theta - S \times 2a \sin \theta - \frac{1}{2}S \times 2a \cos \theta = 0$ (1)

B) $R \times 2a \cos \theta - \frac{1}{2}R \times 2a \sin \theta - 300 \times a \cos \theta = 0$ (2)

→ $S - \frac{1}{2}R = 0$ (3)

From (1) and (2), dividing each by $a \cos \theta$,

$$300 = S(2 \tan \theta + 1) = R(2 - \tan \theta)$$

But $R = 2S$

Therefore $(2 \tan \theta + 1) = 2(2 - \tan \theta)$

and $\tan \theta = \frac{3}{4}$

Therefore the ladder is inclined at an angle $36° 52'$ to the horizontal.

From equation (1) $S = \dfrac{300}{2 \tan \theta + 1} = \dfrac{300}{2.5}$

Therefore the normal reaction at the wall is 120 N.

3) O is the centre of a circular disc of weight W which rests in a vertical plane on two rough pegs A and B, the coefficient of friction with each being 0.5. AO makes $60°$ and BO makes $30°$ with the vertical. Find, in terms of W, the maximum force which can be applied tangentially at the highest point of the disc without causing rotation in the sense from A to B.

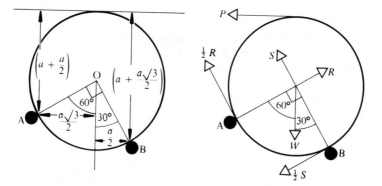

When P has its maximum value the frictional forces at A and B are $\frac{1}{2}R$ and $\frac{1}{2}S$. Let the radius of the disc be a.

Taking moments about axes through A, B and O (which are not collinear) we have:

$$\text{A)} \quad P \times \frac{3a}{2} + Sa - \tfrac{1}{2}Sa - W\frac{a\sqrt{3}}{2} = 0 \tag{1}$$

$$\text{B)} \quad P\left(a + a\frac{\sqrt{3}}{2}\right) + W\frac{a}{2} - Ra - \tfrac{1}{2}Ra = 0 \tag{2}$$

$$\text{O)} \quad Pa - \tfrac{1}{2}Ra - \tfrac{1}{2}Sa = 0 \tag{3}$$

From (1) $S = \sqrt{3}W - 3P$

From (2) $3R = W + P(2 + \sqrt{3})$

From (3) $2P = R + S$

Therefore $2P = \tfrac{1}{3}[W + 2P + \sqrt{3}P] + \sqrt{3}W - .3P$

Hence $(13 - \sqrt{3})P = (1 + 3\sqrt{3})W$

and $$P = \left(\frac{1 + 3\sqrt{3}}{13 - \sqrt{3}}\right)W = \frac{(1 + 3\sqrt{3})(13 + \sqrt{3})}{166}W$$

The greatest force is therefore $\dfrac{(11 + 20\sqrt{3})}{83}W$

Note: The limitation to three independent equations is vital. If, mistakenly, a fourth equation is introduced (e.g. by resolving twice and taking moments twice) then, in the subsequent working, it will be found that everything cancels out and some useless result such as $P = P$ will emerge. If, in a problem, there seem to be four unknown quantities so that three equations are not sufficient the fourth necessary equation must come from a different source e.g. mensuration, Hooke's Law etc. Further examples on the equilibrium of coplanar forces are given in Chapter 17.

EXERCISE 14d

In questions 1–4 a uniform rod **AB** whose mid-point is **M**, is in equilibrium in a vertical plane as shown in each diagram.

1)

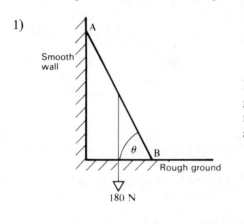

If the coefficient of friction at the ground is $\frac{1}{3}$, calculate the normal reactions at **A** and **B** and find the angle θ.

2)

The rod rests on a rough peg at **C** and a force F acts at **A** as shown. If $BC = CM$ and $\tan\alpha = \frac{4}{3}$ find the coefficient of friction at **C** and the force F.

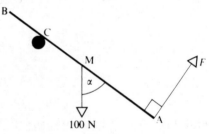

3)

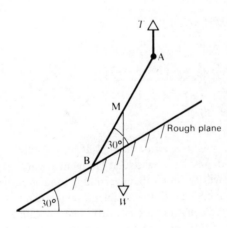

A vertical string is attached to **A**. Find T in terms of W and calculate the value of μ, the coefficient of friction at **B**.

4)

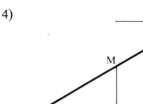

The rod rests on a rough peg at A and a smooth peg at C.

MC = CB

Find the coefficient of friction at A and the normal reaction at C (in terms of W)

5) A disc of mass m and radius a is free to turn in a vertical plane about a smooth pivot through a point P on the circumference. A particle, also of mass m is attached to the point Q on the rim of the disc diametrically opposite to the pivot. What force should be applied to the lowest point of the disc to keep PQ horizontal if:

(a) the force is tangential,

(b) the force is vertical.

Find, in each case, the magnitude of the reaction at the pivot.

Questions 6–8 show sets of coplanar forces which are in equilibrium.

6)

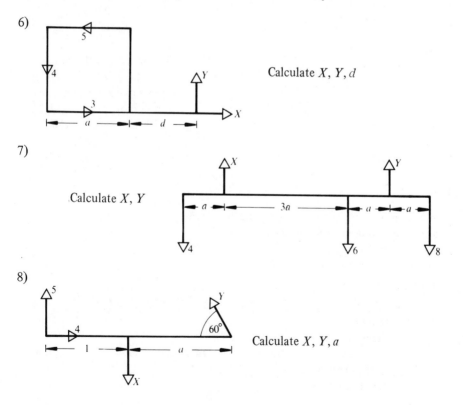

Calculate X, Y, d

7)

Calculate X, Y

8)

Calculate X, Y, a

MULTIPLE CHOICE EXERCISE 14

The instructions for answering these questions are given on page (xii)

TYPE I

1)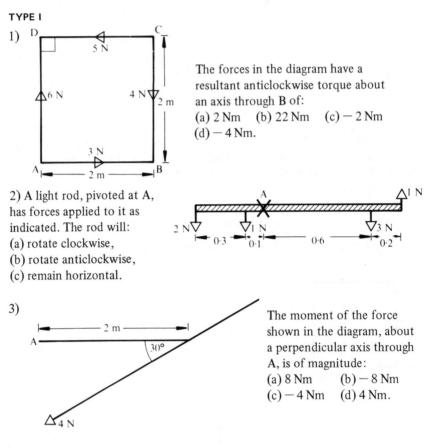

The forces in the diagram have a resultant anticlockwise torque about an axis through B of:
(a) 2 Nm   (b) 22 Nm   (c) − 2 Nm
(d) − 4 Nm.

2) A light rod, pivoted at A, has forces applied to it as indicated. The rod will:
(a) rotate clockwise,
(b) rotate anticlockwise,
(c) remain horizontal.

3)

The moment of the force shown in the diagram, about a perpendicular axis through A, is of magnitude:
(a) 8 Nm   (b) − 8 Nm
(c) − 4 Nm   (d) 4 Nm.

TYPE II

4) The moment of a force about a specified axis is:
(a) measured in newton metres,
(b) a scalar quantity,
(c) measured in joules,
(d) a vector quantity.

5) A force $F_1 = 2i - 3j$ acts through a point $i - 2j$ and a force $F_2 = 4i + 5j$ acts through a point $2i + j$.
(a) The magnitude of F_1 is $\sqrt{13}$ units.
(b) The moment of F_1 about the origin is of magnitude 1 unit.
(c) The magnitude of F_2 is 3 units.
(d) F_1 and F_2 are coplanar.

TYPE III

6) (a) The resultant torque of a set of forces is zero.
   (b) A set of forces is in equilibrium.

7) (a) A rod AB whose mid-point is M is in equilibrium.
   (b) The forces acting on a rod AB have zero resultant torque about axes through each of the points A, B and the mid-point M of AB.

8) (a) The moment of a force F about an axis through A is zero.
   (b) A force F acts through a point A.

TYPE IV

9) A non uniform rod AB rests horizontally on two supports at points C and D. Calculate the forces at the supports if:
(a) AC = 0.4 m,
(b) DB = 0.7 m,
(c) the weight of the rod is 40 N,
(d) the length of the rod is 2 m.

10) Calculate the moment of a force about an axis through a point A:
(a) The magnitude of the force is 10 N.
(b) The sense of rotation is clockwise.
(c) The axis is perpendicular to the force.

11)

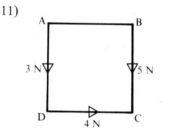

ABCD is a square of side 2 m. Find the position of the point X through which a perpendicular axis passes if, about that axis:
(a) the moment of the 3 N force is 4.5 Nm,
(b) the moment of the 4 N force is 2 Nm,
(c) the resultant moment is 4 Nm.

12) A uniform rod AB is hinged to a vertical wall at A. The mid-point is attached by an inelastic string to a point on the wall above A. Find the tension in the string if:
(a) the weight of the rod is 20 N,
(b) the rod and the string have the same length,
(c) the rod is horizontal,
(d) the string is inclined at 30° to the wall.

TYPE V

13) A square ABCD is rotating in a vertical plane about the side AB.

14) The resultant moment of a set of forces about an axis is independent of the axis.

15) If a set of forces is in equilibrium the resultant moment about any two axes is zero.

16) If a body is kept in equilibrium by four unknown forces, these forces can be found by resolving in two perpendicular directions and taking moments about two different axes.

MISCELLANEOUS EXERCISE 14

1) A uniform bar AB, 1 m long can be balanced about a point 0.2 m from A by hanging a weight of 5 N at A. Find the weight of the bar. What additional weight should be hung from A if the point of support is moved 0.1 m nearer to A?

2) A uniform rod BC, of length 0.6 m and weight 2 N, is hinged to a fixed point at B. It is supported in equilibrium by a string 0.8 m long attached to C and to a point A vertically above B. If AB = 1 m calculate the tension in the string.

3) A uniform plank AB rests on a horizontal roof and B overhangs by 2 m. If the length of the plank is 10 m and its weight is 560 N, find how far a man of weight 1400 N can walk along the overhanging section without causing the plank to tip up. Find also what weight should be placed at A to allow the man to walk to the end B in safety.

4)

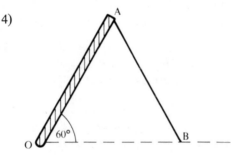

A loft door OA of weight 100 N is propped open at 60° to the horizontal by a light strut AB. The door is hinged at O. If OA = OB = 1.2 m and the weight of the door acts through C where OC = 0.4 m, find the force in the strut.

5) A uniform beam AB, 5 m long and of weight 60 N is supported in a horizontal position at A and at one other point. A load of 10 N is suspended from B and loads of 50 N and 40 N are suspended from points distant 1.8 m and 3 m respectively from B. If the supporting force at A is 40 N find the position of the other support.

6) A diving board of mass 150 kg is clamped at one end. A diver of mass 75 kg walks gently along the board which is 3 m long. What torque is exerted on the clamp when the diver is:
(a) 1 m from the free end,
(b) at the free end.

7) A rod XY is of length $(x + y)$ and its weight acts through a point distant x

from X. It rests on two supports equidistant from X and Y and distant z apart. Prove that the forces exerted by the supports are in the ratio

$$(x - y + z) : (y - x + z).$$

8) Forces of magnitudes 1, 2, 3, 6, 5, 4 N act respectively along the sides $\overrightarrow{AB}$, $\overrightarrow{CB}$, $\overrightarrow{CD}$, $\overrightarrow{ED}$, $\overrightarrow{EF}$, $\overrightarrow{AF}$ of a regular hexagon of side a. Find their resultant moment about axes perpendicular to the hexagon through (i) A   (ii) B   (iii) the centre of the hexagon.

9) With reference to perpendicular axes Ox and Oy, A and B are points with coordinates $(2a, 0)$ and $(2a, 4a)$. A force with components X and Y parallel to Ox and Oy passes through a point P on the x axis. Its anticlockwise moments about axes perpendicular to the xy plane through O, A and B are respectively $+ 4Fa$, $- 4Fa$ and $+ 10Fa$. Find, in terms of F and a, the magnitude and direction of the force and the distance OP.

10) A uniform rod AB, 2 m long and of weight 200 N, is suspended horizontally by two vertical ropes one attached 0.2 m from A and the other 0.3 m from B. If the first rope snaps when its tension exceeds 140 N and the second snaps when its tension exceeds 160 N find where on the rod a load of 100 N can be placed without snapping either rope.

11) A non uniform beam AB rests on two supports in a horizontal line, one at A and one at a point C. AB = 5 m, AC = 4 m and the weight of the beam is 350 N. If the supports exert equal forces on the beam find the point on the beam where the weight acts. If an extra weight W is then attached to B find the value of W if:
(a) the supporting force at C is twice the supporting force at A,
(b) the beam is just about to rotate.

12) A uniform plank of mass 80 kg and length 4 m overhangs a horizontal roof by 1.5 m A man can walk to within 0.5 m of the overhanging end when a mass of 12 kg is placed on the opposite end. What is the mass of the man and how much bigger a load must be placed at the end of the plank to enable the man to walk right to the overhanging end.

13) A ladder rests with its foot on smooth horizontal ground and its upper end against a smooth vertical wall. The ladder is uniform, weighs 300 N and is inclined to the wall at an angle θ. What horizontal force must be applied to the foot of the ladder to prevent it slipping if (a) $\theta = 30°$ (b) $\theta = \arctan \frac{3}{4}$.

14) A uniform rod AB of length $2a$ and weight W has its lower end A on rough horizontal ground. It is supported at 60° to the horizontal by a string attached to its upper end B and at right angles to the rod. Find the tension in the string and the frictional and normal forces at the ground.

15) AB and BC are two light rods of length $3a$ and $2a$ respectively smoothly jointed at B. Bodies of weights P, Q and R are attached at A, at the mid-point

of AB and at C respectively. The system rests in equilibrium with the rods in a horizontal line on supports at the two points of trisection of AB and at the mid-point of BC. Show that $Q \geqslant 2P + 4R$.

If the two supports of the rod AB are replaced by a single support, find its distance from B, in terms of a, P, Q and R, for equilibrium to be maintained.   (U of L)

16) If XYZ is any triangle, prove that any system of forces acting in the plane of the triangle can be replaced by a force acting along XY, a force acting along YZ and a force acting along ZX.

ABCDEF is a regular hexagon, lettered in an anticlockwise direction. A system of forces in the plane of the hexagon has total anticlockwise moment p about A, q about B and r about C. Show that the moment of the system about D is $p - 2q + 2r$, and find the moments about E and F.   (Cambridge)

17) A uniform rod AB of weight W has its end A on rough horizontal ground and rests at $45°$ to the vertical against a small smooth peg at C, where $AC = \frac{3}{4} AB$. If the rod is on the point of slipping in the vertical plane containing the rod, calculate μ, the coefficient of friction between the rod and the ground.

If $\mu = \frac{3}{4}$, calculate the largest vertical downward force which can be applied to the rod at C without disturbing the equilibrium.   (A.E.B.)

CHAPTER 15

RESULTANTS OF COPLANAR FORCES.
EQUIVALENT FORCE SYSTEMS

The resultant of a set of forces is the simplest possible force system which has the same effect in all respects as the original set.

The resultant of forces in one plane may be either a single force or a torque.

COPLANAR FORCES REDUCING TO A SINGLE FORCE

When the resultant of a set of coplanar forces is a single force, it is fully defined only when its magnitude, direction and line of action are known.

The *magnitude* and *direction* can be found by collecting the components, in each of two perpendicular directions, of the original forces (see Chapter 2).

The *position* of the resultant is determined by comparing its turning effect about a specified axis with that of the original forces.

In this way three independent equations are obtained.

EXAMPLES 15a

1) Find the magnitude and direction of the resultant of forces of magnitudes 6 N, 2 N, 2 N and 1 N which act along the sides $\overrightarrow{AB}$, $\overrightarrow{BC}$, $\overrightarrow{CD}$ and $\overrightarrow{AD}$ of a square ABCD and find where the line of action of the resultant cuts AB (produced if necessary).

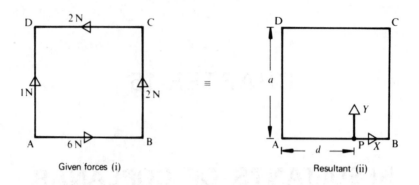

Given forces (i)   Resultant (ii)

Let the side of the square be a. Diagram (ii) shows the resultant, represented by a pair of components X and Y parallel to **AB** and **AD** respectively and cutting **AB** at an unknown point P where $AP = d$.

Comparing the original forces (shown in diagram (i)) with the resultant we have:

$\rightarrow$ $\quad\quad\quad\quad\quad\quad\quad\quad\quad 6 - 2 = X$

$\uparrow$ $\quad\quad\quad\quad\quad\quad\quad\quad\quad 2 + 1 = Y$

$A\}$ $\quad\quad\quad\quad\quad\quad\quad\quad 2a + 2a = Yd$

Hence $\quad\quad\quad\quad X = 4\,\text{N}; \ \ Y = 3\,\text{N}; \ \ d = \dfrac{4a}{3}$

Therefore the resultant is of magnitude $\sqrt{4^2 + 3^2} = 5\,\text{N}$.

Its line of action makes $\arctan \frac{3}{4}$ with **AB** and cuts **AB** produced at P where $3AP = 4AB$.

2) Find the equation of the line of action of the resultant of forces of magnitudes $4\sqrt{2}\,\text{N}$, $13\,\text{N}$ and $3\,\text{N}$ which act as shown along lines whose equations are $y = x$, $12y = 5x + 24$ and $x = 2$ respectively.

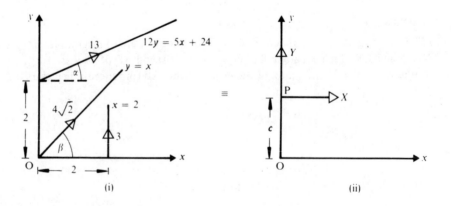

(i)   (ii)

Let the resultant have components X and Y parallel to Ox and Oy respectively and let it cut Oy at a point $P(0, c)$.

From the gradients of the given lines it can be seen that

$$\tan \alpha = \tfrac{5}{12}$$

$$\tan \beta = 1$$

Comparing the given forces (diagram (i)) with the resultant we have:

$\rightarrow$
$$13 \cos \alpha + 4\sqrt{2} \cos \beta = X \tag{1}$$

$\uparrow$
$$13 \sin \alpha + 4\sqrt{2} \sin \beta + 3 = Y \tag{2}$$

$O\curvearrowright$
$$13 \cos \alpha \times 2 - 3 \times 2 = Xc \tag{3}$$

Hence
$$13 \times \frac{12}{13} + 4\sqrt{2} \times \frac{1}{\sqrt{2}} = X \tag{1}$$

$$13 \times \frac{5}{13} + 4\sqrt{2} \times \frac{1}{\sqrt{2}} + 3 = Y \tag{2}$$

$$13 \times \frac{12}{13} \times 2 - 3 \times 2 = Xc \tag{3}$$

Giving
$$X = 16\,\text{N}; \quad Y = 12\,\text{N}; \quad c = \frac{18}{16} = \frac{9}{8}$$

The line of action of the resultant has gradient $\dfrac{Y}{X} = \dfrac{3}{4}$ and its y intercept is $+\dfrac{9}{8}$

Therefore the equation of the line of action of the resultant is
$$y = \frac{3}{4}x + \frac{9}{8} \quad \text{or} \quad 8y = 6x + 9.$$

(*Note.* When the equation of the line of action is wanted it is best to take a point P on the *y axis* as the unknown point through which the resultant passes. In this way the distance OP is also the y intercept of the line of action of the resultant and can be used directly in the general equation $y = mx + c$).

3) ABCD is a square in which L bisects $\overrightarrow{AB}$ and M bisects BC. Forces of magnitudes 4, 8, P (newton) act respectively along $\overrightarrow{AB}$, $\overrightarrow{BC}$, $\overrightarrow{CD}$ and their resultant is parallel to $\overrightarrow{LM}$. Find the magnitude and position of the resultant and the value of P.

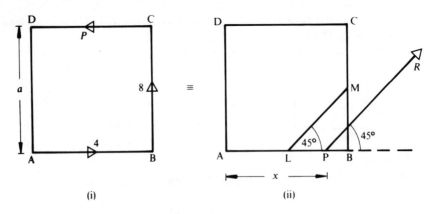

(i)   (ii)

Since LM makes an angle of $45°$ with **AB**, the resultant, of magnitude R, is also at $45°$ with **AB**. Let the resultant cut **AB** at P where $AP = x$.
Comparing the resultant with the original forces:

$\rightarrow$ $4 - P = R \cos 45°$ (1)

$\uparrow$ $8 = R \sin 45°$ (2)

$A\downarrow$ $8a + Pa = Rx \sin 45°$ (3)

From (2) $R = 8\sqrt{2}$

From (1) $P = 4 - 8 = -4$

From (3) $x = \dfrac{8a - 4a}{8} = \dfrac{a}{2}$

Therefore the resultant is of magnitude $8\sqrt{2}\,\text{N}$ and cuts **AB** at a point $\frac{1}{2}$**AB** from A. i.e. the resultant is along **LM**.

4) Forces $2P$, $3P$, $4P$ act respectively along the sides $\overrightarrow{AB}$, $\overrightarrow{BC}$, $\overrightarrow{CA}$ of an equilateral triangle ABC of side a. Find the magnitude and direction of their resultant and the distance from A of the point where it cuts AC.

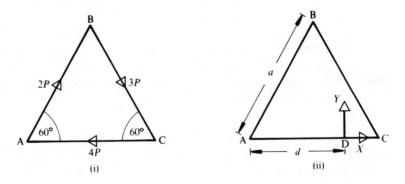

(i)   (ii)

Comparing the original three forces with the resultant (made up of components X and Y as shown in diagram (ii), passing through a point D on AC where $AD = d$) we have:

$\rightarrow$ $\qquad\qquad 2P \cos 60° + 3P \cos 60° - 4P = X$ $\qquad\qquad$ (1)

$\uparrow$ $\qquad\qquad\quad 2P \sin 60° - 3P \sin 60° = Y$ $\qquad\qquad$ (2)

$\underset{\curvearrowright}{A}$ $\qquad\qquad\qquad 3P (a \sin 60°) = -Yd$ $\qquad\qquad$ (3)

(*N.B.* When comparing torque about an axis through A, care must be taken to use the same sense for both force systems. In this problem the *clockwise* moment of the resultant is negative).

From (1) and (2) $\qquad X = -\dfrac{3P}{2}$ and $Y = -\dfrac{\sqrt{3}P}{2}$

In (3) $\qquad\qquad\qquad 3Pa\dfrac{\sqrt{3}}{2} = -\left(-\dfrac{\sqrt{3}P}{2}\right)d$

Giving $\qquad\qquad\qquad\qquad d = 3a.$

The resultant is therefore of magnitude $\sqrt{X^2 + Y^2} = \sqrt{3}P$ and its direction is at an angle α to AC where $\tan \alpha = \dfrac{Y}{X} = \dfrac{1}{\sqrt{3}}$. The line of action of the resultant passes through a point on AC produced distant $3a$ from A and is at $30°$ to AC.

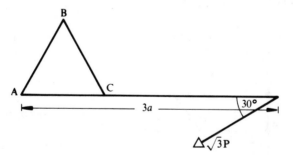

5) A, B and C are points with coordinates $(0, 0)$, $(0, a)$ and $(a, 0)$ referred to rectangular axes. The clockwise moments of a system of forces in the plane ABC about perpendicular axes through A, B and C are $6M$, $9M$ and $2M$ respectively. Find in terms of M and a the magnitude of the resultant of the system and the equation of its line of action.

(*Note.* Although in this problem none of the original forces are specified individually, their resultant can still be determined by comparing its effect with that of the original system).

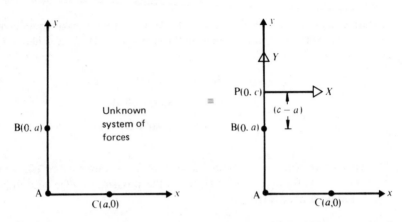

If the resultant has components X and Y and passes through a point $P\,(0, c)$ then comparing the moment of the original system with that of the resultant about each of three axes through A, B and C (which are not collinear) we have:

A	$6M = Xc$	(1)
B	$9M = X\,(c - a)$	(2)
C	$2M = Xc + Ya$	(3)

(1) and (3) give $2M = 6M + Ya$ $Y = -\dfrac{4M}{a}$

(1) and (2) give $9M = 6M - Xa$ $X = -\dfrac{3M}{a}$

In (1) $6M = \left(-\dfrac{3M}{a}\right)c$ $c = -2a$

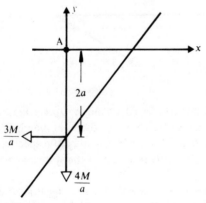

The magnitude of the resultant is

$$\sqrt{X^2 + Y^2} = \frac{5M}{a}$$

Its line of action makes an angle α with the x axis where

$$\tan \alpha = \frac{Y}{X} = \frac{4}{3}$$

Therefore the equation of its line of action is $y = \tfrac{4}{3}x - 2a$ or $3y = 4x - 6a$.

6) Forces of magnitudes 3, 4, 2, 1, P, Q act along the sides $\overrightarrow{AB}, \overrightarrow{BC}, \overrightarrow{CD}, \overrightarrow{DE}, \overrightarrow{EF}$, $\overrightarrow{FA}$ respectively of a regular hexagon ABCDEF. Find the values of P and Q if the resultant of the six forces acts along CE.

[Since the resultant is known to act along CE, a diagram in which CE is either horizontal or vertical makes the solution simpler.]

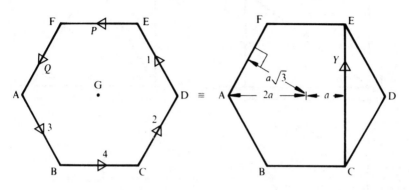

Taking G as the centre of the hexagon and $2a$ as the length of each side, comparison gives:

$$\rightarrow \qquad 4 - P + (2 - 1 - Q + 3) \cos 60° = 0 \qquad (1)$$

$$\uparrow \qquad (2 + 1 - Q - 3) \sin 60° = Y \qquad (2)$$

$$G \curvearrowright \qquad (3 + 4 + 2 + 1 + P + Q) a \sqrt{3} = Ya \qquad (3)$$

From (2) and (3)
$$(P + Q + 10) \sqrt{3} = -Q \frac{\sqrt{3}}{2}$$

Hence
$$2P + 3Q + 20 = 0$$

From (1)
$$2P + Q - 12 = 0$$

Therefore
$$Q = -16 \quad \text{and} \quad P = 14$$

N.B. An alternative method of solution is to take moments about axes through C and E. The resultant moment is zero in both cases since the resultant force passes through both C and E.

EXERCISE 15a

In questions 1–5, find the magnitude, direction and equation of the line of action of the resultant of the given forces (units are newton and metre throughout).

1)

2)

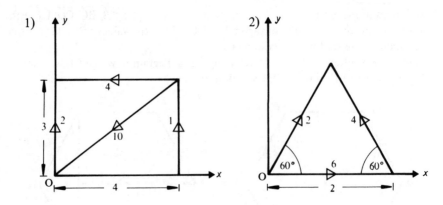

3)

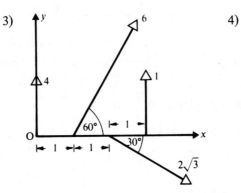

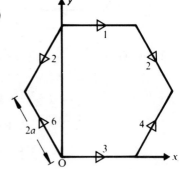

4)

5)

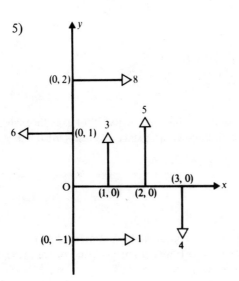

6) Forces of magnitudes 4, 3, 2, 1, P, Q act along the sides $\overrightarrow{AB}$, $\overrightarrow{BC}$, $\overrightarrow{CD}$, $\overrightarrow{AD}$, $\overrightarrow{AC}$, $\overrightarrow{BD}$ respectively of a square ABCD of side a.
(i) Find P and Q if the resultant acts along AB.
(ii) Find the magnitude of the resultant if its line of action passes through B and is parallel to AC.

7) ABC is an equilateral triangle of side $2a$. A system of forces act in the plane of the triangle. About axes through A, B and C perpendicular to this plane, the forces exert anticlockwise torques of magnitudes $+ 2Pa$, $+ 3Pa$ and $- Pa$ respectively. Find, in terms of P and a, the magnitude of the resultant of the system and the distance from A of the point where it crosses AC.

8) Forces of magnitudes $9F$, $2F$, nF, mF and $10F$ act along the sides $\overrightarrow{AB}$, $\overrightarrow{BC}$, $\overrightarrow{CD}$, $\overrightarrow{DA}$ and the diagonal $\overrightarrow{DB}$ of a rectangle ABCD in which $AB = 4a$ and $BC = 3a$.
If AB and AD are taken as the x and y axes respectively and the equation of the line of action of the resultant is $12y + 5x = a$ find the values of n and m.

9) A, B and C are points with coordinates $(2, 0)$, $(2, 1)$ and $(0, 1)$ respectively referred to perpendicular axes Ox and Oy. Forces which act in the plane ABC have anticlockwise turning effects about axes through A, B and C of $+3$, $+5$, $+4$ units respectively (the axes are perpendicular to the plane ABC). Find the equation of the line of action of their resultant.

10) Forces of magnitudes 2, 3, P and Q act along the sides $\overrightarrow{AB}$, $\overrightarrow{BC}$, $\overrightarrow{CD}$ and $\overrightarrow{DA}$ of a square. Find the magnitudes of P and Q if the line of action of the resultant of the four forces:
(a) bisects AB and DC,
(b) bisects AB and passes through C.

RESULTANT OF PARALLEL FORCES

(a) Like Parallel Forces (i.e. forces in the same sense).

Consider two forces P and Q whose lines of action are parallel and distant d apart.

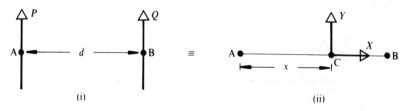

(i)   (ii)

If A and B are two points on the lines of action of P and Q respectively such that AB is perpendicular to both forces, then $AB = d$.

Diagram (ii) shows the resultant represented by components X and Y and passing through a point C on **AB** where $\text{AC} = x$.

Comparing the given forces with their resultant we have:

$\uparrow$ $P + Q = Y$ (1)

$\rightarrow$ $0 = X$ (2)

$A\mathbf{\}$ $Qd = Yx$ (3)

From (3) $x = \left(\dfrac{Q}{P+Q}\right)d = \text{AC}$

Therefore $\text{BC} = d - x = \left(\dfrac{P}{P+Q}\right)d$

Hence the resultant of two like parallel forces P and Q is parallel to P and Q, is of magnitude $(P + Q)$ and divides **AB** (the distance between the parallel forces) in the ratio $Q : P$.

N.B. Because of the geometric properties of parallel lines, it is not only **AB** but *any* transversal between P and Q which is divided by the resultant in the ratio $Q : P$.

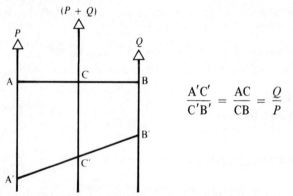

$$\dfrac{A'C'}{C'B'} = \dfrac{AC}{CB} = \dfrac{Q}{P}$$

Now let us consider what happens to the resultant if P and Q are each rotated in the same sense about A and B respectively through equal angles so that the forces are still parallel.

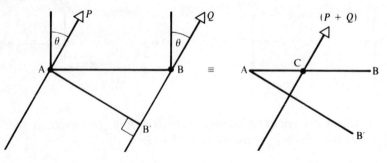

If AB$'$ is perpendicular to P and Q in their new positions, the resultant, as we have just shown, is a force parallel to P and Q, of magnitude $(P + Q)$ and dividing AB$'$ in the ratio $Q : P$.

But the line of action of the resultant also divides any other transversal, one of which is AB, in the ratio $Q : P$.

Therefore the new resultant passes through the same point C as the original resultant did (before P and Q were rotated).

This argument can be applied successively to include further forces and to establish the general principle that:

If any number of like parallel forces each pass through a fixed point, their resultant passes through a fixed point regardless of the orientation of those forces.

(b) Unlike Parallel Forces (i.e. forces in opposite senses).

Consider two forces P and Q whose lines of action are parallel and distant d apart and suppose $Q > P$.

Again taking points A and B on the lines of action of P and Q respectively where $AB = d$ and representing the resultant by components X and Y as shown, comparison gives:

$\uparrow$ $Q - P = Y$

$\rightarrow$ $0 = X$

A$\curvearrowright$ $Qd = Yx$

This time $$AC = x = \left(\frac{Q}{Q - P}\right) d$$

so that $$BC = d - x = \left(\frac{-P}{Q - P}\right) d$$

Therefore $AC : CB = Q : -P$ showing that the resultant, which is of magnitude $Q - P$, divides AB *externally* in the ratio $Q : P$.

(*Note*. When parallel forces occur in problems it is frequently simpler to locate the resultant by using the principle of moments than to quote the results derived above).

(c) Equal Unlike Parallel Forces

This is a special case of (b) above when $P = Q$. The magnitude of the resultant, $(Q - P)$, is now zero.

The turning effect however is not zero as can be seen by taking moments about an axis through A.

A pair of equal and opposite parallel forces therefore have a resultant which is pure torque.

Such a pair of forces is known as a *Couple*.

When a couple acts on a body there is no change in the linear movement of the body but there is a change in its rotation.

Constant Moment of a Couple

Consider a couple comprising two equal and opposite forces of magnitude P whose lines of action are distant d apart.

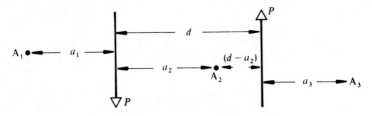

Axes perpendicular to the plane of action of the couple could be taken between the two forces (e.g. through A_2) or outside the lines of action of the two forces (e.g. through A_1 or A_3).

We shall now determine the torque exerted by the couple about each of these axes in turn.

A_1 Anticlockwise torque $= P(a_1 + d) - Pa_1 = Pd$

A_2 Anticlockwise torque $= P(d - a_2) + Pa_2 = Pd$

A_3 Anticlockwise torque $= P(d + a_3) - Pa_3 = Pd$

Therefore the moment of a couple is the same about all axes perpendicular to its plane.

The magnitude of the moment of a couple is often referred to as the magnitude of the couple.

Characteristics of a Couple

1. The *linear resultant* of a couple *is zero.*

2. The *moment* of a couple is *not zero* and is independent of the position of the axis so long as the axis is perpendicular to the plane in which the couple acts. *These characteristics are also those of a force system whose resultant is a couple*, a property which can be used in solving many problems.

EXAMPLES 15b

1) ABCDEF is a regular hexagon of side 2*a*. Forces of magnitudes 5*P*, *P*, 3*P*, 4*P*, 2*P* and 2*P* act respectively along the sides $\overrightarrow{AB}$, $\overrightarrow{BC}$, $\overrightarrow{CD}$, $\overrightarrow{DE}$, $\overrightarrow{EF}$ and $\overrightarrow{FA}$. Prove that they reduce to a couple, and find its magnitude.

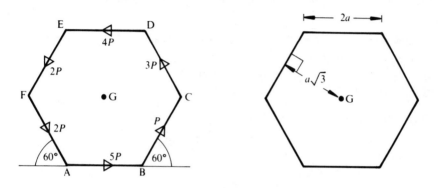

[The resultant is a couple if the six forces have a linear resultant which is zero and a resultant moment which is not zero].

Resolving parallel and perpendicular to **AB** and taking moments about an axis through G we have:

$\rightarrow$ $$5P - 4P + (P - 3P - 2P + 2P) \cos 60° = 0 \qquad (1)$$

$\uparrow$ $$(P + 3P - 2P - 2P) \sin 60° = 0 \qquad (2)$$

G $\circlearrowleft$ $$(5P + P + 3P + 4P + 2P + 2P) a \sqrt{3} = 17Pa\sqrt{3} \qquad (3)$$

(1) and (2) show that the linear resultant is zero. Therefore the six forces reduce to a couple of magnitude $17Pa \sqrt{3}$ in the sense ABC.

2) ABCD is a square. Forces of magnitudes 1, 2, 3, *P* and *Q* units act along $\overrightarrow{AB}$, $\overrightarrow{BC}$, $\overrightarrow{CD}$, $\overrightarrow{DA}$ and $\overrightarrow{AC}$ respectively. Find values for *P* and *Q* so that the resultant of the five forces is a couple.

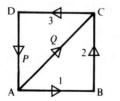

If the resultant is a couple, the linear resultant is zero.

Therefore   → $1 + Q \cos 45° - 3 = 0$

and   ↑ $2 + Q \sin 45° - P = 0$

Hence, when $Q = 2\sqrt{2}$ and $P = 4$, the linear resultant of the given forces is zero. This is *not sufficient* to ensure that the forces reduce to a couple. We must also show that their *turning effect is not zero*.

If AB = a,   A↲· $2a + 3a \neq 0.$

Therefore the forces reduce to a couple if $P = 4$, $Q = 2\sqrt{2}$ units.

3) Show that the following forces reduce to a couple and find its magnitude.
$F_1 = -4i + 3j$ acting through the point $2i - j$
$F_2 = 6i - 7j$,, ,, ,, ,, $-3i + j$
$F_3 = -2i + 4j$,, ,, ,, ,, $4j$

The resultant force is $Xi + Yj$ where $X = -4 + 6 - 2 = 0$
$$\text{and } Y = 3 - 7 + 4 = 0$$

The resultant force is therefore zero.

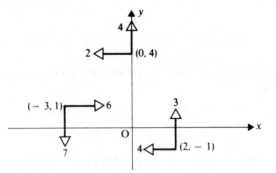

The resultant turning effect about an axis through O (taking anticlockwise as positive) is:

$$(3 \times 2 - 4 \times 1) + (7 \times 3 - 6 \times 1) + (2 \times 4) = 25$$

Since the resultant force is zero but the resultant turning effect is not zero, the forces reduce to a couple of magnitude 25 units anticlockwise.

4) Forces acting along the sides $\overrightarrow{AB}$, $\overrightarrow{BC}$ and $\overrightarrow{CA}$ of a triangle ABC have magnitudes proportional to the lengths of those sides. Prove that the three forces reduce to a couple.

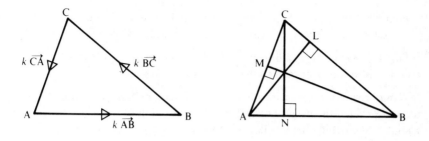

[It is more convenient in this problem to use the constant moment property of a couple].

Taking moments about axes through A, B and C we have:

A}

$$\text{Torque} = |k\ \overrightarrow{BC}| \times AL$$

$$= k \times BC \times AL$$

$$= 2k \times \text{area of triangle ABC}$$

B}

$$\text{Torque} = |k\ \overrightarrow{CA}| \times BM$$

$$= 2k \times \text{area of triangle ABC}$$

C}

$$\text{Torque} = |k\ \overrightarrow{AB}| \times CN$$

$$= 2k \times \text{area of triangle ABC}.$$

Since about each of three axes the turning effect of the given forces is the same, the forces reduce to a couple.

EXERCISE 15b

1) Show that forces of magnitudes $6F, 7F, F, 3F, 4F, 4F$ acting along the sides $\overrightarrow{AB}, \overrightarrow{CB}, \overrightarrow{DC}, \overrightarrow{DE}, \overrightarrow{FE}, \overrightarrow{AF}$ of a regular hexagon are equivalent to a couple and find its magnitude.

2) Forces $1, 2, 3, 4, P, Q$ act along the sides of a regular hexagon taken in order. Find values for P and Q for which the six forces reduce to a couple.

3) ABC is an equilateral triangle and D is the mid-point of BC. Forces P and $3P$ acting along $\overrightarrow{AB}$ and $\overrightarrow{AC}$ together with a third force in the plane ABC whose line of action passes through D, reduce to a couple. Find the magnitude and direction of the force through D.

4) Forces proportional to the sides of a quadrilateral taken in order act respectively along those sides. Prove that the resultant of the system is a couple whose magnitude is represented by twice the area of the quadrilateral.

*In questions 5–8, ABCD is a square of side $2a$. Forces of magnitudes F and $2F$ act along $\overrightarrow{AB}$ and $\overrightarrow{BC}$ respectively.

*5) Find the magnitudes of two forces which, acting along AC and AD, combine with the two given forces to form a couple and find the magnitude of the couple.

*6) Find the magnitude and direction of a force acting through D which, together with the given forces, form a couple.

*7) A third force, together with the two given forces, reduce to a couple of magnitude $2Fa$. Find the magnitude and direction of the third force and the distance from A of the point where its line of action cuts AB (produced if necessary).

*8) Two forces both of magnitude nF are added to the system. One acts along AC and the other passes through B.
Calculate n if the new system reduces to a couple.

9) Four forces are represented by $i - 4j$, $3i + 6j$, $- 9i + j$ and $5i - 3j$, and their points of application are given by $3i - j$, $2i + 2j$, $- i - j$ and $- 3i + 4j$ respectively.
(a) Show that the forces reduce to a couple and find its magnitude.
(b) If the fourth force is removed and the first force is moved to the point $i - 8j$ show that the system is now in equilibrium.

10) ABC is a right angled triangle in which $AB = 4a$; $BC = 3a$. Forces of magnitudes P, Q and R act along the sides $\overrightarrow{AB}$, $\overrightarrow{BC}$ and $\overrightarrow{CA}$ respectively. Find the ratios of $P : Q : R$ if their resultant is a couple.
If the force along $\overrightarrow{AC}$ is now reversed, find in terms of P, the magnitude of the resultant of the new system.

11) Forces of magnitudes 1, 6, 8, 2 and 5 units act along the sides $\overrightarrow{AB}$, $\overrightarrow{BC}$, $\overrightarrow{DC}$, $\overrightarrow{DE}$ and $\overrightarrow{EF}$ respectively of a regular hexagon and another force acts along FA.
Give as much information as you can about the resultant of the six forces if the sixth force is:
(a) 1 unit along $\overrightarrow{FA}$,
(b) 7 units along $\overrightarrow{AF}$.

IDENTIFICATION OF FORCE SYSTEMS

A set of coplanar forces may:
(a) be in equilibrium,
(b) reduce to a couple,
(c) reduce to a single force.
In order to establish which of these applies to a particular set of forces, *three independent facts* are needed (since coplanar forces have three degrees of freedom). These three facts are derived from various combinations of resolving and taking moments.
Suppose that X and Y represent the collected components in two perpendicular directions and that M_A, M_B and M_C represent the resultant moments about axes

through any three non collinear points A, B and C in the plane of the forces then:

(a) the system is in equilibrium if:

(i) $X = 0$ $Y = 0$ $M_A = 0$
or (ii) $X = 0$ $M_A = 0$ $M_B = 0$
or (iii) $M_A = 0$ $M_B = 0$ $M_C = 0$

(b) the system reduces to a couple if:

(i) $X = 0$ $Y = 0$ $M_A \neq 0$
or (ii) $M_A = M_B = M_C \neq 0$.

(c) the system reduces to a single force if X and Y are not both zero. The value of M_A is then required to locate this force.

Partial Identification

When less than three independent facts are given the coplanar force system to which they apply cannot be identified precisely.

EXAMPLES 15c

In these examples X, Y, M_A, M_B, M_C have the same significance as in the preceding paragraph.

1) What is the state of a set of coplanar forces for which $X = 0$ and $Y = 0$?

If $X = 0$ and $Y = 0$ there is no linear resultant. Therefore the set of forces is either in equilibrium or reduces to a couple. (Without further information there is no way of differentiating between the two possibilities).

2) What is the resultant of a set of coplanar forces for which $M_A = M_B \neq 0$?

Since the turning effects about two different axes are equal the resultant could be a couple.
On the other hand, points A and B could be equidistant from a linear resultant.

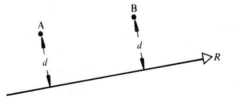

Therefore the set of forces reduces either to a couple or to a single force parallel to **AB**.

3) A set of coplanar forces is such that $X = 0$ and $M_A = 0$. To what simple forms is it possible for the forces to reduce?

Since $X = 0$, the linear resultant, if
there is one, is in the direction of Y.
Then $M_A = Yd$ and can be zero either
if $Y = 0$ or if $d = 0$.

The resultant cannot be a couple since $M_A = 0$. Therefore either the system
reduces to a single force in the direction of Y and passing through A (i.e. $d = 0$)
or the system is in equilibrium (i.e. $Y = 0$).

EXERCISE 15c

Describe carefully the resultant of a set of coplanar forces if:

1) The turning effect about each of three non-coplanar axes perpendicular to the
plane of the forces is zero.

2) The turning effect about each of two axes perpendicular to the plane of the
forces is zero.

3) The collected components of the forces are zero in both directions Ox and Oy.

4) The collected components in (3) are not zero but the total moment about an
axis through a point A in the plane of the forces is zero.

5) The system of forces causes a body to rotate while its centre of gravity remains
stationary.

6) The forces are all parallel and in the same sense.

THE RESULTANT OF FORCES REPRESENTED BY LINE SEGMENTS

Suppose that two forces are represented completely (i.e. in magnitude, direction
and *position*) by $p\overrightarrow{AB}$ and $q\overrightarrow{AC}$ where p and q are constants.

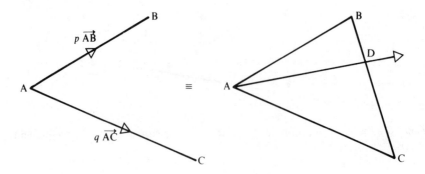

The resultant passes through A (the point of intersection of the given forces) and
will cut the line through B and C at some unknown point D.

$p\overrightarrow{AB}$ can be replaced completely by components which intersect at A and are represented in magnitude and direction by $p\overrightarrow{AD}$ and $p\overrightarrow{DB}$ (treating ADB as a vector triangle).

Similarly $q\overrightarrow{AC}$ can be replaced completely by components through A represented in magnitude and direction by $q\overrightarrow{AD}$ and $q\overrightarrow{DC}$.

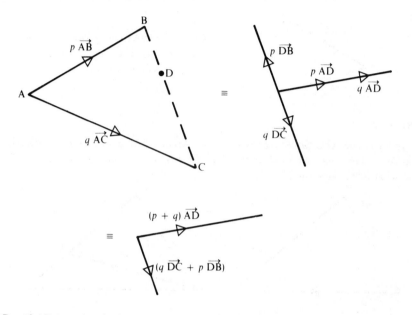

But if AD is to be the line along which the resultant force acts, the component which is not in this direction must be zero.

i.e.
$$q\overrightarrow{DC} + p\overrightarrow{DB} = \vec{0}.$$

Therefore $q\overrightarrow{DC}$ and $p\overrightarrow{DB}$ are equal and opposite and the position of D is such that

$$DB : DC = q : p.$$

Therefore *the resultant of forces represented completely by $p\overrightarrow{AB}$ and $q\overrightarrow{AC}$ is represented completely by $(p + q)\,\overrightarrow{AD}$ where D divides BC in the ratio q : p.* This important *Resultant Vector Theorem* applies to any two vectors which have the same sense relative to their point of intersection.

e.g.

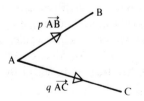

Both forces are *going away from A* therefore the theorem applies.

$p\overrightarrow{AB} + q\overrightarrow{AC} = (p + q)\,\overrightarrow{AD}$ where BD : DC $= q : p$.

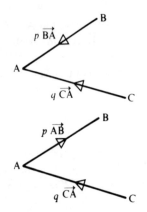

Both forces are *going towards A* therefore the theorem applies.

$p\vec{BA} + q\vec{CA} = (p+q)\,\vec{DA}$ where $BD : DC = q : p$

(the resultant also goes towards **A**).

But

One force $(p\vec{AB})$ goes away from **A** and the other $(q\vec{CA})$ goes towards **A** so the theorem does not apply.

EXAMPLE

In a triangle ABC forces represented by $2\vec{AB}$ and $3\vec{AC}$ act along the sides **AB** and **AC** respectively. Where does the line of action of the resultant force cut **BC** and what is its magnitude.

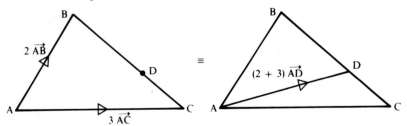

Using the Resultant Vector Theorem:

$$2\vec{AB} + 3\vec{AC} = (2+3)\,\vec{AD} \text{ where BD : DC } = 3 : 2$$

Therefore the resultant is represented in magnitude by 5AD and its line of action divides BC in the ratio 3 : 2.

Sometimes a pair of forces whose resultant cannot at first be found by using this theorem, can be alternatively represented so that the theorem can be applied.

EXAMPLE

In a triangle ABC, M is the mid-point of **AC**. Two forces are represented completely by $2\vec{AC}$ and $3\vec{MB}$. Find their resultant.

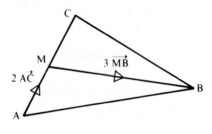

Since M is the point of intersection of the two forces, the Resultant Vector Theorem can be used only if each force is represented by a line segment, one end of which is M. An alternative form must therefore be found for the force $2\vec{AC}$.

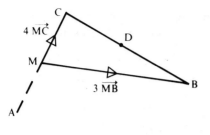

But $AC = 2MC$ therefore $2\overrightarrow{AC} = 4\overrightarrow{MC}$.
Now the theorem can be applied giving:
$4\overrightarrow{MC} + 3\overrightarrow{MB} = (4 + 3) \overrightarrow{MD}$ where
$CD : DB = 3 : 4$
Therefore the resultant of $2\overrightarrow{AC}$ and
$3\overrightarrow{MB}$ is represented completely by
$7\overrightarrow{MD}$ where D divides CB in the
ratio $3 : 4$

Successive applications of this theorem can be used to find the resultant of more
than two forces given in line segment form.

EXAMPLES 15d

1) Forces represented completely by $2\overrightarrow{AB}$, $\overrightarrow{CB}$, $2\overrightarrow{CD}$ and $4\overrightarrow{AD}$ act along the sides
of a quadrilateral ABCD. Find their resultant in vector form and find the points
where its line of action intersects the diagonals of the quadrilateral.

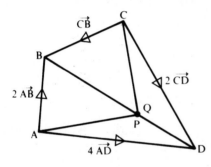

Applying the vector theorem we have:
$$2\overrightarrow{AB} + 4\overrightarrow{AD} = (2 + 4) \overrightarrow{AP}$$
where $BP : PD = 4 : 2$
and $\overrightarrow{CB} + 2\overrightarrow{CD} = (1 + 2) \overrightarrow{CQ}$
where $BQ : QD = 2 : 1$
P and Q divide BD in the same ratio,
therefore they are the same point and
$3\overrightarrow{CQ} \equiv 3\overrightarrow{CP}$.

Therefore

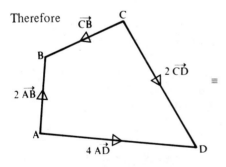 $\equiv$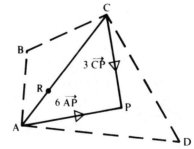

Again $3\overrightarrow{CP} + 6\overrightarrow{AP} = (3 + 6) \overrightarrow{RP}$ where $CR : RA = 6 : 3 = 2 : 1$.
Therefore the resultant is represented completely by $9\overrightarrow{RP}$ where R is a point on
the diagonal AC dividing it in the ratio $1 : 2$ and P is a point on the diagonal
BD dividing it in the ratio $2 : 1$.

2) Forces represented completely by $2\overrightarrow{AB}$, $3\overrightarrow{BC}$, $4\overrightarrow{AC}$ act along the sides of a triangle ABC. Express their resultant in vector form and find where its line of action cuts AB and BC.

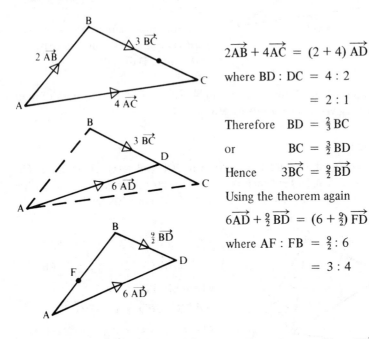

$2\overrightarrow{AB} + 4\overrightarrow{AC} = (2 + 4)\,\overrightarrow{AD}$

where $BD : DC = 4 : 2$

$\qquad\qquad\qquad = 2 : 1$

Therefore $\quad BD = \tfrac{2}{3}BC$

or $\qquad\qquad BC = \tfrac{3}{2}BD$

Hence $\qquad 3\overrightarrow{BC} = \tfrac{9}{2}\overrightarrow{BD}$

Using the theorem again

$6\overrightarrow{AD} + \tfrac{9}{2}\overrightarrow{BD} = (6 + \tfrac{9}{2})\,\overrightarrow{FD}$

where $AF : FB = \tfrac{9}{2} : 6$

$\qquad\qquad\qquad = 3 : 4$

The resultant of $2\overrightarrow{AB}$, $3\overrightarrow{BC}$ and $4\overrightarrow{AC}$ is therefore represented by $\tfrac{21}{2}\,\overrightarrow{FD}$ where F divides AB in the ratio 3 : 4 and D divides BC in the ratio 2 : 1.

3) ABC is a triangle and G is its centroid. Show that forces represented completely by $\overrightarrow{PA}$, $\overrightarrow{PB}$, $\overrightarrow{PC}$, where P is any point in the plane of the triangle, have a resultant represented completely by $3\overrightarrow{PG}$.

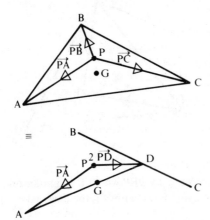

$\overrightarrow{PB} + \overrightarrow{PC} = (1 + 1)\,\overrightarrow{PD}$
where $BD : DC = 1 : 1$
Therefore AD is a median of triangle
ABC and G is on AD where
$AG : GD = 2 : 1$

Now $\overrightarrow{PA} + 2\overrightarrow{PD} = (1 + 2)\,\overrightarrow{PG}$
since $AG : GD = 2 : 1$
Therefore the resultant of $\overrightarrow{PA}$, $\overrightarrow{PB}$
and $\overrightarrow{PC}$ is $3\overrightarrow{PG}$.

EXERCISE 15d

In questions 1—4 find, in vector form, the resultant of the given forces. The positions of any additional points which are introduced must be carefully defined.

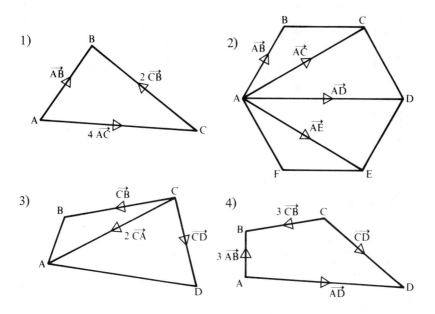

5) The circumscribed circle of an equilateral triangle ABC is drawn. From any point P on the circumference of the circle, forces $\overrightarrow{PA}$, $\overrightarrow{PB}$ and $\overrightarrow{PC}$ act along PA, PB and PC. Show that the magnitude of their resultant is independent of the position of P.

6) Forces represented completely by $\overrightarrow{AB}$, $\overrightarrow{AC}$ and $\overrightarrow{BM}$ act in the plane of a triangle ABC in which L and M are the mid-points of BC and AC respectively. Show that the resultant force is represented completely by $9\overrightarrow{GP}$ where P is on LM and divides it in the ratio 1 : 2, and G is the centroid of the triangle.

GENERAL PROBLEMS ON COPLANAR FORCE SYSTEMS

1. Equivalent Force Systems

Two sets of forces are equivalent if, in all respects, they have the same effect. When the forces are coplanar their equivalence is defined by three independent relationships based on comparing components and/or torque.

EXAMPLE

OABC is a square. Forces of magnitudes 3, 4, 2, 5 and $\sqrt{2}$ N act along $\overrightarrow{OA}$, $\overrightarrow{AB}$, $\overrightarrow{CB}$, $\overrightarrow{OC}$ and $\overrightarrow{OB}$ respectively. If this force system is to be replaced by two forces of equal magnitude acting along $\overrightarrow{OA}$ and $\overrightarrow{OC}$ and a third force whose line of action passes through **A**, find the magnitudes of these forces and the direction of the third force.

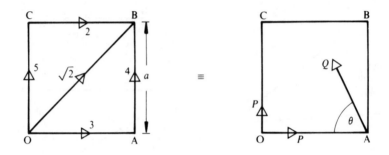

Using P and Q for the unknown magnitudes and θ as the unknown angle, comparison gives:

$\rightarrow$ $\qquad\qquad 3 + \sqrt{2}\cos 45° + 2 = P - Q\cos\theta$ (1)

$\uparrow$ $\qquad\qquad 5 + \sqrt{2}\sin 45° + 4 = P + Q\sin\theta$ (2)

$O\!\!\uparrow$ $\qquad\qquad 4a - 2a = Qa\sin\theta$ (3)

From (3) $\qquad\qquad\qquad Q = \dfrac{2}{\sin\theta}$

In (2) $\qquad\qquad\qquad P = 10 - 2 = 8$

In (1) $\qquad\qquad\qquad Q\cos\theta = 8 - 6 = 2$

Hence $\qquad\qquad\qquad \tan\theta = 1$

and $\qquad\qquad\qquad Q = 2\sqrt{2}$

The replacement force system therefore comprises two forces of 8 N along $\overrightarrow{OA}$ and $\overrightarrow{OC}$ and a force of $2\sqrt{2}$ N passing through **A** and making an angle of $45°$ with AO.

2. The Combination of a Force and a Couple

Consider a force of magnitude F and a couple of moment M which act in one plane. With reference to perpendicular axes Ox and Oy which, for convenience, are chosen to be parallel and perpendicular to the given force, the original system and its resultant can be represented in a diagram as shown.

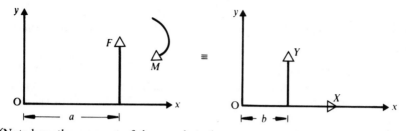

(Note how the moment of the couple is shown as a curved arrow indicating turning effect. This must not be mistaken for a force).

Comparing in the usual way we have:

$\rightarrow$ $\qquad\qquad\qquad\qquad\qquad 0 = X$ $\qquad\qquad\qquad\qquad$ (1)

$\uparrow$ $\qquad\qquad\qquad\qquad\qquad F = Y$ $\qquad\qquad\qquad\qquad$ (2)

$0\,\rangle$ $\qquad\qquad\qquad\qquad Fa - M = Yb$ $\qquad\qquad\qquad$ (3)

From (1) and (2) we see that, in magnitude and direction, the resultant is identical to the original force.

From (2) and (3), $\qquad\qquad\qquad (a - b) = \dfrac{M}{F}$

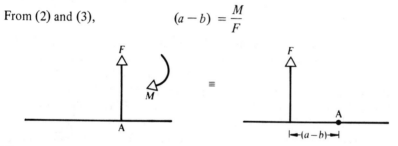

The very useful conclusion reached therefore is:

A couple M together with a coplanar force F are equivalent to an equal force F displaced through a distance $\dfrac{M}{F}$.

Because the direction of the displacement of the line of action depends on the sense of the couple it is advisable to calculate the displacement, rather than to quote it, in each problem.

SUMMARY

1) The resultant of any force system which is not in equilibrium is either a single force or a couple and has exactly the same linear and turning effects as the given system.

2) The resultant of two like parallel forces P and Q is of magnitude $P + Q$ and acts in a line parallel to P and Q dividing them internally in the ratio $Q : P$.

3) The resultant of two unlike, unequal, parallel forces P and Q is of magnitude $|P - Q|$ and acts in a line parallel to P and Q dividing them externally in the ratio $Q : P$.

4) If each member of a set of parallel forces passes through a fixed point, then their resultant also passes through a fixed point which is independent of their orientation.

5) A couple is a pair of equal and opposite non-collinear forces. It has zero linear resultant and produces pure rotation. The magnitude of a couple is its moment which is Fd where F is the magnitude of each force and d the distance between them.

6) The moment of a couple is the same about all axes perpendicular to its plane.

7) The combination of a force and a couple in the same plane is an equal force whose line of action is displaced.

8) The resultant of two forces represented completely by $p\overrightarrow{AB}$ and $q\overrightarrow{AC}$ is represented completely by $(p + q)\overrightarrow{AD}$ where $BD : DC = q : p$.

9) Complete specification of a force system in one plane requires three independent facts. When fewer than three are given or used, incomplete or ambiguous results arise.

EXAMPLES 15e

1) Forces P, $2P$, $3P$ act along the sides $\overrightarrow{AB}$, $\overrightarrow{BC}$, $\overrightarrow{CA}$ of an equilateral triangle of side a. Find the magnitude and direction of their resultant and the distance from A of the point where its line of action cuts AC (produced if necessary).
A couple of magnitude $\sqrt{3}\,Pa$ acting in the sense ABC and in the plane of the triangle is added to the system. Find the intersection with AC of the line of action of the resultant of the new system.
What single force must now be introduced to reduce the system to equilibrium?

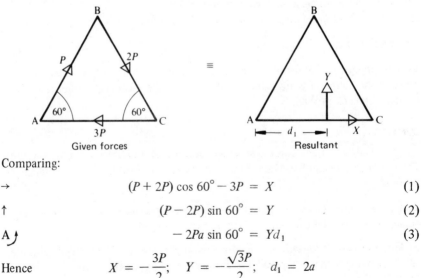

Given forces   Resultant

Comparing:

$\rightarrow$ $(P + 2P)\cos 60° - 3P = X$ (1)

$\uparrow$ $(P - 2P)\sin 60° = Y$ (2)

$A\big\}$ $-2Pa\sin 60° = Yd_1$ (3)

Hence $X = -\dfrac{3P}{2}; \quad Y = -\dfrac{\sqrt{3}P}{2}; \quad d_1 = 2a$

Therefore the resultant of the three forces has magnitude $\sqrt{X^2 + Y^2} = \sqrt{3}P$; its direction makes an angle

$\arctan \dfrac{Y}{X}(= 30°)$ with CA, and its line of action cuts AC produced at a distance $2a$ from A.

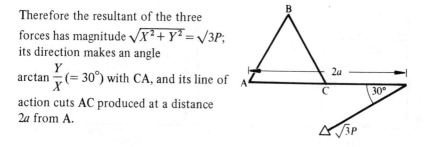

When a couple of magnitude $\sqrt{3}Pa$ is introduced, we have the combination of a force and a couple which is equivalent to an equal force in a different position. Let the new line of action cut AC at a point distant d_2 from A, then:

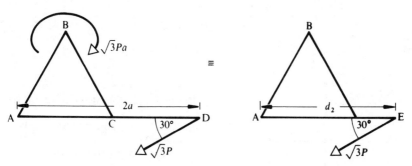

Old Resultant plus Couple   New Resultant

Comparing turning effect only (since magnitude and direction of the new resultant are known)

$$\sqrt{3}P\, 2a \sin 30° + \sqrt{3}Pa = \sqrt{3}P\, d_2 \sin 30°$$

Hence
$$d_2 = 4a$$

Therefore the new resultant cuts AC produced at E, distant $4a$ from A.
To reduce the system to equilibrium, a force equal and opposite to and collinear with this resultant must be added.

i.e. a force $\sqrt{3}P$ at 30° to AC and cutting AC produced at E.

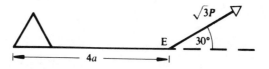

2) Forces $7P$, $5P$, $3P$ and $2P$ act along the sides, $\overrightarrow{AB}$, $\overrightarrow{BC}$, $\overrightarrow{CD}$ and $\overrightarrow{DA}$ of a square ABCD of side a. Find the equation of the line of action of the resultant of the system using AB and AD as x and y axes respectively.
A force F along AB and a couple of moment M are added to the system so that the new resultant passes through B and D. Find the magnitude and sense of the force and the couple.

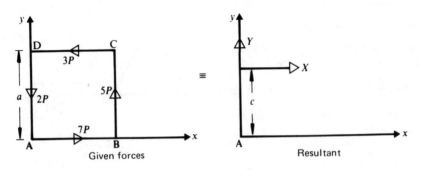

Given forces   ≡   Resultant

Comparing, we have:

→ $7P - 3P = X$ (1)

↑ $5P - 2P = Y$ (2)

A ↻ $-5Pa - 3Pa = Xc$ (3)

Therefore $X = 4P; \quad Y = 3P; \quad c = -2a.$

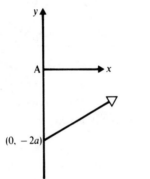

The line of action of the resultant has gradient $\dfrac{Y}{X} = \dfrac{3}{4}$ and cuts the y axis at $(0, -2a)$. Its equation is therefore

$$y = \frac{3}{4}x - 2a$$

or $4y = 3x - 8a$.

Adding the force F and couple M to this resultant (which is equivalent to the original system) gives:

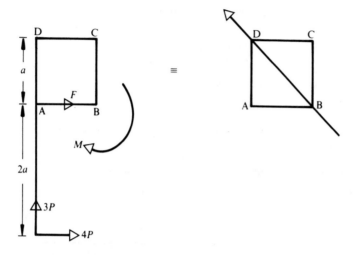

As the new resultant passes through B and D the turning effect of the system about axes through B and D is zero.

B $\circlearrowleft$ $M + 3Pa - 4P(2a) = 0$

D $\circlearrowleft$ $M - 4Pa(3a) - Fa = 0$

Therefore $M = 5Pa$ and $F = -7P$

The force is of magnitude $7P$ in the sense $\overrightarrow{BA}$ and the couple is of magnitude $5Pa$ in the sense **CBA**.

3) Forces $3P$, $7P$, P, $2P$, mP and nP act along the sides $\overrightarrow{AB}, \overrightarrow{BC}, \overrightarrow{CD}, \overrightarrow{DE}, \overrightarrow{FE}$ and $\overrightarrow{FA}$ of a regular hexagon. Find the values of m and n if:
(a) the six forces reduce to a couple,
(b) the system reduces to a single force along AD.

(a)

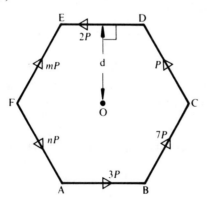

When the resultant is a couple the linear resultant is zero but the resultant moment is not.

Therefore → $3P - 2P + (7P - P + mP + nP) \cos 60° = 0$

and   ↑ $(7P + P + mP - nP) \sin 60° = 0$

These give $m = -8$ and $n = 0$

With these values, and taking O as the centre of the hexagon,

O ↻ $(3P + 7P + P + 2P + 8P)d \neq 0$

Therefore when $m = -8$ and $n = 0$ the system does reduce to a couple.

(b)

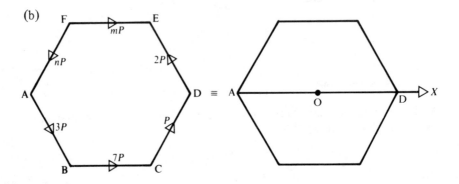

[If the resultant is along AD it is simpler if this line is horizontal (or vertical) in the diagram.]

Comparing:

↑ $(P + 2P - nP - 3P) \sin 60° = 0$

O ↻ $(3P + 7P + P + 2P - mP + nP)d = 0$

These give: $n = 0$ and $m = 13$

With these values

→ $X = 7P + 13P + (P - 2P + 3P) \cos 60° \neq 0$

Therefore when $n = 0$ and $m = 13$ the system does reduce to a single force along AD.

4) OABC is a rectangle in which $OA = 2a$ and $OC = a$. Forces of magnitudes P, Q and R act along $\overrightarrow{OA}$, $\overrightarrow{AB}$ and $\overrightarrow{BC}$ respectively. When OA and OC are taken as x and y axes respectively, the line of action of the resultant of these forces has equation $x = 4(y + a)$.
Find the ratio of the magnitudes of P, Q and R. Find also in terms of P and a, the moment of the couple necessary to transfer the line of action of the resultant to the line with equation $4y = x + 2a$.

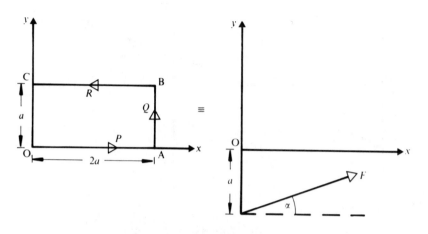

[If the resultant makes an angle α with Ox then

$\tan \alpha = $ gradient of line of action $= \dfrac{1}{4} \Rightarrow$]

Comparing:

$\rightarrow$ $$P - R = F \cos \alpha \tag{1}$$

$\uparrow$ $$Q = F \sin \alpha \tag{2}$$

O $$2aQ + aR = Fa \cos \alpha \tag{3}$$

From (3) $$R = F \cos \alpha - 2F \sin \alpha = \frac{F}{\sqrt{17}}(4 - 2)$$

From (1) $$P = F \cos \alpha + R = \frac{F}{\sqrt{17}}(4 + 2)$$

Therefore $$P : Q : R = \frac{6F}{\sqrt{17}} : \frac{F}{\sqrt{17}} : \frac{2F}{\sqrt{17}}$$

i.e. $$P : Q : R = 6 : 1 : 2.$$

The resultant must now be transferred to act along a parallel line whose y-intercept is the point $\left(0, \dfrac{a}{2}\right)$. Let the necessary couple be of magnitude kPa then:

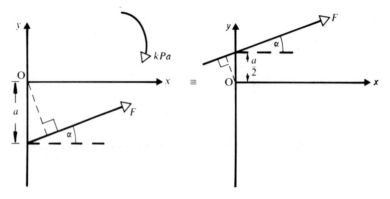

Comparing moments only:

$$kPa - Fa \cos \alpha = F\frac{a}{2} \cos \alpha$$

Hence

$$kP = 3\frac{F}{2} \cos \alpha$$

But $P = \dfrac{6F}{\sqrt{17}}$ therefore $k = 1$

Therefore the required couple is of magnitude Pa and acts in the sense **CBA**.

EXERCISE 15e

1) Forces of magnitudes $3F$, $4F$, $2F$, F act along the sides $\overrightarrow{AB}$, $\overrightarrow{BC}$, $\overrightarrow{CD}$, $\overrightarrow{DA}$ of a rectangle ABCD in which $AB = 4a$ and $AD = 3a$. If two more forces pF and qF act along $\overrightarrow{AC}$ and $\overrightarrow{BD}$ respectively, find the values of p and q for which the six forces:
(a) reduce to a couple,
(b) reduce to a force through B parallel to AC.
Explain why it is impossible to find values of p and q for which the system is in equilibrium.

2) Forces P, $2P$, $2P$ act along the sides $\overrightarrow{AB}$, $\overrightarrow{BC}$, $\overrightarrow{CA}$ of an equilateral triangle of side $2a$. Find the magnitude and direction of their resultant and find the point where its line of action cuts AC (produced if necessary).
The system is to be reduced to equilibrium by introducing a couple in the plane ABC and a force which acts through A. Find the magnitude and direction of the force and the magnitude and sense of the couple.

3) ABCD is a square of side 1 m. Forces F_1, F_2 and 4 N act along $\overrightarrow{AB}$, $\overrightarrow{BC}$ and $\overrightarrow{CD}$ respectively. The equation of the line of action of their resultant, referred to AB and AD as x and y axes respectively, is $3y = 2x + 6$. Calculate the values of F_1 and F_2.

A couple of magnitude 3 Nm in the plane of the square is now added to the system. Find the equation of the line of action of the new resultant.

4) Forces F, $2F$, $3F$ and $4F$ acting along the sides $\overrightarrow{AB}$, $\overrightarrow{BC}$, $\overrightarrow{CD}$ and $\overrightarrow{DA}$ of a square ABCD of side $2a$ are to be replaced by three forces acting along the sides of the triangle ABC. Find, in terms of F, the magnitude and sense of each of these forces. If the force acting along AC is now reversed find the distance from A of the point where the line of action of the resultant now cuts AB (produced if necessary).

5) Three forces which act along the sides $\overrightarrow{AB}$, $\overrightarrow{BC}$ and $\overrightarrow{CD}$ of a regular hexagon ABCDEF of side $2a$, have a resultant which acts along DF.
When a couple $4Pa$ in the sense CBA is added in the plane of the hexagon, the resultant acts along CA. Find the magnitudes of the three forces in terms of P.

6) Two forces in the same plane act as shown in the diagram.

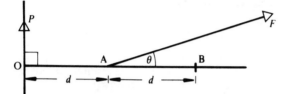

What can be added to the system in order to:
(a) reduce it to a single force equal in magnitude and direction to F but acting
    through (i) O   (ii) B,
(b) reduce it to equilibrium,
(c) reduce it to a clockwise couple of magnitude Pd.

MULTIPLE CHOICE EXERCISE 15

The instructions for answering these questions are given on page (xii)

TYPE I

1)

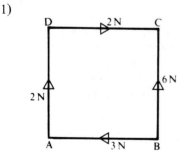

Forces act as shown round the sides of a square ABCD of side $2a$. The resultant force cuts AB at a point P.
(a) P is on AB produced and $AP = 4a$.
(b) P bisects AB.
(c) P is on BA produced and $AP = 2a$.
(d) P is on BA produced and $AP = a$.

2) The resultant moment of a set of coplanar forces about each of two axes through points A and B is zero. The set of forces reduces to:
(a) equilibrium,

(b) a force through A and a couple,
(c) a couple,
(d) a force through A and B,
(e) either equilibrium or a force through **A** and **B**.

3)

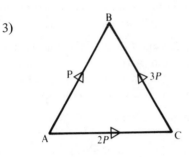

ABC is an equilateral triangle. The resultant of the three given forces intersects
AC:
(a) on AC produced,
(b) on CA produced,
(c) between A and C,
(d) at C.

4)

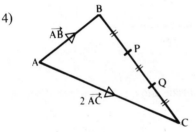

The resultant of $\overrightarrow{AB}$ and $2\overrightarrow{AC}$ is:
(a) $3\overrightarrow{AP}$,
(b) $3\overrightarrow{BC}$,
(c) $3\overrightarrow{AQ}$,
(d) $3\overrightarrow{PA}$.

0).

5)

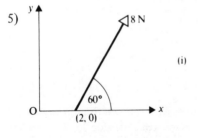

(i)

The force in figure (i), together with a
couple are equivalent to the force in
figure (ii). The couple is:
(a) 4 Nm clockwise,
(b) $8\sqrt{3}$ Nm anticlockwise,
(c) $4\sqrt{3}$ Nm clockwise,
(d) 16 Nm anticlockwise.

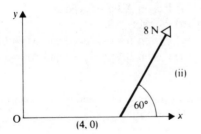

(ii)

TYPE II

6)

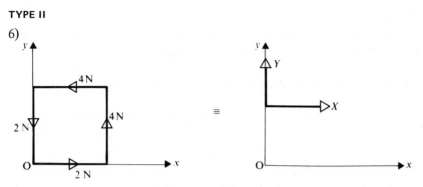

The diagrams represent a set of forces and their resultant.
(a) $X = -2$.
(b) The resultant is a couple.
(c) The resultant is a force at $45°$ to Oy.
(d) The resultant is a force at $45°$ to Ox.

7)

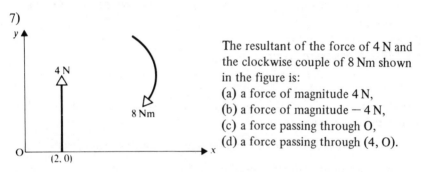

The resultant of the force of 4 N and the clockwise couple of 8 Nm shown in the figure is:
(a) a force of magnitude 4 N,
(b) a force of magnitude -4 N,
(c) a force passing through O,
(d) a force passing through (4, O).

TYPE III

8) (a) A set of coplanar forces has zero linear resultant.
   (b) A set of coplanar forces reduces to a couple.

9) (a) A set of coplanar forces is in equilibrium.
   (b) The moment of a set of coplanar forces about each of two different axes is zero.

10) (a) A set of coplanar forces reduces to a couple.
    (b) A set of like parallel forces acts in a plane.

11) (a) Forces represented by $2\overrightarrow{AB}$ and $3\overrightarrow{AC}$ have a resultant represented by $5\overrightarrow{AD}$.
    (b) In a triangle ABC, D is a point on BC where BD : DC = 3 : 2.

12) (a) The moment of a set of coplanar forces about each of three axes which are not in line, is zero.
    (b) A set of coplanar forces is in equilibrium.

TYPE IV

13) Find the magnitude and direction of the resultant of a set of coplanar forces.

(a) The resultant anticlockwise torque about an axis through a point $2i + 3j$ is 10 Nm.

(b) The resultant anticlockwise torque about an axis through a point $5i - j$ is 8 Nm.

(c) The resultant anticlockwise torque about an axis through a point $-4i + j$ is -4 Nm.

(d) The forces are not concurrent.

14) Find the resultant of forces represented by $\overrightarrow{AB}$, $2\overrightarrow{BC}$, $3\overrightarrow{AD}$ and $6\overrightarrow{DC}$.

(a) ABCD is a quadrilateral.

(b) AB = 2 m.

(c) BÂC = 60°.

15) Six forces act round the sides of a hexagon. Find the equation of the line of action of their resultant.

(a) Their magnitudes are P, $2P$, $4P$, $3P$, P, $2P$ along $\overrightarrow{AB}$, $\overrightarrow{BC}$, $\overrightarrow{CD}$, $\overrightarrow{ED}$, $\overrightarrow{FE}$, $\overrightarrow{AF}$ respectively.

(b) The hexagon is regular.

(c) The co-ordinates of vertex B are (1, 1).

TYPE V

16) The resultant of a set of forces is a force **F**. When a couple is added to the system the new resultant also is **F**.

17) A set of forces whose linear resultant is zero must be in equilibrium.

18) The moment of a couple depends upon the axis of rotation.

19) If a set of coplanar forces is not in equilibrium they reduce either to a force or to a couple.

20) If an axis is chosen passing through a point on the resultant of a force system, the resultant torque of the system about that axis is zero.

MISCELLANEOUS EXERCISE 15

1) If ABC is any triangle and PQRS is a square of side $3a$, *write down* a complete specification of the resultant of each of the following sets of forces:

(a) Three forces which act on a particle and are represented in magnitude and direction by $\overrightarrow{AB}$, $\overrightarrow{BC}$ and $\overrightarrow{CA}$.

(b) Three forces represented completely by $\overrightarrow{AB}$, $\overrightarrow{BC}$ and $\overrightarrow{CA}$.

(c) Two forces of magnitudes F and $2F$ acting along $\overrightarrow{PQ}$ and $\overrightarrow{SR}$.

(d) Two forces of magnitudes F and $2F$ acting along $\overrightarrow{PQ}$ and $\overrightarrow{RS}$.

(e) Two forces each of magnitude F acting along $\overrightarrow{PQ}$ and $\overrightarrow{RS}$.

(f) Two forces represented completely by $\overrightarrow{AB}$ and $\overrightarrow{AC}$.

(g) Two forces represented completely by $\overrightarrow{AB}$ and $\overrightarrow{CA}$.

2) Prove that a couple, together with a force in the same plane, is equivalent to a single force. Describe completely the possible resultants of a force of 10 N acting in the same plane as a couple of magnitude 20 Nm.

3)

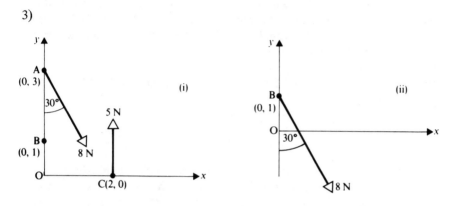

Two forces act as shown in diagram (i).

A third force is added to the system and the resultant of the three forces is shown in diagram (ii).

Find the magnitude, direction and position of the third force.

4) Replace forces F, $2F$, $3F$, $4F$ acting in order round the sides of a square ABCD of side a, by three forces acting along the sides of triangle AEB where E is the mid-point of CD.

5) Show that the resultant of forces $\overrightarrow{AB}$, $\overrightarrow{CB}$, $2\overrightarrow{CD}$ and $2\overrightarrow{AD}$ acting along the corresponding sides of a quadrilateral ABCD, is represented completely by $6\overrightarrow{QP}$ where P divides BD in the ratio 1 : 2 and Q bisects AC.

6) A rod AB is loaded and supported as shown in the figure. Find the largest torque which can be applied to the rod in a vertical plane without causing the rod to overturn if the torque is:

(a) clockwise,

(b) anticlockwise.

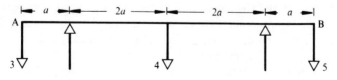

7) A system of coplanar forces has anticlockwise moments M, $2M$ and $5M$ respectively about the points $(a, 0)$, $(0, a)$ and (a, a) in the plane. Find the magnitude of the resultant of the system and the equation of its line of action.

(U of L)

8) A non-uniform rigid beam AB, of length $3a$ and weight nW, rests on supports P and Q at the same level, where $AP = PQ = QB = a$. When a load of weight W is hung from A, the beam is on the point of tilting about P. Find the distance of the centre of gravity of the beam from A. When an additional load of weight W_1 is hung from B, the forces exerted on the supports at P and Q are equal. Find W_1 in terms of n and W.
If a couple, of moment L and acting in the vertical plane through AB, is now applied to the loaded beam, the reaction at P is increased in the ratio 3 : 2. Show that:

$$L = \tfrac{1}{3}(n + 1)Wa \qquad \text{(J.M.B.)}$$

9) (a) Forces 3, 2, 7 and 5 newton act along the sides OX, XP, PY and YO respectively of a square OXPY of side 2 m in the sense indicated by the letters. Calculate the magnitude of the resultant of this system of forces and the distance from O of the point at which the line of action of this resultant cuts XO produced.

(b) A uniform rigid beam ABCD, of length $5a$ and weight W, rests horizontally on supports at B and C at the same level where $AB = a$, $CD = 2a$ as shown in the figure. Calculate the forces exerted by the beam on the supports.

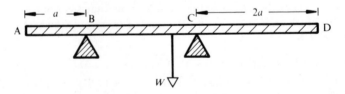

A clockwise couple of moment L is now applied to the beam tending to rotate the beam in the vertical plane through AD. If the beam remains in equilibrium in the horizontal position, calculate, in terms of W, L and a the force exerted by the beam on the support B.   (U of L)

10) A system of coplanar forces consists of forces of 4, 3, 2, 5 and 6 newton acting along the sides AB, BC, CD, DE and EF respectively of a regular hexagon ABCDEF of side 2 m, the forces acting in the directions indicated by the order of the letters. Find, in magnitude and direction, the force P newtons, acting at F, which will reduce the system to a couple and find the magnitude and sense of this couple. If the force P newtons is replaced by a force of 7 newton along AF, show that the system now reduces to a single force and find the magnitude of this resultant and the point of intersection of its line of action with AB, produced if necessary.

(A.E.B.)

11) Forces $\mathbf{i} + 3\mathbf{j}$, $-2\mathbf{i} - \mathbf{j}$, $\mathbf{i} - 2\mathbf{j}$ act through the points with position vectors $2\mathbf{i} + 5\mathbf{j}$, $4\mathbf{j}$, $-\mathbf{i} + \mathbf{j}$ respectively. Prove that this system of forces is equivalent to a couple, and calculate the moment of this couple. (U of L)

12) A system of forces acting in the plane of perpendicular axes Ox and Oy consists of:

a force $10P$ along Ox,

a force $-9P$ along Oy,

a force $13P$ along OA, where A is the point $(12a, 5a)$,

a force $20P$ along AB, where B is the point $(8a, 8a)$.

Find the magnitude, direction and equation of the line of action of the resultant of this system.

A clockwise coplanar couple of magnitude $240Pa$ is added to the system. Find the magnitude, direction and equation of the line of action of the resultant of the new system. A.E.B.

13) A rectangle ABCD has $AB = a$ and $AD = 2a$, and M is the mid-point of AD. Forces W, $2W$, $4W$, $6W$, $3W\sqrt{2}$, $W\sqrt{5}$ act along CB, DA, BA, CD, MB, DB respectively, the direction of the forces being indicated by the order of the letters. Reduce the system to a single force acting through A and a couple; state the magnitude and direction of the force, and show that the couple has moment $6aW$. Where does the resultant of the system cut AD?

Find two parallel forces through B and D which are together equivalent to the system. (Cambridge)

14) Find the magnitude and direction of the resultant of each of the following two systems of forces which act in the plane of a rectangle ABCD, in which $AB = 4a$ and $BC = 3a$.

(a) Forces $4P$ along AB, P along AD and $10P$ along DB.

(b) Forces which have total moment $-Pa$, $+15Pa$ and $-5Pa$ about A, B and D respectively ($+$ indicates the sense ABC).

Find also, in each case, the point of intersection of the line of action of the resultant with the line AB (produced if necessary). (A.E.B.)

15) Forces of magnitude $2P$, P, $2P$, $3P$, $2P$ and P act along the sides AB, BC, CD, ED, EF and AF respectively of a regular hexagon of side $2a$ in the directions indicated by the letters. Prove that this system of forces can be reduced to a single force of magnitude $2P\sqrt{3}$ acting along AC together with a couple. Find the magnitude of the couple.

Show that the system can be reduced to a single force without a couple. If the line of action of this force cuts FA produced at X, calculate the length of AX. (U of L)

16) ABCDEF is a regular hexagon with sides of length a. Forces of magnitudes 3, 5, 5, 8, 1, 4, 5 and 4 units act along AB, BC, DC, DE, EF, FA, AD and EB respectively, the order of the letters indicating the sense. Find:

(a) the magnitude and inclination to **AB** of the direction of the single force equivalent to the system, indicating clearly the direction and sense in a figure;

(b) the cartesian equation of the line of action of this force, taking the centre O of the hexagon as origin and the x-axis parallel to **AB**;

(c) the magnitude and sense of the couple that would have to be added to the system to make it equivalent to a single force through O.   (W.J.E.C.)

17) A lamina is in the shape of an equilateral triangle ABC, and D, E, F are the mid-points of BC, CA, AB respectively. Forces of magnitude 4 N, 8 N, 4 N, 3 N, 3 N act along **AB**, **BC**, **CA**, **BE**, **CF** respectively, the direction of each force being indicated by the order of the letters. Find the magnitude of the resultant force on the lamina, and show that its line of action cuts AD produced at G, where DG = AD.

The lamina is kept in equilibrium by three forces acting along FE, DF, ED. Find the magnitudes of these forces.   (Cambridge)

18) (a) State the result known as the parallelogram of forces.

Calculate the magnitude and direction of the resultant of two forces whose magnitudes are 7.5 N and 5.3 N and whose lines of action are inclined at 35°.

(b) Six equal forces *F* newton act in order along the sides of a regular hexagon of side 2*a* m. Show that the six forces are equivalent to a couple and find its magnitude.

(c) ABCD is a rectangle in which AB = CD = 2*a* and BC = DA = *a*. CED is an equilateral triangle constructed on CD lying outside the rectangle. Equal forces *P* act along the following lines in senses indicated by the orders of the letters; DE, EC, BC, BA, DA. Find whether the system is equivalent to a single force or a couple.   (S.U.J.B.)

19) The points A, B, C, D, E, F are the verticles of a regular hexagon. Forces each of 2 newtons act along **AB** and **DC**, and forces each of 1 newton act along **BC** and **ED**, in the directions indicated by the order of the letters. Forces *P* newtons and *Q* newtons act along EF and AF respectively. Find *P* and *Q*:

(a) if the system reduces to a couple,

(b) if the resultant of the system is a force acting along EB.   (U of L)

20) (a) A uniform rod AB, of length 2*a* and weight *W*, rests with its lower end A on a smooth horizontal plane and a point C of its length on a rough horizontal rail fixed at a height *a* above the plane. The rod is perpendicular to the rail and inclined at θ to the horizontal. Determine the direction of the resultant reaction on the rod at C, and prove that $\theta \leqslant \lambda$, where $\lambda\ (> 30°)$ is the angle of friction at C.

When $\theta = 45°$ a force *P* is applied to the rod at A in the direction AD, where D is on the plane vertically below C. Prove that the rod will not move upwards if

$$P < W \frac{(1 + \tan \lambda)}{2\sqrt{2}}$$

(b) A system of forces in the plane of a triangle ABC has anticlockwise moments of G, $2G$ and $-2G$ about the points A, B and C respectively. State why the system reduces to a single force and not a couple. Find the point of intersection of the line of action of this force with the side BC, and calculate the moment about the centroid of the triangle ABC.

(J.M.B.)

21) State one set of conditions sufficient to ensure that a system of coplanar forces is in equilibrium.

Three points, A, B and C, have coordinates $(2a, 0)$, $(2a, 2a)$ and $(0, 2a)$ respectively referred to perpendicular axes Ox, Oy. A system of forces in the plane xOy has anti-clockwise moments of $40Pa$ and $60Pa$ about A and C respectively and a clockwise moment of $20Pa$ about B. Calculate the magnitude and direction of the resultant of this system and the equation of its line of action.   A.E.B.

22) A triangle ABC has $AB = 4$ m, $BC = 5$ m, $CA = 3$ m, and D, E, F are the mid-points of BC, CA, AB respectively. Forces of magnitude 4 N, 5 N, 3 N, x N, y N act along AB, BC, CA, ED, CF respectively, the direction of the forces being indicated by the order of the letters. The resultant of the system acts along EF. Calculate x and y, and show that the magnitude of the resultant is 20 N.

The system is equivalent to a force P acting along AC, a force Q acting along CF and a couple of moment M. Find P, Q and M.   (Cambridge)

23) Forces $\lambda\overrightarrow{OA}$ and $\mu\overrightarrow{OB}$ act along the lines AO and OB respectively. Show that the resultant is a force $(\lambda + \mu)\overrightarrow{OC}$ where C lies on AB and AC : CB $= \mu : \lambda$. Forces $3\overrightarrow{AB}$, $2\overrightarrow{AC}$ and $\overrightarrow{CB}$ act along the sides AB, AC and CB respectively of a triangle ABC. Their resultant meets BC in P and AC in Q and its magnitude is kPQ. Find BP : PC, AQ : QC and k.   (U of L)

24) (a) Prove that, if forces represented by $\lambda\overrightarrow{OL}$ and $\mu\overrightarrow{OM}$ act along sides OL and OM of triangle OLM then the resultant force is $(\lambda + \mu)\overrightarrow{OX}$ where X is the point of LM such that $\lambda LX = \mu XM$.

Consider the case when $\lambda + \mu = 0$.

(b) Forces $10\overrightarrow{AB}$, $15\overrightarrow{AC}$, $4\overrightarrow{CB}$ act along the sides AB, AC and CB respectively of triangle ABC. The line of action of the resultant cuts AC at Y and BC at X. Find the ratios BX : XC and AY : YC and show that the magnitude of the resultant is 35 YX.

(c) D, E and F are the mid-points of the sides QR, RP and PQ respectively of triangle PQR whose circumcentre is O. Forces of magnitude kQR, kRP and kPQ act at O in directions $\overrightarrow{OD}$, $\overrightarrow{OE}$ and $\overrightarrow{OF}$ respectively.

Prove that the forces are in equilibrium.   (S.U.J.B.)

25) The diagonals of the plane quadrilateral ABCD intersect at O and X and Y are the mid-points of the diagonals AC and BD respectively (see figure). Show that:

(a) $\overrightarrow{BA} + \overrightarrow{BC} = 2\overrightarrow{BX}$,

(b) $\overrightarrow{BA} + \overrightarrow{BC} + \overrightarrow{DA} + \overrightarrow{DC} = 4\overrightarrow{YX}$,

(c) $2\overrightarrow{AB} + 2\overrightarrow{BC} + 2\overrightarrow{CA}$ reduces to a couple, and state its magnitude in terms of the triangle ABC.

If $\overrightarrow{OA} + \overrightarrow{OB} + \overrightarrow{OC} + \overrightarrow{OD} = 4\overrightarrow{OM}$, find the locations of the point M.

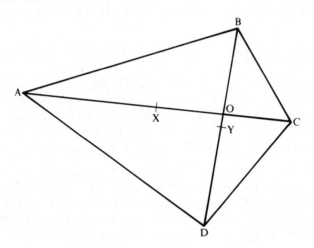

(A.E.B.)

CHAPTER 16

CENTRES OF GRAVITY

WEIGHT AND CENTRE OF GRAVITY

A solid body is made up of a number of particles rigidly held together by forces of attraction where each particle has a mass and therefore a weight which acts vertically downward. The weight of a solid body is the resultant of the weights of its constituent particles, i.e. the resultant of a set of parallel forces. It was seen in Chapter 15 p 413 that such a resultant passes through a fixed point whatever the orientation of the forces, so the weight of a body passes through a fixed point whatever the orientation of that body. This fixed point is called the centre of gravity of the body or (with certain limitations which are discussed later) the centre of mass of the body.

Thus the weight of a body is equal to the algebraic sum of the weights of its constituent particles and acts vertically downward through a fixed point in the body (called the centre of gravity) where that fixed point is independent of the orientation of the body.

To find the centre of gravity of a body we can use the fact that the *sum of the moments of the weights of the constituent particles about any line is equal to the moment of the resultant weight about the same line:* This will give the distance of the centre of gravity from that line and to locate the centre of gravity completely it may be necessary to take moments about two non-parallel lines (and, in the case of certain three dimensional problems, about three non-parallel lines, although such problems do not concern us at this stage but are covered in the second volume.

THE CENTRE OF GRAVITY OF A SET OF PARTICLES IN A PLANE

Consider three particles of weights $5g$ N, $2g$ N, $3g$ N which are at points

$(3, -1), (2, 3), (-2, 5)$ referred to co-ordinate axes Ox and Oy.

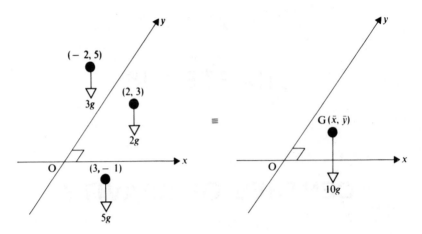

The centre of gravity of these particles will be in the xy plane — let this point be $G(\bar{x}, \bar{y})$.

Suppose that the xy plane is horizontal so the weights of the particles act vertically downward perpendicular to the xy plane and the total weight $(10g)$ acts in the same direction through G.

Using the principle of moments:

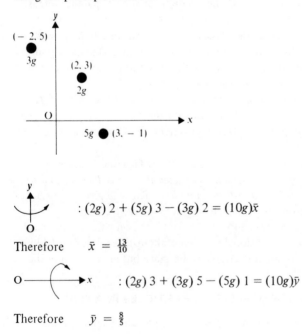

$: (2g) 2 + (5g) 3 - (3g) 2 = (10g)\bar{x}$

Therefore $\bar{x} = \frac{13}{10}$

$: (2g) 3 + (3g) 5 - (5g) 1 = (10g)\bar{y}$

Therefore $\bar{y} = \frac{8}{5}$

so the centre of gravity is at the point $(\frac{13}{10}, \frac{8}{5})$

In general consider particles of mass m_1, m_2, m_3 ..... at the points (x_1, y_1), $(x_2, y_2), (x_3, y_3)$ ..... in the xy plane. The weights of these particles are m_1g, m_2g, m_3g ..... so the total weight is $\Sigma\, mg$, acting at a point $G(\bar{x}, \bar{y})$ in the xy plane.

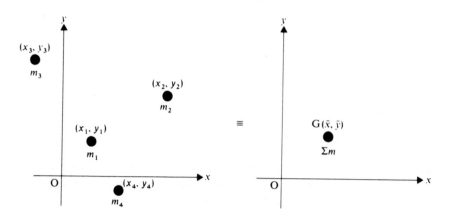

Supposing that the xy plane is horizontal (i.e. the weights act perpendicularly to the xy plane) then using the principle of moments we have

$: (m_1g)x_1 + (m_2g)x_2 + (m_3g)x_3 + ... = (m_1 + m_2 + m_3 + ...)g\bar{x}$

$$\Sigma mx = \bar{x}\, \Sigma m$$

$$\text{Therefore } \bar{x} = \frac{\Sigma mx}{\Sigma m}$$

Similarly:

$$\bar{y} = \frac{\Sigma my}{\Sigma m}$$

These two equations may now be used to find the centre of gravity of any set of coplanar particles. (The centre of gravity of a set of non-coplanar particles will be found in Volume 2).

This result may also be expressed in vector terms: let the particles be at the points whose position vectors are $\mathbf{r}_1, \mathbf{r}_2, \mathbf{r}_3$, ...

Then $\mathbf{r}_1 = x_1\mathbf{i} + y_1\mathbf{j}, \quad \mathbf{r}_2 = x_2\mathbf{i} + y_2\mathbf{j}, \quad \mathbf{r}_3 = x_3\mathbf{i} + y_3\mathbf{j}, ...$

As before $\bar{x} = \dfrac{\Sigma mx}{\Sigma m}$ and $\bar{y} = \dfrac{\Sigma my}{\Sigma m}$

Therefore the position vector of G is $\mathbf{r}$ where $\mathbf{r} = \bar{x}\mathbf{i} + \bar{y}\mathbf{j}$

$$= \frac{\Sigma mx\mathbf{i} + \Sigma my\mathbf{j}}{\Sigma m}$$

$$= \frac{(m_1x_1\mathbf{i} + m_2x_2\mathbf{i} + ...) + (m_1y_1\mathbf{j} + m_2y_2\mathbf{j} + ...)}{\Sigma m}$$

$$= \frac{m_1(x_1\mathbf{i} + y_1\mathbf{j}) + m_2(x_2\mathbf{i} + y_2\mathbf{j}) + ...}{\Sigma m}$$

$$= \frac{m_1\mathbf{r}_1 + m_2\mathbf{r}_2 + m_3\mathbf{r}_3 + ...}{\Sigma m}$$

$$= \frac{\Sigma m\mathbf{r}}{\Sigma m}.$$

Reconsidering the first example in vector terms we have particles of masses 2 kg, 5 kg and 3 kg at points whose position vectors are $2\mathbf{i} + 3\mathbf{j}$, $3\mathbf{i} - \mathbf{j}$ and $-2\mathbf{i} + 5\mathbf{j}$. Using the result above, the position vector of G is

$$\frac{2(2\mathbf{i} + 3\mathbf{j}) + 5(3\mathbf{i} - \mathbf{j}) + 3(-2\mathbf{i} + 5\mathbf{j})}{10}$$

$$= \tfrac{1}{10}(13\mathbf{i} + 16\mathbf{j}).$$

When the number of particles involved is small the summing can be done by simple addition but when there is a continuous distribution of particles (as in the case of a rigid body) the summing may have to be done by integration. The position of the centre of gravity of certain rigid bodies can be found from considerations of symmetry.

UNIFORM BODIES

A uniform body is made from uniform material, i.e. any given quantity of the material (measured by length, area or volume as appropriate) will have the same mass as any equal quantity of the same material: so a uniform body will have mass equally distributed about any line of symmetry: therefore *the centre of gravity of a uniform body lies on each line of symmetry that the body possesses.*

Therefore the centre of gravity of a uniform rod, circular lamina, sphere etc, lies at the centre of the body. The centre of gravity of a cylinder (hollow or solid) lies at the mid-point of its axis.

We can extend this argument to find the centre of gravity of some other simple bodies:

Centre of Gravity of a Uniform Triangular Lamina

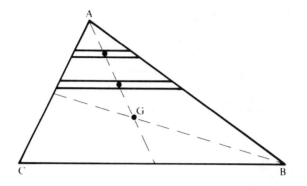

Consider the triangle as being made from a series of rods parallel to the side BC. As each rod is uniform, its centre of gravity is at its mid-point: so the centre of gravity of the triangle (G) must lie on the line joining the mid-points of these rods: i.e. on the median through A. Similarly by considering the triangle as being made from a series of rods parallel to AC, G also lies on the median through B. Therefore the position of *the centre of gravity of any triangle is at the point of intersection of the medians.* (The medians of a triangle intersect at a point which is $\frac{2}{3}$ of the length of each from a vertex). By a similar argument the centre of gravity of a lamina in the form of a rectangle or parallelogram is at the point of intersection of the diagonals.

Note: We have considered centre of gravity and centre of mass as being the same and for all practical purposes this is true. (They differ in the case of a very large body – so large that the weights of the constituent particles are not parallel. The centre of gravity of such a body is still the point through which the resultant weight acts but it can not be found from the formulae derived on p. 447 – these formulae would give the centre of mass). A term which is frequently confused with centre of gravity is centroid. The centroid of a body is the geometric centre of area or volume and in the case of a *uniform* body the centroid and centre of gravity coincide.

EXAMPLE 16a

Show that the centre of gravity of a uniform triangular lamina ABC is at the same position as the centre of gravity of three particles of equal mass placed at the vertices A, B, C of the triangle.

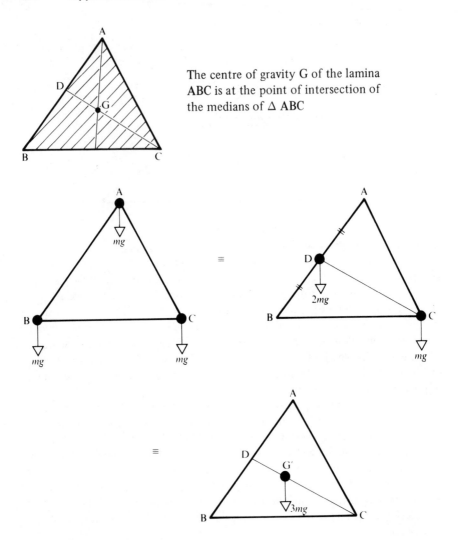

The centre of gravity G of the lamina ABC is at the point of intersection of the medians of △ ABC

Let the particles each have a mass m.

Considering the weights at A and B, their resultant passes through the point D, the mid-point of AB.

Considering the weights $2mg$ at D and mg at C, their resultant passes through the point G′ on the median DC such that $DG' : G'C = 1 : 2$.

Similarly we can show that G′ lies on the median through A and on the median through B, therefore G and G′ are the same point.

Thus the centre of gravity of the three particles at A, B and C is the same point as the centre of gravity of the lamina ABC.

(Incidentally, as it can also be shown that G divides the median through A and the median through B in the ratio $2 : 1$, this proves that the medians of a triangle intersect at a point of trisection).

EXERCISE 16a

1) Three particles A, B, C of mass 2, 3, 4 kg are at the points $(1, 4)$, $(3, 6)$, $(2, 1)$ in the xy plane. Find the co-ordinates of their centre of gravity.

2) Four particles A, B, C, D of mass 3, 5, 2, 4 kg are at the points $(1, 6)$, $(-1, 5)$, $(2, -3)$, $(-1, -4)$. Find the co-ordinates of their centre of gravity.

3) Three particles of mass 5, 3, 7 kg are at the points A, B, C, whose position vectors are $i - 2j$, $7i + j$, $-3i + 5j$. Find the position vector of their centre of mass. Find also the position vector of the centroid of the points A, B, C. (The centroid coincides with the centre of mass of three particles of equal mass at the points A, B, C).

4) Four particles of mass 3, 2, 5, 1 kg are at the points A, B, C, D whose position vectors are $2i - j$, $3i + 5j$, $-2i - j$, $i - 3j$. Find:
(a) the position vector of the centre of mass of the particles,
(b) the position vector of the centroid of the points A, B, C, D.

5) A uniform lamina is in the form of a trapezium ABCD where AB and DC are the parallel sides. Show that the centre of gravity of the trapezium lies on the line joining the mid-points of AB and DC.

6) The vertices of a triangle are at the points $i + j$, $3i - j$, $2i + j$. Find the position vector of the centre of gravity of the triangle, assuming it to be a uniform lamina.

7) Show that the centre of gravity of a uniform lamina in the form of a parallelogram is at the point of intersection of the diagonals.

8) By dividing a parallelogram into two triangles show that the centre of gravity of a lamina in the form of a parallelogram is the same point as the centre of gravity of four particles, two of mass m at one pair of opposite vertices and two of mass $2m$ at the other pair of opposite vertices.

COMPOSITE BODIES

When a body is made up from two or more parts, each of which has a known weight and centre of gravity, then as the weight of the complete body is the resultant of the weights of its parts we can again use the principle of moments to find the centre of gravity of the body.

EXAMPLES 16b

1) A uniform lamina ABCDE is made from a square ABDE and an equilateral triangle BCD. Find the centre of gravity of the lamina.

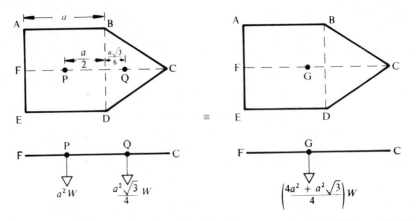

As the body is made from uniform material its centre of gravity (G) is on the line of symmetry CF, also the weight of any part of the body is proportional to the area of that part.

Let the length of a side of the lamina be a and the weight per unit area be W.

Thus the weight of the square ABDE is $a^2 W$ and its centre of gravity is at P, $\frac{1}{2}a$ from AE.

The weight of the triangle BCD is $\dfrac{a^2\sqrt{3}}{4} W$ and its centre of gravity is at Q, $\dfrac{a\sqrt{3}}{6}$ from BD.

Supposing the plane of the lamina is horizontal, we can find G by taking moments about any line in the plane of the lamina perpendicular to CF. It helps if the information required is listed in a table.

Choosing to take moments about AE

BODY	WEIGHT	DISTANCE OF CENTRE OF GRAVITY FROM AE
square ABDE	$a^2 W$	$\dfrac{a}{2}$
triangle BCD	$\dfrac{a^2\sqrt{3}}{4} W$	$a + \dfrac{a\sqrt{3}}{6}$
complete lamina	$\dfrac{(4a^2 + a^2\sqrt{3})}{4} W$	FG

$$(a^2 W)\frac{a}{2} + \left(\frac{a^2\sqrt{3}}{4} W\right)\left(a + \frac{a\sqrt{3}}{6}\right) = \left(\frac{4a^2 + a^2\sqrt{3}}{4}\right) W \times FG$$

$$\left(\frac{5 + 2\sqrt{3}}{8}\right)a = \left(\frac{4 + \sqrt{3}}{4}\right) FG$$

$$\text{Therefore } FG = \frac{14 + 3\sqrt{3}}{26}\, a$$

2) A thin uniform wire is bent to form the two equal sides AB and AC of triangle ABC, where AB = AC = 5 cm. The third side BC, of length 6 cm, is made from uniform wire of twice the density of the first. Find the centre of gravity of the framework.

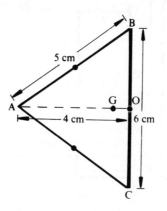

AO = 4 cm (Pythagoras)
Let w be the weight per unit length of AB and AC.
Then $2w$ is the weight per unit length of BC.
From symmetry the centre of gravity of the body lies on AO, so we will take moments about BC.

BODY	WEIGHT	DISTANCE OF CENTRE OF GRAVITY FROM BC
wire AB	$5w$	2
wire AC	$5w$	2
wire BC	$12w$	0
framework ABC	$22w$	OG

$$(5w)\,2 + (5w)\,2 + (12w)\,0 = (22w)\,OG$$

$$\text{Therefore } OG = \tfrac{5}{11}$$

Therefore the centre of gravity is $\tfrac{5}{11}$ cm from side BC on the line of symmetry AO.

3) A uniform lamina is in the form of a rectangle ABCD where AB = $2a$ and BC = $4a$. E and F are points on BC and AD such that BE = AF = a, and H and J are the midpoints of EF and CD. A cut is made through the lamina along the line EH, and the rectangular section HECJ is folded along HJ so as to lie on top of FHJD. Find the centre of gravity of the resulting body.

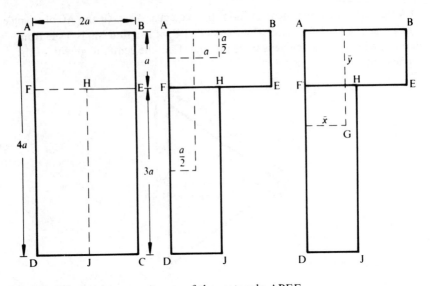

Let W be the weight per unit area of the rectangle ABEF.

Then $2W$ will be the weight per unit area of the rectangle FHJD as it is of double thickness.

There are no lines of symmetry so we will have to take moments about two lines to find the position of G, the centre of gravity of the resulting lamina.

(Even if the lamina were symmetrical in shape it would be dangerous to use the properties of symmetry to locate G because the different densities of the parts prevent the lamina from being mechanically symmetrical).

BODY	WEIGHT	DISTANCE OF CENTRE OF GRAVITY FROM AB	DISTANCE OF CENTRE OF GRAVITY FROM AD
rectangle ABEF	$2a^2 W$	$\dfrac{a}{2}$	a
rectangle FHJD	$3a^2(2W)$	$\dfrac{5a}{2}$	$\dfrac{a}{2}$
complete body	$8a^2 W$	$\bar{y}$	$\bar{x}$

$$(2a^2 W)\frac{a}{2} + (6a^2 W)\frac{5a}{2} = 8a^2 W\bar{y}$$

$$\bar{y} = 2a$$

$$(2a^2 W)a + (6a^2 W)\frac{a}{2} = 8a^2 W\bar{x}$$

$$\bar{x} = \tfrac{5}{8}a$$

Therefore the centre of gravity is at the point which is $2a$ from AB and $\frac{5}{8}a$ from AD.

4) A uniform lamina is in the form of a square ABCD of side $3a$. E is a point on BC and F is a point on DC such that $CE = CF = a$. A square FCEH is removed from the lamina. Find the centre of gravity of the remainder.

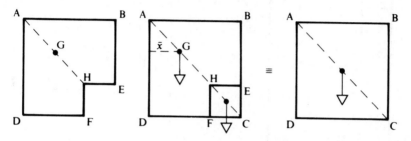

The weight of the complete square ABCD is the resultant of the weight of the square HECF and the remainder ABEHFD.

From symmetry all centres of gravity lie on AH, so AD is a convenient line axis.

BODY	WEIGHT	DISTANCE OF CENTRE OF GRAVITY FROM AD
Square ABCD	$9a^2W$	$\dfrac{3a}{2}$
Square FHEC	a^2W	$\dfrac{5a}{2}$
Remainder	$8a^2W$	$\bar{x}$

$$(9a^2W)\frac{3a}{2} = (a^2W)\frac{5a}{2} + (8a^2W)\bar{x}$$

Therefore $\bar{x} = \frac{11}{8}a$

Therefore the centre of gravity of the remainder lies on AH at a distance of $\frac{11}{8}a$ from AD.

5) A uniform solid is in the form of a cylinder of radius $2a$ and height $2h$ with a cylindrical hole of radius a and height h drilled centrally at one plane end. Find the centre of gravity of the solid.

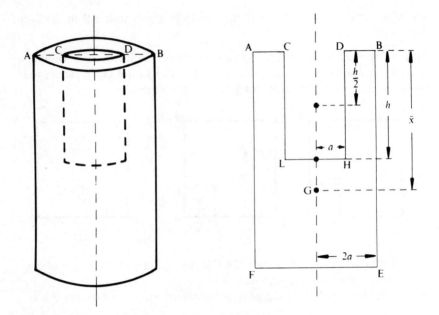

From symmetry the centre of gravity of the solid lies on the axis of the cylinder. The complete cylinder and the cylinder removed from it are similar bodies so their volumes (and therefore their weights) are in the ratio $8:1$, (the cube of the ratio of corresponding lengths). Let W be the weight of the portion removed.

BODY	WEIGHT	DISTANCE OF CENTRE OF GRAVITY FROM AB
solid cylinder ABEF	$8W$	h
solid cylinder CDHL	W	$\dfrac{h}{2}$
remainder	$7W$	$\bar{x}$

A——(——B

$$(8W)h = (W)\frac{h}{2} + (7W)\bar{x}$$

$$\bar{x} = \tfrac{15}{14}h$$

Therefore the centre of gravity of the solid lies on the axis at a distance of $\tfrac{15}{14}h$ from the end with the hole in it.

This method for determining the relationships between the weights of similar bodies is quicker than using 'weight per unit volume' and should be used whenever possible.

6) A uniform lamina ABCD is in the form of a trapezium where AB is parallel

to DC and AB $= a$, DC $= b$. Show that the centre of gravity of the lamina is at the same point as the centre of gravity of four particles placed at the vertices of the triangle where the mass at B is am, the mass at D is bm, and the mass at both A and C is $(a + b)m$.

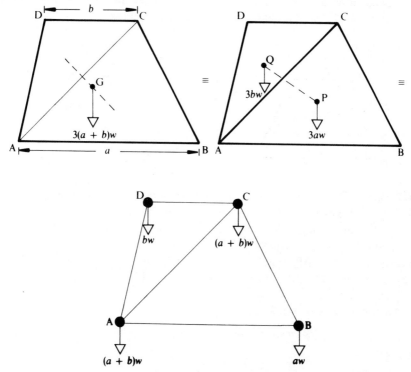

The weight of the lamina ABCD acting through its centre of gravity G is the resultant of the weight of the lamina ABC and the weight of the lamina ADC acting through the centres of gravity P and Q.

Weight of $\triangle$ABC : weight of $\triangle$ADC $= a:b$ (equal height)

Therefore G is on PQ and divides PQ in the ratio $b:a$.

If the lamina ABC is replaced by three particles of equal weight at the points A, B, C, the centre of gravity of these particles is at P (see example 16a). If the weight of each of these particles is aw their total weight is $3aw$ acting through P. Similarly if the lamina ADC is replaced by three particles each of weight bw at A, D, C, the resultant weight of these three particles is $3bw$ acting through Q. The resultant of the weights $3aw$ at P and $3bw$ at Q divides PQ in the ratio $b:a$ i.e. it passes through G.

Therefore the centre of gravity of a mass am at B, bm at D, $(a + b)m$ at A and $(a + b)m$ at C is the same point as the centre of gravity of the uniform lamina ABCD. This is a very useful result as it is usually easier to find the centre of gravity of four particles than it is to find the centre of gravity of a lamina in the form of a trapezium.

7) A uniform lamina is in the form of a triangle ABC where AB = 3*a*. D and E are points on AC and BC such that DE is parallel to AB and DE = *a*. The portion CDE is removed. Find the centre of gravity of the remainder.

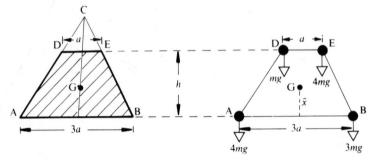

The centres of gravity of △ABC and △CDE lie on the median through C: therefore the centre of gravity G of the remainder also lies on the median through C. (G can be found using the methods in examples 4 and 5, but an alternative method using the result from example 6 follows).

Replace the lamina ABED with four particles, two of mass 4*m* at A and E, one of mass 3*m* at B and one of mass *m* at D. (The parallel sides DE and AB are in the ratio 1:3).

If AB and DE are distance *h* apart:

$$mgh + 4\,mgh = 12\,mg\,\bar{x}$$

Therefore $\bar{x} = \dfrac{5}{12}h$

The centre of gravity of these four particles is the same as the centre of gravity of the lamina ABED.

Therefore G is on the line joining the mid-points of AB and DE at a point which is $\frac{5}{12}$ of its length from AB.

EXERCISE 16b

Find position of the centre of gravity of each uniform lamina in questions 1–3

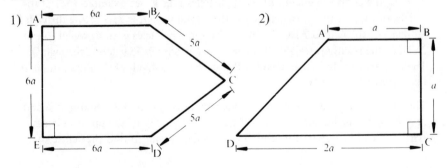

3)

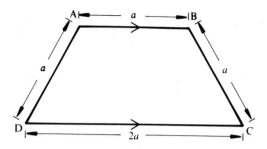

4) A uniform solid body consists of a cylinder of radius $2a$ and height $2h$ with another cylinder of radius a and height h with one plane face placed centrally on one plane face of the first cylinder. Find the position of the centre of gravity of the solid.

5) A uniform wire is bent to form an equilateral triangle. Locate its centre of gravity.

6) A uniform wire is bent to form two adjacent sides of a square and another uniform wire of three times the density of the first is bent to form the other two adjacent sides of the square. Find the position of the centre of gravity of the complete square framework.

7) A uniform lamina is in the form of a square of side 2 m and has a weight of W per square metre. Two particles each of weight W are attached to two adjacent vertices. Find position of the centre of gravity of the resulting body.

8) A uniform lamina is in the form of an isosceles right angled triangle. The equal sides of the triangle are of length 4 m and the lamina has a weight W per unit area. A particle of weight $3W$ is attached to the right angled vertex. Find the centre of gravity of the resulting body.

9) A uniform lamina consists of a square of side a with a circle of diameter a (made from the same material) glued on to the square so that a diameter of the circle coincides with one edge of the square. Locate the centre of gravity of the lamina.

10) A uniform lamina ABCD is in the form of a square and a uniform wire is placed round the circumference of the square. Locate the centre of gravity of the complete body.

The rectangular laminas illustrated in questions 11 and 12 are uniform and part of the lamina has been folded back upon itself to form a section of double thickness. Locate the centre of gravity in each case.

11)

12)

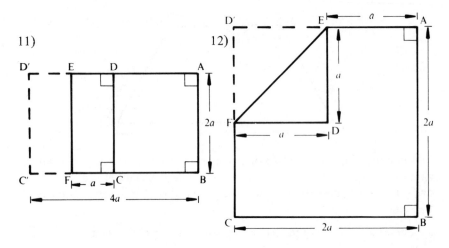

Find the position of the centre of gravity of the uniform laminas in questions 13–15.

13)

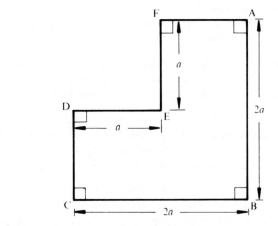

14)

15)

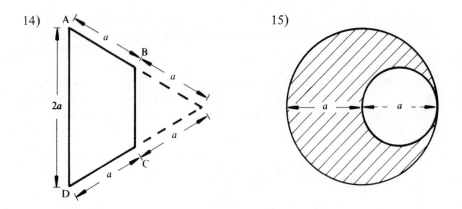

16) A uniform lamina is in the form of a rectangle of sides 2 m and 3 m. A circle of diameter 1 m with its centre equidistant from the sides of length 3 m, and $\frac{1}{2}$ m from one of the sides of length 2 m is cut from the lamina. Find the position of the centre of gravity of the remainder.

17) A uniform solid is in the form of a cylinder of radius a and height $2a$. A hole, whose cross section is a square of side a, is cut centrally from one end to a depth of a. Find the centre of gravity of the remainder.

CENTRE OF GRAVITY BY INTEGRATION

When a body cannot be divided into a small finite number of parts whose weights and centres of gravity are known, it may be divided into a large number of very small parts whose weights and centres of gravity are known. The position of the centre of gravity of the body can then be found by taking moments about suitable axes although the summing of the moments of the parts will have to be done by integration.

The examples which follow are particularly important because as well as demonstrating the use of integration to locate the centre of gravity they deal with objects which occur frequently in problems.

EXAMPLES 16c

1) Find the position of the centre of gravity of a *uniform semicircular lamina* of radius a.

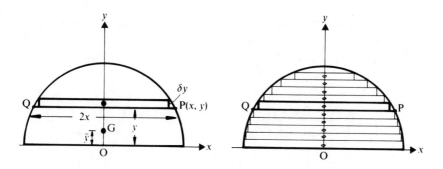

Let W be the weight per unit area of the lamina.
Taking axes as shown, as the lamina is uniform, its centre of gravity (G) lies on Oy.
If we divide the lamina into thin strips parallel to Ox, each strip is approximately a rod with its centre of gravity at its mid-point.
Considering the element PQ where P is the point (x, y) on the circumference of the lamina:

BODY	WEIGHT	DISTANCE OF CENTRE OF GRAVITY FROM Ox
Element PQ	$(2x\delta y)W$	y
Semi-circle	$\dfrac{\pi}{2}a^2\ W$	$\bar{y}$

$$\sum_{y=0}^{a}(2x\delta y W)y \simeq \left(\frac{\pi}{2}a^2W\right)\bar{y}$$

$$\therefore \int_0^a 2xy\,Wdy = \left(\frac{\pi}{2}a^2W\right)\bar{y}$$

P is a point on the circumference of a circle, centre O, radius a, therefore
$x^2 + y^2 = a^2$

$$\frac{4}{\pi a^2}\int_0^a y(a^2-y^2)^{\frac{1}{2}}dy = \bar{y}$$

$$\frac{4}{\pi a^2}\left[-\frac{1}{3}(a^2-y^2)^{\frac{3}{2}}\right]_0^a = \bar{y}$$

$$\frac{4a}{3\pi} = \bar{y}$$

2) Find the position of the centre of gravity of a *uniform solid right circular cone* of base radius a and height h

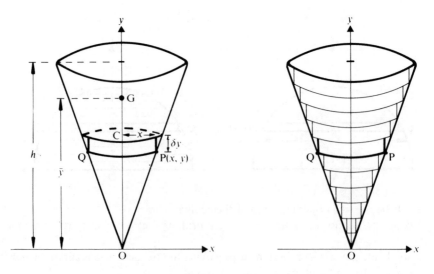

Let W be the weight per unit volume of the cone.
Taking axes as shown, as the cone is uniform its centre of gravity G lies on Oy.
If we divide the solid into sections parallel to its plane face, each section is

approximately a disc with its centre of gravity at its centre.

Considering the element PQ where P is the point (x, y) on the surface of the cone:

BODY	WEIGHT	DISTANCE OF CENTRE OF GRAVITY FROM Ox
Element PQ	$\pi x^2 \delta y W$	y
cone	$\frac{1}{3}\pi a^2 h W$	$\bar{y}$

$$\sum_{y=0}^{h} \pi x^2 \delta y \ Wy \simeq \frac{1}{3}\pi a^2 h \ W\bar{y}$$

Therefore $$\int_0^h \pi x^2 y \ W \, dy = \frac{1}{3}\pi a^2 h \ W\bar{y}$$

From similar triangles $$\frac{x}{a} = \frac{y}{h}$$

Therefore $$\int_0^h \frac{a^2 y^3}{h^2} \, dy = \frac{1}{3}a^2 h\bar{y}$$

$$\frac{3}{h^3}\left[\frac{y^4}{4}\right]_0^h = \bar{y}$$

Therefore $$\bar{y} = \frac{3h}{4}$$

3) Find the position of the centre of gravity of a uniform solid formed by rotating the section of the curve $y^2 = 4ax$ between $x = 0$ and $x = 2a$ about the x axis.

Let W be the weight per unit volume.

Taking axes as shown the centre of gravity G of the solid lies on Ox.

If we divide the solid into discs parallel to its plane face then each disc is approximately a cylinder with its centre of gravity at its centre.

Considering a typical element distant x from O and of thickness δx, its volume is $\pi\, y^2\, \delta x$

BODY	WEIGHT	DISTANCE OF CENTRE OF GRAVITY FROM Oy
Element	$\pi\, y^2 \delta x\, W$	x
Solid	$\Sigma\, \pi\, y^2 \delta x\, W$	$\bar{x}$

$$\sum_{x=0}^{2a} (\pi y^2 \delta x\ W)\, x \;\simeq\; \left(\sum_{x=0}^{2a} \pi y^2 \delta x\ W\right) \bar{x}$$

Therefore
$$\int_0^{2a} \pi\, W\, x y^2 dx \;=\; \bar{x}\ \int_0^{2a} \pi\, W\, y^2 dx$$

But $P(x, y)$ is a point on the curve $y^2 = 4ax$

Therefore
$$\int_0^{2a} 4ax^2 dx \;=\; \bar{x}\ \int_0^{2a} 4ax\, dx$$

$$\left[\frac{4a}{3} x^3\right]_0^{2a} = \bar{x}\ \left[2ax^2\right]_0^{2a}$$

Therefore
$$\bar{x} = \frac{4a}{3}$$

Therefore the centre of gravity lies on the line of symmetry at a point which is distant $\dfrac{2a}{3}$ from the plane face.

4) Find the position of the centre of gravity of a uniform lamina in the form of a *sector of a circle* of radius a subtending an angle 2α at the centre.

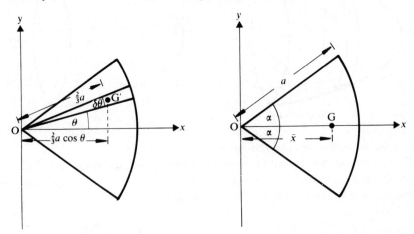

Let W be the weight per unit area of the lamina.

Taking axes as shown, the centre of gravity G of the sector lies on Ox.

If we divide the lamina into sectors, then each sector is approximately a triangle with centre of gravity G' at a distance $\frac{2}{3}a$ from O.

BODY	WEIGHT	DISTANCE OF CENTRE OF GRAVITY FROM Oy
Element	$(\frac{1}{2}a^2\delta\theta\,W)$	$\frac{2}{3}a\cos\theta$
Whole sector	$(\frac{1}{2}a^2\,2\alpha W)$	$\bar{x}$

$$\sum_{\theta=-\alpha}^{+\alpha} (\tfrac{1}{2}a^2\,\delta\theta\,W)(\tfrac{2}{3}a\cos\theta) \simeq (\tfrac{1}{2}a^2\,2\alpha\,W)\bar{x}$$

$$\therefore \quad \int_{-\alpha}^{+\alpha} \tfrac{1}{3}a^3\,W\cos\theta\;d\theta = a^2\alpha\,W\bar{x}$$

$$\frac{a}{3\alpha}\Big[\sin\theta\Big]_{-\alpha}^{\alpha} = \bar{x}$$

$$\frac{2a\sin\alpha}{3\alpha} = \bar{x}$$

The position of the centre of gravity of a semi-circular lamina can be obtained from this result by substituting $\alpha = \pi/2$, thus giving an alternative method for example 1.

5) Find the position of the centre of gravity of a uniform wire bent into the form of an *arc of a circle* of radius a and subtending an angle 2α at the centre.

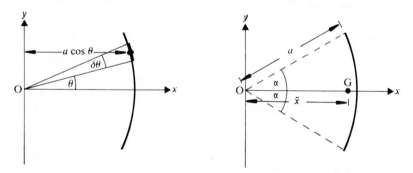

Let the weight per unit length of the wire be W.

Taking axes as shown the centre of gravity of the arc lies on Ox.

If we divide the wire into small arcs subtending an angle $\delta\theta$ at O then each element of length $a\delta\theta$ is approximately a particle.

BODY	WEIGHT	DISTANCE OF CENTRE OF GRAVITY FROM Oy
Element	$(a\,\delta\theta)\,W$	$a\cos\theta$
Arc	$(a\times 2\alpha)\,W$	$\bar{x}$

$$\sum_{\theta=-\alpha}^{\alpha}(aW\,\delta\theta)a\cos\theta \simeq (a\times 2\alpha\times W)\bar{x}$$

$$\therefore\quad \int_{-\alpha}^{\alpha} a^2 W\cos\theta\,d\theta = 2a\alpha W\bar{x}$$

$$\frac{a}{2\alpha}\Big[\sin\theta\Big]_{-\alpha}^{\alpha} = \bar{x}$$

$$\frac{a\sin\alpha}{\alpha} = \bar{x}$$

6) Find the position of the centre of gravity of a uniform hemispherical shell of radius a.

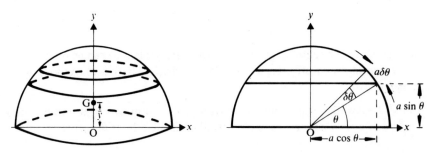

From symmetry the centre of gravity G of the hemisphere lies on Oy.
If we divide the hemisphere into rings parallel to its plane face then each ring is approximately a circular wire with its centre of gravity at its centre.
Considering the ring shown in the diagram, this is approximately a cylinder of radius $a\cos\theta$ and width $a\,\delta\theta$ and so has a surface area of $(2\pi a\cos\theta)\,(a\,\delta\theta)$
Let W be the weight per unit area of the hemisphere.

BODY	WEIGHT	DISTANCE OF CENTRE OF GRAVITY FROM Ox
Element	$(2\pi a^2\cos\theta\,\delta\theta)W$	$a\sin\theta$
Hemisphere	$2\pi a^2\,W$	$\bar{y}$

$$\sum_{\theta=0}^{\frac{\pi}{2}}(2\pi a^2\cos\theta\,\delta\theta\,W)\,a\sin\theta \simeq 2\pi a^2\,W\bar{y}$$

Therefore $\int_0^{\frac{\pi}{2}} 2\pi a^3 W \cos\theta \sin\theta \, d\theta = 2\pi a^2 W\bar{y}$

$$\frac{a}{2}\left[-\tfrac{1}{2}\cos 2\theta\right]_0^{\frac{\pi}{2}} = \bar{y}$$

$$\bar{y} = \frac{a}{2}$$

The temptation with this body is to take the ring of width δy and radius x, but this gives a bad approximation to its surface area as can be seen from the cross section through the shell.

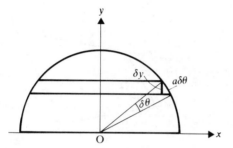

7) Find the position of the centre of gravity of a *uniform solid tetrahedron*.

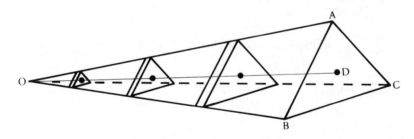

If we divide the tetrahedron into plane sections parallel to the base ABC these sections are approximately triangular laminas with their centres of gravity at the point of intersection of the medians. Thus the centre of gravity of the complete tetrahedron lies on the line joining O to D, the centre of gravity of the base ABC.

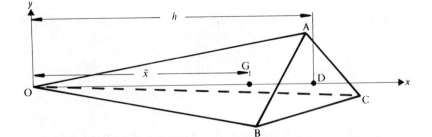

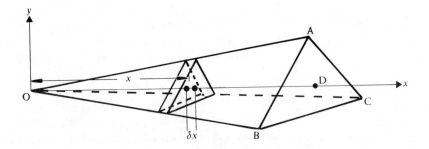

With axes as shown and taking the weight per unit volume as W, the height h, and the area of $\triangle$ ABC as A then:

BODY	WEIGHT	DISTANCE OF CENTRE OF GRAVITY FROM Oy
Element	$(x/h)^2 \, A W \, \delta x$	x
Tetrahedron	$\frac{1}{3} A h W$	$\bar{x}$

$$(\tfrac{1}{3}AhW)\bar{x} \simeq \sum_{x=0}^{h} \left(\frac{x^2}{h^2} A W \, \delta x \right) x$$

Therefore

$$\int_0^h \frac{x^2}{h^2} x A W \, dx = \tfrac{1}{3} A h W \bar{x}$$

$$\frac{3}{h^3} \left[\frac{x^4}{4} \right]_0^h = \bar{x}$$

$$\tfrac{3}{4} h = \bar{x}$$

Therefore

$$\text{OG} = \tfrac{3}{4} \text{OD}$$

Therefore the centre of gravity of a uniform solid tetrahedron lies one quarter of the way up the line joining the centre of gravity of the base to the vertex. We deduce the position of the centre of gravity of a uniform solid pyramid from this result. (The base of a pyramid can be any plane figure bounded by straight lines, the remaining faces of the pyramid are triangular and meet in a common vertex).

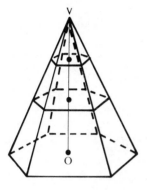

If the pyramid is divided into sections parallel to the base, as all such sections are similar it can be seen that the centre of gravity G of the pyramid lies on the line joining the vertex V to O, the centre of gravity of the base.

If the pyramid is divided into tetra-hedrons each having the same height as the pyramid, the centre of gravity of each tetrahedron is at a point which is $\frac{1}{4}$ of the height of the pyra-mid above the base.

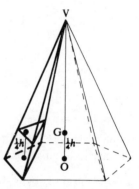

Therefore the centre of gravity of a uniform solid pyramid lies on the line joining the vertex to the centre of gravity of the base at a point which is $\frac{1}{4}$ of the length of this line from the base.

As the number of sides of a pyramid becomes infinitely large the sloping faces tend to form a curved surface and the pyramid becomes a cone. So the centre of gravity of a cone lies on the line joining its vertex to the centre of gravity of its base at a point $\frac{1}{4}$ of the length of this line from the base.

8) Find the position of the centre of gravity of a rod AB of length l where the weight per unit length of the rod at a point distant x from A is $(1 + x)g$.

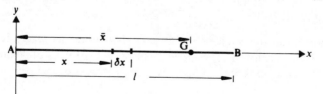

Consider a small section of the rod of length δx. This is approximately a particle of weight $(1 + x)g\,\delta x$.

BODY	WEIGHT	DISTANCE OF CENTRE OF GRAVITY FROM Oy
Element	$(1 + x)g\,\delta x$	x
Rod	$\displaystyle\sum_{x=0}^{l} (1 + x)g\,\delta x$	$\bar{x}$

$$\sum_{x=0}^{l}\{(1 + x)g\,\delta x\}x \simeq \left[\sum_{x=0}^{l}(1 + x)g\,\delta x\right]\bar{x}$$

Therefore

$$\int_0^l x(1 + x)g\,dx = \bar{x}\int_0^l (1 + x)g\,dx$$

$$\left[\frac{x^2}{2} + \frac{x^3}{3}\right]_0^l = \bar{x}\left[x + \frac{x^2}{2}\right]_0^l$$

$$\bar{x} = \left(\frac{3 + 2l}{6 + 3l}\right)l$$

EXERCISE 16c

1) Find the position of the centre of gravity of a uniform solid hemisphere by dividing it into discs parallel to its plane face.

2) A uniform right circular solid cone has a base radius of $3r$ and a height h. A cone of base radius r is cut from the top, find the distance from the plane face of radius $3r$ of the centre of gravity of the remaining frustum by dividing it into discs parallel to the plane faces.

3) Find the position of the centre of gravity of a uniform shell in the shape of the curved surface of a right circular cone of base radius a and height h.

4) Find by integration the position of the centre of gravity of a uniform wire bent into the form of a semicircle of radius a.

5) A solid sphere of radius a is cut into two sections by a plane. The maximum depth of the smaller section is h. Find the distance of the centre of gravity of the smaller cap from its plane face.

6) A section is cut from a uniform solid hemisphere of radius $3a$ by two cuts, parallel to its plane face. If the radii of the plane faces of the section are $2a$ and a find the distance of its centre of gravity from the larger plane face.

7) Find the position of the centre of gravity of a section similar to that in No.6 cut from a uniform hemispherical shell.

8) A rod AB is of length l and has a weight Wx per unit length at a point distant x from A. Find the distance of the centre of gravity from A.

9) A lamina in the form of a semicircle of radius a has a weight per unit area of Wr where W is a constant and r is the distance from the centre of the straight edge. By dividing the lamina into semicircular rings find the distance of the centre of gravity of the lamina from the centre of its straight edge.

STANDARD CENTRES OF GRAVITY

When the centre of gravity of a body is required in order to solve a problem it is useful to be able to quote the position of G (unless the problem specifically asks that the position of G be found). A list of the positions of the centres of gravity of some standard bodies follows:

UNIFORM BODY	POSITION OF CENTRE OF GRAVITY ON AXIS OF SYMMETRY.
Solid hemisphere	$\dfrac{3a}{8}$
Hollow hemisphere	$\dfrac{a}{2}$ from plane face
Arc subtending an angle 2α at the centre	$\dfrac{a \sin \alpha}{\alpha}$ from centre
Semicircular arc	$\dfrac{2a}{\pi}$ from centre
Sector subtending an angle 2α at the centre	$\dfrac{2a \sin \alpha}{3\alpha}$ from centre
Semicircular lamina	$\dfrac{4a}{3\pi}$ from centre
Solid $\begin{cases} \text{tetrahedron} \\ \text{pyramid} \\ \text{cone} \end{cases}$	$\dfrac{h}{4}$ from base
Hollow (without base) $\begin{cases} \text{tetrahedron} \\ \text{pyramid} \\ \text{cone} \end{cases}$	$\dfrac{h}{3}$ from base

Bodies Hanging Freely from One Point

Consider a body freely suspended from one point **A**:

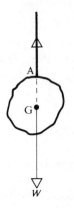

There are only two forces acting on the body: the tension in the tie at **A** and the weight acting through the centre of gravity G. If the body is in equilibrium under the action of these two forces then as the weight acts vertically downward so the tension must be vertically upwards and as there is no torque **AG** *must be vertical.*

Bodies Resting on Planes

Consider a body resting with its base in contact with a smooth horizontal plane.

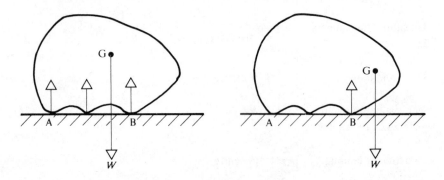

The forces acting on the body are its weight and the normal reaction forces at the points of contact between the body and the plane. These reaction forces are vertical and parallel, so the resultant normal reaction force must be between **A** and **B**, the extreme points of contact with the plane. If the body is resting in equilibrium the weight and the normal reaction force must be acting in opposite senses: therefore *the vertical through the centre of gravity must fall between A and B.*

If the vertical through G falls outside **AB** then there is a turning effect about **A** or **B** and the body will topple.

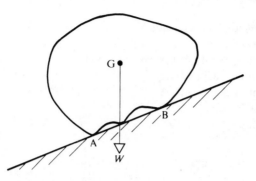

Similarly if the only forces on a body on an inclined plane are the contact forces between the body and the plane (which may include friction) and the weight of the body, then again the vertical through G must fall between A and B to prevent toppling.

EXAMPLES 16d

1) A thin uniform wire AB is bent into the form of a semicircle. Find the inclination of AB to the vertical when the wire is freely suspended from A.
A particle equal to the weight of the wire is now attached to B, find the new inclination of AB to the vertical.

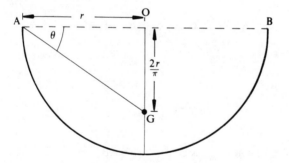

If O is the mid-point of AB and G is the centre of gravity of the wire then
$$OG = \frac{2r}{\pi}$$
When the wire is freely suspended from A, AG is vertical.
Therefore the angle between AB and AG is the angle made by AB with the vertical.
From the diagram $\tan \theta = \dfrac{2}{\pi}$

Therefore AB makes an angle $\arctan \dfrac{2}{\pi}$ with the vertical.

Let W be the weight of the wire and the particle attached to B.

If G' is the centre of gravity of the wire plus the particle then AG' is vertical.

Also the moment of the weight of particle about AG' is equal to the moment of the weight of the wire about AG':

i.e. $\qquad\qquad GC = BD$

From the diagram $BD = 2r \sin \alpha$

$$OE = r \tan \alpha$$

Therefore $\qquad EG = \dfrac{2r}{\pi} - r \tan \alpha$

so $\qquad GC = \left(\dfrac{2r}{\pi} - r \tan \alpha\right) \cos \alpha$

Therefore $\qquad 2r \sin \alpha = \left(\dfrac{2r}{\pi} - r \tan \alpha\right) \cos \alpha$

$$2 \sin \alpha = \dfrac{2}{\pi} \cos \alpha - \sin \alpha$$

$$3 \tan \alpha = \dfrac{2}{\pi}$$

$$\tan \alpha = \dfrac{2}{3\pi}$$

Therefore AB makes an angle $\arctan \dfrac{2}{3\pi}$ with AB.

2) A frustum of a uniform solid right circular cone is of height $3a$ and the radii of the plane faces are $2a$ and a. The frustum is freely suspended from a point on the edge of the smaller plane face and a particle is attached to the lowest point of this face so that the generator through the point of suspension is horizontal. If W is the weight of the frustum find the weight of the particle in terms of W.

We must first find the centre of gravity of the frustum.

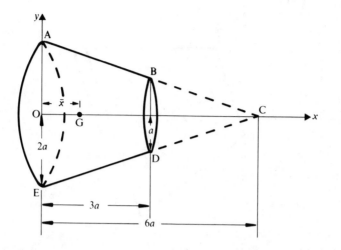

The complete cone and the cone removed are similar figures with corresponding lengths in the ratio 2 : 1.

Let W be the weight of the cone BCD.

BODY	WEIGHT	DISTANCE OF CENTRE OF GRAVITY FROM Oy
Cone ACE	$8W$	$\dfrac{6a}{4}$
Cone BCD	W	$\left(3a + \dfrac{3a}{4}\right)$
Frustum	$7W$	$\bar{x}$

$$8W\left(\frac{6a}{4}\right) = W\left(\frac{15a}{4}\right) + (7W)\bar{x}$$

Therefore $\quad \bar{x} = \dfrac{33}{28}a$

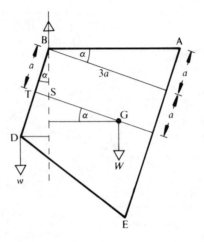

Let w be the weight of the particle at D.

From the diagram

$$\tan \alpha = \tfrac{1}{3}, \quad TS = a \tan \alpha, \quad TG = \frac{51}{28}a, \text{ therefore } SG = \frac{125}{84}a$$

$\overset{\frown}{B}$ $w \times 2a \sin \alpha - W \times \dfrac{125}{84}a \cos \alpha = 0$

Therefore $w = W \times \dfrac{125}{84} \times \dfrac{3}{2}$

$$= \frac{125}{56}W$$

3) A uniform lamina is in the form of a square ABCD of side $2\,m$. E is a point on AD such that $ED = x$ metre and the portion EDC is removed. Show that if the lamina is placed in a vertical plane with AE on a rough horizontal surface it will topple if $x > 3 - \sqrt{3}$. If $x = 1.5$ and the weight of the lamina is W find the least force which must be applied to the lamina to stop it toppling.

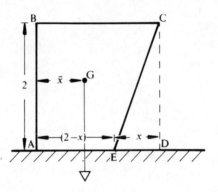

If G is the centre of gravity of the lamina, the lamina will rest in equilibrium in the position shown if the vertical through G falls within AE and it will topple about E if the line of action of the weight falls outside AE. So we must first find the distance of G from AB.

Let w be the weight per unit area.

BODY	WEIGHT	DISTANCE OF CENTRE OF GRAVITY FROM AB
Square ABCD	$4w$	1
$\triangle$ CDE	xw	$2 - \frac{1}{3}x$
remainder	$(4-x)w$	$\bar{x}$

$$(4w)\,1 - xw\,(2 - \tfrac{1}{3}x) = (4-x)\,w\bar{x}$$

$$\frac{12 - 6x + x^2}{3(4-x)} = \bar{x}$$

The lamina will topple if $\bar{x} > $ AE

i.e. if

$$\frac{12 - 6x + x^2}{3(4-x)} > 2 - x$$

$$x^2 - 6x + 6 > 0$$

$$[x - (3 + \sqrt{3})]\,[x - (3 - \sqrt{3})] > 0$$

i.e.

$$x > 3 - \sqrt{3}$$

When $x = 1.5$, $\bar{x} = \frac{7}{10}$

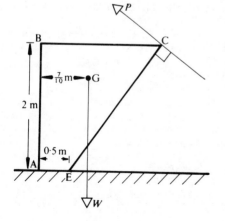

To stop the lamina toppling about E a force must be applied to the lamina to counteract the moment of W about E: the minimum force necessary to do this is the one whose line of action is at the maximum possible distance from E, i.e. a force applied at C perpendicular to CE.

$$\curvearrowright E \quad : P\sqrt{4 + \frac{9}{4}} - W \times \frac{1}{5} = 0$$

$$P = \frac{2W}{25}$$

Therefore the least force which will stop the lamina toppling is $\dfrac{2W}{25}$ applied at C in a direction perpendicular to CE.

4) A uniform solid consists of a hemisphere of radius r and a right circular cone of base radius r fixed rogether so that their plane faces coincide. If the solid can rest in equilibrium with any point of the curved surface of the hemisphere in contact with a horizontal plane find the height of the cone in terms of r.

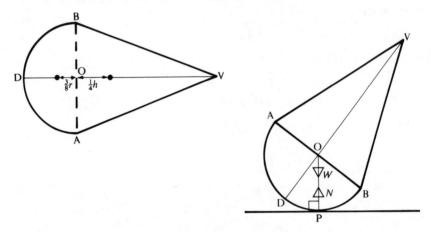

From symmetry the centre of gravity G of the solid lies on DOV.
The body can rest in equilibrium with any point P of the curved surface of the hemisphere in contact with a horizontal surface. The forces acting on the body are the normal reaction N and the weight W: these are both vertical forces so their lines of action coincide, therefore G also lies on PO. Therefore G is at the point O.

BODY	WEIGHT	DISTANCE OF CENTRE OF GRAVITY FROM AB
Hemisphere	$\frac{2}{3}\pi r^3 W$	$\frac{3}{8} r$
Cone	$\frac{1}{3}\pi r^2 h W$	$\frac{1}{4} h$
Complete body	$\frac{2}{3}\pi r^3 W + \frac{1}{3}\pi r^2 h W$	0

$$\tfrac{1}{4}h\left(\tfrac{1}{3}\pi r^2 h W\right) - \tfrac{3}{8}r\left(\tfrac{2}{3}\pi r^3 W\right) = 0$$

$$h = r\sqrt{3}$$

SUMMARY

The weight of a body is the resultant of the weights of its parts.

The centre of gravity of a body is the fixed point through which the line of action of its weight passes whatever the orientation of the body.

The position of the centre of gravity of a body is found by using the fact that the sum of the moments of the weights of its parts about any axis is equal to the moment of the weight of the body about the same axis.

MULTIPLE CHOICE EXERCISE 16

The instructions for answering these questions are given on page (xii).

TYPE I

1) Three particles of masses 1 kg, 2 kg, 1 kg are at the points whose position vectors are $\mathbf{i} + \mathbf{j}$, $2\mathbf{i} - \mathbf{j}$, $3\mathbf{i} + \mathbf{j}$. The position vector of their centre of mass is:

(a) $\frac{1}{4}(6\mathbf{i} + \mathbf{j})$ (b) $2\mathbf{i}$ (c) $\frac{1}{3}(6\mathbf{i} + \mathbf{j})$ (d) $8\mathbf{i}$ (e) $2\mathbf{i} + \mathbf{j}$.

2) A lamina is in the shape of an isosceles trapezium. The two parallel sides are 5 m apart and their lengths are 3 m and 2 m. The distance of the centre of gravity of the trapezium from the longer of the parallel sides is:

(a) $\frac{8}{3}$m   (b) $\frac{8}{15}$m   (c) 6 m   (d) $\frac{5}{2}$m   (e) $\frac{7}{3}$m.

3)

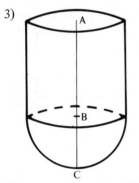

A child's drinking cup is made from a uniform solid hemisphere surmounted by a uniform hollow cylinder as shown in the diagram. If the cup is tilted on a horizontal surface it will always right itself (return to the position such that AC is vertical). The centre of gravity of the cup is:

(a) between B and C   (b) at A   (c) at B   (d) between B and A   (e) at C.

4)

The area between the curve $y = f(x)$, the x-axis and the ordinates 0 and x_1 represents a uniform lamina. The x coordinate of its centre of gravity is given by:

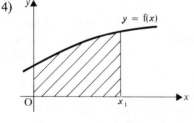

(a) $\dfrac{\displaystyle\int_0^{x_1} xy\,dx}{\displaystyle\int_0^{x_1} x\,dx}$
(b) $\dfrac{\displaystyle\int_0^{x_1} xy^2\,dx}{\displaystyle\int_0^{x_1} y^2\,dx}$
(c) $\dfrac{\displaystyle\int_0^{x_1} yx\,dx}{\displaystyle\int_0^{x_1} y\,dx}$
(d) $\displaystyle\int_0^{x_1} xy\,dx$
(e) $\dfrac{x_1}{2}$

5) A uniform solid cone has a base radius r and height $4r$. It rests with its plane face on an inclined plane which is rough enough to prevent sliding. The cone will topple when the inclination of the plane to the horizontal is greater than:

(a) $45°$ (b) arctan $\frac{1}{4}$ (c) arctan $\frac{3}{4}$ (d) $90°$ (e) arctan $\frac{1}{2}$.

TYPE V

6) The centre of mass of a non-uniform triangular lamina coincides with its centroid.

7) The centre of gravity of three particles of equal weight placed at the vertices of a triangle ABC coincides with the centroid of the triangle ABC.

8) A uniform wire is bent to form the sides of a triangle ABC. If the centre of gravity of the wire coincides with the centroid of the triangle ABC, triangle ABC must be equilateral.

9) The centre of gravity of a uniform lamina in the form of a quadrilateral coincides with the centre of gravity of four particles of equal weight placed at the vertices of the quadrilateral.

10) A uniform lamina in the form of a rectangle has one corner bent over as in the diagram. The centre of gravity of the resulting lamina lies on the diagonal AC.

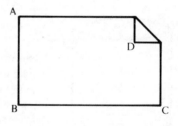

MISCELLANEOUS EXERCISE 16

1) A lamina ABCD is in the form of a trapezium in which DC is parallel to AB, AB $= 2a$, CD $= a$, AD $= h$ and the angle BAD is $90°$. Find the distance of the centroid of this lamina from the edges AD and AB.
The lamina is placed vertically with the edge BC on a horizontal plane. Find the minimum value of h for the lamina to remain in this position without toppling in its own vertical plane.   (AEB)

2) ABCD is a uniform square metal plate of side 3 m. Points E, F are taken on AB, BC respectively such that BE $=$ BF $= x$ m and the portion BEF is removed. Find the distance of the centroid of the remainder from AD. Show that the remainder cannot stand in equilibrium on AE as base with AD vertical unless
$2x^3 - 54x + 81 \geqslant 0$.
If the mass of the remainder is 14 kg, find in newtons the least horizontal force applied at C required to maintain it in equilibrium in this position when $x = 2$.
(Take g as 9.8 m/s^2).   (U of L)

3) A uniform circular disc of radius a and centre O is cut in half along a diameter. Show that the centre of mass of one of the halves is at a distance $4a/3\pi$ from O. A uniform circular cone of height a has a plane base of radius a. The cone is cut in half along a plane passing through its axis. Find the distances of the centre of mass of one of the halves from its plane faces.　　(WJEC)

4) The diagonals AC, BD of a uniform quadrilateral lamina ABCD of weight W cross at right angles at O where $2AO = OC = 2b$ and $OB = OD = a$. Find the position of the centre of gravity of this lamina.

The lamina is placed in a vertical plane with CD resting on a horizontal table and a particle of weight kW is attached at A. If $a < b\sqrt{2}$ and the lamina is on the point of toppling in its own plane, find the value of k in terms of a and b.　　(AEB)

5) Prove that the centre of mass of a uniform solid right circular cone, of height h and semi-vertical angle α is at a distance $\frac{3}{4}h$ from its vertex.

A frustum is cut from the cone by a plane parallel to the base at a distance $\frac{1}{2}h$ from the vertex. Show that the distance of the centre of mass of this frustum from its larger plane end is $11h/56$.

This frustum is placed with its curved surface in contact with a horizontal table. Show that equilibrium is not possible unless $45\cos^2\alpha \geqslant 28$.　　(JMB)

6) Prove that the centre of gravity of a uniform thin hemispherical shell of radius r is at a distance $r/2$ from the centre.

The body of a cocktail shaker consists of a frustum of a right circular cone, the diameters of the ends being 4 cm and 8 cm and the height 12 cm. The lid is in the form of a hemisphere of diameter 8 cm. Both the body and the lid are made out of the same uniform thin material. Ignoring overlap find the position of the centre of gravity of the cocktail shaker with its lid on.　　(AEB)

7) Show that the centroid of a uniform solid hemisphere of radius a is at a distance $3a/8$ from O, the centre of the plane face.

The figure below shows the central cross-section of a casting made in the form of a uniform solid hemisphere of radius a and centre O, with a hemispherical cavity of radius $\frac{1}{2}a$ and centre A. If this solid rests in equilibrium with its curved surface in contact with a horizontal plane, find the angle made by OA with the horizontal.

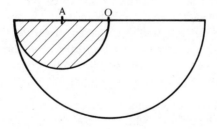

(U of L)

8) Prove that the centre of gravity of a uniform triangular lamina is the same as that of three equal particles placed at the vertices of the lamina.

A uniform lamina of weight W is in the shape of a quadrilateral ABCD. The diagonals AC, BD meet at P, where $AP < PC$, $BP < PD$, and O, R are points on AC, BD respectively such that $QC = AP$, $RD = BP$. By replacing triangles ABD, BCD by equivalent systems of particles, or otherwise, prove that the centre of gravity of the lamina is the same as that of a particle of weight $\frac{1}{3}W$ at Q and a particle of weight $\frac{2}{3}W$ at the mid-point of BD.

Deduce that the centre of gravity of the whole lamina is the same as that of the triangle PQR.   (Cambridge)

9) Show that the centre of mass of a uniform right circular solid cone of height h is at a distance $3h/4$ from the vertex.

A uniform solid spinning top has the shape of an inverted right circular cone of radius $3r$ and height $4r$ surmounted by a cylinder of base radius $3r$ and height $6r$. Find the position of the centre of mass of the spinning top and hence show that if it is placed with the curved surface of the cone on a horizontal plane, the top will topple.   (U of L)

10) In a uniform rectangular lamina ABCD the lengths AB and BC are $4a$ and $3a$ respectively and E is the point in CD such that $CE = \lambda a$. The portion BCE is removed. Find the distance of the centroid of the remainder from (i) AD, (ii) AB. When this remainder is freely suspended from the corner A, the line AM, where M is the mid-point of BE is vertical. Find the value of λ.   (AEB)

11) A heavy uniform circular disc centre X and radius R has a circular hole centre Y and radius r cut from it, where $r < R$. If $XY = R - r$, and the centre of gravity of the crescent-shaped lamina is at a distance $\dfrac{4r}{9}$ from X, show that $R = \dfrac{5r}{4}$.

The lamina is now suspended from a point on its outer rim lying on the perpendicular to XY through X. Find the angle which XY makes with the vertical. If the weight of the crescent is W, find the smallest weight which must be attached to the lamina to maintain XY in a horizontal position.   (U of L)

12) A triangle ABC with $AB = BC = 2a$ and $AC = 2a\sqrt{2}$ is drawn on a uniform lamina. A semi-circle is drawn on BC as diameter, on the opposite side of BC from A, and the area enclosed by the triangle and the semi-circle is cut out. The resulting lamina is suspended freely from B. Show that AB makes an angle $\tan^{-1}(2 + \frac{3}{4}\pi)$ with the vertical. A point P is taken on AB and the triangle APC is cut off. If the remaining lamina hangs with BC vertical, find the distance BP. (The centre of gravity of a uniform semi-circular lamina of radius a is at a distance $\frac{4}{3}(a/\pi)$ from the centre).   (Cambridge)

13) Show that the distance of the centroid of a uniform circular sector AOB from the centre O is $(2a\sin\theta)/3\theta$, where 2θ is the angle AOB and a is the radius. Find the distance from O of the centroid of the segment of which AB is the chord,

given that $\theta = \pi/6$. If a uniform lamina in the shape of this segment hangs at rest freely suspended from A, show that the tangent of the angle which AB makes with the downward vertical equals $(11 - 2\pi\sqrt{3})/(2\pi - 3\sqrt{3})$. (U of L)

14) A uniform lamina of weight W is in the shape of a triangle ABC with AB = AC = $2a$ and the angle BAC equal to 2α. The side AB is fixed along a diameter of uniform solid hemisphere of radius a, the plane of the lamina being perpendicular to the flat surface of the hemisphere. The body rests in equilibrium with a point of the curved surface of the hemisphere in contact with a horizontal table and with BC vertical. Show that the wieght of the hemisphere is $\frac{8}{9}W \cot \alpha$.
A particle of weight W is attached to a point P of AB where AP $= \frac{2}{3}a$ and the body now settles in equilibrium with the mid-point of BC vertically above A. Prove that $\tan \alpha = \frac{1}{2}$. (Cambridge)

15) Prove by integration that the centre of gravity of a uniform solid right circular cone of vertical height h and base radius a is at a distance $3h/4$ from the vertex of the cone. Such a cone is joined to a uniform solid right circular cylinder of the same material and of height h and base radius a, so that the plane base of the cone coincides with a plane face of the cylinder. Find the distance of the centre of gravity of the solid from the centre of the base of the cone.
When the solid hangs in equilibrium from a point A on the circumference of the base of the cone, the line joining A to the vertex of the cone is horizontal. Prove that $4a = h\sqrt{5}$ and find the angle of inclination of the steepest inclined plane on which the solid can stand in equilibrium on its plane face, the plane being sufficiently rough to prevent sliding. (JMB)

16) ABCD is a uniform square lamina of side $2a$ and weight W per unit area; E is the mid-point of CD and F is the point on AD distant $\frac{1}{2}a$ from A. The triangular portion DEF is removed.
Find the distances of the centre of gravity of the remaining area ABCEF from AB and BC. The portion ABCEF is suspended so that AC is horizontal, by vertical strings at A and C. Find the tensions in the strings. (SU)

17) Show that the centre of mass of a uniform solid right circular cone of height h is at a distance $\frac{1}{4}h$ from its base.
From a uniform solid right circular cylinder, of radius r and height h, a right circular cone is bored out. The base of the cone coincides with one end of the cylinder and the vertex O is at the centre of the other end. Show that the centre of mass of the remainder of the cylinder is at a distance $3h/8$ from O.
The bored-out cylinder is placed with O uppermost on a horizontal plane which is rough enough to prevent slipping; the plane is then gradually tilted. Show that the cylinder topples when the inclination of the plane to the horizontal exceeds $\tan^{-1}(8r/5h)$. (JMB)

18) Show by integration that the centre of gravity of a uniform solid hemisphere of radius r is at a distance $3r/8$ from the centre of its plane face.

Such a hemisphere is joined to a solid, uniform right circular cylinder, of different density but with the same base-radius r, so that the plane face of the hemisphere coincides with a plane face of the cylinder.

The resulting solid can rest in equilibrium, as shown with the hemi-
-spherical surface in contact with a
rough plane inclined at $30°$ to the
horizontal. The axis of symmetry
of the solid makes an angle of $30°$ with
the line of greatest slope of the inclined
plane. Find, in terms of r, the distance
of the centre of gravity of the solid
from the centre of the hemisphere.

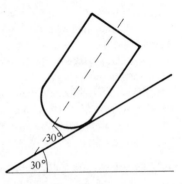

The solid can also just rest in equilibrium, without toppling, when placed with its plane face on the inclined plane, but if the angle of the inclined plane were to be slightly increased the solid would topple over. Prove that the height of the cylinder is $r(1 + \sqrt{3})$, and show that the ratio of the weight of the hemisphere to that of the cylinder is $4(\sqrt{3} - 1) : 11$.   (JMB)

CHAPTER 17

PROBLEMS INVOLVING RIGID BODIES

EQUILIBRIUM OF RIGID BODIES

There are several general considerations which are important when solving problems concerned with a rigid body which is in equilibrium under the action of a set of coplanar forces. These points have all been explained in previous chapters and a summary of the main points is set out below.

1) When a body is in equilibrium under the action of three forces, the lines of action of the forces are concurrent. Useful methods for calculating unknown forces are Lami's Theorem and the Triangle of Forces. When determining angles the cotangent rule for a triangle is useful (see below).

2) When a body is in equilibrium under the action of more than three forces, only three independent equations can be found by various combinations of resolving and taking moments for the forces acting on that body. If more than three equations are needed they must come from other sources, such as the mensuration of the figure, Hooke's Law etc.

3) The choice of axes about which moments are taken or the direction in which forces are resolved should be made with the following considerations in mind:
   (a) to keep the number of quantities in any one equation down to a minimum,
   (b) to eliminate as many as possible of the unknown quantities that are *not* required.

4) In problems involving frictional forces, when equilibrium is about to be broken by slipping, the friction is limiting at the point or points of contact at which slipping is likely to occur.

485

5) If equilibrium is about to be broken by topping the normal reaction force between the objects in contact acts through the point (or line) about which the body will topple.

Cotangent Rule for a Triangle

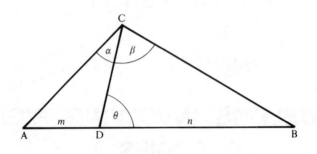

If, in any triangle ABC, D divides AB in the ratio $m : n$, there is a relationship between m, n and the angles in the triangle which is known as the *Cotangent Rule*. It can be expressed in two forms:-

$$(m + n) \cot \theta = m \cot \alpha - n \cot \beta$$

and $$(m + n) \cot \theta = n \cot A - m \cot B$$

(the proof of this rule can be found in any standard A Level Pure Mathematics textbook).

EXAMPLES 17a

1) A rod **AB** of length l has its centre of gravity at a point **G** where $AG = \frac{1}{4}l$. The rod rests in equilibrium in a vertical plane at an angle β to the horizontal, with its ends in contact with two inclined planes whose line of intersection is perpendicular to the rod.
If the planes are smooth and are equally inclined at an angle α to the horizontal show that $2 \tan \alpha \tan \beta = 1$.

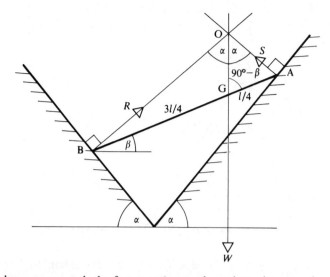

As the planes are smooth the forces acting on the rod are the normal reactions at A and B and the weight at G: as only three forces act on the rod, they must be concurrent. Let their lines of action meet at O.

In $\triangle$ OAB, $\hat{BOG} = \alpha$, $\hat{AOG} = \alpha$, $\hat{OGA} = 90° - \beta$.

Using the cotangent formula on this triangle:

$$\tfrac{3}{4}l \cot \alpha - \tfrac{1}{4}l \cot \alpha = (\tfrac{3}{4} + \tfrac{1}{4})l \cot (90° - \beta)$$

Therefore

$$\tfrac{1}{2} \cot \alpha = \tan \beta$$

Therefore

$$2 \tan \alpha \tan \beta = 1$$

2) A ladder whose centre of gravity is at a point of trisection leans in a vertical plane with one end on rough horizontal ground and the other end against a rough vertical wall such that the centre of gravity of the ladder is nearer to the wall. If the coefficient of friction at each point of contact is μ and the ladder is on the point of slipping when it is inclined at an angle θ to the vertical prove that

$$\tan \theta = \frac{3\mu}{2 - \mu^2}$$

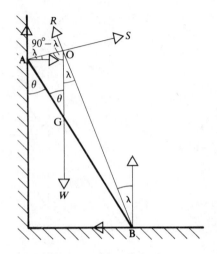

[When the ladder is on the point of slipping the end B will tend to slip away from the wall so the total reaction R at B makes an angle λ (where $\mu = \tan \lambda$) with the normal reaction at B as shown in the diagram. The end A will tend to slide down the wall so the total reaction S at A makes an angle λ with the normal reaction at the wall as shown in the diagram.]

Considering the total reactions at A and B the ladder is in equilibrium under the action of three forces: if the lines of action of these forces meet at O, in $\triangle$ AOB, G divides AB in the ratio 1:2. Using the cotangent rule on $\triangle$ AOB:

$$3 \cot \theta = 2 \cot \lambda - \cot (90° - \lambda)$$

$$3 \cot \theta = \frac{2}{\mu} - \mu$$

$$3\mu \cot \theta = 2 - \mu^2$$

$$\tan \theta = \frac{3\mu}{2 - \mu^2}$$

3) A cylinder of radius a and weight W rests in equilibrium between two rough planes which are both inclined at 30° to the horizontal. The axis of the cylinder is parallel to the line joining the two planes and the coefficient of friction at the points of contact with both planes is $\frac{1}{2}$. Find the least couple that must be applied to the cylinder to make it rotate about its axis if:

(a) the cylinder is uniform,

(b) the centre of gravity of the cylinder is midway along its length but distant $\frac{a}{2}$ from the axis on a horizontal diameter.

a)

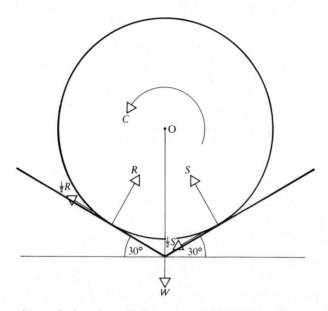

If a torque C is applied to the cylinder and friction is limiting then

$\rightarrow$: $R \sin 30° - \frac{1}{2}R \cos 30° - \frac{1}{2}S \cos 30° - S \sin 30° = 0$ (1)

$\uparrow$: $\frac{1}{2}R \sin 30° + R \cos 30° + S \cos 30° - \frac{1}{2}S \sin 30° - W = 0$ (2)

If the cylinder is to rotate about its axis then

$\curvearrowright$: $C - \frac{1}{2}Sa - \frac{1}{2}Ra > 0$ (3)

or $2C > (R + S)a$

Simplifying (1) and (2) we have:

$$2(R - S) - \sqrt{3}(R + S) = 0$$

and $(R - S) + 2\sqrt{3}(R + S) = 4W$

Hence $(R + S) = \dfrac{8\sqrt{3}\,W}{15}$

Then in equation (3) $2C > \dfrac{8\sqrt{3}}{15}Wa$

Therefore the least couple required is of magnitude slightly greater than $\dfrac{4\sqrt{3}}{15}Wa$

(N.B. It is always wise to assemble *all the equations* which are to be used before beginning their solution. The form of equation (3) suggests that $(R + S)$ be found from equations (1) and (2) rather than R and S separately. In practice this is a much shorter process.)

b)

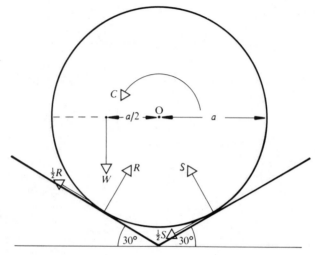

In this case the weight W has an anticlockwise moment about O, so the least couple that will make the cylinder rotate should have a moment about O in the same sense as W. Applying a couple of moment C about O and resolving vertically and horizontally we get equations (1) and (2) as found in (a).

$$\widehat{O} \quad : \qquad C + W\frac{a}{2} - \tfrac{1}{2}Sa - \tfrac{1}{2}Ra > 0$$

$$C > \tfrac{1}{2}a(R + S) - \tfrac{1}{2}aW$$

$$C > \tfrac{1}{2}a\frac{(8\sqrt{3}\,W)}{15} - \tfrac{1}{2}aW$$

$$C > \frac{aW}{30}(8\sqrt{3} - 15)$$

Therefore the least couple required has a moment slightly greater than $\dfrac{Wa}{30}(8\sqrt{3} - 15)$.

4) A uniform solid hemisphere of radius a rests with its curved surface in contact with a vertical wall. The hemisphere is supported by a light inextensible string of length a one end of which is fixed to the wall and the other end to the highest point of the plane face of the hemisphere. If the hemisphere is on the point of slipping down the wall when its plane face is inclined at arctan $\tfrac{4}{3}$ to the horizontal find the coefficient of friction between the hemisphere and the wall.

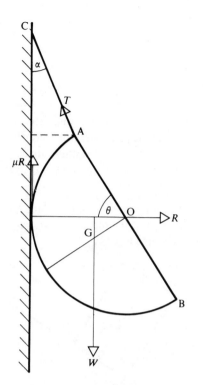

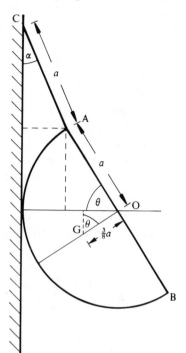

If α is the inclination of the string to the vertical,
from the diagram $a \sin \alpha + a \cos \theta = a$
i.e. $\sin \alpha = 1 - \cos \theta$

Now $\tan \theta = \dfrac{4}{3}$ therefore $\sin \alpha = \dfrac{2}{5}$

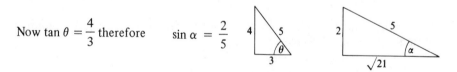

[The tension T in the string is not asked for in this problem so, by choosing
equations carefully so as to avoid T, only two equations will be necessary as only
two other unknown quantities (μ and R) are now involved.]

$\overset{\curvearrowleft}{C}$: $W(a - \tfrac{3}{8}a \sin \theta) - R(a \cos \alpha + a \sin \theta) = 0$ (1)

$\overset{\curvearrowright}{A}$: $\mu Ra \sin \alpha - Ra \sin \theta + W(a \cos \theta - \tfrac{3}{8}a \sin \theta) = 0$ (2)

(1) $\Rightarrow$ $7W = 2R(\sqrt{21} + 4)$

(2) $\Rightarrow$ $3W = 2R(4 - 2\mu)$

Hence
$$\frac{3}{7} = \frac{4 - 2\mu}{\sqrt{21} + 4}$$

Therefore
$$\mu = \frac{16 - 3\sqrt{21}}{14}$$

Certain types of problems concerning a rigid body involve a variable quantity (such as the inclination of a plane or a force) which, as it increases, will eventually reach a point where it disturbs the equilibrium of the body. This equilibrium can be broken either by sliding or by overturning. Each of these possibilities is analysed separately and the results compared.

5) A uniform solid cylinder of radius a and height $3a$ is placed with one plane face in contact with a rough inclined plane. The inclination of the plane is slowly increased. Show that equilibrium will be broken by sliding if $\mu < \frac{2}{3}$

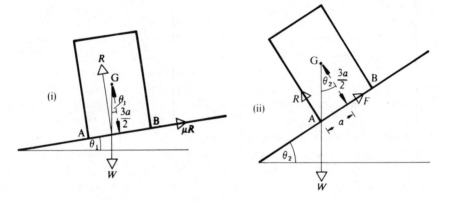

If the inclination of the plane is θ_1 to the horizontal and equilibrium is about to be broken by sliding (diagram (i)) then
resolving perpendicular to the plane:

$\nwarrow :$ $R - W \cos \theta_1 = 0$

resolving parallel to the plane:

$\nearrow :$ $\mu R - W \sin \theta_1 = 0$

Therefore $\mu = \tan \theta_1$

If the plane is inclined at θ_2 to the horizontal and equilibrium is about to be broken by overturning (diagram (ii)) then the line of action W passes through A

Therefore $\tan \theta_2 = \frac{2}{3}$

If sliding is to occur before overturning, $\theta_1 < \theta_2$

i.e. $\mu < \frac{2}{3}$

6)

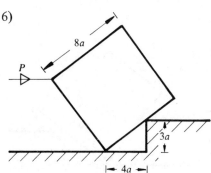

The diagram shows a cross-section through a uniform solid cube which is resting with an edge on the ground and its base on the edge of a step. The coefficient of friction between the cube and the ground and the cube and the step is $\frac{1}{3}$. An increasing force P is applied horizontally to the centre of the edge shown in the diagram. Determine how equilibrium will be broken.

Equilibrium will be broken either by the cube sliding at both points of contact or by the cube turning about the edge of the step.

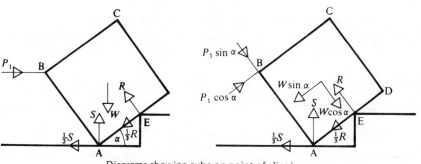

Diagrams showing cube on point of slipping.

If the cube slides, friction is limiting at E and A

→: $$P_1 - \tfrac{1}{3}S - \tfrac{1}{3}R \cos \alpha - R \sin \alpha = 0 \qquad (1)$$

↑: $$S + R \cos \alpha - W - \tfrac{1}{3}R \sin \alpha = 0 \qquad (2)$$

$\widehat{\text{A}}$: $$P_1 \cos \alpha.8a + W \cos \alpha.4a - W \sin \alpha.4a - R.5a = 0 \qquad (3)$$

(using the components of P_1 and W parallel to BC and BA)

$$(1) \Rightarrow \quad 15P_1 - 10S - 13R = 0$$

$$(2) \Rightarrow \quad 5S + 3R - 5W = 0$$

$$(3) \Rightarrow \quad 32P_1 + 4W - 25R = 0$$

$$\text{giving} \qquad P_1 = 3W$$

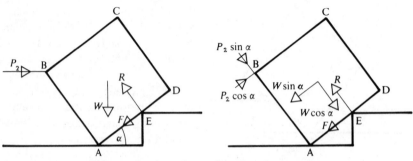

Diagrams showing cube on the point of overturning.

If the cube overturns about the step E, there will be no reaction at A.

$$\widehat{E} \quad : \quad P_2 \cos \alpha \cdot 8a - P_2 \sin \alpha \cdot 5a - W \cos \alpha \cdot a - W \sin \alpha \cdot 4a = 0$$

giving $P_2 = \dfrac{16}{17} W$

Now $P_2 < P_1$

Therefore the cube will tilt about the step before it slides.

EXERCISE 17a

1) A uniform rod rests in equilibrium with one end against a smooth vertical wall and the other end against a smooth plane inclined at $30°$ to the horizontal. Find the inclination of the rod to the horizontal.

2) A uniform ladder rests with one end against a rough wall and the other end on rough horizontal ground. When the ladder is inclined at $30°$ to the vertical it is on the point of slipping. The coefficient of friction between the ladder and the wall and the ladder and the ground is μ. Find the value of μ.

3) A smooth hemispherical bowl of radius a is fixed with its rim uppermost and horizontal. A smooth uniform rod of length $2l$ $(l > a)$ rests with one end inside the bowl and leaning on the rim. Find the length of the rod that overhangs the bowl.

4) A uniform cylinder of weight W rests with its axis horizontal and its curved surface in contact with a rough vertical wall and with a rough plane inclined at $45°$ to the horizontal. The coefficient of friction between the cylinder and wall and the cylinder and the plane is μ. If the radius of the cylinder is a, find in terms of a, μ and W the least couple that will rotate the cylinder.

5) A uniform solid cone of base radius a and height $2a$ is placed with its plane surface in contact with a rough plane which is initially horizontal. The coefficient of friction between the cone and the plane is $\frac{1}{4}$. Determine how equilibrium will

be broken if:

(a) the plane is gradually tilted so that its inclination to the horizontal increases slowly,

(b) the plane is kept horizontal but a gradually increasing horizontal force is applied to the cone half-way up its height.

6) A uniform sphere of radius a rests against a vertical wall supported by a string of length $2a$ fixed to a point of its surface and to a point of the wall.

(a) If the wall is smooth find the inclination of the string to the vertical.

(b) If the wall is rough and the sphere is on the point of sliding down the wall when the string is inclined at $30°$ to the vertical find the coefficient of friction between the sphere and the wall.

7) A uniform lamina in the form of a semicircle of radius a rests in a vertical plane with its curved edge in contact with a smooth vertical wall and rough horizontal ground. If the coefficient of friction between the lamina and the ground is $\frac{1}{6}$ find the inclination of its straight edge to the horizontal when it is on the point of slipping.

EQUILIBRIUM OF BODIES IN CONTACT

When two or more bodies in contact are in equilibrium under the action of a set of coplanar forces, the complete system is in equilibrium under the action of the external forces and each separate body is in equilibrium under the action of the forces acting on that body (these will include contact forces with other bodies). If the system is made up of two bodies, each body has three degrees of freedom so six independent equations may be derived for the system. The equilibrium either of the individual bodies or of the system as a whole may be considered when resolving or taking moments to form these equations.

It must be remembered that six is the *maximum* number of independent equations but that many problems can be solved by using fewer than six. This occurs when some of the unknown quantities are not required and in this case their introduction into any equation should be avoided if this is possible. Careful choice of axes when taking moments, and direction when resolving, helps to keep the number of unknown quantities (and therefore equations) to a minimum.

If there are more than two bodies in contact, the number of independent equations is three times the number of bodies in the system and these equations can be formed by considering the equilibrium of individual bodies or of two bodies or of any number of bodies, but the general principles mentioned above are important so that the number of equations is always kept to a minimum.

EXAMPLES 17b

1) A uniform rod of length $2a$ and weight W rests at an angle of $60°$ to the horizontal with one end hinged to a horizontal plane and resting on a cylinder of

radius a and weight W which is itself resting on the horizontal plane. The axis of the cylinder is perpendicular to the vertical plane containing the rod. The contacts between the rod and the cylinder and the cylinder and the ground are rough. Find the ratio of the frictional force to the normal reaction force at both points of contact.

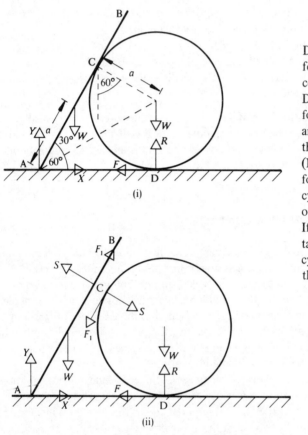

(i)

(ii)

Diagram (i) shows the forces acting on the complete system.
Diagram (ii) shows the forces acting on the rod and the forces acting on the cylinder.
(Note that the contact forces between rod and cylinder are equal and opposite).
If C is the point of contact of the rod with the cylinder
then $AC = a \cot 30°$
$\qquad = a\sqrt{3} = AD$

$\overset{\curvearrowright}{A}$ for complete system: $Wa \cos 60° + Wa \sqrt{3} - Ra \sqrt{3} = 0$ (1)

$\overset{\curvearrowright}{C}$ for the cylinder only: $(W - R)a \sin 60° + Fa \sqrt{3} \sin 60° = 0$ (2)

(1) gives: $R = \dfrac{(\sqrt{3} + 6)}{6} W$

$\left. \right\} \Rightarrow \dfrac{F}{R} = \dfrac{6 - \sqrt{3}}{33}$

Then (2) gives: $F = \tfrac{1}{6} W$

$\overset{\curvearrowright}{D}$ for the cylinder only: $Sa \sin 60° - F_1 a \sqrt{3} \sin 60° = 0$ $\qquad$ (3)

Therefore $\qquad\qquad\qquad\qquad\qquad \dfrac{F_1}{S} = \dfrac{1}{\sqrt{3}} = \dfrac{\sqrt{3}}{3}$

2) A uniform rod AB of length $2l$ and weight $2W$ rests with the end A on rough ground. The rod is supported at an angle of 45° to the horizontal by a string of length l attached to the end B. A small ring of weight W is attached to the other end of the string and the ring is free to slide on a rough horizontal wire. The rod and the wire are both in the same vertical plane and the coefficient of friction between the rod and the ground and the ring and the wire is $\frac{1}{2}$. The wire is at a height h above the ground. Find the two possible values of h for the system to be in limiting equilibrium.

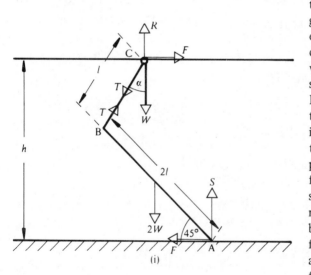

(i)

This is an example of a type of problem in which there are two possible geometric configurations, each leading to slightly different force systems which must be analysed separately.

Diagrams (i) and (ii) show the two possible positions of the string relative to the rod. In each position, resolving the forces acting on the system of the rod and ring horizontally, it can be seen that the frictional force acting on the rod at A is equal to the frictional force acting on the ring. Let the string be inclined at an angle α to the vertical.

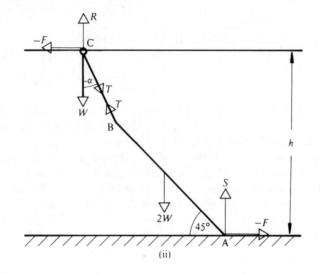

(ii)

Considering position (i):

For the forces acting on the system: ↑ $\qquad\qquad\qquad S + R - 3W = 0$ (1)

For the forces acting on the ring:

$B\!\!\uparrow$: $Wl \sin \alpha + Fl \cos \alpha - Rl \sin \alpha = 0 \qquad (R - W) \tan \alpha = F$ (2)

For the forces acting on the rod:

$B\!\!\uparrow$: $2Wl \cos 45° + F \cdot 2l \cos 45° - S \cdot 2l \cos 45° = 0 \quad W + F = S$ (3)

Solving equations (1), (2), (3) for S, R, F in terms of W and α:

$$R = \frac{W(2 + \tan \alpha)}{\tan \alpha + 1}$$

$$F = \frac{W \tan \alpha}{\tan \alpha + 1}$$

$$S = \frac{W(2 \tan \alpha + 1)}{\tan \alpha + 1}$$

$$\left.\begin{array}{l} \dfrac{F}{R} = \dfrac{\tan \alpha}{2 + \tan \alpha} \\[2mm] \text{and} \quad \dfrac{F}{S} = \dfrac{\tan \alpha}{2 \tan \alpha + 1} \end{array}\right\}$$
if no slipping is to occur at either point then
$$\frac{F}{R} \leqslant \tfrac{1}{2} \text{ and } \frac{F}{S} \leqslant \tfrac{1}{2}$$

Therefore $\left.\dfrac{F}{R} = \dfrac{\tan \alpha}{2 + \tan \alpha} \leqslant \tfrac{1}{2}\right\}$ and $\left\{\dfrac{F}{S} = \dfrac{\tan \alpha}{2 \tan \alpha + 1} \leqslant \tfrac{1}{2}\right.$

$$2 \tan \alpha \leqslant 2 + \tan \alpha \Bigg\} \quad \text{and} \quad \Bigg\{ \begin{array}{l} 2 \tan \alpha \leqslant 2 \tan \alpha + 1 \\ \text{this is true for all values of } \alpha \end{array}$$

$$\tan \alpha \leqslant 2$$

Therefore the system is in limiting equilibrium when $\tan \alpha = 2$ with the ring on the point of slipping.

$$h = 2l \sin 45° + l \cos \alpha$$

when $\tan \alpha = 2$

$$h = l\sqrt{2} + \frac{l}{\sqrt{5}}$$

$$= \frac{l}{5}(5\sqrt{2} + \sqrt{5})$$

Considering position (ii)

The frictional forces at A and C have been reversed with respect to diagram (i) and so has the inclination of the string to the vertical, but otherwise the directions of the other forces remain the same. Therefore the ratio of the frictional force to the normal reaction force at A and C can be found by using the equations derived for position (i) and replacing F by $-F$ and α by $-\alpha$

Now

$$\frac{F}{R} = \frac{\tan \alpha}{2 + \tan \alpha}$$

Therefore

$$-\frac{F}{R} = \frac{-(\tan(-\alpha))}{2 + \tan(-\alpha)} = \frac{\tan \alpha}{2 - \tan \alpha}$$

and

$$\frac{F}{S} = \frac{\tan \alpha}{1 + 2 \tan \alpha}$$

Therefore

$$-\frac{F}{S} = \frac{-(\tan(-\alpha))}{1 + 2 \tan(-\alpha)} = \frac{\tan \alpha}{1 - 2 \tan \alpha}$$

if no slipping is to occur at either point then

$$-\frac{F}{R} \leqslant \tfrac{1}{2} \quad \text{and} \quad -\frac{F}{S} \leqslant \tfrac{1}{2}$$

i.e.

$$\frac{\tan \alpha}{2 - \tan \alpha} \leqslant \tfrac{1}{2} \Bigg\} \quad \text{and} \quad \Bigg\{ \frac{\tan \alpha}{1 - 2 \tan \alpha} \leqslant \tfrac{1}{2}$$

$$\tan \alpha \leqslant \tfrac{2}{3} \qquad\qquad \tan \alpha \leqslant \tfrac{1}{4}$$

Therefore the system is in limiting equilibrium when $\tan \alpha = \tfrac{1}{4}$, with the rod on the point of slipping.

$$h = 2l \sin 45° + l \cos \alpha,$$

when $\tan \alpha = \frac{1}{4}$ $\qquad h = l\sqrt{2} + \dfrac{4l\sqrt{17}}{17}$

$$h = \frac{l}{17}(17\sqrt{2} + 4\sqrt{17})$$

EXERCISE 17b

1) A uniform rod AB of length $3l$ is freely hinged to level ground at A. The rod rests inclined at an angle of $30°$ to the ground resting against a uniform solid cube of edge l. Contact between the rod and cube is smooth and contact between the cube and the ground is rough. Find the reaction between the rod and cube and the coefficient of friction between the cube and the ground if the cube is on the point of slipping. The weight of the cube is twice the weight of the rod.

2) A uniform plank AB of length $4l$ and weight W rests with one end on level ground and leans against a cylinder of radius l such that the point of contact between the plank and cylinder is distant $3l$ from A. The cylinder is uniform and of weight W and rests on the ground with its axis perpendicular to the vertical plane containing the plank. Find the frictional force at each point of contact and if μ is the coefficient of friction at each point of contact show that for equilibrium to be possible $\mu \geqslant \frac{8}{21}$.

3) A uniform sphere of radius a and weight W has a light inelastic string of length a attached to a point on its circumference. The other end of the string has a small ring of weight W attached to it and the ring is free to slide on a rough horizontal wire. The sphere hangs below the wire and a horizontal force is applied to the sphere at a point level with its centre. The line of action of the force, the string and the centre of the sphere are all in the same vertical plane. If the coefficient of friction between the ring and wire is $\frac{2}{3}$ find the maximum force that can be applied to the sphere without upsetting equilibrium. Find also the inclination of the string to the vertical when the ring is about to slide along the wire.

4) Two uniform spheres of radius a and weight W rest on rough horizontal ground with their centres distant $2\sqrt{2}a$ apart. A third sphere of radius a and weight W is balanced on top of the other two spheres such that the centres of all three spheres lie in the same vertical plane. If the coefficient of friction, μ, is the same at all points of contact, find the minimum value of μ if equilibrium is to be maintained.

CONNECTED BODIES

When two bodies are connected by a smooth light hinge, which offers no resistance to their relative rotation, the bodies are said to be *freely jointed*.

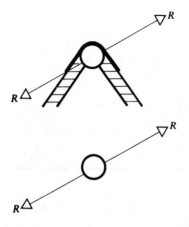

If the system is in equilibrium, the forces acting on the hinge are in equilibrium. Unless an external force acts at the hinge the only forces affecting it are the reactions which the two jointed bodies exert on each other. For equilibrium these forces are equal and opposite and so can be treated in the same way as contact forces.

(If an external force acts at the hinge however this is *not* the case).

Because the direction of hinge forces is usually unknown it is most convenient to show these forces in component form as in the diagram.

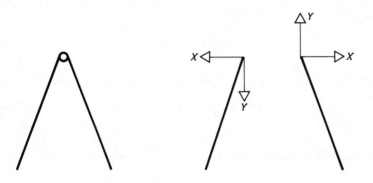

EXAMPLES 17c

1) Two uniform rods **AB** and **BC** of equal length but of weights W and $3W$ are freely jointed together at **B**. The rods stand in a vertical plane with the ends **A** and **C** on rough horizontal ground. If one rod is on the point of slipping when they are inclined at $60°$ to each other find the coefficient of friction μ between the rods and the ground, μ being the same at both points of contact. Find also the reaction at the hinge **B** when the rods are in this position.

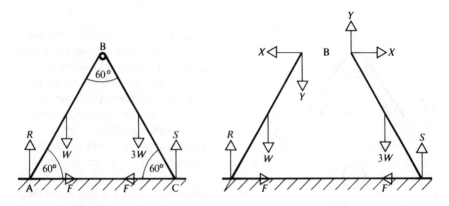

The greater of the ratios of frictional force to normal reaction at the ends A and C determines which rod is in limiting equilibrium.

It is clear from resolving horizontally for the whole system that the frictional forces at A and C are equal and opposite.

$\overset{\frown}{A}$ for whole system $S(4l \cos 60°) - 3W(3l \cos 60°) - W(l \cos 60°) = 0$

Hence $$S = \frac{5W}{2} \qquad (1)$$

$\overset{\frown}{C}$ for whole system $R(4l \cos 60°) - W(3l \cos 60°) - 3W(l \cos 60°) = 0$

Hence $$R = \frac{3W}{2} \qquad (2)$$

[Check: ↑ for whole system $R + S - 4W = \dfrac{3W}{2} + \dfrac{5W}{2} - 4W = 0$]

$\overset{\frown}{B}$ for BA alone $F(2l \sin 60°) + W(l \cos 60°) - R(2l \cos 60°) = 0$

Hence $$F = \frac{W\sqrt{3}}{3} \qquad (3)$$

Therefore at the end A $$\frac{F}{R} = \frac{2\sqrt{3}}{9} \leqslant \mu$$

and at the end C $$\frac{F}{S} = \frac{2\sqrt{3}}{15} \leqslant \mu$$

Therefore it is the rod AB which is about to slip and $\mu = \dfrac{2\sqrt{3}}{9}$

To find the reaction at B we must consider the equilibrium of either rod alone.

For the rod $AB \rightarrow$: $F - X = 0$ $X = \dfrac{W\sqrt{3}}{3}$ (4)

$\uparrow : R - W - Y = 0$ $Y = \dfrac{W}{2}$ (5)

Therefore the reaction at B has magnitude $\sqrt{X^2 + Y^2} = \dfrac{W}{2}\sqrt{\dfrac{7}{3}}$

Its line of action makes an angle α with the vertical where

$\tan \alpha = \dfrac{Y}{X} = \dfrac{\sqrt{3}}{2}$

(In this problem the maximum number of independent equations (six) have been used. Five of them are numbered and the sixth was used in stating initially that the frictional forces at A and C are equal).

2) Four uniform rods each of length l and weight W are freely jointed at their ends to form a framework. The ends of a light spring of modulus $3W$ are attached to two opposite vertices of the framework. The framework is freely suspended from one of the other vertices and when hanging in equilibrium takes the form of a square. Find the force in the spring and hence its natural length. Find also the reaction at the lowest joint.

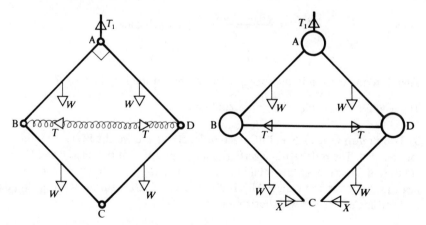

There are two points to consider in this problem:
(a) The external forces acting on the framework are symmetrical about the line AC, so the reactions at the hinges will also be symmetrical about the line AC. Thus the reaction at C will have no vertical component.

(b) There are external forces acting on the joints A, B and D, so the reactions on the ends of the rods at these joints will not be equal and opposite. It is usually possible to avoid introducing the internal forces at these joints into the analysis either by (1) considering the equilibrium of sections of the framework which include the complete joint at A, B or D, or (2) by choosing an axis through A, B or D when taking moments.

The forces at the joints A, B and D have not been entered but the joints have been circled to indicate that there are forces acting there.

For the forces acting on AB and BC:

$$A \quad : \quad W\left(\frac{l}{2}\cos 45°\right) + W\left(\frac{l}{2}\cos 45°\right) - Tl\cos 45° + X \cdot 2l\cos 45° = 0$$

$$W - T + 2X = 0 \quad (1)$$

For the forces acting on BC only:

$$B \quad : \qquad\qquad Xl\cos 45° - W\frac{l}{2}\cos 45° = 0$$

$$2X - W = 0 \quad (2)$$

Hence $$X = \frac{W}{2}$$

and $$T = 2W$$

The length of the spring BD is $\sqrt{2}l$

Let x be the natural length of the spring

Then $$2W = \frac{3W(x - \sqrt{2}l)}{x} \quad \text{(Hooke's Law)}$$

$$x = 3\sqrt{2}l$$

Therefore the tension in the spring is $2W$ and its natural length is $3\sqrt{2}l$

The reaction at the joint C is $\frac{W}{2}$ horizontally.

3) Two uniform rods AB and BC, each of length $2l$ and weight W are smoothly jointed at B. The rods rest in a vertical plane supported on two pegs P and Q which are distant l apart in a horizontal line. The coefficient of friction between each peg and the rod is $\frac{2}{3}$ and angle ABC is $90°$. If the rod AB is on the point of slipping find the angle it makes with horizontal.

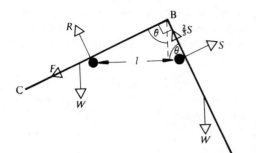

[In this problem the components of reaction at B are marked parallel to the rods since the majority of the other forces act in these directions.]

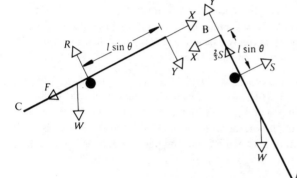

For the rod AB alone	$\circlearrowleft$ B	: $Sl \cos \theta - Wl \cos \theta = 0$	(1)
	$\uparrow$	$Y + \tfrac{2}{3}S - W \sin \theta = 0$	(2)
For the rod BC alone	$\circlearrowleft$ P	: $Wl(1 - \sin \theta) \sin \theta - Yl \sin \theta = 0$	(3)
From (1)		$S = W$	
From (3)		$Y = (1 - \sin \theta)W$	
In (2)		$\tfrac{2}{3}W = W \sin \theta - W(1 - \sin \theta)$	

Therefore $\sin \theta = \tfrac{5}{6}$ and the rod AB makes an angle of $56° 24'$ with the horizontal. (Only three of the possible six equations were used because R, F and X have not been introduced).

EXERCISE 17c

1) Two uniform rods AB and BC of equal weight W but of lengths a and $2a$ are freely jointed together at B. The rods stand in a vertical plane with their ends A

and C on rough horizontal ground, such that the angle ABC = 90°. If one of the rods is in limiting equilibrium find the minimum value of the coefficient of friction between the rods and the ground, it being the same for both rods. Find also the reaction at the hinge.

2) Two uniform rods AB and BC each of length l and weight W are freely jointed together at B. The rods rest in a vertical plane with A against a smooth vertical wall and C standing on rough horizontal ground. The coefficient of friction between the end C and the ground is $\frac{1}{2}$. Find the angle between the rods when they are resting in limiting equilibrium.

3) Three uniform rods each of length a and weight W are freely jointed together to form a triangle. The framework is freely suspended from one vertex. Find the reactions at the ends of the horizontal rod.

4) Four uniform rods of equal length l and weight W are freely jointed to form a framework ABCD. The joints A and C are connected by a light elastic string of natural length a. The framework is freely suspended from A and takes up the shape of a square. Find the modulus of the string.

5) Two uniform rods AB and BC of lengths l and $2l$ and of weights W and $2W$ are freely jointed together at B. The rods rest in a vertical plane with BC horizontal and resting on a rough peg at a point which is distant $\frac{3}{2}l$ from B. The end A of the rod AB rests on a rough horizontal plane such that the angle ABC is 120°. The coefficient of friction between BC and the peg and between A and the ground is μ. Find the minimum value of μ for equilibrium to be possible.

6) Three uniform rods AB, BC, CA of equal length a and weight W are freely jointed together to form a triangle ABC. The framework rests in a vertical plane on smooth supports at A and C so that AC is horizontal and B is above AC. A mass of weight W is attached to a point D on AB where AD = $a/3$. Find the reaction between the rods AB and BC.

MISCELLANEOUS EXERCISE 17

1) A uniform ladder of weight W rests with one end on rough horizontal ground and with the other end against a smooth vertical wall. The ladder is at an angle $\tan^{-1} 2$ to the ground and is in a vertical plane perpendicular to the wall. The coefficient of friction between the ladder and the ground is $\frac{1}{3}$. Find how far up the ladder a boy of weight $2W$ can climb without disturbing equilibrium. Find also the least horizontal force which must be applied to the foot of the ladder to enable the boy to climb to the top of the ladder without it slipping.

(AEB)

2) A uniform rod AB of length $2l$ and weight W is in limiting equilibrium at an angle of 45° to the horizontal with its end A on a rough horizontal plane and with a point C in its length against a horizontal rail. This rail is at right angles to

the vertical plane containing **AB**. The coefficient of friction between the rod and the plane is $\frac{1}{2}$ and between the rod and the rail is $\frac{1}{3}$. Calculate:

(a) the magnitude and direction of the resultant reaction at **A**,

(b) the length **AC**.

(AEB)

3) A uniform cylinder of radius a and weight W rests with its curved surface in contact with two fixed planes, each of which is inclined at $45°$ to the horizontal, the line of intersection of the planes being horizontal and parallel to the axis of the cylinder. A couple is applied to the cylinder in a plane perpendicular to its axis. If the angle of friction between the cylinder and each plane is $15°$ show that the cylinder will rotate if the moment of the couple exceeds $Wa/(2\sqrt{2})$.

(U of L)

4) The diagram shows a uniform circular lamina, of weight W, in contact with a smooth horizontal floor and a rough vertical wall, with its plane perpendicular to both. A force P is applied as shown at the point of the lamina furthest from the wall, in the plane of the lamina and at an angle θ above the horizontal. The coefficient of friction is $\sqrt{3}$. Show that for equilibrium to be possible θ must not exceed $60°$.

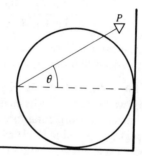

Show that, when $\theta = 30°$, W is the largest value of P for which equilibrium is possible. In this case and with this value of P a couple, whose moment is of magnitude G and whose sense is anticlockwise in the diagram, is applied to the lamina. Find, in terms of W and the radius a of the lamina, the greatest value of G for which equilibrium is possible.

(JMB)

5) Two points, **A**, **B** on a horizontal ceiling are at a distance $2a$ apart. A uniform rod **CD** of length a and weight W is suspended from **A** and **B** by two light strings **AC**, **BD**. A particle of weight $\frac{2}{5}W$ is attached to the rod at **D**, and the system hangs in equilibrium with the rod horizontal and **AC** inclined at an angle arctan $\frac{4}{3}$ to the horizontal. Prove that the rod is at a distance $\frac{6}{7}a$ below the ceiling, and find the inclination of **BD**. If both strings are elastic and of natural length $\frac{1}{2}a$, find the modulus of each string in terms of W.

(Cambridge)

6) A heavy thin rod **AB** of length l can be made to balance across a small smooth peg **C** when a weight $2W$ is suspended from **A**. Alternatively, it can be made to

balance across the peg with a weight $3W$ suspended from B. If the distance AC in the first case is the same as the distance BC in the second, show that the distance of the centre of gravity of the rod from A lies between $\frac{2}{5}l$ and $\frac{1}{2}l$. If the two equal distances above are each $\frac{1}{4}l$ and if the weights $2W$ and $3W$ are suspended from A and B respectively, find the distance from A to the peg when the rod balances.

(U of L)

7) A circular disc of radius a and mass m has its centre of mass G in the plane of the disc and at a distance $\frac{a}{2}$ from the geometric centre O. The disc rests in contact with a vertical wall and a horizontal floor, the plane of the disc being perpendicular to the wall and the floor, and the line OG makes an acute angle θ with the downward vertical:

(a) If the wall is smooth, the coefficient of friction between disc and floor is μ and no external forces except the weight of the disc are present, show that $\sin\theta \leqslant 2\mu$.

(b) If the coefficients of friction between disc and floor and between disc and wall are both equal to μ and if an additional vertical force $\mathbf{F}$ acts at O, show that the friction is limiting at both points of contact provided that

$$|\mathbf{F}| = mg\left| \left\{ 1 - \left(\frac{1+\mu^2}{\mu+\mu^2}\right)\frac{\sin\theta}{2} \right\} \right|$$

If $\mathbf{F} = \mathbf{0}$ show that the angle θ can be chosen so as to make the friction limiting at both points of contact, provided that $\mu \leqslant (\sqrt{2}-1)$.

(WJEC)

8) A uniform block in the form of a cube stands on a plane inclined at an angle α to the horizontal in such a way that four of its edges are parallel to the line of greatest slope. A gradually increasing horizontal force is applied to the uppermost edge of the block at right angles to it and in a vertical plane through the centre of mass of the block, in the direction which would tend to move the block down the plane. If μ ($> \tan\alpha$) is the coefficient of friction between the block and the plane, show that the block will tilt without sliding provided that

$$\mu > \frac{2\tan^2\alpha + \tan\alpha + 1}{\tan^2\alpha + \tan\alpha + 2}.$$

(Oxford)

9) A square table has a uniform top with sides of length $2a$. At the corners are four light straight legs, of height h, perpendicular to the top. The table rests in equilibrium on a rough plane, inclined at an angle α to the horizontal, with two of the edges of the top parallel to lines of greatest slope. If the coefficient of friction between the plane and the two lower legs is μ_1 and between the plane and the two upper legs is μ_2, show that $h\tan\alpha \leqslant a$ and
$\{2a - (\mu_1 - \mu_2)h\}\tan\alpha \leqslant (\mu_1 + \mu_2)a$.
If the slope of the plane is slowly increased and equilibrium is broken by slipping, show that $\mu_1 \leqslant a/h$.

(WJEC)

10)

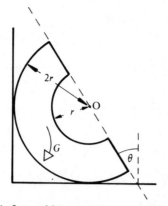

A uniform plane lamina is formed by removing a semicircle of radius r from a concentric semicircle of radius $2r$ as shown in the diagram. Prove that the centroid of the lamina is at a distance $(28r)/(9\pi)$ from the common centre O. (You may assume that the centroid of a semicircle of radius a is at a distance $(4a)/(3\pi)$ from its centre).

The lamina is placed with a curved edge in contact with both a rough horizontal plane and a smooth vertical plane, the plane of the lamina being perpendicular to both of these planes and its straight edges making an angle θ with the vertical where $\cos \theta = 3/4$. The weight of the lamina is W and the coefficient of friction between the lamina and the horizontal plane is $1/4$.

A couple of moment G is applied to the lamina in the sense shown in the diagram. Find, in terms of r, π and W, the range of values of G for which equilibrium is maintained.

(JMB)

11)

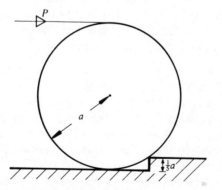

The diagram shows a uniform sphere of radius a and weight W resting on horizontal ground in contact with a step of height $\frac{1}{5}a$. The coefficient of friction between the sphere and the ground is $\frac{3}{4}$, and that between the sphere and the step is $\mu \ (< 2)$. A gradually increasing horizontal force P is applied to the highest point of the sphere in a direction perpendicular to the edge of the step. If equilibrium is broken by the sphere rotating about the step (rather than by slipping against the step and the ground) show that this happens when $P = \frac{1}{3}W$.

If on the other hand, equilibrium is broken by slipping, show that this happens when $P = \frac{1}{6}W(3 + \mu)/(2 - \mu)$.

For what range of values of μ is equilibrium broken by slipping?   (Cambridge)

12)

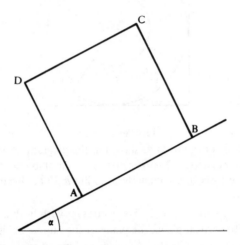

A uniform cube of weight W is placed as shown in the figure on a rough plane of inclination α ($< \frac{\pi}{4}$), the centre of mass of the cube lying in the plane ABCD and the edges perpendicular to this plane being horizontal. If the coefficient of friction between the cube and the plane is μ show that the cube cannot remain in equilibrium unless $\mu \geqslant \tan \alpha$.

If $\tan \alpha = 1/2, \mu = 2/3$ and a horizontal force P, steadily increasing in magnitude from zero is applied at D (acting from left to right and with line of action lying in the plane ABCD) show that equilibrium will be broken by the cube turning about the edge through B before it slides up the plane.   (U of L)

13) A rough heavy uniform sphere of radius a and centre C rests in contact with a horizontal floor at D. A uniform rod AB of length $2b$ and weight W is smoothly hinged at A to a fixed point on the floor and rests on the sphere, touching it at E. The rod is inclined at an angle 2θ to the horizontal (with $2b > a \cot \theta$) and is in the vertical plane ACD. If the contacts at D and E are rough enough to prevent slipping, prove that the mutual action and reaction at E act in the line ED and are each of magnitude $Wb \sin \theta (1 - \tan^2 \theta)/a$.

The angle of friction at both D and E is λ. Prove that if $\lambda > \theta$ the friction is not limiting at either contact but that if $\lambda = \theta$ then the friction is limiting at E and not at D.   (JMB)

14) Two equal uniform circular cylinders B and C lie on a horizontal plane, in contact with each other along a generator, and a third equal cylinder A lies on them with its axis parallel to theirs. Show that the frictional force between B and C is zero and that the frictional forces at the four other contacts all have the same magnitude, say F.

If, when the normal thrust between B and C is N_1, that between A and C is N_2, show that

$$F = \frac{W + 2\sqrt{3}\,N_1}{4 + 2\sqrt{3}}, \quad N_2 = \frac{(2 + \sqrt{3})\,W - 2\,N_1}{4 + 2\sqrt{3}},$$

where W is the weight of each cylinder. Hence find the smallest value of the coefficient of friction between the cylinders for which equilibrium is possible.

(JMB)

15) A uniform sphere of radius a and mass M rests on a rough horizontal plane. A uniform rod AB of length $2a$ and mass M rests with its end A on the plane and with a point of the rod (not B) in contact with the sphere. The rod and the centre of the sphere are in the same vertical plane. AB makes an angle of $60°$ with the horizontal.

(a) Show that the frictional force has the same magnitude at all three contacts.
(b) Show that the normal reaction between the rod and the sphere has magnitude $Mg/2\sqrt{3}$.
(c) If the coefficient of friction is the same at all three contacts and friction is limiting at one of them, show that it must be at the point of contact between the rod and sphere and find the coefficient of friction. (SUJB)

16) Two equal uniform circular cylinders B and C, each of weight W, rest side by side on a rough horizontal plane; their axes are horizontal and parallel and the cylinders are almost in contact. A third equal cylinder A is gently placed so as to rest in equilibrium upon them and in contact with each of them along a generator. Show, by considering the equilibrium of C, that the force of friction between C and A and that between C and the plane are equal in magnitude. Show also that their common magnitude is $\frac{1}{2}W(2 - \sqrt{3})$.

If μ is the coefficient of friction at all contacts, show that $\mu > 2 - \sqrt{3}$. (JMB)

17)

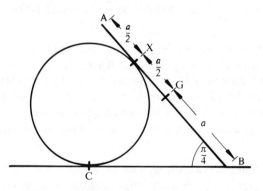

In the diagram, AB is a uniform ladder of length $2a$ and weight W, and G is the centre of mass of the ladder. The ladder is resting against a *fixed* cylindrical roller with circular cross-section whose axis is perpendicular to the vertical plane containing AB. The ladder is inclined at an angle $\frac{1}{4}\pi$ to the horizontal. The point of contact X of the ladder with the roller is at a distance $\frac{1}{2}a$ from the end A and the contact at X is smooth. Show that in order that equilibrium be maintained in this position the coefficient of friction μ at B must not be less than $\frac{1}{2}$.

A man of weight W stands at X and then starts walking slowly up the ladder. Show that if $\mu = \frac{11}{13}$ the ladder is on the point of slipping when he has moved a distance of $\frac{1}{4}a$.   (Oxford)

18) A uniform rod AB of weight W and length $2a$ is freely hinged at A to a fixed point on a rough horizontal table. A uniform rough sphere of radius a and weight $W\sqrt{3}$ rests on the table. The rod leans against the sphere so that the point of contact is at a distance $a\sqrt{3}$ from A and so that the rod and the centre of the sphere lie in a vertical plane. Show that the frictional force between the rod and the sphere is $\frac{1}{6}W$. If the coefficient of friction at each point of contact is μ find the smallest value of μ which makes equilibrium possible.   (Cambridge)

19) Two equal uniform planks AB, CD have their lower ends B, D on rough horizontal ground and their upper ends A, C resting against one another. A third equal plank is now inserted between A and C and is held in a vertical position, not touching the ground, by friction at A and C. The coefficient of friction at A and C is μ, that at B and D is μ', and AB, CD are inclined to the horizontal at an angle θ. Find, in terms of μ and μ' the limits between which $\tan\theta$ must lie. Deduce that equilibrium in this position is possible only if $\mu\mu' \geqslant 1/3$.   (JMB)

20) A uniform rod of weight $4W$ and length $2a$ is maintained in a horizontal position by two light inextensible strings each of length a attached to the ends of the rod. The other ends of the strings are attached to small rings each of weight W which can slide on a fixed rough horizontal bar with which the coefficients of friction are each $\frac{1}{2}$. Show that in equilibrium the distance between the bar and the rod cannot be less than $4a/5$, and find the greatest and least possible distances apart of the rings.   (U of L)

21) Two uniform rods, AB and BC are of the same length and weigh $3W$ and W respectively. They are smoothly jointed at B and stand in a vertical plane with A and C on a rough horizontal plane. The coefficient of friction between each rod and the plane is $\frac{2}{3}$. Equilibrium is about to be broken by one of the rods slipping on the plane. Find which rod will slip and calculate the angle each rod makes with the plane. Calculate also the reaction at the hinge B in magnitude and direction.   (AEB)

22) Two equal uniform rods AB, AC each of weight W and length $2a$ and a third uniform rod of weight W_1, are freely hinged together to form a triangle ABC in which the angle BAC is 2θ. The triangle hangs in a vertical plane from a smooth pivot at B, and a couple is applied to the rod AB so as to keep the triangle in equilibrium with BC horizontal and A below BC. Find:

(a) the moment of the couple, showing its sense in a diagram,

(b) the horizontal and vertical components of the forces exerted on AC by BC and AB.   (JMB)

23) Two uniform straight rods AB, CD are of mass $2m$, m respectively and of length $4a$, $2a$ respectively. The end C of CD is freely hinged to the mid-point of AB and the rods stand in equilibrium in a vertical plane with A, D resting on a smooth horizontal plane and the angle ACD maintained a right-angle by a light string connecting the mid-points of AC, CD. Find the tension in the string. A mass M is now attached to the end B of AB and the tension in the string is found to be four times the weight of CD. Show that $M = \frac{3}{4}m$, and find the magnitude of the reaction at C in this case.   (WJEC)

24) The diagram shows two uniform rods AB, BC, each of length $2a$ and weight W which are smoothly hinged at B. The end A is smoothly hinged to a point on a fixed rough horizontal bar, the hinges allowing the rods to rotate in the vertical plane through the bar. The end C is fastened to a small ring of weight w which is threaded on the bar.

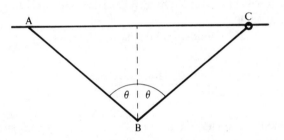

The rods are in equilibrium with each inclined at an angle θ to the vertical. Find the force of friction at C and the components of the reaction of the hinge on the rod AB at A.
Show that, when $W = 2w$ and the coefficient of friction at C is 1/4 the greatest possible distance AC in an equilibrium position of the rods is $12a/5$.   (JMB)

25)

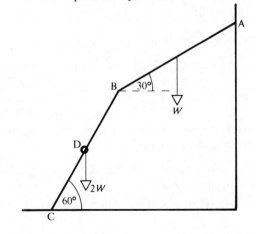

The diagram shows two uniform rods AB and BC smoothly jointed at B and resting in equilibrium with A against a smooth vertical wall, C on rough horizontal ground and BC passing through a fixed smooth ring at its mid-point D. The plane of the rods is perpendicular to both the wall and the ground. The rods have the same length; the rod AB is of weight W and inclined at $30°$ to the horizontal; the rod BC is of weight $2W$ and inclined at $60°$ to the horizontal. Prove that the reaction of the wall at A is $W\sqrt{3}/2$. Find:
(a) the reaction of the ring,
(b) the horizontal and vertical components of the reaction of the ground at C.
Show that the coefficient of friction at C must not be less than $3\sqrt{3}/11$.
(JMB)

26) A uniform rod AB of weight W_1 is attached at A to a fixed smooth pivot and is freely hinged at B to a uniform rod BC of weight W_2. The system is in equilibrium in a vertical plane with AB resting on a smooth peg P below the level of A and the end C of the rod BC on a smooth horizontal plane. The distance AP is x, the length AB is $2a$ and the acute angle which AB makes with the horizontal is θ. Prove that the force between the rods at B is vertical and equal to $\frac{1}{2}W_2$, and find the reaction at the peg.
If the reaction at A is horizontal, find its magnitude in terms of W_1, W_2 and θ, and prove that

$$x = \frac{2a\,(W_1 + W_2)\cos^2\theta}{2W_1 + W_2}$$

(JMB)

27) A rough circular cylinder of radius a is fixed with its axis horizontal. Two uniform rods AB and AC, each of weight W and length $4a$ are rigidly jointed together at A to enclose an angle of $60°$ and rest on the cylinder in a plane perpendicular to the axis with A uppermost and vertically above the axis. The coefficient of friction at each contact is $\frac{3}{4}$. A pull of magnitude P is applied at A in the plane ABC at an angle θ with the upward drawn vertical. If the rods are about to slip, show that

$$P(3\cos\theta + 4\sin\theta) = 6W$$

and find the magnitude and direction of the least possible pull.   (U of L)

28) Four uniform heavy rods AB, BC, CD, DA, each of weight W and length $2a$ are smoothly jointed at their ends to form a framework ABCD. The framework is suspended from A and is held in the shape of a square by a light inextensible string whose ends are attached to the mid-points of AD and CD. Find the horizontal and vertical components of the force exerted by AB on BC and show that the tension in the string is of magnitude $4W$.   (JMB)

29) Four equal uniform rods, each of weight W, are smoothly jointed together at their ends to form a rhombus ABCD. The rhombus is suspended from A and is maintained in equilibrium, with C below A and with $\angle DAB = 2\theta$ by a light string

connecting the joints at A and C. Find the horizontal and vertical components of the force exerted by AB on BC. Hence, or otherwise, find the tension in the string.

(JMB)

CHAPTER 18

FRAMEWORKS

A framework consists of a number of light rods which are smoothly jointed together at their ends to form a rigid construction.

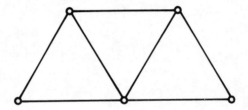

[Note that the term 'light' rods means that the weights of the rods are negligible compared to the loads that they bear.]

If a framework has external forces acting on it, each rod can perform one of two functions:

either they stop the framework from collapsing inwards

or they prevent the joints from flying apart.

A rod which is preventing a collapse exerts a push at either end, is described as a strut and is said to be *in thrust* or *in compression*.

rod in thrust

A rod which is preventing the framework from coming apart exerts a pull at either end, is described as a tie and is said to be *in tension*.

rod in tension

In both cases the forces exerted at the ends of the rod are equal and opposite. Consider a framework of three light rods smoothly jointed as shown in the diagram.

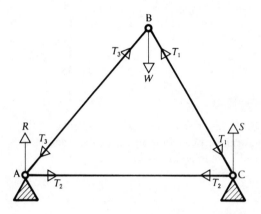

If the framework carries a load at B and is supported at A and C, then the forces acting at B are the weight W and the forces T_1 and T_3 in the rods BC and BA. The forces acting at A are the supporting force R and forces T_2 and T_3 in rods AC and AB. Similarly forces S, T_1, and T_2 act at C as shown.

If the whole system is in equilibrium *the forces acting at each joint are in equilibrium.*

As the forces in the rods occur in equal and opposite pairs they are internal forces, therefore *the external forces acting on the framework are in equilibrium.*

When solving problems it is not always as obvious as in the problem above which rods are in tension and which are in thrust, so we will adopt the policy of marking all rods in thrust so that negative answers indicate the rods which are in tension.

EXAMPLE

A framework consists of three light rods each of length $2a$ smoothly jointed together to form a triangle ABC. The framework is smoothly hinged at B to a smooth vertical wall and carries a weight W at A, and rests in equilibrium with C below B. Find the reaction at B and the force in each rod.

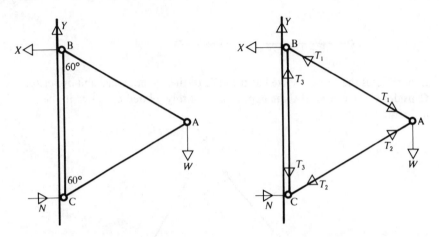

As the wall is smooth, the reaction at C is perpendicular to the wall. Take X and Y as the horizontal and vertical components of the reaction at B.

As the external forces are in equilibrium:

$\uparrow$ $$Y = W \tag{1}$$

$\rightarrow$ $$X = N \tag{2}$$

$\widehat{C}$ $$Wa\sqrt{3} = 2aX$$
$$X = W\sqrt{3}/2 \tag{3}$$

The reaction at B is $$\sqrt{X^2 + Y^2} = \frac{W}{2}\sqrt{7}$$

at $\arctan \dfrac{X}{Y}$ to CB $\qquad = \underline{\arctan \sqrt{3}/2 \text{ to CB}}$

Each joint is in equilibrium
Therefore considering the forces acting at C:
from (2) and (3) $$N = \frac{W\sqrt{3}}{2} \tag{4}$$

$\rightarrow$ $$N = T_2 \cos 30° \tag{5}$$

$\downarrow$ $$T_3 + T_2 \cos 60° = 0 \tag{6}$$

giving $$T_2 = W \tag{7}$$

$$T_3 = -\frac{W}{2} \tag{8}$$

Considering the forces acting at A:

$\rightarrow$ $$T_2 \cos 30° + T_1 \cos 30° = 0 \tag{9}$$

From (7) and (9): $T_1 = -W$

Therefore there is a <u>tension W in AB</u>, a tension $\dfrac{W}{2}$ in BC and a <u>thrust W in AC</u>.

EXERCISE 18a

1) Two light rods AB and BC of length $2a$ and a respectively are smoothly jointed at B. The ends A and C are smoothly hinged to a vertical wall with A above C such that BC is horizontal, and a weight W is hung from B. Find the forces in the rods and the reaction at C.

2) The light rods AB, BC and CA of lengths $4a$, $3a$ and $5a$ respectively are smoothly jointed at their ends to form a triangle ABC. A weight W is hung from B and the triangle is supported at A and C, with AC horizontal and B vertically above AC. Find the reactions at A and C and the force in each rod.

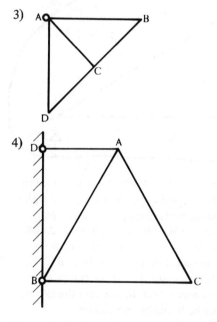

3) A framework consists of five light rods as shown in the diagram.
$AC = CB = CD = a$, $AB = AD = \sqrt{2}a$.
The framework carries a weight W at B and is smoothly hinged at A with D resting against a smooth support. Find the reaction at D and show that there is no force in AC.

4) A framework consists of four light rods as shown in the diagram.
$AB = BC = CA = 2a$, and $AD = a$.
It is smoothly hinged to a vertical wall at B and D with BC horizontal, and carries a weight W at C. Find the reaction at D and the force in each rod.

The method for finding the force in the members of a framework used in the previous section is not practical for a large number of joints as the number of equations involved is too large to handle easily. There are two alternative methods which simplify the work, one is graphical and the other involves calculation.

GRAPHICAL METHOD (BOW'S NOTATION)

This method is basically drawing a force polygon for each group of forces that are in equilibrium, i.e. the set of forces acting at each joint. A specialised notation makes this process easier by allowing each polygon to be superimposed on the previous one.

Consider a framework of three light rods as shown in the diagram.
The framework is smoothly jointed, rests in a vertical plane on smooth blocks at A and C and carries a weight 200 N at B. $AB = a$, $AC = 2a$ and $BC = \sqrt{3}a$.
As the supports at A and C are smooth the forces at A and C are vertical.

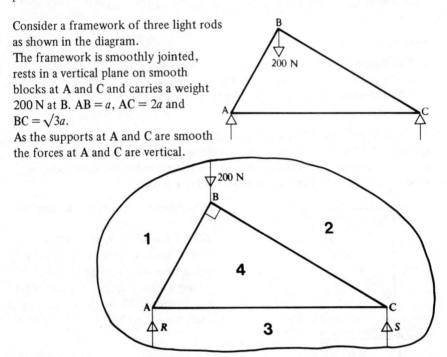

A boundary is drawn round the diagram and the line of action of each external force is drawn outside the framework and extended to the boundary so creating a number of closed spaces. Each space is numbered, so that each force line is identified by a pair of numbers, one on either side of the force. Thus 1, 2 identifies the load at B, 2, 4 the force in the rod BC and so on. Also each vertex of the framework can be identified by the set of numbers in the spaces around it. Thus 1, 4, 2 identifies the vertex B, 2, 4, 3 the vertex C and 1, 3, 4 the vertex A.
The force polygon for the external forces is drawn first. In this case the external forces are parallel so their magnitudes must be found by calculation:

$$\uparrow \qquad R + S = 200$$
$$(A) \qquad S \times 2a = 200 \times \frac{a}{2}$$

therefore $S = 50$, $R = 150$

and the force polygon is a straight line.

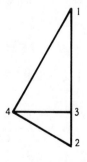

The polygon is numbered so that the figures which identify a force on the space diagram are used to represent the force on the polygon of forces. Therefore $\overrightarrow{1-2}$ represents the weight 200 N, $\overrightarrow{2-3}$ the force S and $\overrightarrow{3-1}$ the force R

The next stage is to draw the force polygon for one of the vertices where an external force acts and not more than two forces are unknown. Choosing A, we construct the triangle of forces for the forces acting at A. $\overrightarrow{3-1}$, representing R, is already drawn.

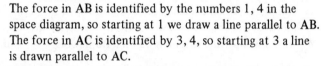

The force in AB is identified by the numbers 1, 4 in the space diagram, so starting at 1 we draw a line parallel to AB. The force in AC is identified by 3, 4, so starting at 3 a line is drawn parallel to AC.

The point of intersection of these two lines is the vertex 4. As the triangle 1, 3, 4 represents three forces which are in equilibrium, the vertices of this triangle taken in order indicate the directions of the forces;
as $\overrightarrow{3-1}$ represents R, $\overrightarrow{1-4}$ represents the force in AB acting at A: this is towards the joint A,

therefore the rod AB is in thrust.
Similarly $\overrightarrow{4-3}$ represents the force in AC acting at A, and thus is away from A. Therefore AC is in tension.
By measurement from the diagram: the force in AB is a thrust of 170 N
the force in AC is a tension of 86 N

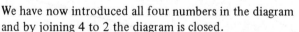

We have now introduced all four numbers in the diagram and by joining 4 to 2 the diagram is closed.
Thus 4, 2, 3 represents the triangle of forces for the joint C.
Now $\overrightarrow{2-3}$ represents the force S,
therefore $\overrightarrow{3-4}$ represents the force in AC at C
and $\overrightarrow{4-2}$ the force in BC at C: this is towards C.
Therefore BC is in thrust.
By measurement from the diagram the force in BC is a thrust of 100 N.

The triangle 1, 4, 2 represents the forces acting at **B**.
Thus the line $\overrightarrow{4-1}$ represents the force in the rod **AB** acting on the joint **B**,
but the line $\overrightarrow{1-4}$ (in triangle 1, 4, 3) represents the force in the same rod
acting on **A**.
So the line joining 1 and 4 represents a pair of equal but opposite forces. For
this reason the sense of each force along its line of action is *not* entered in the
construction.
Summarising: the steps to follow when using Bow's Notation are:
(1) Draw a boundary round the diagram and extend each external force line
    away from the framework to the boundary.
(2) Number each space. (Make sure there is only *one* number in each space).
(3) Draw the polygon of forces for the external forces (these may have to be
    calculated first).
(4) Superimpose the force polygon for a joint where an external force acts
    and not more than two forces are unknown.
(5) Superimpose the force polygon for each remaining joint until the figure is
    complete. (When choosing the order in which to do this, make sure that
    there are not more than two unknown forces at any joint selected).
We will now illustrate this method on a framework with more joints.

EXAMPLE

A framework consists of seven light rods smoothly jointed together as shown
in the diagram. The framework is smoothly hinged at **A** and carries a weight
of 400 N at **C**. It is held in a vertical plane with **BC** horizontal by a horizontal
force at **B**. Find the reaction at **A** and the force in each rod.

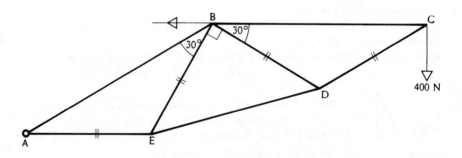

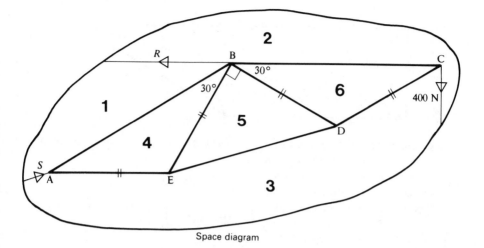

Space diagram

As the framework is in equilibrium under the action of three forces, their lines of action are concurrent: therefore the line of action of S is along AC (i.e. 15° to the horizontal).

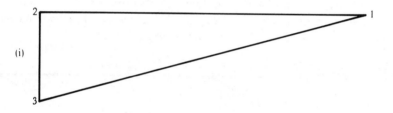

(i)

Diagram (i) shows the triangle of forces for the external forces: the line $\overrightarrow{3-1}$ represents S.

By measurement the reaction S at A is 1550 N at 15° to the horizontal.

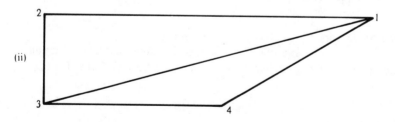

(ii)

In diagram (ii) the triangle of forces for the forces acting at A is superimposed. As S acts along $\overrightarrow{3-1}$, the force in AB (1, 4) acts along $\overrightarrow{1-4}$ and the force in AE is represented by $\overrightarrow{4-3}$.

By measurement, the force in **AB** is a <u>thrust</u> of 800 N
the force in **AE** is a <u>thrust</u> of 800 N.

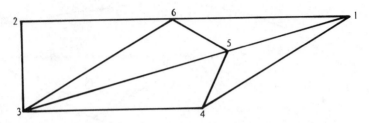

Superimposing the force triangles for the vertices E, then D, the figure is completed.
By measurement from the diagram:
the force in EB is a tension of 290 N
the force in ED is a thrust of 970 N
the force in DC is a thrust of 800 N
the force in DB is a tension of 290 N
the force in BC is a tension of 690 N.

METHOD OF SECTIONS

This method involves dividing the framework into two or more sections by
drawing a line through *not more than three rods*. The forces in the *cut* rods are
then treated as external forces for the section being considered. We will illustrate
this method by working through the example on page (522).

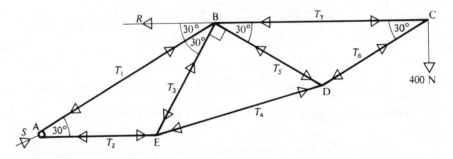

The external forces (R and S) are calculated first.
There are only three external forces acting: therefore their lines of action are
concurrent: therefore the line of action of S goes through C (i.e. $15°$ to the horizontal).

$\uparrow$
$$S \sin 15° = 400$$

Therefore
$$S = 1560 \text{ N}$$

$\rightarrow$
$$R = S \cos 15°$$
$$= 1490 \text{ N}$$

We now *cut* the framework through the rods AB, BE and ED and consider the section from **A** to this cut.

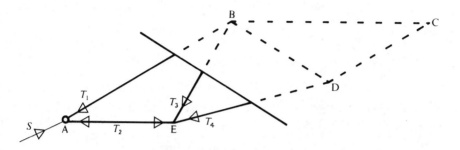

For this section T_2 is an internal force, so the section is in equilibrium under the action of external forces S, T_1, T_3, T_4. Let the length of the equal rods (AE, EB, BD, DC) be a.

Considering the equilibrium of these forces:

$\widehat{\text{E}}$ $\qquad\qquad T_1 \times a \sin 30° - S \times a \sin 15° = 0$

$\qquad\qquad\qquad \underline{T_1 = 800}$ (AB is in thrust)

$\widehat{\text{B}}$ $\qquad\qquad T_4 \times a \sin 45° - S \times \sqrt{3}a \sin 15° = 0$

$\qquad\qquad\qquad \underline{T_4 = 980}$ (ED is in thrust)

$\widehat{\text{A}}$ $\qquad\qquad T_3 \times a \sin 60° + T_4 \times a \sin 15° = 0$

$\qquad\qquad\qquad \underline{T_3 = -293}$ (EB is in tension)

The force in AE can be found easily by considering the equilibrium of the forces acting at A: $\leftarrow$ $\qquad\qquad T_2 + T_1 \cos 30° - S \cos 15° = 0$

$\qquad\qquad\qquad \underline{T_2 = 800}$ (AE is in thrust)

This leaves the forces in BC, BD and DC to be found. If we cut the framework through BC, BD and DE and consider the section from C to this cut we can find the forces in BC and BD.

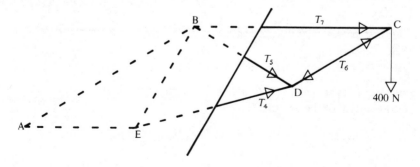

T_6 is an internal force, so this section is in equilibrium under the action of T_4, T_5, T_7 and the weight 400 N. Considering the equilibrium of these forces

$\widehat{D}$ $400 \times a \cos 30° + T_7 \times a \sin 30° = 0$

Therefore $T_7 = -693$ (BC is in tension)

$\widehat{C}$ $T_4 \times a \sin 15° + T_5 \times a \sin 60° = 0$

$T_5 = -293$ (BD is in tension)

The remaining force, T_6, can be found by considering the equilibrium of the forces acting at C: ↑ $T_6 \cos 60° = 400$

$T_6 = 800$ (DC is in thrust)

This method is particularly appropriate when forces in only a few rods are required. To find the force in one particular rod the framework is cut into sections by a line through that rod. It must be remembered, though, that the dividing line must not go through more than three rods whose forces are unknown.

EXAMPLE

The framework in the diagram consists of seven equal light rods, each of length $2a$, smoothly jointed together. The framework rests in a vertical plane on smooth supports at A and D so that BC is horizontal. Loads of 500 N and 200 N are carried at B and C. Find the forces in the rods AB, BC and CE.

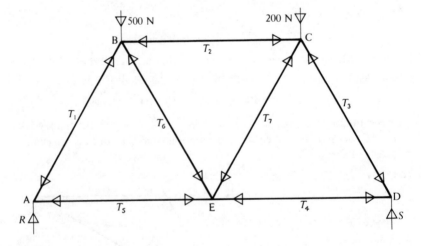

As the supports at A and D are smooth the reactions will be vertical: considering the equilibrium of the external forces:

↑ $R + S = 700$

↶A $S \times 4a = 500 \times a + 200 \times 3a$

Therefore $S = 275$ and $R = 425$

The stress in AB can be found easily by considering the equilibrium of the forces acting at A.

↑ (for joint A): $425 = T_1 \sin 60°$

Therefore $T_1 = 491$

The forces in BC and CE can be found by dividing the framework into two sections with a cut through BC, CE and ED and considering the left hand section. (Analysing the right hand section works just as well).

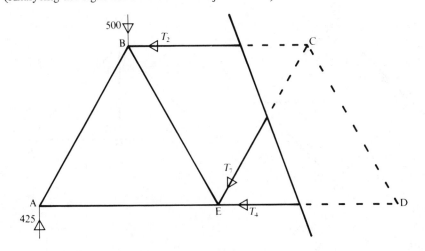

The forces in the rods AB, AE and BE are internal, so this section is in equilibrium under the action of the forces T_2, T_4, T_7, the reaction at A and the weight at B.

So for these forces: ↑ $T_7 \cos 30° + 500 - 425 = 0$

$$T_7 = -87$$

↶E $T_2 \times a\sqrt{3} + 500 \times a - 425 \times 2a = 0$

$$T_2 = 202$$

Therefore the force in AB is a thrust of 491 N,
the force in BC is a thrust of 202 N,
the force in EC is a tension of 87 N.

SUMMARY

If a framework of light rods which are smoothly jointed together is in equilibrium then:

(a) the external forces acting on it are in equilibrium,
(b) the forces at each joint are in equilibrium.
When solving problems on light frameworks always find the external forces first.
The method of sections will usually give the shortest solution unless the framework
consists of many rods *and* all the forces are required.

EXERCISE 18b

The frameworks in questions 1–4 consist of light rods smoothly jointed together
and rest in a vertical plane as shown. The frameworks are either supported by
forces as shown or smoothly hinged to a fixed support as shown. Find the external
forces and calculate the force in each rod.

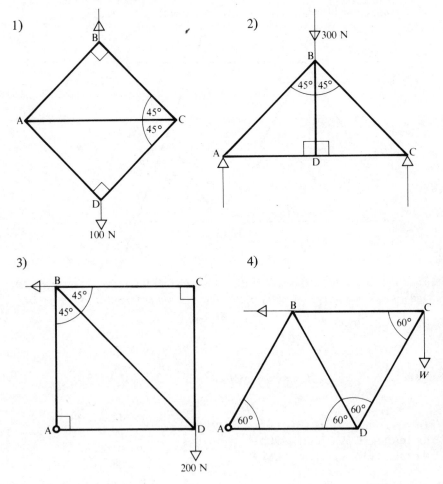

1)

2)

3)

4)

In questions 5 – 10 find the external forces and find the force in each rod graph-
cally.

5)

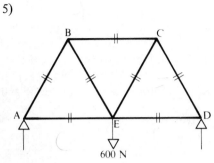

6)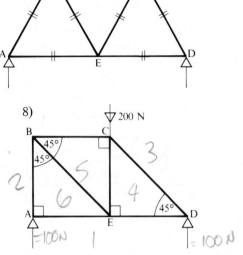

7)

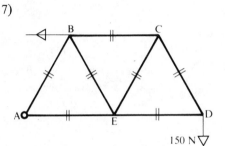

8)

9)

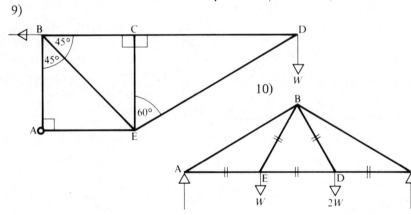

10)

11)

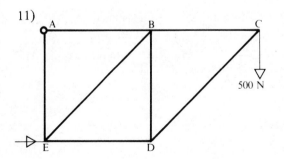

The framework in the diagram is smoothly hinged at A and is held with AE vertical by a horizontal force at E. The rods AB, BC, BD, ED, EA are all equal and ABC is horizontal. The framework carries a load of 500 N at C. Find the reaction at A and the forces in the rods ED, BD and BC.

12)

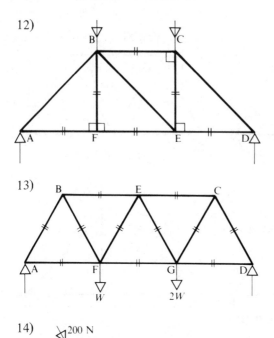

The framework ABCDEF is smoothly supported at A and D and carries weights of 200 N and 100 N at B and C. Find the forces in the rods FE, BE and CD.

13)

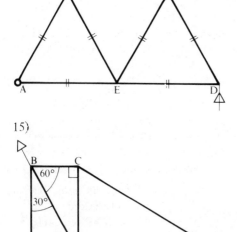

The framework BECDGFA is smoothly supported at A and D carries weights W and $2W$ at F and G. Find the forces in the rods BE, BF and FG.

14)

The framework ABCDE is smoothly hinged at A and is held with AD horizontal by a vertical force at D. A force of 200 N in the direction BE is applied at B. Find the stress in the rods BE, EC and ED.

15)

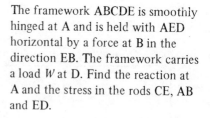

The framework ABCDE is smoothly hinged at A and is held with AED horizontal by a force at B in the direction EB. The framework carries a load W at D. Find the reaction at A and the stress in the rods CE, AB and ED.

16)

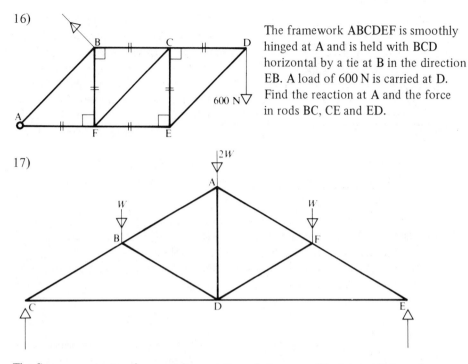

The framework ABCDEF is smoothly hinged at A and is held with BCD horizontal by a tie at B in the direction EB. A load of 600 N is carried at D. Find the reaction at A and the force in rods BC, CE and ED.

17)

The figure represents a framework consisting of nine smoothly jointed light rods. AD is vertical, CD = DE and the acute angles in the figure are either 30° or 60°. The framework carries weights $2W$ at A, W at B and W at F and rests on smooth supports at C and E. Determine the stresses in the rods, specifying which are tensions and which are thrusts. (Oxford)

18) The smoothly jointed framework ABCDEF consisting of eight light rods, is in equilibrium in a vertical plane, smoothly hinged to a vertical wall at A and B and carrying loads $2W$ and $3W$ at C and D respectively. The rod AF is of length a and all the other rods are of length $2a$. The rods AF, FE, BC and CD are horizontal. Calculate the force exerted by the framework on the wall at A. Find graphically, or otherwise, the forces in the rods CD, CE, CF and BC, stating which rods are in compression.

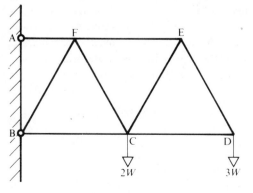

(AEB)

19)

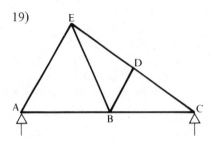

ABCDE is a smoothly pinjointed framework of light rods. AB = BC, CD = DE and the perpendicular from E to AC meets AC at a point one fifth of its length from A; the angle ACE = 36°. The framework is supported at A and C with AC horizontal and equal loads W are applied at E and D. Calculate (or find graphically) the supporting forces at A and C and find *graphically* the stress in each rod, indicating which rods are in tension and which in compression.

(SUJB)

20) A framework consists of three light rods AB, BC, CA of lengths $a, a\sqrt{3}, a$ respectively, smoothly jointed at A, B, C. The framework is suspended freely from A and carries weights $2W$ at B and W at C. Show that, in the equilibrium position with B below A, the thrust in the rod BC is $2W$ and that the tensions in the rods AB, CA are $2W\sqrt{3}, W\sqrt{3}$ respectively.   (Oxford)

21)

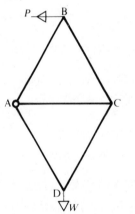

A light framework ABCD consists of 5 smoothly jointed rods of equal length. The framework carries a load W at D and is smoothly hinged and fixed at A. The framework is kept in equilibrium in a vertical plane with AC horizontal by a force P applied at B in a direction parallel to CA. Find the magnitude of P and the magnitude and direction of the reaction at A. Find, graphically or otherwise, the forces in the five rods and state which rods are in compression.

(AEB)

22) The light smoothly jointed framework shown is hinged to a vertical wall at A and B and carries a load of 400 N at D, AD being horizontal. AE = ED = AC = CD = 10 m, EC = 5 m, BC = 15 m. By means of a force diagram find the forces in all the members, stating which are in tension and which are in compression. Use the method of sections to check the magnitude of the force in AE.

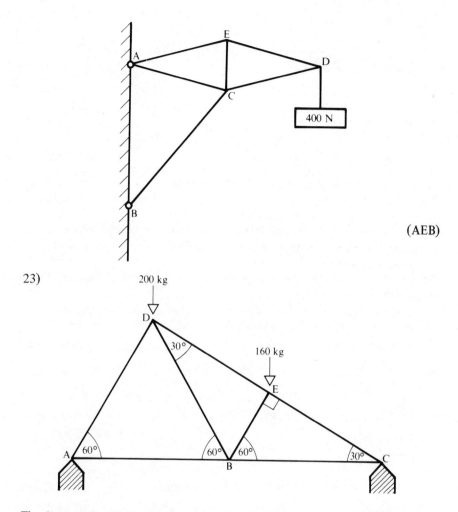

(AEB)

23)

The diagram shows a framework of seven freely jointed light rods resting on fixed supports at A and C, with AB and BC horizontal. Loads 200 kg, 160 kg are carried at D, E respectively. Find the reactions at A and C.

It is necessary to strengthen any rod subjected to a stress exceeding 250 kg. By drawing a force diagram, or otherwise, find which rods require strengthening, and state the magnitude and nature of the stresses in each of these rods.

(Cambridge)

24)

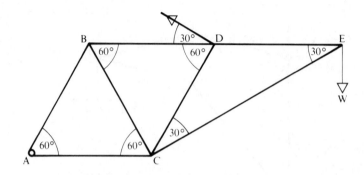

The diagram shows a framework of seven freely jointed light rods, AC, BD and DE being horizontal. The framework is freely pivoted to a fixed support at A and carries a load W at E, equilibrium being maintained by a rope at D in the direction shown. Find, in terms of W, the tension in the rope and the magnitude of the reaction at A.

By drawing a force diagram, or otherwise, find the magnitude and nature of the stress in the rod BC.

Find also the largest permissible value of W if no rod can withstand a stress exceeding 1000 kg. What is likely to happen if this value is slightly exceeded?

(Cambridge)

25)

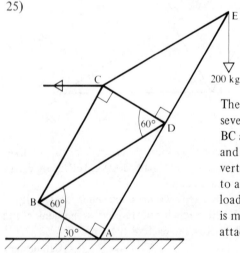

The diagram shows a framework of seven freely jointed light rods. AD, DE, BC are inclined at $30°$ to the vertical and AB, DC, BD, CE at $60°$ to the vertical. The framework is freely pivoted to a fixed support at A and carries a load of mass 200 kg at E. Equilibrium is maintained by a horizontal rope attached to C.

Find graphically or otherwise:
(a) the tension in the rope,
(b) the magnitude and direction of the reaction at A,
(c) the stresses in CB and CD, stating their nature.   (Cambridge)

APPENDIX

Quotable Formulae, Using Standard Symbols

MOTION WITH CONSTANT ACCELERATION

$$v = u + at$$
$$2s = (u + v)t$$
$$s = ut + \tfrac{1}{2}at^2$$
$$s = vt - \tfrac{1}{2}at^2$$
$$v^2 - u^2 = 2as$$

PROJECTILES

$$\ddot{x} = 0 \qquad\qquad \ddot{y} = -g$$
$$\dot{x} = u \cos \alpha \qquad \dot{y} = u \sin \alpha - gt$$
$$x = ut \cos \alpha \qquad y = ut \sin \alpha - \tfrac{1}{2}gt^2$$
$$y = x \tan \alpha - \frac{gx^2}{2u^2 \cos^2 \alpha}$$

SIMPLE HARMONIC MOTION

$$\ddot{x} = -n^2 x$$
$$\dot{x} = n \sqrt{a^2 - x^2}$$

$$x = a \cos nt$$

$$\text{Period} = \frac{2\pi}{n}$$

CENTRES OF GRAVITY

Uniform Body	Position of G on axis of symmetry
Solid hemisphere	$\dfrac{3a}{8}$ from plane face
Solid {pyramid cone	$\dfrac{h}{4}$ from base
Hollow hemisphere	$\dfrac{a}{2}$ from plane section
Hollow {pyramid cone (no base)	$\dfrac{h}{3}$ from base
Circular arc subtending an angle 2α	$\dfrac{a \sin \alpha}{\alpha}$ from centre
Circular sector subtending an angle 2α	$\dfrac{2a \sin \alpha}{3\alpha}$ from centre

PROPERTIES OF MOTION ETC.

Momentum	$= mv$
Kinetic Energy	$= \frac{1}{2}mv^2$
Potential Energy	$= mgh$
Elastic Energy	$= \frac{1}{2}\dfrac{\lambda x^2}{l}$
Work done	by a constant force $= Fs$ by a variable force $= \int F ds$
Impulse	of a constant force $= Ft$ of a variable force $= \int F dt$

ANSWERS

Exercise 1a – p. 4

1)a) 6 m, $3\sqrt{3}$ m in the direction AC
   b) 10.5 m, 5.41 m from A to the midpoint of DE
2) $3\sqrt{3}$ m in the direction AC
3)a) 2 ms^{-1} along DE
   b) 2 ms^{-1} along AB
4) No
5) The straight sections AB and CD.

Exercise 2a – p. 18

1) $3\sqrt{2}$ m NE
2)i) $\overrightarrow{AC}$ ii) $\overrightarrow{BD}$ iii) $\overrightarrow{AD}$ iv) $\overrightarrow{DB}$
3) $\mathbf{a}$; $\mathbf{b} - \mathbf{a}$; $2(\mathbf{b} - \mathbf{a})$
6) (ii),   (iii),   (v),   (vi)

Exercise 2b – p. 23

1)a) 5.64 N, 2.0 N   b) 10 ms^{-1}, 17.3 ms^{-1} c) 6.4 N, 4.8 N
2) 2 N,   3.5 N
3) $P \sin 20°$, $W \cos 20°$, T; $P \cos 20°$, $W \sin 20°$
4) $4\mathbf{i}$; $3\sqrt{3}\mathbf{i} + 3\mathbf{j}$; $3\mathbf{j}$; $-2\mathbf{i}$; $-2\sqrt{2}\mathbf{i} - 2\sqrt{2}\mathbf{j}$
6) East: 7.07, -6 North: 7.07, 24

Exercise 2c – p. 28

1) 5 N at arctan $\frac{3}{4}$ to 4 N force.
2) 14 N at 21° 45′ to 10 N force.
3) ± 5;   67° 23′, 112° 37′
4) 445 kmh^{-1}

5)a) 75° 31′   b) 138° 36′
6)a) 15   b) 11.5
7)a) 104° 29′   b) 0   c) 180°

Exercise 2d – p. 34

1) $\sqrt{7}$ N at arctan $3\sqrt{3}$ with BA
2) $9\mathbf{i} + 5\mathbf{j}$
3) 292 N at 6° to centre rope
4) 261 m N 54° 54′ W
5) $\sqrt{3}\mathbf{i} \pm 6\mathbf{j}$
6) 7.1 kmh^{-1} S 46° E
7) 139 kmh^{-1}
8)a) 11.95 N at 3° 30′ to AD
   b) 12.13 N at 64° 51′ to AB

Multiple Choice Exercise 2 – p. 36

1) c   2) c   3) a   4) d
5) c   6) a   7) c, d   8) b, d
9) a c   10) A   11) B   12) E
13) c   14) I   15) A   16) I
17) F   18) T   19) F   20) F
21) F

Miscellaneous Exercise 2 – p. 38

1) 24 N;   36° 52′
3) 8.1 N   4) $3\mathbf{i} - 3\mathbf{j}$
5) 6° 44′
6)i) 8 ms^{-1} South West   ii) 4.3 ms^{-1} N 48° W   iii) 21 ms^{-1} S 82° 17′ W
7)a) (i) $\overrightarrow{AC}$ (ii) $\overrightarrow{EB}$
8) $\overrightarrow{BD}$

10) $2(\sqrt{3}-1)$ N

11) $P\sqrt{39}$ at $\arctan\sqrt{3/7}$ to AE

12) $-8\mathbf{i}+10\mathbf{j}$

13) $\dfrac{7\sqrt{3}-2}{13}$

14)a) $\sqrt{3}P$　b) $150°$　c) $120°,60°$

15) $5.14P$ at $76°\ 30'$ to Ox

16) 17.03 knots; 1 hour 34 minutes

17) Mid-point of XY

18) AB and CD bisect each other.

Exercise 3a — p. 44

1) $-2\sqrt{2};2$

2) 8.7 N at $46°40'$ to BA

3) 1.15 N or 0.35 N.

Exercise 3b — p. 52

1)a) 26 N; 10 N　b) 25.5 N; 8.7 N

2) 5 N　3) 10 N; $22°\ 37'$

4)a) $30°$　b) $18°\ 26'$

5)a) 5 N　b) 5.77 N　6) $W;\sqrt{2}W$

7) $12\sqrt{3}$ N; 24 N

8) $W/\sqrt{2}$ perp. to BC where W is the weight of the rod.

Exercise 3c — p. 61

1)a) 0.364　b) $2(6+5\sqrt{3})$ N　c) $15°$
  d) 2.8 N at $13°\ 26'$ to the horizontal

2)a) 5·72 N　b) 19·34 N　3) 1009 N

4) $61°\ 49'$

5)a) 1 N, no　b) 4 N, no　c) 4 N, yes

6) $\frac{3}{4}a; W/\sqrt{3}$　7) $60°$　8) 173.2 N; $60°$
  or 86.6 N; $19°\ 5'$

Multiple Choice Exercise 3 — p. 62

1) c	2) b	3) b	4) d
5) d	6) b d	7) a b	8) c
9) a d	10) B	11) B	12) B
13) E	14) A	15) I	16) a
17) I	18) a c	19) F	20) F
21) T	22) F	23) T	

Miscellaneous Exercise 3 — p. 65

1) $\sqrt{10}$ units at $18°\ 26'$ to BA; $\sqrt{10}$ units at $18°\ 26'$ to BA produced

3) $45°$; $W\sqrt{5}/2$

4) Either $3W,1/\sqrt{3}$ or $5W,\sqrt{3}/5$

5) 8640 N　7) $10^3/16$ N

8)a) 10 N, $10\sqrt{3}$ N
  b) $24-4\sqrt{3},12\sqrt{3}-8$
  c) 5.73 N, 8.73 N　d) $51°\ 54'$, 33.04 N

9) $20\sqrt{3}$ N, 40 N　11)a) 13 N　b) 4.5 N
  c) $3\sqrt{13}$ N　d) 3.6 N; 10.25 N

12) $100\sqrt{3}$; 200　13) $W\sqrt{3}$; W

14)a) $\sqrt{3}/3$　b) $\sqrt{3}/4$

15)a) $49°\ 6'$　b) $58°\ 22'$

16) $W\cot\alpha/2$; $W\cos\alpha/2$

19)ii) $82°\ 48'$

20)i) $W\sqrt{5}/4$ at $26°\ 34'$ to horizontal
  ii) $4l/3$

21) $1.2W$; $36°\ 52'$　22) $\arctan a/(h-\mu a)$

23)i) $2W$　ii) $\arctan\sqrt{7}/7$　iii) $3\sqrt{2}W/2$

24) $60°$; $\sqrt{3}/3$; $\sqrt{3}W/3$

Exercise 4a — p. 73

1) 7.875 ms^{-1}　2) 1.481 ms^{-1}

3) 2.32 ms^{-1}, -0.387 ms^{-1}

4) 1.54 ms^{-1},　0.769 ms^{-1}

5)a) 2 ms^{-1}, b) 0, c) -1.5 ms^{-1}

Exercise 4b — p. 75

1)a) 2 ms^{-1}　b) -2 ms^{-1}

2)a) 0,　b) 1 ms^{-1}

3)a) -3 m,　b) 15 m,　c) 5 ms^{-1}
  d) -1 ms^{-1}, -16 ms^{-1}

4)a) -34 ms^{-1},　b) -39 ms^{-1},　c) $\frac{1}{10}$ s

5)a) 2.5 m,　b) 6 m,　c) 1 ms^{-1},
  d) t = $+\frac{1}{2}$

Exercise 4c — p. 77

1) -2 ms^{-2}　2) 8 ms^{-1}

3)a) 3 ms^{-1},　b) 0,　c) -3 ms^{-1}

4) 2 ms^{-1}　5) 2 ms^{-2}

Exercise 4d — p. 80

1) 3 ms^{-2}, 250 m　2) 360 m

3) 96 m　4) -3 ms^{-2}, 114 m

5)a) -11 ms^{-1},　b) 46.5 m,　c) 14 m

6)a) $+1.5$ ms^{-2},　b) 16.5 m,　c) -4.5 m

Exercise 4e — p. 86

1) 17 ms^{-1}, 47.5 m　2a) 12 m,　b) 8 m

3) 2.5 ms^{-2}, 40 m　4) 2.5 ms^{-2}, 45 m

5) 5 m　6) 3 s later

7) 6.67 s　8) 5 ms^{-2}

9) $-\frac{1}{30}$ ms^{-2}　10)a) $5\pm\sqrt{15}$ s,
  b) $5+\sqrt{35}$ s

11) $6+3\sqrt{2}$ s　12) 5.71 m

13) 8 s　14) 360 m

15) 111 s

Exercise 4f — p. 90

1) $14\sqrt{10}$ ms^{-1}　2) 5.1 m

3) 1.43 s, 14 ms^{-1}　4) 4.08 s

5) 4.547 s　6) 26.1 m

7) 15.45 ms^{-1}　8) 6.8 s

9) 0.82 m　10) 1.275 m above the
  initial position

11) 60 m

Exercise 4g — p. 93

1) $\dfrac{11\pi}{10}$ rad s^{-1}, $\dfrac{3\pi}{2}$ rad s^{-1} 2) $\dfrac{\pi}{30}$ rad s^{-1}

3) 40 ms^{-1} 4) 1600 $\pi/3$ km/h

5) 15.16 hours

Exercise 4h — p. 94

1) 6 rad s^{-1} 2) π rad s^{-2}

3) 15 rad, $\frac{2}{5}$ rad s^{-2} 4) -84π rad s^{-2}

5) $\dfrac{10\pi}{9}$ rad s^{-2} 6) $\dfrac{5\pi}{8}$

Multiple Choice Exercise 4 — p. 95

1) c	2) b	3) d
4) a	5) b	6) b
7) a, b	8) a, c	9) A
10) B	11) D	12) c
13) A	14) I	15) c
16) F	17) T	18) T
19) F	20) T	21) T
22) F	23) F	

Miscellaneous Exercise 4 — p. 99

1) 0.591 s   2) 0.5 rad s^{-2}, 24 m

3) $\dfrac{2\pi}{3}$ ms^{-1}, 2 m at 60° to the vertical

4) 1.2 s   5) 10.8 s, 37 ms^{-1}

6) 5 ms^{-2} 7) 20.6 m

8) 0.837 m   10) $2\sqrt{2}$ ms^{-1}

11) 9.64 ms^{-1} 13) 440 m

14) $l/24$, $4l/3$

15) 16 km/hr/min, $\frac{5}{3}$ km beyond C

17) 40 rev, 3 min

18) $\left(\dfrac{N-300}{60}\right)$ min, 80 rev/min/min, 150.

Exercise 5a — p. 103

1) No   2) Yes

3) Yes   4) Yes

5) $2\sqrt{13}$ N, 123° 41′

Exercise 5b — p. 108

1) 10 N   2) $\frac{8}{3}$ ms^{-2}

3) 15 N   4) $g(1 + 5\sqrt{3})$

5) $\dfrac{5\sqrt{3}}{8}$ ms^{-2} 6) $(25 - g)/5$ ms^{-2}

7) $2\sqrt{35}/175$ 8) $15(g - 4)$ N

9) $(3g - 5)/3$ ms^{-2} downwards

10) 16 000 N   11) 750g, 500g, 0

12) 1500 N   13) $50(5g - 1)$ N

14) $(11 - 3\sqrt{3})g/70$ ms^{-2}

Exercise 5c — p. 115

1) $g/3$, $20g/3$ 2) $g/19$, $180g/19$

3) $\dfrac{(M - m)g}{M + m}$, $\dfrac{2Mmg}{M + m}$

4) $\dfrac{g}{3}$ $(\sqrt{3} - 1)$, $\dfrac{2g}{3}$ $(2 + \sqrt{3})$

5) $g/3$, $4g/3$ 6) $13g/33$, $40g/11$

7)a) $2\sqrt{2}g/9$, $20\sqrt{2}g/9$

b) $\dfrac{g}{36}$ $(6\sqrt{2} - 5)$, $\dfrac{5g}{9}$ $(3\sqrt{2} + 2)$

8)a) $g\sqrt{3}/6$, $10g\sqrt{3}/3$

b) $\dfrac{g}{60}$ $(10\sqrt{3} - 3)$, $10g\sqrt{3}/3$

9) $\dfrac{80g}{13}$, $\dfrac{80g}{13}$ 10) $\dfrac{7g}{4}$ $(\sqrt{6} + \sqrt{2})$

11)a) $\dfrac{11g}{36}$,   b) $\dfrac{50g\sqrt{2}}{9}$,   c) $\dfrac{1}{2}\left(\sqrt{\dfrac{11g}{3}}\right)$

12) $2\sqrt{g/7}$ 13) $\dfrac{13}{12}$ m

14)a) $\left(\dfrac{4\sqrt{2g}}{35}\right)^{\frac{1}{2}}$, b) $\dfrac{g}{\sqrt{2}}$, c) $\dfrac{3}{35}$ m

Exercise 5d — 123

1) $8g/11$, $15g/11$ 2) $3g/19$, $48g/19$

3) $13g/25$, $48g/25$ 4) $5g/11$, $12g/11$

5) $g/5$, $12g/5$, $6g/5$ 6) $11g/49$, $120g/49$,

240g/49

7) $14g/29$, $36g/29$, $72g/29$ 8) $g\sqrt{3}/17$

9) $\dfrac{g}{14}\sqrt{106}$ 10) $\dfrac{g}{19}$, $\dfrac{15\sqrt{2}}{8}$ g

11) $\dfrac{3g\sqrt{505}}{217}$, $\dfrac{10\sqrt{2g}}{7}$

Multiple Choice Exercise 5 — p. 124

1) b	2) a	3) e
4) c	5) d	6) b
7) a, b	8) a, c	9) a, b
10) a, b, c	11) C	12) D
13) E	14) A	15) A
16) c	17) I	18) b
19) c	20) a	21) I
22) T	23) T	24) F
25) F	26) T	27) F

Miscellaneous Exercise 5 — p. 128

1) $\dfrac{R}{2m}$ 2) $\sqrt{3}/6$

3) $\dfrac{147\sqrt{2}}{8g}$, $\dfrac{21}{4g}$ $(2 + \sqrt{2})$ 4) $-\dfrac{R}{m}$, $\dfrac{R}{M}$

5) $T = 0$

6) $g/3, \frac{2}{3}mg$

7) $\frac{6}{17}$

8) $4\sqrt{\frac{2}{11g}}$

9) $\frac{g}{4}$ ms^{-2}, $\frac{15g}{4}$ N, 4.7 ms^{-2} down, 1.3 ms^{-2} down, 25.5 N

10) $\frac{g}{2}(\cos\theta - \sin\theta), \frac{mg}{2}(\cos\theta + \sin\theta),$

$Mg + \frac{mg}{2}(3 + \sin 2\theta)$

11) $\frac{21}{5}$ kg

12) $\frac{g}{9}, \frac{40}{9}mg, \frac{5}{3}mg$

13)a) $\frac{6k\,Mg}{k+8}$ b) $\frac{3k\,Mg}{k+8}$

14) $\frac{1}{3}mg(1 + \sqrt{3})$

15) $R_1 = \frac{m}{4a}(u^2 - v^2), R_2 = \frac{mv^2}{2a}, \frac{5a}{4}$

17) $\frac{g}{8}$

Exercise 6a – p. 137

1) $Tx, 0, 0, -Fx$ 2) $0, Tl\cos(\alpha+\beta),$
$Wl\sin\alpha, -Fl$

3) 49 000 J   4) 126.8

5) 3×10^6 J   6) 8844×10^3 J

7) 1400×10^3 J   8) 11 300 J, 17 300 J

9) 20 N   10) 250 J

11) 1330 N   12) 0.13

Exercise 6b – p. 143

1) 1110 kW   2) 1800 N

3) 4950 kW   4) 51.4 N

5)a) 37.5 ms^{-1},   b) 19.5 ms^{-1},
c) 461.5 ms^{-1} 6) 33.6 ms^{-1}

7) 60 N   8) 180 J, 32.9 W

9) 8 ms^{-2} 10) 5.51 ms^{-2}

11) 0.127 ms^{-2} 12) 3.3 ms^{-2}, 1420 N

13) 0.121 ms^{-2} 14) 6000 N

Multiple Choice Exercise 6 – p. 145

1) d   2) b   3) e   4) a
5) d   6) E   7) D   8) a
9) I   10) A   11) c   12) T
13) F   14) F   5) F   16) T
17) T

Miscellaneous Exercise 6 – p. 146

1) 125 kW   2) 4800 N, 35.7 ms^{-1}

3) 70 kW   4) 132 W, 0.275 ms^{-2}

5) $\frac{24\,000}{g}$ kg, 9.14 ms^{-2}

6) $0.83v^2$, 5.34 ms^{-2} 7) 892.5 N, 81 800 N

8) 2.4 ms^{-2}, 13.9 kW

9) 45 ms^{-1}, 1.715 ms^{-2}

10) $73\frac{1}{3}$ kW, 50 km/h

11) 3270 W,   a) 40 km/h,   b) 24 km/h

12) 0.833 ms^{-2}, 86.2 km/h

13) 2160 N, 79.7 m   14) $\frac{3W}{n}, \frac{2g}{n}$

Exercise 7a – p. 157

1)a) 23 m   b) 6 m   c) 4.5 m

2) 0.625 m

3) 40 N

4) $\frac{Mgl}{\lambda}$

5) $\frac{a_1 M_2 - a_2 M_1}{M_2 - M_1}, \frac{g(M_1 a_2 - M_2 a_1)}{a_1 - a_2}$

6) 1.5 kg

7) $\frac{9a}{4}$

8) 0.5 m

9) $\frac{16a}{7}$

10) $3mg, 3g$

Exercise 7b – p. 162

1) 9 J, 10 m

2) 2.4 m

3) $\frac{27}{14}$

4) $\pi \times 10^{-2}$ J

Exercise 7c – p. 167

1) 54 J, 5 m/s, 1 kg

2)a) 0.16 J   b) 0.25 J

3) 5.72 kJ

4) 3 J

5) $10m(2gh + v^2)$

Exercise 7d – p. 172

1) 2.5 m

2) $M\left(\frac{dg}{2} + 4u^2\right)$

3) $\frac{1}{2}\sqrt{gl}$

4) $\sqrt{gl}$

5) 6 m

6) $(3 + \sqrt{5})\frac{l}{2}$

7) $\frac{3l}{4}$

8) 0.45 m

Multiple Choice Exercise 7 — p. 173

1) c	2) a	3) c	4) c
5) d	6) b, c	7) c, d	8) d
9) B	10) C	11) B	12) D
13) I	14) I	15) A	16) b, c
17) F	18) F	19) T	20) F

Miscellaneous Exercise 7 — p. 175

1) $\sqrt{\dfrac{2gl}{3}}$

2) 0.96 m   1.04 m

3) i) 3 m   ii) $\sqrt{5}$ m

4) 3.17×10^5 J

5) 0.3 m

6) a) $30°$ b) $W\sqrt{3}, \dfrac{W\sqrt{3}}{2}, 30°$

7) $\sqrt{\dfrac{5ga}{2}}$

8) i) $8g$ N   ii) 0.128 m   iii) 0.36 m

9) 1.5 m; 2.82 m

10) 1 m   0.577 m,   16.97 N

11) a) $(2\sqrt{2ga})^{\frac{1}{2}}$ b) $2\sqrt{ga}$
 c) $2\sqrt{ga(\cos\theta - \cos 2\theta)}$

12) $W\sqrt{3}/3$

13) a) $2a$ b) $\dfrac{3\sqrt{2ga}}{4}$

14) $5\sqrt{3} - 8$

15) 2880 J

16) $\dfrac{W}{2}(2\sqrt{3} - 3)$

17) mg

20) arctan 1/3, $\dfrac{2\sqrt{10}}{3}, \dfrac{3g\sqrt{10}}{10}$ N, $\dfrac{3\sqrt{10}}{5}$

Exercise 8a — p. 183

1) 17 ms^{-1}

2) $5\frac{5}{8}$ s

3) 18 Ns

4) 24 N

5) 10.4 Ns

6) 40 N

7) $20\sqrt{5}$ Ns at arctan $\frac{1}{2}$ to the direction of the initial velocity.

8) a) $\dfrac{12}{5}\sqrt{7}$ Ns   b) $\dfrac{12}{5}\sqrt{13 - 3\sqrt{3}}$ Ns

9) 2000 litre

Exercise 8b — p. 188

1) a) $\frac{1}{2}$ ms^{-1} b) $\frac{7}{2}$ ms^{-1}

2) 600 kg

3) a) 486 ms^{-1} b) 480 ms^{-1}

4) 50 kg

6) a) $\dfrac{u}{50}$ b) $\dfrac{2u}{51}$

7) $\dfrac{mv}{M+m}$; $\dfrac{m^2v^2 + 2gh(M+m)^2}{2h(M+m)}$

Exercise 8c — p. 195

1) a) $\dfrac{u}{2}; \dfrac{mu}{2}$ b) $\dfrac{u\sqrt{13}}{8}; \dfrac{mu\sqrt{13}}{8};$

 c) $\dfrac{u\sqrt{3}}{4}; \dfrac{mu\sqrt{3}}{4}$

2) 1.12 ms^{-1}; 3.36 Ns.

3) $\dfrac{J\sqrt{3}}{15}; \dfrac{4J\sqrt{3}}{15}$; A: $\dfrac{J\sqrt{3}}{15m}$ along $\overrightarrow{AB}$;

 B: $\dfrac{2J\sqrt{21}}{15m}$ at arctan $3\sqrt{3}$ with $\overrightarrow{AB}$;

 C: $\dfrac{4J\sqrt{3}}{15m}$ along $\overrightarrow{CB}$

4) a) $\dfrac{3m\sqrt{6g}}{5}$ b) $\dfrac{\sqrt{6g}}{10}$

5) a) $\dfrac{mv}{2}$ b) $\dfrac{v}{2}$ c) $\dfrac{v}{3}$

6) i) 4.2 ms^{-1} ii) 2.8 Ns   iii) 1.4 ms^{-1}
 iv) 0.99 ms^{-1} v) 0.99 Ns; No

Exercise 8d — p. 201

1) 6 ms^{-1}; 16 ms^{-1}; 100 Ns

2) 5.4 ms^{-1}; 3.9 ms^{-1}; 1.05 J

4) 0.2 kg; 2.5 ms^{-1}; 0.5 Ns

5) $\dfrac{u}{5}$ $\dfrac{2u}{5}$ $\dfrac{8u}{5}$

6) a) $Mm(1+e)(V+v)/(M+m)$
 b) $Mm(1+e)(V-v)/(M+m)$

7) 2.5 m

8) $\sqrt{\dfrac{5}{6}}; \dfrac{2g}{5}$ J

9) $44°$ $3'$

10) $e^2h, c^4h, e^6h; h\left(\dfrac{1+e^2}{1-e^2}\right)$

Multiple Choice Exercise 8 – p. 202

1) d   2) d   3) c   4) c
5) c   6) a, d   7) a, d   8) c
9) c, b   10) b, c   11) B 12) C
13) B 14) B 15) D 16) A
17) c   18) a or b or c   19) I 20) d
21) T 22) F 23) T 24) T
25) F

Miscellaneous Exercise 8 – p. 206

1) 65 ms^{-1}
2) 60 ms^{-1} upwards; 120 ms^{-1} downwards
3) $10^3 v^2 c$ N
4) 14.6 ms^{-1}
5) 1.2 ms^{-1}
6) $\dfrac{\sqrt{2}}{2}$; $m\sqrt{gh}(1+\sqrt{2})$; $\dfrac{mgh}{2}$
8) $\dfrac{m_1 u}{m_2}$; $\dfrac{m_1}{m_2}$; $\dfrac{(m_2)^2}{m_1}$
9) $\dfrac{u(2-e)}{3}$; $\dfrac{2u(1+e)}{3}$; $\dfrac{u}{9}(e^2+8e-2)$
10) $\dfrac{V}{2}(1-e)$, $\dfrac{V}{4}(1-e^2)$; $\dfrac{V}{4}(1+e)^2$
11) 8175 J; 502.7 N
12) $\dfrac{V}{16}$, $\dfrac{3V}{16}$
13) $\dfrac{15u^2}{32g}$
14)i) $2\sqrt{\dfrac{gh}{13}}$ ii) $\dfrac{2h}{9}$ iii) $\sqrt{\dfrac{13}{15}}$;

$m\sqrt{\dfrac{2gh}{13}}(\sqrt{15}+\sqrt{13})$

15) $\dfrac{4a}{V}$; $\dfrac{V}{6}$; $\dfrac{5mV^2}{12}$
16) $\dfrac{m}{2}\sqrt{u^2-ga}$; $\sqrt{7ga}$; $\dfrac{mg}{4}$
17) $\dfrac{4V}{3}$; $\dfrac{4V}{3(n+1)}$
19) $\frac{5}{7}$
20) mu^2; $\sqrt{gh}$
22) $4\frac{4}{9}$ m; 14.12 kg ms^{-1}
23) $9u$ North, u South; u, $u\sqrt{3}$
24) $\dfrac{3mg}{2}$; $\dfrac{g}{2}$; $\dfrac{3mgt}{14}$; $\dfrac{5gt}{7}$
26) $\dfrac{2\sqrt{2}J}{7}$
27) $\dfrac{20m}{7}$; $\dfrac{7u}{54}$

28) $4Mm(M+m)^2$; $4Mm(M-m)^2$;
$(M-m)^4$

Exercise 9a – p. 215

1) $v=\left(\dfrac{t^2}{2}-6t\right)$, -18 ms^{-1}, $s=\left(\dfrac{t^3}{6}-3t^2\right)$;
-72 m
2) $v=t^2$, $s=\dfrac{t^3}{3}$
3) $v=\frac{3}{2}t^2-t-1$, 31.5 ms^{-1} 4) 18 m
5) 3 m   6) $v=\frac{1}{2}-\dfrac{1}{2t^2}$, $s=\dfrac{1}{2t}+\dfrac{t}{2}-1$,
$\frac{3}{8}$ ms^{-1}, $\frac{1}{4}$ m
7) 2 ms^{-1}, $s=2t-\dfrac{1}{t}+c$
8) $v=\frac{1}{2}(1-\cos 2t)$, $s=\frac{1}{2}(1+t-\frac{1}{2}\sin 2t)$,
π s
9) $\dfrac{9}{4}$ ms^{-1} 10) $\dfrac{32}{3}$ ms^{-1}, $13\frac{1}{3}$ m
11) $\dfrac{1}{\omega}$ 12) 0, 0, $\dfrac{2}{\pi^2}$ m
13) $v=\dfrac{2}{9}t^2$ 14) $s=\dfrac{32t^2}{15(t+1)}$

Exercise 9b – p. 219

1) $v=\sqrt{6t}$, $s=\dfrac{2\sqrt{6}}{3}t^{\frac{3}{2}}$ $45\frac{1}{3}$ ms^{-1}
2) $\dfrac{2\sqrt{73}}{73}$ ms^{-1}, $\dfrac{1}{6}(\sqrt{73}-1)$ m
3) -1 m   4) 8 ms^{-1}

Exercise 9c – p. 222

1)i) 0.5 ms^{-2},   ii) 39.6 m   2) 5 s, 14.3 m
3)a) 8 ms^{-2},   b) 2.46 s
4)a) 3.5 ms^{-2},   b) 3.6 s
5) 1.2 ms^{-1}, 6.2 ms^{-1} 6) $113\frac{1}{3}$ m

Exercise 9d – p. 227

1) $6t\mathbf{i}+4\mathbf{j}$, $6\mathbf{i}$, $24\mathbf{i}+4\mathbf{j}$, $6\mathbf{i}$
2) $(t^2+3)\mathbf{i}+(1-\frac{1}{2}t^2)\mathbf{j}$
3) $18\mathbf{i}+\mathbf{j}$, $27\mathbf{i}+\frac{3}{2}\mathbf{j}$ 5) $3t\mathbf{i}-2t\mathbf{j}$
6) $\sqrt{5}$ ms^{-1} at arctan $\frac{1}{2}$ to Ox
7) ω at $\left(\dfrac{\pi}{2}+\omega t\right)$ to Ox, ω^2 at $-(\pi-\omega t)$
to Ox
8) $2\sqrt{10}$ ms^{-1} at arctan $\frac{1}{3}$ to Ox
9) $\ddot{x}=x$, $\ddot{y}=2\sqrt{y}$
10) $\dot{x}=2t^{\frac{1}{2}}$, $\dot{y}=3t^{1/2}$

Multiple Choice Exercise 9 – p. 232

1) a   2) c   3) d   4) b
5) d   6) d   7) e   8) c

9) a 10) d 11) a, b, c 12) b, c
13) a, b 14) b, c 15) a, b 16) B
17) C 18) A 19) D 20) a
21) c 22) A 23) I 24) b
25) T 26) F 27) T 28) T

Miscellaneous Exercise 9 – p. 235

1) $-k \sin 3t, \frac{1}{3}k (\cos 3t - 1) + u,$
$\frac{k}{9} (\sin 3t - 3t) + ut$

2) $(u^2 - a^2)^{\frac{1}{2}}$

3) $6mi$

4) $\frac{1}{2}(t^2 + 2t + 2)i + \frac{1}{2}(2 - 2t - 3t^2)j$

5) $\frac{1}{m} [e^{-t} (mu + k) - k]$

6) 0.223 s, 1.61 s

7) 2.07 ms^{-1}, 5.84 ms^{-1}

8)i) 3 ms^{-2}, 0.5 ms^{-2}, ii) $\frac{1}{3}(24 + 13\sqrt{3})$ ms^{-2},
$\frac{1}{3}(24 - 13\sqrt{3})$ ms^{-2}, iii) 258 m

9) 84.8 kmh^{-1}

10) $2u$

14) 4 m, $2\lambda/(e^\lambda - 1)$ ms^{-1}, 5 ms^{-1}

15) $\frac{u}{k} (1 - e^{-kt}), ue^{-kt}, \frac{1}{k} \ln \left(\frac{g + ku}{g} \right)$

16)i) $\frac{v_0}{a_0}, \frac{v_0^2}{2a_0}$, ii) $\frac{v_0^2}{6a_0} + \frac{1}{3a_0v_0} \{2a_0v_0t - v_0^2\}^{\frac{3}{2}}$,
4 ms^{-2}, 16.25 s

17) $\left\{ 2g \left(\frac{k}{a} - \frac{k}{b} + \mu a - \mu b \right) \right\}^{\frac{1}{2}}$,

19) $3y^2 = 8x$

20) $\frac{1}{4}(30i + 75j)$

22) $r = (2T^2 - 1)i + (T^4 + 1)j, 7i + 6j$

24) $\frac{\pi}{4}$ to Ox

25)a) mk^2h at $-(\pi - kt)$ to Ox
b) $\left(\frac{1}{2}gt^2, \frac{F}{m} \left\{ \frac{t^2}{2} - \frac{t}{n} - \frac{e^{-nt}}{n^2} + \frac{1}{n^2} \right\} + Ut \right)$

26) $\frac{2\pi}{\omega}$

27) $\frac{5}{v} - \frac{v}{80}$, 70.2 m

28) $\frac{m}{2k} \ln (\frac{4}{3})$

29) $m \left[k^2 \ln \left(\frac{k}{k - u} \right) - ku \right]$

Exercise 10a – p. 250

1) 28 ms^{-1} at 44° 55' above the horizontal
2) 4.5 m 3) 3.67 s 4) 9° 24'
5) 1.79 s, 12.63 m

6) $\frac{15\sqrt{3}}{g}, \frac{15\sqrt{3}}{2g}$ 7) 29.25 m

8) 1.7 s, arctan -0.712
9) 22° 33' 10) $16g/(4 - \sqrt{3})$ ms^{-1}
11) $16g/(4 + \sqrt{3})$ ms^{-1}
12) 1.43 s 13) 4.52 s, 181 m
14) 30.4 ms^{-1}
15) $v = i + (2 - gt)j, i - 13j,$
$r = ti + (2t - \frac{1}{2}gt^2)j, \frac{3}{4}(2i - 11j)$
16) $\frac{1}{6} (16i + 49j)$
17) arctan 7 below the horizontal,
$9y = -3x - 5x^2$
19) $2(3\sqrt{2} - \sqrt{6})$
20) $\sqrt{2}$ s after projection, 20.2 m
21) 48.2 ms^{-1} at arctan 1/12 below the
horizontal
22) 2 s after projection of the first particle,
arctan $-\frac{16}{9}$, arctan $\frac{91}{250}$

Exercise 10b – p. 258

1) 44.7 ms^{-1} at 45° to the horizontal
2) 38.7 ms^{-1}, 37.5 m
3) 22.4 ms^{-1} at 45° to the horizontal, 12.5 m
4) 75.2 ms^{-1} 5) 9.8 m
6) 20° 54', 69° 6' 7) 76° 29', 40° 5'
8) 19° 37' 9) 61 ms^{-1}
10) 5°8', 178 m 11) 82° 46'
13) arctan 4/5 15) 19° 54', 70° 6', 10 m
16) 25 ms^{-1} at arctan 4/3 to the horizontal
17) 2830 m, 14.1 s
18) arctan $(4 - \sqrt{3})/13$

Multiple Choice Exercise 10 – p. 260

1) e 2) c 3) b 4) b
5) d 6) a 7) c 8) a, b
9) a, c 10) a, b, c 11) a, b 12) b
13) b 14) I 15) A 16) I
17) b

Miscellaneous Exercise 10 – p. 262

1) 4.74 m
4) $2\sqrt{2g}, (\sqrt{7} - 1)$ m
6) arctan $\left(\frac{u \sin \alpha - gt}{u \cos \alpha} \right)$
7) 10 ms^{-1}, arctan $\frac{3}{4}$ to the horizontal,
2.8 s, 9.6 m
8) 26.2 ms^{-1}, 13.2 m
9) arctan $\frac{1}{4}$, 1.13 s
10) 64 m, arcsin 4/5, 36 m, arcsin 3/5
11) 18° 26', 71° 34' 12) 26° 34', 74° 3'

14) $26° 34' \leqslant \alpha \leqslant 63° 26'$, 98 m, 10.7 m

15) $h \sqrt{\dfrac{1 + \sin \theta}{2}}$

17) $35° 16'$, $7h/3$

18) $\dfrac{gT(\cos \alpha + \cos 2\alpha)}{2 \sin \alpha}$ 19) $2/3$

Exercise 11a – p. 270

1) 32 ms^{-2}; 6 m   2) 8 N
3) $0.63 \leqslant \mu < 0.99$ 4) $7 \sqrt{2}/2$
5)a) 42.7 N; 3.92 N   b) 14.4 rads^{-1}

Exercise 11b – p. 275

1) $7 \sqrt{3}/3$ rads^{-1} 2) $5 \sqrt{6}/3$
3) $\sqrt{g/l} \cos \theta$
4)i) $21\sqrt{5}/25$ ii) 17.9 N
5)a) $2m\omega^2 l$, mg b) $2m\omega^2 l$, $m(g - \omega^2 l)$
6) $M{:}m = 2{:}1$; $\omega^2 = g/l$ 7) $7\sqrt{10}/5$ rads^{-1}
8) $49m/4$ N   9) $3a/5$; $5/6$

Exercise 11c – p. 282

1) 11 ms^{-1} 2) $18° 47'$ 3) 15.34 ms^{-1}
4) $21° 48'$ 5) 44.27 ms^{-1}; 76.68 ms^{-1}
6) 8230 N; 0.0147 m   7) $32°$
8)a) 88×10^3 N (inner) b) 113×10^3 N
                                                              (outer)

   c) 202×10^3 N (inner)

Exercise 11d – p. 290

1)i) $\sqrt{2g}$, $4g$ ii) $\sqrt{3g}$, $7g$ iii) $2\sqrt{g}$, $10g$
2)i) $11g/2$ ii) $15g/2$ iii) $19g/2$
3) $u > \sqrt{32gl}$ 4)i) $2mg$, $\sqrt{2ga}$, $g\sqrt{5}$
ii) $7mg/2$, $\sqrt{3ga}$, $g\sqrt{39}/2$
iii) $5mg$, $2\sqrt{ga}$, $4g$
5) $5/6$ m   6) a; $a/4$

Exercise 11e – p. 299

1) $v \geqslant \sqrt{3g}$ 2) $\frac{1}{2}\sqrt{ga}$
3)a) oscillates   b) loses contact
c) describes complete circles
4) $7mg$: mg a) $6g$ b) $2g$ c) $g\sqrt{17}$
5)a) $J \geqslant 21\sqrt{2}/4$ Ns b) $3\sqrt{7g}/4$
6) $a/2$; 11 : 5

Multiple Choice Exercise 11 – p. 300

1) c   2) b   3) c   4) c
5) d   6) a,c   7) c,d   8) a,c
9) a,b,d 10) D   11) C   12) D
13) I   14) b   15) b   16) F
17) F   18) F   19) F

Miscellaneous Exercise 11 – p. 302

1) $8.8 \text{ ms}^{-1} \leqslant v \leqslant 37.6 \text{ ms}^{-1}$
2) $2a\sqrt{3}/3$; $8a\sqrt{6}/9$
3) $\dfrac{3mg}{2} (2 \cos \theta - 1)$

5) $3l/8$; $4\sqrt{g/3l}$ 6) $5a/4$ 7) $n \geqslant 14$
9) $30°$; $\sqrt{2g/3l}$ 12) $\sqrt{3ga}/2 \tan \alpha$
13) $\frac{1}{2}m(3g - a\omega^2)$ 14) $12mg$
15) $mlv^2/(l^2 - h^2)$ i) 15.85 N
ii) 2.29 ms^{-1}; 32.7 N
16) $\frac{1}{2}l$; $\frac{1}{2}l$; $\frac{3}{2}mg$; $3mg$ 17) $\sqrt{g/3a}$
18)i) $m\sqrt{2ga} \cos^3 \alpha$ ii) $\sin \alpha \sqrt{2ga} \cos \alpha$
iii) $\cos^3 \alpha$
19) $[u^2 - 2ga(1 + \cos \theta)]^{\frac{1}{2}}$;
    $mu^2/a - mg(2 + \frac{3}{2} \cos \theta)$;
    $[ga/2(3\sqrt{2} + 4)]^{\frac{1}{2}}$
20) $\arccos (2g/l\omega^2)$
21)i) $10mg$, $6mg$ iii) $2\pi\sqrt{a/6g}$
22) $gb(1 - \sec \alpha + \frac{b}{a} \sec^2\alpha)$; $gb(1 + \sec \alpha)$
23) $\sqrt{ga}$ 24) $mg/2$
25) $m(r\omega^2 \cos \theta - g \sin \theta)$;
    $m(r\omega^2 \sin \theta + g \cos \theta)$; $4\pi\sqrt{3a/35g}$

Exercise 12a – p. 314

1)a) $\pi \sqrt{2}$ s   b) $4\pi/3$

2)a) 6 ms^{-1} b) 24 ms^{-2} c) $\dfrac{\pi}{2}$ s

3) $2\sqrt{3}$ rad s^{-2}

4) $2\pi \left(\dfrac{x_2{}^2 - x_1{}^2}{v_1{}^2 - v_2{}^2} \right)^{\frac{1}{2}}$

5) $\dfrac{\pi}{3}$; $\dfrac{\pi\sqrt{3}}{3}$ rad s^{-1}

6) 1·2 m;   0·27 ms^{-1};   0·18 ms^{-2}
7) 0.023 m   3.7 ms^{-2};   0.26 ms^{-1}

Exercise 12b – p. 318

1)a) $\dfrac{\pi\sqrt{3}}{12}$ s   b) $\dfrac{\pi\sqrt{3}}{8}$ s   c) $\dfrac{\pi\sqrt{3}}{12}$ s

2)i) $\dfrac{a\sqrt{3}}{2}$ ii) $\dfrac{a}{2}$ iii) $a \dfrac{\sqrt{3}}{2}$

3) $2T$
4)a) 38.2 s   b) 9.1 s

5)a) 1 m   b) 0.28 ms^{-2} c) $\dfrac{\pi\sqrt{3}}{12}$ ms^{-1}

Exercise 12c – p. 321

1) 0.0018 m
2) 9.803
3) 431 seconds in 24 hours in both cases

Exercise 12d — p. 325

2) $10g$; E, $\frac{2}{7}\pi\sqrt{2}$ s; $\frac{7}{10}\sqrt{2}$ ms^{-1}; 0.2 m

3) $6a$; $2\pi\sqrt{\frac{2a}{5g}}$

4) $5a$

5) 800 N; a) 80 ms^{-2} b) $\frac{\pi}{40}$ s

 c) $2\sqrt{3}$ ms^{-1}

6) $2\pi\sqrt{\frac{ml}{\lambda}}$; $\frac{mgl}{\lambda}$

Exercise 12e — p. 339

1) $\frac{1}{3\sqrt{5g}}(2\pi + 3\sqrt{3})$

2)a) $\sqrt{5ga}$ b) $\sqrt{7ga}$

3) $2\sqrt{10}$ ms^{-1}; $\frac{1}{2\sqrt{10}}\left(\frac{\pi}{\sqrt{2}} + 2\sqrt{2}\right)$ s

4)a) $\frac{\pi}{2}\sqrt{\frac{a}{g}}$ b) $\sqrt{\frac{a}{g}}\left(\frac{\pi}{2} + 1\right)$

 c) $\sqrt{\frac{a}{g}}\left(2\pi + 4\right)$

5) $\frac{5a}{4}$; $\frac{a}{4}$; $\sqrt{\frac{a}{g}}\left(\frac{2\pi}{3} + \sqrt{3}\right)$

Multiple Choice Exercise 12 — p. 340

1) c 2) a 3) d 4) a, c
5) c, d 6) a, b, c 7) b, c 8) b
9) A 10) F 11) F 12) T
13) F 14) F 15) T

Miscellaneous Exercise 12 — p. 341

1) $\lambda\sqrt{d^2 - x^2}$; $\frac{\pi}{\lambda}$; $\frac{\pi}{3\lambda}$

2) $\frac{3}{4}$ m; $\frac{\pi}{\sqrt{2g}}$

3) 2 : 7; 1.3 s

4) $4\sqrt{\frac{2}{5}}$ m; $2\pi\sqrt{\frac{3}{5}}$ s; $4\sqrt{\frac{2}{3}}$ ms^{-1}

5) $4\sqrt{6}$ cms^{-1}; $12\sqrt{10}$ cms^{-2}
 i) 0.13 s ii) 225×10^{-7} J

6) $2\pi\sqrt{\frac{ma}{\lambda}}$; $\sqrt{\left(2gc + \frac{\lambda c^2}{ma}\right)}$

7) $\left(3 - \frac{3\sqrt{2}}{4}\right)l$

8) $\frac{2\pi}{3}\sqrt{\frac{b}{g\sin\theta}}$; $\sqrt{3bg\sin\theta}$

9) $\frac{a}{12}$; a) $\frac{5a}{12}$ b) $5\sqrt{\frac{ag}{12}}$; $5g$

10) $2\sqrt{2}$ m; $\frac{1}{2}\sqrt{2}$ ms^{-1} in direction PO

11) 3; $\frac{l}{2}$ 12) $3a$

13)a)i) $\frac{4}{3}$ m ii) 75 ms^{-1} iii) $\frac{1}{9}$
 b)i) 3 m ii) $\sqrt{5}$ m

14) $\frac{40b}{9}$; $\frac{4\pi}{3}\sqrt{\frac{b}{g}}$

15) $\left(a + \frac{amg}{\lambda}\right)$ below A; $2\pi\sqrt{\frac{am}{\lambda}}$;
 $\left(b - \frac{amg}{\lambda}\right)$; $|b| \leqslant \frac{2amg}{\lambda}$

16) $\sqrt{\frac{\lambda a}{3m}}$

18) $\frac{l}{4}$

19) $4\pi\sqrt{\frac{c}{g}}$; $\sqrt{cg}$

20) $2\pi\sqrt{\frac{6ml}{11\lambda}}$; $\sqrt{\frac{\lambda l}{22m}}$

21) $\pi\sqrt{\frac{a}{g}}$; $\frac{a}{4}$

Exercise 13a — p. 354

1) 5.83 kmh^{-1} 2) 38.4 kmh^{-1}
3) S 87° 15′ W or N 7° 15′ W
4) 13.3 kmh^{-1}, 5.6 kmh^{-1}
5) 8.9 kmh^{-1} 6) S 30° W

Exercise 13b — p. 361

1) 5 ms^{-1}, S 53° 8′ E, 16 m
2) 34° 16′ with V_A produced, 2.66 s or
 85° 42′ with V_A, 1.5 s
3) 5.32 km, 21.3 kmh^{-1}, S 41° 49′ E
4) 151 m 5) 12.27
6) 2.27 km 7) 6.94 kmh^{-1}, 9.23 kmh^{-1}
8) 12.46 hours

Exercise 13c — p. 365

1) 34.2 N 47° 3′ E 2) 888.9 m, $d \leqslant 814.1$
3) S 34° 15′ E 4) N 38° 25′ E
5) 440 kmh^{-1}, 1.8 km

Exercise 13d — p. 368

1) $v\sqrt{2}$, $2v$, $v\sqrt{3}$
2)a) $\sqrt{37}$ at arctan 6 to Ox
 b) $\sqrt{145}$ at arctan (-12) to Ox

3) $2\omega (5 + 4 \sin 3\omega t)^{\frac{1}{2}}$, $\pi/2\omega$,
   $2\omega^2 (17 - 8 \sin 3\omega)^{\frac{1}{2}}$

4)a) $u\sqrt{(2t^2 - 2t + 1)}$ at arctan $\dfrac{t-1}{t}$ to Ox

 b) $2\sqrt{(u^2 - 4u + 8)}$

Miscellaneous Exercise 13 − p. 369

1) 1754 s

2)a) $11\frac{1}{2}$ minutes later, 2.9 nautical miles, 349° 36′

 b) 28 minutes later, 4 nautical miles, north east

3) 13.75 km, 24.7 s   4) 20 knots, N 45° W

5)i) 36.6, 136.5 or 71.8, 121.8
   ii) $193 + 102t$

6) 3.2 ms^{-1}, $5\frac{1}{3}$ ms^{-1} perpendicular to the bank, $5\frac{1}{3}$ ms^{-1}

7) $10(11 + 6\sqrt{3})^{\frac{1}{2}}$

8) 20 knots, 0.9 hours, N 85° 29′ E

9) S 44° 30′ E, N 60° E

10) 12 knots, arcsin 7/9 west of north, $\dfrac{2\sqrt{2}}{3}$ hours, 24/7 knots

11)i) 709 kmh^{-1} ii) 1029 kmh^{-1}

12)i) $\sqrt{13}\,\omega r$, arctan 3/2 with OB produced

 ii) $\sqrt{7}\,\omega r$, arctan $3\sqrt{3}$ with BO, $\cos\theta = 2/3$, $7r/\sqrt{13}$

13) arcsin $\dfrac{u}{2v}$

14)a) $V_0 = 10$, 11.5 hours
   b) arcos 3/5

15)i) 6.72 km
   ii) 2.94, arcsin 7/15 east of north

16) 69 s, 58 s   17)i) $\dfrac{6a}{\sqrt{35\,V}}$ ii) $a/6, a/V$

18) $u/\sqrt{2}$, $v = u(1 - 1/\sqrt{2})$

Exercise 14a − p. 379

1) 0; 8 Nm; − 6 Nm; 0

2) $6Fa\sqrt{3}$; $-2Fa\sqrt{3}$; $4Fa$

3) 0; 4 Nm; $\sqrt{3}$ Nm; −4 Nm

4) $6Fa$; $-2Fa$; $2Fa$; $-Fa\sqrt{3}$

5) 1 Nm anticlockwise

6) −2, −7, −12, −6 units

Exercise 14b − p. 385

1) Fa clockwise

2) $(7 - 4\sqrt{3})a$ Nm anticlockwise

3) $\dfrac{Pa}{2} (12 - \sqrt{3})$ clockwise

4) $\frac{1}{2}(3 + \sqrt{3})$ Nm anticlockwise

5) 23 units, 47 units, both clockwise

6) 11 N; − 4 N; 3 N

Exercise 14c − p. 389

1) $\dfrac{200}{19}$ N   2) 30 N

3) 1.35 m from the end

4) $\dfrac{180}{7}$; $\dfrac{100}{7}$ 5) 1.39 m

6) 52; 66   7) 10   8) 15; $\dfrac{75}{2}$

Exercise 14d − p. 396

1) 60 N; 180 N; arctan 3/2

2) 9/8; $26\frac{2}{3}$ N

3) $W/2$; $1/\sqrt{3}$ 4) $\sqrt{3}$; $W/\sqrt{3}$

5)a) $3mg$; $\sqrt{13}\,mg$ at arctan 2/3 to PQ
   b) $3mg$; mg vertically downwards

6) 2; 4; $-\dfrac{9a}{4}$ 7) 9/2; 27/2

8) $(4\sqrt{3} + 5)$; 8; $\dfrac{5\sqrt{3}}{12}$

Multiple Choice Exercise 14 − p. 398

1) c   2) a   3) d   4) a,d
5) a,b,d   6) B 7) A 8) C
9) I 10) I 11) A 12) d
13) F 14) F 15) T 16) F

Miscellaneous Exercise 14 − p. 400

1) $\dfrac{10}{3}$ N; $\dfrac{25}{3}$ N   2) 0.8 N

3) 1.2 m; 140 N   4) $\dfrac{100\sqrt{3}}{9}$ N

5) $\dfrac{11}{3}$ m from A   6) 375g Nm; 450g Nm

8)i) $\dfrac{3\sqrt{3}}{2}a$ ii) $\dfrac{3\sqrt{3}}{2}a$

 iii) $\dfrac{3\sqrt{3}}{2}a$, all in the sense CBA

9) $\dfrac{F}{2}\sqrt{113}$ making arctan 8/7 with the x-axis; a

10) 1 m from A

11) 2 m from A; 100 N; 700 N

12) 70 kg; 14 kg   13) $50\sqrt{3}$; 112.5

14) $W/4$; $\sqrt{3}W/8$; $7W/8$

15) $\dfrac{3a(2P + Q)}{2(P + Q - R)}$

16) $2p - 3q + 2r$; $2p - 2q + r$

17) 1/2; $4W/3$

Exercise 15a – p. 409

1) $3\sqrt{17}$ at $\arctan\frac{1}{4}$ to Ox; $12y = 3x + 16$

2) $2\sqrt{13}$ at $\arctan\dfrac{3\sqrt{3}}{5}$ to Ox;

   $5y = 3\sqrt{3}x - 4\sqrt{3}$

3) 10.4; $y = 1.4x - 0.8$

4) 6; $y = \sqrt{3}x$ 5) 5; $3y = 4x + 8$

6)i) $P = \sqrt{2}; Q = -5\sqrt{2}$ ii) $4\sqrt{2}$

7) $P\sqrt{13/3}$; $4a/3$

8) $n = 5, m = 1$ 9) $4y + x + 4 = 0$

10)a) $P = 2; \; Q = -7$

   b) $P = -\frac{1}{2}; \; Q = -2$

Exercise 15b – p. 417

1) $7\sqrt{3}Fa$ where $2a$ is the length of one side

2) $P = -1; \; Q = 6$

3) $\sqrt{13}\,P$; $\arctan 2\sqrt{3}$ with DB

5) $\sqrt{2}F$; F along CA and DA

6) $F\sqrt{5}$ at $\arctan\frac{1}{2}$ to DA

7) $\sqrt{5}F$ at $\arctan 2$ to BA; a

8)a) 0   b) $\dfrac{5\sqrt{2}}{2}$ 9) 26 units

10) $4 : 3 : 5$; $\dfrac{35P}{12}$

11)a) A force of magnitude 8 units

   b) A couple

Exercise 15c – p. 420

1) Equilibrium

2) Either equilibrium or the resultant is a force passing through both axes

3) Either a couple or in equilibrium

4) A force passing through A

5) A couple

6) A force parallel to the given forces

Exercise 15d – p. 425

(N.B. There are alternative ways of expressing the answers to this exercise)

1) $15\overrightarrow{PQ}$ where AP:PC = 2:1 and BQ:QC = 4:1

2) $2\overrightarrow{AM} + 2\overrightarrow{AN} = 4\overrightarrow{AL}$; M bisects BC; N bisects DE; L bisects MN

3) $4\overrightarrow{CL}$ where L is the mid-point of MN, M bisects AB and N bisects AD

4) $8\overrightarrow{MN}$ where M bisects AC and BN:ND = 1:3

Exercise 15e – p. 434

1)a) $p = -25/8; \; q = -15/8$

   b) $p = 25/6; \; q = -15/8$

2) P parallel to BA cutting AC produced at D where AD = $4a$; P parallel to AB; $2Pa\sqrt{3}$ in sense CBA

3) $5/2; -1$; $3y = 2x$ or $3y = 2x + 12$

4) $5F$ along $\overrightarrow{AB}$; $5F$ along $\overrightarrow{BC}$;

   $7\sqrt{2}F$ along $\overrightarrow{CA}$; $5a/6$

5) $\dfrac{4P}{\sqrt{3}}$ $(\overrightarrow{AB})$; $\dfrac{8P}{\sqrt{3}}$ $(\overrightarrow{CB})$; $2P\sqrt{3}$ $(\overrightarrow{CD})$

Multiple Choice Exercise 15 – p. 435

1) b	2) e	3) c	4) c
5) b	6) a,c	7) a,c	8) B
9) A	10) D	11) A	12) C
13) d	14) b,c	15) I	16) T
11) F	18) F	19) T	20) T

Miscellaneous Exercise 15 – p. 438

1)a) Equilibrium

   b) Couple of magnitude twice area ABC

   c) $3F$ parallel to $\overrightarrow{SR}$ and dividing SP in the ratio 1:2

   d) F parallel to $\overrightarrow{RS}$ cutting PS produced $3a$ from S

   e) Couple of magnitude $3Fa$

   f) $2\overrightarrow{AD}$ where D bisects BC

   g) A force passing through A and represented by $\overrightarrow{CB}$

2) A force of 10 N parallel to the original force and distant 2 m from it on either side of it.

3) 5 N in a direction parallel to the negative y-axis and through (2/5, 0).

4) $4F$ along AB; $\dfrac{5\sqrt{5}}{2}F$ along BE:

   $\dfrac{7\sqrt{5}}{2}F$ along EA

6)a) $18a$ b) $30a$

7) $5M/a$; $4y + 3x = 2a$

8) $\dfrac{a(1 + n)}{n}$; $\dfrac{W(1 + n)}{3}$

9)a) 5; 6 m   b) $\frac{1}{4}W$; $\frac{3}{4}W$; $\frac{1}{4}W - L/2a$

10) $\sqrt{13}$; $\arctan\sqrt{3/7}$ to AB; $19\sqrt{3}$ Nm, ABC; $2\sqrt{19}$ N, distant $7\frac{2}{3}$ m from A

12) $10P$ at $\arctan 4/3$ to Ox;

   $3y = 4x - 112a$

   $10P$ at $\arctan 4/3$ to Ox;

   $3y = 4x + 8a$

13) $10W$ at $\arctan 3/4$ to DA produced; at M; $7W$; $3W$

14)a) $13P$ at $\arctan 5/12$ to AB; $4a/5$ from B on AB produced

b) $\dfrac{4P}{3}\sqrt{10}$ at arctan 3 to BA; $a/4$ from

A on AB

15) $Pa\sqrt{3}$; $a/2$ 16)a) $4\sqrt{3}$; $30°$

b) $\sqrt{3}y + x + 4a = 0$ c) $8a\sqrt{3}$

17) 5, 6, 10 + $\sqrt{3}$, 10 − $\sqrt{3}$

18)a) 12.2 at $20° \ 36'$ to the 5.3 N force

b) $6\sqrt{3}Fa$ c) couple

19) $P = 4$; $Q = 5$; $P = 4$; $Q = 4$

20)a) vertical b) Mid-point of BC; $G/3$

21) $50P$; $3y + 4x = 12a$

22) $X = 8$ N; $Y = 4\sqrt{13}$ N; $M = 24$ Nm;

$P = 12$ N; $Q = 8\sqrt{13}$ N

23) BP : PC = 2 : 3; AQ : QC = 1 : 3;

$k = 20/3$

24)b) AY : YC = 2 : 5; BX : XC = 3 : 2

c) $4\triangle$ABC

25) M is the mid-point of XY

Exercise 16a − p. 451

1) $\left(\dfrac{19}{9}, \dfrac{10}{3}\right)$ 2) $\left(-\dfrac{1}{7}, \dfrac{3}{2}\right)$

3) $\dfrac{1}{15}(5\mathbf{i} + 28\mathbf{j})$, $\dfrac{1}{3}(5\mathbf{i} + 4\mathbf{j})$

4) $\dfrac{1}{11}(3\mathbf{i} - \mathbf{j})$, $\mathbf{i}$ 6) $2\mathbf{i} + \frac{1}{3}\mathbf{j}$

Exercise 16b − p. 458

1) $\dfrac{71}{12}a$ from C

2) $\dfrac{7}{9}a$ from BC, $\dfrac{4}{9}a$ from DC

3) $\dfrac{5a\sqrt{3}}{18}$ from AB

4) $\dfrac{7h}{6}$ from the base of the larger cylinder

5) centroid of the triangle

6) $\frac{3}{8}$ of the side of the square from each of the heavier sides

7) $\frac{2}{3}$ m from the edge joining the particles

8) $\dfrac{32\sqrt{2}}{33}$ m along the median through the right angled vertex

9) $\left(\dfrac{2 + \pi}{4 + \pi}\right)a$ from the straight edge

10) centre of the square

11) $\dfrac{a}{4}$ from DC

12) $\dfrac{a\sqrt{2}}{12}$ from D on BD

13) $\dfrac{5a}{6}$ from AB and BC

14) $\dfrac{2a\sqrt{3}}{9}$ from AD

15) $\dfrac{a}{6}$ from the centre of the largest circle

16) $\dfrac{24}{24 - \pi}$ from the centre of the hole

17) $a\left(\dfrac{4\pi - 3}{4\pi - 2}\right)$ from the solid base

Exercise 16c − p. 470

1) $\frac{3}{8}$ of the radius from the plane face

2) $\dfrac{3h}{13}$ 3) $\dfrac{h}{3}$ from the base

4) $\dfrac{2a}{\pi}$ from the centre 5) $\dfrac{4ah - h^2}{4(3a - h)}$

6) $\dfrac{45a}{4(19\sqrt{8} - 22\sqrt{5})}$ 7) $\frac{a}{2}(\sqrt{8} - \sqrt{5})$

8) $2l/3$ 9) $3a/2\pi$

Multiple Choice Exercise 16 − p. 479

1) b   2) e   3) a   4) c

5) a   6) F   7) T   8) T

9) F   10) F

Miscellaneous Exercise 16 − p. 480

1) $\dfrac{7a}{9}$, $\dfrac{4h}{9}$, $\dfrac{a\sqrt{10}}{5}$ 2) 12.0 N

3) $\dfrac{a}{4}$, $\dfrac{a}{\pi}$

4) $\dfrac{b}{3}$ from O on OC, $\dfrac{3a^2 + 2b^2}{6b^2 - 3a^2}$

6) 8.57 cm from the base   7) $10° \ 5'$

9) $\dfrac{73r}{33}$ from the joint face

10) $\dfrac{(\lambda^2 - 12\lambda + 48)a}{3(8 - \lambda)}$, $\dfrac{2(6 - \lambda)a}{8 - \lambda}$, 4

11) $70° \ 26'$, $\dfrac{16W}{45}$ 12) $a\sqrt{2}$

13) $\dfrac{a}{(2\pi - 3\sqrt{3})}$ 15) $\dfrac{5h}{16}$, arctan $\dfrac{4\sqrt{5}}{11}$

16) $\dfrac{23a}{26}$, $\dfrac{11a}{13}$, $\dfrac{51}{32}a^2 W$ at A and $\dfrac{53}{32}a^2 W$ at B

18) r

Exercise 17a − p. 494

1) $40° \ 52'$ 2) $2 - \sqrt{3}$

3) $\dfrac{7l - \sqrt{l^2 + 32a^2}}{4}$ 4) $\dfrac{\mu(1 + \sqrt{2} - \mu)aW}{1 + \mu^2}$

5)a) by sliding,   b) by sliding

6)a) arcsin $\frac{1}{3}$,   b) 1

7) arcsin $\dfrac{\pi}{8}$

Exercise 17b – p. 500

1) $\dfrac{3\sqrt{3}W}{8}$ where W is the weight of the rod, $3\sqrt{3}/41$

2) $\dfrac{8W}{45}$ at all points of contact

3) $\dfrac{4W}{3}$, arctan $\frac{4}{3}$ 4) $\sqrt{2}-1$

Exercise 17c – p. 505

1) $\dfrac{4}{7}, \dfrac{W}{2}$ at arctan $\frac{3}{4}$ to the horizontal

2) $150°\ 16'$

3) $\dfrac{\sqrt{21}}{6} \dfrac{W}{}$ at arctan $\dfrac{\sqrt{3}}{2}$ to the horizontal

4) $\dfrac{2aW}{l\sqrt{2}-a}$

5) $\dfrac{7\sqrt{3}}{24}$

6) $\dfrac{W\sqrt{57}}{18}$ at arctan $\dfrac{\sqrt{3}}{4}$ to the horizontal

Miscellaneous Exercise 17 – p. 506

1) $\dfrac{3}{4}, \dfrac{W}{4}$

2)a) $\dfrac{\sqrt{5}}{4} W$ at arctan $\frac{1}{2}$ to the vertical,

   b) $\dfrac{4l}{3}$ 4) $2aW$

5) arctan $\dfrac{12}{5}$ to the horizontal, $\dfrac{35}{64}W, \dfrac{91}{80}W$

6) $\dfrac{11l}{20}$

10) $Wr\left(\dfrac{7}{3\pi}-\dfrac{1}{2}\right) \leqslant G \leqslant \dfrac{7Wr}{3\pi}$

11) $\mu < \dfrac{1}{3}$

14) $2-\sqrt{3}$

15) $\dfrac{1}{\sqrt{3}}$

18) $\dfrac{1}{\sqrt{3}}$

19) $\dfrac{2}{3\mu'} \leqslant \tan\theta \leqslant 2\mu$

20) $\dfrac{16a}{5}, \dfrac{4a}{5}$

21) BC, $45°$, $\dfrac{\sqrt{5}W}{2}$ at arctan $\frac{1}{2}$ to the horizontal

22)a) $2a(2W + W_1)\sin\theta$,

   b) $\frac{1}{2}(W + W_1)\tan\theta, \frac{1}{2}W_1, \frac{1}{2}(W + W_1)\tan\theta, \frac{1}{2}(2W + W_1)$

23) $\dfrac{5mg}{2}, \dfrac{\sqrt{73}mg}{2}$

24) $\frac{1}{2}W\tan\theta$, W vertically, $\frac{1}{2}W\tan\theta$ horizontally

25) $\dfrac{W}{2}, \dfrac{3\sqrt{3}W}{4}, \dfrac{11W}{4}$

26) $\dfrac{a\cos\theta}{x}\ [W_1 + W_2], \frac{1}{2}[2W_1 + W_2]\tan\theta$

27) $\dfrac{6W}{5}$ at arctan $\dfrac{4}{3}$ with the vertical

28) $\frac{1}{2}W, 0$

29) $\frac{1}{2}W\tan\theta, 0, 2W$

Exercise 18a – p. 519

1) AB $-\dfrac{2\sqrt{3}}{3}W$, BC $\dfrac{\sqrt{3}}{3}W$,

   $\dfrac{\sqrt{3}}{3}W$ in the direction CB

2) $9W/25, 12W/25$, AB $3W/5$, BC $4W/5$, AC $-12W/25$

3) W in the direction AB

4) $4\sqrt{3}W/3$ in the direction AD; AB $2\sqrt{3}W/3$, BC $\sqrt{3}W/3$; CA $-2\sqrt{3}W/3$, AD $-4\sqrt{3}W/3$

Exercise 18b – p. 528

1) 100 N at B, AB, BC, CD, AD $-50\sqrt{2}$ N, AC 100 N

2) 150 N, 150 N, AB, BC $150\sqrt{2}$ N; AD, DC -150 N; BD 0

3) 200 N at B, $200\sqrt{2}$ N at A at $45°$ to AD; AB, AD 200 N; BD $-200\sqrt{2}$ N; BC, CD 0

4) $W\sqrt{3}$ at B, $2W$ at A at $30°$ to AD; AB, DC $W\sqrt{3}/3$, BD $-W\sqrt{3}/3$, AD $5W\sqrt{3}/6$, BC $-W(\sqrt{3}-1)$

5) 300 N, 300 N, AB, CD 170 N; AE, ED -150 N; BE, CE -170 N; BC 170 N

6) 225 N at A, 75 N at D, AB 260 N; BC, BE, CD 87 N; AE -130 N; CE -87 N, ED -43 N

7) 378 N at $23°\ 16'$ to AD at A, 346 N at B; CD, BC, BE -173 N; CE, AB 173 N, ED 87 N, AE 260 N

8) 100 N at A and D; AB, BC, CE 100 N,
ED − 100 N, CD 141 N, AE 0,
BE − 141 N

9) 2.7W at B, 2.9W at A at 20° 6′ to AE;
CD, BC − 1.7W, ED 2W, CE 0
BE − 1.4W, AB W, AE 2.7W

10) 5W/3 at C, 4W/3 at A, AB 8W/3,
AD − 4$\sqrt{3}W$/3, BD −2$\sqrt{3}W$/3,
DE − $\sqrt{3}W$, BC 10W/3,
EC − 5$\sqrt{3}W$/3, BE − 4$\sqrt{3}W$/3

11) 112 N at 26° 34′ below the horizontal,
500 N, − 500 N, − 500 N

12) − 167 N, 47.1 N, 186 N

13) 4$\sqrt{3}W$/9, − 8$\sqrt{3}W$/9, − $\sqrt{3}W$

14) 100 N, − 100 N, − 50 N

15) 3.80W at 52° 26′ below AD, W,
− 3.01W, 1.73W

16) 948 N at 18° 25′ below AE, − 1200 N,
− 600 N, 600$\sqrt{2}$ N

17) Thrusts: AB, FA 3W; BC, EF 4W;
BD, DF W

Tensions: CD, DE 2$W\sqrt{3}$; AD W

18) $\dfrac{8W\sqrt{3}}{3}$ horizontally, $\sqrt{3}W$, 2$\sqrt{3}W$,
$\dfrac{-10\sqrt{3}W}{3}$, $\dfrac{11W\sqrt{3}}{3}$

19) 1.2W, 0.8W, DC 1.4W, BC − 1.1W,
AE 1.27W, AB −0.4W, DB 0.8W
DE W, EB − 0.9W

21) $\sqrt{3}W$/3, 2$\sqrt{3}W$/3 along AB;
AD, DC − $\sqrt{3}W$/3, AB $\sqrt{3}W$/3,
BC − $\sqrt{3}W$/3, AC $\sqrt{3}W$/3

22) CD 800 N; ED, AE − 800 N,
EC 400 N, BC 860 N, AC 230 N

23) 210 kg, 150 kg, BC 260 kg, tension,
CE 300 kg, thrust

24) 5W/3, $W\sqrt{19/3}$, $W\sqrt{3}$/9 tension,
500 kg, CE would buckle

25)a) 100$\sqrt{3}$ kg,   b) 100$\sqrt{7}$ kg
arctan 2/$\sqrt{3}$ with the horizontal,
c) tension 50$\sqrt{3}$ kg, tension 50 kg.

INDEX

Acceleration 3, 76, 212
    angular 93
    as a function of distance 217
    as a function of time 212
    as a function of velocity 217
    Cartesian components of 223
    constant 76, 81
    due to gravity 88
    related accelerations 117
Acceleration-displacement graph 236
Acceleration-time graph 223
Acceleration-velocity graph 236
Air resistance 1
Amplitude of simple harmonic motion 311
Angle of friction 56
Angular acceleration 93
Angular velocity 290
    relation to linear velocity 92
Associated circular motion of simple
      harmonic motion 315
Average velocity 72

Banking 277
Bob 1, 320
Bow's Notation 519

Centre of gravity 445
    of composite bodies 451
    calculus methods for finding 461
    standard results 471, 536
Centre of mass 449
Centroid 449
Circular motion 91, 267
    constant speed 268

    variable speed 283
    radial acceleration 268, 269
    tangential acceleration 283
Closest approach 359
Coefficient of friction 56
Coefficient of restitution 197
Components
    Cartesian 21
    of acceleration 224, 225, 283
    of displacement 224, 225
    of a force 19, 21
    of a vector 15, 19
    of a velocity 224, 225
Compression
    light rods 516
    springs 150
Concurrent forces 35, 48
Conditions for equilibrium 391, 392
Conical pendulum 271
Connected particles 110
Conservation of mechanical energy 167
    use in problem solving 168
Conservation of linear momentum 185
Contact forces 6, 53, 109
Coplanar vectors 16
Coplanar forces 376, 390, 403, 418
Cotangent Rule 486
Couples 414
    constant moment of 414

Degrees of freedom 391, 418, 495
Direct Impact 180
    elastic 196
    inelastic 196

Displacement 3
  relative 355
Displacement-time graph 71

Elastic impact 196
Elastic limit 150
Elastic strings 149
Energy 162
  conservation of 167
  elastic potential 164
  gravitational potential 163
  kinetic 163
Equilibrant 44
Equilibrium 41
  conditions for 419
  limiting 56
  of bodies in contact 495
  of concurrent forces 41
  of coplanar forces 419
  of connected bodies 500
  of three forces 45
Equivalent sets of forces 425
External forces 54, 55, 495, 517
External impact 197

Force 5, 102
  components of 19, 21
  equivalent to a couple and a force 427
  external 54, 55, 495, 517
  frictional 7, 56
  internal 54, 109
  moment of 275
  resultant (and see resultant vector) 420
Forces 5, 102
  coplanar systems of 391, 403, 418
  contact 6, 53, 109
  equivalent systems of 425
  in light rods 517
  parallel 411
  polygon of (see polygon of vectors)
  triangle of 45
  which do no work 134, 168
Frameworks
  light 516
  heavy 503
Free vector 15
Freely jointed bodies 500
Friction 7, 55
  angle of 56
  coefficient of 56
  limiting 56

Graphical methods
  Bow's notation for light frameworks 519
  for constant acceleration 74, 78
  for relative velocity 348
  for variable acceleration 220
Gravitation, acceleration due to 88

Hinge 500
Hooke's Law 149

Impact
  direct 196
  elastic 196
  inelastic 196
  internal 184
Impulse 180
  external 197
  instantaneous 181
  of a constant force 180
  of a variable force 230
  relation to momentum 180
Impulsive tension 189
Interception 362
Internal forces 54, 109

Jointed rods
  heavy 501
  light 516

Kinetic energy 163
  relation to work 163

Laws of Mechanics 1
Lami's Theorem 46
Lamina 2
Light 2
Light rods, frameworks of 516
Limiting friction 56
Line of action 5, 403, 404
  of resultant force 405
Load 516, 517

Mass 5, 105
Mechanical Energy 163
Method of sections 524
Modulus of elasticity 150
Moment 375
  of a couple 414
  of a force 375
  resultant 386
Moments, Principle of 381
Momentum 180
  conservation of 185
  relation to impulse 180
Motion in a circle 267
  radial acceleration 269
  tangential acceleration 283
  with constant speed 286
  with variable speed 283
Motion in two dimensions 223
  equation of path 224
Motion, Newton's Laws of 102

Newton's Law of Motion 102
Newton's Law of Restitution 196

Normal contact force 53
Normal reaction 53

Overturning 472

Parabolic flight 245, 252
Parallel forces 411
    resultant of like 411
    resultant of unlike 413
Particle 1
Period of oscillation (S.H.M.) 311
Plane of rotation 374
Polygon of vectors 15, 29
Position vector 378
Potential Energy 163
    gravitational 163
    elastic 164
Power 138
    of a moving vehicle 138
Principles
    conservation of mechanical energy 167
    conservation of momentum 185
    friction 55
    impulse-momentum 180
    moments 381
    work-energy 162
Projectiles 242
    angle of projection 253
    equation of path 245, 254
    greatest height 252
    impact of 258
    maximum range on a horizontal plane
        253
    range on a horizontal plane 253
    time of flight 252
Pulley systems 110, 118

Range on a horizontal plane 253
Reaction
    normal 53
    total 57
Recoil of guns 186
Relative
    displacement 355
    path 358, 360
    position 354
    velocity 347
Resolving 19
Resultant
    displacement 16
    force 420
    moment 386
    of parallel forces 411
    vector 15, 24
    velocity 31
Restitution
    coefficient of 197
    Newton's Law of 196

Retardation 79
Rigid body 109
    centre of gravity of 445
    equilibrium of 485

Scalar quantity 12
Seconds pendulum 320
Sections, method of 524
Sideslip of a vehicle 277
Simple Harmonic motion 309
    amplitude 311
    centre 311
    equations of motion 311
    forces causing 321
    incomplete oscillations 326
    period of 311
    relation to motion in a circle 315
Simple pendulum 319
Space diagram 520
Speed 3, 70
    average 72
Smooth 2
Spring 150
Systems of connected particles 110
Strut 516

Tension
    impulsive 189
    in a light rod 516
    in a string 7
    in elastic strings 149
    in springs 150
Three forces in equilibrium 45
Thrust
    in a light rod 516
    in a spring 150
Tie 516
Tied Vector 15
Toppling 472
Torque 375
    graphical representation of 376
    resultant 381
Triangle
    of forces 45
    of velocities 348
    of vectors 15
Turning effect 35, 375

Uniform
    acceleration 76, 81
    body 448
    velocity 70
Units 2

Variable acceleration 212
Vector 12
    addition 15
    Cartesian components of 21

components of 15, 19
differentiation with respect to time 225
free 15
integration with respect to time 226
multiplication by a scalar 14
negative 14
position 378
resultant 15, 24
subtraction 14
tied 15
Vector quantity 12
Vectors 12
    angle between 24
    coplanar 16
    equal 13
    parallel 14
    polygon of 15, 29
    resolving 19
    triangle of 15

Velocity 3, 70
    angular 93
    at an instant 73
    average 72
    relative 347
    uniform 70
    variable 212
Velocity-displacement graph 220
Velocity-time graph 77, 220
Vertical motion under gravity 88

Weight 5, 105
Work 133
    relation to mechanical energy 162
    done against gravity 134
    done by a constant force 133
    done by a variable force 230
    done extending an elastic string or spring
        158
    done by a moving vehicle 135
Wind direction 351